MW00855785

Big Game Hunter's Guide to™

COLORADO

Titles Available in This Series

Big Game Hunter's Guide to Montana

Big Game Hunter's Guide to Idaho

Big Game Hunter's Guide to Colorado

Big Game Hunter's Guide to™
COLORADO

John Axelson

Wilderness
Adventures
Press, Inc.™

Belgrade, Montana

This book was made with an easy opening, lay flat binding.

© 2002 John Axelson

Cover Photograph © 2002 Ron Spomer
Photographs contained herein © 2002 John Axelson, unless otherwise noted.
Art Today Photographs pages xiv, 5, 33, 38, 65, 69, 72, 74, 81, 112, 114, 115, 122, 124, 147, 153, 156, 163, 167, 192, 199, 203, 258, 260, 266, 281, 289, 297, 321, 346, 347, 349, 444

Maps, book design and cover design © 2002 Wilderness Adventures Press, Inc.™
Big Game Hunter's Guide to™

Published by Wilderness Adventures Press, Inc.™
45 Buckskin Road
Belgrade, MT 59714
800-925-3339
Website: www.wildadv.com
email: books@wildadv.com

10 9 8 7 6 5 4 3 2 1

All rights reserved, including the right to reproduce this book or portions thereof in any form or by any means, electronic or mechanical, including photocopying, recording, or by any information storage and retrieval system, without permission in writing from the publisher. All inquiries should be addressed to: Wilderness Adventures Press, Inc.™, 45 Buckskin Road, Belgrade, MT 59714.

Printed in the United States of America

Library of Congress Cataloging-in-Publication Data

Axelson, John, 1965-
   Big game hunter's guide to Colorado / by John Axelson.
   p. cm.
   ISBN 1-885106-55-6 (pbk. : alk. paper)
   1. Big game hunting--Colorado--Guidebooks. 2. Colorado
--Guidebooks.   I. Title.
SK57.A94 2002
798.2'6'09788--dc21

2002012729

00-043318

Acknowledgments

I would like to thank the Colorado Division of Wildlife for providing information on hunting regulations, licensing, animal populations, and hunting statistics. Special thanks to all of the Division of Wildlife personnel who took the time to answer my never-ending questions. I would also like to thank the Boone and Crockett Club for granting permission to reprint scoring sheets for the big game species listed in this book and all of my friends who contributed pictures. Lastly, I want to thank Chuck and Blanche Johnson and Darren Brown of Wilderness Adventures Press for giving me the opportunity to write this book.

Table of Contents

Colorado's 2002 fire season was the worst in recent history, but only a small fraction of the public land open to big game hunting was affected.

Wildfire

Although there are several wildfires in Colorado every year, the extreme media coverage during the summer of 2002 led some people to believe that the entire state was on fire. News programs that called it the "Summer of Fire" propagated this misconception. Governor Bill Owens even added fuel to the fire when he said something to the effect that *all of Colorado is burning.* It is true that the summer of 2002 was one of the worst years for wildfires in Colorado's history. Four major fires, mostly on national forest land, burned about 230,000 acres by the beginning of July. This is a tremendous amount of land, but overall it's less than one percent of the public land acreage in the state available for big game hunting.

The effect on wildlife in the burn areas is not completely known yet and likely won't be for several years. In general, most big game animals are able to survive wildfires. The most significant documented loss of wildlife was in the Hayman Fire where two small herds of elk, each numbering 20 to 30 animals, were unable to escape.

The bright side of this situation for big game hunters is that the recent fires will have very little effect on the big game hunting seasons, unless you are specifically hunting in units ravaged by the fire. In these cases areas may be closed while restoration efforts are underway. If you hunt due west of Glenwood Springs (Coal Seam Fire), north of Lake George (Hayman Fire), north of Durango (Missionary Ridge Fire), or north of New Castle (Spring Creek Fire), you should contact the Colorado Division of Wildlife and the National Forest Service for closure information. It is possible that state wildlife areas in these regions could be closed, and access could be restricted in the burn areas. If dry conditions continue there may be more major fires, and you can also expect fire restrictions that will limit all open fires in most areas.

Of greater concern to big game hunters should be the drought conditions and the long-term impact those conditions could have on wildlife. With any luck the drought conditions will end before any harm has been done. In the meantime, Colorado's big game populations are very strong with an all-time high number of elk estimated at over 300,000 animals.

Wildfires will continue to burn in Colorado each year, and for those of us who love to pursue big game, we will continue to hunt, even if we have to alter our plans a little. Savvy hunters willing to spend some time watching the burn areas over the next few years just might find themselves a hot spot (no pun intended) for big game as the new vegetation attracts all types of wildlife.

One of Colorado's major hunting assets is that all the big game species may be hunted on public land.

Introduction

With the largest population of elk in North America, 10 species of big game animals, and over 25 million acres of public land, Colorado is truly one of the premier big game hunting states in the country. Colorado also has the distinction of being the only state that still offers over-the-counter hunting licenses for elk. For the time being a hunter can still buy an elk license at a sporting goods store prior to hunting season and go hunting in any of the game management units open to unlimited licenses. In addition, all of the big game species can be hunted on public land. This is one of the appealing aspects of hunting in Colorado; do-it-yourself hunts are well within reach of novice and expert hunters alike. If you prefer, there are also numerous outfitters that can help you plan and execute a hunt. Hopefully, the information provided in this book will lead you to an exceptional hunting experience.

Colorado Elevations

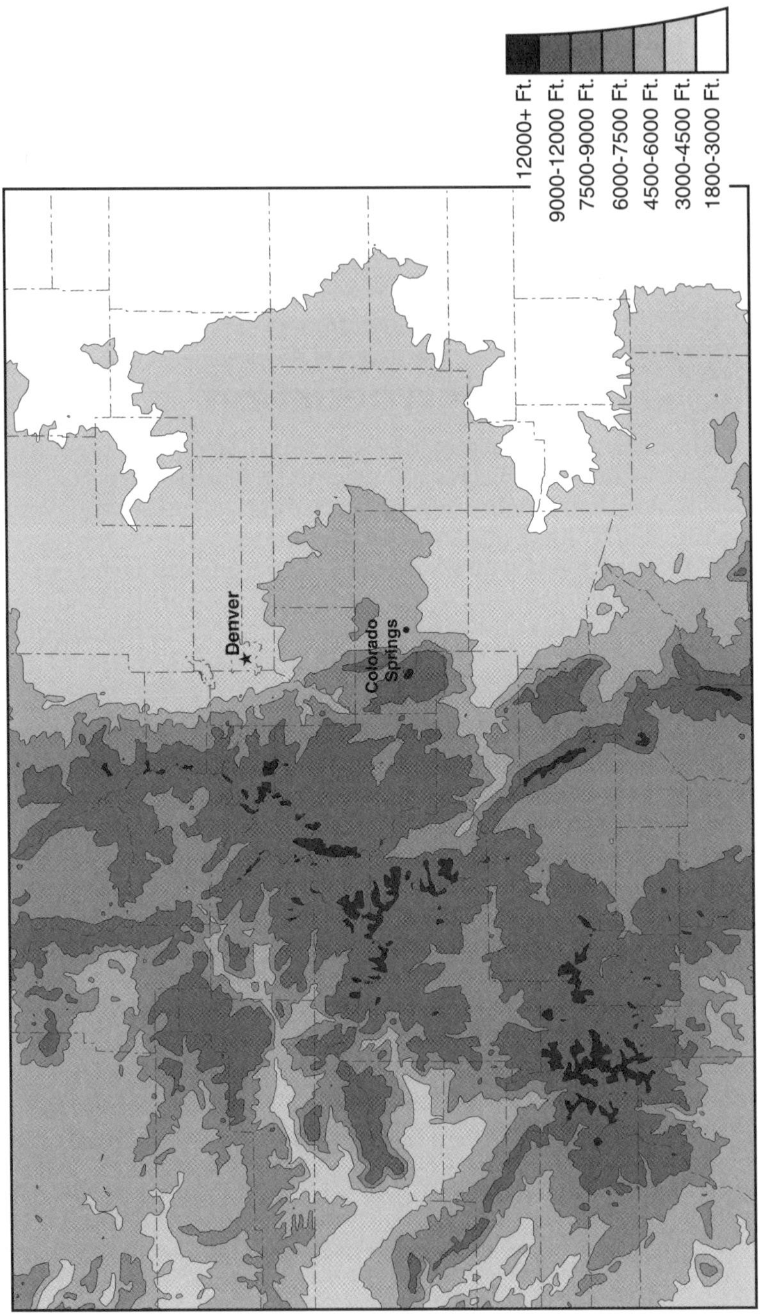

	12000+ Ft.
	9000-12000 Ft.
	7500-9000 Ft.
	6000-7500 Ft.
	4500-6000 Ft.
	3000-4500 Ft.
	1800-3000 Ft.

Denver

Colorado Springs

© WILDERNESS ADVENTURES PRESS, INC.

Tips on Using This Book

This guide is divided into four regional sections. The information presented for each region includes:

- Distribution maps for each big game species present in the region;
- Maps of federal lands, ecosystems, mountain ranges, and game management units;
- Descriptions of physical terrain, land use, local weather patterns, big game populations, and harvest rates;
- Descriptions that detail regional hunting opportunities, including guides and outfitters;
- Information on regional hub cities, including accommodations, camping, restaurants, veterinarians, sporting goods, gun sales, gunsmiths, taxidermists, meat processors, auto repair and rental, air service, and medical services.

This information is current at the time of printing, but always check in advance of your trip.

A good way to use this book to do preliminary scouting is to refer to the big game distribution maps and population statistics and compare them to the public land maps for each region. In this way you can determine which areas have large acreages of public land and good populations of the various big game animals. From there you can refer to the game management unit (GMU) maps to determine which units or herds you are interested in. For more detailed information on the units you can refer to the regional highlights. If you have already hunted in Colorado for many years and you would only like information on a specific unit, the GMUs discussed in each regional highlight area are shown in parenthesis next to the highlight area title.

The units discussed in each highlight area often correspond to Data Analysis units (DAU) used by the Colorado Division of Wildlife (DOW) to define herds of big game in the state. Herds are generally named for a prominent geographic feature and are composed of all animals in one or more GMU. For example, the Bookcliffs deer herd is named after the Book Cliffs located outside of Rifle, Colorado. It is made up of two GMUs (21 and 30), which comprise a DAU in northwest Colorado. The population of the herd was estimated at 10,230 deer based on 2001 big game population statistics published by the DOW. Please understand that there are not 10,230 deer running around in a single herd in this area. The population estimate includes all of the separate groups of animals that are found within the two-unit geographic area that makes up the DAU.

Animal distributions are subject to change over the course of years based on migrations, weather patterns, predation, development, and disease; as a result, the maps contained herein are only approximations. In addition, hunting regulations, license costs, and season structure can all change from one year to the next. The Colorado Wildlife Commission sets big game hunting seasons in five-year increments. The season dates listed within are based on the 2002 to 2004 Big Game Season

Structure. However, special management objectives, as demonstrated in the recent past, may cause certain seasons to change from year to year. Please verify season dates, license costs, and regulations each year by contacting the Colorado Division of Wildlife (DOW) or refer to the big game hunting brochures published by the DOW each year.

Hunting big game on private land without permission is illegal in Colorado. Always ask permission before hunting or fishing on private land. Also, keep in mind that landowners do not have to mark the boundaries of their property, so always verify property boundaries prior to entering.

Yankee Boy Basin near Ouray.

Getting Around Colorado

Colorado is the eighth largest state in the country. Even though it is relatively large, access throughout the state is good via the 9,000 miles of interstate and state highways. County roads account for over 57,000 miles of paved and unpaved roads while Forest Service roads add another 6,200 miles to the system. City roads add up to another 11,000 miles.

The major route of travel across the entire state from west to east is Interstate 70. From north to south, Interstate 25 crosses the state just east of the leading edge of the mountains. These two major interstates meet in Denver. Other highways that make up important travel routes for hunters include Highway 40, which provides good access across the northwestern quarter of the state, and Interstate 76, which transects the northeastern plains. Highway 50 travels from the eastern plains all the way to Montrose in southwestern Colorado. Finally, Highway 160 provides access to the southern part of the state extending from the Four Corners region to the Kansas state line.

Colorado's highways are generally kept in very good condition. Most secondary roads are paved, while unpaved roads receive frequent grading and often have a gravel road base. It should be noted that unpaved roads often become muddy or snow-packed in the winter with washboard, ruts, and potholes. These conditions can make travel into the backcountry difficult during the hunting seasons. Due to frequent snowstorms and uncertain road conditions, four-wheel-drive vehicles are recommended. Furthermore, it is always good to have tire chains along when traveling over the high mountain passes. At a minimum, it doesn't hurt to have a good towrope and shovel in case you find yourself in a road ditch.

Colorado spends a great deal of money on snow removal every year. In 1995 the state expended over 18 million to remove snow from the state's roads. If you are hunting in the backcountry during a bad storm you must realize that snow removal generally occurs on the most heavily traveled roads first and on emergency routes. Then, as time allows, less frequently used roads are plowed. If you are in a remote area and the snow begins to pile up, you may want to consider heading out before you get snowed in.

Denver International Airport (DIA) is an important travel hub for the entire country. Hunters traveling by air will likely fly into DIA or the Colorado Springs Municipal Airport. Commuter flights from both airports provide service to many of the smaller communities throughout Colorado. Popular hunter destinations in the west such as Steamboat Springs, Grand Junction, Montrose, Gunnison, and Durango (to name a few) all have airports that receive commuter flights daily. If you intend to hunt the eastern plains most areas are within a 4-hour drive from the Denver or Colorado Springs airports.

Colorado also has rail and bus service. Although probably not the best form of travel for hunters, Amtrak does provide service with several stops from east to west across the state. There are also bus stops in most of the major towns throughout the state, but busses generally do not allow the transport of firearms.

There are currently four area codes in Colorado. The 303 and 702 area codes cover the Denver area. Western and northern Colorado uses the 970 prefix, and southeast Colorado uses 719. All in-state local and long distance calls must be dialed with the area code prefix.

Road Conditions

To get current road and weather information, call the Colorado Department of Transportation's road, weather, and construction hotline at (303) 639-1111. For local road conditions or emergency numbers refer to the listings presented below.

Location	Emergency Phone #	Road/Weather Phone
Alamosa	(719) 589-5807	(719) 589-9024
Burlington	(719) 346-8703	(719) 346-8778
Canon City	(719) 275-1558	(719) 275-1637
Colorado Springs	(719) 635-3581	(719) 635-7623
Cortez	(970) 565-8454	(970) 565-4511
Craig	(970) 824-6501	(970) 824-4765
Denver	(303) 239-4501	(303) 639-1111
Durango	(970) 247-4722	(970) 247-3355
Frisco	(970) 668-3133	(970) 668-3133
Fort Collins	(970) 484-4020	(970) 482-2222
Glenwood Springs	(970) 945-6198	(970) 945-2222
Grand Junction	(970) 245-7911	(970) 245-8800
La Junta	(719) 336-3444	(719) 336-4326
Limon	(719) 775-2354	(719) 775-2000
Montrose	(970) 249-9611	(970) 249-9363
Pueblo	(719) 544-2424	(719) 545-8520
Sterling	(970) 522-4693	(970) 522-4848
Trinidad	(719) 846-2227	(719) 846-9262

Additional numbers of importance are the Colorado State Patrol at (303) 239-4500 and the Emergency Direct Dispatch (303) 239-4501.

Major Roads and Rivers

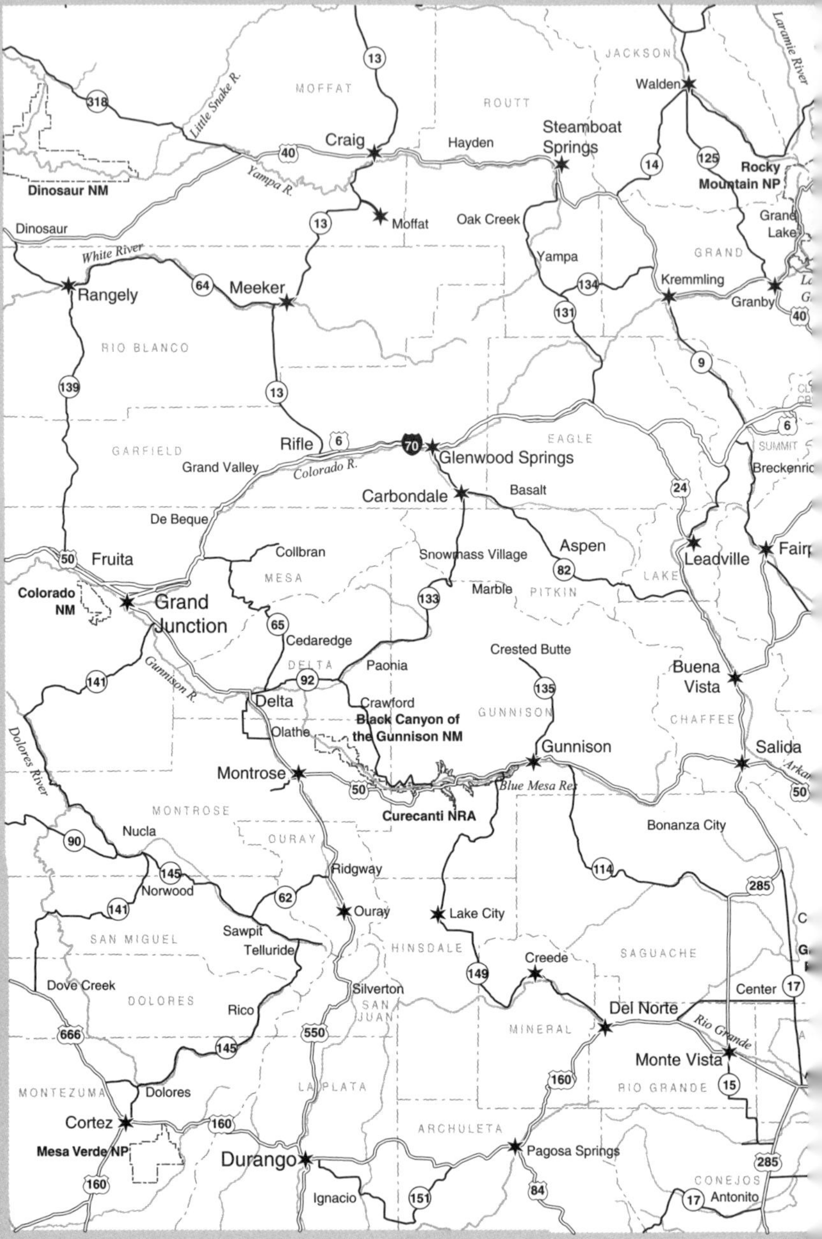

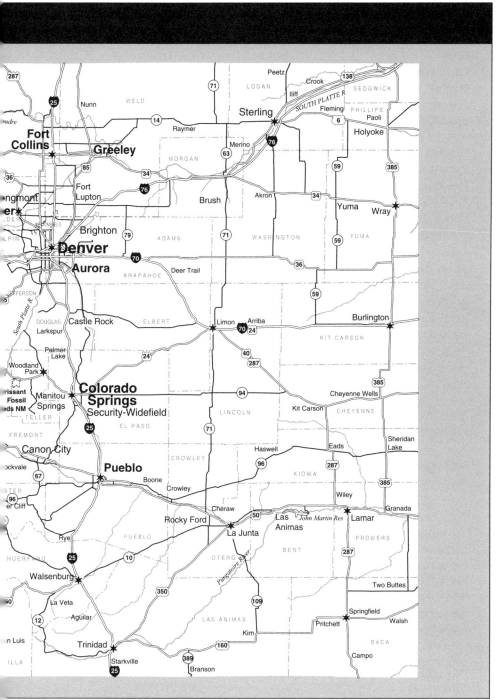

© WILDERNESS ADVENTURES PRESS, INC.

Colorado Facts

State Features

Size	Eighth largest state in the union
Land Area	104,247 square miles or 66,624,000 acres
Width	380 miles east to west
Length	280 miles north to south
Elevations	3,350 feet to 14,433 feet
	54 mountains over 14,000 feet in elevation
Highest Point	Mount Elbert, 14,433 feet
Lowest Point	Arkansas River at the Town of Holly, 3,350 feet
Counties	64
Towns and Cities	1,544
Population (April 2000)	4,301,261
Nicknames	Centennial State, Colorful Colorado
Capital	Denver
State Bird	Lark Bunting
State Flower	Rocky Mountain Columbine
State Tree	Blue Spruce
State Animal	Rocky Mountain Bighorn Sheep
State Gemstone	Aquamarine
State Fish	Greenback Cutthroat Trout
State Fossil	Stegosaurus
State Grass	Blue Grama

The Land

Indian Reservations	Southern Ute Reservation, 310,000 acres
	Ute Mountain Reservation, 7,634 acres
National Parks	Rocky Mountain, Mesa Verde
National Monuments	Dinosaur, Colorado, Black Canyon of the Gunnison, Great Sand Dunes
National Grasslands	612,000 acres
National Recreation Areas	Arapaho: Total 36,086
National Forests	Eleven for a total of 16.15 million acres
State Recreation Areas	23
State Forests	120,708 acres
Wilderness Areas	Thirty-three for a total of 3.2 million acres
State Parks	Eleven for a total of 160,000 acres
State Wildlife Areas	241

Primary Industries

Manufacturing, government, tourism, agriculture, aerospace, electronics equipment.

© WILDERNESS ADVENTURES PRESS, INC.

Colorado Mountain Ranges

Colorado Land Ownership

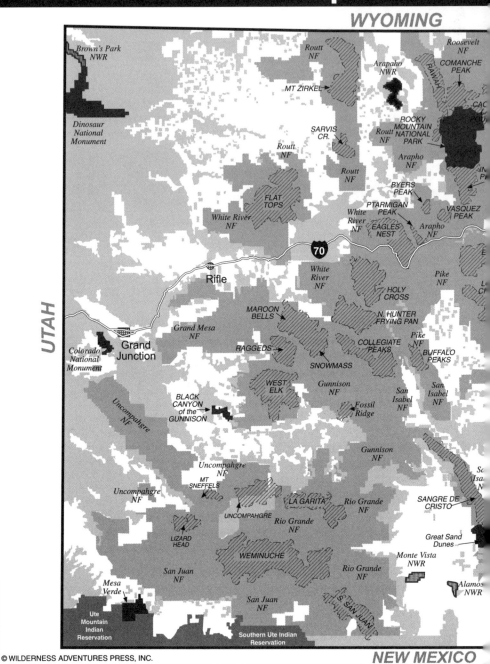

WYOMING

UTAH

NEW MEXICO

© WILDERNESS ADVENTURES PRESS, INC.

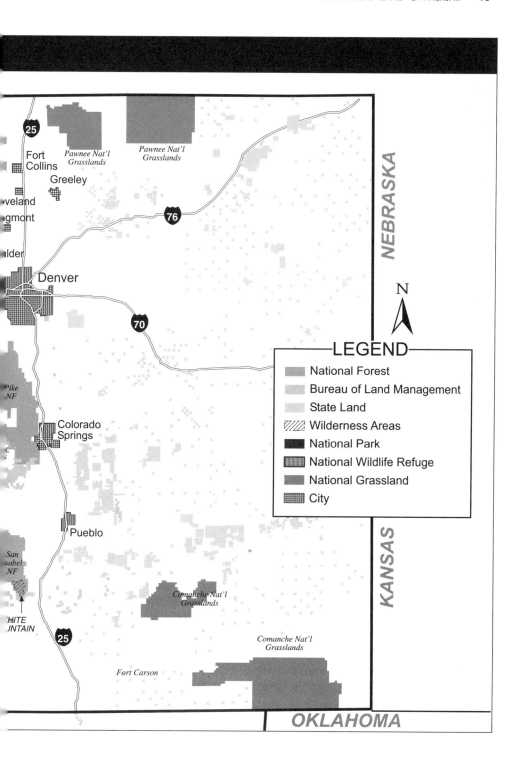

Ecosystems

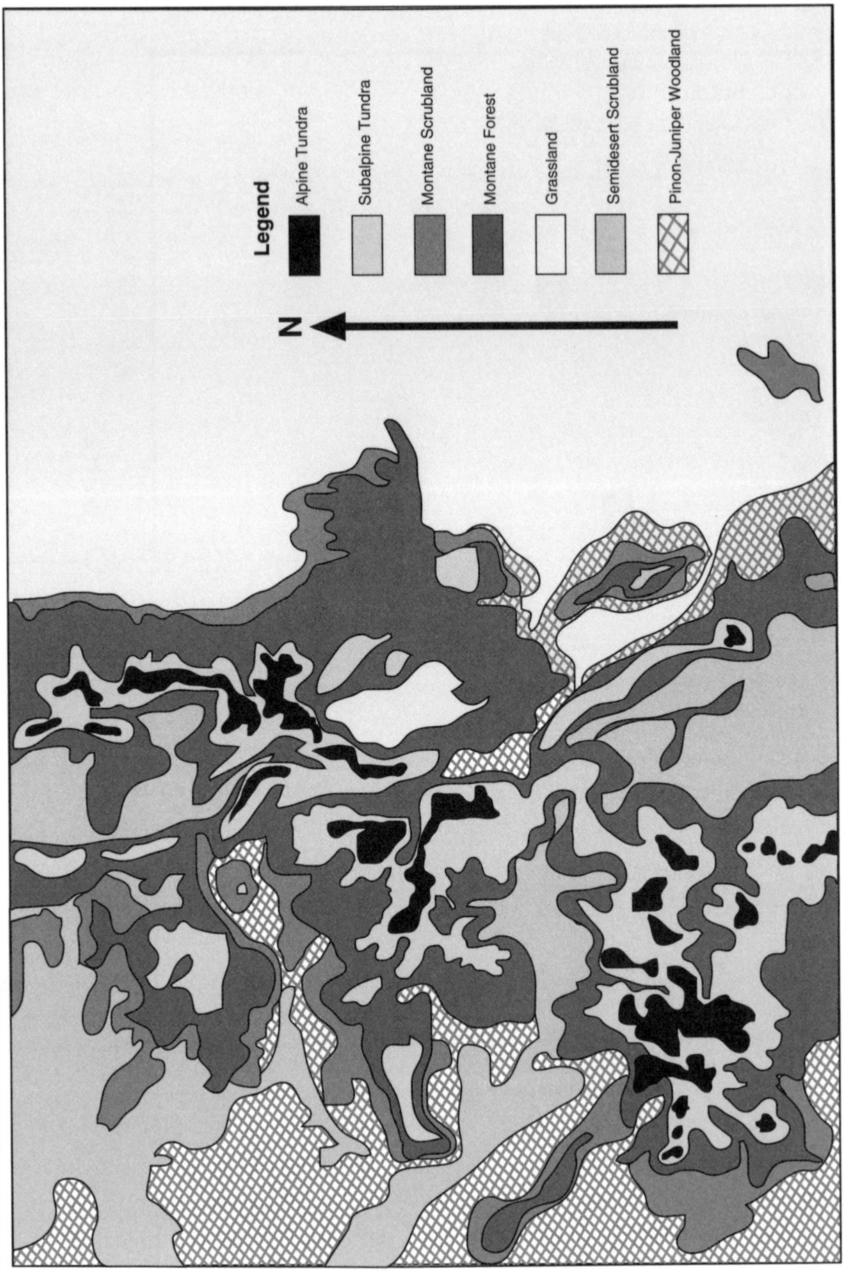

Legend

- Alpine Tundra
- Subalpine Tundra
- Montane Scrubland
- Montane Forest
- Grassland
- Semidesert Scrubland
- Pinon-Juniper Woodland

N

© WILDERNESS ADVENTURES PRESS, INC.

Ecosystems

Throughout the regional highlight sections of this book there are references to various ecosystems. There are eight prominent ecosystems in Colorado, although they can be split further. An ecosystem is characterized by several factors, including altitude, precipitation, temperature, plant life, and animal life. At a glance, the ecosystem map presented here will allow you to identify the prominent characteristics in different areas of the state. As a reference, the basic defining characteristics of each ecosystem depicted on the map are discussed below.

Riparian Land

Riparian areas provide some of the richest and most diverse wildlife habitat in the state. Most riparian areas are found along major river drainages, but they can also exist around lakes, marshes, or other bodies of water. Riparian lands account for 1 to 2 percent of the land area in the state. These areas are often characterized by various cottonwood trees that utilize the abundance of water. In terms of big game species this ecosystem is most important for mule deer and white-tailed deer. Nearly all of the state's white-tailed deer live in, or utilize to a large extent, riparian areas on the eastern plains. They also seem to be moving into western Colorado along riparian corridors.

Characteristic Plants: Plains cottonwood, narrowleaf cottonwood, mountain willow, box-elder, broad-leaved cattail, bulrush, sedges, bittercress, cow parsnip, Geyer willow, field horsetail, sand dropseed, river birch, salt-grass.

Elevation Range: All elevations, but commonly below 10,000 feet

Average Annual Precipitation: Variable based on elevation and location

Average Temperature: Variable, generally above 50 degrees at lower elevations

Mule deer are often found feeding on vegetation in montane shrubland.

Pronghorn are typically found on grasslands or semi-desert shrubland.

GRASSLANDS

Most of Colorado's grasslands are found on the eastern plains. There are also a few scattered areas in western Colorado most commonly found in intermountain valleys such as South Park. The topography of the grasslands is generally flat to gently rolling terrain. Much of the grassland on the eastern plains is characterized by shortgrass prairie consisting of buffalo grass and blue grama. Most of the grasslands in Colorado are found at an elevation between 4,000 and 6,000 feet; however, it is possible to have grasslands at much higher elevations. Low precipitation and strong winds characterize these areas. The most common big game species you will find on the grasslands in Colorado are pronghorn and mule deer. Whitetail deer will occasionally use grassland areas adjacent to river drainages and agricultural areas.

Characteristic Plants: Blue grama, buffalograss, western wheatgrass, needle-and-thread, silver sage, broom snakeweed, yucca, prickly pear cactus, and prairie coneflower.

Elevation Range: 4,000 to 10,000 feet (most commonly 4,000 to 6,000 feet)

Average Annual Precipitation: 14 inches

Average Temperature: 52 degrees

Semi-Desert Shrublands

Dispersed throughout western Colorado, semi-desert shrublands are characterized by open landscapes with low vegetation and hilly terrain. Large tracts of semi-desert shrubland are found in, but not limited to, northwest Colorado, North Park, Middle Park, the San Luis Valley, and the Gunnison River valley. Semi-desert shrublands occupy about 15 percent of the land area in the state. These areas are very arid, receiving small amounts of annual precipitation, and often consist of large tracts of sagebrush. The most common big game species you will find on semi-desert shrublands are pronghorn, mule deer, and elk. Deer and elk often migrate to lower elevations and winter in areas of semi-desert shrubland. Moose also utilize semi-desert shrubland in northern Colorado. Several other big game species utilize this ecosystem at various times throughout the year to a lesser extent.

Characteristic Plants: Big sagebrush, mountain sagebrush, rabbitbrush, greasewood, four-winged saltbrush, squirrel tail, galleta grass, arrowleaf balsamroot, paintbrush, shadscale.

Elevation Range: 4,000 to 8,000 feet

Average Annual Precipitation: 10 inches

Average Temperature: 43 degrees

Pinon-Juniper Woodlands

As the name implies, this ecosystem is characterized by stands of pinon and juniper, often with little understory. The largest areas of this ecosystem are found in the western third of Colorado, but they are distributed throughout the state, accounting for 10 to 15 percent of the land area. They often occur between semi-desert shrubland or grassland and montane shrubland. The terrain is generally made up of hills and slopes, with canyons, plateaus, and mesas dominant features of the landscape. These areas are also very arid, receiving small amounts of rain and snow. In terms of the big game species, mule deer are often found in pinon-juniper woodlands as well as elk, and occasionally bighorn sheep. Desert bighorns utilize this ecosystem in the southwestern part of the state, and mountain lions often haunt these areas.

Characteristic Plants: Pinon pine, Utah juniper, one-seed juniper, red cedar, mountain-mahogany, bitterbrush, junegrass, Indian ricegrass, prickly pear, blue grama.

Elevation Range: 5,500 to 8,000 feet

Average Annual Precipitation: 14 inches

Average Temperature: 50 degrees

Montane Shrublands

Montane shrublands are commonly found above pinon-juniper woodlands and below tracts of montane forests. These areas often occur in rocky terrain along ridges, and on hills and slopes. This ecosystem is distributed throughout western Colorado and covers 5 to 10 percent of the state. Oakbrush is often the dominant plant in the ecosystem, and bears are particularly fond of montane shrublands. Other big game species that commonly occur here are mule deer, elk, and mountain lion.

Characteristic Plants: Gambel oak, mountain-mahogany, serviceberry, skunkbrush, smooth sumac, snowberry, scarlet gilia, lupine, needle-and-thread, wild rose, wax currant, choke cherry, rabbitbrush, western wheat-grass.

Elevation Range: 5,500 to 8,500 feet

Average Annual Precipitation: 15 inches

Average Temperature: 45 degrees

Montane Forests

The montane forests are found at higher elevations than the pinon-juniper woodlands and montane shrublands. Much of the western mountains are covered by montane forest consisting of large stands of ponderosa pine and Douglas fir. Montane forests account for roughly 10 percent of the land area in the state. Most of the big game species, including mule deer, elk, moose, black bear, mountain lion, and bighorn sheep, utilize montane forest.

Characteristic Plants: Ponderosa pine, Douglas-fir, white fir, lodgepole pine, limber pine, Colorado blue spruce, quaking aspen, Rocky Mountain juniper, wax currant, mountain maple, kinnikinnik, golden banner, mountain muhly

Elevation Range: 5,600 to 9,000 feet

Average Annual Precipitation: 20.4 inches

Average Temperature: 45 degrees

Subalpine Forests

Subalpine forests cover large expanses of mountainous areas throughout western Colorado. Some of the largest tracts of subalpine forest are found in central and southwest Colorado. This ecosystem represents 15 percent of the land area in the state and is characterized by higher precipitation and colder temperatures than the ecosystems at lower elevations. Dense stands of spruce, fir, and pine with intermingled aspen stands are dominant in subalpine forests. It is also important to many of the big game species in the state, especially elk, but mule deer, black bear and bighorn sheep are also primary animals found here. Mountain lion, moose, and mountain goats also utilize this ecosystem.

One of Colorado's montane forest ecosystems.

Characteristic Plants: Engelmann spruce, subalpine fir, quaking aspen, lodgepole pine, limber pine, bristlecone pine, blueberry, wild rose, Colorado columbine, fairy slipper, broom huckleberry, heart-leaved arnica.

Elevation Range: 9,000 to 11,400 feet

Average Annual Precipitation: 30 inches

Average Temperature: 36 degrees

ALPINE TUNDRA

The highest ecosystem in the state, alpine tundra is generally characterized as treeless areas above 11,400 feet in elevation. Alpine tundra consists of isolated areas at the tops of mountains surrounded by subalpine forest. These areas are prone to extreme weather conditions including heavy snowfall, strong winds, and extremely cold temperatures. Much of the snow is redistributed by the wind to lower elevations. Although this ecosystem accounts for less than 5 percent of the land area in the state, there is more alpine tundra in Colorado than in any other state. Alpine tundra is where mountain goats live, but bighorn sheep and elk also utilize this ecosystem frequently.

Characteristic Plants: Arctic willow, alpine avens, kobresia, tufted hairgrass, sedges, alpine sandwort, American bistort, marsh-marigold, alpine forget-me-not, moss campion

Elevation Range: 11,400 feet and higher

Average Annual Precipitation: 30 inches

Average Temperature: 27 degrees

Colorado Division of Wildlife Service Centers

Denver Headquarters
6060 Broadway
Denver, CO 80216
(303) 297-1192

Southeast Region Service Center
2126 N. Weber
Colorado Springs, CO 80907
(719) 227-5200

Northeast Region Service Center
6060 Broadway
Denver, CO 80216
(303) 291-7227

Lamar Service Center
1204 E. Olive
Lamar, CO 81052
(719) 336-6600

Fort Collins Service Center
317 West Prospect Avenue
Fort Collins, CO 80526
(970) 472-4300

Monte Vista Service Center
0722 South Road 1 East
Fort Monte Vista, CO 81144
(719) 587-6900

West Region Service Center
711 Independent Ave.
Grand Junction, CO 81505
(970) 255-6100

Brush Service Center
122 E. Edison, Box 128
Brush, CO 80723
(970) 842-6300

Glenwood Springs Service Center
50633 Hwys. 6 and 24
Glenwood Springs, CO 81601
(970) 947-2920

Montrose Service Center
2300 S. Townsend Ave.
Montrose, CO 81401
(970) 252-6000

Durango Service Center
151 E. 16th St.
Durango, CO 81301
(970) 247-0855

Gunnison Service Center
300 W. New York Ave.
Gunnison, CO 81230
(970) 641-7060

Hot Sulphur Springs Service Center
346 Grand County Rd. 362
Hot Sulphur Springs, CO 80451
(970) 725-6200

Meeker Service Center
Box 1181
Meeker, CO 81641
(970) 878-4493

Steamboat Springs Service Center
925 Weiss Drive
Steamboat Springs, CO 80477
(970) 870-3324

Pueblo Service Center
600 Reservoir Rd.
Pueblo, CO 81005
(719) 561-4909

Salida Service Center
7405 Hwy. 50
Salida, CO 81201
(719) 530-5520

Colorado Hunting Regulations, Seasons, and Licensing

Like many other states, Colorado has a vast number of hunting regulations, and season structure and licensing requirements can seem complicated. In order to become a successful big game hunter in Colorado you must do more than rely on your outdoor skills. You must be aware of and understand the litany of regulations. You must also understand the season structure and licensing system in order to increase your chances to hunt quality units in the appropriate season.

The Colorado Division of Wildlife (DOW) is charged with managing the state's wildlife resources and enforcing the regulations that apply to hunting, fishing, and wildlife. Since regulations change from year to year, and it would be impossible to include every regulation, you should always refer to the *Big Game Hunting Regulations* each year. These regulations are provided in the various hunting season brochures published by the DOW on an annual basis. To obtain the brochures for big game hunting contact the DOW by phone at (303) 297-1192 or via the Internet at www.dnr.state.co.us/wildlife. You can also contact one of the DOW Service Centers listed in the previous section.

The regulations, seasons, and licensing information presented herein are based on the *Colorado Hunting Season Information* brochures for the 2002 hunting season.

Understanding the season structure and licensing system will better your chances for taking a nice buck.

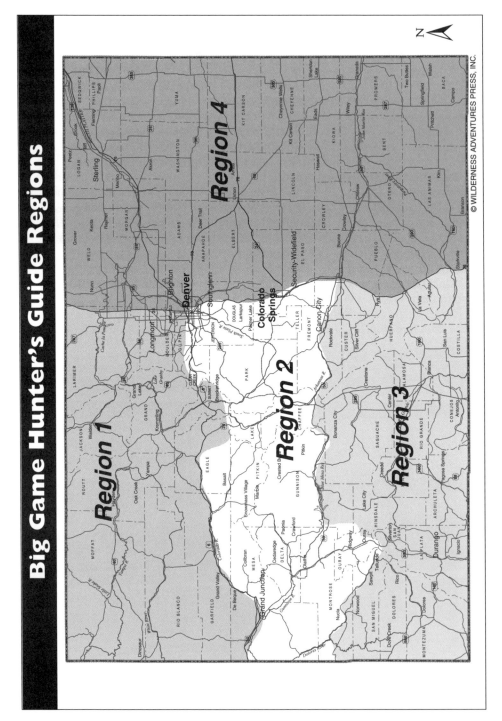

© WILDERNESS ADVENTURES PRESS, INC.

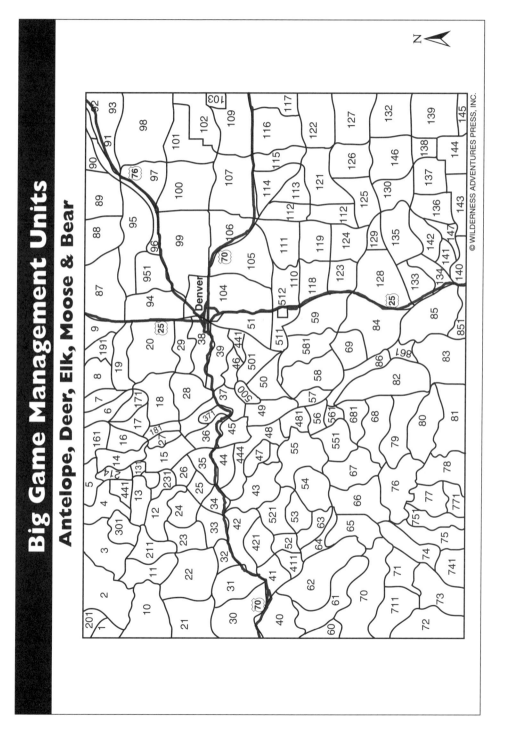

Big Game Management Units
Antelope, Deer, Elk, Moose & Bear

© WILDERNESS ADVENTURES PRESS, INC.

Bighorn Sheep Management Units

© WILDERNESS ADVENTURES PRESS, INC.

Mountain Goat Management Units

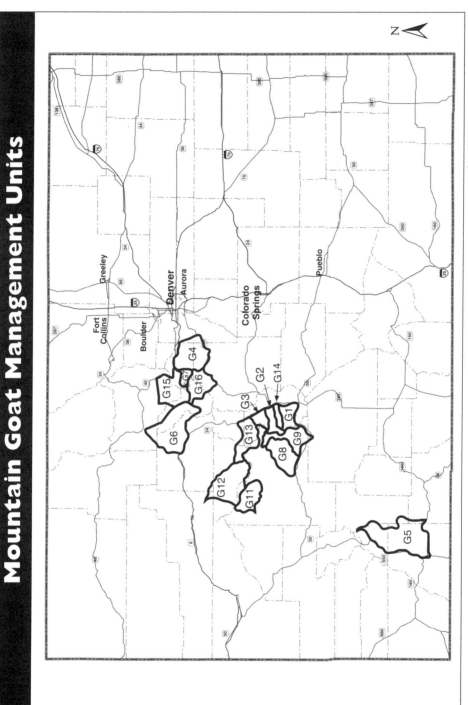

© WILDERNESS ADVENTURES PRESS, INC.

General Regulations

BASIC HUNTING REGULATIONS

Every big game hunter in Colorado should have an understanding of the following basic hunting regulations. In order to eliminate any confusion in translation or interpretation, the following basic hunting regulations are quoted from the *2002 Deer, Elk, Antelope, Black Bear and Moose, Colorado Hunting Information* brochure published by the Colorado Division of Wildlife.

It is against the law to:

- Have a loaded (in the chamber) rifle or shotgun in or on a motor vehicle, including a motorcycle. Muzzleloading rifles cannot be primed, that is, cannot have a percussion cap on the nipple or powder in the flashpan.

- Carry on an OHV (Off Highway Vehicle) during deer, elk, antelope and bear seasons, firearms (except handguns) unless they are unloaded in the chamber and magazine. Firearms (except handguns) and bows carried on an OHV must be fully enclosed in a hard or soft case. Scabbards or cases with open ends or sides are prohibited. This regulation does not apply to landowners or their agents carrying a firearm on an OHV for the purpose of taking depredating wildlife on property owned or leased by them.

- Hunt carelessly or discharge a firearm or release an arrow disregarding human life or property.

- Operate or ride a snowmobile with a firearm unless it's completely unloaded and cased, or with a bow unless it's unstrung or cased. Compound bows must be cased, not unstrung.

- Shoot from or use a motor vehicle, motorcycle, all-terrain vehicle, snowmobile or aircraft to hunt, harass, or drive wildlife.

- Use aircraft to hunt, to direct hunters on the ground or to hunt the same day or day after a flight was made to locate wildlife.

- Hunt under the influence of alcohol or controlled substance.

- Use artificial light to hunt wildlife. Having a firearm with cartridges in the chamber or magazine, or loaded with powder or a ball, or a strung, uncased bow while trying to project artificial light into an area where wildlife can be found is prima facie evidence of a violation.

- Use dogs or bait to hunt bears, deer, elk, antelope or moose. Bait means to put, expose, deposit, distribute or scatter salt, minerals, grain, animal parts or other food so as to constitute a lure, attraction or enticement for big game on or over any area where hunters are attempting to take big game.

- Use poison, drugs or explosives to hunt or harass wildlife.

- Leave a fire that is not completely extinguished.
- Not make a reasonable attempt to track and kill an animal you wounded. If the animal goes on private property, you must try to contact the landowner or person in charge before pursuing it.
- Not wear at least 500 square inches of solid Daylight Fluorescent Orange material in an outer garment above the waist while hunting deer, elk, antelope, bear or moose during a muzzleloading or rifle season. Part of the fluorescent orange must be a hat or head covering visible from all directions. Camouflage orange does not meet this requirement. Mesh garments are legal but not recommended. Bowhunters are not required to wear fluorescent orange during an archery season. The DOW strongly recommends wearing daylight fluorescent orange clothes in the field even if you're not hunting.
- Fail to use edible wildlife meat for human consumption. At a minimum, the four quarters, tenderloins and backstraps are edible meat. Internal organs are not considered edible meat.
- Shoot from, across or on a public road with a firearm, bow or crossbow. People firing a bow, rifle, handgun or shotgun with a single slug must be at least 50 feet from the centerline of the road.
- Party hunt (kill someone else's game or let someone kill your game).
- Interfere with hunters. That includes alarming, distracting or frightening prey; causing prey to flee by using light or noise; chasing prey on foot or by vehicle; throwing objects; making movements; harassing hunters by using threats or actions; erecting barriers to deny access to hunting areas and intentionally injecting yourself into the line of fire. Violators face criminal prosecution and may have to pay damages to the victim, as well as court costs.
- (Felony) Kill and abandon big game wildlife. Taking big game, removing only the hide, antlers or other trophy parts and leaving the carcass in the field are illegal.
- (Felony) Sell, purchase or offer to sell or purchase big game.
- (Felony) Solicit someone to illegally take big game for commercial gain or providing outfitting services without required registration.

If convicted of these felony violations, you may face a lifetime license suspension in Colorado.

LEGAL FIREARMS AND BOWS

Centerfire Rifles—must be .24 caliber (6mm) or larger. The barrel must be at least 16 inches in length, and the entire length of the rifle must be at least 26 inches. Semiautomatic rifles cannot hold more than 6 rounds in the magazine and chamber combined. Fully automatic rifles are prohibited. Bullets must be an expanding type and weigh at least 70 grains for deer, antelope and bear, 85 grains for elk and moose. There is a minimum 1,000 foot/pound requirement for the amount of energy that the bullet expends at impact at 100 yards as rated by the manufacturer.

Note: it is illegal to hunt game birds, small game mammals or furbearers during the combined deer and elk rifle seasons west of Interstate 25 with a centerfire rifle larger than .23 caliber unless you have a deer or elk license for the current combined season.

Muzzleloading Rifles and Smoothbore Muskets—must be single-barrel and fired from the shoulder. They must only be capable of firing a single roundball or conical projectile the length of which does not exceed twice the diameter of the bore. Sabots are prohibited in Colorado, but cloth patches are not considered to be sabots. The minimum caliber requirement for muzzleloaders is .40 caliber for deer, antelope, bear, sheep and goat, and .50 caliber or larger for elk and moose. Bullet weights must be a minimum of 170 grains if fired from a .40 caliber to .50 caliber muzzleloader and 210 grains if fired from a muzzleloader larger than .50 caliber. In-line muzzleloaders are legal in Colorado as long as the appropriate caliber and bullet requirements are followed. However, muzzleloaders that load from the breech are not allowed in Colorado. It is also unallowable to use pelletized powder systems, and a muzzleloader or musket may only have open or iron sites. It is legal to use fiber optic site paints on open sites. In addition to the muzzleloader season, it is legal to use a muzzleloader or musket during the general rifle seasons for the various big game species as long as the minimum caliber and bullet weight requirements are met. In 2002, a new rule was adopted which prohibits smokeless powder during the muzzleloading seasons.

Hand-Held Bows—or compound bows with a string cannot be drawn mechanically or held mechanically under tension. The minimum draw weight to legally hunt big game in Colorado is 35 pounds and the maximum let off allowable on compound bows is 80 percent. No part of the bow's riser (handle) or track, trough, channel, arrow rest or other device (excluding cables and bowstring) that attaches to the riser can contact support and/or guide the arrow from a point rearward of the bow's brace height. Bows can propel only a single arrow at a time, and no mechanism for automatically loading arrows is permitted. Electronic or battery-powered devices cannot be incorporated into or attached to the bow. Hydraulic or pneumatic technology cannot be used to derive or store energy to propel arrows. Finally, it is illegal to use explosive arrows. (Please note, that it is legal to use hand held release aids to draw and release the string.)

Shotguns—must have a barrel at least 18 inches in length, and the overall length must be at least 26 inches. Shotguns must be 20-gauge or larger and fire a single slug. There are currently no separate shotgun seasons in Colorado; shotguns can only be used during the rifle seasons.

Crossbows—must have a minimum draw weight of 125 pounds and a minimum draw length of 14 inches from the front of the bow to the nocking point on the string. Bolts must be at least 16 inches in length and tipped with a broadhead meeting the requirements listed for hand held bows. There are currently no separate crossbow seasons in Colorado. It is illegal to use a crossbow during the archery or muzzleloader seasons. The only time you can hunt big game with a crossbow in Colorado is during one of the rifle seasons.

Handguns—must have a barrel with a minimum length of 4 inches. They must use a .24 caliber or larger expanding bullet. Handguns cannot have a shoulder stock or attachment. There is a minimum energy requirement of 550 foot/pounds at 50 yards. It is legal to carry a handgun while hunting big game as long as it is not concealed. There are currently no separate handgun seasons in Colorado. Handguns can only be used to hunt big game during the rifle seasons.

Duane Redford with a spike in Unit 500 that
had a broken antler. Region 2, South Park GMU.

Residency Qualifications

In order to obtain a resident hunting license in Colorado you must have lived in the state continuously for at least six months prior to applying for or buying a hunting license. Children (under the age of 18) are considered to have the same residency status as their custodial parent or legal guardian.

You may also qualify for a resident license if you are in the U.S. Armed Services, military personnel of U.S. allies, or U.S. Diplomatic Service personnel stationed in Colorado on permanent active duty orders. Also, if you were a resident of the state prior to joining military service and you have not changed the record of your permanent home to another state, you can obtain a resident license. Dependants of military personnel who meet the criteria listed above can also qualify for resident licenses. Reserve status in the armed services does not qualify you for resident licenses, and non-resident National Guard personnel who might be stationed in the state aren't eligible for resident licenses.

Full-time students who are enrolled and attending a Colorado college, university or trade school can also be eligible for resident hunting licenses. They must have been enrolled and attending for at least six months prior to applying for a resident license. Students who are temporarily absent from the state are still eligible if they are still enrolled.

Hunting Hours

Legal hours for hunting big game in Colorado are one-half hour before sunrise to one half-hour after sunset. Hunting is legal seven days a week. Certain state and federal properties may have specific regulations that limit the number of days you can hunt and the legal hours.

Season Participation and Bag Limits

Colorado has specific rules concerning season participation that you need to be aware of before applying for limited licenses, or buying over-the-counter (unlimited) licenses. If you are planning to hunt deer and elk in a combined rifle season, both species must be hunted in the same season (unless exceptions apply). For example, you could not hunt deer in the second combined season and elk in the third combined season. You would have to choose one season to hunt them both. The first rifle season is a limited season for elk only. If you draw an elk tag for this season you would be allowed to hunt deer only in one of the following combined rifle seasons. Also, new for 2002, if you have a fourth-season elk license for units that are open only for elk, you may hunt deer in another combined season.

If you choose to hunt an early season, such as archery, you have the option to hunt both deer and elk then or choose one species and then hunt the second species in one of the later rifle seasons. However, you are limited to only one license per species per year (unless exceptions apply). For example, you could not hunt deer during the archery season and hunt deer again in one of the later rifle seasons even if you didn't fill your archery tag (unless you obtained an "additional license," which will be explained later). Once archery season is over, you would be done deer hunting for the year.

In general the bag limit for big game animals in Colorado is no more than one of each species per year. However, there are exceptions to the one animal bag limit. When available, a hunter can purchase additional licenses each year. An "additional license" can include licenses for special damage hunts or Southern Ute Tribal Land permits if they are available. Chronic Wasting Disease (CWD) management licenses and auction or raffle licenses are also considered "additional." Also, if an animal were harvested during a January or February hunting season established as part of the previous calendar year's hunting season, it would be considered a part of the annual bag limit for the previous year.

The most recent change to the "additional license" designation will go into effect during the 2002 big game hunting seasons. You will be allowed to buy two licenses a year for the same species if at least one of them falls under the following categories: private-land-only bear licenses; private-land-only antelope licenses; private-land-only antlerless deer licenses; and private-land-only antlerless elk licenses.

Also new in 2002 there will be limited antlerless elk licenses designated as "additional licenses." (Remember that in this context "limited" refers to licenses you must apply for in the application process before the hunting season and "unlimited" means licenses that are available to purchase over the counter at sporting goods stores.) These "additional" limited antlerless elk licenses will be available in the following units: 3, 4, 5, 6, 7, 8, 9, 11, 12, 13, 14, 15, 16, 17, 18, 19, 21, 22, 23, 24, 24, 26, 27, 28, 30, 31, 32, 33, 34, 35, 36, 37, 38, 43, 44, 45, 47, 50, 53, 59, 63, 68, 74, 75, 76, 79, 80, 81, 82, 83, 128, 131, 132, 133, 134, 135, 136, 137, 138, 139, 141, 142, 143, 144, 145, 147, 161, 171, 181, 191, 211, 214, 231, 301, 371, 441, 444, 471, 500, 501, 511, 512, 581, 591, and 681.

There will also be unlimited either-sex elk licenses designated as "additional licenses" in the following units: 87, 88, 89, 90, 91, 92, 93, 94, 95, 96, 97, 98, 99, 100, 101, 102, 951.

In 2002 there are also "additional licenses" for antlerless deer in the following units: 7, 8, 9, 19, 20, 29, 191. (Remember you must apply for all deer licenses unless special exceptions apply.) Each antlerless deer license for these units will include two carcass tags.

Unlimited antlerless deer licenses are available in Unit 9 during 2002, and there will be leftover late-season licenses in Units 19 and 191 this year.

Although variable from season to season there may be the opportunity to purchase more than one "additional license" for specific units. For the 2002 season a person could buy an unrestricted number of leftover, private-land-only, antlerless elk licenses for Units 391 and 461. Obviously you would have to have permission to hunt private land in Unit 391 or 461 to legally use one of those licenses.

The DOW also generates a list of leftover licenses after the official drawing each year. If you didn't get a tag through the big game drawing, leftover licenses offer another opportunity to get a tag. In order to purchase one of these licenses you will have to go to a DOW office in person. The licenses are usually sold on a first-come, first-served basis.

Many of the "additional" deer licenses have been made available in an effort to control the spread of CWD, and many of the "additional" elk licenses have been made available to meet management objectives where elk numbers are high.

Since management objectives change from year to year be sure to check the hunting brochures carefully to determine where "additional licenses" apply. For 2002 at least, there will be opportunities to bag more animals than normally allowed in previous hunting seasons.

New Licensing System

As early as fall 2002 the DOW may begin selling hunting and fishing licenses through a new system referred to as the "Total Licensing System." This system should expedite the purchase of hunting and fishing licenses from license agents. It will also make licenses available over the Internet as early as 2003. Check with the DOW for updates on the new system.

Two-Way Radio Communication

Air to ground radio communication during big game hunting is illegal; however, there is currently no regulation that addresses two-way radio communication on the ground. Hunters can legally use hand-held radios to communicate with each other on the ground when hunting in Colorado. This does bring up an ethics issue, and hunters will have to decide for themselves if the use of radios to help guide hunters to animals is fair chase. There is some discussion of amending the current regulations to address two-way radio communications. Check the regulations each year prior to hunting.

OHV (Off Highway Vehicle) Restrictions and Registration

OHVs, often referred to as all-terrain vehicles (ATVs), must be registered in Colorado. Residents and non-residents can obtain an OHV permit through the Colorado State Parks Registration Unit, 13787 S. Highway 85, Littleton, CO 80125, (303) 791-1920. It is also possible to register at state park regional offices as well as most OHV dealers. Non-residents who possess a valid OHV registration or license from another state can use their OHV for 30 consecutive days in Colorado before obtaining a permit. After that they need to obtain a non-resident OHV permit. The permit fee for both residents and non-residents is $15.25. For more information concerning valid registrations or licenses from another state please contact the State Parks Registration Unit.

OHV use is regulated the same as motor vehicles on DOW, Forest Service, and BLM lands. Motor vehicles and OHVs are only allowed on established roads and trails that are marked open for use. They are illegal in wilderness areas. The only time an OHV or motor vehicle can be driven off an established road or trail is when the governing land management agency allows it. Hunting, harassing, pursuing, or chasing wildlife with an OHV is illegal.

Starting in 2000, it became illegal to carry a firearm or bow on an OHV unless it was unloaded and cased. (This regulation does not apply to handguns.) Unloaded means no ammunition in the magazine or the chamber. Furthermore, the case has to be fully enclosed, although it can be a hard or soft case. Scabbard type cases with open ends are not legal. These regulations do not apply to landowners or their agents who use an OHV while taking depredating wildlife on property that they own or lease.

BEAR HUNTING RESTRICTIONS

It is illegal to use dogs or baits to aid in hunting black bears. (Refer to the Basic Hunting Regulations section for a definition of bait.) Scents are not considered baits. It is illegal to sell or trade bear gallbladders or meat. It is also illegal to kill cubs or any bear that is accompanied by one or more cubs. A cub is defined as a bear less than one year in age. Although there are currently no known populations of grizzly bears in Colorado, it is illegal to kill a grizzly bear.

Black bears can vary dramatically in color from light brown to cinnamon to black.

Mandatory Inspections and Seals

If you are lucky enough to harvest a bear you must present it (unfrozen hide and skull) in person to the DOW for inspection and sealing within five working days of the kill. It is illegal to possess a bear hide after five days without a seal from the DOW. If you fail to get the seal the bear becomes the property of the state, even if you had a valid hunting license to harvest the bear. It is also illegal to transport a bear out of the state prior to obtaining a seal. The seal should remain on the hide until it is tanned.

If you need to transport the bear out of the country after getting the DOW seal, you must get a CITES document through the U.S. Fish and Wildlife Service. They can be reached in Denver at (303) 236-7540.

Mandatory inspections are also required for mountain lion, mountain goats, and bighorn sheep. Inspections for these species must also be made within five working days of the kill. Bighorn sheep and mountain goat hunters will also be required to remit a completed questionnaire to the DOW within 30 days of the end of the hunting season that they participated in. This questionnaire is required whether you harvest a sheep or goat or not. If you fail to fill it out and return it, you will not be eligible for future sheep or goat licenses.

It is illegal to possess any part of a bear or mountain lion unless the animal was taken by a licensed hunter in an established season or unless you have authorization from the DOW.

Starting in 2002 it will not be mandatory for moose hunters who kill an antlered moose to personally present the antlers to a DOW office or officer. However, a completed questionnaire must be provided by successful as well as unsuccessful moose hunters within 30 days after the season ends. As is the case with sheep and goat surveys, if you don't provide the survey you won't be eligible for future moose hunts.

The lifetime bag limit for antlered moose is one unless you are able to obtain an auction or raffle license.

Chronic Wasting Disease

As many hunters are aware, Chronic Wasting Disease (CWD) has been a growing concern over the past few years. The recent media attention both locally and nationally has put some hunters in a panic mode. The facts are that CWD has been around for decades, and there have been no cases of the disease being transmitted to humans. There is also no evidence that CWD infects domestic cattle. This doesn't mean you should ignore it. A better approach is to use common sense and follow the precautions listed in the DOW hunting brochures.

The first and best method to avoid contacting an animal with CWD is not to shoot an animal that appears to be sick. If you see an animal that exhibits unusual symptoms such as emaciation, abnormal behavior, or excessive salivating, simply don't shoot it. Secondly, the DOW suggests wearing rubber gloves when cleaning a deer or elk that has been harvested in a unit where CWD has been identified. This is a good idea anyway. The pathogen responsible for the disease is not known to reside in muscle tissue, but is probably most prevalent in the brain and spinal tissue of the animal. As a result, the DOW recommends that hunters avoid handling the brain or spinal tissue, and although most of us wouldn't in the first place, don't eat the brain, spinal cord, eyes, spleen, tonsils, or lymph nodes. Lastly, bone out the meat instead of cutting bone-in steaks.

In order to help prevent the spread of CWD the DOW is requiring hunters to leave the gut-pile and other inedible portions in the field where you harvested the animal in units where CWD is known to exist. Only remove the meat, cleaned hides, and cleaned skull plates in these units. The bottom line is we don't want to spread the disease, so don't transport a carcass from a CWD area and field dress it or dispose of the parts in a non-CWD area.

In an attempt to control the disease and learn more about the extent of infection, the DOW is taking several steps. There is a voluntary CWD surveillance program in place for several units and there are new regulations under review that could limit the transportation of deer and elk carcasses out of CWD affected areas. There will also be special CWD hunts during the 2002 season. Unlimited antlerless licenses are available in Unit 9 from September 1 to January 31.

The primary units of concern are in the northeastern part of the state and include 7, 8, 9, 191, 19, 20, 29, 88, 89, 91, 93, 94, 95, 951, and 96. If you have a license for deer or elk in one of these units, the DOW may contact you by mail before the hunting season concerning a voluntary surveillance program for CWD.

If you want to conduct your own research on CWD a good source of information is the Colorado Department of Public Health and Environment (303) 692-2700. If you think you have seen or harvested an animal with CWD contact the DOW at (970) 472-4300. The DOW web site also has a great deal of information on CWD at wildlife.state.co.us/hunt/Hunter Education/chronic.asp.

Rules, regulations, and management objectives will go through many changes in the next few years in regard to CWD. Check the hunting brochure each year for more details.

CHECK STATIONS AND DECOY EFFORTS

The DOW sets up several check stations during the big game hunting seasons each year. The stations are often located at state boundaries and are sometimes operated in cooperation with other states. These stations are generally found in areas where hunters are likely to be traveling. The DOW operates the stations to gather biological information and enforce laws. According to the *2002 Deer, Elk, Antelope, Black Bear and Moose* brochure, "All vehicles must stop whether or not they are transporting big game." If you are stopped, the DOW will check you thoroughly. Among other things, they will want to verify that you have the appropriate license, that the carcass tag is correctly attached, that the appropriate weapon was used, that there is evidence of sex, and that there was no waste of meat.

The DOW also sets up lifelike decoys every year to tempt big game hunters into making mistakes. Regardless of whether you believe this is entrapment or not, be aware that it is done. You need to make some decisions before you go hunting because temptation can sway even honest sportsmen into making a mistake. It is not hard to understand why hunters are ensnared by decoy efforts. Many people save all of their vacation time for one hunt each year. Then after hunting hard and legally all season without any luck they happen to see a nice buck out in a field off the road. They're not sure if the property is private or public, but the thought doesn't even cross their mind when they see the big buck they've been looking for. They get out of the vehicle and begin to shoot before the animal runs. Suddenly, several DOW officers appear and apprehend the new criminal.

In 1999 the DOW made 33 decoy efforts. Out of 649 vehicles, 70 stopped and 34 individual charges were written for a total of $3,600 in fines. If you have already decided that you won't road hunt, and you won't pursue an animal on property that you don't have permission to hunt on, then you won't be tempted when you run across that big buck decoy standing out in a field.

Horses and Hay

Hunters who bring horses into the state need to obtain a Certificate of Health Inspection 30 days prior to entering Colorado. Horses must also have a Coggins Blood Test for equine infectious anemia within a year before entering the state. For more information contact the Colorado State Veterinarian's office at (303) 239-4161.

If you bring hay, straw, or mulch onto federal lands or DOW properties to feed your horse, the materials must be certified as noxious weed-free. For more information contact the Colorado Department of Agriculture at (303) 239-4140.

Colorado is a certified weed-free state.

GUIDES AND OUTFITTERS

In order to operate legally on federal lands, guides and outfitters must have the appropriate permit. They are also required to register with the Office of Outfitter Registration. If you have retained an outfitter to help you with a hunt you can contact the Office of Outfitter Registration to find out if the outfitter has ever incurred any violations. Always ask for their license number prior to booking a hunt. You can contact the Office of Outfitter Registration at 1560 Broadway, Suite 1340, Denver, CO 80202, (303) 894-7778, or on the Internet at www.dora.state.us/outfitters.

DAYLIGHT FLUORESCENT ORANGE

You must wear at least 500 square inches of solid, daylight fluorescent orange material in an outer garment while hunting during the rifle and muzzleloader seasons for deer, elk, bear, antelope, and moose in Colorado. It must be worn above the waist and part of it must be worn on the head in the form of a hat or head covering. Orange camouflage does not meet the requirement. However, fluorescent orange mesh garments can be worn, although the DOW does not recommend them.

Bowhunters are not required to wear fluorescent orange during the archery seasons. You should be aware that muzzleloader season for deer and elk overlaps with the archery season. Bowhunters still don't have to wear orange during this overlap, but muzzleloader hunters do. If you choose to use a bow during a rifle season you must still wear fluorescent orange.

SCENTS AND CALLS

Scent attractants are legal to use in Colorado to hunt big game, but bait is not legal. Please refer to the section on *Basic Hunting Regulations* for a description of bait. Mechanical calls, such as mouth calls, are legal to use in Colorado. However, electronic calls, such as amplified cassette recordings, are not legal to use while hunting big game.

ACCIDENTAL KILL OF A BIG GAME ANIMAL

The DOW considers a big game animal to be accidentally taken if the kill was unintentionally made and was not due to carelessness or negligence. If you accidentally shoot the wrong species or sex of a big game animal while hunting you are supposed to report the incident to the DOW as soon as practical prior to continuing to hunt. The DOW will investigate the incident to determine if it was an accident. They will look at the circumstances involved, which may include the number of shots fired, the species and number of animals present, the firearms and ammunition used, shot angle and distance, topography, and weather.

If any of the circumstances of the incident indicate that there was carelessness or negligence you will likely receive a ticket. Much of the decision will be left to the discretion of the investigating officer. If you accidentally kill a big game animal and you do not report it to the DOW, you will face much more severe penalties if caught.

MOST COMMON HUNTING VIOLATIONS

According to an article by Brad Frano in a recent years issue of *Colorado Outdoors*, the ten most common hunting violations and associated fines were as follows:

Hunting Violation	Fine	*Points
1. Loaded firearm in a vehicle	$68	15
2. Hunting without a proper or valid license	$342	15
3. Trespassing–hunting without permission on private property	$137	20
4. Shooting from a public road	$ 68	5
5. Failure to tag a harvested animal	$ 68	10
6. Unlawful weapon	$ 68	5
7. Failure to wear daylight fluorescent orange	$137	10
8. Failure to leave evidence of sex (big game)	$137	10
9. Waste of game meat (big game)	$411	15
10. Hunting before or after legal hours	$68	5

*Colorado uses a point system similar to that used for a driver's license. If you receive a hunting violation you will receive a fine and a number of points will be deducted from your license. If you receive violations amounting to 20 points or more, your hunting license will be suspended.

Mule deer in the Great Sand Dunes National Monument in the San Luis Valley.

Procedures to Follow After Harvesting an Animal

Carcass Tag

When hunting in Colorado you will have a license, which is a stamp that is affixed to a Conservation Certificate. (Detailed information on Conservation Certificates is included in the section on General Licensing Information). In addition to the license you will receive a carcass tag. The tag can be separated into two pieces along a perforated line. Immediately upon harvesting an animal you are required to detach the validation strip along the perforated line and sign the back of the tag. You must also punch out the correct sex, month, and day of the kill on the tag. Be sure to do this before you do anything else.

According to the instructions on the back of the carcass tag, once you have validated your license you can place it back in your pocket while you process the animal. This means that you are not required to affix the carcass tag until you have cleaned the animal and/or drug it out. This stipulation was included so that people would not attach the tag then lose it while cleaning or packing the animal out. Keep in mind that if you have to leave the carcass for any reason you must affix the tag before you leave, even if you have to temporarily leave it at the kill site. This is considered storage.

Prior to transporting the carcass by vehicle or storing it you must attach the tag. The DOW recommends using wire or cord, and the tag must be attached in a way that makes it readily visible for inspection. Furthermore, the tag is supposed to be attached to the carcass, not the antlers.

It should go without saying, but once you have validated the tag you cannot use it again. Also, if your tag is lost, destroyed, or inadvertently detached at the perforation you can't hunt until you get a replacement tag. The only way to do this is to go to a DOW service center and prove that the loss, destruction, or detachment was accidental.

You should be aware that once the carcass tag is attached to the big game animal it should remain attached to the meat until processing. If you choose to have the meat processed by a commercial butcher they will require the carcass tag when you drop the meat off. If you try to drop off game meat without a tag, a call will probably be made to the DOW since there is no way to prove that the animal wasn't poached.

Properly attaching the carcass tag is a relatively straightforward and uncomplicated process. Still, failure to properly tag a big game animal was the fifth most common violation during the 1999 big game hunting season. In your excitement after harvesting an animal, don't forget to validate the tag, and when appropriate, properly affix it to the carcass.

EVIDENCE OF SEX

Another common violation each hunting season is failure to leave evidence of sex naturally attached. As stated in the *2002 Deer, Elk, Antelope, Black Bear and Moose* brochure published by the DOW, evidence of sex is:

Buck/Bull: Head attached to carcass with antlers or horns, or attached testicle, scrotum or penis.

Doe/Cow: Head attached to carcass, udder (mammary) or vulva.

Black Bear: Male bear: testicles or baculum. Female bear: vulva.

Please keep in mind that the DOW does not consider an unattached head evidence of sex.

If the carcass has been cut up or de-boned prior to transportation, evidence of sex should remain on a quarter or on another major part of the carcass. You must transport all of the individual pieces together.

ANTLER POINT RESTRICTIONS

You should be aware that many of the game management units in Colorado have antler point restrictions for elk. In units that have antler point restrictions bull elk are required to have four points or more on at least one antler. It is also legal to harvest a bull in a 4-point area that has a brow tine at least five inches in length. Antler point restrictions can change in units each year. Be sure to refer to the big game hunting brochure to determine if you are hunting in a unit that has a 4-point minimum requirement for elk. During the 2000 hunting season antler point restrictions were eliminated for deer.

Count the antler points and check the regulations carefully
for the game management unit you are hunting.

TRANSPORTING GAME

To legally transport harvested game animals in Colorado the carcass tag must be properly attached to the meat and evidence of sex must be naturally attached. Since Colorado has point restrictions for bull elk, the head must also accompany the carcass even if the testicle, scrotum, or penis is attached for evidence of sex. The antlers should remain naturally attached to the skull plate during transportation. If you want to drop the head off at a taxidermists shop before transporting the rest of the carcass home or to a butcher, you must get a receipt from the taxidermist that lists the date of delivery and describes the antlers. The carcass tag should also remain with processed meat during transportation. If you are transporting game for another hunter, you could be held liable if the carcass tag, evidence of sex, or antler point requirements are not met.

If you transport illegally taken game animals across state lines, it is a violation of the Federal Lacy Act. Violation of this act could result in fines up to $20,000 and up to five years in prison.

DONATING GAME MEAT

It is possible to donate game meat to a hunter or non-hunter, but there are several requirements. To understand the rules you must know that the definition of a "like license," which is a license for exactly the same species, sex, season and method of hunting as a donor's licenses. With that understood, the following rules apply:

A person without a like license can receive up to 20 pounds of unprocessed meat at any location. Over 20 pounds of unprocessed meat can only be donated at the recipient's home.

A person with a like license can receive up to 20 pounds of unprocessed meat at any location. You can donate over 20 pounds of unprocessed meat to a person with a like license at any location as long as the following conditions are met. The recipient's license must be unfilled, and the recipient must place his/her own carcass tag on the meat. If this is done the recipient has in effect validated the tag and given up the opportunity to continue hunting for that particular species in that season. The donor's carcass tag should remain with the portion of meat that he/she keeps.

An entire carcass can be donated to a person with a like license if the donor's tag and the recipient's tag are both attached to the carcass. Both the donor and recipient are done hunting for that species in that season.

It is legal to donate any amount of processed and packaged meat to anybody at any location.

All donations require a donation certificate from the donor to the recipient. There is no standard form, so a handwritten note from the donor is appropriate. At a minimum the note should contain the names, addresses and telephone numbers of donor and recipient, the hunting license number of the donor, the species and amounts of meat donated, and the date the animal was killed. Finally, the donor must sign the note to make it valid. This note must be kept with the meat until it is all consumed.

Hunter Education

In order to legally obtain a hunting license in Colorado you must have completed an approved hunter education course if you were born after January 1, 1949. If you were born before January 1, 1949, you can get a license without a hunter education card. Since Colorado currently does not require mandatory bowhunter education classes, you can obtain either a rifle or archery license after completing an approved hunter education course. An approved bowhunter education course will only allow you to purchase an archery license.

Non-residents can obtain a Colorado hunting license if they have completed an approved hunter education course sanctioned by another state or province. Regardless of your residency status, you are required to present your hunter's safety card when purchasing an over-the-counter license. Presenting a license from another state or a previous hunting season that lists your hunter's safety card number is not adequate to obtain an over-the-counter license.

When hunting in Colorado you are required to have your hunter's safety card with you at all times. The only time this doesn't apply is if the words "Proof of Hunter Education Verified" are printed by the DOW on your Conservation Certificate.

Property Laws

Permission to Hunt Big Game

It is illegal to hunt on private property without first obtaining permission from the landowner or the person in charge of the land. For your own protection, it is recommended that you receive permission in writing. Also, if you are seeking permission to hunt on private land you should do it in advance of the hunting season or before applying for limited licenses.

Trespass

In 1999, trespassing was the third most common violation that hunters committed. Trespassing is a serious infraction. If you are caught you will likely receive a $137 fine and a 20-point violation, which will cause suspension of your hunting license. It is the hunter's responsibility to ensure that he/she is not trespassing. Ignorance is not a valid excuse.

Posting Requirements

Although there is no lack of private property signs in Colorado, landowners are not required to post the boundaries of their property. It is up to you to determine where public and private property boundaries are. This can be very difficult to determine. The best approach is to refer to the BLM Surface Management Status Maps that depict many of the public land boundaries. Be aware that property boundaries can change over time, so be sure to refer to a recent map. If the maps are not detailed enough to determine whether or not property is public or private, you will either have to stay off the property or do additional research. County land plats may be helpful, or you may want to try to contact property owners in the area you intend to hunt.

Although it is rare, if you find land that you believe is inaccurately posted, contact the local authorities. It is illegal to improperly post public lands as private. Furthermore, it is illegal to prevent people from accessing public lands on public roads. If you find a public road with a locked gate and there is no signage to explain the closure, contact the authorities. In both cases you will want to contact the authorities before trying to gain access to the property in question.

LAND-USE RESTRICTIONS

It is illegal to hunt on State Land Board properties unless the DOW has obtained the property and opened it to hunting. A list of state trust lands open to hunting or fishing is provided in the *Supplement to the Colorado Wildlife Property Directory STATE TRUST LANDS 1997-2000*. An updated directory was available as of 2001. These directories are available at DOW service centers and at some license agents.

National Parks and National Monuments are closed to big game hunting. State wildlife areas that allow big game hunting may have special restrictions. A complete list of state wildlife areas is available in the *2002 Colorado Fishing Season Information and Wildlife Property Directory* at DOW service centers or license agents.

State Parks and State Recreation Areas may or may not be open to big game hunting. Contact each park directly to determine if hunting is allowed. You can also contact the Colorado Division of Parks and Recreation at 1313 Sherman Street, Room 618, Denver, CO 80203; (303) 866-3437.

There are four national wildlife refuges in Colorado. Big game hunting may be allowed during certain seasons, but special restrictions may apply. For more information contact each refuge directly:

Alamosa NWR – Box 1148, Alamosa, CO 81101, (719) 589-4021

Arapaho NWR – Box 457, Walden, CO 80480, (970) 723-8202

Browns Park NWR – 1318 Hwy. 318, Maybell, CO 81640, (970) 365-3613

Monte Vista NWR – c/Alamosa NWR, Box 1148, Alamosa, CO 81101, (719) 589-4021

There are two Indian Reservations in Colorado. Hunting by non-tribal members is currently not allowed on either Reservation. For more information see the section on Hunting on Indian Reservations.

According to the *2002 Deer, Elk, Antelope, Black Bear and Moose* brochure published by the DOW, the following closures and land-use restrictions also apply:

Hunting is prohibited ½ mile either side of the centerline of the Mt. Evans Hwy. (Colo. 5) from Echo Lake to the summit, all of Summit Lake Cirque and most of Summit Lake flats.

Hunting is prohibited within 50 feet of the centerline of a federal, state, or county road or highway. Lands between divided highways are closed to hunting.

Hunting is prohibited in the Gore Creek drainage south of I-70 from the Lions Head ski lift at Vail, to I-70 and US 24. Hunting is also prohibited north of I-70 and within ½ mile of I-70 between Vail and I-70 and US 24.

Moose hunting is prohibited ¼ mile north and ½ mile south of Hwy. 14 in Jackson County from Cameron Pass west to Forest Rd. 740 at Gould.

Patience and stealth will pay dividends when stalking big game animals.

General Licensing Information

When hunting big game in Colorado every hunter is required to have a Conservation Certificate (CC). The CC is not a license, but it is a document containing pertinent information about the hunter. It contains much of the same information as a driver's license plus your hunter education certification number. You can obtain a CC by presenting your hunter education card at a licensing agent or at a DOW service center. You must have a CC in order to obtain hunting and fishing licenses in Colorado. If you are a non-resident you can fill out a CC application and mail it to the DOW.

Once you have a CC you can purchase over-the-counter big game licenses or apply for limited licenses. Once you receive a license it will consist of a stamp that you affix to your CC and a carcass tag. You must possess the CC, the license, the carcass tag, and your hunter's safety card while hunting in Colorado. The only exception is that you are not required to possess a hunter's safety card if you were born before January 1, 1949, or your CC has "Proof of Hunter Education Verified" printed on it by the DOW.

OVER-THE-COUNTER LICENSES

"Unlimited" refers to big game licenses that are sold over the counter at DOW service centers and license agents. Starting in 2000 there have been no unlimited licenses for deer. In addition to deer, bighorn sheep, mountain goat, and moose licenses were totally limited. In order to obtain one of these licenses you had to fill out an application and submit it for the limited license drawing.

Depending on the unit, weapon, sex, and season there were unlimited licenses available for elk, antelope, and bear. To determine what seasons and which units had unlimited licenses you must refer to the big game hunting brochure published by the DOW. Mountain lion licenses are unlimited, but there is a quota system that determines how many animals may be harvested from each unit. Prior to hunting mountain lions you must first contact the DOW at 1-888-940-LION (5466) to determine if there are still quotas available in the unit you wish to hunt.

The advantage of obtaining an unlimited license is that it does not restrict you to a specific unit. You can hunt any unit open to unlimited licenses as listed in the big game hunting brochure.

LIMITED LICENSES AND PREFERENCE POINTS

Limited licenses are obtained through the annual drawing. The DOW uses harvest data and population statistics to determine how many licenses will be available for certain GMUs. Because habitat and management practices often lead to higher quality in these units, demand is very high for the limited number of licenses. As a result, there are often fewer licenses available than the number of hunters applying. When this happens you will generally need one or more preference points before drawing the license. For limited deer, elk, antelope, and bear licenses a hunter receives one preference point every time he/she is unsuccessful in the drawing. Depending on the demand for limited licenses in a given unit, it could take anywhere from 0 to 10 points to draw. If there are more licenses available for a unit than applicants, this unit is considered undersubscribed. Leftover licenses from undersubscribed units are sometimes offered to hunters after the general drawing. To find out what licenses are left over you can contact the DOW at (303) 291-7519 to hear a recorded listing.

Moose hunters can accrue no more than three preference points under the current system. Once a hunter gets three points his/her name is basically thrown into a hat with the rest of the hunters who have three points and the licenses are assigned based on a random drawing.

Prior to 2001, the bighorn sheep and mountain goat preference point system was the same as the moose system. You still accumulate three points, but every year after three you get a weighted point that is also tracked. In effect, the more times you put in after three years, the more likely you will draw. It is possible to draw a goat or sheep tag with fewer than three points in certain units if you are willing to apply for a ewe tag as a first choice. You may also draw with fewer than three points in the unlikely event that you applied for an undersubscribed unit.

Each application allows you to choose a first choice and second choice hunt code. If you are unsuccessful in the first choice you have a chance to draw the second unit you have applied for. Another catch is that you can apply for only a preference point. There is a special hunt code that allows this. You still have to send in the application and the cost of the license, but you are guaranteed one preference point. The license fee is refunded to you after the drawing if you apply for only a preference point, or if you are unsuccessful in the draw.

A good approach for hunters who have not accumulated enough preference points to hunt the unit they desire is to apply for a first choice preference point, then apply for a unit with better chances of drawing as a second choice. If you draw a second choice license you do not lose any of your preference points. However, if you draw a license with a first choice you lose all of your accumulated points. Many hunters make the mistake every year of applying for a license as a first choice that only requires one or two points, even though they have already accumulated several points. When this happens they still lose all of their points. Also keep in mind that you lose any accrued preference points if you do not apply for that species in a period of five years.

If you're not familiar with Colorado's limited license system, you are probably wondering how to determine how many preference points it takes to draw a license for a certain unit. This information is available on the DOW website www.dnr.state.co.us/wildlife. There is also a product available from the DOW on CD-ROM known as *Colorado Outdoors Big Game CD* that provides several years of DOW hunting statistics.

If you're new to the limited licenses system and you're not thoroughly confused already, hang in there, it's not quite as bad as it may seem. You just need to understand that the point system is a game that all hunters have to play in Colorado each year to get the licenses they want.

LANDOWNER PREFERENCE

A way to beat the limited license game is to obtain a tag through a private landowner. As many as 15 percent of the antelope, deer, and elk licenses available for totally limited units are allocated to landowners each year. In order to be eligible a landowner must have a minimum of 160 acres, and the land must be used primarily for agricultural purposes. The species for which preference is sought must also use the land for the greater portion of the year. The land must also be within the GMU for which the application is made. Once you have identified a private landowner with property that conforms to the requirements, you must obtain an affidavit and application from the DOW and have the landowner fill them out. This may sound complicated, but it is one method that could allow you to hunt a limited unit more frequently than if you applied for it in the limited drawing. See the DOW big game hunting brochure for additional stipulations for Landowner Preference.

YOUTH BIG GAME LICENSES
AND YOUTH PREFERENCE

Youths must be at least 12 years old to legally hunt in Colorado, and they must meet the hunter education requirements. License fees for youths between the ages of 12 and 15 are reduced. An 11-year-old can apply for a big game license as long as he will turn 12 before he goes hunting. A mentor must accompany a youth, and the mentor must be able to see and hear the youth at all times during the hunt. Mentors do not have to hunt to accompany a youth, but they must be at least 18 years of age. Furthermore, they must meet hunter education requirements.

As many as 15 percent of the doe antelope and antlerless deer and elk licenses are set aside for youths between the ages of 12 and 15. Youths must apply for these licenses through the regular limited license drawing. Any licenses that aren't drawn by youths are provided to the general public.

*A twelve-year-old
with his first deer.*

Seasons and Licenses by Species

In June of 1999, the Colorado Wildlife Commission made policy decisions for the five-year big game hunting season structure for the period from 2000 to 2004. The final text of the season structure was adopted on November 18, 1999. The following season dates for deer, elk, antelope, moose, and bear were obtained from the *5-Year Big Game Season Structure Final Policy Statements.* Please be aware that season dates are subject to change in the case that special management objectives are required. As demonstrated in the past three years, several season structure changes have taken place to meet management objectives.

Early Deer and Elk Season

Archery Deer and Elk Seasons – West of I-25 and Unit 140

2002:	August 31 through September 29
2003:	August 30 through September 28
2004:	August 28 through September 26

Note: All archery deer licenses are limited either sex or limited buck only assigned by GMU or DAU. This means that you will have to choose the GMU you want to hunt in and apply through the annual drawing to obtain a deer license. Elk archery licenses include unlimited either-sex or limited either-sex licenses, which are issued by GMU or DAU. Again, if you want a limited archery elk license you will have to apply.

Muzzleloading Deer and Elk Seasons – West of I-25 and Unit 140

2002:	September 14 through September 22
2003:	September 13 through September 21
2004:	September 11 through September 19

Note: All muzzleloading deer and elk licenses are limited and you must apply through the drawing to get a license.

High Country Deer Seasons

2002:	September 7 through September 15
2003:	September 6 through September 14
2004:	September 4 through September 12

Note: The High Country Deer Season is a good opportunity to hunt with a rifle in an early season. A few GMUs in high country areas and wilderness areas have this season. Licenses for this season are completely limited.

Regular Rifle Deer and Elk Season

For the five-year season structure there will be four separate rifle seasons each year. These will include a Separate Limited Elk season followed by three combined deer and elk seasons. Season dates are as follows:

2002:	Separate Limited Elk Season	October 12 - October 16
	First Combined Deer and Elk Season	October 19 - October 25
	Second Combined Deer and Elk Season	November 2 - November 8
	Third Combined Deer and Elk Season	November 9 - November 13
2003:	Separate Limited Elk Season	October 11 - October 15
	First Combined Deer and Elk Season	October 18 - October 24
	Second Combined Deer and Elk Season	November 1 - November 7
	Third Combined Deer and Elk Season	November 8 - November 12
2004:	Separate Limited Elk Season	October 9 - October 15
	First Combined Deer and Elk Season	October 16 - October 22
	Second Combined Deer and Elk Season	October 30 - November 5
	Third Combined Deer and Elk Season	November 6 - November 10

Note: Deer licenses are completely limited regardless of the season. Elk licenses are totally limited for the first Separate Elk Season. There are both unlimited (over-the-counter) and limited licenses available for the three combined rifle seasons. Check the big game hunting brochure each year to determine which units can be hunted with over-the-counter licenses and which units require a limited license obtained through the drawing.

Plains Muzzleloading Deer – East of I-25 except Unit 140

2002:	October 12 through October 20
2003:	October 11 through October 19
2004:	October 9 through October 17

Note: All Plains Muzzleloading Deer licenses are limited.

Plains Regular Rifle Deer Season – East of I-25 except Unit 140

2002:	October 26 through November 5
2003:	October 25 through November 4
2004:	October 23 through November 2

Note: All Plains Regular Rifle Deer licenses are limited.

Late Deer and Elk Season

In order to avoid overlap between late plains archery and rifle deer hunting, there will be two or three splits in the late plains archery deer season depending on which GMU you choose to hunt. Refer to the big game hunting brochure each season to determine which splits apply to which units. The following season dates for Late Plains Archery Deer include the three split season scenario followed by the two split season scenario. All late season archery deer tags are limited.

Late Plains Archery Deer Season – East of I-25 except Unit 140

2002: October 1 – October 25 and November 6 – November 30 and December 15 – December 31, or
October 1 – October 25 and November 6 – December 31

2003: October 1 – October 24 and November 5 – November 30 and December 15 – December 31, or
October 1 – October 24 and November 5 – December 31

2004: October 1 – October 22 and November 3 – November 30 and December 15 – December 31, or
October 1 – October 22 and November 3 – December 31

Late Plains Rifle Deer Season

2002 to 2004: December 1 through December 14 annually.

Note: All Late Plains Rifle Deer licenses are limited. The season will be the same each year for the five-year season structure.

Late Rifle Elk Seasons

2002 to 2004: November 16 through January 31.

Note: The late rifle elk season licenses are for antlerless elk only and completely limited. This season is specifically designed to achieve population objectives on an as-needed basis. Different GMUs may or may not be open to this season each year. The length of the season will be variable, but will fall within the dates listed above. Refer to the big game hunting brochure each year to determine the availability of late season rifle elk licenses.

Private Land Only Deer and Elk Season

There are two season scenarios for Private Land Only (PLO) licenses. The first is for limited antlerless or either-sex deer and limited antlerless or either-sex elk. The second is for antlered deer and either-sex elk. These seasons are variable by GMU/DAU from year to year and are used to achieve population goals and/or distribute the opportunity to hunt bucks/bulls between private and public lands.

Private Land Only Deer and Elk

2002 to 2004: September 1 through January 31 (season length is variable and set annually). Applies to antlerless, either-sex deer and elk, issued by GMU/DAU.

2002 to 2004: Concurrent with the regular rifle seasons, including plains regular rifle seasons (units variable and set annually). Applies to deer and either-sex elk.

Antelope Season

Archery Antelope

2002 to 2004: August 15 through August 31, annually for bucks only, September 1 through September 20, annually for either sex.

Note: Some archery antelope licenses are limited, and others are unlimited. Refer to the big game hunting brochure each year to determine which units have limited or unlimited licenses. An over-the-counter archery antelope license allows you to hunt for bucks only during the first part of the season. If you haven't harvested a buck by September 1, you can hunt for either sex until the end of the season. You must choose which sex you want to hunt for limited antelope licenses in units that offer both buck and doe tags.

Muzzleloading Antelope

2002 to 2004: October 21 through October 29, annually.

Note: All muzzleloader licenses are limited for bucks or does. The licenses are good statewide except in closed units. Refer to the big game hunting brochure each year to determine which units are closed.

Rifle Antelope

The Rifle Antelope season dates vary between two geographic regions in the state. Rifle licenses are completely limited for buck or doe and issued by GMU/DAU.

North of I-70 and US 36		South of I-70 and US 36	
2002:	September 28 – October 4	2002:	October 5 – October 11
2003:	September 27 – October 3	2003:	October 4 – October 10
2004:	September 25 – October 1	2004:	October 2 – October 8

Moose Season

Archery Moose Season
      2002:   September 7 through September 29
      2003:   September 6 through September 28
      2004:   September 11 through September 26

Muzzleloading Moose Season
      2002:   September 14 through September 22
      2003:   September 13 through September 21
      2004:   September 11 through September 19

Rifle Moose Season
      2002 to 2004:   October 1 through October 9 annually.

Note: All moose licenses (regardless of season) are limited

Black Bear Season

You can obtain a bear license one of two ways. First, you can apply for a limited license for a specific GMU through the drawing. Second, you can buy an unlimited license (over-the-counter) during your archery, muzzleloading, or regular rifle deer or elk season in the same units as you are hunting deer or elk.

Archery Bear
      2002:   September 2 through September 29
      2003:   September 2 through September 28
      2004:   September 2 through September 26

Note: The archery bear license is unlimited, but you must also have an archery deer or elk license. The bear license is only good for the same units you are hunting deer or elk.

Muzzleloading Bear
      2002:   September 14 through September 22
      2003:   September 13 through September 21
      2004:   September 11 through September 19

Note: The muzzleloader bear license is unlimited, but you must also have a muzzleloading deer or elk license. The bear license is only good for the same unit you are hunting deer of elk.

Limited Rifle Bear
2002 to 2004:   September 2 through September 30, annually.

Note: Limited bear licenses are issued by GMU/DAU. If you do not harvest a bear during the limited season, you can continue to hunt bear in the same unit(s) during a regular rifle deer or elk season provided you have a deer or elk license for that season and unit(s).

Mountain Lion Season

The mountain lion season is set annually. Refer to the mountain lion hunting brochure each year for the specific season dates. In 2002 the hunting season is January 1st to March 31st and the day after the close of the last combined rifle deer and elk season through December 31st.

Bighorn Sheep and Mountain Goat Season

Bighorn sheep and mountain goat archery and rifle seasons are set annually and vary from unit to unit. To determine specific seasons for each unit, refer to the DOW hunting brochure for sheep and goats each year. Generally, sheep hunting begins in August or September. Most of the later seasons begin near the end of September and extend into early October. During the 2000 hunting season there were a few units that had November hunting seasons for sheep, and there was even a December season for at least one unit. Goat seasons usually start in September or October and end in October. The two units that had desert bighorn sheep licenses had a November 4 to December 3 hunting season in 2000.

Mature male bighorn sheep usually stay apart from females and young for most of the year in separate bachelor herds. They migrate seasonally, using larger upland areas in the summer and concentrating in sheltered valleys during the winter.

LICENSE COSTS

Colorado had not changed its big game license fees for several years, and had some of the lowest non-resident fees in the nation. Non-resident bear and mountain lion fees are currently the same, but they could also be adjusted after the 2002 hunting season. Resident license fees are also likely to increase in the near future. Residents and non-residents should check the regulations for current license costs each year.

LICENSE	$ RESIDENT	$ NON-RESIDENT
Elk* (bull)	$30.25	$470.25
Elk* (cow)	30.25	250.25
Elk* (either sex)	30.25	470.25
Deer*	20.25	285.25
Antelope*	20.25	285.25
Moose	203.25	1583.25
Mountain Lion	30.25	250.25
Bear*	30.25	250.25
Mountain Goat	153.25	1583.25
Bighorn Sheep	153.25	1583.25
Desert Bighorn	203.25	Residents Only
Youth Big Game	10.00	100.00

*Indicates that an application processing fee of $3 is required in addition to the price of the license if applied for through the drawing.

LICENSE SALES CUTOFF DATES
AND APPLICATION DEADLINES

At this time there is no cutoff date for over-the-counter archery elk licenses. This means you can purchase an archery elk license at any time during the season. Still, it is illegal to hunt without the appropriate license. Don't try to hunt during the archery or muzzleloader season without a license thinking you can buy one after you have harvested an animal. If a DOW officer checks you in the field, you will likely be ticketed for hunting without a proper or valid license.

For the second, third, and fourth combined deer and elk rifle seasons the cutoff date for over-the-counter licenses is at midnight on the day before the season opens. For example, during the 2002 season the following cutoff dates apply:

2nd season, combined rifle, October 19-25: cutoff is October 18 at midnight.

3rd season, combined rifle, November 2-8: cutoff is November 1 at midnight.

4th season, combined rifle, November 9-13: cutoff is November 8 at midnight.

(These dates are really only relevant to elk licenses since deer licenses are completely limited at this time.)

If you forgot to get your rifle elk license for one of the combined deer and elk rifle season before the cutoff date you can still obtain a license, but you have to buy it in person at a DOW office.

Also starting in 2002 bear licenses will be sold only in person at DOW offices after midnight September 1.

For limited licenses during the 2002 hunting season applications had to be submitted to the DOW by April 2. This date can change from year to year. Please refer to the DOW big game hunting brochures each year to determine the appropriate application deadline.

Practicing your shot from a tree stand will improve your chances for a clean kill.

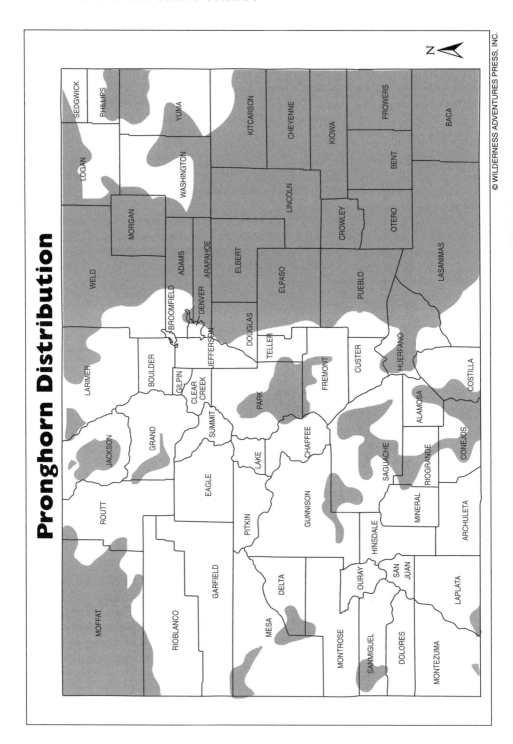

Pronghorn Distribution

© WILDERNESS ADVENTURES PRESS, INC.

Pronghorn
Antilocapra americana

Although the pronghorn is the smallest big game animal in Colorado, it makes up for its size with tenacity and speed. It survives in relatively desolate landscapes often with little water or cover. Based on current Colorado Division of Wildlife estimates, there are over 60,000 pronghorn in the state. The largest concentrations are found in the northwest quarter of Colorado and on the eastern plains. With large, high-set eyes, jet-black horns, and prominent black cheek patches, a mature buck antelope is one of the most distinct and handsome big game animals in North America.

Fascinating Facts

- The name antelope, in reference to pronghorns, is actually a misnomer. Pronghorn are members of a distinct family known as Antilocapridae, which evolved in North America. Antelope is more accurate for African animals such as gazelle.
- Pronghorn are the fastest North American land animal. They can achieve speeds in excess of 60 miles per hour. The evolution of this incredible speed may be due to the fact that cheetahs also inhabited pronghorn range during the Pleistocene Epoch.
- Pronghorns have incredible eyesight. Peripheral vision is excellent as well as distance vision. Pronghorns may be capable of seeing small objects as far as four miles away.
- Pronghorns shed their horns every year.
- Pronghorns will generally go underneath barbed wire fences even though they have the ability to jump them.
- The fossil record shows 13 extinct genus of pronghorn, one of which had four horns.
- The lifespan of a pronghorn in the wild is generally less than nine years.

Local Names
Antelope, goat, prairie goat, prairie ghost, lopes

Size
An adult buck pronghorn will generally weigh between 110 and 135 pounds and stand 36 to 40 inches at the shoulder. Does are smaller with average weights between 85 and 110 pounds and heights of 32 to 36 inches at the shoulders.

Coat and Color
The coat of a pronghorn is made up of coarse, somewhat bristly, hollow hairs that provide excellent insulation in extreme weather conditions. The hair on the back of the neck is slightly longer on mature bucks and forms something of a short dark

Notice the dark cheek patch and snout on this buck.

mane. Coloration over much of the coat varies from a light, dusty tan, to a darker reddish-brown. The tan coloration covers more than half of the body from the top of the neck, down the back, along the sides, and outsides of the legs. The coat changes to white along the sides of the pronghorn from the back of the front shoulder to the front of the back leg. The white continues on the underbelly and along the inside of the legs. White also covers the rump as well as portions of the neck and mouth. Bucks exhibit a black cheek patch two to three inches below the eye and ear that covers a scent gland. Finally, it almost appears that the black of the horns has leaked down and stained the top of the snout. Does do not exhibit the black cheek patch or the dark snout.

Horns

The horns of both male and female pronghorns originate from a bony core. The core of a mature buck appears dagger-like, and extends five to six inches from the top of the skull directly above the eye. The horn is made up of keratinous, fused hairs that form a sheath around the bony core. The prong is a flattened extension that comes to a point on the front of the horn. There are often irregular bumps and small protrusions along the horn, especially in the vicinity of the prong where it forks away from the main body of the horn. Above the prong, the horn narrows and curves inward, or sometimes backwards. Bigger, mature bucks often have deep curves at the top of their horns, which end in nearly translucent ivory tips. Although the configuration of horns vary from animal to animal, when looked at straight on, the outline of symmetrical horns will often form a heart-like shape.

Does commonly have very small, short, black nubs protruding one or two inches above the hair on the top of the head. Occasionally a doe will grow horns up to four or five inches in length. These horns do not exhibit the prong and are generally not as rigid as a buck's horns.

Pronghorns shed their horns each year after the mating season. The shed doesn't occur in the classic sense that most antlered animals drop their antlers. Instead, a new sheath forms around the bony core replacing the existing horn. This sheath gradually pushes off the old horn as it grows. By summer the new horn has finished growing and has reached its size potential for the year. Winter conditions can affect the size of the horn. Mild temperatures with plentiful food sources often lead to better horn growth.

Voice and Communications

Both male and female pronghorns have an arsenal of communicative skills. They include voice, scent, and visual displays. Voice communication includes grunts, bleats, and barks. If you spook a pronghorn, it will often run off a couple of hundred yards and emit a high-pitched bark (*pshoooowf*) that carries great distances. This bark, or blow, is loud and persistent. The frightened animal (usually a doe) will often remain within a quarter of a mile randomly blowing and stamping its feet until it has determined what the danger is. If you are set up at a waterhole, this display can ruin your hunting for several hours since animals anywhere within earshot will be warned of danger in the area. In addition to the bark, bucks will commonly grunt and smack their lips during the rut.

Does and fawns often make high-pitched whines, bleats, and blats.

Pronghorn will often flare their rump hairs when alarmed. Feet stamping and posture also make up visual communicative displays. Finally, pronghorns have several scent glands. They are located on the cheek, between the hooves, on the rump and hock. Communication through scent marking is poorly understood, but at a minimum, bucks may rub scent glands and urinate on scrapes to mark territories.

Senses

Pronghorns are probably known best for their incredible vision. They can see detail at long distances, sometimes compared to the vision that certain birds of prey have. Since they generally live in wide-open landscapes, their incredible vision is usually their best defense against predators. Often overlooked is their excellent hearing and sense of smell. Muzzleloader hunters and bowhunters are often thwarted by these two senses when trying to get within adequate shooting range. Just like a whitetail deer, a pronghorn will be far out of range once he hears you or smells you at close range. At greater distances a pronghorn will often hang around until it verifies the danger with its eyes. Still, wind direction and a silent approach should be considered before making a stalk.

Tracks and Sign

Pronghorns have heart-shaped hoof prints comprised of two teardrop-shaped components. They vary in size from about two inches to over three inches in length and 2.5 inches in width. Pronghorn tracks are smaller than deer tracks, but it is easy to confuse the tracks of the two animals. One important difference is that pronghorns do not have dewclaws.

When browsing, the resulting droppings are generally small, individual pellets, but when they eat succulent vegetation the droppings are stringy and segmented. Mature bucks often mark areas by scraping the ground with their front hooves and urinating and defecating in the resulting scrape mark.

Additional signs of antelope are not dissimilar to whitetail deer. Pronghorns will rub the scent glands in their cheeks on sticks and bushy vegetation leaving a pungent odor. They will also rub and thrash their horns on bushes, leaving broken vegetation as evidence of their presence.

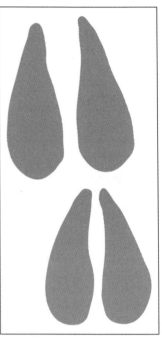

Pronghorn tracks. Above, front, 3¼" long; below, rear, 2¾" long.

Reproduction and Young

Breeding generally occurs in September and into the beginning of October. Yearling bucks are capable of breeding does, but they usually don't due to competition from more mature bucks. Does generally start breeding as yearlings and carry their young for about 250 days. The fawns are dropped in May and June. When the habitat is productive, most does will drop twins. Like many other species, predation can be high on fawns. Most predation at this time comes from coyotes and large birds of prey such as golden eagles. Like most successful species, the young of the pronghorn adapt and develop quickly. They spend their first week of life developing balance and strength walking and running. At this time they are left hidden in tall grass to avoid predators. By the second week of a fawn's life, it is usually capable of running with the herd, although the female and her fawn(s) generally stay segregated from the herd for the first three to six weeks.

Habitat

There are two major ecosystems that comprise important pronghorn habitat in Colorado: semi-desert shrubland and grassland. Most of the semi-desert shrubland exists in northwestern Colorado and throughout the western part of the state in mountain parks and valleys. Most of the grassland occurs on the eastern plains, and areas of shortgrass prairie are best suited for antelope. The terrain is generally hilly to flat with wide-open spaces where they can utilize their incredible eyesight and speed to avoid predators.

Home Range

The home range of an antelope is dependent on the quality of the habitat and can vary from less than one square mile to nine or ten square miles. In general, antelope will not travel more than six miles in any given day. Depending on the quality of forage, some herds of antelope will migrate from summer to winter ranges.

Generally, young bucks form bachelor herds in the spring and summer while mature, dominant bucks remain solitary. After fawns are dropped in May and June, does will usually travel together in nursery bands. During the winter all ages and sexes come together to form large herds.

Forage Plants

The diet of antelope changes with the seasons. In semi-desert shrubland antelope primarily feed on browse such as sagebrush and bitterbrush during the winter, whereas forbs (broadleaf plants) make up the majority of their diet in the spring and summer. In the grasslands, pronghorns subsist on nearly equal amounts of browse and forbs. In both ecosystems, pronghorns also eat cactus on a regular basis, but eat very little grass. Where agriculture is present, antelope will also feed on wheat and alfalfa, to the frustration of ranchers and farmers. These are good areas to target for permission to hunt on private property.

Pronghorns have excellent distance and peripheral vision.

Daily Patterns

Pronghorn are active at any time during the day, but when temperatures are very high, they spend more time foraging during the early and late hours. They will generally seek water at waterholes, seeps, or rivers at least once a day, sometimes more frequently. Pronghorns generally bed down through much of the night, but they have also been known to forage during the night.

Rutting Behavior

Pronghorns generally go into rut in September in Colorado. The rut will last into October. At this time of the year, just like other big game species, mature buck pronghorns will display aggressive tendencies toward other bucks. Depending on habitat conditions, bucks may mark and maintain territories or gather harems of does. Generally if habitat conditions are good, a buck will mark out a territory by scent marking and scraping. He will then defend the territory by chasing off other bucks. The buck will either breed the does that are within his territory, or he will try to maintain a harem within the territory. Typically, bucks will establish and maintain their territory for several months before the rut.

In areas where habitat conditions are poor, bucks are more apt to gather harems of does and move more readily. This pattern seems to be more prevalent on the eastern plains. Similar to a bull elk, a dominant pronghorn buck will keep the harem together and chase off rival bucks. This can lead to fights between bucks where they lock horns and push each other. There are often younger bucks, or "satellite" bucks, that follow the harems looking for opportunities to breed the does when the dominant buck is busy. Depending on population dynamics it is also possible for more than one dominant buck to run with large groups of does during the rut.

Trophy Dimensions

According to the 11th edition of the *Boone and Crockett Club Records of North American Big Game*, the largest antelope ever recorded scored an incredible 93 4/8. Michael O'Haco, Jr., took this buck in Coconino County, Arizona in 1985. If you are looking to enter a buck in Boone and Crockett it will have to have a minimum score of 82. (Please refer to the scoring sheet to determine measuring and scoring criteria). Most of the bucks that make the Boone and Crockett minimum score have horns with lengths of 15 to 18 inches. Most commonly the horns will be in the 17-inch range with good symmetry, mass, and long prongs.

Bob Schneidmiller took the biggest buck ever recorded from Colorado in Weld County in 1965. This buck still ranks fifth all time in Boone and Crockett with an incredible score of 91 4/8. The impressive thing about this buck is that the horns were only slightly over 15 inches, but it had incredible mass with 7 7/8-inch circumference measurements at the base of each horn. In addition, the symmetry was outstanding with very few deductions, and the prongs were very long at 7 inches each.

The Pope and Young Club, which uses the same scoring system as Boone and Crockett, requires a minimum score of 67 to enter an animal harvested with archery equipment into the record book. This is a much more attainable goal if you're after record-book animals. Generally, a buck with 13-inch horns, good symmetry, moder-

Records of
North American
Big Game

250 Station Drive
Missoula, MT 59801
(406) 542-1888

BOONE AND CROCKETT CLUB®
OFFICIAL SCORING SYSTEM FOR NORTH AMERICAN BIG GAME TROPHIES

MINIMUM SCORES

AWARDS	ALL-TIME
80	82

PRONGHORN

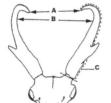

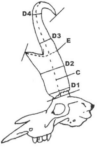

SEE OTHER SIDE FOR INSTRUCTIONS		COLUMN 1	COLUMN 2	COLUMN 3
A. Tip to Tip Spread		Right Horn	Left Horn	Difference
B. Inside Spread of Main Beams				
C. Length of Horn				
D-1. Circumference of Base				
D-2. Circumference at First Quarter				
D-3. Circumference at Second Quarter				
D-4. Circumference at Third Quarter				
E. Length of Prong				
TOTALS				

ADD	Column 1		Exact Locality Where Killed:	
	Column 2		Date Killed:	Hunter:
	Subtotal		Owner:	Telephone #:
SUBTRACT Column 3			Owner's Address:	
FINAL SCORE			Guide's Name and Address:	
			Remarks: (Mention Any Abnormalities or Unique Qualities)	

I, _____ , certify that I have measured this trophy on _____

PRINT NAME   MM/DD/YYYYY

at _____

STREET ADDRESS   CITY   STATE/PROVINCE

and that these measurements and data are, to the best of my knowledge and belief, made in accordance with the instructions given.

Witness: _____ Signature: _____ I.D. Number ☐☐☐☐

B&C OFFICIAL MEASURER

COPYRIGHT © 2002 BY BOONE AND CROCKETT CLUB®

Reprinted courtesy of the Boone and Crockett Club, 250 Station Dr., Missoula, MT 59801, 406-542-1888

INSTRUCTIONS FOR MEASURING PRONGHORN

All measurements must be made with a 1/4-inch wide flexible steel tape to the nearest one-eighth of an inch. Enter fractional figures in eighths, without reduction. Official measurements cannot be taken until horns have air dried for at least 60 days after the animal was killed.

A. Tip to Tip Spread is measured between tips of horns.

B. Inside Spread of Main Beams is measured at a right angle to the center line of the skull, at widest point between main beams.

C. Length of Horn is measured on the outside curve on the general line illustrated. The line taken will vary with different heads, depending on the direction of their curvature. Measure along the center of the outer curve from tip of horn to a point in line with the lowest edge of the base, using a straight edge to establish the line end.

D-1. Circumference of Base is measured at a right angle to axis of horn. **Do not** follow irregular edge of horn; the line of measurement must be entirely on horn material.

D-2-3-4. Divide measurement C of longer horn by four. Starting at base, mark **both** horns at these quarters (even though the other horn is shorter) and measure circumferences at these marks. If the prong interferes with D-2, move the measurement down to just below the swelling of the prong. If D-3 falls in the swelling of the prong, move the measurement up to just above the prong.

E. Length of Prong: Measure from the tip of the prong along the upper edge of the outer side to the horn; then continue around the horn to a point at the rear of the horn where a straight edge across the back of both horns touches the horn, with the latter part being at a right angle to the long axis of horn.

ENTRY AFFIDAVIT FOR ALL HUNTER-TAKEN TROPHIES

For the purpose of entry into the Boone and Crockett Club's® records, North American big game harvested by the use of the following methods or under the following conditions are ineligible:

I. Spotting or herding game from the air, followed by landing in its vicinity for the purpose of pursuit and shooting;

II. Herding or chasing with the aid of any motorized equipment;

III. Use of electronic communication devices, artificial lighting, or electronic light intensifying devices;

IV. Confined by artificial barriers, including escape-proof fenced enclosures;

V. Transplanted for the purpose of commercial shooting;

VI. By the use of traps or pharmaceuticals;

VII. While swimming, helpless in deep snow, or helpless in any other natural or artificial medium;

VIII. On another hunter's license;

IX. Not in full compliance with the game laws or regulations of the federal government or of any state, province, territory, or tribal council on reservations or tribal lands;

I certify that the trophy scored on this chart was not taken in violation of the conditions listed above. In signing this statement, I understand that if the information provided on this entry is found to be misrepresented or fraudulent in any respect, it will not be accepted into the Awards Program and 1) all of my prior entries are subject to deletion from future editions of **Records of North American Big Game** 2) future entries may not be accepted.

FAIR CHASE, as defined by the Boone and Crockett Club®, is the ethical, sportsmanlike and lawful pursuit and taking of any free-ranging wild, native North American big game animal in a manner that does not give the hunter an improper advantage over such game animals.

The Boone and Crockett Club® may exclude the entry of any animal that it deems to have been taken in an unethical manner or under conditions deemed inappropriate by the Club.

Date:_____ Signature of Hunter:_____
(SIGNATURE MUST BE WITNESSED BY AN OFFICIAL MEASURER OR A NOTARY PUBLIC.)

Date:_____ Signature of Notary or Official Measurer:_____

Reprinted courtesy of the Boone and Crockett Club, 250 Station Dr., Missoula, MT 59801, 406-542-1888

ate mass, and moderate prongs will meet the minimum score requirement. Judd Cooney harvested the largest antelope taken in Colorado with a bow in 1983 in Moffat County. This buck had an impressive score of 85.

The simplest way to begin to judge trophy quality in the field is to compare the horns to the ears. Generally, a pronghorn's ears are about six inches long from the top of the head. If the buck appears to have horns twice as long as the ears, you're probably looking at a 12-inch buck. Another good gauge is to note where the prong is in relation to the ear. If the prong is above the top of the ear, you're probably looking at a very respectable buck. In addition to length, good mass and long prongs add significantly to the score. Finally, the more symmetrical the horns, the less deduction it will have from the overall score.

Compare the size of the ears to the horns to determine a trophy quality buck.

Hunting Tactics

The best way to rifle hunt antelope is to spot and stalk. You can generally spot antelope at great distances with the help of good optics. The goal is to spot the animal before it's aware of your presence. In this way you can take your time and plan out an appropriate stalk. Before pursuing the pronghorn, try to determine the direction of travel and good sources of cover between you and the prey. Also, try to choose landmarks on long stalks so that you can gauge your progress in relation to the animal. A productive scenario is to watch a pronghorn feed over the top of a hill, then quickly move up on it and try to get into rifle range before it has traveled too far down the other side. If you can get permission to hunt agricultural land where pronghorns are actively feeding you will have good success taking a stand within rifle range of the field.

Bowhunters will have the greatest success hunting at waterholes. Building a blind or using a portable blind at a waterhole will be the most efficient way to harvest a pronghorn. Taking a perch in a windmill overlooking a water source will also be very effective. Consider where the majority of the tracks are and how the wind moves around the waterhole. At close range, an antelope will spook from human scent just like any other prey animal. Situating the blind properly will help you get clean shots at unspooked animals. Also, if you are new to bowhunting, be sure to let the animal drink before drawing the bow. Pronghorns will often false drink one or two times before drinking in earnest. They put their head down like they are about to drink then suddenly snap it up to double check for danger. If you're in the process of drawing your bow when the animal snaps its head up, it will probably catch the movement, even in a well-constructed blind.

Bowhunters can also have good success hunting antelope during the rut with decoys. This usually works best in teams of two, a hunter and another person to position the decoy. Try to locate a dominant, territorial buck and get the decoy close enough for the buck to see it. Grunting or snorting can get the buck's attention, causing him to charge in to drive off the competitor. If the buck stops within bow range you will only have a short time to get a shot. Since the buck is alert and looking at the decoy, select your shot carefully. This is a scenario that could result in a poor shot if you are not an ethical and patient hunter. Don't take the shot unless the buck is broadside and stationary. Decoying should only be used by bowhunters, since at long range, a rifle hunter could easily mistake the decoy for a real buck.

Pronghorns are small animals and make small targets. Regardless of whether you choose to hunt with a bow, muzzleloader, or rifle, spend a great deal of time becoming proficient with your weapon of choice. Also, know your effective range and stick to it. Wait for a good broadside shot at a stationary animal and you will have your highest percentage for making an ethical harvest.

Rifle Caliber Suggestions

Due to their low body weight and thin skin, any high-powered rifle that meets the minimum caliber requirements for hunting big game in Colorado will be adequate to bring down a pronghorn. Optimal calibers include the .243, 6mm, .25-06, and .270.

Shot Placement:

Top: Broadside shot.
Aim for the center of the chest just behind the bend of the front leg or shoulder; this should penetrate the lungs.

Below: Quartering shot.
Aim for the off-side shoulder by drawing an imaginary line from your rifle or bow to the far-side shoulder; aim slightly behind the shoulder if you don't wish to damage any meat.

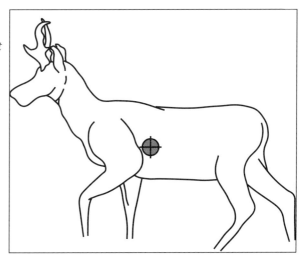

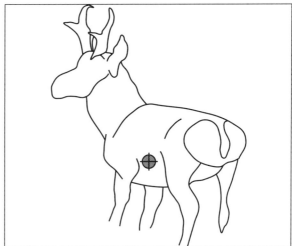

Crazy from the Heat

It can be very hot during the antelope hunting season, especially during the early archery and muzzleloader seasons. Bowhunters often have their best success hunting out of blinds at waterholes. If you plan on using this technique, make sure to build a blind that provides ample shade from the sun. One of the biggest problems when hunting from a blind is beating the heat. In late August temperatures are likely to push over the 90-degree mark. No matter how well prepared you are, or how much water you drink, if you sit in the direct sun for several hours you're going to get a little crazy from the heat. In fact, heat stress is a real concern.

Some hunters believe that antelope quit moving during the hottest hours of the day. This may be true some of the time, but my experience is that pronghorns will move to water at any time during the day, no matter how hot it gets. The longer you can stay in the blind the better your chances of filling your tag. There are several ways to beat the heat in addition to building a good blind that offers plenty of shade. Wetting a bandana or cloth with water and placing it around your neck is a good start. I've even taken a spray bottle filled with water to mist over my face, head, and neck. The evaporating water helps dissipate the heat, although it probably doesn't help with scent dispersion. There are also small, battery-operated, hand-sized fans with rubber blades that are virtually silent to operate. It may sound funny, but one of these little fans can be a godsend when you're sweltering in an antelope blind.

*Does generally start breeding as yearlings and
carry their young for about 250 days.*

Antelope buck.

White-tailed Deer Distribution

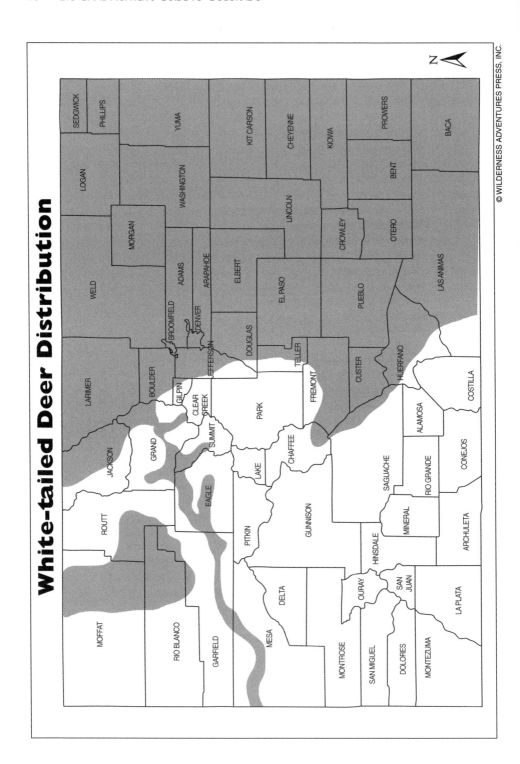

© WILDERNESS ADVENTURES PRESS, INC.

White-tailed Deer
Odocoileus virginianus

Often referred to as the most sought after big game animal of North America, the white-tailed deer is slowly becoming popular to hunters in Colorado. Although population statistics are lacking, there may be over 12,000 of these wary animals living on the eastern plains of Colorado.

Fascinating Facts

- Although not considered to be a major part of their diet, whitetail deer seem to have a great fondness for mushrooms.
- When alarmed, whitetails will snort, stamp their front hooves, and flag their long tails to communicate prevailing danger to other deer.
- Most white-tailed deer are found along the major river drainages on the eastern plains of Colorado; however, they have also been found in the mountains along the Colorado River drainage, Rocky Mountain National Park, the San Luis Valley, and the White River drainage.
- Interbreeding between mule deer and whitetails occasionally occurs in Colorado. In addition to unusual antlers, the telltale sign of a hybrid is often a long tail with a black stripe.
- The coat of a whitetail changes dramatically from reddish brown in the summer to gray in the winter.
- White-tailed deer are amazing athletes capable of jumps eight feet high and 30 feet long. They can also attain speeds of up to 40 mph.
- Whitetails are excellent swimmers, crossing rivers and lakes when necessary.

Local Names
Whitetail, flagtail

Size
Age and habitat conditions play a large role in size. On average, does and younger bucks will stand 3 feet at the shoulders and weigh 120 to 160 pounds. Mature bucks will stand 3½ feet at the shoulders and often weigh over 200 pounds. Extremely large bucks in Colorado will push over the 300-pound mark.

Coat and Color
The coat of a whitetail is reddish-brown in summer and grayish-brown in winter. They generally have a prominent white patch on their upper throat, which continues up the lower jaw and forms a ring near the end of the muzzle. The eyes are ringed with white and the inner ears, belly, inner legs, rump, and the underside of the famous tail are all white. There is also a prominent black strip near the end of the muzzle just behind the nose that continues down to the lower jaw.

*Look for the brow tines that rise vertically near the base
of each antler on white-tailed bucks.*

Antlers

The continuous main beams characterize the antlers of a whitetail. They rise upward and outward from the head, generally curving back in towards the tips. Stiletto-like brow tines rise vertically near the base of each antler and generally three or four more tines grow up from the beam. Irregular, or "non-typical," whitetail antlers often display drop tines and/or smaller tines and bumps sometimes referred to as sticker-points.

Age, genetics, and nutrition all play a role in antler size. Antlers are shed each year in February or March and grow back by the following August.

Voice and Communications

Whitetail deer communicate with each other in a number of ways. Voice communication includes bleats, snorts, and grunts. They also communicate largely through scent produced by various glands. These glands are located on the forehead, in front of the eyes, in the mouth, between the hooves, and on the hock. Whitetails also communicate through physical signs such as flagging the tail when they run. They also erect the white hair on the rump, snort, and stamp their hooves when threatened. During the rut the bucks and does communicate through a complicated system of scent, voice, and posturing. Bucks often emit low, hoarse, grunts, sometimes referred to as the tending grunt, when in pursuit of does during the rut.

Senses

Hearing, smell, and vision of the whitetail are extremely acute. Since heavy cover often limits visual observation, the whitetail depends greatly on hearing and sense of smell to avoid predators. Their excellent sense of smell has given rise to the array of cover scents, scent neutralizers, and scent eliminating clothing available to hunters today. Even with the help of modern technology, the best way to stay undetected by whitetail deer is to keep the wind in your favor.

Tracks and Sign

Like other deer and pronghorns, the track of a whitetail is composed of two tear- dropped hooves that form a heart shape. Typically the hoof is 3 to 3.5 inches long and 1.5 to 2.5 inches in width. Whitetails have dewclaws, which show up when tracks are made in soft ground or snow. The individual hooves are often splayed wider apart when the deer runs to give it better footing.

Whitetails leave an abundance of sign. Droppings include pellets and cakes, depending on the season and type of vegetation being consumed. During the rut, bucks make scrapes by pawing the ground with their hooves. These scrapes are almost always placed under hanging branches that the buck will lick and rub with the glands in his eyes to leave scent. Bucks also urinate on the scrape over their hocks where the metatarsal gland is located to mark territories and leave scent for does during the rut. Bucks will also rub trees and bushes with their antlers to remove velvet and mark territories. These rubs are easily identified where bucks have removed the bark from the lower sections of trees or broken branches on bushes.

Reproduction and Young

When does go into heat there is a chemical change in the urine that is believed to alert mature bucks that the doe is ready to breed. Estrus usually lasts a day, and if breeding is unsuccessful, the doe will go into estrus again in three to four weeks. Whitetail does are often bred as yearlings, but bucks generally don't breed until their second year. The gestation period is about 200 days, at which time does

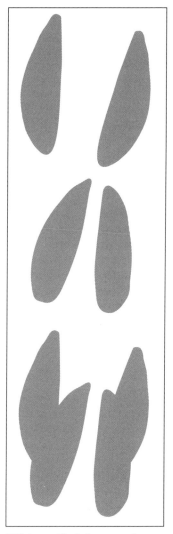

White-tailed deer tracks.
Top: *Front foot, average length of 2¾"; notice the spread of the hooves.*
Middle: *Rear foot; notice the traditional heart shape.*
Bottom: *Often the tracks double-register, overlapping by an inch or more.*

can give birth to single fawns, twins, or even triplets. Fawns grow rapidly and begin to forage within two to three weeks of birth. By five months the fawn is usually weaned, and by seven to nine months the young deer often ways over 100 pounds. Adult bucks are considered fully-grown after four years; does after three.

Habitat

In Colorado white-tailed deer are most commonly found in riparian habitat along river bottoms and the accompanying farmlands on the eastern plains. Riparian habitat is extremely rich in wildlife due to the abundance of water, cover, and food. Whitetails prefer heavy cover for protection and thick brushy river bottom is perfect. These areas often contain plant life such as cottonwood trees, tamarack, willow, cattail, box elder, and sedges.

Home Range

Since whitetails live predominantly along the river bottoms, their home ranges are somewhat narrow and long. In studies (performed by Kufeld in 1992) on the South Platte and Arkansas River drainages, whitetails generally had a home range of three square miles. Due to the narrow width of the river bottoms the home ranges can be anywhere from 5 to 12 miles in length. Mature bucks often have larger ranges than does.

Whitetails generally inhabit the same areas year-round, but there is some indication that they make short seasonal movements. In spring and summer they will sometimes move from the river bottoms to agricultural lands. They return to the river

Whitetails prefer lower elevation, river-bottom habitat.

bottoms in the fall where they form small herds of up to 20 animals after the breeding season. These herds are usually made up of does and their offspring along with immature bucks.

Forage Plants

In agricultural areas white-tailed deer derive a large percentage of their diet from corn, wheat, and alfalfa. Most of the prominent river bottoms on the eastern plains are surrounded by irrigated croplands. When crops aren't available, they seem to prefer grasses and forbs to browse. Unlike many areas in the east, whitetail habitat in Colorado is lacking in mast production. Crops and the abundant forbs and grasses on the river bottom offset the absence of acorns and other nuts.

Whitetails have a fondness for mushrooms and fruit, including wild grapevines. Cottonwood probably makes up a great deal of their diet when browsing.

Daily Patterns

Whitetails are most active at dawn and dusk (referred to as crepuscular). They generally have specific bedding areas in heavy cover that they seek during most of the day. As the sun goes down, the deer become active and start moving to feeding areas. They will often feed well into the night before bedding again. They also feed and water early in the morning. Some hunters believe that wise old bucks become nocturnal in nature. This may be true, or it may simply be that wise old bucks are fewer in number and better at living a secret existence.

To the hunters' advantage, mature bucks abandon their secretive lifestyle during the rut. At this time of year they may move at any time of the day and all day long pursuing does.

Rutting Behavior

The rutting behavior of the white-tailed deer has been studied thoroughly by scientists and hunters alike. The rut is like a chink in the armor of a mature buck. It is the one time when bucks will ignore their acute senses and throw caution to the wind in pursuit of does.

The rut is usually at its peak by early to mid-November in Colorado. The peak of the rut is preceded and followed by lesser phases in October and December. Common signs of the rut are scrapes on the ground and rubs on trees and bushes. In both instances bucks will leave scent as a way to mark their territory. They often urinate over the metatarsal gland onto scrapes and rub scent on overhanging branches with the glands in front of their eyes. Just prior to and during the rut, mature bucks will often fight by locking antlers and pushing each other. Fights can be violent, and bucks sometimes entangle their horns to the point that they can't release, which results in death.

Older does will become more solitary during the rut. When in heat they urinate more frequently and also leave a scent trail through glands in their hooves. Bucks pick up this trail and actively follow until the estrus doe is found. When necessary the buck will interrupt his pursuit to fend off other bucks. Bucks commonly grunt when following does, and they exhibit a swollen neck during this time of the year.

Trophy Dimensions

The largest typical whitetail ever recorded by Boone and Crockett scored an immense 213 5/8 points. Milo Hanson took the buck in Saskatchewan, Canada in 1993. There have only been a handful of typical whitetail racks recorded by Boone and Crockett that scored over 200 points. The minimum score for Boone and Crockett is 170 and for Pope and Young it's 125. For non-typical whitetail, it will have to score 195 for Boone and Crockett and 155 for Pope and Young.

Although Colorado may not have a reputation as a trophy whitetail state, it produces some exceptional bucks each year. The South Platte, Arkansas, and Republican River drainages in eastern Colorado are becoming known as trophy producers. As always the word trophy is relative. One man's average buck may be another mans Holy Grail. Regardless of your definition of "trophy," it is very possible to harvest a mature typical buck in Colorado that scores in the 120 to 130 range. Although much more difficult, typical bucks in the 140 to 150 class are taken every year. There are also bigger bucks in the 160 and up category, but tagging one of these is going to take plenty of patience, persistence, and probably some luck.

What will it take to get a typical whitetail into Boone and Crockett? The short answer is a lot. More specifically the buck will need to be a minimum 5x5 with long main beams in the neighborhood of 24 inches. The inside spread will probably need to be at least 18 to 20 inches. Throw in long points, good symmetry, and mass and you will likely meet the 170-point minimum score – an exceptional buck in anybody's book.

Although the Pope and Young 125-point minimum for typical whitetail deer is much more attainable, it is still no easy task. The antlers will generally need to contain a minimum of 4 points on each side. The longer the main beams the better, and the spread will probably need to be 16 to 18 inches. Finally two of the points will need to exceed six inches in length, and mass and symmetry must be good. In Colorado there have only been a handful of typical whitetails taken with a bow that scored over 160 points. Stuart Clodfelder took the state record typical buck in 1981 according to the *Fourth Edition of the Colorado Bowhunting Records of Big Game*. This impressive buck scored 194 points and was taken in Logan County.

Records of
North American
Big Game

250 Station Drive
Missoula, MT 59801
(406) 542-1888

BOONE AND CROCKETT CLUB®
OFFICIAL SCORING SYSTEM FOR NORTH AMERICAN BIG GAME TROPHIES

TYPICAL
WHITETAIL AND COUES' DEER

MINIMUM SCORES		
	AWARDS	ALL-TIME
whitetail	160	170
Coues'	100	110

KIND OF DEER (check one)
☐ whitetail
☐ Coues'

Detail of Point Measurement

Abnormal Points	
Right Antler	Left Antler

SUBTOTALS		
TOTAL TO E		

SEE OTHER SIDE FOR INSTRUCTIONS			COLUMN 1	COLUMN 2	COLUMN 3	COLUMN 4
A. No. Points on Right Antler		No. Points on Left Antler	Spread Credit	Right Antler	Left Antler	Difference
B. Tip to Tip Spread		C. Greatest Spread				
D. Inside Spread of Main Beams		SPREAD CREDIT MAY EQUAL BUT NOT EXCEED LONGER MAIN BEAM				
E. Total of Lengths of Abnormal Points						
F. Length of Main Beam						
G-1. Length of First Point						
G-2. Length of Second Point						
G-3. Length of Third Point						
G-4. Length of Fourth Point, If Present						
G-5. Length of Fifth Point, If Present						
G-6. Length of Sixth Point, If Present						
G-7. Length of Seventh Point, If Present						
H-1. Circumference at Smallest Place Between Burr and First Point						
H-2. Circumference at Smallest Place Between First and Second Points						
H-3. Circumference at Smallest Place Between Second and Third Points						
H-4. Circumference at Smallest Place Between Third and Fourth Points						
		TOTALS				

ADD	Column 1	
	Column 2	
	Column 3	
	Subtotal	
SUBTRACT Column 4		
FINAL SCORE		

Exact Locality Where Killed:

Date Killed: Hunter:

Owner: Telephone #:

Owner's Address:

Guide's Name and Address:

Remarks: (Mention Any Abnormalities or Unique Qualities)

COPYRIGHT ©2002 BY BOONE AND CROCKETT CLUB®

Reprinted courtesy of the Boone and Crockett Club, 250 Station Dr., Missoula, MT 59801, 406-542-1888

I, _____ , certify that I have measured this trophy on _____
      PRINT NAME   MM/DD/YYYYY

at _____
   STREET ADDRESS   CITY   STATE/PROVINCE

and that these measurements and data are, to the best of my knowledge and belief, made in accordance with the instructions given.

Witness: _____ Signature: _____ I.D. Number [ ][ ][ ][ ]
                                              B&C OFFICIAL MEASURER

INSTRUCTIONS FOR MEASURING TYPICAL WHITETAIL AND COUES' DEER

All measurements must be made with a 1/4-inch wide flexible steel tape to the nearest one-eighth of an inch. (Note: A flexible steel cable can be used to measure points and main beams only.) Enter fractional figures in eighths, without reduction. Official measurements cannot be taken until the antlers have air dried for at least 60 days after the animal was killed.

A. Number of Points on Each Antler: To be counted a point, the projection must be at least one inch long, with the length exceeding width at one inch or more of length. All points are measured from tip of point to nearest edge of beam as illustrated. Beam tip is counted as a point but not measured as a point.

B. Tip to Tip Spread is measured between tips of main beams.

C. Greatest Spread is measured between perpendiculars at a right angle to the center line of the skull at widest part, whether across main beams or points.

D. Inside Spread of Main Beams is measured at a right angle to the center line of the skull at widest point between main beams. Enter this measurement again as the Spread Credit if it is less than or equal to the length of the longer main beam; if greater, enter longer main beam length for Spread Credit.

E. Total of Lengths of all Abnormal Points: Abnormal Points are those non-typical in location (such as points originating from a point or from bottom or sides of main beam) or extra points beyond the normal pattern of points. Measure in usual manner and enter in appropriate blanks.

F. Length of Main Beam is measured from the center of the lowest outside edge of burr over the outer side to the most distant point of the main beam. The point of beginning is that point on the burr where the center line along the outer side of the beam intersects the burr, then following generally the line of the illustration.

G-1-2-3-4-5-6-7. Length of Normal Points: Normal points project from the top of the main beam. They are measured from nearest edge of main beam over outer curve to tip. Lay the tape along the outer curve of the beam so that the top edge of the tape coincides with the top edge of the beam on both sides of the point to determine the baseline for point measurements. Record point lengths in appropriate blanks.

H-1-2-3-4. Circumferences are taken as detailed in illustration for each measurement. If brow point is missing, take H-1 and H-2 at smallest place between burr and G-2. If G-4 is missing, take H-4 halfway between G-3 and tip of main beam.

ENTRY AFFIDAVIT FOR ALL HUNTER-TAKEN TROPHIES

For the purpose of entry into the Boone and Crockett Club's® records, North American big game harvested by the use of the following methods or under the following conditions are ineligible:

I.   Spotting or herding game from the air, followed by landing in its vicinity for the purpose of pursuit and shooting;
II. Herding or chasing with the aid of any motorized equipment;
III. Use of electronic communication devices, artificial lighting, or electronic light intensifying devices;
IV. Confined by artificial barriers, including escape-proof fenced enclosures;
V.   Transplanted for the purpose of commercial shooting;
VI. By the use of traps or pharmaceuticals;
VII. While swimming, helpless in deep snow, or helpless in any other natural or artificial medium;
VIII. On another hunter's license;
IX. Not in full compliance with the game laws or regulations of the federal government or of any state, province, territory, or tribal council on reservations or tribal lands;

I certify that the trophy scored on this chart was not taken in violation of the conditions listed above. In signing this statement, I understand that if the information provided on this entry is found to be misrepresented or fraudulent in any respect, it will not be accepted into the Awards Program and 1) all of my prior entries are subject to deletion from future editions of **Records of North American Big Game** 2) future entries may not be accepted.

FAIR CHASE, as defined by the Boone and Crockett Club®, is the ethical, sportsmanlike and lawful pursuit and taking of any free-ranging wild, native North American big game animal in a manner that does not give the hunter an improper advantage over such game animals.

The Boone and Crockett Club® may exclude the entry of any animal that it deems to have been taken in an unethical manner or under conditions deemed inappropriate by the Club.

Date: _____ Signature of Hunter: _____
                                              (SIGNATURE MUST BE WITNESSED BY AN OFFICIAL MEASURER OR A NOTARY PUBLIC.)

Date: _____ Signature of Notary or Official Measurer: _____

Reprinted courtesy of the Boone and Crockett Club, 250 Station Dr., Missoula, MT 59801, 406-542-1888

Records of
North American
Big Game

250 Station Drive
Missoula, MT 59801
(406) 542-1888

BOONE AND CROCKETT CLUB®
OFFICIAL SCORING SYSTEM FOR NORTH AMERICAN BIG GAME TROPHIES

MINIMUM SCORES		NON-TYPICAL	KIND OF DEER (check one)

	AWARDS	ALL-TIME
whitetail	185	195
Coues'	105	120

WHITETAIL AND COUES' DEER

KIND OF DEER (check one)
☐ whitetail
☐ Coues'

Abnormal Points	
Right Antler	Left Antler

Detail of Point
Measurement

SUBTOTALS	
E. TOTAL	

SEE OTHER SIDE FOR INSTRUCTIONS

		COLUMN 1	COLUMN 2	COLUMN 3	COLUMN 4
A. No. Points on Right Antler	No. Points on Left Antler	Spread Credit	Right Antler	Left Antler	Difference
B. Tip to Tip Spread	C. Greatest Spread				
D. Inside Spread of Main Beams	SPREAD CREDIT MAY EQUAL BUT NOT EXCEED LONGER MAIN BEAM				
F. Length of Main Beam					
G-1. Length of First Point					
G-2. Length of Second Point					
G-3. Length of Third Point					
G-4. Length of Fourth Point, If Present					
G-5. Length of Fifth Point, If Present					
G-6. Length of Sixth Point, If Present					
G-7. Length of Seventh Point, If Present					
H-1. Circumference at Smallest Place Between Burr and First Point					
H-2. Circumference at Smallest Place Between First and Second Points					
H-3. Circumference at Smallest Place Between Second and Third Points					
H-4. Circumference at Smallest Place Between Third and Fourth Points					
	TOTALS				

ADD	Column 1		Exact Locality Where Killed:
	Column 2		Date Killed: Hunter:
	Column 3		Owner: Telephone #:
	Subtotal		Owner's Address:
SUBTRACT Column 4			Guide's Name and Address:
	Subtotal		Remarks: (Mention Any Abnormalities or Unique Qualities)
	ADD Line E Total		
	FINAL SCORE		

COPYRIGHT © 2002 BY BOONE AND CROCKETT CLUB®

Reprinted courtesy of the Boone and Crockett Club, 250 Station Dr., Missoula, MT 59801, 406-542-1888

Hunting Tactics

There are a variety of ways to hunt whitetails. One of the most common practices is to hunt from treestands or blinds during the peak of the rut. Grunting can sometimes lure in a curious buck, and right before and during the rut, rattling and grunting are good techniques to attract dominant bucks. Bowhunters can also increase their odds by using decoys and scent attractants. Taking stands over green fields or other feeding areas is also a good way to harvest a whitetail. This technique is very suited to rifle hunters who can cover long ranges from one stand. Setting up on travel corridors is also a good way to get into range of a wary whitetail. Finally, in the rare instances in Colorado where you find whitetails in open and broken country, stalking may be an option; however, thick cover in the river bottoms makes stalking and still-hunting a very difficult proposition.

Regardless of the method you must always stay downwind of the whitetail. Once they smell you they'll be gone. The numerous scent-elimination and scent-cover systems on the market will help, but you will still be detected if you try to hunt upwind of a whitetail.

Shot Placement:
Broadside shot.
Aim for the center of the chest just behind the bend of the front leg or shoulder; this should penetrate the lungs.

Rifle Caliber Suggestions

Since most of your hunting is likely to take place at relatively close range on brush-choked river bottoms; short rifles will be effective. A .30-30, while not as widely used as it once was, makes a good caliber for a river-bottom rifle. Calibers such as .25-06, .270, .280, or .30-06 are also ideal for whitetail, and would be better suited for fields or large meadows where longer shots may be required.

White-tailed deer yearling and doe.

Look for the distinctive "flag" on a running white-tailed deer that clearly distinguishes it from a mule deer.

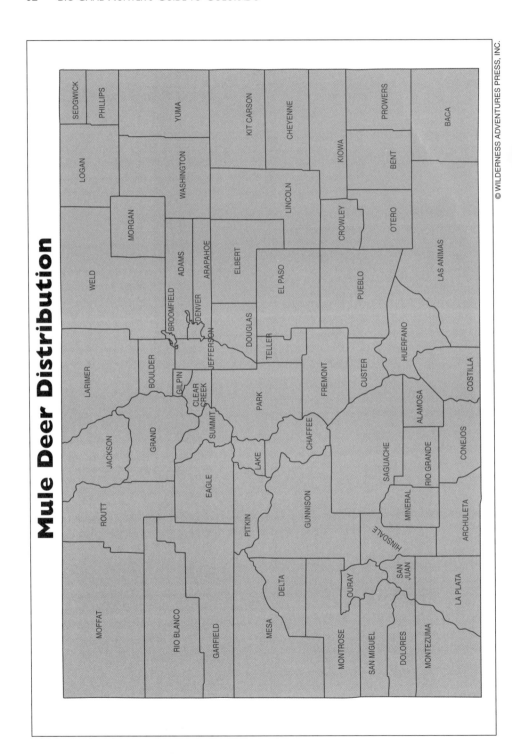

Mule Deer Distribution

© WILDERNESS ADVENTURES PRESS, INC.

Mule Deer

Odocoileus hemionus

Mule deer are the most abundant big game animal in Colorado with a current population over 500,000. There are large numbers of mule deer on public land, and they exist in every ecosystem in the state. Not only are numbers good, but the state is known for producing exceptionally large bucks. A mature timberline buck is considered by many to be the most elusive big game animal.

Fascinating Facts

- Over one-third of the top 100 typical mule deer entries listed in Boone and Crockett came from Colorado.
- Mule deer bound when they run with all four feet leaving the ground simultaneously. This characteristic gait is sometimes referred to as stotting.
- Antler growth accelerates in the summer and often exceeds over 1 cm per day.
- Mule deer may be the descendants of whitetail and Pacific coast blacktails that crossbred thousands of years ago.
- Large bucks will often remain motionless when hidden, even as predators approach within close proximity. If the predator makes eye contact, though, the buck will bolt.
- Whitetail deer and mule deer often inhabit the same sections of river bottom in eastern Colorado. Rare crossbreeding has resulted in hybrid deer.
- Mule deer typically make seasonal migrations from summer grounds to wintering areas at lower elevations.
- Although a lifespan of 6 to 8 years is more common, mule deer are capable of living to 20 years in the wild.

Local Names

Muley, blacktail

Size

Mature bucks commonly stand 3½ feet at the shoulders and weigh 150 to 200 pounds. Big bucks can weigh over 400 pounds. Mature does are generally about 3 feet at the shoulders and weigh up to 160 pounds.

Coat and Color

Mule deer normally have a light brown or reddish-brown coat in the summer, which becomes thicker and changes to gray in the winter. Portions of the belly, rump, tail, throat, muzzle, and inner ears are white. The tail is black-tipped, and the top of the head and end of the muzzle are often black or dark gray on mature bucks. A patch on the throat and the chest can also appear nearly black on mature bucks. The hair on most of the coat is fine and smooth, but the hair on the underbelly is longer and somewhat woolly.

Mule deer's oversized ears enables it to detect faint sounds over great distances.

Antlers

Unlike the continuous main beams of the white-tailed deer, the antlers of a mule deer are characterized by branching. A typical rack of a mature buck will branch equally (dichotomously) forming two tines on each branch, or a basic 4x4. If the antlers continue to grow there may be another branch resulting in additional tines. Brow tines are usually only a few inches in length if they are present. Some bucks will grow non-typical racks with irregular configurations and numerous points extending from the beams in different directions. These racks are sometimes palmated and can be very massive.

Young bucks generally have spikes or fork horns. The antlers usually fork into a 4-point rack by 2½ to 3½ years of age. As long as nutrition is good and the buck is healthy, the antlers will grow larger each year. Mule deer bucks continue to grow until they are 9 or 10 years of age. If they survive this long they can produce huge antlers with long beams, numerous points, and spreads of 30 inches.

Mule deer usually drop their antlers in February or March, but in some areas it can be as early as January. They begin to re-grow the antlers in April and rub the velvet off by August or September.

Voice and Communications

A mule deer buck will grunt and sometimes blatt, and both bucks and does will snort and stamp their feet when danger is present. Does and fawns often bleat in high-pitched tones. Posture and scent are also largely used by mule deer for communication. Scent glands are present on the face, legs, and feet. Bucks will sometimes lay their ears back and erect their tail and body hair to communicate aggression. They will also urinate on the metatarsal gland to broadcast scent. Big bucks rub bushes and trees with their antlers not only to remove velvet in the fall, but also to communicate dominance.

Senses

Mule deer possess keen senses of smell, sight, and hearing. Their oversized ears can detect faint sounds over great distances, but they probably rely on their senses of smell and sight just as much to warn them of impending danger. Since mule deer inhabit all types of habitat, they live in wooded areas, open country, and even densely vegetated river bottoms. As a result, they may rely on one sense over another depending on the terrain. Thick vegetation may necessitate a reliance on smell and hearing over sight. In open prairie country the mule deer may rely more heavily on its keen vision to assess danger.

In heavy cover a mule deer will often slink away at the slightest noise. Another conspicuous trait occurs when a well-hidden buck will remain stationary at the approach of a predator. While elk hunting near timberline in GMU 500 a few years ago I took a lunch break next to a large spruce. I was tired from hiking and rested there for about 20 minutes. When I got ready to leave I swung my pack on and happened to step forward towards an adjacent spruce tree no more than 10 yards away. There, bedded in the shadows of the drooping limbs, was one of the largest muleys I've ever seen. The moment I made eye contact with the buck he sprang from his bed and bounded out of sight. He had remained hunkered down the whole time I ate lunch. I couldn't believe it, but it taught me a valuable lesson about mule deer.

Tracks and Sign

Like white-tailed deer, mule deer have heart-shaped tracks that are well rounded in the back and pointed in the front. The track usually shows the two hooves, but in soft ground or snow the dewclaws are often visible. Also like a whitetail deer a muley will often splay the toes apart when running. This allows them to contact more surface area on the ground and gives them more stability. Mule deer bound up and down with all four feet leaving and contacting the ground simultaneously (referred to as stotting). This results in clusters of four tracks with distances of 9 to 19 feet between sets. If you find stotting tracks 15 feet apart, you probably won't get a chance to see the deer that left them since he is likely in the next county. Tracks are generally 2 to 3.5 inches in length and 1.6 to 2.5 inches wide. Older deer will often have worn and blunted hooves resulting in a rounder track.

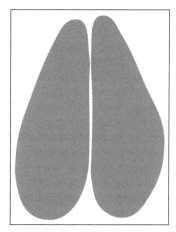

Mule deer track, running to 3¼″ in length.

Muleys leave piles of individual pellets when

browsing and cakes when eating lush vegetation. Additional sign includes beds that result in oval-shaped depressions in thick grass. Beds are also visible as depressions and scraped areas in dirt and pine needles. A good way to determine if a bed was made by a buck is to smell for urine. Does do not generally urinate in their beds like bucks do. During the rut bucks will also rub trees and shrubs leaving broken vegetation behind. Bucks also urinate over the tarsal glands on their hocks during the rut. If you find a spot with overlapping track and urine in a small area, it may indicate a mature buck in rut.

Reproduction and Young

Mule deer breed in November and December. Does go into estrus for short durations, often less than a day in length. If they are not bred they repeat the cycle every few weeks until they are bred. The gestation period is about 200 days. Does are bred as yearlings and generally produce a single fawn. Older does tend to give birth to two fawns. Fawns are usually 8 pounds at birth and rely exclusively on mothers' milk for the first two to three weeks after birth. During this time the fawns will remain hidden much of the time. They begin to forage with their mother after three weeks and are completely weaned by fall. The doe will remain isolated from other deer after fawning. As winter approaches she will take the fawns and rejoin larger groups of does and their young.

Habitat

Mule deer inhabit every major ecosystem in Colorado. They are very adaptable to settings as variable as semi-desert shrubland to alpine tundra and everything in between; however, they have the greatest population densities in shrublands. The shrublands provide an abundance of browse, which makes up a large part of their diet throughout the year. Generally they subsist on over 70 percent browse during the winters. During the other seasons browse from trees and shrubs accounts for about half of their diet while forbs and grasses make up the rest.

Home Range

Mule deer often migrate in the fall to wintering grounds. Generally these areas are at lower elevations where deep snows are less likely to accumulate. Often the wintering grounds are found on south-facing slopes with good shrub growth. Mule deer may migrate as far as 50 miles to wintering grounds, but distances are generally much less and may be only a mile or two. Two primary factors cause mule deer to migrate, snowfall and range quality. Snowpack at higher elevations can limit the ability of mule deer to forage; as a result, the first significant snow accumulations often cause them to move lower to wintering grounds. Also, if the range is in poor condition, they may start migrations prior to any snow. Unless habitat conditions change dramatically, mule deer will return to the same summer and winter ranges year after year.

Seasonal home ranges are variable and dependant on the quality of the habitat. They range anywhere from 100 acres in size to well over 2,000 acres in size. Mule deer that do not make lengthy seasonal migrations have annual home ranges anywhere from 3 to 10 square miles.

A buck scent-checks a doe during the rut.

Forage Plants

Mule deer have a variable diet that often includes sagebrush, scrub oak, mountain-mahogany, serviceberry, bitterbrush, fir, aspen, rabbitbrush, and various grasses. In agricultural areas mule deer will supplement or sometimes completely subsist on crops such as corn, milo, and alfalfa when available.

Daily Patterns

Mule deer change their daily patterns depending on the season. They are usually most active at sunrise and sunset during the warmer months. They can also be largely nocturnal at this time of year. During the winter, especially during very cold temperatures, they are much more active during the day.

During most of the hunting seasons mule deer will be most active feeding in the early and late hours of the day. They can survive by utilizing the moisture in forage, but more often seek water each day, especially in hot and arid ecosystems.

Deer will often bed during the heat of the day. They choose high vantage points in open prairie country, high covered exposures in rimrock settings, and will often bed under trees or in grassy areas in forests. If forage is good, muleys will often move less than a mile in a given day; however, hunting pressure and poor habitat may cause them to travel several miles a day.

Rutting Behavior

Bucks often roam together in bachelor herds until the rut starts. At this time dominant bucks split up and follow groups of does during November and December.

When the buck senses that a doe has gone into estrus he will single her out of the group and attempt to breed with her. He will often stay with the group until all of the does have been bred.

During the rut bucks will rub or horn vegetation and mark it with scent. They will also urinate on their metatarsal glands to broadcast scent. If other bucks approach, the tending buck will often show an aggressive posture by walking stiff legged with bristled hair and snorting. When two mature bucks meet up a fight can ensue. The bucks will clash their antlers together and push each other. The more powerful buck can often push the weaker animal back until it loses its footing. If it doesn't escape from this dangerous situation the stronger buck may gore the opponent with his antlers. Once the battle is won the victor will chase the loser away and return to his does.

Trophy Dimensions

Colorado has bragging rights to the world record typical mule deer. Doug Burris, Jr. killed the buck in Dolores County in 1972. This buck scored 226 4/8 points under the Boone and Crockett scoring system, beating the second place buck in the world by over 9 points. The buck sported a symmetrical 5x6 rack with a 30 7/8-inch spread and the longest beam pushing over the 30-inch mark.

Additional bragging rights include Pope and Young world records for both typical and non-typical racks. Bill Barcus shot the Pope and Young world record typical muley in 1979 while hunting in the White River National Forest. The buck scored 203 1/8. The non-typical world record (274 7/8) came out of Morgan County and was harvested by bowhunter Ken Plank.

A look at the Boone and Crockett records shows that Colorado accounts for a large percentage of the entries listed for the top 100 typical (and to a lesser extent non-typical) mule deer ever recorded. In fact, Colorado is one of the most prolific producers of trophy mule deer.

Many hunters consider trophy mule deer to be one of the most difficult animals to take. This is especially true for people hunting public land in the high country in Colorado. Trophy timberline muleys are extremely wary and hard to find. Many hunters are discovering that it is much easier to take trophy mule deer off private land on the eastern plains. Either way, it will be a hard-earned trophy.

In order to enter a typical buck into Boone and Crockett it will have to have a minimum score of 190. Non-typical bucks will have to be at least 230. The Pope and Young minimum score for typical bucks is 145, and for non-typical bucks it is 170. Pope and Young also has categories for antlers in velvet.

A Boone and Crockett typical buck will need at least 5 good points on each side. In addition to good symmetry you need to look for a spread of 25 inches or more and main beams of similar length.

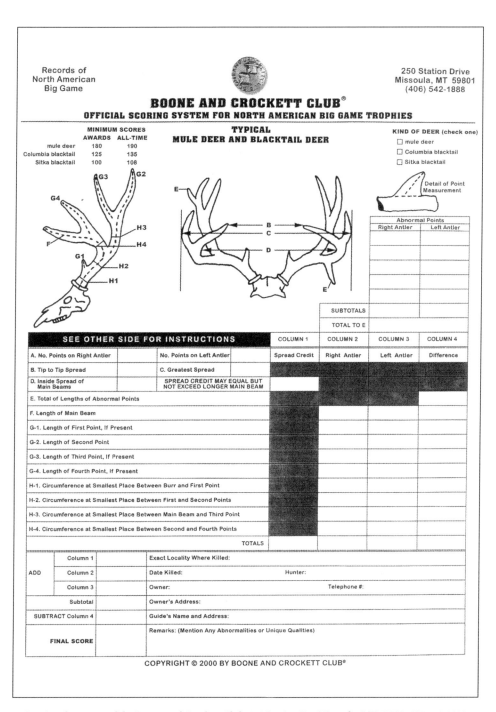

Reprinted courtesy of the Boone and Crockett Club, 250 Station Dr., Missoula, MT 59801, 406-542-1888

I, _____ , certify that I have measured this trophy on _____
PRINT NAME   MM/DD/YYYYY

at _____
STREET ADDRESS   CITY   STATE/PROVINCE

and that these measurements and data are, to the best of my knowledge and belief, made in accordance with the instructions given.

Witness: _____ Signature: _____ I.D. Number □ □ □ □
B&C OFFICIAL MEASURER

INSTRUCTIONS FOR MEASURING TYPICAL MULE AND BLACKTAIL DEER

All measurements must be made with a 1/4-inch wide flexible steel tape to the nearest one-eighth of an inch. (Note: A flexible steel cable can be used to measure points and main beams only.) Enter fractional figures in eighths, without reduction. Official measurements cannot be taken until the antlers have air dried for at least 60 days after the animal was killed.

- **A. Number of Points on Each Antler:** To be counted a point, the projection must be at least one inch long, with length exceeding width at one inch or more of length. All points are measured from tip of point to nearest edge of beam. Beam tip is counted as a point but not measured as a point.
- **B. Tip to Tip Spread** is measured between tips of main beams.
- **C. Greatest Spread** is measured between perpendiculars at a right angle to the center line of the skull at widest part, whether across main beams or points.
- **D. Inside Spread of Main Beams** is measured at a right angle to the center line of the skull at widest point between main beams. Enter this measurement again as the Spread Credit **if** it is less than or equal to the length of the longer main beam; if greater, enter longer main beam length for Spread Credit.
- **E. Total of Lengths of all Abnormal Points:** Abnormal Points are those non-typical in location such as points originating from a point (exception: G-3 originates from G-2 in perfectly normal fashion) or from bottom or sides of main beam, or any points beyond the normal pattern of five (including beam tip) per antler. Measure each abnormal point in usual manner and enter in appropriate blanks.
- **F. Length of Main Beam** is measured from the center of the lowest outside edge of burr over the outer side to the most distant point of the Main Beam. The point of beginning is that point on the burr where the center line along the outer side of the beam intersects the burr, then following generally the line of the illustration.
- **G-1-2-3-4. Length of Normal Points:** Normal points are the brow tines and the upper and lower forks as shown in the illustration. They are measured from nearest edge of main beam over outer curve to tip. Lay the tape along the outer curve of the beam so that the top edge of the tape coincides with the top edge of the beam on both sides of point to determine the baseline for point measurement. Record point lengths in appropriate blanks.
- **H-1-2-3-4. Circumferences** are taken as detailed in illustration for each measurement. If brow point is missing, take H-1 and H-2 at smallest place between burr and G-2. If G-3 is missing, take H-3 halfway between the base and tip of G-2. If G-4 is missing, take H-4 halfway between G-2 and tip of main beam.

ENTRY AFFIDAVIT FOR ALL HUNTER-TAKEN TROPHIES

For the purpose of entry into the Boone and Crockett Club's® records, North American big game harvested by the use of the following methods or under the conditions are ineligible:

- I. Spotting or herding game from the air, followed by landing in its vicinity for the purpose of pursuit and shooting;
- II. Herding or chasing with the aid of any motorized equipment;
- III. Use of electronic communication devices, artificial lighting, or electronic light intensifying devices;
- IV. Confined by artificial barriers, including escape-proof fenced enclosures;
- V. Transplanted for the purpose of commercial shooting;
- VI. By the use of traps or pharmaceuticals;
- VII. While swimming, helpless in deep snow, or helpless in any other natural or artificial medium;
- VIII. On another hunter's license;
- IX. Not in full compliance with the game laws or regulations of the federal government or of any state, province, territory, or tribal council on reservations or tribal lands;

I certify that the trophy scored on this chart was not taken in violation of the conditions listed above. In signing this statement, I understand that if the information provided on this entry is found to be misrepresented or fraudulent in any respect, it will not be accepted into the Awards Program and 1) all of my prior entries are subject to deletion from future editions of **Records of North American Big Game** 2) future entries may not be accepted.

FAIR CHASE, as defined by the Boone and Crockett Club®, is the ethical, sportsmanlike and lawful pursuit and taking of any free-ranging wild, native North American big game animal in a manner that does not give the hunter an improper advantage over such game animals.

The Boone and Crockett Club® may exclude the entry of any animal that it deems to have been taken in an unethical manner or under conditions deemed inappropriate by the Club.

Date: _____ Signature of Hunter: _____
(SIGNATURE MUST BE WITNESSED BY AN OFFICIAL MEASURER OR A NOTARY PUBLIC.)

Date: _____ Signature of Notary or Official Measurer: _____

Reprinted courtesy of the Boone and Crockett Club, 250 Station Dr., Missoula, MT 59801, 406-542-1888

Records of
North American
Big Game

250 Station Drive
Missoula, MT 59801
(406) 542-1888

BOONE AND CROCKETT CLUB®
OFFICIAL SCORING SYSTEM FOR NORTH AMERICAN BIG GAME TROPHIES

MINIMUM SCORES

AWARDS	ALL-TIME
215	230

NON-TYPICAL MULE DEER

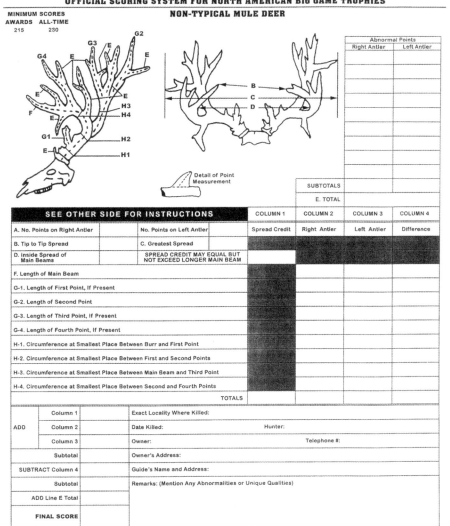

	Abnormal Points	
	Right Antler	Left Antler
SUBTOTALS		
E. TOTAL		

Detail of Point Measurement

SEE OTHER SIDE FOR INSTRUCTIONS		COLUMN 1	COLUMN 2	COLUMN 3	COLUMN 4
		Spread Credit	Right Antler	Left Antler	Difference
A. No. Points on Right Antler	No. Points on Left Antler				
B. Tip to Tip Spread	C. Greatest Spread				
D. Inside Spread of Main Beams	SPREAD CREDIT MAY EQUAL BUT NOT EXCEED LONGER MAIN BEAM				
F. Length of Main Beam					
G-1. Length of First Point, If Present					
G-2. Length of Second Point					
G-3. Length of Third Point, If Present					
G-4. Length of Fourth Point, If Present					
H-1. Circumference at Smallest Place Between Burr and First Point					
H-2. Circumference at Smallest Place Between First and Second Points					
H-3. Circumference at Smallest Place Between Main Beam and Third Point					
H-4. Circumference at Smallest Place Between Second and Fourth Points					
TOTALS					

ADD	Column 1		Exact Locality Where Killed:
	Column 2		Date Killed: Hunter:
	Column 3		Owner: Telephone #:
	Subtotal		Owner's Address:
SUBTRACT Column 4			Guide's Name and Address:
	Subtotal		Remarks: (Mention Any Abnormalities or Unique Qualities)
	ADD Line E Total		
	FINAL SCORE		

COPYRIGHT © 2002 BY BOONE AND CROCKETT CLUB®

Reprinted courtesy of the Boone and Crockett Club, 250 Station Dr., Missoula, MT 59801, 406-542-1888

Hunting Tactics

Hunting big mule deer bucks versus small bucks and does is almost like hunting two different species. Younger bucks and does are much easier to stalk, even in open country. Just make sure the wind is right, and wait to move until the deer has its head down feeding or is turned away from you. Look for objects between you and the deer that will block the line of sight then proceed with extreme caution, not making any noise. When stalking big bucks one of the most effective approaches is to watch them from a distance until they bed down. Once bedded you can map out an appropriate stalk taking the necessary time to close the distance.

Since mule deer inhabit every type of ecosystem in Colorado, the terrain will play greatly in how you pursue them. Hunting big bucks near timberline will require long

Shot Placement:
Top: Broadside shot.
Aim for the center of the chest just behind the bend of the front leg or shoulder; this should penetrate the lungs.

Below: Quartering shot.
Aim for the off-side shoulder by drawing an imaginary line from your rifle or bow to the far-side shoulder; aim slightly behind the shoulder if you don't wish to damage any meat.

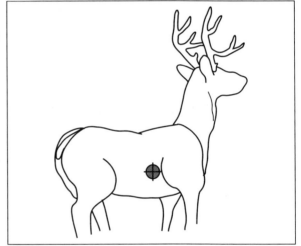

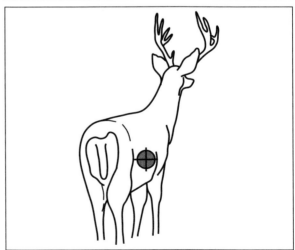

periods of glassing, then cautious stalks. Hunting in the timber will necessitate patient still-hunting. In areas with abundant sign, move slowly a couple of steps at a time then stop and spot. Don't forget to use your binoculars in the timber. Sometimes you will be able to see a small portion of a deer behind trees with the help of your optics that wouldn't be visible otherwise. The key is to spot the deer before it sees, hears, or smells you.

I've had good success hunting mule deer using several different techniques. Again, the key is to fit the method to the country. Stalking has worked very well for me in open sagebrush country. Hunting from blinds constructed near meadows, agricultural fields, and along travel routes has also worked. Treestands are also very effective for mule deer in the river bottoms of eastern Colorado, but don't forget about your treestand when hunting in the mountains. If you can locate areas with high population densities, a stand set in a pine or aspen tree along a prominent trail can be a good bet. Blinds and treestands erected near water sources are also effective.

Another good tactic often used in eastern states but forgotten about in the west is driving deer. Target brushy draws and small mountain valleys. Position hunters at the head of the draw and at obvious escape routes. As another hunter moves up the draw be ready for animals to move. As in any hunting scenario practice extreme caution to identify your target, especially when other hunters are moving in an area. Drives are best suited for rifle hunters. Mini-drives can also be effective for bedded bucks. As often as not the deer will spook right before adequate range is achieved. In these situations try to determine the direction the buck will flee and position a hunter in that direction. Hopefully, one of you will get a close shot.

During the rut don't overlook the use of grunt calls and rattling to attract bucks. This is commonly done when hunting whitetails, but can also be effective for mule deer. Finally, some bowhunters are starting to find that decoys effectively attract mule deer as well as whitetail deer.

Rifle Caliber Suggestions

As with hunting tactics, the terrain will dictate what the best calibers are for mule deer. In wide-open prairie, plains, and even mountain terrain, fast flat-shooting calibers with good knock-down power such as the .270, .280, or 7mm will be ideal. Since many hunters will be pursuing elk in Colorado during the same season they pursue deer, the versatility of a .30-06 is ideal. In thick cover on river bottoms or in wooded areas shorter rifles with good knock-down power are preferable. The old standby .30-30 is a good choice.

There is no better time to have a variable scope than when hunting mule deer. Backing your power down to 3x or 4x is great for up-close conditions. Midrange optics with 5x or 6x magnification are good when hunting in the mountains. If you are an accurate shot, long range situations in open country may necessitate higher magnification. The variable scope is so versatile for mule deer because you could potentially hunt in any of the situations described above in a single day.

Declining Mule Deer

Since many of the rural communities in Colorado derive significant boosts to their local economies during the hunting season, the decline of mule deer populations in the state has become a serious and sometimes emotional issue. In an attempt to more adequately manage deer herds, the Colorado Division of Wildlife recently went to a completely limited licensing system for mule deer hunting. Prior to changing the over-the-counter licensing, the DOW held public meetings concerning the five-year hunting season structure for 2000 to 2004. I attended meetings held in Denver in which there was a great turnout by concerned sportsmen. At one of the meetings there were over 200 people, almost entirely made up of sportsmen. While the greater public is generally unaware that there is even a problem, sportsmen supported a process that could ultimately restrict their chances to hunt mule deer.

Deer populations in the state are believed to have peeked in the 1940s when there may have been as many as one million animals. Over the last six decades the DOW estimates that the population has declined to about half a million animals. It should be noted that many herds in the state have stable populations that still exhibit growth, but there is a problem. Not only is Colorado experiencing the problem, but also many of the western states show similar situations with mule deer declines.

There don't seem to be any easy answers to the cause of the decline or quick fixes for the problem. Nature is a complicated process with countless variables. Key issues concerning the declining mule deer populations include lost habitat, changes in range management practices, disease, competition from other species, predation, and road kill to name a few. The positive side is that through modern management methods paid for by sportsmen, the DOW was able to recognize that a problem existed. As a result, several studies have been launched to determine the causes of the problem, and what the potential remedies may be. In the meantime there are still excellent opportunities to hunt mule deer in Colorado even though you have to apply for a limited license in the annual drawing.

Colorado mule deer trophies hold several world records.

Look for mule deer bedded under trees during the heat of the day.

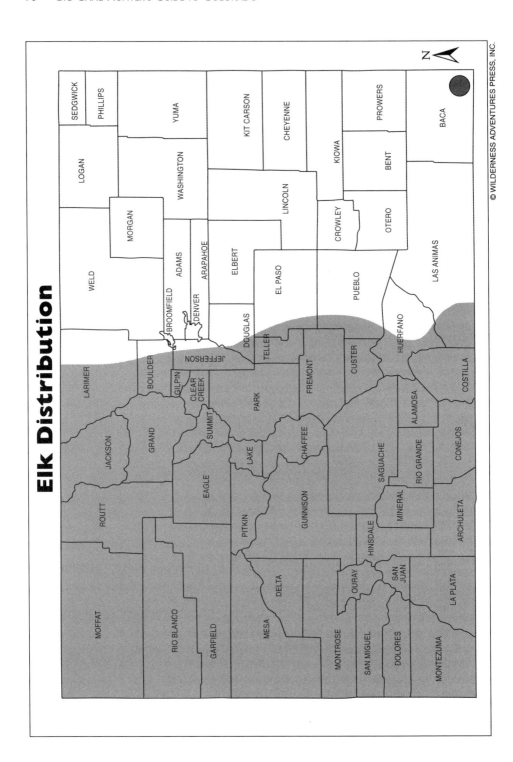

Elk Distribution

© WILDERNESS ADVENTURES PRESS, INC.

Elk

Cervus elephus

The majestic elk not only inhabits the wild places of Colorado, but it lives in the wild places of every big game hunter's imagination. A mature bull elk is often considered one of the most prized big game animals in North America, and hunters spend extraordinary amounts of energy, time, and money in their pursuit each year.

Fascinating Facts

- Colorado is home to the largest population of elk in North America. Population statistics provided by the Colorado Division of Wildlife indicate that there are over 300,000 elk in the state.
- Market hunting for meat and their upper canine teeth (buglers) nearly extirpated elk from the state by the early 1900s. Populations at this time may have been as low as 500. Transplants of Yellowstone elk helped refurbish the population.
- Like white-tailed deer, elk seem to have a fondness for the taste of mushrooms, which often grow in areas of dark timber that the elk like to haunt.
- Elk are capable of living up to 20 years in the wild, but more commonly they survive 3 to 7 years.
- Sheep and elk don't seem to get along. Elk are known to abandon areas being grazed by domestic sheep, and bighorn sheep tend to avoid areas being used by elk.
- Historically, elk lived in the mountains and on the eastern plains, but they now live primarily in the mountainous areas in the western half of Colorado.
- In the scientific name, *Cervus* is Latin for stag, and *elaphus* originated from the Greek word elaphos for deer.

Local Names
Wapiti

Size
Elk are large animals, but hunters probably overestimate their size more than any other big game animal. The average size for a mature bull is somewhere between 500 and 800 pounds. They will stand 5 feet at the shoulders. Exceptionally large bulls can weigh 1,000 pounds and measure up to 9 feet in length from the nose to the tail. Cows and younger bulls stand 4½ feet at the shoulder and weigh 450 to 600 pounds.

Coat and Color
The body of the elk is tan or light brown. The neck is a dark brown with longer hair often referred to as the mane. Much of the legs are also covered with dark brown hair, although much shorter in length than the rest of the coat or the mane. The rump is light tan or cream with a tail of the same color.

An elk's massive antlers can weigh up to 50 pounds.

Antlers

The antlers of a bull elk sweep back from the top of the head. They consist of a continuous main beam that generally doesn't fork. From each main beam several tines protrude upward. The antlers often curve inward towards the back. The size of the antlers is dependent upon several factors including genetics, age, and nutrition. The quality of summer forage may be the single most important factor in determining how big the antlers get.

Typically a 1½-year-old bull will be a spike. By the second or third year the bull will grow racks with 3 or 4 points on each side, often referred to as raghorns. By the fourth year the antlers will be developing into larger racks with 5 or even 6 points per side. Five point bulls and small 6x6s are sometimes referred to as brush bulls. Antler growth will reach its peak when a bull is 7 or 8 years of age. Just like its age, the antlers will often have six to eight points on each beam at this stage. Informally, six point bulls are known as Royal, seven points are Imperial, and eight points are called Monarchs. Depending on the health of a bull and the quality of forage it may continue to grow more massive racks until it reaches 10 to 12 years of age. If the bull lives past its prime the antlers will often dwindle in size in ensuing years.

The dimensions of large elk antlers are impressive. Big bulls can have main beams that reach to five feet in length. Individual tines may grow to 2 feet and the spread between the beams may be over 4 feet. A huge set of antlers with these dimensions may weigh 40 or 50 pounds.

Voice and Communications

In addition to their large antlers, elk are well-known for their vocal communication. Bulls, cows, and calves often mew in high-pitched tones to communicate with one another. Cows and calves sometimes make calls resembling a chirping bird when in heavy cover to stay in contact with one another. Cows will also announce danger with startlingly loud, high-pitched barks that resonate through the forest. Probably best known, though, is the bugle of a bull. The bugle often starts low and raspy, then escalates into a series of higher pitched tones often ending in a series of grunts. From a distance the bugle can almost sound flute-like. Bulls will also make low, bellowing grunts that echo through the woods. Bugling may be done for a variety of reasons, but it is thought that bulls try to attract cows and also show dominance through their bugles. Elk also communicate largely through scent and posturing. Large bulls will urinate on their underbelly, legs, and neck during the rut, broadcasting a distinctive musky odor everywhere they go.

Senses

The elk has highly developed senses of hearing, smell, and sight. Most notable to hunters is the incredible ability of an elk to smell human scent at great distances. When in heavy timber elk probably rely on their sense of smell to the greatest extent. If alarmed by scent they won't hesitate to vacate the area. In open country elk will sometimes stop after running some distance to visually identify the danger, but they don't usually stick around very long. Although their eyesight is good, elk will often walk within close proximity of a hunter as long as he is completely still; however, the slightest movement will send an alert elk fleeing.

Tracks and Sign

Distinctive by their size, a bull elk track will often reach up to 5 inches in length and 4.5 inches in width. The track is generally rounder than that of a mule deer or white-tailed deer. In soft earth or snow the two dewclaws show up in the print. Like mule deer, the hooves on each foot are often splayed apart when an elk runs to give it better stability.

Droppings are characterized by the current food sources being utilized. Segmented cakes are left when there is an abundance of lush forbs and grasses. As the percentage of browse and drier food sources increases individual pellets are left.

Elk are big animals and they leave a lot of sign. Herds will often travel single file, leaving well-worn and chewed up trails. Elk beds are very obvious in grassy areas where large oval-shaped depressions are left. The musky scent of elk is usually very strong in bedding areas. Bulls also leave an abundance of sign. When their antlers mature they begin rubbing the velvet off. This results in broken vegetation and rub marks on trees. As the rut kicks in, bulls often wallow in creeks, bogs, marshes, or muddy areas. They commonly urinate in the area and roll about in the concoction of mud, water, and urine. Their rank smell

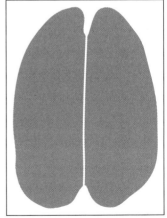

Elk track. Usually, an adult elk print runs around 4" in length.

and the black mud covering their coats easily identifies these bulls.

In the winter elk will often eat the bark of aspen trees, which leaves black scars on the trunks in the years to come. Elk will also seek out natural mineral sources and leave an abundance of sign at licks. Depending on the source of the minerals, the lick may result in deep concave depressions in weathered rock or hard dirt.

Reproduction and Young

Elk usually breed during late September and early October. Cows will go into estrus up to three times if necessary, about 20 days apart. The gestation period is approximately 250 days and calves are dropped in May and June. Cows will breed as yearlings and bulls are capable of breeding as yearlings but don't have much luck due to competition from older more dominant bulls. Most bulls are at least three years of age before they start breeding the cows.

Cows almost always have a single calf, but may occasionally have twins. The calves are large at birth and often weigh 25 to 30 pounds. The cows choose calving grounds with good forage, cover, and water. After birthing the cow will stay isolated with the calf for two or three weeks before rejoining the herd. At this time of year the herd is comprised of cows, calves, and young bulls. The mature bulls usually stay away from the bands of cows and calves until fall.

Habitat

Elk utilize several ecosystems in Colorado on a seasonal basis. In general elk will inhabit higher elevations in the summer. These areas often include subalpine forest and alpine tundra. As winter encroaches elk will often move to lower elevations and winter in montane forest and montane shrubland as well as semi-desert shrubland.

Home Range

If forage is good elk will often stay in a relatively small area for weeks at a time, moving less than a mile on any given day. Generally they migrate from summer ranges to wintering grounds each year. Migrations may be as short as a couple of miles downslope to over 25 miles long.

Summer ranges include high alpine valleys and meadows surrounded by dark timber. Elk migrate to summer ranges in early spring, following the snow line to higher elevations. They may also spend large amounts of time above timberline during the summer where temperatures are lower and bugs are less troublesome. Poor forage or significant accumulations of snow often trigger migrations to wintering grounds. Wintering grounds are often found on shrubland slopes.

Forage Plants

Elk are both grazers and browsers, eating a variety of grasses, forbs, shrubs, and trees. They are seasonal opportunists, taking advantage of lush grasses and forbs in the spring and summer and switching to more browse in the fall and winter. Although they will eat aspen twigs and bark during any season, it is a more common food source in winter when other foods are scarce. Aspen groves often show years of scars on the trunks from feeding elk. Agricultural fields also provide a food source for elk, but due to the damage they can inflict on crops, landowners are quick to get help in deterring elk from their property.

Daily Patterns

Elk generally move less than a mile on a given day, unless they are traveling during seasonal migrations. They may also travel several miles in a day when threatened by predators. They are most active in early morning and late evening. They are also nocturnal, feeding on and off through the night. A daily routine in the summer may include bedding in dark timber or grassy wooded areas on ridges during the heat of the day. As evening approaches they make there way back to feeding areas where they eat on off into the night. They feed again in the morning then make their way back to bedding areas. Elk tend to be more active during the daytime on overcast or rainy days.

A cow elk will occasionally produce twins.

Rutting Behavior

The rutting behavior of elk has been studied by wildlife biologists for decades. Still of debate is the exact trigger that causes the rut. Some believe that elk go into rut because of some habitual sense of timing. Others think that changes in temperature, forage, and the phase of the moon have something to do with it. Still others believe that an increase in the production of testosterone triggers the bull. In all likelihood it is a combination of things. Regardless of the cause, the rut usually starts in the late part of September in Colorado and extends into early October. This can vary slightly from year to year.

At a glance bull elk display several unique characteristics during the rut. They bugle, wallow, and rub their antlers when they're not busy trying to maintain harems of cows. Dominant bulls generally stay in close proximity to the cows during the rut

A bull elk bugling during the rut.

and step in to take control when the cows start to go into estrus. They spend all of their time breeding and fending off rival bulls. Often, a herd bull will simply round up his cows and move to a new area if another dominant bull is encroaching, but when two dominant bull cross paths it can result in violent fights. Younger bulls, or satellite bulls, will often stay near the harems in hopes of breeding cows when the dominant bull is pre-occupied. Mature bulls often lose significant percentages of their body weight during the rut. Throughout the rut the cows remain nearly unchanged in their daily patterns. They feed and bed normally within the confines of the bull's watchful stare.

Trophy Dimensions

Trophy is a subjective word, but most hunters will agree that a 6x6 bull elk is a trophy animal. Colorado has produced a number of huge bulls over the past 100 years, including the former world record typical American elk, which still stands as the second largest bull ever recorded by Boone and Crockett. The bull was shot by a hunter named John Plute in 1899 west of Crested Butte, Colorado. The antlers weren't officially scored until the 1950s, and Boone and Crockett didn't certify it as the world record until 1961. The antlers had incredible dimensions with the longest main beam just short of five feet in length. It was a 7x8 rack with a spread of 45 4/8 inches. What makes it stand out is the astonishing mass and length of the individual tines. The circumference measured between the first and second point was 12 1/8 inches, one of the biggest circumference measurements ever recorded from an American elk. The final score tallied 442 3/8 points under the Boone and Crockett scoring system. It stood as the world record for over three decades. The current world record came from the White Mountains of Arizona, nixing out the Plute bull by 2/8 of a point. Bulls of these dimensions are extremely rare. In fact, Boone and Crockett only lists three bulls over 440 points. From here there is a big drop of 20 points to the fourth place bull, and only 30 bulls have broken the elusive 400-point mark as listed in Boone and Crockett.

The minimum score for a typical American (also referred to as Yellowstone) elk to make Boone and Crockett is 375 points, and 385 for a non-typical. The Pope and Young minimums are 260 for typical and 335 for non-typical elk. Taking a Boone and Crockett class elk is rare, but if you're after the records, here's what you will need to make the minimum for a typical bull. The main beam will have to be at least 50 inches, but probably closer to 55 inches. A 6x6 rack will make it with great mass, spread, and symmetry, but it is more likely if it has seven or eight points on each side. The spread will probably have to be in the neighborhood of four feet.

A typical Pope and Young bull is no easy proposition either. In all likelihood it will have to possess a 5x6 or 6x6 rack with a minimum of a 30-inch spread. The main beams will probably have to extend beyond three feet, and the points will have to be well-defined and long. Good mass and symmetry will help. Wayne Bradley took the state record Pope and Young typical elk in 1986 from Montrose County; the bull scored 393 1/8.

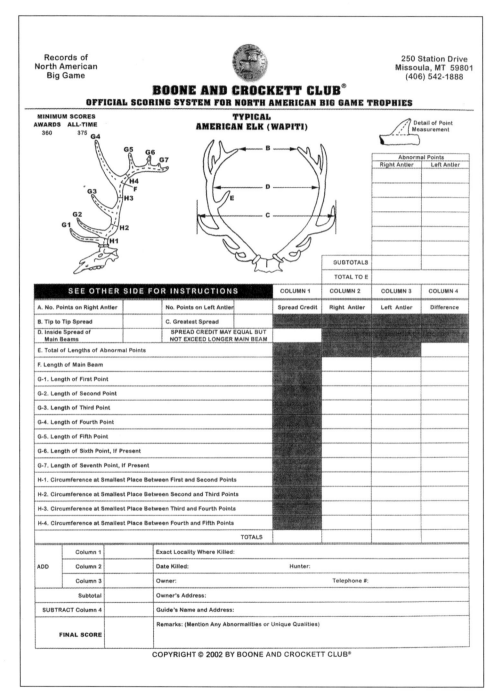

I, _____ , certify that I have measured this trophy on _____
PRINT NAME   MM/DD/YYYYY

at _____
STREET ADDRESS   CITY   STATE/PROVINCE

and that these measurements and data are, to the best of my knowledge and belief, made in accordance with the instructions given.

Witness: _____ Signature: _____ I.D. Number [ ][ ][ ]
B&C OFFICIAL MEASURER

INSTRUCTIONS FOR MEASURING TYPICAL AMERICAN ELK (WAPITI)

All measurements must be made with a 1/4-inch wide flexible steel tape to the nearest one-eighth of an inch. (Note: A flexible steel cable can be used to measure points and main beams only.) Enter fractional figures in eighths, without reduction. Official measurements cannot be taken until the antlers have air dried for at least 60 days after the animal was killed.

A. Number of Points on Each Antler: To be counted a point, the projection must be at least one inch long, with length exceeding width at one inch or more of length. All points are measured from tip of point to nearest edge of beam as illustrated. Beam tip is counted as a point but not measured as a point.

B. Tip to Tip Spread is measured between tips of main beams

C. Greatest Spread is measured between perpendiculars at a right angle to the center line of the skull at widest part, whether across main beams or points.

D. Inside Spread of Main Beams is measured at a right angle to the center line of the skull at widest point between main beams. Enter this measurement again as the Spread Credit if it is less than or equal to the length of the longer main beam; if greater, enter longer main beam length for Spread Credit.

E. Total of Lengths of all Abnormal Points: Abnormal Points are those non-typical in location (such as points originating from a point or from bottom or sides of main beam) or pattern (extra points, not generally paired). Measure in usual manner and record in appropriate blanks.

F. Length of Main Beam is measured from the center of the lowest outside edge of burr over the outer side to the most distant point of the main beam. The point of beginning is that point on the burr where the center line along the outer side of the beam intersects the burr, then following generally the line of the illustration.

G-1-2-3-4-5-6-7. Length of Normal Points: Normal points project from the top or front of the main beam in the general pattern illustrated. They are measured from nearest edge of main beam over outer curve to tip. Lay the tape along the outer curve of the beam so that the top edge of the tape coincides with the top edge of the beam on both sides of point to determine the baseline for point measurement. Record point length in appropriate blanks.

H-1-2-3-4. Circumferences are taken as detailed in illustration for each measurement.

ENTRY AFFIDAVIT FOR ALL HUNTER-TAKEN TROPHIES

For the purpose of entry into the Boone and Crockett Club's® records, North American big game harvested by the use of the following methods or under the following conditions are ineligible:

I. Spotting or herding game from the air, followed by landing in its vicinity for the purpose of pursuit and shooting;
II. Herding or chasing with the aid of any motorized equipment;
III. Use of electronic communication devices, artificial lighting, or electronic light intensifying devices;
IV. Confined by artificial barriers, including escape-proof fenced enclosures;
V. Transplanted for the purpose of commercial shooting;
VI. By the use of traps or pharmaceuticals;
VII. While swimming, helpless in deep snow, or helpless in any other natural or artificial medium;
VIII. On another hunter's license;
IX. Not in full compliance with the game laws or regulations of the federal government or of any state, province, territory, or tribal council on reservations or tribal lands;

I certify that the trophy scored on this chart was not taken in violation of the conditions listed above. In signing this statement, I understand that if the information provided on this entry is found to be misrepresented or fraudulent in any respect, it will not be accepted into the Awards Program and 1) all of my prior entries are subject to deletion from future editions of **Records of North American Big Game** 2) future entries may not be accepted.

FAIR CHASE, as defined by the Boone and Crockett Club®, is the ethical, sportsmanlike and lawful pursuit and taking of any free-ranging wild, native North American big game animal in a manner that does not give the hunter an improper advantage over such game animals.

The Boone and Crockett Club® may exclude the entry of any animal that it deems to have been taken in an unethical manner or under conditions deemed inappropriate by the Club.

Date: _____ Signature of Hunter: _____
(SIGNATURE MUST BE WITNESSED BY AN OFFICIAL MEASURER OR A NOTARY PUBLIC.)

Date: _____ Signature of Notary or Official Measurer: _____

Reprinted courtesy of the Boone and Crockett Club, 250 Station Dr., Missoula, MT 59801, 406-542-1888

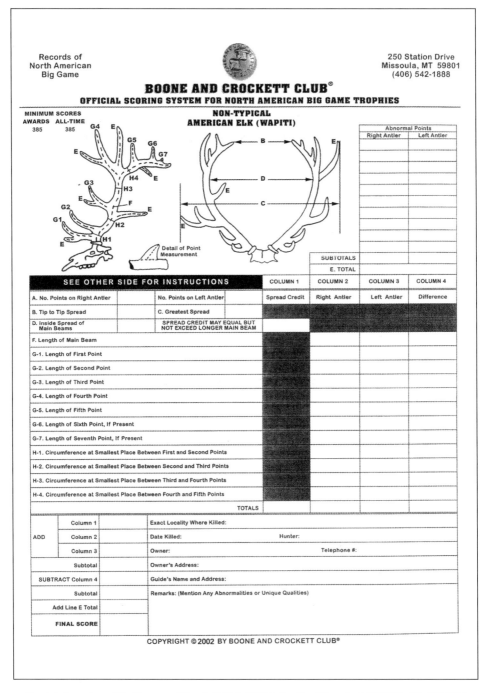

Hunting Tactics

One of the biggest challenges in hunting elk is finding them. Some people may go a whole hunting season without seeing an elk if they haven't done any scouting in advance. As with every big game species, preseason scouting will greatly increase your chances of filling your tag. Once found, elk can often be located in the same areas year after year. If you have found such an area, hunting tactics will vary greatly depending on the type of weapon you are hunting with.

Archery season generally starts before elk have gone into rut. At this time calling can still be an effective approach. Experiment with your calls, and try to concentrate on cow and calf noises. Bulls or cows will often come in silently to these calls, so be patient and don't give up if you don't hear a response. As the rut kicks in later in September many hunters like to run and gun. That is, they bugle and cow call waiting for responses. If nothing calls back they cover country, calling intermittently until a bull answers back. This can be an effective approach, but if you're already in an area where you know there are elk, you might be better off to patiently hunt travel routes, feeding, or watering areas. Treestands can be very effective for elk in these situations. Also, if you find an active wallow or natural mineral lick, a treestand or portable blind might be the ticket to ambush a dominant bull.

Many hunters believe that elk have been educated by over-calling during the last 10 to 20 years. In my experience I've found that the effectiveness of aggressive calling to dominant bulls is a function of timing. If you're too early or too late, it probably won't work well. But if you time it right, you might be in for some of the most exciting and action-packed elk hunting of your life. If you're not having success with bugling and aggressive calling, tone it back a bit and rely more on cow calls. If you get that big bull to come in, quit calling. If you continue to call when they're in close proximity they will very likely pinpoint your location and spook. If they hang up for some reason out of range, then you have nothing to lose, try calling again, minimally, until they come into range.

During the early rifle seasons in October there is a good chance that elk will still be in the rut. I've heard stories of many hunters successfully calling in aggressive bulls at this time of the year. At a minimum, calling should still be in your arsenal when hunting the later rifle seasons. Even if you can't bugle in a bull, you might be able to reassure a spooked group of elk with a cow call and stop them long enough to get a good shot. Rifle hunters will also want to concentrate on feeding areas early in the morning and in the late evening. Sometimes the most effective way is to simply watch meadows within rifle range. Still-hunting dark timber during the day can be effective, and watching prominent trails might get you a shot.

If the weather is fortuitous, you might get some good tracking snow. Look for tracks in fresh snow and start tracking. Realistically, this often results in a worn-out hunter who never sights an elk, but depending on the timing the tracks might also take you right to an old bull. Heavy snowfall can also trigger migrations. If you can find the routes of travel or the wintering areas you will have a good chance to fill your tag. Finally, don't forget to use your binoculars when rifle hunting for elk. In big country at great distances even large elk can be difficult to see. Spend the time to thoroughly glass meadows and mountainsides. This approach can save miles of wear and tear on your legs.

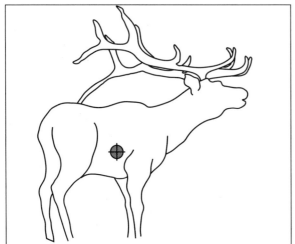

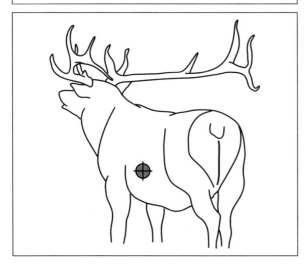

Shot Placement:
Top: Broadside shot.
Aim for the center of the chest just behind the bend of the front leg or shoulder; this should penetrate the lungs.

Below: Quartering shot.
Aim for the off-side shoulder by drawing an imaginary line from your rifle or bow to the far-side shoulder; aim slightly behind the shoulder if you don't wish to damage any meat.

Rifle Caliber Suggestions

The size of an elk dictates heavier bullets from more powerful cartridges than smaller big game animals. Optimal calibers for elk include the .270, .280, 7mm Mag, .300, and .338. Again, since many people will be hunting combined seasons for deer and elk, the .30-06 is a versatile caliber for both. Regardless of the caliber, you should use a premium bullet that will transfer all of the energy to the target without disintegrating on impact.

Trophy Quality

In recent years many people have complained that the trophy quality of Colorado elk is poor in comparison to other western states. The Colorado Division of Wildlife tries to monitor bull-to-cow ratios to determine the health of individual herds. It also manages many big game units as quality areas where the bull harvest is strictly controlled. In many areas point restrictions are in effect in an attempt to allow younger bulls to have better chances of reaching 3 to 4 years of age. In these areas a bull must have at least 4 points or one brow tine at least 5 inches in length to be a legal animal to harvest.

The facts are that several GMUs in Colorado have reputations for producing trophy-class bulls. To name a few, some of the best units are 2, 10, 201, 20, 39, 46, 61, 76, and 851. And even if you don't get lucky and draw a limited license for a quality area, there is still a very good chance to find a good bull on public land in an unlimited unit. The Division of Wildlife is charged with a difficult task. Should they further limit hunters from pursuing elk in certain areas to increase trophy potential, or should they only maintain adequate herd health to provide large numbers of hunters with the greatest chance to harvest any bull? Through questionnaires and hunter surveys the DOW seems to be taking a balanced approach concentrating on maintainable herds with good bull-to-cow ratios. They continue to limit hunting in certain areas to maintain good numbers of mature bulls while providing unlimited opportunities in units with higher populations.

Whatever your take on management scenarios, as hunters and conservationists, we should all be happy with the number of elk in the state, and the excellent opportunities that still exist for taking mature bulls.

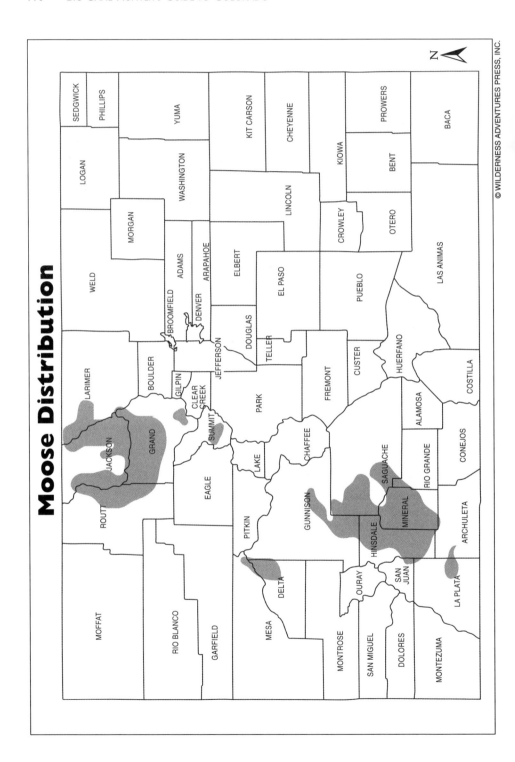

Moose Distribution

© WILDERNESS ADVENTURES PRESS, INC.

Moose

Alces alces

Although considered an introduced animal to Colorado, moose were known to wander into the northern reaches of the state from Wyoming prior to introduction. Once introduced in 1978, moose have increased their numbers and range dramatically. Today, Colorado is home to an estimated 1,100 Shiras moose.

Fascinating Facts

- Moose calves do not bare white spots as elk and mule deer young do.
- Often referred to as the beard, the skin hanging from the neck of a moose is more accurately known as the bell or the dewlap. The bell is not known to perform any specific function.
- Depending on winter range conditions an adult moose may increase its body weight by nearly 50 percent between spring and fall.
- Moose calves may gain over two pounds of body weight each day after they are born in May or June. By the following October healthy calves may weigh over 300 pounds.
- Although rare, moose are capable of living over 20 years in the wild.
- Even with their enormous size, adult moose are capable of running at 35 mph. They are also excellent swimmers capable of traveling over 5 mph through the water.
- Moose can sometimes be aggressive, especially cows with calves and bulls during the rut. Although rare, they have been known to charge people, cars, horses, and livestock.
- Moose will sometimes get down on their front knees while feeding on low vegetation.

Size

Even though it is smaller than its Alaskan and Canadian counterparts, the Shiras moose is the biggest wild animal in Colorado. It is 7 to 9 feet in length from its nose to its tail. Bulls can stand 6½ feet at the shoulders and weigh 800 to 1,110 pounds. Cows generally weigh between 600 and 900 pounds. If you draw a coveted tag and harvest a moose, you better be well prepared to get all of the meat out.

Coat and Color

The coat is chocolate brown to black over most of the body. The belly can be paler in color and the legs are light brown. The coat is longest on the neck and shoulders, but in general it's made up of long, coarse, somewhat brittle hair. The pelage may be slightly grayer during the winter. Calves have no white spots when they are born and a reddish-brown coat.

Antlers

More distinctive than any other member of the deer family, mature bulls generally have heavy palmate antlers that extend away from the top of the head outward and backward. Each palm may have several individual points varying from small protrusions from the ends of the palm to long well formed tines closer to the head. Brow tines can be present as individual points or a part of the palm. Each palm will vary in length from 20 inches to over 30 inches, with widths of 6 to 15 inches. Antlers are shed in December or February.

Voice and Communications

Moose are not nearly as vocal as elk, but they do moan and grunt loudly during the rut, and calves bleat. Cows generally moan to attract the bulls and the bulls make a distinctive nasal-toned grunt. Unlike other members of the deer family, moose don't have as many scent glands and probably don't use scent to communicate as readily as deer or elk. However, bull moose will wallow similar to a bull elk by urinating and rolling in mud. Bulls will also communicate through postural stances and unusual walks, sometimes characterized by a slow stiff-legged gait and a swaying head. This may communicate dominance or aggression. The lack of more advanced communicative traits may stem from their reclusive nature.

Between spring and fall an adult moose may increase its body weight by 50 percent.

Senses

Moose are generally considered to have poor eyesight. They depend more heavily on their excellent sense of smell and ability to hear. A quiet hunter who stays perfectly still downwind from a moose will probably remain undetected. Like elk, moose will also mistake a hunter's movement for another moose as long as they don't smell you.

Tracks and Sign

Comparable to their body size, moose leave the biggest tracks ranging in length from 4 to 7 inches and 3.5 to 5.5 inches wide. Due to their weight they almost always leave the imprint of their dewclaws when running, unless the ground is very hard. With the dewclaw visible the length of the track can reach 10 inches.

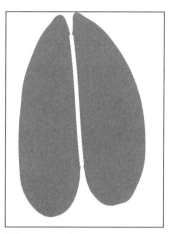

Moose track. Average length is 5".

The shape and size of moose droppings varies greatly depending on current food sources. They are bigger than deer or elk droppings. When eating willow or drier vegetation droppings consist of individual pellets, sometimes showing strands of woody vegetation. Sagebrush results in segmented pellets or strands, and aquatic vegetation and forbs results in small cakes.

Moose also leave a lot of sign in areas where they feed. Beaver ponds and small drainages can be tracked up, and water will be muddy from recent feeding on aquatic plants. Feeding areas also show signs of clipped vegetation and beds. During August and September bulls will rub trees and shrubs with their antlers just as other antlered animals do. This results in trees and shrubs with rub marks and broken branches. Bulls will also wallow in mud holes similar to an elk.

Reproduction and Young

Moose breed in late September and early October, although they may continue into November. Unlike an elk, a mature bull moose will only successfully impregnate two or three cows during the rut. As a result, bull-to-cow ratios must be substantially higher than in elk herds to maintain stable populations. A ratio of 50 bulls to every 100 cows is probably the minimum necessary to maintain consistent populations.

The gestation period is approximately 240 days and calves are dropped in May or June. Cows normally give birth to a single calf, but occasionally twins, and rarely triplets, are born. The occurrence of twins may be dependent upon forage quantity and quality. Unlike other members of the deer family, calves don't have spots when they're born. They often weigh over 20 pounds at birth and gain weight rapidly putting on as much as two pounds per day. By the following October healthy calves can weigh over 300 pounds. The calf will stay with the cow up to the following year when calving occurs again.

A calf born in May can weigh up to 300 pounds the following October.

Habitat

Moose often spend the summer at higher elevations in montane and subalpine forest consisting of spruce, fir, aspen, and willow. They are especially fond of areas that support new growth or lush vegetation. This type of habitat often occurs in areas of logging or where recent burns have occurred. Moose will also habituate high mountain valleys with plenty of water and vegetation in the summer. During the winter they generally move to lower elevations along streams and creeks that provide plenty of forage. In North Park, Colorado, where moose were first introduced, many of the drainages are choked with willows, making up ideal wintering areas for moose. They also frequent tributaries dammed by beavers.

Home Range

Once established in suitable habitat the home range of a moose is relatively small covering a seasonal area of three to five miles. As long as forage is abundant moose will return to the same areas year after year. Young moose will often cover long distances in search of their own territories.

Snow is the common motivator that moves moose to lower elevations in the winter. Once snow of 15 to 20 inches accumulates the animals will often move, even though their long legs give them the ability to survive in much deeper snow. They will seek out valleys sheltered from weather with abundant browse.

Unlike deer and elk, moose will often spend the winter solitary, especially cows with calves. Occasionally mixed groups will come together to form small herds during this time of the year.

Forage Plants

Moose take in a lot of food to keep their big bodies in motion. During the winter months they will eat up as much as 10 to 12 pounds of vegetation each day, and in the summer they nearly double the intake. Moose are predominantly browsers, especially in the winter, subsisting on the leaves, buds, stems, and bark of various trees and shrubs. Willow often makes up a large part of the winter diet along with other shrubs and trees such as sagebrush, dogwood, cottonwood, birch, and aspen. In the spring and summer moose will rely more upon lush vegetation and water plants such as sedges, various forbs, algae, and pondweed. Willow continues to be a mainstay in the diet even in the warmer months.

Daily Patterns

Moose are most active during early morning and late evening. As long as forage is abundant they will often travel less than a mile in a day. In both summer and winter they will bed in or near areas where they are feeding. During hot days in the summer they may move into dark timber for shade, away from feeding areas. During the rut, bulls will travel long distances in search of cows.

The largest member of the deer family, an adult Shiras moose may stand as tall as 6½ feet at the shoulders and weigh up to 1,1000 pounds.

Rutting Behavior

When the rut reaches its peak a bull moose will exhibit a swollen neck and forget about everything but breeding. They hardly forage and show aggression toward other bulls, sometimes resulting in fights. They also thrash and rub trees and shrubs with their antlers.

Moose are most vocal during this time of the year. Cows will moan loudly to attract bulls, and the bulls reciprocate with a nasal-toned grunt. They also bark and make croaking noises during the rut. Dominant bulls paw up wet earth and urinate in it creating mud holes that they wallow in. Once covered in urine-soaked mud the strong scent is broadcast to the cows. Younger bulls that aren't capable of producing the strong urine sometimes scavenge a dominant bull's wallow when vacant to use the scent of the mature bull.

Although a bull may breed with several cows, it seldom impregnates more than two or three in a season. The cows seem to understand this and will become possessive of their bull by chasing other cows away.

Trophy Dimensions

Considering that Shiras moose have only been a legal big game animal on a very limited basis in Colorado since 1985, the state has produced some fine bulls. In 1995, Jack Anderson harvested the number eight moose entered in the Boone and Crockett records. The antlers had a spread of 58½ inches with 9 points on one side and 11 points on the other. The palms were 39 and 40 inches in length and had a width of 13 inches or more. This monster bull scored 194 4/8 and was harvested in Jackson County.

The Boone and Crockett minimum score is 155 and Pope and Young requires a minimum of 125 under the same scoring system. Boone and Crockett class bulls will be very difficult to find in Colorado, but several lucky hunters have done it. Most of these bulls were taken in Jackson County in north-central Colorado. To meet the minimum score of 155 a bull will need to possess 28- to 30-inch palms with 8 to 11 points on each side. The width of each palm will probably have to be at least 10 inches and the spread will need to be over 40 inches, more likely in the 45-inch range. Pope and Young class bulls will need a minimum spread of 35 inches with good palms and 5 to 8 points on each side.

Regardless of trophy dimensions, it is exciting that Colorado has sufficient numbers of moose to hunt on a limited basis. Hopefully, populations will remain healthy and grow where adequate habitat is available.

Hunting Tactics

Archery season for moose during the 2002 hunting season runs from September 7-29. Bowhunters will miss the peak of the rut late in September and early October, but calling may still be an effective approach to lure in a bull. Try scraping trees and brush with branches to imitate a rubbing bull while you call. This approach will probably be more effective at the peak of the rut, which is likely to fall during the rifle season from October 1-9. If calling isn't productive spend time glassing in good habitat. Once an animal is spotted, make a careful stalk keeping the wind in your favor at all times. If you find a feeding area stay close to it during the morning and evening.

Shot Placement:
Top: Broadside shot.
Aim for the center of the chest just behind the bend of the front leg or shoulder; this should penetrate the lungs.

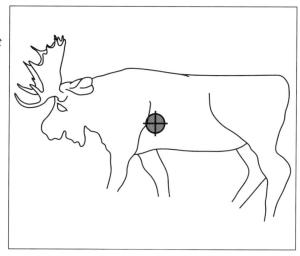

Rifle Caliber Suggestions

Moose have large bodies with big bones. Most calibers used on elk will also be sufficient for moose. Still, you probably want to go with a minimum of a premium 160-grain slug, and a 180-grain or 200-grain slug is better. Good calibers for moose include the 7mm Mag, .30-06, .300, or .338.

Moose eat 10 to 12 pounds of twigs, bark, roots and the shoots of woody plants each day in the winter and nearly double that in the summer.

Records of
North American
Big Game

250 Station Drive
Missoula, MT 59801
(406) 542-1888

BOONE AND CROCKETT CLUB®

OFFICIAL SCORING SYSTEM FOR NORTH AMERICAN BIG GAME TROPHIES

MOOSE

	MINIMUM SCORES	
	AWARDS	ALL-TIME
Canada	185	195
Alaska-Yukon	210	224
Wyoming	140	155

KIND OF MOOSE (check one)
☐ Canada
☐ Alaska-Yukon
☐ Wyoming

Detail of Point
Measurement

	Abnormal Points	
	Right Antler	Left Antler
NUMBER OF POINTS		
TOTAL TO B.		

SEE OTHER SIDE FOR INSTRUCTIONS	COLUMN 1	COLUMN 2	COLUMN 3	COLUMN 4
		Right Antler	Left Antler	Difference
A. Greatest Spread				
B. Number of Abnormal Points on Both Antlers				
C. Number of Normal Points				
D. Width of Palm				
E. Length of Palm Including Brow Palm				
F. Circumference of Beam at Smallest Place				
TOTALS				

ADD	Column 1		Exact Locality Where Killed:
	Column 2		Date Killed: Hunter:
	Column 3		Owner: Telephone #:
	Subtotal		Owner's Address:
SUBTRACT Column 4			Guide's Name and Address:
FINAL SCORE			Remarks: (Mention Any Abnormalities or Unique Qualities)

I, _____ , certify that I have measured this trophy on _____
   PRINT NAME   MM/DD/YYYYY

at _____
   STREET ADDRESS   CITY   STATE/PROVINCE

and that these measurements and data are, to the best of my knowledge and belief, made in accordance with the instructions given.

Witness: _____ Signature: _____ I.D. Number ☐☐☐☐
                                                     B&C OFFICIAL MEASURER

COPYRIGHT © 2002 BY BOONE AND CROCKETT CLUB®

Reprinted courtesy of the Boone and Crockett Club, 250 Station Dr., Missoula, MT 59801, 406-542-1888

INSTRUCTIONS FOR MEASURING MOOSE

Measurements must be made with a 1/4-inch wide flexible steel tape to the nearest one-eighth of an inch. Enter fractional figures in eighths, without reduction. Official measurements cannot be taken until antlers have air dried for at least 60 days after animal was killed.

A. Greatest Spread is measured between perpendiculars in a straight line at a right angle to the center line of the skull.

B. Number of Abnormal Points on Both Antlers: Abnormal points are those projections originating from normal points or from the upper or lower palm surface, or from the inner edge of palm (see illustration). Abnormal points must be at least one inch long, with length exceeding width at one inch or more of length.

C. Number of Normal Points: Normal points originate from the outer edge of palm. To be counted a point, a projection must be at least one inch long, with the length exceeding width at one inch or more of length. Be sure to verify whether or not each projection qualifies as a point.

D. Width of Palm is taken in contact with the under surface of palm, at a right angle to the inner edge of palm. The line of measurement should begin and end at the midpoint of the palm edge, which gives credit for the desirable character of palm thickness.

E. Length of Palm including Brow Palm is taken in contact with the surface along the underside of the palm, **parallel** to the inner edge, from dips between points at the top to dips between points (if present) at the bottom. If a bay is present, measure across the open bay if the proper line of measurement, parallel to **inner edge**, follows this path. The line of measurement should begin and end at the midpoint of the palm edge, which gives credit for the desirable character of palm thickness.

F. Circumference of Beam at Smallest Place is taken as illustrated.

ENTRY AFFIDAVIT FOR ALL HUNTER-TAKEN TROPHIES

For the purpose of entry into the Boone and Crockett Club's® records, North American big game harvested by the use of the following methods or under the following conditions are ineligible:

I. Spotting or herding game from the air, followed by landing in its vicinity for the purpose of pursuit and shooting;

II. Herding or chasing with the aid of any motorized equipment;

III. Use of electronic communication devices, artificial lighting, or electronic light intensifying devices;

IV. Confined by artificial barriers, including escape-proof fenced enclosures;

V. Transplanted for the purpose of commercial shooting;

VI. By the use of traps or pharmaceuticals;

VII. While swimming, helpless in deep snow, or helpless in any other natural or artificial medium;

VIII. On another hunter's license;

IX. Not in full compliance with the game laws or regulations of the federal government or of any state, province, territory, or tribal council on reservations or tribal lands;

I certify that the trophy scored on this chart was not taken in violation of the conditions listed above. In signing this statement, I understand that if the information provided on this entry is found to be misrepresented or fraudulent in any respect, it will not be accepted into the Awards Program and 1) all of my prior entries are subject to deletion from future editions of **Records of North American Big Game** 2) future entries may not be accepted.

FAIR CHASE, as defined by the Boone and Crockett Club®, is the ethical, sportsmanlike and lawful pursuit and taking of any free-ranging wild, native North American big game animal in a manner that does not give the hunter an improper advantage over such game animals.

The Boone and Crockett Club® may exclude the entry of any animal that it deems to have been taken in an unethical manner or under conditions deemed inappropriate by the Club.

Date:_____ Signature of Hunter:_____

(SIGNATURE MUST BE WITNESSED BY AN OFFICIAL MEASURER OR A NOTARY PUBLIC.)

Date:_____ Signature of Notary or Official Measurer:_____

Reprinted courtesy of the Boone and Crockett Club, 250 Station Dr., Missoula, MT 59801, 406-542-1888

Bighorn Sheep Distribution

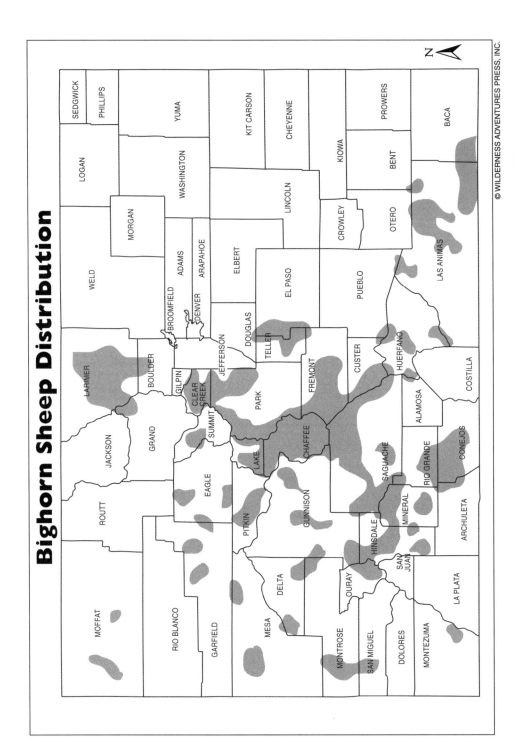

© WILDERNESS ADVENTURES PRESS, INC.

Bighorn Sheep
Ovis canadensis

Designated as the state animal in 1961, the bighorn sheep truly symbolizes the essential quality of the Colorado high country. Currently, the state is home to an estimated 6,500 bighorn sheep. There are also about 400 desert bighorns found in five herds in the Colorado River and Dolores River drainages.

Fascinating Facts

- Bighorn sheep are indigenous to Colorado although early settlers over-hunted them to critically low numbers by the late 1800s. Sheep hunting was closed between 1887 and 1953 to reestablish populations.
- Although dominant rams butt heads frequently during the breeding season, they also display this ritual periodically throughout the year to maintain orders of dominance.
- Rams may reach speeds of 20 mph just prior to butting heads.
- A ram's horns are said to be "broomed" when the sharp points have been blunted by head butting and wear, usually most evident on older rams.
- Sheep habitually use the same seasonal ranges, calving grounds, and bedding areas year after year.
- Historically, bighorn sheep lived at lower elevations in Colorado, including the eastern plains in close proximity to the foothills.
- One bighorn sheep hunting license for Colorado is raffled off each year at the Foundation for North American Sheep banquet. A record bid of $93,000 took the license for the 1999 season, and a bid of $73,000 captured it for the 2000 season.
- It is possible to determine the age of rams by counting annual growth ridges on the horns.

Local Names
Bighorns, mountain sheep, sheep, rams

Size
Sheep are compact and muscular averaging 3 to 3.5 feet at the shoulders and 4 to 6.5 feet in length. Rams vary in weight from 175 to 275 pounds. Ewes are generally about 20 percent smaller than rams. Desert bighorns are generally smaller weighing between 140 and 200 pounds.

Coat and Color
The bighorn pelage is brown to grayish-brown with a white muzzle and rump. The tail is brown or black and the white along the rump extends down the back of the back legs. The underbelly is also lighter in color. Long dense hairs give the bighorn an insulating coat to protect them from the cold and wind. The pelage of desert bighorn is similar, but generally paler.

A ram in its prime has massive, thick, ridged horns that curve backward, spiraling to encircle the ear. These horns continue to grow throughout its life.

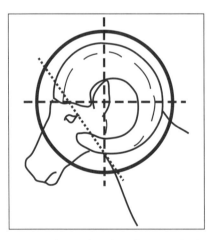

A sheep has a legal curl (¾ curl) if you can draw a straight line from the horn base through any part of the eye to the tip. A full curl would reach past the eye, creating a circle.

Horns

Maybe more coveted by serious big game hunters than any other animal's headgear; the horns of a mature bighorn ram are impressive. The horns grow from bony cores on the skull extending upward, outward and back. As the horns grow they curve downward and back up, forming a curl. Mature rams can grow massive sets of horns reaching over 40 inches in length with basal circumferences over 16 inches. The horns are made up of keratin and are never shed. They are usually light brown with prominent ridges that reflect periods of growth. Mature rams are distinguished by heavy mass and broomed horns with blunted tips. The horns of a mature desert bighorn ram often form wider curls with the ends farther from the head. The tips are generally sharper, displaying less brooming.

Ewes also have horns, although they are usually much thinner than a ram's. Ewe horns grow straight up from the skull sweeping back and out slightly, usually no more than 6 or 8 inches in total length.

Voice and Communications

Bighorn sheep occasionally make the characteristic *baaaa* of domestic sheep. This is usually reserved for ewes and lambs. Rams are vocally quiet but make up for their silence with loud head butting. Most communication between sheep is thought to be postural, especially between rams. Head butting takes place throughout the year, but the impressive bouts between dominant rams usually take place in November and December when the rams fight for ewes. Sheep may also communicate through scent to some degree, but not as readily as members of the deer family.

Senses

All of the senses of a bighorn are finely tuned. In open country where they spend much of their time they rely greatly on vision to detect danger. They can also hear and smell danger that they can't see, running from unseen danger when detected by these acute senses.

Tracks and Sign

Like deer and elk, sheep have two prominent weight-bearing hooves and two dewclaws. Unlike deer and elk, the tracks are less rounded at the back and less pointed at the front, resulting in a squarish imprint. The track is 2.5 to 3.5 inches in length and 1.8 to 2.5 inches wide. Sheep will also splay the weight-bearing hooves on each foot apart to give them better stability when running and climbing. The hooves are hard on the outside and softer on the inside, an adaptation that helps them climb rocky terrain.

One of the most identifiable signs of sheep is their bedding area. Bighorns bed in the same places year after year. The beds are often scratched out of the dirt or snow and the sheep urinate and defecate in the same areas resulting in accumulations of droppings. Well-worn trails often lead to the bedding areas.

Sheep droppings consist of tapered pellets ½-inch in length. They will also leave cakes about 3 inches in size when feeding on more succulent vegetation.

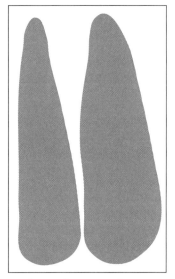

Bighorn sheep track. On average, they run 3½″ in length.

Reproduction and Young

Breeding takes place in November and December each year. A few dominant males breed most of the ewes, although younger males may occasionally step in when opportunities arise. It is thought that most males are 7 to 8 years of age before they breed. Ewes generally begin breeding by 2½ years of age. Typically, there will only be one ewe in estrus in a herd at any given time, causing several rams to pursue her. This is when the rams initiate their head butting fights to gain the right to breed the ewe.

The gestation period is about 180 days and ewes normally give birth to a single lamb 7 to 10 pounds in size. Like bedding areas, sheep return to specific lambing grounds year after year. Ewes and their young return to the herd a week after birthing. The lamb develops quickly and begins to forage on its own within a few weeks, although it isn't weaned for several months.

Mortality rates in lambs can be high not only from predation but from diseases such as lungworm, which causes pneumonia. This disease is carried by domestic sheep and can kill all ages of sheep in a herd. Wildlife managers have combated the disease by inoculating wild sheep and transplanting sheep in remote areas away from domestic animals.

Habitat

Sheep call the high country home, utilizing steep, open, rocky, exposed slopes in alpine tundra, subalpine forest, and montane forest ecosystems. These areas are often found at or above timberline, but sheep frequently utilize wooded areas, and may be found at much lower elevations (seasonally) in valleys or along river bottoms.

As the name implies, desert bighorns inhabit desert-like terrain at lower elevations. They are most often found in rocky, river canyons in southwest Colorado.

Home Range

Sheep are known to migrate between summer and winter ranges. They may also utilize several areas in a given year, moving short distances at a time as they migrate to seasonal grounds. Seasonal movements of 3 to 10 miles are typical, but can be much longer. Once on a seasonal range sheep will often move less than a mile on any given day. Sheep are very social and stay together in small herds. The rams generally separate themselves, forming bachelor groups in spring and summer.

Forage Plants

Sheep diets consist mostly of grasses and browse from various shrubs. They also eat forbs and sedges when available. When grasses are covered in the winter they will paw through shallow snow to feed or turn to more available shrubs such as sagebrush, willow, and rabbitbrush.

Daily Patterns

Sheep are diurnal, meaning they are active by day. If content on a seasonal range they will feed up to five times a day, bedding between feeding periods to chew their cud. At these times daily movements are often less than a mile. Depending on the seasonal range sheep may also travel long distances in a day to reach better food sources, water, or mineral licks. Sheep will often climb down several thousand feet to drink at a river when no other water sources are available. When threatened, sheep prefer to head upslope to rocky cover. They like to bed in rocky areas with open views, and their feeding areas are usually close to good escape cover.

Rutting Behavior

The rut is a busy time of the year for bighorn sheep. Mature rams move to breeding grounds in October with the rut generally starting in November. Rams follow bands of ewes waiting until one ewe comes into estrus. Unlike members of the deer family, ewes will only go into estrus one time during a breeding season. The rams are very attentive, though, and continually scent-check the ewe's urine to determine when it has gone into estrus.

At this time younger rams will also pursue the females. Chases can ensue, but mature rams generally drive the younger suitors away. When more than one dominant ram pursues a ewe serious head-butting fights can occur. The ram's rear up on their hind legs, lower their heads and drive forward towards each other. The two rams collide with a resounding crack as their horns meet. After the collision the rams tilt their heads back, maintaining a stiff pose while they regroup for another assault. Finally, often after many hours of head butting, the victorious ram will drive the opponent away and seek out the ewe. Sometimes younger rams have already bred

Sheep are very social and travel in small herds.

the ewe while the dominant rams were fighting.

The rut continues on into December as mature rams continue to tend groups of ewes one by one as they come into estrus. The rut usually tails off by the end of December or early in January.

Trophy Dimensions

Sheep from Colorado are listed sporadically in the Boone and Crockett records. A large percentage of Boone and Crockett sheep come from Montana and Alberta, Canada, but Colorado has produced some fine specimens. In fact, several large rams have been taken in the past few years. During the 1999 hunting season Wes Ward took the state record bighorn while hunting the Forbes Trinchera Ranch in southern Colorado. This exceptional ram scored 197 7/8. The Pope and Young world record bighorn was taken by Gene Moore in El Paso County, Colorado in 1983. This ram had incredible horns scoring over 191 points.

Any ram that makes the 180-point minimum for Boone and Crockett is truly a unique specimen. Pope and Young requires a minimum score of 140 points. A ram with 2/3 curls and decent mass will likely meet the Pope and Young requirement. To attain a score of 180, a ram will have to possess horns in the neighborhood of 38 inches in length with basal measurements of 15 inches and good mass continuing around the curl.

Sheep are often described and judged by the size of their curl. Horns that extend back and down and curve all the way back up to the eye are said to be full curls. Horns with broomed tips often indicate an older ram. While the horns may be slightly shorter due to the blunted tips, the mass that comes with age often makes up for the missing length.

When threatened, sheep prefer to travel upslope.

Records of
North American
Big Game

250 Station Drive
Missoula, MT 59801
(406) 542-1888

BOONE AND CROCKETT CLUB®
OFFICIAL SCORING SYSTEM FOR NORTH AMERICAN BIG GAME TROPHIES

SHEEP

	MINIMUM SCORES	
	AWARDS	ALL-TIME
bighorn	175	180
desert	165	168
Dall's	160	170
Stone's	165	170

KIND OF SHEEP (check one)
- ☐ bighorn
- ☐ desert
- ☐ Dall's
- ☐ Stone's

PLUG NUMBER

_____

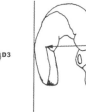

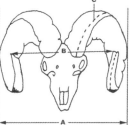

Measure to a
Point in Line
With Horn Tip

SEE OTHER SIDE FOR INSTRUCTIONS	COLUMN 1	COLUMN 2	COLUMN 3
A. Greatest Spread (Is Often Tip to Tip Spread)	Right Horn	Left Horn	Difference
B. Tip to Tip Spread			
C. Length of Horn			
D-1. Circumference of Base			
D-2. Circumference at First Quarter			
D-3. Circumference at Second Quarter			
D-4. Circumference at Third Quarter			
TOTALS			

ADD	Column 1		Exact Locality Where Killed:
	Column 2		Date Killed: Hunter:
	Subtotal		Owner: Telephone #:
SUBTRACT Column 3			Owner's Address:
FINAL SCORE			Guide's Name and Address:
			Remarks: (Mention Any Abnormalities or Unique Qualities)

I, _____ , certify that I have measured this trophy on _____
            PRINT NAME   MM/DD/YYYYY

at _____
   STREET ADDRESS   CITY   STATE/PROVINCE

and that these measurements and data are, to the best of my knowledge and belief, made in accordance with the instructions given.

Witness: _____ Signature: _____ I.D. Number ☐☐☐☐
                                                     B&C OFFICIAL MEASURER

COPYRIGHT © 2002 BY BOONE AND CROCKETT CLUB®

Reprinted courtesy of the Boone and Crockett Club, 250 Station Dr., Missoula, MT 59801, 406-542-1888

INSTRUCTIONS FOR MEASURING SHEEP

All measurements must be made with a 1/4-inch wide flexible steel tape to the nearest one-eighth of an inch. Enter fractional figures in eighths, without reduction. Official measurements cannot be taken until horns have air dried for at least 60 days after the animal was killed.

A. Greatest Spread is measured between perpendiculars at a right angle to the center line of the skull.

B. Tip to Tip Spread is measured between tips of horns.

C. Length of Horn is measured from the lowest point in front on outer curve to a point in line with tip. **Do not** press tape into depressions. The low point of the outer curve of the horn is considered to be the low point of the frontal portion of the horn, situated above and slightly medial to the eye socket (not the outside edge). Use a straight edge, perpendicular to horn axis, to end measurement on "broomed" horns.

D-1. Circumference of Base is measured at a right angle to axis of horn. **Do not** follow irregular edge of horn; the line of measurement must be entirely on horn material.

D-2-3-4. Divide measurement C of longer horn by four. Starting at base, mark both horns at these quarters (even though the other horn is shorter) and measure circumferences at these marks, with measurements taken at right angles to horn axis.

ENTRY AFFIDAVIT FOR ALL HUNTER-TAKEN TROPHIES

For the purpose of entry into the Boone and Crockett Club's® records, North American big game harvested by the use of the following methods or under the following conditions are ineligible:

I. Spotting or herding game from the air, followed by landing in its vicinity for the purpose of pursuit and shooting;

II. Herding or chasing with the aid of any motorized equipment;

III. Use of electronic communication devices, artificial lighting, or electronic light intensifying devices;

IV. Confined by artificial barriers, including escape-proof fenced enclosures;

V. Transplanted for the purpose of commercial shooting;

VI. By the use of traps or pharmaceuticals;

VII. While swimming, helpless in deep snow, or helpless in any other natural or artificial medium;

VIII. On another hunter's license;

IX. Not in full compliance with the game laws or regulations of the federal government or of any state, province, territory, or tribal council on reservations or tribal lands;

I certify that the trophy scored on this chart was not taken in violation of the conditions listed above. In signing this statement, I understand that if the information provided on this entry is found to be misrepresented or fraudulent in any respect, it will not be accepted into the Awards Program and 1) all of my prior entries are subject to deletion from future editions of **Records of North American Big Game** 2) future entries may not be accepted.

FAIR CHASE, as defined by the Boone and Crockett Club®, is the ethical, sportsmanlike and lawful pursuit and taking of any free-ranging wild, native North American big game animal in a manner that does not give the hunter an improper advantage over such game animals.

The Boone and Crockett Club® may exclude the entry of any animal that it deems to have been taken in an unethical manner or under conditions deemed inappropriate by the Club.

Date:_____ Signature of Hunter:_____

(SIGNATURE MUST BE WITNESSED BY AN OFFICIAL MEASURER OR A NOTARY PUBLIC.)

Date:_____ Signature of Notary or Official Measurer:_____

Reprinted courtesy of the Boone and Crockett Club, 250 Station Dr., Missoula, MT 59801, 406-542-1888

Hunting Tactics

The most common method of hunting bighorns is spotting and stalking. Several areas in Colorado allow hunters to glass large areas of terrain from long distances. Once sheep are spotted a stalk can be mapped out. If you have drawn a coveted sheep tag the best approach is to scout your area thoroughly prior to the season. By locating the sheep early you can confine your hunting time to productive areas. Sheep hunters have good success rates in Colorado. During a typical hunting season the success rate for sheep hunters is about 50% for all manners of take.

When stalking sheep it's best to approach from above when possible. Due to the steep rocky terrain this can be a difficult task. Still, it can optimize your chance to close within adequate range. You must be cautious of the wind at all times and move slowly and silently as the sheep are feeding. If you sneak in from above, the wind will ruin the stalk if it's moving downhill. Many times the direction of the stalk will be dictated by the direction of the wind. If you locate sheep in wooded areas a good approach is still-hunting. Bowhunters sometimes have success using treestands where wooded areas surround feeding areas. Another approach is to set up near active trails or bedding areas. Regardless of the approach, good optics will help greatly in pursuit of bighorn sheep.

Rifle Caliber Suggestions

Most calibers used for deer will also work well for sheep. Bullet weights of 140 to 160 grains fired from a 7mm, .270, .280, or .30-06 will work well. Due to the open terrain and long distances across valleys and slopes, good scopes with magnification of at least 6x will work well. This is also a good time to utilize a quality rangefinder.

Shot Placement:
Top: Broadside shot.
Aim for the center of the chest just behind the bend of the front leg or shoulder; this should penetrate the lungs.

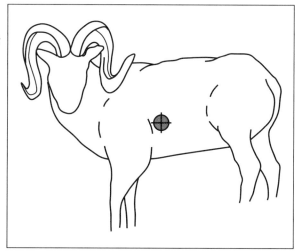

Transplants at Work

Since hunting was closed in the late 1800s, the population of sheep has cycled. As herds were being reestablished a high population estimated over 7,000 was reached by about 1915. Hunting was reopened in 1953, but populations declined due to several factors until there were an estimated 2,200 sheep in 1970. Through the work of the Colorado Division of Wildlife and several conservation organizations such as the Rocky Mountain Bighorn Society, sheep populations have rebounded to current estimates of 6,500. Much of the success has been attributed to treating sheep for lungworm disease and transplanting animals.

Many transplants have led to well-established populations of sheep in remote areas of Colorado. Recently the DOW released fifteen sheep in the Holy Cross Wilderness Area below Homestake Peak. This area is believed to have supported historic populations that were decimated by poaching, disease, and severe weather. Biologists believe that this area could support 80 sheep, and there are several other locations in the wilderness area suitable for sheep transplants. Another transplant of 20 bighorn sheep was carried out in 2001 north of Durango in the Animas River Gorge. Only time will tell if the sheep will utilize the Homestake Peak or Animas River Gorge, but for now the future of bighorn sheep in Colorado is bright.

Sheep country is rough and unforgiving.

Mountain Goat Distribution

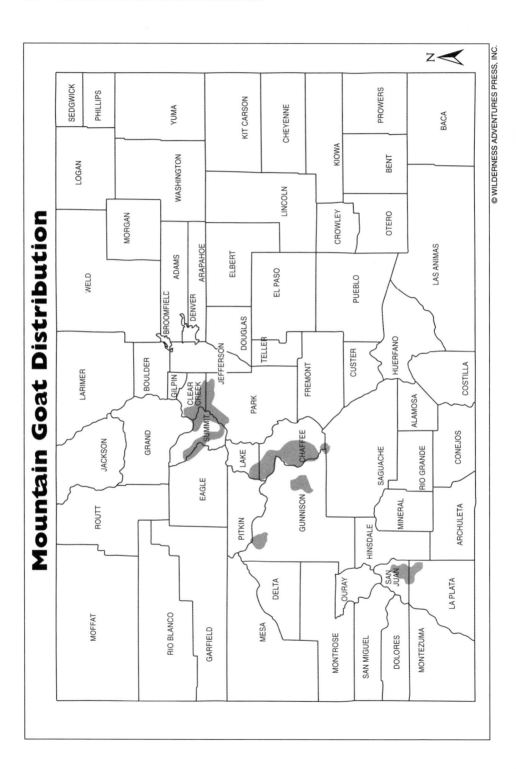

© WILDERNESS ADVENTURES PRESS, INC.

Mountain Goat

Oreamnos americanus

With its thick white coat, a mountain goat is well-suited to its snowy environment above timberline. The terrain it inhabits is extremely harsh with severe climate conditions and limited food supplies. Most other hoofed mammals wouldn't even survive well during the summer months where the mountain goat resides.

Fascinating Facts

- Although historic accounts indicate that mountain goats were native to Colorado, current herds are the result of transplants from Montana, Idaho, South Dakota, and British Columbia starting in 1947.
- Colorado is now home to an estimated 1,100 mountain goats.

Newborn mountain goats (known as kids) adapt to their environments rapidly. Kids begin foraging within one week and start climbing right after birth. Their first ascent is sometimes to the top of their mothers' back as she recovers from birthing.

- Unlike other big game species, fighting or sparring between adult males is rare. When fights do occur serious injuries are often inflicted with their sharp horns.
- Mountain goats derive their excellent ability to climb through a combination of a compact muscular build, low center of gravity, and specially adapted hooves that have a hard outer edge and softer inner pad that provides excellent traction on hard surfaces.
- One of the most prevalent causes of mountain goat mortality is falling due to lost footing, avalanches, and sometimes rockslides.

Local Names

Goat, nanny, billy

Size

Adult mountain goats are commonly 3 to 3.5 feet at the shoulders and can often exceed 5 feet in length from their nose to their tail. Weight varies greatly from 100 to 300 pounds. Nannies are slightly smaller than billies.

Coat and Color

The distinct feature of the mountain goat is its shaggy white to yellowish-white coat. The fur is thick and long with guard hairs up to 7 inches in length. The under-fur forms a woolly layer of insulation. Hair on the back of the neck is longer, forming a mane, and the upper portions of the legs are covered in longer hair. Long hair in the chin region on the underside of the neck forms a beard. The thick winter coat is shed

Grass, lichen, and moss make up much of the diet of mountain goats.

in the summer, resulting in a patchy irregular coat until shedding is complete. With a slight hump at the shoulders and black hooves, horns, and nose, the mountain goat is a very distinctive animal unlike any other big game species in Colorado.

Horns

The horns of the mountain goat grow from bony cores that protrude from the top of the skull. Both males and females have horns, although the billies' horns sometimes carry more mass with larger circumferences. The horns extend up and curve slightly back and out towards the ends where they come to a sharp point. Growth rings are present along the bottom portion of the horns, but the upper portions are generally smooth. Aging a goat is not as simple as counting growth ridges on bighorn sheep horns. Accurate aging is more commonly based on dental traits and the length of the horn. Mountain goat horns are generally 7 to 9 inches in length with exceptionally long horns pushing the 12-inch mark.

Voice and Communications

Most voice communication occurs as bleats between a nanny and her kid. Postural stances and physical displays are more common methods for goats to communicate. Mature males display dominance by flaring their body hairs and thrusting their horns in a mock display of fighting. If the potential contender doesn't back off a fight can ensue. These contests are rare but can be violent, resulting in serious wounds or even death. Goats also communicate to some extent through scent dispersion.

Senses

As a function of their open environment, goats are probably most dependant on sight to detect and avoid danger. This is not to say that they can't hear or smell well, but they aren't as dependent upon these senses as much as other big game species. Hunters should still stalk these animals with stealth and use the wind to their advantage.

Tracks and Sign

The tracks of the mountain goat are distinct due to the wide spread between the toes of the hoof. The tracks are square-like in outline and generally three inches in length. Mountain goats also have dewclaws, which show up in snow and mud. When walking the goat will stride 10 to 19 inches, leaving the impression of its hind hoof in the imprint of its front hoof.

Goats leave both cakes and pellet-like droppings depending on the food supply at hand. In spring and summer when more succulent vegetation is available goats will leave cakes, and drier food sources result in individual piles of tapered pellets.

One of the best signs of mountain goats is the white hair they leave behind. Places heavily used by goats will be evident even in rocky terrain where tracks might not stand out. Careful observation will reveal white hairs on rocks where they scratch and in bedding areas. Goats also dust, pawing out shallow swales in areas of loose soil during the summer months – something of a dry version of an elk wallow.

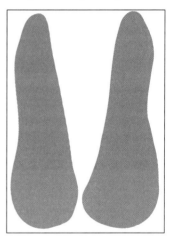

Mountain goat print. Average length is 3".

Reproduction and Young

The breeding season begins in November and generally ends by early December. Females will breed starting in their second year. The gestation period is approximately 180 days, and kids are born in May or June. It is most common for a single kid to be born, although twins can occur. Kids develop rapidly, walking and climbing within a short time after birth and foraging within a week. This accelerated development is due to the harsh environment and short duration of warm days seasonally available in goat habitat. By the end of summer kids are usually weaned. Kids will stay with their nanny until the following birthing season. Kids display a playful quality, chasing each other, climbing boulders, and generally bothering the more stoic elders of nursery bands. Although rare, nannies can show aggressive tendencies towards people or other animals that get too close to their young, including bothersome billies.

Habitat

Areas of alpine tundra (greater than 11,400 feet in elevation) make up the most important habitat for mountain goats, but they also rely on subalpine forest ecosystem, as well. Goat habitat is dominated by talus slopes, cliffs, ledges, and alpine

Females give birth on steep cliffs to avoid predators. The young are mobile shortly after birth and weaned after 3-4 months.

meadows. Unlike most other big game animals that utilize terrain at high elevations, goats will often remain above tree line throughout the winter. They feed on grassy slopes that remain snow-free due to high winds, and seek shelter in rocky slopes with windbreaks and shallow caves. When free water supplies are frozen, they can subsist off of snow to meet their watering needs. In areas where there are insufficient food sources during the winter months goats will migrate to lower elevations at or just below tree line in subalpine forest.

Home Range

The normal home range for mountain goats varies between 10 and 20 square miles. When seasonal migrations occur, they are relatively short, with movements of three to four miles. Similar to bighorn sheep, mountain goats will sometimes travel long distances to reach mineral licks. Sometimes these journeys can be significantly longer than their seasonal migrations.

During the summer months nannies, kids, and young billies congregate together to form small herds. These herds generally contain less than 20 animals, but certain ranges support larger groups with 30 or 40 animals. The billies remain separated from the nannies and kids until the breeding season begins. Mixed herds also assemble on winter ranges.

Forage Plants

The mainstay of the mountain goat diet in summer and winter is grass. This diet is supplemented seasonally by forbs, sedges, and browse. Browse from willows and various trees become important during the winter when deep snow can cover grasses. Goats also eat lichen throughout the year as well as mosses.

Daily Patterns

Mountain goats generally feed for long periods in the mornings and afternoons, taking time out to rest during the middle of the day. They generally forage throughout their range, eating, resting, and bedding in the same area. Depending on the terrain and weather conditions they may also bed on ledges or seek shelter in shallow caves. If food sources and water are adequate, goats may move less than half a mile on any given day, but they will travel long distances of several miles to access mineral licks.

Rutting Behavior

A sure sign of the rut is when the snowy white winter coat of the billies becomes dirty and stained along the belly and the back legs. This often occurs when billies wallow in shallow pits that they paw out with their hooves. In November, when the breeding season starts, billies will wander long distances searching out groups of females. The females are often less than happy to see the male suitors and it takes a patient and persistent billy to find a receptive mate.

Unlike bighorn sheep, goats seldom fight, and due to rather fragile skulls they don't butt heads. Instead, dominant males make postural stances to intimidate lesser goats. On rare occasions two stubborn males refuse to back down. This can end up in a head-swinging fight where the goats try to gore each other with their sharp horns. Goats have been killed in these battles, often from falling to their death during the fight.

Thick skin in the flank area helps protect the male mountain goat from serious damage when fighting during the rut.

Trophy Dimensions

As always, I would point out that trophy, in big game hunting, is a subjective concept. I have put in for goat tags in Colorado for several years without drawing one. Just to draw a tag and get to hunt these beautiful animals in my home state would be something of a trophy in itself.

The Boone and Crockett Club records indicate that there have only been a few goats harvested in Colorado that made the minimum all-time score of 50 points. One of these goats was taken by bowhunter Lyle Willmarth in Park County, Colorado during the 1988 hunting season. The goat ties several others for the 55th spot in the Boone and Crockett records as the largest representative of the species taken in Colorado. It also stands as the Pope and Young Club world record with a score of 52 4/8.

Taking a goat with a score over 50 Boone and Crockett points will be a rare accomplishment. The horns will most likely have to be over 10 inches in length, unless the mass is outstanding. The basal circumference measurements will need to exceed 5½ inches with good mass up the horn. The mass is important since the horns are rather short and four circumference measurements are taken along the horn to compile the total score. The largest mountain goat currently listed in Boone and Crockett has 12-inch horns with bases of 6½ inches. This monster of a goat had a total score of 56 6/8.

The Pope and Young minimum for mountain goats is 40. There are well over 100 mountain goats listed in the Pope and Young records from Colorado. Probably the most prolific producer of Pope and Young class goats is Clear Creek County, with Chaffee County coming in a close second. Goat Units G4 and G7 are popular areas in portions of Clear Creek County and several units (G1, G2, G3, G13, and G14) are found along the Collegiate Range in Chaffee County. Taking a Pope and Young class mountain goat will not be an easy task, but serious bowhunters will find that there are reasonable chances.

Judging goat horns isn't an easy task, either. Friends that have successfully hunted goats tell me one of the most important indicators of a mature goat is the circumference of the bases. It often appears that the bases are very close together on heavy horned goats. Another technique is to judge the length of the horn in relation to the length of the face, which is about 8 inches from the nose to the base of the horns.

Hunting Tactics

Spotting and stalking is probably the most common method to hunt mountain goats. Some hunters also have success working in teams in difficult areas where one person may try to push goats into an escape area where a hunter is waiting. Good optics will be a valuable tool in goat hunting. Finding prominent ridges to glass the surrounding country will save miles of climbing in steep rocky terrain. Once spotted, a stalk can be planned taking prevailing winds into account. Most unsuccessful stalks are the result of terrain. Cliffs, ledges, or unstable talus slopes can stop the hunter from getting into adequate range. If you're patient, you may be able to find a pattern in the direction goats are feeding and set up to ambush them. By most accounts, goats are approachable if reasonable caution is used in the approach. The 1999 harvest statistics support this assertion when you consider that 162 of the 175 available licenses were filled (nearly a 93 percent success rate).

Many hunters maintain that stalking from above is the best approach since goats are often looking downslope for danger. This may be true, but don't pass up an uphill stalk if there is a good concealing route. Finally, concentrate on your physical conditioning and mountaineering skills well in advance of the season.

Rifle Caliber Suggestions

I have heard many stories of hunters who shot their goat only to have it run and fall off a cliff or down a talus slope before dying. This can result in smashed skulls and broken horns, not to mention a difficult recovery. If I were rifle hunting mountain goats, I would use a caliber that would most likely put the animal down in its tracks. While lesser loads may work, I would use a .270 or .280. A 7mm or even a .30-06 would also be a good choice for goat hunting, although rifles in these calibers may be somewhat heavy to lug around the mountains. Premium bullets in the 130- to 150-grain range should be adequate to bring a goat down.

Goat country is rough, and weather conditions can be extreme. Lightweight rifles with synthetic stalks and weatherproof optics will be a plus.

Shot Placement:

Top: Quartering to Shooter
Aim for the off-side shoulder. Draw an imaginary line from your rifle to the farside shoulder, or slightly behind it if you don't want to damage any meat. Aim accordingly, which in this case would be in front of the near-side shoulder. (It would be better to wait for a higher percentage broadside or quartering-away shot.)

Records of
North American
Big Game

250 Station Drive
Missoula, MT 59801
(406) 542-1888

BOONE AND CROCKETT CLUB®
OFFICIAL SCORING SYSTEM FOR NORTH AMERICAN BIG GAME TROPHIES

MINIMUM SCORES
AWARDS   ALL-TIME
47   50

ROCKY MOUNTAIN GOAT

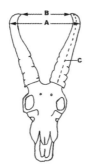
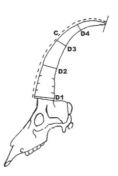

SEE OTHER SIDE FOR INSTRUCTIONS		COLUMN 1	COLUMN 2	COLUMN 3
A. Greatest Spread		Right Horn	Left Horn	Difference
B. Tip to Tip Spread				
C. Length of Horn				
D-1. Circumference of Base				
D-2. Circumference at First Quarter				
D-3. Circumference at Second Quarter				
D-4. Circumference at Third Quarter				
TOTALS				

ADD	Column 1		Exact Locality Where Killed:	
	Column 2		Date Killed:	Hunter:
	Subtotal		Owner:	Telephone #:
SUBTRACT Column 3			Owner's Address:	
FINAL SCORE			Guide's Name and Address:	
			Remarks: (Mention Any Abnormalities or Unique Qualities)	

I, _____ , certify that I have measured this trophy on _____
PRINT NAME   MM/DD/YYYYY

at _____
STREET ADDRESS   CITY   STATE/PROVINCE
and that these measurements and data are, to the best of my knowledge and belief, made in accordance with the instructions given.

Witness: _____   Signature: _____   I.D. Number
                                             B&C OFFICIAL MEASURER

COPYRIGHT © 2002 BY BOONE AND CROCKETT CLUB®

Reprinted courtesy of the Boone and Crockett Club, 250 Station Dr., Missoula, MT 59801, 406-542-1888

INSTRUCTIONS FOR MEASURING ROCKY MOUNTAIN GOAT

All measurements must be made with a 1/4-inch wide flexible steel tape to the nearest one-eighth of an inch. Wherever it is necessary to change direction of measurement, mark a control point and swing tape at this point. Enter fractional figures in eighths, without reduction. Official measurements cannot be taken until horns have air dried for at least 60 days after the animal was killed.

A. Greatest Spread is measured between perpendiculars at a right angle to the center line of the skull.

B. Tip to Tip spread is measured between tips of the horns.

C. Length of Horn is measured from the lowest point in front over outer curve to a point in line with tip.

D-1. Circumference of Base is measured at a right angle to axis of horn. Do not follow irregular edge of horn; the line of measurement must be entirely on horn material.

D-2-3-4. Divide measurement C of longer horn by four. Starting at base, mark both horns at these quarters (even though the other horn is shorter) and measure circumferences at these marks, with measurements taken at right angles to horn axis.

ENTRY AFFIDAVIT FOR ALL HUNTER-TAKEN TROPHIES

For the purpose of entry into the Boone and Crockett Club's® records, North American big game harvested by the use of the following methods or under the following conditions are ineligible:

    I.   Spotting or herding game from the air, followed by landing in its vicinity for the purpose of pursuit and shooting;

    II.   Herding or chasing with the aid of any motorized equipment;

    III.   Use of electronic communication devices, artificial lighting, or electronic light intensifying devices;

    IV.   Confined by artificial barriers, including escape-proof fenced enclosures;

    V.   Transplanted for the purpose of commercial shooting;

    VI.   By the use of traps or pharmaceuticals;

    VII.   While swimming, helpless in deep snow, or helpless in any other natural or artificial medium;

    VIII.   On another hunter's license;

    IX.   Not in full compliance with the game laws or regulations of the federal government or of any state, province, territory, or tribal council on reservations or tribal lands;

I certify that the trophy scored on this chart was not taken in violation of the conditions listed above. In signing this statement, I understand that if the information provided on this entry is found to be misrepresented or fraudulent in any respect, it will not be accepted into the Awards Program and 1) all of my prior entries are subject to deletion from future editions of **Records of North American Big Game** 2) future entries may not be accepted.

FAIR CHASE, as defined by the Boone and Crockett Club®, is the ethical, sportsmanlike and lawful pursuit and taking of any free-ranging wild, native North American big game animal in a manner that does not give the hunter an improper advantage over such game animals.

The Boone and Crockett Club® may exclude the entry of any animal that it deems to have been taken in an unethical manner or under conditions deemed inappropriate by the Club.

Date:_____ Signature of Hunter:_____
                                     (SIGNATURE MUST BE WITNESSED BY AN OFFICIAL MEASURER OR A NOTARY PUBLIC.)

Date:_____ Signature of Notary or Official Measurer:_____

Reprinted courtesy of the Boone and Crockett Club, 250 Station Dr., Missoula, MT 59801, 406-542-1888

Black Bear Distribution

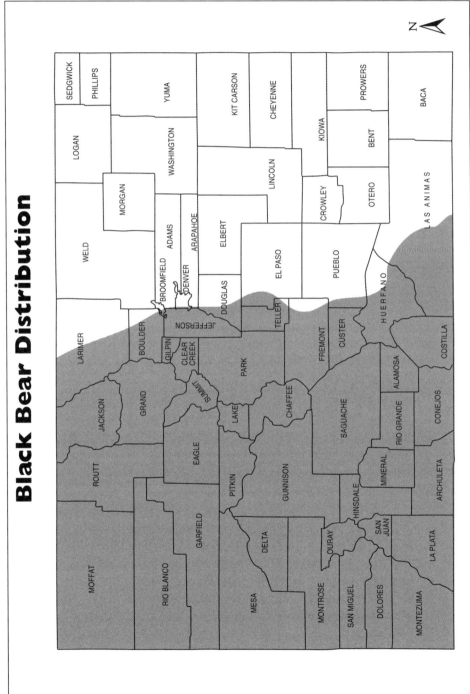

© WILDERNESS ADVENTURES PRESS, INC.

Black Bear

Ursus americanus

The largest carnivore in the state, black bears keep our wild places wild. Even though attacks are very rare, just knowing a bear might be lurking in the woods keeps the anxiety level high for many outdoor enthusiasts who enter bear country. Ancient cultures revered the bear as a symbol of strength and power. With its sharp teeth and long claws, the black bear pads through much of Western legend. Even today, bear stories, whether fact or fiction, are some of the most entertaining tales circulated in the big game hunting community.

Fascinating Facts

- According to studies conducted by the Colorado Division of Wildlife, over 70 percent of Colorado black bears are brown in coloration.
- Dry years often result in more bear/human encounters in Colorado because bears are forced to forage in unlikely areas when food sources are short. During these times bears are often attracted to campgrounds or homes where food smells are prominent.
- Black bears are omnivores relying on meat and plant matter to make up their diet. Depending on seasonal abundance of certain foods, bears may rely almost completely on plant material for the bulk of their diet, although they are known to be skilled hunters for newborn fawns and elk calves in the spring.
- Although not true hibernation by scientific standards, black bears go into a deep sleep for six to seven months out of the year where their metabolic rates and heart rates decrease. They utilize fat stores for energy during this time.
- When emerging from hibernation black bears go through a walking hibernation phase for two to three weeks. During this time they rarely eat as their body readjusts to normal active rhythms.
- Black bears often shed the outer layer of their footpads during hibernation.
- Female bears give birth to cubs during hibernation in their dens. Cubs are often less than half a pound at birth.
- Adult males will kill and eat cub black bears.
- Although difficult to estimate due to low population densities, the population of black bears in Colorado is thought to be between 8,000 and 12,000.

Local Names

Black bear, blackie

Size

Blacks bears stand 36 to 40 inches at the shoulders. Weight varies greatly based on maturity and the quality of annual food sources. Mature bears average 250

Black bears are not active predators, feeding primarily on insects.
(Colorado Division of Wildlife)

pounds, but weights may range from 180 to over 500 pounds. Bears over 400 pounds are rare in Colorado. Most Colorado bears are about 5½ feet in length. Females are generally about 20 percent smaller than males, and yearling cubs are about half the size of an adult.

Coat and Color

Black bears, as most hunters know, are not always black. They can have several different color phases, and their color can change slightly throughout the year due to fading. Color can also change as the bear ages. The basic color phases include black, brown, or blonde. Many people refer to variations of the brown phase as cinnamon or chocolate, tasteful descriptions I'm sure the bear would appreciate. In studies conducted by the Colorado Division of Wildlife, specific populations exhibited over 80 percent brown phase, and statewide hunter harvest data indicate that nearly 75 percent of the bears in Colorado are brown. The next most common color is black, and blonde-phased bears are the most rare in the state. Black bears can also have a white blaze on their chest, and their muzzles are generally lighter in color than the rest of their bodies.

The coat of the black bear is made up of thick soft to coarse hair several inches long. When the bear emerges from the den in spring the coat is often in good condition, although shedding and rubbing rapidly change the quality of the coat. As summer continues into fall the coat becomes denser until about the beginning of September when it reaches prime condition.

Voice and Communications

Black bears are mostly quiet in terms of voice communication. When they do use voice it often accompanies times of threat or fighting. Bears may make growling noises or bawl, and they often make "woofing" sounds before charging. They also pop their teeth when threatened. Cubs can be boisterous, whimpering and grunting as they play or when they can't find their mother.

Once, while bowhunting black bear, a large boar repeatedly made a loud distinctive hissing or snarl that sounded more like a big cat than a bear. I can assure you this wasn't a comforting sound considering I was only about 30 feet from the bear and there was no chance for a clear shot. Time stood still for a while as I wondered if the bear would charge, but ultimately he circled and retreated leaving me wondering why I had chosen to pursue black bear with a bow.

Much of the communication between bears is thought to be through visual signs and scent. Bears rub trees and shrubs, depositing scent. They also break tree branches and bite and claw trees leaving visual signs of their presence in the area.

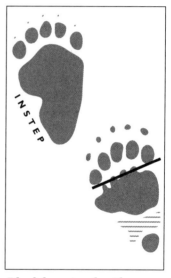

Senses

The black bear's most acute sense is smell. As backpackers and campers who have made the mistake of leaving food items out in bear country can tell you, a bear can smell food from long distances. They utilize their sense of smell to help them identify food sources such as berry patches, carrion, and even the newborn young of deer and elk. Deer and elk quickly clean the newborn immediately after birth to prevent predators from scenting the young. Bears also have very good hearing and good eyesight, although it's a common misconception that they can't see very well.

Black bear tracks. Above, right rear foot, approx. 7" long by 3½" wide; below, front foot, approx. 4½" from toes to rear of palm print and 3¾" wide. Note: the rear foot registers ahead of the front. The toes of the front foot should arc forward from a line drawn from big toe to little toe. The rear foot will have a wedge in the instep.

Tracks and Sign

Black bear tracks are similar in shape to a human footprint, although wider. The dimensions of their feet vary from 3.5 to 5.5 inches wide and 4.5 to 7 inches in length. The rear feet are slightly longer than the front. The paw has two pads, a large forward pad and smaller rear pad. The rear pad on the front foot is noticeably smaller than the rear pad on the back foot. Each foot has five toes with claws that register in the track. Due to the size, or possibly the way the bear distributes its weight, the smallest inner toe rarely shows up in the track.

Since there are no hard edges, the track usually

doesn't register unless the bear is walking through mud, snow, or very soft earth. I've often found bear tracks in muddy areas along creeks, in boggy willow patches between beaver ponds, and in snow near timberline during early spring. When bears walk, their back feet register on, or slightly in front of, the front feet. This is pronounced when they run, with the rear track often well in advance of the front.

Often more prominent than tracks are areas where bears have been foraging. Black bears are attracted to rotten stumps and logs that hold insects or insect larvae, often clawing the wood apart to find food. They also dig up anthills and dig for rodents. Bears will also leave abundant sign in berry patches where they are actively feeding. There will often be an abundance of bear scat containing seeds in the area. Also, while stripping the fruit from the limbs berries often fall through their clutch, which are subsequently trampled. Depending on the surface of the ground, the staining from the berries will remain until the first precipitation washes it away. Obvious bear sign also includes scratch and bite marks on trees.

Depending on diet, bears leave loose piles of scat similar to that of a dog but usually larger in diameter. Indigestible portions of prey animals also show up in bear droppings, but during premium berry-producing seasons, scat often contains an abundance of seeds.

Reproduction and Young

Black bears breed in the summer during June, July, and the beginning of August. The gestation period is between 200 and 240 days. An interesting characteristic in the reproduction process of black bears is that the fertilized egg(s) are not implanted to the wall of the uterus until November or December. Then in January or February the cub(s) are born while the sow is still in the den. Studies conducted in Colorado by the Division of Wildlife indicate it is most common for sows to give birth to two cubs. Although rare, three cubs can also make up a litter. Most female black bears are at least three years of age before they have their first litter, and they generally skip at least one year between each litter.

At birth cubs are miniature, hairless creatures that can't see. They often weigh less than half a pound. They are weaned from mothers' milk by the first fall, and stay with the sow for 1½ years.

Habitat

With the exception of the grasslands of the eastern plains, black bears utilize just about every major ecosystem in Colorado. The most productive ecosystem for black bears in the state is montane shrubland, but montane forest, subalpine forest, and pinon-juniper woodland also make up important areas. Some of the most well-known and highly publicized bear areas are located in the southern portion of the state. These include areas surrounding the town of Trinidad, west to the Sangre De Cristo and San Juan Mountains.

Home Range

Depending on age, sex, and habitat, the size of home ranges can be extremely variable. Mature male bears seem to have the largest home ranges. Studies con-

A female black bear is at least 3 years old before producing its first litter.

ducted by the Colorado Division of Wildlife indicate annual home ranges between 1.5 and 56 square miles. In *Black Bears of West-Central Colorado*, Technical Publication #39 of the Colorado Division of Wildlife, Tom Beck documented seasonal migrations of bears in the Black Mesa area to specific food sources. In this case the bears were traveling to areas of oakbrush where abundant mast was available in the fall. In a matter of a few days bears would travel between 8 and 22 miles to reach these food sources.

Forage Plants and Other Food Sources

Black bears are seasonal opportunists. During the spring they take advantage of emerging vegetation and forbs. Bears are omnivorous, and a substantial part of their diet consists of vegetative matter. With that said, black bears are also known to be effective hunters of newborn deer and elk. The frequency of successful kills is unknown, but a study in Idaho showed significant predation by black bears on elk calves. Of course, variables such as winter weather, the quality of habitat, and prevalence of disease, which affect the overall health of an elk herd, probably play a big role in the success or failure of the bears. The overlap of elk and bear range and bear populations also play a role in newborn deer and elk predation. Bears also take domestic livestock on occasion.

Another popular food source is carrion. Whether it's an elk carcass or domestic animal, a bear will smell it and eat it. Mature male bears will also kill and eat the

*Prime black bear habitat is characterized by thick understory vegetation
and abundant sources of food in the form of shrub or trees.
(Colorado Division of Wildlife)*

young of their own species, although a protective sow will have something to say about it. Bears also consume insects, insect larvae, small mammals, grasses, sedges, forbs, berries, and mast on a regular basis. In the fall bears go through what is known as a "hyperphagic phase" in which they gorge themselves in preparation of the oncoming winter.

Of importance to bear hunters in Colorado is the habit of bears to utilize berry patches and mast as prominent food sources in the fall. Fruit-bearing plants such as currant, serviceberry, and chokecherry are common food sources at this time. The main mast producers in Colorado are Gambel oak and pinon.

Daily Patterns

Bears are active during dawn and dusk, but depending on temperature and food sources, can also be active throughout the day. They are also highly nocturnal, especially in the spring and fall. Bears are solitary animals except family groups of a sow and her cubs. Occasionally when there is an abundant food source available bears will congregate together to feed.

Sows with cubs generally maintain separate home ranges away from male bears. A common trend when bears come out of their dens in the spring is to follow emerging plant growth up in elevation as the snowline recedes. They will also spend several days in small areas if there are abundant food sources such as berry patches, mast, or carrion.

Breeding Behavior

During the breeding season in the summer, male bears will travel great distances in search of a female, trailing her until she comes into estrus. Males may increase their marking activities, clawing trees and breaking branches during this time of the year. Occasionally two male bears will fight over a female. These can be violent episodes in which serious injuries occur. Sometimes these fights even result in death.

Trophy Dimensions

Since bears don't have antlers or horns, the Boone and Crockett Club and Pope and Young Club use the skull as a measuring stick for the trophy status of a bear. For many hunters, though, the trophy status of a bear is often measured in terms of the quality and size of the pelt. A black bear with a thick coat and stretching to 6 feet in length would be considered by many as a prize trophy. Many hunters consider the overall weight of the bear to be an important aspect. While bears between 200 and 300 pounds are common in Colorado, a bear over 400 pounds is often considered to be a rare trophy even if the skull is small relative to record book dimensions.

In terms of body size, Colorado bears are generally smaller than those in eastern states; however, Colorado does produce a significant number of record-book bears. The Boone and Crockett Club and Pope and Young Club use a simple measurement system to score a black bear. The combined measurements of the length and width of the skull determine the score. The minimum score to make the B&C all-time record book is 21 inches. The Pope and Young minimum is 18 inches.

By my count there are 32 black bear entries in Boone and Crockett from Colorado. Two Colorado bears tie several others for the 40th spot in Boone and Crockett with scores of 22 inches. One of these bears was taken on Hahns Peak in northwestern Colorado, and the other was taken in Garfield County. If you are interested in trophy black bears, it should be noted that Garfield County produced several of the Boone and Crockett bears as well as numerous Pope and Young entries. It's straightforward math to figure out what the dimensions of a black bear's skull will have to be to make Boone and Crockett. A width of 8 inches and a length of 13 inches will get the minimum.

The largest black bear from Colorado entered in Pope and Young was taken in 1978 by Ray Cox. This large bear scored 22 4/16 and was taken in San Miguel County. Judging a trophy bear in terms of skull measurements can be difficult. If the bear's head looks large in proportion to the rest of its body, or if it appears to have very small ears in relation to its head, it's probably a pretty good bear. Still, getting a bear in the trophy books will probably take some degree of luck.

Records of
North American
Big Game

250 Station Drive
Missoula, MT 59801
(406) 542-1888

BOONE AND CROCKETT CLUB®
OFFICIAL SCORING SYSTEM FOR NORTH AMERICAN BIG GAME TROPHIES

BEAR

	MINIMUM SCORES	
	AWARDS	ALL-TIME
black bear	20	21
grizzly bear	23	24
Alaska brown bear	26	28
polar bear	27	27

KIND OF BEAR (check one)
- ☐ black bear
- ☐ grizzly
- ☐ Alaska brown bear
- ☐ polar

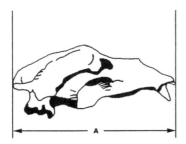
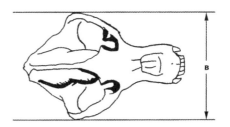

SEE OTHER SIDE FOR INSTRUCTIONS	MEASUREMENTS
A. Greatest Length Without Lower Jaw	
B. Greatest Width	
FINAL SCORE	

Exact Locality Where Killed:

Date Killed: Hunter:

Owner: Telephone #:

Owner's Address:

Guide's Name and Address:

Remarks: (Mention Any Abnormalities or Unique Qualities)

I, _____ , certify that I have measured this trophy on _____
     PRINT NAME   MM/DD/YYYYY

at _____
   STREET ADDRESS   CITY   STATE/PROVINCE

and that these measurements and data are, to the best of my knowledge and belief, made in accordance with the instructions given.

Witness: _____ Signature: _____ I.D. Number ☐☐☐☐
                             B&C OFFICIAL MEASURER

COPYRIGHT © 2002 BY BOONE AND CROCKETT CLUB®

Reprinted courtesy of the Boone and Crockett Club, 250 Station Dr., Missoula, MT 59801, 406-542-1888

INSTRUCTIONS FOR MEASURING BEAR

Measurements are taken with calipers or by using parallel perpendiculars, to the nearest **one-sixteenth** of an inch, without reduction of fractions. Official measurements cannot be taken until the skull has air dried for at least 60 days after the animal was killed. All adhering flesh, membrane and cartilage must be completely removed **before** official measurements are taken.

    A. Greatest Length is measured between perpendiculars parallel to the long axis of the skull, without the lower jaw and excluding malformations.

    B. Greatest Width is measured between perpendiculars at right angles to the long axis.

ENTRY AFFIDAVIT FOR ALL HUNTER-TAKEN TROPHIES

For the purpose of entry into the Boone and Crockett Club's® records, North American big game harvested by the use of the following methods or under the following conditions are ineligible:

    I.   Spotting, or herding game from the air, followed by landing in its vicinity for the purpose of pursuit and shooting;

    II.   Herding or chasing with the aid of any motorized equipment;

    III. Use of electronic communication devices, artificial lighting, or electronic light intensifying devices;

    IV. Confined by artificial barriers, including escape-proof fenced enclosures;

    V.   Transplanted for the purpose of commercial shooting;

    VI. By the use of traps or pharmaceuticals;

    VII. While swimming, helpless in deep snow, or helpless in any other natural or artificial medium;

    VIII. On another hunter's license;

    IX. Not in full compliance with the game laws or regulations of the federal government or of any state, province, territory, or tribal council on reservations or tribal lands;

Please answer the following questions:

Were dogs used in conjunction with the pursuit and harvest of this animal?

    ☐ Yes   ☐ No

If the answer to the above question is yes, answer the following statements:

    1. I was present on the hunt at the times the dogs were released to pursue this animal.
       ☐ True ☐ False

    2. If electronic collars were attached to any of the dogs, receivers were not used to harvest this animal.
       ☐ True ☐ False

To the best of my knowledge the answers to the above statements are true. If the answer to either #1 or #2 above is false, please explain on a separate sheet.

I certify that the trophy scored on this chart was not taken in violation of the conditions listed above. In signing this statement, I understand that if the information provided on this entry is found to be misrepresented or fraudulent in any respect, it will not be accepted into the Awards Program and 1) all of my prior entries are subject to deletion from future editions of **Records of North American Big Game** 2) future entries may not be accepted.

FAIR CHASE, as defined by the Boone and Crockett Club®, is the ethical, sportsmanlike and lawful pursuit and taking of any free-ranging wild, native North American big game animal in a manner that does not give the hunter an improper advantage over such game animals.

The Boone and Crockett Club® may exclude the entry of any animal that it deems to have been taken in an unethical manner or under conditions deemed inappropriate by the Club.

Date:_____ Signature of Hunter:_____

                              (SIGNATURE MUST BE WITNESSED BY AN OFFICIAL MEASURER OR A NOTARY PUBLIC.)

Date:_____ Signature of Notary or Official Measurer:_____

Hunting Tactics

Bear baiting and running bears with dogs are both illegal hunting practices in Colorado. There is no spring season for bears, so hunters will need to understand the traits of black bears in the fall. The fall is a productive time to hunt bears since they spend so much time feeding for the onset of winter. Instead of a few hours of activity in the morning and evening, bears may stay active up to 20 hours a day in the fall. Finding prominent food sources during this time of the year is probably the best way to find a bear. Berry patches and oakbrush are two of the best places to look. Since bears consume large quantities of food during this time of the year, they also leave numerous piles of scat in feeding areas. Once you find a good berry patch or stand of oakbrush with good bear sign, it might be productive to hang a treestand and wait out a hungry bear. Also, look for prominent trails into feeding areas if the vegetation is too thick to get a clear shot.

I know hunters who have had good success taking bears at water sources near feeding areas. These hunters used treestands and waited the bears out. If you don't have the patience to sit for long periods of time near feeding areas or water sources, spot-and-stalk techniques can be productive although most areas in Colorado don't have a high enough population density of bears to successfully spot them on a regular basis. If you have access to a very productive bear area, glassing mountain meadows may give you the chance to plan a stalk. Calling for bears has been effective for some hunters. Mimicking a cub in distress or using a predator call can attract a bear into close range. If you plan on using this technique be prepared for an aggressive bear coming in fast. This technique can result in a dangerous situation. Finally, if you find an animal carcass that naturally died or was killed, you may take a stand near it in hopes of ambushing a bear coming to feed. Many hunters also wait near gut piles during the various big game seasons in hopes that a bear will be attracted.

Bear hunters in Colorado should be aware that even though licenses are either sex, according to the DOW, "It is illegal to kill cubs or a black bear accompanied by one or more cubs. A cub is a bear less than a year old." This rule is in effect to protect sows with cubs. So if you see a big bear accompanied by one or more small bears, it's a no- shoot situation.

Shot Placement:
Broadside shot.
Unlike ungulates, the heart and lungs are directly between the shoulders. Aim high on the shoulder. This should hit the scapular or spine and drop the bear instantly.

Aim high on the shoulder with a rifle.

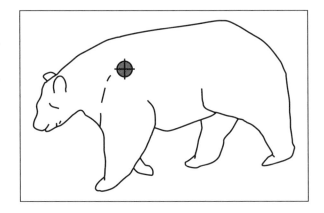

Rifle Caliber Suggestions

If you're hunting elk during one of the rifle seasons in Colorado and you also have a bear tag; your elk gun will be more than sufficient for a bear. I would recommend a .270, .30-06, 7mm Mag, or .300 to take a bear. The .30-06 utilizing a 160- to 180-grain premium bullet will be a very effective choice for those of you hunting deer, elk, and bear in the same season.

A black bear.

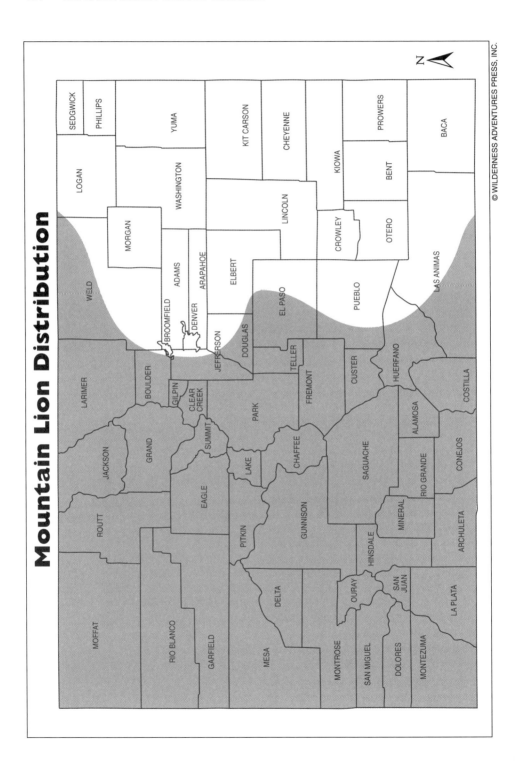

Mountain Lion Distribution

© WILDERNESS ADVENTURES PRESS, INC.

Mountain Lion

Felis concolor

Stealth, cunning, and power define the attributes of this ultimate predator. Seldom seen by most, this elusive hunter commands respect and awe from all who enter his domain. Just seeing his track in the soft earth can raise the hairs on the back of your neck because it is possible that he is out there, somewhere nearby, watching.

Fascinating Facts

- In 1965 Colorado changed the status of the mountain lion from a nuisance predator, which $50 bounties were paid on, to a big game animal. Quotas are now set for each unit, and once met, the unit is closed to additional hunting for that season. A total of 315 lions were harvested in 2000.
- Mountain lion populations are very difficult to determine, but some estimates put the state population at 1,500 to 3,500.
- Mountain lions hunt through stealth and stalking versus active chasing. Once the big cat is close enough to the prey, it will spring for the final pursuit and kill.
- Although rare, mountain lions do attack humans. Two deaths have been reported in Colorado, one in January 1991 in which a high school student was killed while jogging near Idaho Springs. The second occurred in July 1997 when a young boy was killed in Rocky Mountain National Park.
- After successfully killing and feeding on a large prey animal such as a deer, a mountain lion will often cover the remains with dirt, leaves, and branches and return to feed on it again later.
- Mountain lions have the tools they need for their trade with sharp retractable claws and a jaw that is capable of opening to nearly 90 degrees.
- Other than tracks, evidence of a mountain lion is often hard to find. They even bury or partially bury their droppings.

Local Names

Cougar, catamount, lion, puma, panther, painter

Size

Male lions generally weigh about 150 pounds and can be 8 to 9 feet in length (including the tail). The tail is usually about 30 percent the overall length of the body and head. They stand 30 to 36 inches at the shoulder, and large individuals may weigh as much as 250 pounds. Females are smaller, weighing on average 90 pounds, but larger females can weigh up to 150 pounds. They are generally less than three feet in height at the shoulder and a foot shorter in overall length than a male.

Coat and Color

The color of the mountain lions coat is often referred to as tawny or tan. Regardless of the shade of brown, the underbelly, chest, and inner legs are generally lighter than the rest of the coat. The chest area, muzzle, and inner ears are often white. The back of the ears, sides of the nose on the muzzle, and tip of the tail are black. Kittens are born with black spots, which fade away as they get older. The coat of a lion is made up of very dense short hairs.

Voice and Communications

Mountain lions are seldom heard, but they will purr, growl, and snarl. Kittens often purr or mew. Females are known to make noises when they are in estrus to attract males who may be listening. Lions also communicate through scent marking. They will spray trees and brush with urine and partially cover droppings and urine with piles of dirt, leaves, or pine needles. They also scratch trees.

Senses

The senses of a mountain lion are extremely acute. It utilizes excellent eyesight to aid it in hunting. Both hearing and sense of smell are well-developed and allow the mountain lion to detect unseen danger.

Once a mountain lion is close enough to its prey, it will spring for the kill.

Tracks and Sign

Mountain lions bear most of their weight on their toes as they walk; however, the pad is usually visible in tracks that register in snow and very soft earth or mud. The front paws have five toes, although one is non-weight bearing and doesn't appear in the track, and the back paw has four toes. The claws are generally retracted when walking and don't register in the print. The four toes in a track surround a single pad that is triangular in shape. The narrower end is toward the toes and the rear portion of the pad expands with three lobes. The track is generally wider than longer with the length 3 to 4 inches and the width 3.5 to 4.5 inches. When thick fur surrounds the paw in the winter, a track left in snow can appear larger. The front paw is slightly larger than the back, and when the cat walks the rear paw registers in or slightly in front of the front track. When walking through deep snow the lion often leaves drag marks with its tail.

Mountain lion tracks. Above, front, 3″ long and 3½″ wide; below, rear, 3″ long and 3″ wide.

Lynx leave a track very similar to mountain lions. With the recent reintroduction of lynx in the state it is possible to come across their tracks, although very few have been released. The lynx track doesn't exhibit the prominent three lobes at the back of the pad as the lion track does.

Other sign left by mountain lion are dog-like droppings, which often contain fur and undigested portions of prey animals. Cats generally cover their droppings. They also claw and scratch trees. Sometimes the most prominent sign left by mountain lions are their kills. Drag marks and partially eaten carcasses of deer or elk that have been covered are indicative.

Reproduction and Young

Unlike the other big game species, mountain lions don't have a specific breeding season. Females can be in estrus during any time of the year. Still there seems to be a trend where most kittens are born between April and July. The gestation period is a short three months. Litter sizes vary from one to six kittens, but two or three is more common. The kittens, like bear cubs, are blind at birth, but unlike a bear they have fur at birth. The fur is covered with black spots and there are rings around the tail. They develop quickly, being weaned in two months. Through instinct, play, and observation of their mother they learn the skills to hunt, and start hunting as early as six or seven months, but they still rely on kills made by their mother. The young usually stay with their mother about 18 months before striking out on their own.

Habitat

Like the black bear, mountain lions are widespread and capable of living in most ecosystems in Colorado. Although rare, there are occasional reports of mountain lion sightings on the eastern plains. These are usually in canyon-like country or areas with broken terrain. The highest population densities are found in western Colorado. The most suitable ecosystems for lions seem to be pinon-juniper woodlands, montane shrubland, and montane forest where there are good populations of deer.

Home Range

Lions roam far and wide. Various studies indicate that males may have home ranges as small as 40 square miles or as big as 320 square miles. Females generally have smaller home ranges than males. One crucial factor in the size of the home range is the population density of prey animals within a lion's territory. If prey is abundant and concentrated into smaller geographic areas, the cat's home range will probably be smaller. The home range can change from year to year in response to population fluctuations in prey animals. Fewer and more dispersed prey animals means the lion will have to travel farther between kills. In areas where deer herds make significant winter/spring migrations, the mountain lion home range may shift seasonally in response to these migrations.

Adult male lions are very territorial. They will allow female lions to overlap the boundaries of their territories, but they won't tolerate other males. Young males must find their own territories. The territorial nature of these big cats helps support the premise that their populations are self-regulating. If suitable habitat with abundant

A treed mountain lion can be a tough target. (Rudy Meyers)

prey animals is not available to additional cats, they won't survive. If they try to move into another dominant cat's territory there is likely to be a fight, sometimes to the death.

Food Sources

Mountain lions almost exclusively eat the meat of animals of prey that they have killed. It is thought that they rarely eat carrion, but in severe conditions, they may take advantage of it as a food source. Their most common food item is thought to be deer and occasionally elk, although where their ranges overlap lions will also hunt bighorn sheep, mountain goats, and antelope. Smaller animals such as rabbits, ground squirrels, porcupines, birds, and small predators also make up a portion of their diets. Finally, they may also occasionally eat fish, insects, and berries. Lions also get into trouble when they take domestic animals. Like a male bear, a male mountain lion will kill and eat the young of its own species.

Daily Patterns

Mountain lions are active both at night and during the day, hunting when opportunities arise. They may travel 20 to 25 miles on any given day in search of prey. They drink from streams, seeps, or lakes, but probably don't frequently water in the same spots. When they kill a large animal they often stay near to feed on it several times until it's gone. Unless you find a fresh lion kill, there is probably no good way to pattern a big cat on a daily basis.

Breeding Behavior

Females are thought to first breed at 2½ years of age. They generally only breed with one male, but the male will seek out several females to breed with. When in heat a female will attract a male by making what we can only assume are seductive sounds. She also leaves her scent, which attracts the male. Once a male finds her, they may spend a few days together. After breeding the male will search out other females or resume his solitary life. Lions are almost completely solitary except when breeding, or when females have kittens. Females generally have a litter every 2½ years.

Trophy Dimensions

Like the black bear, the cumulative length and width of the skull determines if the cat makes Boone and Crockett or Pope and Young. A mountain lion will have to score a minimum of 15 to qualify for the all-time Boone and Crockett Club record book while the Pope and Young Club minimum is 13½.

President Theodore Roosevelt took one of the biggest mountain lions recorded in Boone and Crockett. He killed the cat in 1901 near Meeker, Colorado. It scored 15 12/16 and is still number seven, tied with several other cats including another Colorado lion that was taken by Robert Meyer in Mesa County, Colorado. In fact, Colorado has produced its fair share of Boone and Crockett entries over the last century and has a reputation for big lions. The benchmarks for a Boone and Crockett mountain lion are a skull 9 inches in length and 6 inches in width.

Records of
North American
Big Game

250 Station Drive
Missoula, MT 59801
(406) 542-1888

BOONE AND CROCKETT CLUB®
OFFICIAL SCORING SYSTEM FOR NORTH AMERICAN BIG GAME TROPHIES

COUGAR AND JAGUAR

	MINIMUM SCORES		KIND OF CAT (check one)
	AWARDS	ALL-TIME	☐ cougar
cougar	14 - 8/16	15	☐ jaguar
jaguar	14 - 8/16	14 - 8/16	

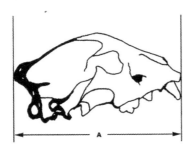

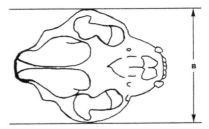

SEE OTHER SIDE FOR INSTRUCTIONS	MEASUREMENTS
A. Greatest Length Without Lower Jaw	
B. Greatest Width	
FINAL SCORE	

Exact Locality Where Killed:

Date Killed: Hunter:

Owner: Telephone #:

Owner's Address:

Guide's Name and Address:

Remarks: (Mention Any Abnormalities or Unique Qualities)

I, _____ , certify that I have measured this trophy on _____
PRINT NAME   MM/DD/YYYYY

at _____
STREET ADDRESS   CITY   STATE/PROVINCE

and that these measurements and data are, to the best of my knowledge and belief, made in accordance with the instructions given.

Witness: _____ Signature: _____ I.D. Number ☐☐☐☐
                                              B&C OFFICIAL MEASURER

COPYRIGHT © 2002 BY BOONE AND CROCKETT CLUB®

Reprinted courtesy of the Boone and Crockett Club, 250 Station Dr., Missoula, MT 59801, 406-542-1888

INSTRUCTIONS FOR MEASURING COUGAR AND JAGUAR

Measurements are taken with calipers or by using parallel perpendiculars, to the nearest **one-sixteenth** of an inch, without reduction of fractions. Official measurements cannot be taken until the skull has air dried for at least 60 days after the animal was killed. All adhering flesh, membrane and cartilage must be completely removed **before** official measurements are taken.

   A. Greatest Length is measured between perpendiculars parallel to the long axis of the skull, without the lower jaw and excluding malformations.

   B. Greatest Width is measured between perpendiculars at right angles to the long axis.

ENTRY AFFIDAVIT FOR ALL HUNTER-TAKEN TROPHIES

For the purpose of entry into the Boone and Crockett Club's® records, North American big game harvested by the use of the following methods or under the following conditions are ineligible:

   I.   Spotting or herding game from the air, followed by landing in its vicinity for the purpose of pursuit and shooting;
   II. Herding or chasing with the aid of any motorized equipment;
   III. Use of electronic communication devices, artificial lighting, or electronic light intensifying devices;
   IV. Confined by artificial barriers, including escape-proof fenced enclosures;
   V.   Transplanted for the purpose of commercial shooting;
   VI. By the use of traps or pharmaceuticals;
   VII. While swimming, helpless in deep snow, or helpless in any other natural or artificial medium;
   VIII. On another hunter's license;
   IX. Not in full compliance with the game laws or regulations of the federal government or of any state, province, territory, or tribal council on reservations or tribal lands;

Please answer the following questions:

Were dogs used in conjunction with the pursuit and harvest of this animal?
   ☐ Yes   ☐ No

If the answer to the above question is yes, answer the following statements:

   1. I was present on the hunt at the times the dogs were released to pursue this animal.
      ☐ True ☐ False

   2. If electronic collars were attached to any of the dogs, receivers were not used to harvest this animal.
      ☐ True ☐ False

To the best of my knowledge the answers to the above statements are true. If the answer to either #1 or #2 above is false, please explain on a separate sheet.

I certify that the trophy scored on this chart was not taken in violation of the conditions listed above. In signing this statement, I understand that if the information provided on this entry is found to be misrepresented or fraudulent in any respect, it will not be accepted into the Awards Program and 1) all of my prior entries are subject to deletion from future editions of **Records of North American Big Game** 2) future entries may not be accepted.

FAIR CHASE, as defined by the Boone and Crockett Club®, is the ethical, sportsmanlike and lawful pursuit and taking of any free-ranging wild, native North American big game animal in a manner that does not give the hunter an improper advantage over such game animals.

The Boone and Crockett Club® may exclude the entry of any animal that it deems to have been taken in an unethical manner or under conditions deemed inappropriate by the Club.

Date:_____ Signature of Hunter:_____
                                    (SIGNATURE MUST BE WITNESSED BY AN OFFICIAL MEASURER OR A NOTARY PUBLIC.)

Date:_____ Signature of Notary or Official Measurer:_____

Reprinted courtesy of the Boone and Crockett Club, 250 Station Dr., Missoula, MT 59801, 406-542-1888

Randell Thompson took the state record Pope and Young lion in 1992 in Montrose County. This impressive animal scored 15 11/16. Judging a trophy class mountain lion may be harder than any other animal. After years of hunting lions, some guides can judge the head of a trophy animal. Body size is also a good indicator, but it doesn't mean the skull will make a record book. Still, if you take a mature tom that weighs in the 200-pound range, it's a trophy in most anyone's book.

Hunting Tactics

Almost all hunting in Colorado is done with the use of dogs. Various breeds of hounds are usually used to track lions in the snow. Once treed, the hunter dispatches the lion. It sounds simple and straightforward, but most hunts require days of searching to find a fresh track. Once on the track it can take several hours of following the baying hounds until a cat is treed. Even then the hunt is not assured as the cat may escape before the hunters arrive. Mountain lion hunting can be physically challenging, and it generally occurs during winter months when temperature and weather conditions can be extreme.

I know of one instance (second hand) of a hunter who followed the drag marks of a fresh mountain lion kill that led him to a feeding cat and a successful hunt, but these situations are rare. There are also a handful of mountain lions that have been taken by chance when a hunter was out during another hunting season and happened to have a lion license. Again, these instances are rare. If you are serious about getting a mountain lion and you don't have your own dogs; your best bet will be to retain a local guide who specializes in lion hunting.

Shot Placement:
Broadside shot.
Aim for the center of the chest just behind the bend of the front shoulder; this should penetrate the lungs.

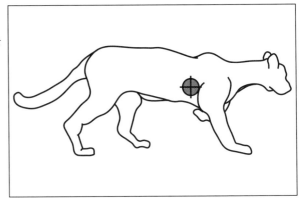

Rifle Caliber Suggestions

Any of the popular calibers used to hunt big game in Colorado will be effective to take a mountain lion. Since most lions are treed and shots are taken at close range, using a lightweight rifle will save you the burden of lugging a big gun over countless miles. Many lion hunters prefer lever action rifles such as Winchester or Marlin in .30-30. Due to the close range of most shots on treed lions, many hunters use handguns, bows, or muzzleloaders when hunting lions. Regardless of your choice you must be competent with the weapon. Mountain lions are dangerous, and a bad shot could endanger you, the dogs, or anybody else in the group.

The most suitable ecosystems for lions seem to be pinon-juniper woodlands, montane shrubland, and forests where there are good deer populations.

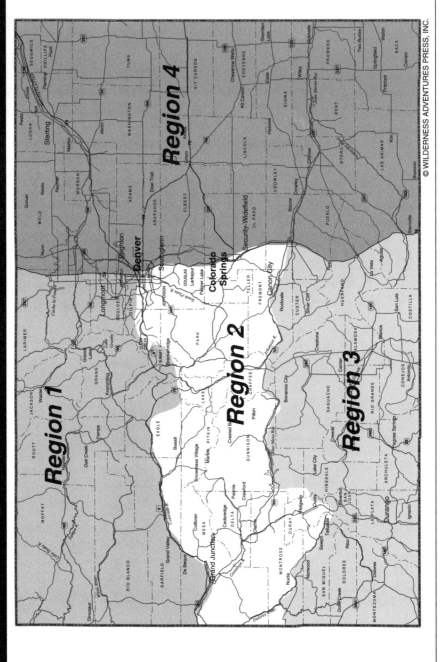

Big Game Hunter's Guide Regions

© WILDERNESS ADVENTURES PRESS, INC.

Discussion of Regions

When determining a logical division of regions for this book, several considerations had to be made. First of all the Colorado Division of Wildlife (DOW) uses Game Management Units (GMUs) to define specific hunting areas in the state. There are 173 GMUs, and it would be confusing if the dividing lines of the regions cut through these GMUs. As a result, GMU boundaries were followed when selecting the regions.

There are also prominent geographic regions, herds, and political boundaries within the state that I didn't want to dissect with regional boundaries. In general, Colorado is comprised of three basic physiographic regions: the Great Plains, the Southern Rocky Mountains, and the Colorado Plateau. The Great Plains extend from the mountains to the east and comprise 30 to 40 percent of the state. The Southern Rockies generally trend north-south and make up the central 30 to 40 percent of the state. Finally, the Colorado Plateau is found along the western edge of the state accounting for the remaining 20 to 30 percent of the total area in Colorado. Within each physiographic region are numerous political boundaries such as national forests, state parks, county lines, and other federal lands. Often the prominent herds of big game animals overlap one or more of the boundaries listed above.

After much consideration, four regions were selected. The first and most obvious distinction made is that Colorado is mountainous to the west and generally flat to the east. Interstate 25 (I-25) runs north to south and divides the state in two. It forms an important boundary in regard to hunting season structure, and as a result, was chosen as the east/west boundary. The mountainous areas to the west of I-25 were broken down into three distinct regions that provide smaller, more manageable areas to discuss in detail. Each of these three regions contains a portion of the Rockies and Colorado Plateau. The four regions are briefly defined on the following page:

Region 1
The northwest part of the state bounded to the east by I-25; the north by the Wyoming state line; the west by the Utah state line; and the south by Interstate 70 (I-70) and the Colorado River drainage.

Region 2
The central and western part of the state bounded to the east by I-25; the north by I-70 and the Colorado River drainage; the west by the Utah state line; and the south by Highway 50 from Pueblo to Montrose and the southern boundaries of GMUs 60, 61, and 62 to the Utah state line.

Region 3
The southwest part of the state bounded to the east by I-25; the north by Highway 50 from Pueblo to Montrose and the southern boundaries of GMUs 60, 61, and 62; the west by the Utah state line; and the south by the New Mexico state line.

Region 4
The eastern part of the state bounded to the east by the Kansas and Nebraska state lines; the north by the Nebraska and Wyoming state lines, the west by I-25; and the south by the New Mexico and Oklahoma state lines.

Region I Major Roads, Rivers & Hub Cities

© WILDERNESS ADVENTURES PRESS, INC.

REGION I

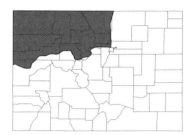

Starting at the eastern edge of Region 1, where the Front Range rises abruptly from the eastern plains, Longs Peak stands as a prominent landmark—just one of fifty- four, 14,000-foot peaks found in Colorado. The region is geographically diverse with several prominent mountain ranges, parks, plateaus, and rivers. An abundance of public land is available to hunt, consisting of national forests, wilderness areas, and thousands of acres of BLM land that cover a large percentage of the northwest corner of the state.

The best opportunity to bag a moose in Colorado exists in the North Park area, and if you want terrific antelope hunting the Great Divide herd is the largest in the state. There are also large populations of elk and deer in this part of the state and quality opportunities for bear, mountain lion, mountain goat, and bighorn sheep exist locally. Whether you have hunted Colorado all of your life or you are planning your first trip, this region of the state is one of the best, and should not be overlooked.

Long's Peak, the prominent landmark in Region 1.

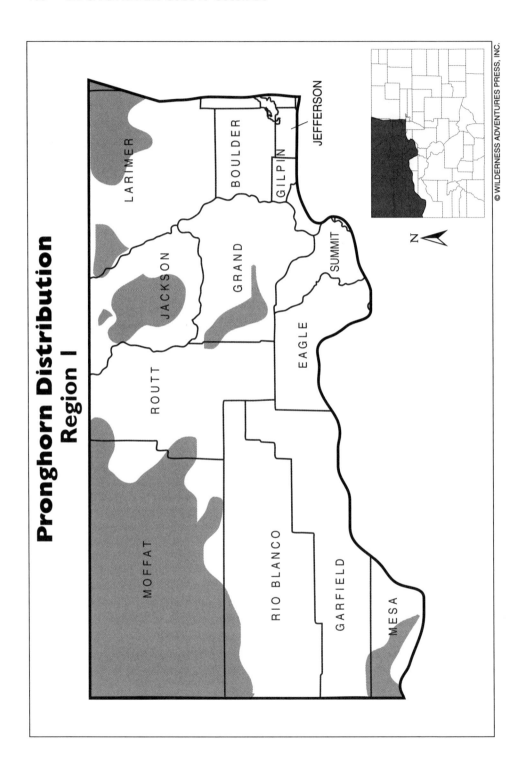

Pronghorn Distribution
Region I

© WILDERNESS ADVENTURES PRESS, INC.

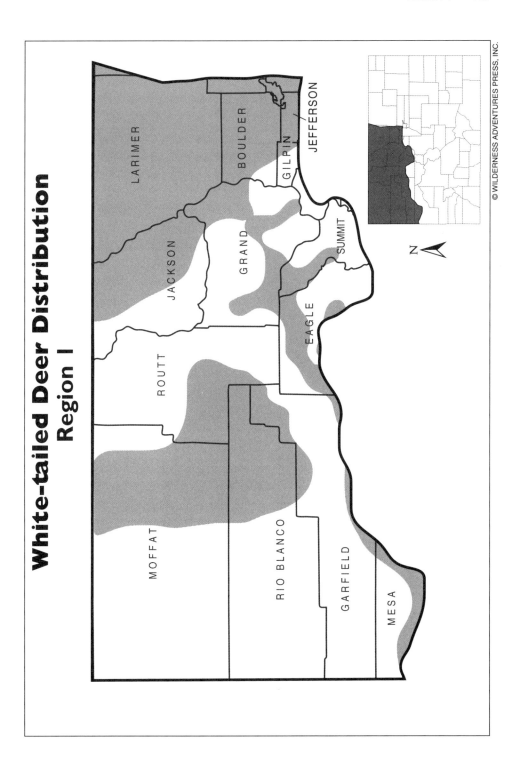

White-tailed Deer Distribution
Region 1

© WILDERNESS ADVENTURES PRESS, INC.

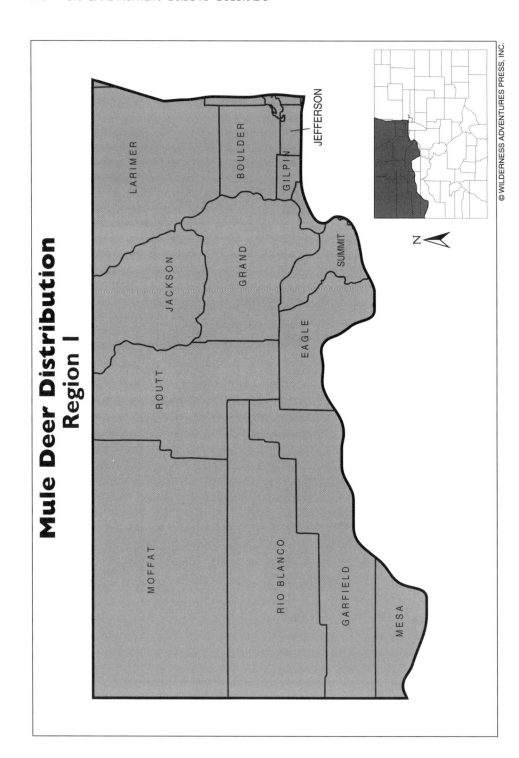

Mule Deer Distribution
Region I

© WILDERNESS ADVENTURES PRESS, INC.

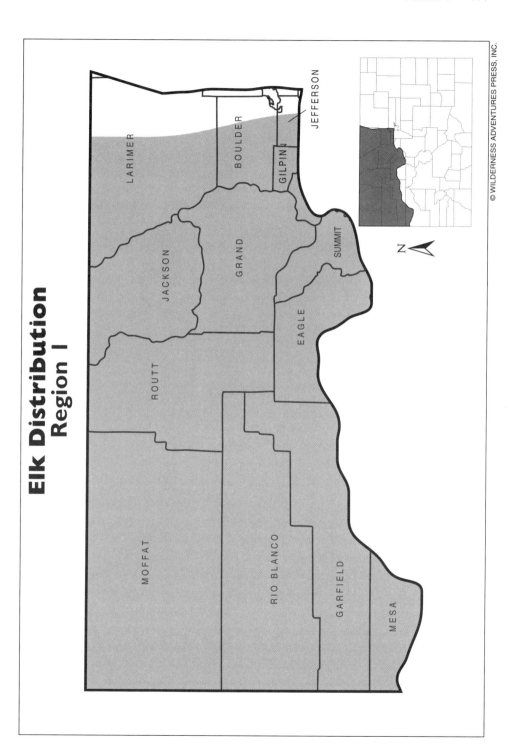

Elk Distribution
Region 1

© WILDERNESS ADVENTURES PRESS, INC.

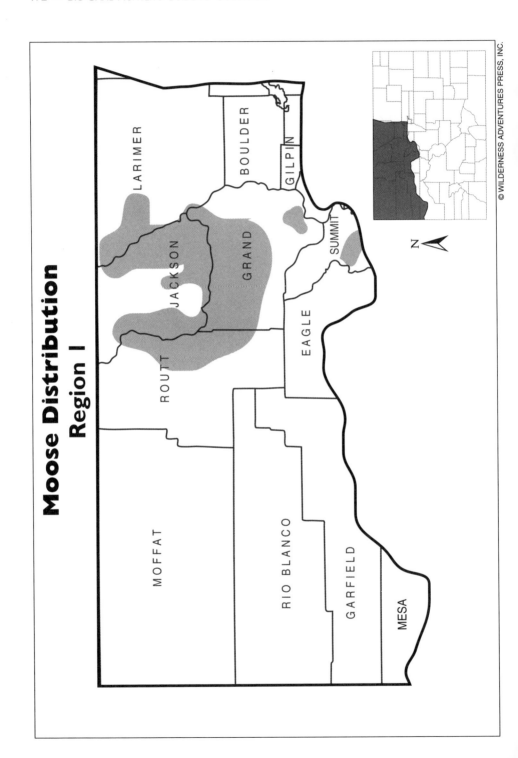

Moose Distribution Region I

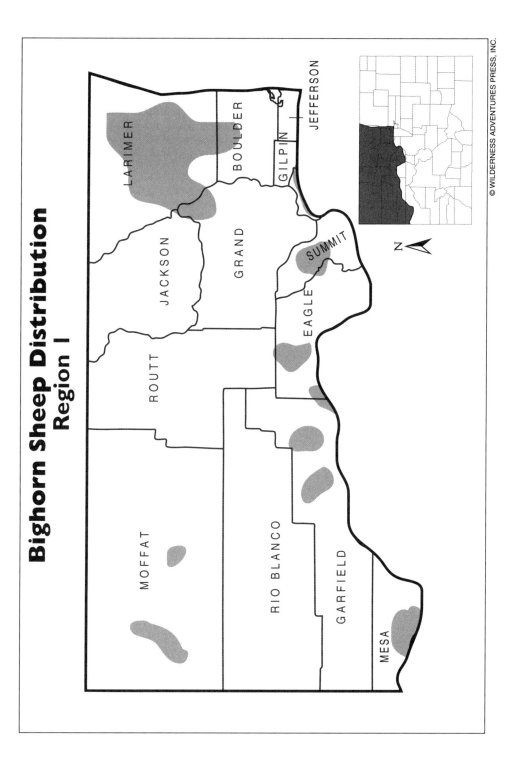

Bighorn Sheep Distribution Region 1

© WILDERNESS ADVENTURES PRESS, INC.

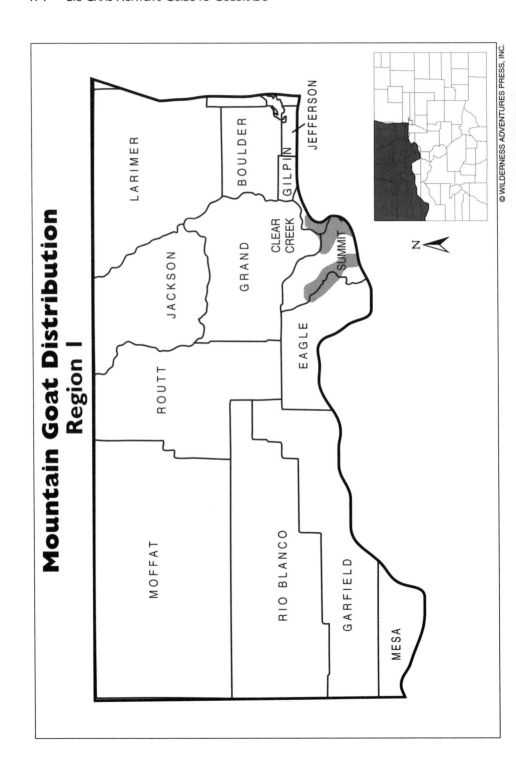

Mountain Goat Distribution
Region I

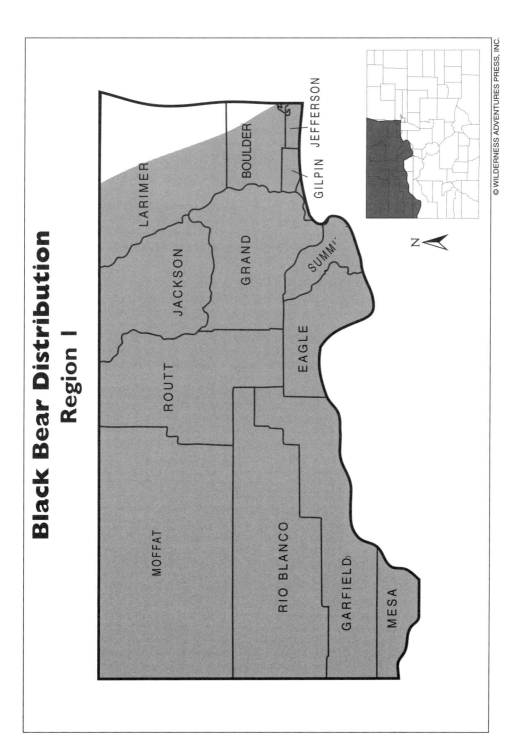

Black Bear Distribution
Region 1

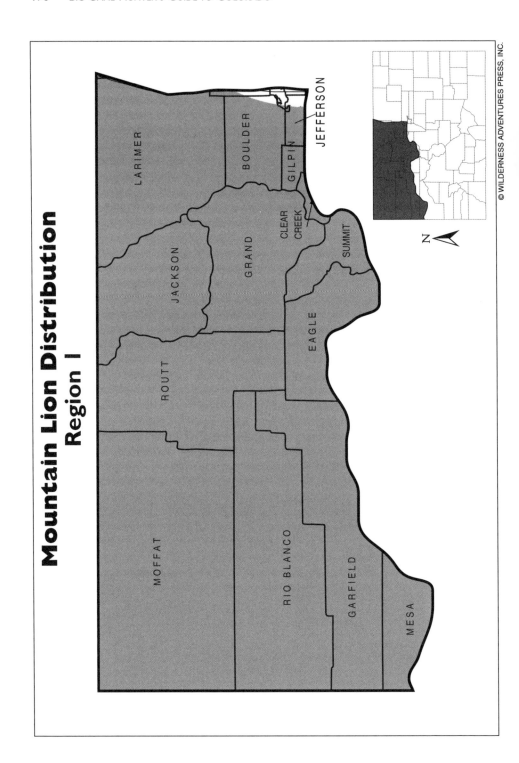

Mountain Lion Distribution
Region I

© WILDERNESS ADVENTURES PRESS, INC.

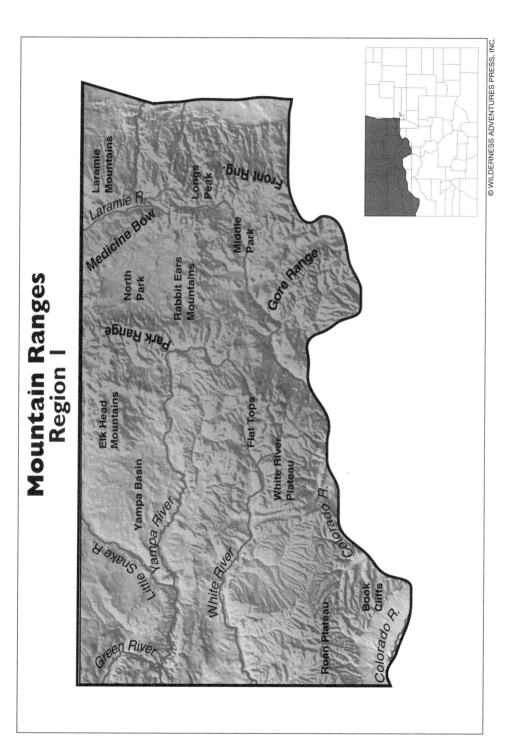

Mountain Ranges
Region 1

Laramie Mountains

Laramie R.

Longs Peak

Front Rng.

Medicine Bow

Middle Park

North Park

Rabbit Ears Mountains

Gore Range

Park Range

Elk Head Mountains

Flat Tops

White River Plateau

Yampa Basin

Yampa River

Little Snake R.

White River

Colorado R.

Roan Plateau

Book Cliffs

Colorado R.

Green River

© WILDERNESS ADVENTURES PRESS, INC.

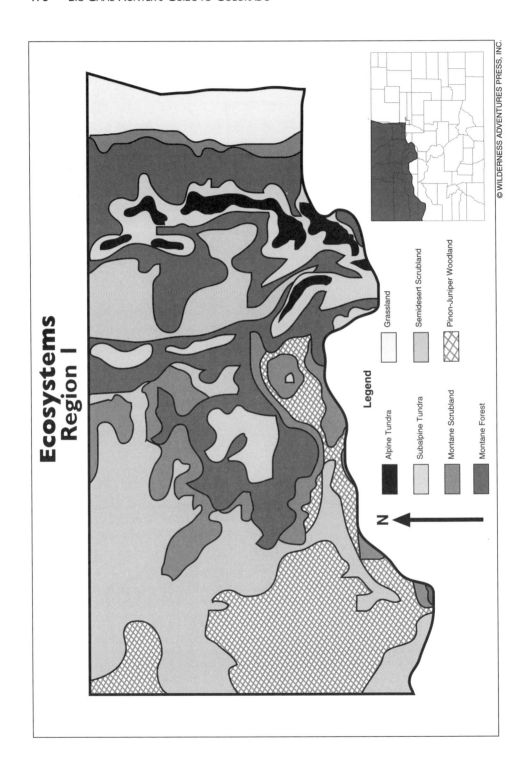

Ecosystems
Region I

Legend

Alpine Tundra

Subalpine Tundra

Montane Scrubland

Montane Forest

Grassland

Semidesert Scrubland

Pinon-Juniper Woodland

N

© WILDERNESS ADVENTURES PRESS, INC.

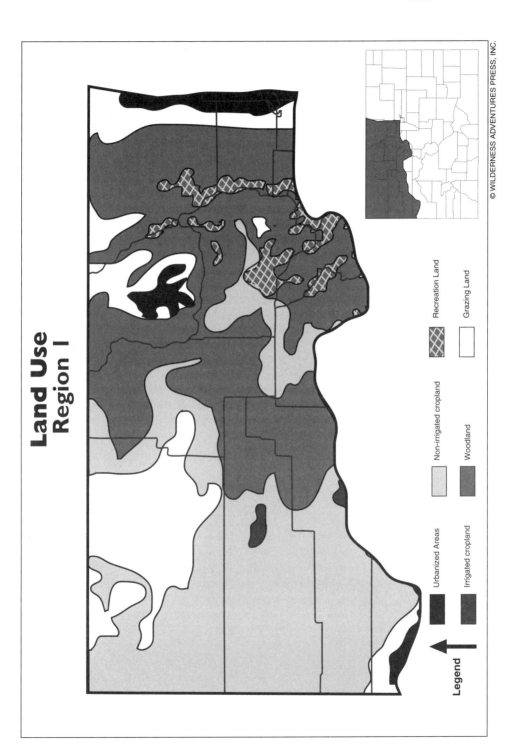

Land Use
Region 1

Legend

Urbanized Areas

Irrigated cropland

Non-irrigated cropland

Woodland

Recreation Land

Grazing Land

© WILDERNESS ADVENTURES PRESS, INC.

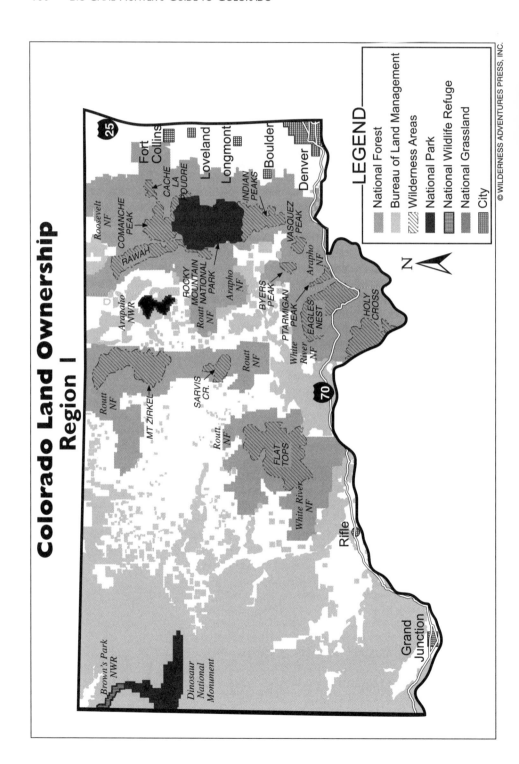

Colorado Land Ownership
Region 1

LEGEND

National Forest
Bureau of Land Management
Wilderness Areas
National Park
National Wildlife Refuge
National Grassland
City

© WILDERNESS ADVENTURES PRESS, INC.

GAME SPECIES AND NUMBERS

Region 1 has fourteen recognized herds of deer amounting to over 245,000 animals in all. Nearly one-third of all the elk in Colorado roam this area, including the White River herd at over 53,380 animals. The state's largest herd of antelope is found here, as well. If you're after one or all three of the prominent big game species in Colorado, Region 1 is a good area to plan a hunting trip—and it even gets better. Most of Colorado's moose population is also found in Region 1 in addition to good numbers of bear, mountain lion, and bighorn sheep. If this region has a weakness, it might be the lack of opportunities to hunt mountain goat. However, the one goat unit in the region (GMU 7) generally offers more licenses than any other goat unit in the state.

Population statistics are a valuable asset to the hunter and the Colorado Division of Wildlife prepares official population and harvest statistics available to the public each year. This information is gathered from license sale statistics, field research, including aerial population counts, and hunter harvest surveys. Obviously, it would be impossible to count every animal in the state, so the populations are to some extent estimated using population models. However, this is the best information available, and in my opinion, it is quality information.

The following tables provide the herd name, the GMUs where the herd ranges and the population of the herd. This information is current at the time of publishing, but populations change over time. Still, the distribution of populations in each area has remained relatively consistent over the years.

ELK HERD	UNITS	POPULATION
Green River	1	180
Bear's Ear	3, 4, 5, 14, 214, 301, 441	30,360
Cold Springs	2, 201	1,000
North Park	6, 16, 17, 161, 171	6,700
Poudre River	7, 8, 9, 19, 191	4,280
Rangely	10	1,650
White River	11, 12, 13, 23, 24, 25, 26, 33, 34, 131, 211, 231	53,380
Gore Pass	15, 27	5,350
Troublesome	18, 181	3,590
St. Vrain	20	4,370
Yellow Creek	21, 22, 30, 31, 32	9,770
William's Fork	28, 37, 371	3,490
Clear Creek	29, 38	1,290
Piney River	35, 36	6,970
TOTAL ELK POPULATION REGION I = 132,380		

DEER HERD	UNITS	POPULATION
Little Snake	1, 2, 201	13,600
Bears Ear	3, 4, 5, 14, 214, 301, 441	39,650
North Park	6, 16, 17, 161, 171	4,870
Red Feather	7, 8, 9, 19, 191	9,720
Rangely	10	7,100
White River	11, 12, 13, 22, 23, 2, 131, 211, 231	84,170
State Bridge	15, 35, 36, 45	19,730
Middle Park	18, 27, 28, 37, 181, 371	12,250
Big Thompson	20	6,470
Bookcliffs	21, 30	10,230
Sweetwater Creek	25, 26, 34	8,200
Boulder	29, 38	7,270
Logan Mountain	31, 32	13,260
Rifle Creek	33	8,820
TOTAL DEER POPULATION REGION I =		*245,340*

ANTELOPE HERD	UNITS	POPULATION
Vermillion Bluffs	1, 2, 201	3,140
Great Divide	3, 4, 5, 13, 14, 214, 301, 441	13,350
North Park	6, 16, 17, 161, 171	1,300
Laramie River	7, 8	630
Cherokee	9, 19, 191	1,060
Dinosaur	10, 21	350
Maybell	11	1,340
Axial Basin	12, 23, 211	290
Middle Park	18, 181, 27, 28, 37, 371	670
TOTAL ANTELOPE POPULATION REGION I = 22,130		

Populations of bear and mountain lion are not as well documented. There is specific statewide information for the other big game species.

SPECIES	STATEWIDE POPULATION
Black Bear	Unknown (estimates from 8,000 to 12,000)
Mountain Lion	Unknown (estimates from 1,500 to 3,500)
Desert Bighorn	400
Rocky Mtn. Bighorn	6,500
Mountain Goat	1,100
Moose	1,175

Harvest Trends

Hunter success rates vary greatly from year to year, season to season, and unit to unit. The Colorado Division of Wildlife publishes the big game hunting statistics each year, which includes success rates for each season in each unit. This information is available online at http://wildlife.state.co.us/huntrecap/index.asp.

The following success rates are based on 2001 DOW statistics averaged for all seasons and manners of take statewide.

SPECIES	SUCCESS RATE	TOTAL ANIMALS HARVESTED
Elk	21%	42,630
Deer	42%	31,634
Antelope	61%	6,417
Black Bear	6%	759
Desert Bighorn	100%	9
Rocky Mtn. Bighorn	51%	175
Mountain Goat	92%	169
Moose	84%	102

It is not possible to estimate the mountain lion success rate because the harvest is based on a quota system instead of limited licenses; however, 315 of the big cats were harvested in Colorado during the 2000 hunting season.

Physical Characteristics

Interstate 25 (I-25) marks the eastern boundary of Region 1. The area between I-25 and the mountains to the west is a heavily developed corridor consisting of relatively flat terrain to rolling hills as you approach the mountains. This area is heavily populated includes the cities of Denver, Boulder, and Ft. Collins. The Front Range Mountains rise from the flat terrain of the eastern plains. At 14,255 feet, Longs Peak stands out as one of the prominent features along the Front Range. It should be noted that Longs Peak is within the boundaries of Rocky Mountain National Park, which is closed to hunting. However, the park is an area with spectacular scenery and an abundance of wildlife. Every fall hordes of photographers flock to the park to capture rutting elk on film. This is a great area to observe big game animals and learn their traits and habits first hand. The areas surrounding the park are also good areas to consider hunting.

Moving to the west across the northern portion of Region 1 is another prominent geographical feature known as North Park. As the name implies, it is a large park-like area bounded by the Medicine Bow Range and Front Range to the east, the Rabbit Ears Mountains to the south and the Park Range to the west. The Arapahoe National Wildlife Refuge is located in North Park just south of the town of Walden. Other prominent features in this area include Middle Park, the beginning of the Colorado River drainage, the Gore Range, and the Blue River.

Continuing west, you cross the continental divide as you cross the Park Range.

Ski enthusiasts are probably familiar with Steamboat Springs, which is located on the west side of the Park Range. Farther to the west, the Elkhead Mountains rise above the Yampa Basin, which is drained by the last truly wild river in Colorado – the Yampa River. It is the only major river within the state that has not been dammed anywhere along its course. The Yampa flows west to meet the Green River within Dinosaur National Monument. South of the Yampa is the White River, another important drainage that originates in the Flat Tops and White River Plateau. If you're familiar with big game hunting in Colorado you've probably heard about the White River elk herd. This herd currently has over 45,000 elk, which rivals the total population of elk found in many of the western states and Canadian provinces.

Other notable geographic features include the Roan Plateau and the Book Cliffs in the southwest portion of Region 1. Finally, Interstate 70 (I-70) parallels the Colorado River, which makes up a large part of the southern boundary of Region 1. The Colorado River drainage provides critical habitat for large populations of deer and elk in the state. Unfortunately, it is also an area that has undergone a significant increase in development over the past 20 years.

Region 1 contains large tracts of public land with 13 federally designated wilderness areas within four national forests, thousands of acres of BLM land, and the Colorado State Forest. There are also numerous state wildlife areas and state trust lands that can be hunted.

In terms of habitat, Region 1 has a diverse mixture, starting with grasslands in the plains area between I-25 and the mountains. The prominent mountainous areas, west of the plains, such as the Front Range, Laramie Mountains, Park Range, Gore Range, and the Flat Tops, contain large tracts of montane and subalpine forest. The higher ranges also contain areas of alpine tundra habitat. North Park, Middle Park, and the Yampa Basin are characterized by semi-desert shrubland with large areas of sagebrush. The Yampa Basin also contains relatively large areas of montane shrubland in transition zones between montane forest and the semi-desert shrubland. The southwest portion of the region, including the Roan Plateau and the Book Cliffs, is predominantly pinon-juniper woodland.

Land Use

The I-25 corridor from Denver to Wyoming is the most heavily populated area in Colorado, and it stands to reason that this is also the most developed area in the state. Urban sprawl is slowly chewing up much of the plains and foothills area between I-25 and the mountains. The undeveloped area is predominantly private agricultural land made up in large part by irrigated cropland. If you don't have contact with a private landowner in this area, it's probably not the best place to consider hunting big game. However, there are some good opportunities for deer, and elk if you're willing to take the time to cultivate a relationship with a farmer – no pun intended.

From the Front Range Mountains to the west are large areas of national forest. Land use in the national forests includes logging, ranching, recreation, and mining. The Forest Service makes large areas of timber available for logging each year. Logging roads provide access into otherwise remote areas. This is an advantage to the big game hunter, and I often take advantage of these roads myself. The downside is that these areas are visited by a wide variety of people who wouldn't normally access locations they couldn't drive to. Large ranching operations are found in the mountains and large tracts of national forest are leased for grazing. There are several ski areas in Region 1 and recreational opportunities abound. Very limited mining for precious metals still occurs on a small scale, but there are several sand and gravel operations as well as crushed stone quarries, and large coal mining operations.

Land use in North Park, Middle Park, and the Yampa Basin includes ranching, oil and gas production, mining, and recreation. For the most part these areas contain wide-open spaces with isolated areas of trees on hills and along river bottoms. All three areas contain large ranching operations with vast amounts of hay meadows. Much of this land, especially areas along river bottoms, is private property and, of course, you will see numerous deer and elk standing behind fences that are plastered with "no trespassing" signs. (Don't even think about it, it's not worth it.) Again, if you can develop a relationship with a landowner, you might find the ideal hunting venue. It seems that more and more ranchers are finding out that hunting can be a windfall to their income. Many ranchers will allow access to their property for a trespass fee.

Land use in the Roan Cliffs and Book Cliffs includes oil and gas production, limited mining, recreation, and ranching. Much of this land is BLM property with various energy companies controlling mineral rights, and to some extent, access. However, there is a great deal of accessible public land in this area with quality deer and elk hunting opportunities.

Weather

If you live in Colorado you've probably heard the saying, "if you don't like the weather now, wait ten minutes and it will change." This is especially true in the high country. Region 1 has a great deal of high country and weather changes can be abrupt.

Bowhunters and muzzleloader hunters are generally hunting in Colorado as early as August through the end of September, depending on what species they pursue. Bowhunters pursuing antelope will experience summer temperatures that can exceed 90 degrees. These hot temperatures are good because antelope, just like people, need to drink more water when it's hot. The downside is that it's hard to stay out all day if you're not prepared for the heat. The secret, if you are bowhunting from a blind at a waterhole is to prepare a blind that offers ample shade.

Afternoon thunderstorms are the common weather pattern in Colorado in the summer months. Mornings are generally calm and clear with sunny blue skies. As the mountains heat during the morning, convection causes clouds to rise in the afternoon. Often by mid-afternoon these systems have enough energy to turn into thunderstorms. This weather pattern is fairly consistent across the state at this time of year.

While bowhunting antelope northwest of Craig, Colorado a few years ago I witnessed a huge storm build up in the west. At the time I had a pickup truck with a camper-shell on it. I was camped out on a flat sagebrush plain near the Little Snake River when the storm approached. My instinct told me to leave the area, but I rationalized that I would be fine in the back of my truck, and it was too much trouble to move to another area. It was late in the evening as the storm approached, and wind began to gently rock my truck as it got dark. Off in the distance there was a drill rig with a tall derrick lit by a row of vertical lights. As the wind picked up I happened to look out just as a thick bolt of lightning struck the rig, blowing out all of the lights on the derrick in a brilliant flash. I began to question my decision to stay, but it was too late, the dry earth turned to mud as the first downpour of rain hit. As the storm passed over my location, violent winds rocked my truck back and forth and lightning flashed constantly. I regretted my decision to stay, and I must admit that I re-affirmed my faith in God that night with several prayers that dealt primarily with self-preservation. This is only one of many severe storms that I have endured while hunting in Colorado. If you're hunting this time of year enjoy the nice weather, but be prepared for cold temperatures, rain, sleet, hail, and/or snow. I've experienced several forms of precipitation in a single day.

More often than not, hunting in late August and September is very pleasant. As summer comes to an end in September, the afternoon thunderstorm weather pattern is usually beginning to change. Cold fronts can push down from the north bringing the first snows to the high country as early as mid-September. Winter snowpack will generally begin to accumulate at the higher elevations in October and November. As the first rifle season begins in October, the weather can be anything from bad snowstorms (usually with relatively mild temperatures and slushy snow) to warm 60-degree days. During the last rifle season in November, temperatures can drop to extreme lows, and snow can be heavy. Again it varies from year to year, depending on the path of the Jet Stream. Some years there are complaints about the hunting because the weather was too nice, other years there are complaints that the weather was too bad. You never know where your next excuse is going to come from, and I commonly utilize weather to rationalize my hunting-related failures.

The high mountain ranges experience extremes in weather and precipitation. If you're hunting above 8,000 feet during any of the rifle seasons in the Front Range, Gore Range, Park Range, or Flat Tops in Region 1, listen to the weather forecasts. If you hear that a Pacific front is headed into Colorado, it could mean that the mountains, especially the high ranges, are in for snow. This might be the time to travel to a lower elevation, as the deer and elk might move down if a significant storm hits. It seems that hunters get stranded in the mountains every year when deep snows fall. This is especially true of hunters who travel into remote areas with large RVs and ignore storm warnings.

The following table provides average high and low temperatures as well as total precipitation and total monthly snowfall for Steamboat Springs, Colorado. Steamboat Springs is centrally located in Region 1 at an elevation of 6,695 feet above mean sea level.

MONTH	AVERAGE HIGH (°F)	AVERAGE LOW (°F)	AVERAGE TOTAL PRECIPITATION (in.)	AVERAGE TOTAL SNOW FALL (in.)
August	80.1	40.0	1.59	0.0
September	72.3	32.5	1.76	0.9
October	60.1	23.8	1.92	7.0
November	43.2	14.2	1.96	19.9
December	30.7	3.3	2.42	32.9

Temperature ranges were based on National Weather Service data for Steamboat Springs. Period of record 9/2/1908 to 7/31/2000. Remember that the ambient temperature decreases with an increase in elevation. It's not exact, but as a general rule there is a 3-degree decrease in temperature per 1,000-foot gain in elevation. As an example, you might be staying in the town of Craig at an elevation slightly over 6,000 feet during your hunting trip. Each morning you drive into the high mountains in the Routt National Forest and hunt at an elevation of 10,000 feet. The temperature is probably going to be about 12 degrees lower at the higher elevation than the temperature in Craig.

Public Lands and Acreage

Region 1 has over eight million acres of public land in the form of national forests, BLM, state lands, and national wildlife refuges. The national forests contain several federally designated wilderness areas. The acreage of these areas is tabled below to help identify the amount of wilderness area in the region. However, the acreage of these areas is part of the total acres listed under the national forests.

State lands include state wildlife areas (SWA) and state trust lands, as well as state parks and recreation areas. State wildlife areas are properties owned by the state managed for wildlife. State trust lands are properties leased by the state and are subject to change based on lease agreements. There are over 430,000 acres of state trust lands open to hunting and fishing in Colorado. Because state trust lands and SWAs are often found within national forest boundaries, the acreage for these lands make up part of the total public lands listed below. Furthermore, while many of these lands have excellent big game hunting opportunities, some of them are only open for fishing or small game hunting. Brochures and maps for all of the state trust lands and SWAs are available from the Colorado Division of Wildlife.

Please note that all of the acres listed are not necessarily within the boundaries of the region. Some of the national forest areas extend beyond the Regional I boundary. Most notably, a large portion of the White River National Forest is in Region 2. As a result, only about 50 percent of the White River N.F. acres are accounted for in Region 1. BLM acreage is given by county, and some of the counties also cross the Region 1 boundary. It should also be noted that there are private lands within the national forests and areas on the BLM lands that are sometimes closed to public use due to various leases.

PUBLIC LAND DESCRIPTION	ACREAGES
Roosevelt National Forest	788,000
Routt National Forest	1,125,000
Arapaho National Forest	1,025,000
White River National Forest (50 Percent)	1,000,000
Bureau Of Land Management	3,978,579
Colorado State Forest	120,708
Arapaho National Wildlife Refuge	14,500
Browns Park National Wildlife Refuge	13,500
TOTAL PUBLIC LANDS IN REGION I	8,065,287

WILDERNESS AREAS (NATIONAL FOREST)		ACREAGES
Indian Peaks	(Arapaho/Roosevelt)	73,391
Comanche Peak	(Roosevelt)	67,791
Cache La Poudre	(Roosevelt)	9,238
Rawah	(Roosevelt)	73,899
Byers Peak	(Arapaho)	8,095
Vasquez Peak	(Arapaho)	12,300
Neota	(Roosevelt)	9,924
Never Summer	(Arapaho/Routt)	20,692
Mount Zirkel	(Routt)	160,568
Sarvis Creek	(Routt)	47,140
Flat Tops	(White River/Routt)	235,035
Ptarmigan Peak	(White River/Routt)	13,175
Eagles Nest	(White River/Arapaho)	133,688
TOTAL WILDERNESS AREA REGION I		864,936

REGION I HIGHLIGHTS

Red Feathers (GMUs 7, 8, 9, 19, 191)

Located in north-central Colorado (Larimer County) within the Roosevelt National Forest, the very small town of Red Feather Lakes sits among a cluster of small lakes including the one that bears its name. The surrounding area holds the Red Feathers deer herd, inclusive of all animals within GMUs 7, 8, 9, 191, and 19. Based on recent deer population estimates there are 9,000 to 11,000 animals with a good buck-to-doe ratio of 33 bucks for every 100 does. The same five GMUs comprise the Poudre River elk herd with an estimated population that normally exceeds 4,000 animals.

The area offers outstanding hunting for deer and elk. There is also a high population density of mountain lions here, especially within the Cache la Poudre River

Canyon. Bighorn sheep also inhabit the area, and there are tags available in Bighorn Sheep Units S1, S18, and S19. There is also a small herd of antelope located in GMUs 7 and 8 at the lower elevations.

The Laramie Mountains make up a large portion of the subject area. Large tracts of montane forest cover these mountains with an abundance of ponderosa pine, Douglas fir, juniper, and lodgepole pine. There are also areas of subalpine forest, to the west in the Medicine Bow Mountains within GMU 7 that contain fir, spruce, and aspen. Weather is generally mild in the early seasons with daytime temperatures between 50 and 70 degrees. During the rifle seasons in October and November the temperatures are lower with highs in the 30s to 50s at average elevations of 8,000 feet. Snow generally begins to accumulate in the higher elevations in mid-October, but like all high country in Colorado, be prepared for significant changes in the weather. It might be warm and sunny one day and cold and snowing the next.

Access is good via State Highway 14, which runs parallel to the Cache la Poudre River. This highway provides access into all five of the GMUs discussed earlier. To get to Highway 14 take US Highway 287 north through the town of Fort Collins and turn left onto 14 at Teds Place. If you want to get to Red Feather Lakes continue north on 287 past Teds Place and turn left onto Road 74E (Red Feather Lakes Road) at Livermore. This road will take you past the Lower Lone Pine Units of Cherokee Park State Wildlife Area on your way to Red Feather Lakes. The upper unit of Cherokee Park SWA is a good place to hunt deer and elk. To get to the upper unit stay on US Hwy 287 past Livermore and turn west onto County Road 80C (Cherokee Park Road). Good north to south access is provided on Road 103, which runs from the Wyoming state line south to Highway 14 at Chambers Lake. There is an abundance of public land in the area. The Fort Collins BLM Surface Management Status Map will help you identify the public lands.

In recent years there have generally been over 3,200 rifle deer licenses available on a limited basis for the five-unit area of 7, 8, 9, 19, and 191. Remember that there will be unlimited antlerless deer licenses available in Unit 9 from September 1 to January 31 during 2002 in an attempt to control CWD in this area.

There were also several licenses available in GMU 7 for the early season High Country Rifle Deer hunt. Elk licenses were unlimited for the three combined rifle seasons for bulls. Hunters also had a very good chance to draw a cow elk tag in these units with 0 to 1 preference points.

My first elk hunt took place in the southwest corner of GMU 19 very close to Cameron Pass many years ago. I was a teenager at the time and had just purchased my first hunting rifle, a Remington Model 700 ADL in .30-06. I didn't get my elk that year, but I will never forget that hunt. Elk camp consisted of a large white canvas tent complete with a gas-fired heater and comfortable cots to sleep on. I was a guest of a high school friend, and his dad took good care of us on the hunt. Each evening he prepared big meals on the camp stove, and I can still remember the smells of cooking in the tent as well as the warmth when coming in from the cold. Although that hunt was long ago, the images are crystal-clear. One afternoon I stumbled into a herd of elk bedded in very dark timber. They rose from their day beds and magically slipped away into the tangle of woods. I was amazed at how fluidly and silently they moved through the thick timber. I was awe-struck and never even raised my rifle to shoot, but that one moment hooked me on elk hunting.

North Park Moose (GMUs 6, 16, 17, 161, 171)

Over the years I have spent a lot of time in North Park hunting and fishing. The small town of Walden is centered in North Park/Jackson County and makes a good base of operations. The area contains a rich mixture of opportunities for the avid sportsman. There are several small lakes and rivers that provide exceptional fishing and good waterfowl hunting. Good populations of blue grouse and sage grouse will keep the wingshooter busy, and big game hunters will have opportunities to take trophy antelope, deer, elk, bear, and moose. The Arapaho National Wildlife Refuge is located just south of Walden and is open in some areas to some types of hunting.

Game Management Units 6, 16, 17, 161, and 171 cover the North Park area. The North Park deer herd has recently been close to 5,000 animals. The area also has a strong elk herd with nearly 7,000 animals and an antelope population that is generally well over 1,000 animals. Although there are not huge numbers of antelope in this region, trophy quality is good. Rudy Meyers (who has operated Tanglewood Taxidermy for nearly 30 years) tells me that many big antelope come out of the North Park area each hunting season. On my many visits to this area I've seen several bucks that would score in the 75 to 80 range.

Deer hunting can be good in the area, even with the relatively low number of mule deer. I've seen some huge bucks (30-inch spread category) when traveling over Willow Creek Pass, and if you're able to get permission to hunt one of the ranches in the area, you might have a good shot at tagging a decent-sized buck. There are also several licenses available in GMUs 6, 16, and 161 for the early season High Country Rifle Deer hunt. Elk hunters will have good opportunities on Independence Mountain located to the north of Walden as well as Willow Creek Pass and the Park Range.

Colorado's moose population is estimated to be 1,100 animals. Half of the total population is concentrated in the North Park area. Through a wildlife trade with Wyoming and Utah, 36 Shiras moose were introduced into North Park over a nine-year period beginning in 1978. Since that time the population has grown and the animals have migrated into new areas including Middle Park, and Rocky Mountain National Park. Although tags are difficult to get, there are approximately 65 licenses issued for the North Park area each year. Most animals are taken from GMU 171, which extends south from Walden to Willow Creek Pass. I usually see moose every year when driving over Willow Creek Pass on my way to Walden. There is also a moose viewing area set up near the town of Gould located to the east of Walden on the edge of the Colorado State Forest within the Medicine Bow Mountains.

If you plan to hunt the North Park area you will find the terrain is very diverse. The actual park area is roughly 25 miles east to west and 30 miles north to south. This region consists of wide-open expanses of semi-desert shrubland, predominantly sagebrush. Mountains with large tracts of montane and subalpine forest bound the park. There is an abundance of BLM land in the park area, but there are also large ranching operations mixed in. Public access is good into the national forests surrounding the park, and there are good hunting opportunities in the Colorado State

Forest to the east of North Park.

To get to the area you can take Highway 14 from Fort Collins. This route will take you through Poudre Canyon and over Cameron Pass. This is a pretty drive, but be aware that the traffic can be tough—especially on the weekends. I prefer to take I-70 from Denver to Highway 40. This will take you over Berthoud Pass through Winter Park and into the town of Granby. From Granby take Highway 125 over Willow Creek Pass into Walden. You will likely see antelope, deer, and elk at various locations along the way. If you're lucky you might even see a moose or two.

Weather can be extreme in North Park and the surrounding mountains. North Park itself has an arid climate with relatively small amounts of snow accumulating in the winter. However, it can get extremely cold and high winds are common. It doesn't take a lot of snow to make big drifts. The mountains surrounding North Park get deep snowpacks in the winter. When hunting the area be prepared for extreme weather conditions and listen to the weather forecasts if you're in remote areas. It seems like hunters get rescued from remote camps every year, and their vehicles stay put until the spring thaw.

To sum it up, North Park is one of the best areas in the state for a wide variety of big game animals. If you're after a moose, this is definitely the place to hunt. Although there are only a handful of Colorado moose listed in the record books, all of those listed in the bowhunting records were taken from Jackson County, with the state record scoring a respectable 161 7/8.

Mistaken Identity

If you find yourself hunting big game in any of the GMUs that contain moose, be extra careful (as you should be anyway) to identify your target before shooting. Every year elk hunters shoot several moose by mistake during the rifle seasons, especially in North Park and the surrounding areas. One of the worst years on record for mistaken identity was 1998 when there were 37 confirmed cases of accidentally and illegally killed moose in Colorado. I am reminded of an old cartoon that depicts a big bull moose standing over two dogs. One of the dogs (named Bruce) has his leg lifted about ready to urinate on the front leg of the moose. The other dog has a caption above his head that reads, "That's a moose, Bruce, not a spruce." In Colorado that caption would be more applicable if it said, "That's a moose, Bruce, not an elk." It doesn't rhyme, but you get the point.

Besides the embarrassment associated with shooting the wrong animal, the DOW will hit you where it counts if you accidentally shoot a moose. You will typically receive a $1,368 fine and a 15-point violation against your hunting license, although the actual penalties can be less severe or much more severe depending on the circumstances. For instance, if you accidentally shoot a moose and immediately report it to the DOW, the penalties will probably be much less severe than if you try to conceal what you have done. Because moose are considered "trophy animals" by the state, poaching a moose could result in as much as a $10,000 fine and up to three years in prison. This stiff penalty was the result of legislation enacted after a non-resident poached a huge bull elk in the town of Estes Park. The residents had affectionately named the bull Sampson, and the legislation became known as the Sampson Bill.

Everyone who has ever taken a hunter safety course knows that you should never shoot until you have properly identified the target. Anyone who hunts also knows how excited a person can become while hunting. My advice is to always take that extra moment to identify the target. If there is any doubt, don't shoot. Even a missed opportunity at an elk is better than an embarrassing and costly mistake.

A moose in thick cover in a Colorado forest.
Be sure you can see your target well.

Greg Gardner with a trophy bull taken in the Middle Park Area -
Reg. 1 Middle Park GMU. (Steve Penrose)

Middle Park (GMUs 18, 27, 28, 37, 181, 371)

Located to the south of North Park within Grand County, Middle Park is conveniently located in the center of excellent big game country. From the town of Granby access is good into the Arapahoe National Forest and the Never Summer Wilderness to the north. Joined by many small feeder creeks in the vicinity of Granby, the Colorado River has its origin in Rocky Mountain National Park to the north. Just north of Granby the Colorado River turns west and begins its run to the Gulf of Mexico. Along the continental divide to the east is the Indian Peaks Wilderness Area. The Arapahoe National Forest wraps back around Middle Park to the south. With large tracts of national forest and abundant BLM to the west, this area offers an excellent opportunity to hunt big game on public land.

Habitat in the park is largely semi-desert shrubland. The surrounding mountains contain a diversity of ecosystems starting with relatively large areas of alpine tundra at the highest elevations in the Front Range to the east. Descending in elevation you will find large tracts of subalpine and montane forest. Weather in this part of the state can be severe during the hunting seasons, as the name of the Never Summer Wilderness implies. The high mountains to the north, east, and south of Middle Park can receive deep snowpack in the winter, often exceeding 150 inches of total snowfall. Generally, the snow doesn't begin to accumulate until late September or early October, but hunters should be prepared for the worst. When hunting this part of the state in late October and November, hunters will almost always encounter snow at elevations above 9,000 feet.

A large portion of Middle Park is covered by GMUs 18 and 28. With a strong population of deer that generally varies from 12,000 to 14,000 animals, the Middle Park deer herd includes GMUs 18, 27, 28, 37, 181, and 371. Much of the river bottom properties along the Fraser and Colorado Rivers hold good numbers of mule deer. Unfortunately, most of this land is privately owned. Don't get discouraged though; if you're willing to pay there are a number of outfitters in the area who can get you onto private land. If you're willing to work a little harder, there are also good opportunities to take mule deer on public lands in the area.

Elk hunting in the area is outstanding with high trophy potential. GMUs 18 and 181 make up the Troublesome elk herd with recent populations approaching 3,600. GMUs 28, 37, and 371 make up the William's Fork elk herd with nearly 3,500 animals. Often overlooked by big game hunters in Colorado, the Middle Park antelope herd has a nominal population that generally contains over 600 animals in GMUs 18 and 181. Good bucks are often visible on the sagebrush-covered hills right outside of the town to the west of Granby. If you want to hunt antelope bucks in this area during the rifle season it will take at least five preference points to draw a tag, but you might be able to get a superb trophy. The mountains surrounding Middle Park also hold a fair number of black bears.

Hunter access to the area is good. To get to Middle Park take Interstate 70 west from Denver to Highway 40 over Berthoud Pass. As you start down the pass you come

Steve Penrose with a trophy mule deer taken in Grand County -
Region 1, Middle Park GMU. (Steve Penrose)

into GMU 28. Berthoud Pass holds some tremendous mule deer. This is another area that hunters often drive through, but fail to hunt. Granted, the terrain is steep and weather can be severe, making the hunting conditions on the pass a tough proposition, but it shouldn't be overlooked. Staying on Highway 40 will take you to the town of Granby, about two hours from Denver. If you continue on 40 heading west, you will find numerous county roads that provide access to large tracts of public land on the north side of the road. Highway 40 will take you to the town of Hot Sulphur Springs and on into Kremmling located farther to the west. Just outside of Granby is Highway 125 that will take you over Willow Creek Pass and into North Park. This is another road that provides good access into public land with good opportunities for deer, elk, and (as discussed in the North Park section) moose.

Sometimes the recreational diversity of an area makes it that much more appealing to hunters. With Rocky Mountain National Park accessible by Highway 34 out of Granby and numerous reservoirs and ski resorts, the area offers a broad array of recreational opportunities. (Please note that Rocky Mountain National Park is closed to hunting.)

Eagles Nest Wilderness (GMUs 36, 37, 371)

While fishing the Blue River north of Silverthorne, I've often looked up in wonder at the jagged peaks of the Gore Range to the west. This is truly a majestic range of glaciated mountains. Thin knife-like ridges connect peaks that overlook cirque basins that hold numerous small alpine lakes.

Sometimes the success of a hunt can be measured by more than just the quantity or quality of animals. The Eagles Nest Wilderness Area has an intangible quality of ruggedness and beauty that can make a hunting adventure a success, regardless of the take. If you're up to it physically, this might be a good area to consider a remote wilderness hunt. Backpacking or on horseback will probably be the most effective way to access the remote areas. Although it will be a lot of work, if you pull it off you might go home with much more than a trophy to remember for the rest of your life.

The Eagles Nest Wilderness is located approximately two hours west of Denver. To get to the area take Interstate 70 west from Denver to the town of Silverthorne. From Silverthorne proceed north on State Highway 9, which runs parallel to the Blue River, a gold medal trout fishery. Highway 9 provides access along the east side of the Gore Range in Summit County within the Arapahoe National Forest. Although much of the land along the river is privately owned, there are several trailheads and a few county roads that will get you into the backcountry. To gain access to the west side, continue west on I-70 from Silverthorne to Vail. County roads from Vail will get you into the south part of the wilderness area on the White River National Forest side of the Gore Range within Eagle County. Additional access to the west side can be gained by traveling Highway 131 north from Wolcott.

Since this area is bounded by I-70 on the south, you might think there would be crowds of people. This is true in the areas with easy access, but if you expend the effort to get into the backcountry, you will be rewarded with a true wilderness hunt.

The actual wilderness area is 133,688 acres with large areas of subalpine and montane forest with alpine tundra habitat at the higher elevations. Elevations range from 8,000 feet to over 13,000 feet at the higher peaks. Weather can be extreme along the Gore Range. Be prepared for cold temperatures, rain, and snow regardless of the season you're hunting. Snow can begin accumulating as early as September at some of the higher elevations.

Game Management Unit 371 covers a large portion of the wilderness area. Units 36 and 37 also cover portions of this area. Deer numbers are good with the chance for some trophy-caliber timberline bucks in the higher elevations. Elk hunting can be very good in this area with the opportunity for large bulls. The William's Fork and Piney River elk herds cover the area with a combined population that has recently grown to over 10,000 animals. With large stands of lodgepole pine, spruce, and aspen, still-hunting will be an effective approach. Taking stands near open parks and meadows can also be effective. At higher elevations you will encounter boggy, alpine meadows with thick tangles of willow. The going may be tough, but you might run into that bull of a lifetime in one of these remote meadows.

If you plan on hunting the Eagles Nest Wilderness don't forget to purchase a bear tag. There are good populations of black bear in this part of Colorado. Mountain goat GMU G6 also covers this area. In recent years there have been 11 goat tags available for this unit with 100% success rates.

Clear Creek Sheep (GMU S32)

Just west of Denver on Interstate 70 (I-70) starting near the town of Idaho Springs is GMU S32. This unit stretches to the Eisenhower Tunnel to the west and lies on the north side of the interstate. It makes up one of the more productive bighorn sheep units in the state. Colorado boasts a population of roughly 6,500 bighorns, which is more than any other state in the U.S.

Interstate 70 runs parallel to Clear Creek all the way to the Eisenhower Tunnel. Justifiably named, Clear Creek County is home to a large population of bighorn sheep. The area also offers decent deer hunting and a moderate population of over 1,200 elk in GMUs 29 and 38. The area also contains mountain lions and bears.

If you travel I-70 on a regular basis, you will see bighorn sheep on a regular basis. Many times the sheep are right down off the side of the highway. This often causes traffic problems as tourists slam on their brakes to get a look at the wild sheep. Abrupt stops often lead to problems when the flow of traffic is usually moving at 65 miles per hour or better. Still it is always entertaining to see the sheep. Occasionally, you will catch a glimpse of a nice ram near the highway, but for the most part the big ones stay well away from the road in the higher elevations.

The terrain in this area is extremely steep. Clear Creek has carved a canyon through this part of the mountains and hunters will need to be in shape. The best way to hunt this area is with high power optics. Scan the mountains for an animal and plan a stalk. You will be much better off if you have a companion to flag you towards the animal once you start your stalk. These mountains can be dangerous to climb, and sometimes the sheep will be in places that you won't be able to get to without technical climbing skills. Best to find an animal in a more approachable location than killing yourself. Be prepared to commit to long stalks of several hours. You're probably not going to get that big ram on a 15-minute hike.

Although sheep tags in general are difficult to draw, this is a good area if you're lucky enough to get the tag. Trophy potential is high and access from Denver is good. Be aware that there are many historic patented mining claims in this area. Although nearly all of these claims are inactive, you can still get run in for trespassing if you stray off the public lands. Generally, you must be more than 50 feet from the center-line of a public road before discharging a weapon, and this includes bows.

Jake Cloyed with a ewe taken in Area S32 - Region 1 Clear Creek Sheep GMU.

Jim Fitzgerald with a ram taken in Area S32 - Region 1, Clear Creek Sheep GMU.

Altitude Sickness

If you take the challenge to hunt bighorn sheep, then you will most likely hunt at extremely high elevations. Since Colorado has more land above 10,000 feet than any other contiguous state, the opportunity to hunt several of the big game species at high elevation exists.

If you live in Colorado and spend much time in the high country, chances are that you won't have to worry much about altitude sickness. However, the sickness is unpredictable and can strike any person of any age group in any physical condition. In my experience, many people are not even aware of the sickness. Knowing some basic information about altitude sickness may improve your comfort while hunting at high elevation, and could even prevent a serious medical problem.

In general, altitude sickness can occur at elevations as low as 5,000 feet, but is more common at altitudes of 8,000 feet and higher. As altitude increases, the pressure of the atmosphere decreases. Although the percentage of oxygen remains constant at 21 percent, there are less molecules of oxygen available to breathe. As a result the body must work harder to maintain normal oxygen levels in the blood. The effects of high altitude on most people include increased breathing rate accompanied by a shortness of breath after exertion. The fluid balance in the body can also change to improve the ability of the blood to carry oxygen resulting in increased urination. Sleeping patterns at high elevation can also become irregular causing people to awake frequently during the night.

Altitude sickness (or more correctly, Acute Mountain Sickness) occurs when the body cannot adequately adjust to the low oxygen. Symptoms of the sickness almost always include a headache along with one or more of the following: nausea, vomiting, dizziness, weakness, difficulty sleeping, tunnel vision, and even confusion. If any of these symptoms occur along with a headache while at high altitude, it's time to head downhill. Descending from elevation is the only sure cure of altitude sickness. Plenty of rest, fluids, and analgesics such as aspirin may also help. If you ignore the symptoms and continue to ascend to higher elevations, serious health problems may result. In severe form, altitude sickness can lead to a swelling of the brain (cerebral edema), which can ultimately lead to death. A prominent symptom of cerebral edema is staggering, just like a person might exhibit when very drunk. In this case, the remedy is again a rapid descent.

Fluid build-up in the lungs (pulmonary edema) is another serious condition that can occur at high altitude. This condition may accompany altitude sickness or it can also occur on its own. Symptoms may include extreme fatigue, a cough that produces frothy pink spit, tightness in the chest, blue/gray discoloration in the lips and fingernails, and wheezing or rattling breaths.

The best way to avoid altitude sickness is to allow the body to adjust to the high altitude over a period of one to three days. This process is known as acclimatization. Also try to avoid rapid ascents to high elevation. If you're flying into Colorado from out of state, it is very possible to leave sea level and arrive in elk camp at 10,000 feet all in the same day. This is going to be a shock to the body and you will need some time to acclimatize. It might make for a much more enjoyable trip if you can plan a couple of extra days on the front end of the hunt to adjust to the elevation. It is also helpful to stay well hydrated by drinking plenty of water and avoiding alcohol and caffeine.

If you have experienced altitude sickness in the past, it might be wise to consult a physician prior to planning your next hunt in Colorado. There is a drug available that will help the body acclimatize to high altitude more rapidly, but it isn't necessarily a cure-all for the sickness.

At an elevation of 14,255 feet, Longs Peak is the prominent landmark in this region. Altitude sickness is a real possibility even at much lower elevations.

Hypothermia

Every avid hunter has gotten cold at some point in time. Simply put, getting cold is the start of hypothermia. Most people have also learned about hypothermia through a hunter safety course or first-aid training, but it deserves special attention for hunters in Colorado. If you already know about hypothermia, this can be a basic refresher. If you don't know about it, the following information could save your life or the life of someone you know.

As mentioned in the discussion of the Park Range, I experienced extremely cold temperatures during my 1993 elk hunt. In such extreme conditions, decisions and actions become critical. A seemingly minor accident such as a sprained ankle can turn into a life or death situation. Hunters constantly face conditions and situations that can result in hypothermia. They hunt during the autumn months when temperatures can get very low. They often hunt when it is raining or snowing, and long hikes over rough and steep terrain can result in perspiration and fatigue that can also contribute to hypothermia.

Generally, hypothermia begins when your core body temperature falls below 96.8 degrees. (The core is generally referred to as that portion of your body beneath the skin.) At this point the prominent symptom is shivering. If heat loss continues, mild hypothermia begins when the core temperature reaches 95 degrees. At this stage your body is not creating enough heat to maintain normal body functions. Symptoms include extreme shivering and loss of coordination. To conserve heat, the body constricts blood vessels, reducing blood supply to the outer extremities. This may not become a desperate situation if the danger is recognized, the heat loss is stopped, and the body is allowed to naturally warm itself back to a normal core temperature.

If heat loss continues and the core temperature falls below 91.4 degrees, moderate hypothermia has set in and the situation has become serious. A person in this condition will generally stop shivering. Mental capacity diminishes and muscles begin to get stiff. Ultimately, the person will begin to have trouble talking clearly, breathing can slow, and drowsiness can set in. Now the person has lost the ability to help him or herself out of the situation. Simple warming may not be adequate once this stage of hypothermia has set in, and a doctor should treat the person.

If the heat loss is not stopped and the core temperature lowers to 87.8°F, severe hypothermia sets in. Symptoms include discoloration of the skin to shades of blue or gray, dilated pupils, loss of coordination, and eventually loss of consciousness. The upside is that people can recover from severe hypothermia with medical assistance. The downside for a hunter is that if you're two miles from camp and severe hypothermia has set in, this will probably be your last hunt.

How do you treat hypothermia? If the person is in the early stages, you may be able to reverse the heat loss by removing them from the cold environment, warming with additional clothing, and administering a warm drink. However, you should never attempt to warm a person with alcoholic beverages, coffee, or tea. A sweetened drink and high-energy food will provide calories that the body can convert into heat.

If moderate hypothermia has occurred, as in all stages, the person must be removed from the cold environment. This may include removing wet clothing once the person is in a warm sheltered location. The body will need to be warmed by applying moderate heat to areas of high blood flow. This can be accomplished with heating pads, warm towels, hot water bottles, or even another body. Applying heat to the head, neck, chest, and groin will best accomplish warming. In this stage, warming may take a long time and a physician should examine the person.

If severe hypothermia has set in, the goal is to prevent any more heat loss and get the person to a doctor as soon as possible. Trying to warm the person back to a normal body temperature too rapidly without medical attention could result in life-threatening complications. Mild heat can be applied as in the case of moderate hypothermia, but only as a way of stopping additional heat loss. The person can also be placed in a sleeping bag with another person to provide heat. If the person is still conscious, try to keep them awake. If they have lost consciousness, monitor their breathing and pulse. If the pulse stops, cardiopulmonary resuscitation (CPR) should be administered.

Once severe hypothermia has set in, the best treatment is done at a medical facility by inhalation warming. This allows the core of the body to slowly warm from the inside out. If the body is warmed too rapidly from the outside, cold blood can flow to the heart and brain creating severe complications.

As is always the case, prevention is always a better alternative than treatment. How do you prevent hypothermia? You prepare for extremely cold temperatures. You wear clothing in layers so you can continually adjust your temperature by shedding or adding layers. You protect areas of the body that lose large amounts of heat such as the head and neck. You carry survival gear so that if necessary, you can build a temporary shelter and start a fire. You carry a dry change of clothing that may include socks, long underwear, and an extra outer garment. You stay well hydrated and intake adequate food to maintain your strength. You hunt with a partner, or if you're by yourself, you tell somebody where you're going and when you plan on returning. Lastly, know your limits.

Don't be fooled by the temperature. Hypothermia can occur at relatively high temperatures starting in the 50-degree range. Also, as most of you know, wind chill can significantly increase the likelihood of hypothermia. As an example, if the temperature is 45 degrees (which might be a common daytime temperature during the third rifle season in Colorado) and the wind is blowing steady at 10 miles per hour, the actual effect is a temperature of 34 degrees.

Nearly every hunting season there are fatalities related to hypothermia in Colorado. This often occurs when a person becomes lost or injured and is forced to spend the night outdoors. With all of the modern survival equipment and space-age fabrics, people still enter the backcountry unprepared. Even if you only intend to walk 100 yards from your vehicle to glass a nearby valley, take your survival gear. The one time you leave it behind will be the time that you spot that bull or a buck of a lifetime, and you proceed on a chase that ends up covering several miles. At the end of the chase you find that you are lost, and you don't have your pack. This is a bad predicament that you don't want to find yourself in.

The Park Range and Mount Zirkel
Wilderness Area (GMUs 5, 14, 214)

The Park Range (located within the Routt National Forest) borders the west side of North Park and runs in a north to south orientation from the Wyoming state line south to the Gore Range. The continental divide runs along the top of the Park Range separating the North Platte River drainage to the east (Jackson County) from the Yampa River drainage to the west (Routt County). Mount Zirkel is the highest mountain in the range at 12,180 feet, and is the namesake of a 160,568-acre wilderness area located in the northern portion of the Routt National Forest just north of Steamboat Springs.

This area boasts exceptional elk hunting and good deer hunting. In fact, if you spend any time in the restaurants, bars, or shops of Steamboat Springs, you will see some fine examples of trophy-caliber elk mounts adorning many of these establishments. There are also good numbers of black bear and the occasional mountain lion in this area. The primary GMUs of concern in this region are 5, 14, and 214; three of seven units that make up the Bear's Ears deer and elk herds with populations of 39,650 and 30,360 animals respectively.

The terrain in this area is quite rugged with highly glaciated mountains along the continental divide resulting in hundreds of small alpine lakes and countless drainages. Originating in the wilderness area, the Elk River is a major tributary of the Yampa River on the west side of the divide. As the name would imply, the upper reaches of the Elk River is a good area to find a few wapiti. Major ecosystems include subalpine forest along the continental divide at the higher elevations with montane forest below. North of Steamboat along Road 129 there are also relatively large areas of montane shrubland consisting of oakbrush surrounding semi-desert shrublands of sagebrush meadows. There are many large ranches at the lower elevations, so be aware of private land. The Walden and Craig BLM Surface Management Status Maps will help identify public/private properties in this area.

Access to the area is good, especially from the west side. Travel to Steamboat Springs via State Highway 40. From the east side you will drive over Rabbit Ears Pass. Once in Steamboat you can top off the tank at the Space Station Gas Station and then head north on Road 129. You can't miss the large signs with arrows pointing the way to Steamboat and Pearl Lakes on the west side of town. From 129 there are numerous county roads and jeep trails to the east that will get you into the high country and provide access to the wilderness area. The wilderness area has an extensive trail system of over 150 miles.

The DOW is very liberal with elk tags in this area. Bull elk licenses have been unlimited in Units 5, 14, and 214 over the past several years. There are also good opportunities to draw limited cow tags with 0 to 1 preference points, depending on which unit and season you choose to hunt. Hunter success for elk is good in the three units with archery hunters averaging close to 15 percent and rifle hunters generally bagging their elk 20 percent to 30 percent of the time in recent years.

As is often the case in Colorado, weather can be extreme in this region. I rifle hunted in GMU 14 in November of 1993. Upon arriving at camp there were eight inches of new snow on the ground. This can be good for hunting, but the clear skies that followed the snowstorm made for extremely cold temperatures. The thermometer dipped well below zero at night and everything I brought to drink (including five gallons of water, pop, and even a six pack of beer) was frozen solid by the first morning of the hunt. Freezing temperatures are dangerous, and if you're unprepared, you may find yourself in a life or death situation. Dress in layers, stay well hydrated, and watch for signs of hypothermia.

The Park Range area north of Steamboat Springs offers some exceptional big game opportunities. In terms of spectacular scenery, abundant access, and a healthy population of elk, this is one of the best locations in the state. Whether you decide to rough it or spend your nights in a luxurious lodge, Steamboat Springs offers all major services.

Elk Hunting

If you've never hunted the area and you want a good opportunity to take an elk, head north from Steamboat Springs to the small town of Clark. Just north of Clark go east on Road 64 for three to four miles. There are three campgrounds along this road and several trailheads. One good area to concentrate on is the South Fork of the Elk River via the North Lake Pack Trail. Get the Farwell Mountain, Mount Ethel, Floyd Peak, and Mount Zirkel 7.5-minute USGS topographic maps and scout this area before your hunting season. In addition to elk, there are also some big muleys in the area as well as numerous bears. Good Luck.

A mule deer pauses in the willows on Rabbit Ears Pass in Region 1.

Rabbit Ears (GMUs 14, 15, 16, 17, 27, 181)

At the top of Rabbit Ears Pass along Highway 40, the continental divide takes a hard turn to the east and follows the Rabbit Ears Range. Although Rabbit Ears Peak is actually located at the eastern edge of the southern portion of the Park Range (which was discussed in the preceding section) it deserves special attention. The Rabbit Ears Range is a distinct range of volcanic mountains that mark the southern end of North Park.

The pass is named for the peak located approximately two miles north of its summit. Rabbit Ears Peak is very prominent because of two large columns of basalt that, with a little imagination, resemble a rabbit's ears. Traveling Highway 40 from the town of Kremmling you will start up Muddy Pass where Highway 14 meets 40 from the east. From this point to the summit of both passes you will travel through exceptional deer and elk habitat with vast areas of montane forest, and at the higher elevations subalpine forest.

Both to the benefit and, at times, the detriment of the wildlife, Rabbit Ears Pass receives large amounts of snow each year resulting in deep snowpacks that can last well into spring. The result of all the moisture is thick, lush vegetation that provides good forage for deer and elk. Good nutrition often results in heavy antlers, and many times I have seen big mule deer bucks while traveling over the pass. If deep snow accumulates too early, however, the animals can be forced to lower wintering ranges before the last rifle season is over. Based on my knowledge of the area, this is usually the exception rather than the rule, and the deer are more likely to move from the heavy snows more readily than the elk.

In order to hunt the Rabbit Ears Pass area you must be aware that the boundaries of six GMUs merge together near the summit of the pass. Game Management Unit 27 bounds Highway 40 on its west side, and GMU 181 bounds it on the east as you approach the summit. GMUs 14, 16, and 17 are all located on the north side of the pass and GMU 15 is found on the south side. If you've set up a nice camp somewhere near the summit of the pass, you could easily access any of these GMUs. This presents no real problem if you hold an unlimited bull elk license, however, if you want to hunt cow elk or deer, you will have to choose one of these units and draw the appropriate tag. My suggestion for deer hunters is GMU 27; it has good harvest rates for archery hunters in the 20 percent range, and rifle hunters generally succeed 25 percent to over 40 percent of the time depending on which season they hunt. Any of the units in this area can be good for elk. My suggestion here is that you spend some time scouting the area before you decide on a GMU for elk. Remember, if you want to rifle hunt deer and elk in one of the three combined rifle seasons, you must hunt both species in the same season.

Every year, literally thousands of hunters will travel over Rabbit Ears Pass on their way to other hunting locations. It always amazes me that many of these hunters will travel through such a game-rich area only to get to other locations that aren't as good. Of course, the drawback to the Rabbit Ears area is that many hunters *have* realized that it's a good place to stop and hunt. All of the hunting seasons can be crowded in this area, but depending on your knowledge of the country, you may be able to use the crowds to your advantage.

As a side note, this is a great place to visit in the spring. Just as the snow has melted, the parks and meadows are covered in brilliant arrays of wildflowers. Vivid displays of orange, purple, and yellow blossoms contrast sharply with lush green backdrops. Take your camera and an ultra-light spinning rod or light fly rod and fish the creeks and small lakes as you hike the drainages to get the lay of the land. All of the moisture results in mosquitoes so take along some bug juice and enjoy—this is good country!

The Flat Tops (GMUs 12, 13, 23, 24, 25, 26, 33, 34, 131, 211, and 231)

Located within the White River National Forest and the Routt National Forest, the Flat Tops are synonymous with elk hunting in Colorado. The Flat Tops Wilderness Area is slightly over 235,000 acres, making it the largest wilderness area in Region 1 and the second largest in the state. The bulk of this area is located in Garfield and Rio Blanco Counties. The White River Plateau dominates the geography of the area with elevations between 9,000 and 11,000 feet. Several mountains push up over 12,000 feet in elevation and the area is covered with lakes and creeks too numerous to name. Most notably, Trappers Lake is a prominent and scenic landmark located near the center of the wilderness. As a map reference, the area is centered north of Glenwood Springs, east of Meeker, south of Craig and Steamboat, and to the west of Yampa.

A vast area, with the Flat Tops at its core, GMUs 12, 13, 23, 24, 25, 26, 33, 34, 131, 211, and 231 encompass the White River elk herd which is the largest herd in the state with a recent population well over 50,000 animals. Defined by GMUs 11, 12, 13, 22, 23, 24, 131, 211, and 231, the White River deer herd is also the largest in the state with a current population estimate of 84,170 animals.

The terrain on top of the plateaus is relatively flat, as the name indicates. However, drainages can be extremely steep-sided and many of the plateau escarpments are nearly vertical. The predominant ecosystem on the Flat Tops is subalpine forest consisting of spruce and fir interrupted by large parks and meadows, aspen, lodgepole pine, and, locally, bristlecone pine. The area receives heavy snow in the winter with cold temperatures. Snows generally begin to accumulate in October at the higher elevations. Early snows can dictate deer and elk movement to lower elevations, and if you are hunting the third rifle season on the Flat Tops, watch the weather. Winter storms can be severe, and hunters do get stranded in the backcountry.

Access into the national forests surrounding the Flat Tops is good. To get into the Flat Tops, County Road 8 from the town of Meeker provides good access to several trailheads. Most of the land is public (national forest and wilderness area) but you still have to be careful of private property, especially the river bottoms along the North and South Forks of the White River. Once in the wilderness area travel is strictly regulated and most vehicle and ATV use is restricted. Foot travel and horseback are the only means of transportation allowed along most of the 160 miles of trail located in the Flat Tops. If you've never hunted the Flat Tops before, you might be surprised to learn that many of the established campgrounds and popular trails are very crowded with hunters. You will have to work to get away from the crowds, but it will be worth it. The area was made for pack-in hunting, whether you choose a backpack, horse, or llama. If you're interested in getting far back into the wilderness and you don't have horses, there are several qualified outfitters who service the area. If you have never hunted here before, my advice would be to start scouting for elk in one of the following three units: 23, 25, or 26.

There is no mountain goat hunting in this area and only one sheep unit (S67) that generally has a single tag available. However, the Flat Tops have a high density of bears and mountain lions.

Because the area is so large, it is hard to generalize hunter success. (Please refer to the Harvest Trends for Region 1 to evaluate specific units in this area.) If you're willing to spend the time, there are exceptional opportunities to take deer and elk in the Flat Tops. I have known people who consistently take elk each year in this area. I've also talked to people who hunted the area for one season and didn't see a single elk, so they gave up on it. As with all hunting, the key to success is learning the area so your hunting trip doesn't turn into a scouting trip.

Great Divide Antelope (GMUs 3, 4, 13, 301)

The largest herd of antelope in Colorado is known as the Great Divide herd. In recent years 13,000 to 15,000 antelope roam the sagebrush prairie in GMUs 3, 4, 13, and 301 within Moffat County. The namesake of the herd is a ghost town located about 20 miles northwest of the town of Craig. Access to the area is good, with abundant public lands to hunt. The BLM Surface Management Status Map for Craig, Colorado will be a valuable tool in determining public versus private land, as much of the private property is not posted and some of the public is.

To get to the area travel Highway 40 to Craig, Colorado. From Craig you can access the units by traveling north on Highway 13 or west on Highway 40. Moffat County Road (CR) 4 runs east to west parallel to the Little Snake River near the Wyoming state line. This is a good road to access the units from the north. Moffat CR 7 is a prominent road that runs through the middle of Units 3 and 301 from Craig, northwest to CR 4. From any of these roads there are numerous county roads that cross the entire area. Road conditions vary greatly. Prominent county roads are well maintained and have a gravel base that keeps them passable in most seasons. Less traveled roads are simply graded dirt roads that can get extremely muddy during rainstorms. Be cautious when traveling these roads, a passing thunderstorm can turn the roads into greasy mud in a matter of minutes.

The author with a pronghorn taken on public land in Unit 3 -
Region 1, Great Divide Antelope GMU.

The majority of the area is comprised of semi-desert shrublands with an abundance of sagebrush. The landscape consists of rolling hills with prominent drainages that flow intermittently during the spring. Isolated highlands, bluffs, and gulches support stands of pinon and juniper. The elevation throughout this area is generally 6,000 to 7,000 feet above mean sea level. Higher elevations occur in GMU 4 within the Routt National Forest.

Archery season for antelope usually starts in early August. At this time of year temperatures can be extremely hot, with highs in the 90s. The occasional thunderstorms usually build up in the afternoons, and rarely these storms can become violent with strong wind and lighting. For the most part, the area is very dry with average precipitation of 10 inches per year. Much of this precipitation comes in the winter. The rifle seasons take place in late September into November when snowstorms can occur. Accumulations are usually minimal, but drifting can be a problem.

The success rate for antelope hunters in GMUs 3, 4, 13, and 301 is very high. Archery hunters often push 50 percent success in this area with rifle hunters exceeding 80 percent. If you want a chance at filling your tag, regardless of weapon, this is the best area in the state. There are also many big bucks shot in this area each year. Judd Cooney shot and tied the former archery world record in this area in 1983. The horns scored an impressive 85, one of the biggest bucks taken in Colorado. A quick look in the record books shows that many bucks scoring over 70 are taken in Moffat County every year.

A well-constructed blind hides a bowhunter at a waterhole in the Great Divide Antelope GMU.

Antelope licenses are limited in this area for all methods of hunting, so you will have to apply for a license. Archery hunters will generally draw a buck tag with one to three preference points. If you are willing to hunt does during the archery season you will probably draw a license without any preference points. Rifle hunters can draw a doe tag with a minimum of one preference point. Rifle hunters who want a buck tag are going to have to be patient. It will take at least five preference points to pull a buck tag in this area, but once you get the tag, it will be worth it.

I have spent a lot of time in this part of Colorado bowhunting for antelope and deer. Since the area is very dry, waterholes are the key to success for bowhunters. Once you find a waterhole with abundant tracks around it, scout the area for quality of bucks. Build a blind and prepare to be patient. The key to tagging an antelope with a bow when hunting a waterhole is patience. The more time you spend in the blind the greater your chances will be. Antelope will come in to drink at any time during the day, so don't just hunt the mornings or evenings. Take lots of water with you and build the blind so it provides shade. Pit blinds are generally the most effective, but be aware that digging a pit blind on state lands is not allowed. Your blind will have to be a temporary structure completely above surface. It is still allowable to dig pit blinds on most BLM lands. However, that could change in the near future so check the hunting regulations each year. Regardless of what kind of blind you build, please pick up all of your materials at the end of the season. If you have dug a pit blind, remove the blind and fill in the hole. Many of the modern portable blinds will also be very effective to use at waterholes.

If sitting in a blind isn't your style of hunting, try to spot and stalk. This is wide-open country so finding antelope isn't a problem. For bowhunters stalking is going to be a tough proposition since there is very little cover and the senses of antelope are extremely acute. There are a few bowhunters each year that take antelope by stalking. If you're lucky enough to pull it off, it is probably one of the most rewarding ways to take an antelope. Most rifle hunters will not have a problem bagging an antelope. The question is usually how long to hold out for a big buck. Spot-and-stalk methods work very well for rifle hunters since antelope will often let you get into rifle range before spooking. Still you must make a cautious approach. Try to move when the animals have their heads down grazing, and watch the wind.

This area should not be overlooked for mule deer. Again, spot-and-stalk methods of hunting will be your best approach. Certain waterholes will attract deer on a regular basis, but you are going to have to look long and hard to find those waterholes. In my experience spotting and stalking during the early morning and evening is the most effective way to hunt deer in this area with bow or rifle. Most of the deer that you will find in the open sagebrush areas will be does or younger bucks. You will also find elk in this area, but much of the open sagebrush areas are used only as wintering grounds later in the year. Concentrate on GMU 4 within the Routt National Forest for elk.

The Trophy Corner (GMUs 2, 201, 10, 11)

Moving to the far northwest corner of the state, there are several units with reputations as trophy areas. This part of Colorado is much like the Great Divide area in terms of habitat and weather. The primary ecosystem is semi-desert shrubland with large areas of sagebrush. You will also find pinon-juniper woodland at the higher elevations.

Units 2 and 201 comprise the Cold Springs elk herd with a population that has stayed at about 1,000 animals for the past several years. The thing to note about this herd is the high bull-to-cow ratio of 50 bulls to every 100 cows. The DOW manages these units as trophy elk areas, and as a result licenses are completely limited. If you want to hunt this area you're going to have to make your plans many years in advance because it will probably take seven or eight years to draw an archery license and even longer for rifle hunters. If you do draw the tag you might be in for the hunt of a lifetime. If you get a tag in Unit 2, Douglas Mountain is well known for big bulls. In GMU 201, the namesake of the herd, Cold Springs Mountain, is a good place to start scouting.

Units 2 and 201 are also home to the Vermillion Bluffs antelope herd. In recent years the population of this herd has been over 3,000 animals. Some huge antelope have been taken out of Unit 2. Bowhunters will need a minimum of three preference points to draw a tag for this area and rifle hunters will need at least six. It seems like a long wait, but there are many other seasons and units you can hunt as a second choice while you gather the necessary preference points to hunt a trophy unit.

The Rangley elk herd is located in GMUs 10 and 11 with Unit 10 having the trophy reputation. The herd generally numbers between 1,500 and 2,000 animals, again with a high bull-to-cow ratio of 45 bulls to every 100 cows. Archery hunters will have to wait five years minimum to accumulate enough preference points to hunt GMU 10 and rifle hunters are looking at eight or nine years. Again, trophy potential is high and the unit is managed for that potential. If you draw a Unit 10 tag, Blue Mountain is a good area to scout for some exceptional bulls.

Book Cliffs Deer (GMUs 21, 22, 30, 31, 32)

The southwest portion of Region 1 is a great place to concentrate on deer hunting. GMUs 21, 22, 30, 31, and 32 cover an area known as the Book Cliffs, Roan Cliffs and the Roan Plateau. This area is located in Garfield and Rio Blanco Counties. These GMUs are bounded on the north by the White River, the east by the White River Plateau, the south by the Colorado River and the west by the Utah state line. GMUs 21 and 30 cover the Book Cliffs deer herd with a population that generally exceeds 10,000 animals. The Logan Mountain deer herd includes GMUs 31 and 32 with a population that is normally over 13,000 animals. Lastly, GMU 22 is one of nine GMUs that make up the White River herd; the largest deer herd in the state.

The five units mentioned above also contain the Yellow Creek elk herd that has a strong population that normally exceeds 9,000 animals based on DOW statistics. This part of Region 1 also has good numbers of bear and mountain lion.

Access into the area is relatively good from the towns of Rifle, Grand Junction, Rangley, and Meeker. This is a large area with vast amounts of BLM land that are open to hunting. There are mineral leases held by various energy companies that prevent access into certain areas. From my experience, most of these areas are fenced or well marked. Once you're off the blacktop the going can get rough. Clay soils in this part of the state can make for extremely slick and muddy roads when the infrequent rains come. Also, some of the roads that access the higher elevations are narrow, steep, and winding, with areas along sheer drops.

Most of the region is pinon-juniper woodland with areas of montane shrubland. Elevations vary greatly from 5,345 feet at the town of Rifle to over 9,000 feet in the Roan Cliffs just west of town. There are large stands of spruce, fir and aspen at the higher elevations. The lower terrain consists of heavily eroded areas leading to sheer cliffs at the boundaries of mesas and highlands. On top of the mesas the topography can be moderately flat to hilly with steep terrain surrounding drainages.

This part of Colorado has an arid climate averaging 10 to 15 inches of total precipitation per year. During archery season in September, temperatures can be warm with highs in the 80s. Moving into the rifle seasons in October and November the temperatures are lower, but comfortable, with highs generally in the 50s to 60s. As with any other location in Colorado, if you're hunting at high elevations, specific weather systems can dramatically affect local weather. Be prepared for temperatures below freezing at night, and pay attention to weather forecasts. You don't want to be caught on top of the Book Cliffs in a blizzard. You may be there for a while. In most years, snow doesn't begin to accumulate until late November and December.

As mentioned previously, there are good opportunities for elk, mountain lion, and bear in this part of Colorado. Many large lions have been taken in Rio Blanco County and a good number of large bears come out of Garfield County. Deer hunters can expect good success rates, with archers averaging 20 percent or better with a high of 47 percent in Unit 30 in recent years. Rifle hunters will generally have a success rate anywhere from 35 percent to 75 percent in this area. Deer licenses are generally plentiful in this area with good chances to draw on your first or second attempt. If you're new to this area, give GMU 22 a try. There are several tributaries to Piceance Creek west of Meeker that are exceptional deer hunting areas.

Deer hunters can use a variety of techniques in this area. Rifle hunters will have luck with spot-and-stalk hunting along open hillsides. In areas of thicker vegetation still-hunting will work best. For more patient hunters, taking a stand over areas with abundant sign might pay off. Since deer numbers are high in this area it is possible to pattern deer movements in certain areas. If you spend enough time to find these areas during your preseason scouting, a treestand or ground blind might be the way to go. Bowhunters will probably want to still hunt very patiently or hunt from treestands. Don't overlook treestands for elk in this area, either. Although drives are not common hunting methods in most areas of Colorado, keep this technique in mind for some of the steep drainages that you will find.

I was fortunate enough to bowhunt this area for deer in 1994 with my friend Steve Penrose. Steve had hunted the area for several years and knew the productive locations inside and out. It had been an extremely hot and dry year, and we took advantage of the lack of water. I hunted from a treestand overlooking a small spring near the bottom of a long steep draw. I managed to take my deer on the first evening of the hunt as many deer were moving to water.

Region I Hub Cities

Walden

Population — 830 • Elevation — 8,099'

Walden is located in north-central Colorado in the middle of a large basin known as North Park. Surrounded by prominent mountain ranges, the park is bounded on the west by the Park Range, the south by the Rabbit Ears Range, and the east by the Medicine Bow Mountains. Walden is the Jackson County Seat, one of the more sparsely populated counties in the state.

The town of Walden has billed itself as the "Moose Viewing Capital of the World." While the area does offer good viewing and the best moose hunting in the state, it is also an excellent area for antelope, deer, elk, and bear. The North Platte River originates just west of the town and several other small rivers such as the Michigan, Illinois, and Grizzly Creek offer excellent fishing. There are also several lakes in the area such as the Delaney lakes, Lake John, Cowdry Lake, and Big Creek Lakes that have reputations as excellent fisheries. The Arapahoe National Wildlife Refuge is located just south of Walden and it offers limited hunting for small game, upland birds, antelope, and waterfowl. (Please call the refuge directly for more information on specific hunting regulations at 970-723-8202).

ACCOMMODATIONS

Chedsey Motel, 537 Main Street, (970) 723-8201
Hoover Roundup Motel, 361 Main Street, (970) 723-4680
North Park Motel, 625 Main Street, (970) 723-4271
Village Inn Hotel, 409 Main Street, (970) 723 4378
Eagle's Watch Condos, 32296 Highway 14 West, (970) 723-8633

CAMPGROUNDS AND RV PARKS

KOA North Park Campground, 53337 Highway 14, Gould, CO (970) 723-4310
Richard's RV Park, County Road 7A, (17 miles west of Walden) (970) 723- 4407
Lake John Resort, (970) 723-3226
State Park Camping Reservations, 800-678-CAMP
Forest Services Camping Reservations, 877-444-6777

RESTAURANTS

Coffee Pot Inn, 460 Main Street, (970) 723-4670
Elkhorn Café, 486 Main Street, (970) 723-9996
Four Winds Pizza and Subs, 496 Main Street, (970) 723-8668
Paradise Lanes, 680 Main Street, (970) 723-8616
Moose Creek Cookhouse and Saloon, 508 Main Street, (970) 723-8272

VETERINARIANS

North Park Veterinary Clinic, 33725 Highway 125, (970) 723-8314

SPORTING GOODS, GUNS, AND GUNSMITHS

High Country Sports, 491 Main Street, (970) 723-4648
Sportsmans Supply, 466 Main Street, (970) 723-4343
Flies Only Tackle, 524 Main Street, (970) 723-4215

AUTO REPAIR

Grama's Towing, 507 Main Street, (970) 723-8291
Jack's Auto Parts, 528 Main Street, (970) 723-4674

MEDICAL

North Park Medical Clinic, 521 5th Street, (970) 723-4255
Jackson County Pubic Health Nurse, 312 5th Street, (970) 723-8572
Jackson County Ambulance Service, 396 Lafever Street, (970) 723-4586

FOR MORE INFORMATION

Chamber of Commerce, North Park, 416 4th Street, (970) 723-4600

Craig

Population — 7,980 • Elevation — 6,185'

Craig is located in the Yampa River valley within Moffat County in northwestern Colorado. Largely an agricultural community with large ranching operations, there is also a large power generation facility nearby as well as several big coal mines. The area also produces a significant amount of natural gas.

Craig is the last stop with all major services if you're headed west into Dinosaur National Monument. The Yampa River is located just to the south of town and flows west into the monument. The Elkhead Mountains are located just north of Craig and the Routt National Forest is easy to access from Craig to the north, east, and south.

Situated in a vast area of semi-desert shrubland with huge expanses of sagebrush, Craig is well known for the large numbers of antelope in the area. The deer and elk hunting are also excellent in the surrounding areas.

ACCOMMODATIONS

Black Nugget Motel, 2855 W. Victory Way, (970) 824-8161
Colorado Inn, 205 E. Victory Way, (970) 824-3274
Craig Motel, 894 Yampa, (970) 824-4491
El Rancho Motel, 627 W. Victory Way, (970) 824-3233
El Monte Inn Motel, 441 W. Victory Way, (970) 824-6189
Holiday Inn of Craig, 300 S. Colorado Highway 13, (970) 824-4000
Ramada Limited, 262 Commerce Street, Highway 13, (970) 824-9282
Super 8 Motel, 200 Highway 13, (970) 824-3471

CAMPGROUNDS AND RV PARKS

Craig KOA Kampground, 2800 E. US Highway 40, (970) 824-5105
State Park Camping Reservations 800-678-CAMP
Forest Services Camping Reservations 877-444-6777

RESTAURANTS

Bad to the Bone BBQ and Grille, 572 Breeze Street, (970) 824-8588
Cactus Grill, 420 Yampa Ave., (970) 824-9966
Carelli's Italian Restaurant, 465 Yampa Ave., (970) 824-6868
Eagle Watch Inn, 2179 Highway 394, (970) 824-3764
The Galaxy Restaurant, 524 Yampa Ave., (970) 824-8164
Golden Cavvy Restaurant and Lounge, 738 N. Yampa Ave., (970) 824-6038
The La Plaza Restaurant, 994 Yampa Ave., (970) 824-7345
Ling Ling Chinese Restaurant, 1111 W. Victory Way, (970) 824-6560
The OP Bar and Grill, 534 E. Victory Way, (970) 824-8918
Signal Hill Inn, 2705 W. Victory Way, (970) 824-6682
T-K's Truck Stop, 425 W. Victory Way, (970) 824-4150
Village Inn Pancake House, 1103 W. Victory Way, (970) 824-9600
Wallie's Restaurant and Lounge, 410 N. Ranney, (970) 824-7103

VETERINARIANS

Craig Veterinary Hospital, 37451 Highway 13, (970) 824-9629
High Country Veterinary Clinic, 356 Ranney, (970) 824-2243
McCandless Animal Hospital, 2430 E. Victory Way, (970) 824-5964

SPORTING GOODS, GUNS, AND GUNSMITHS

Cashway Distributors, 385 Ranney, (970) 824-3035
Craig Sports, 124 W. Victory Way, (970) 824-4044
Outdoor Connections, 34 E. Victory Way, (970) 824-5510
Sport Stop, Centennial Mall, (970) 824-8661

TAXIDERMISTS

Mountain Man Taxidermy, 460 Barclay, (970) 824-4910
Wapiti Valley Taxidermy Shop and Art Studio, 390 Lincoln, (970) 824-1027

MEAT PROCESSORS

Custom Quality Meats, 1430 Yampa Ave., (970) 824-4668
Mountain Meat Packing, 291 Lincoln, (970) 824-4878

AUTO RENTAL AND REPAIR

Craig Ford Mercury (for Rental) (970) 324-9441
Arrowhead Auto and Equipment Repair, 1481 N. Yampa Ave., (970) 824-4163
Certified Automotive, 345 N. Mack Lane, (970) 824-3084
Chapman Automotive Service Center, 310 E. Victory Way, (970) 824-4912
Cook Chevrolet, 1776 W. Victory Way, (970) 824-2100
Ike's Automatic Transmission and Auto, 96502 US Highway 40, (970) 824-6475
Jim's Tire and Auto Service, 736 W. Victory Way, (970) 824-8585
Precision Auto Service, 1294 W 4th Street, (970) 824-8566
Rocky Mountain Auto and Muffler, 1694 N Yampa Ave. Highway 13 N, (970) 824-5749
Round Bottom Auto Wrecking 24 Hour Towing, 21 S. Ranney, (970) 824-3395
Craig Conoco Service, 140 W. Victory Way, (970) 824-5310
Simpson's Amoco, 430 W. Victory Way, (970) 824-3116

AIR SERVICE

Craig Municipal Airport (970) 824-6335
Hayden Valley Airport, East of Hayden, CO (970) 276-3669
Steamboat Springs Airport, 3495 Airport Circle, Steamboat, CO 80477, (970) 879-1204

MEDICAL

Memorial Hospital, 785 Russell, (970) 824-9411

FOR MORE INFORMATION

Craig Chamber of Commerce, 360 E. Victory Way, (970) 824-5689

Kremmling
Population — 1,280 • Elevation — 7,364'

As a young boy, my family often visited friends in the town of Kremmling. Many good times were had fishing for brook trout in small streams, rafting the Colorado River, fossil hunting, and camping.

A small community with access to a great deal of public land, Kremmling is located in Grand County on the east side of the Gore Range. Prominent bluffs of shale capped with sandstone stand above the town to the north. The Colorado River meets the Blue River and Muddy Creek just outside of town before continuing west through a deep canyon carved through the Gore Range. The recently constructed Wolford Reservoir is located to the north of town and offers good fishing.

If you drive into Kremmling during any of the three rifle seasons, large orange banners that say, "Welcome Hunters," will greet you. Kremmling, like many of the small mountain communities, collects a significant amount of annual revenue by providing services to hunters. For those people hunting in the surrounding Arapahoe National Forest or the BLM lands in the area, Kremmling will make a good base of operations.

ACCOMMODATIONS

Bob's Western Motel, 110 west Park Ave., (970) 724-326
Canyon Motel, Hot Sulphur Springs, (970) 725-3395
Cliffside Inn Hotel, Hwy 9 and Hwy 40, (970) 724-9620
Hotel Eastin, 104 South 2nd, (970) 724-3261
Hot Sulphur Springs Resort/Spa, Hot Sulphur Springs, (970) 725-3306
Modern Hotel and Building, 214 East Park Ave. (970) 724-9968
Stagecoach Country Inn, Hot Sulphur Springs, (970) 725-3910
Ute Trail Motel, Hot Sulphur Springs, (970) 725-0123

CAMPGROUNDS AND RV PARKS

Red Mountain RV Park, CR 22 and Hwy 40, (970) 724-9593
State Park Camping Reservations 800-678-CAMP
Forest Services Camping Reservations 877-444-6777

RESTAURANTS

The Bakers Rack, 104 North 6th, (970) 724-3412
Lone Moose Restaurant and Lounge, 115 West Park Ave., (970) 724-9987
Mrs. Z's Burger Barn, 413 East Park Ave., (970) 724-9300
Quarter Circle Saloon, 106 West Park Ave., (970) 724-9601
The Wagon Restaurant and Sports Bar, 276 Central Ave., (970) 724-9219

VETERINARIANS

John Colburn, 106 Eagle, (970) 724-3633
Diana Matheson, 2057 CR 24, (970) 724-0630

SPORTING GOODS, GUNS, AND GUNSMITHS

Fishin' Hole Sporting Goods, 310 Park Ave., (970) 724-9407
Middle Park Baits, 412 South 5th, (970) 724-0530

TAXIDERMISTS

American West Taxidermy, 45 CR 12, (970) 724-9321

MEAT PROCESSORS

Alpine Wild Game Processing, 115 West Central, (970) 724-9655
Kremmling Wild Game Processing, 5240 CR 22, (970) 724-3759
Wizardry Wild Game, 1802 Jackson, (970) 724-3810

AUTO REPAIR

Cunningham Automotive, 103 North Pine, (970) 724-3660
Fettig Auto Repair, 1105 Eagle, (970) 724-9536
High Country Auto and Off Road/Towing, 112 S. 3rd, (970) 724-0595
T&H Mobile Repair, Hot Sulphur Springs, (970) 725-9534
West Grand Auto Parts, Inc., 605 East Park Ave., (970) 724-3851

AIR SERVICE

Alpine Wings, McElroy Field, (970) 724-0611

MEDICAL

Kremmling Memorial Hospital District, 214 South 4th, (970) 724-3442

FOR MORE INFORMATION

Kremmling Chamber of Commerce, Town Square, P.O. Box 471, Kremmling, CO 80459, (970) 724-3472

Granby

Population — 1,200 • Elevation — 7,935'

Located centrally in Grand County, the town of Granby is surrounded by exceptional big game hunting country, providing access to the Middle Park area. Encompassed by scenic mountains with Winter Park and Silver Creek Ski Resorts nearby, Granby offers four seasons of recreational activity. Snowmobile enthusiasts flock to the area in the winter, and avid fishermen take advantage of opportunities on the Colorado River, Grand Lake, Granby Reservoir, Shadow Mountain Reservoir and Willow Creek Reservoir; not to mention the numerous small creeks and lakes found in the Arapaho National Forest.

Like so many of the communities west of the continental divide in Colorado, Granby depends on hunters for a large percentage of revenue during the months of autumn. As a result, the town caters to hunters and provides all required services. Don't overlook services provided by the surrounding towns of Hot Sulphur Springs, Fraser, Winter Park, and Grand Lake if you plan on hunting this area.

ACCOMMODATIONS

Blue Spruce Motel, (970) 887-3300, 170 E Agate Ave. 80446
Broken Arrow Motel, (970) 887-3532, 509 W Agage Ave. 80446
El Monte Motor Inn, (970) 887-3348, 425 W Agate Ave. 80446
Homestead Motel, (970) 887-3665, 851 W Agate Ave & US Hwy 40 80446
Inn at Silver Creek, (970) 887-4080, 62927 US Hwy 40 80446-9322
Western Riviera Motel, (970) 627-3580, 875 W Agate Ave. 80446
Beacon Landing Motel, (970) 627-36711026 County Rd 64, Grand Lake 80447
Best-Vu Motel, (970) 887-2034, 8042 US Highway 34 80446-9216
North Shore Resort, (970) 627-3220, 928 County Rd 64 80446
Lake Granby Marina, (970) 887-3456, 6862 US Hwy 34
Daven Haven Lodge, (970) 627-8144, 604 Marina Dr, Grand Lake 80447
Rapids Lodge & Restaurant (970) 627-3707, 209- Rapids LN, Grand Lake 80447
River Pines Cottages, (970) 627-3632, 12082 US Hwy 34, Grand Lake 80447-9011
Shadow Mountain Motel, (970) 627-8546, 12365 US Hwy 34, Grand Lake 80447
Winding River Ranch, (970) 586-4212, 5770 State Hwy 7, Estes Park 80517-6403
Rapids Lodge, (970) 627-3707, 209 Rapids LN, Grand Lake 80447
Inn at Silver Creek, (970) 887-2131 or (800) 927-4386

CAMPGROUNDS AND RV PARKS

Elk Creek, (800) 355-2733 or (970) 878-5311
River Pines Cottages (970) 627-3632, 12082 US Hwy 34, Grand Lake 80477
Winding River Resort Village (970) 627-3215, 1447 County Rd 491, Grand Lake 80447
State Park Camping Reservations 800-678-CAMP
Forest Services Camping Reservations 877-444-6777

Restaurants

El Monte, (970) 887-3221, 519 Agage Ave, Granby 80446
Longbranch, (970) 887-220, 185 E Agate Ave, Granby 80446
Paul's Creekside Grill , (970) 887-2484, 62927 US Hwy 40, Granby 80446
Rapids Lodge & Restaurant, (970) 627-3707, 209 Rapids Ln, Grand Lake 80447
Sunrise Grill, (970) 887-9466, 729 W Agate Ave, Granby 80446

Veterinarians

Brooks Veterinary Service, 12 E. Agate Ave., (970) 887-2417
Granby Veterinary Clinic, 458 E Agate Ave., (970) 887-3848

Sporting Goods, Guns, and Gunsmiths

Budget Tackle, (970) 887-9344, 255 E Agate Ave, Granby 80446
Fletcher's Sporting Goods, (970) 887-3747, 843 W Agate Ave, Granby 80446

Taxidermists

Alpine Taxidermy, 813 Maple, Hot Sulphur Springs, (970) 725-3534

Auto Rental and Repair

Avalanche Car Rental, (970) 887-3908, 662 E Garnet Ave, Granby 80446
D J Towing and Automotive, (970) 887-9414, 62429 Hwy 40
Steve's Towing and Repair, (970) 887-3661, 6th and Garnet
Wrangler Tire and Tune Inc., (970) 887-3144, 585 E Agate Ave, Granby 80446

Air Service

Granby-Grand County Airport, (970) 887-2311

Medical

Granby Medical Center, 480 E. Agate Ave., (970) 887-2117

For More Information

Greater Granby Area Chamber of Commerce, P.O. Box 35, Granby, CO 80446, 81 W Casper Ave., (970) 887-2311, Fax (970) 887-3895

Meeker
Population — 2,362 • Elevation — 6,239'

As the county seat of Rio Blanco County, Meeker provides a good location to access the huge tracts of BLM lands to the west, including the Roan Plateau. Meeker is also a good choice for those planning on hunting the White River National Forest and portions of the Routt National Forest.

In addition to the deer and elk hunting the area is famous for, there are also numerous mountain lions taken out of Rio Blanco County each year. In fact, President Theodore Roosevelt shot the former world record lion near the town of Meeker in 1901. Boone and Crockett still lists that mountain lion as the 7th biggest in the world with a formidable score of 15 12/16.

Located in one of the more undeveloped areas in the state, Meeker is one of only a few towns that can provide adequate services to sportsmen hunting in this remote part of Colorado.

ACCOMMODATIONS

Meeker Hotel, 560 Main St., (970) 878-5255
Rustic Lodge, 173 1st St, (970) 878-3136
Stagecoach RV Campground and Motel, 39084 Hwy 13, (970) 878-4334
Valley Motel, 723 Market St., (970) 878-3656
White River Inn, 219 E Market, (970) 878-5031
Sleepy Cat Guest Ranch, 16064 County Rd 8, (970) 878-4413

CAMPGROUNDS AND RV PARKS

Thousand Trails, 20285 County Rd 8, (970) 878-4078
Stagecoach RV Campground and Motel, 39084 Hwy 13, (970) 878-4334
State Park Camping Reservations 800-678-CAMP
Forest Services Camping Reservations 877-444-6777

RESTAURANTS

Clark's Big Burger, 858 Market, (970) 878-3240
Go-Fer Foods and Deli, 812 Market, (970) 878-5381
Meeker Café, 560 Main St., (970) 878-5062
Sleepy Cat Guest Ranch, 16064 County Rd 8, (970) 878-4413

VETERINARIANS

W.R. Veterinary Clinic, (970) 878-5645

SPORTING GOODS, GUNS, AND GUNSMITHS

Rocky Mountain Bowstrings and Guns, 240 7, (970) 878-4300
Wyatt's Sports Center, 223 8, (970) 878-4428

TAXIDERMISTS

Antler Taxidermy, 369 Market, (970) 878-3365

MEAT PROCESSORS

Watt's Ranch Market, 488 Market, (970) 878-5868

AUTO REPAIR

Jack's Automotive Service, 6 and E Market, (970) 878-5606
Reg Nichols Sales and Service, 486 Market, (970) 878-5026
Valley Repair Inc., 431 E Market, (970) 878-3316
We Fix It, 1085 Market, (970) 878-0930

AIR SERVICE

Meeker Airport, 921 E Market, (970) 878-5045

MEDICAL

Pioneers Hospital of Rio Blanco County, 345 Cleveland, (970) 878-5047

FOR MORE INFORMATION

Meeker Chamber of Commerce, 710 Market, (970) 878-5510

Glenwood Springs
Population — 7,829 • Elevation — 5,746'

Located at the confluence of the Roaring Fork River and the Colorado River, the town of Glenwood Springs is strategically located in the middle of excellent big game hunting country. It provides good access into the surrounding White River National Forest and the Flat Tops to the north.

After a long day of hunting, nothing feels better than warming your bones in the hot mineral waters of Glenwood Hot Springs. Even President Theodore Roosevelt used Glenwood Springs as a base of operations during hunting trips in Colorado. The town caters to hunters and provides all of the necessary services. The scenery in the area is spectacular, and the recreational opportunities are abundant.

ACCOMMODATIONS

Ponderosa Lodge, 51793 Hwy 6 and 24, (970) 945-5058
Red Mountain Inn, 51637 Hwy 6 and 24, (970) 945-6353
Riverside Cottages, 1308 CR 129, (970) 945-5509
Affordable Inns, 51823 Hwy 6 and 24, (970) 945-8551
Best Western Antlers, 171 West 6th Street, (970) 945-8535
Best Western Caravan Inn, 1826 Grand Ave., (970) 945-7451
Cedar Lodge, 2102 Grand Avenue, (970) 945-6579
Frontier Lodge, 2834 Glen Ave., (970) 945-5496
Holiday Inn Express, 501 West 1st St., (970) 945-8817
Hot Springs Lodge and Pool, 401 North River Road, (970) 945-6571
Hotel Colorado, 526 Pine Street, (970) 945-6511
Hotel Denver, 402 7th Street, (970) 945-6565
Ramada Inn, 124 West 6th Street, (970) 945-2500

CAMPGROUNDS AND RV PARKS

Ami's Acres, 50235 Hwy 6 and 24, (970) 945-5340
Hideout Cabins and Campground, 1293 Road 117, (970) 945-5621
Rock Gardens, 1308 CR 129, (970) 945-6737
State Park Camping Reservations 800-678-CAMP
Forest Services Camping Reservations 877-444-6777

RESTAURANTS

19th Street Diner, 1908 Grand Ave., (970) 945-9133
Brass Parrot, 3637 Hwy 82, (970) 945-5297
Marshall Dillon's Steakhouse, 51359 Hwy 6 and 24, (970) 945-0605
Sapphire Grille, 710 Grand Ave., (970) 945-4771
Wild Rose Bakery, 310 7th Street, (970) 928-8973
Bayou, 52103 Hwy 6 and 24, (970) 945-1047
Peking Garden, 1512 Grand Ave., (970) 945-8143
Florindo's Italian Cuisine, 721 Grand Ave., (970) 945-1245
Dos Hombres Glenwood, 51783 Hwy 6 and 24, (970) 928-0490

VETERINARIANS

Glenwood Veterinary Clinic, 2514 Grand Ave., (970) 945-5401
Birch Tree Animal Hospital, 1602 Grand Ave., (970) 945-0125
All Cats and Dogs Hospital, 1605 Grand Ave., (970) 945-6762

SPORTING GOODS, GUNS, AND GUNSMITHS

Army and Factory Surplus, 2828 Glen Ave., (970) 945-7796
Roaring Fork Anglers, 2114 Grand Ave., (970) 945-0181
Roaring Fork Outfitters, 2022 Grand Ave., (970) 945-5800
Summit Canyon Mountaineering, 307 8th Street, (970) 945-6994

TAXIDERMISTS

Slims Taxidermy, 7916 Hwy 82, (970) 945-2270

MEAT PROCESSORS

Gross Locker Plant, 140 South 8th Street, Silt, Colorado (970) 876-2334
Rifle Packing Plant, 2140 Whiteriver Ave., Rifle, Colorado (970) 625-1745

AUTO RENTAL AND REPAIR

Glenwood Springs NAPA Auto Parts, 3024 glen Ave., (970) 945-6561
Alpine Tire, 2750 South Glen Ave., (970) 945-6662
Taylor's Auto and RV Center, 51101 Hwy 6 and 24, (970) 945-1500
Glenwood Springs Ford, 55 Storm King Road, (970) 945-2317
John Haines Chevrolet, 130 Center Drive, (970) 945-7444

AIR SERVICE

Eagle County Regional Airport (25 miles east of Glenwood Springs) (970) 524-8246
Glenwood Springs (small municipal airport) (970) 945-2385

MEDICAL

Valley View Hospital, 1906 Blake Ave., (970) 945-6535

FOR MORE INFORMATION

Glenwood Springs Chamber Resort Association, 1102 Grand Avenue, Glenwood Springs, CO 81601, (970) 945-6589.

Steamboat Springs
Population — 8,500 • Elevation — 6,695'

Located near the center of Region 1, Steamboat Springs is one of my favorite mountain towns. Providing hunter access into the Routt National Forest and the Mount Zirkel and Sarvis Creek Wilderness Areas, Steamboat is also well known for its ski resort and hot springs.

Originally a cattle and mining community, Steamboat now owes a large part of its existence to tourism. In addition to excellent hunting opportunities, fishing is also good on the Yampa River and on the surrounding lakes and reservoirs, including Stagecoach, Steamboat Lake, and Pearl Lake. The town has experienced a great deal of growth in the last decade. This has resulted in a community that can provide a broad array of lodging and dining, as well as any of the other necessary services required by hunters.

ACCOMMODATIONS

Alpiner Lodge, (970) 879-1430. 424 Lincoln Ave. 80487-5006
Best Western Inn, (970) 897-1730, 2304 Apres Ski Way 80487-9028
Bunkhouse Lodge, (970) 871-9121, 3155 S. Lincoln St. 80487-1768
Comfort Inn, (970) 879-6669, 1055 Walton Creek Rd. 80487-1767
Fairfield Inn, (970) 870-9000, 3200 S. Lincoln St. 80487-1780
Sheraton, (970) 879-2220, 2200 Village Inn Ct. 80487
Harbor Hotel, (970) 879-1522, 703 Lincoln Ave 80487-5026
Thunderhead Lodge, (970) 879-9000, 1965 Ski Time Square Dr. 80487-9000
Holiday Inn, (970) 879-2250, 3190 S. Lincoln St. 80487-1768
Hotel Bristol, (970) 879-3083, 917 Lincoln Ave. 80487-5002
Inn At Steamboat, (970) 879-2600, 3070 Columbine Dr. 80487-2347
Iron Horse Inn, (970) 879-6505, 333 S. Lincoln Ave. 80487-8907
Nite's Rest Motel, (970) 879-1212, 601 S. Lincoln Ave. 80487-8902
Nordic Lodge Motel, (970) 879-0531, 1036 S. Lincoln Ave. 80487-5013
Rabbit Ears Motel, (970) 879-1150, 201 Lincoln Ave. 80487
Ramada Vacation Suites Hilltop, (970) 879-2900 or (800) 634-6981,
    1000 High Point Dr. 80487-3126
Super 8 Motel, (970) 879-5230, 3195 Lincoln St. 80487-1768
Western Lodge & Condos, (970) 879-1050, 1122 S. Lincoln Ave. 80487-5013

*Steamboat offers many condominiums, houses, and bed and breakfasts too numerous to list here. For a full listing of all available lodging in Steamboat and the surrounding area, please contact the Steamboat Springs Chamber Resort Association at 970-879-0882.

CAMPGROUNDS AND RV PARKS

Ski Town Campground, (KOA Franchise) (970) 879-0273
State Park Camping Reservations, 800-678-CAMP
Forest Services Camping Reservations, 877-444-6777

RESTAURANTS

Alpine Bistro, 521 Lincoln Ave., (970) 879-7757
Blue Moose Pizza, Thunderhead Lodge, (970) 870-8666
The Butcher Shop, 1940 Ski Time Square, (970) 879-2484
Cat House Café, Ski Time Square, (970) 879-2441
Dos Amigos, Ski Time Square, (970) 879-4270
Double Z Bar and BBQ, 1124 Yampa Street, (970) 879-0849
The Grubstake, Gondola Square, (970) 879-4448
Heavenly Daze Brewery and Grill, 1860 Ski Time Square, (970) 879-8080
Johnny B. Good's Diner, 738 Lincoln Ave., (970) 870-8400
The Main Dish, 628 Lincoln Ave., (970) 879-5611
Riverbend Inn, 26795 RC US Hwy 40, (970) 879-1615
Wally's Pizzeria, Central Park Plaza, (970) 879-8600
   *Steamboat offers too many restaurants to fully list here. For a complete listing of all available dining in Steamboat and the surrounding area, please contact the Steamboat Springs Chamber Resort Association at 970-879-0882.

VETERINARIANS

Steamboat Veterinary Hospital, 1878 Lincoln Ave., (970) 879-1041
Mt. Werner Veterinary Hospital, 35825 E US Hwy 40, (970) 879-3486
Steamboat Veterinary Hospital PC, 1878 Lincoln Ave., (970) 879-1041

SPORTING GOODS, GUNS, AND GUNSMITHS

Christy Sports, 1835 Central Park Plaza, (970) 879-1250
Good Times Sports, 730 Lincoln Ave., (970) 879-7818
Shop and Hop Food Stores-Phillips 66, 35775 E US Hwy 40, (970) 879-2489
SportStalker, 36900 Steamboat Village Circle, (970) 879-0371
Straightline Outdoor Sports, 744 Lincoln Ave., (970) 879-7568
Wal-Mart, 1805 Central park Drive, (970) 879-8115

TAXIDERMISTS

All Seasons Taxidermy, 30020 W. Hwy 40, (970) 871-9591
B&L Quality Taxidermy, 30470 W. Hwy 40, (970) 879-1316

MEAT PROCESSORS

OK's Meat Market, 1030 Yampa, (970) 879-1513

AUTO RENTAL AND REPAIR

Avis Rent A Car, 41205 Elk River Rd., (970) 879-3786
Check Point Rent a Car (970) 870-1996
Economy Car Rental (970) 879-1179
Enterprise Rent-A-Car, 40510 Downhill Dr., (970) 871-1900
Steamboat Motors, 2310 Lincoln Ave., (970)-879-8880
Black Diamond Automotive, 2780 Acre Lane, (970) 879-5300

Elk Mountain Automotive, Hwy 40, (970) 870-1871
Baker Auto, Sundance Plaza, (970) 879-4200
Repair Dynamics, Inc., 29585 W US hwy 40, Unit #4, (970) 879-3232
Grama's Towing Unlimited, (970) 879-1178
Four Star Repair Inc., 29579 W US Hwy 40, (970) 879-7557
Automotive Service Center, 500 S. Lincoln, (970) 879-3602

AIR SERVICE

Yampa Valley Regional Airport, (970) 276-3669

MEDICAL

Routt Memorial Hospital and Extended Care Center, 80 park Ave., (970) 879-1322

FOR MORE INFORMATION

Steamboat Springs Chamber Resort Association, P.O. Box 774408, 1255 South Lincoln Avenue, Steamboat Springs, CO 80477, (970) 879-0882

Rangely
Population — 2,596 • Elevation — 5,261'

Located in the western part of Region 1 along the White River, the town of Rangely provides services in a very remote part of Colorado. It is almost completely surrounded by BLM lands and is home to a major oil field, which produces from the Coal Oil Basin on the north side of town.

Rangely is situated at the southern boundary of GMU 10, which is home to a large deer herd of over 7,000 animals. If you lucked out and drew one of the few bull elk tags for GMU 10, Rangely will be a good base of operations for your hunt.

ACCOMMODATIONS

4 Queens Motel, 206 E. Main, (970) 675-5035
Budget Host Inn, 117 S. Grand Ave., (970) 675-8461

CAMPGROUNDS AND RV PARKS

State Park Camping Reservations 800-678-CAMP
Forest Services Camping Reservations 877-444-6777

RESTAURANTS

Ace High Steakhouse, 616 E. Main, (970) 675-8574
Cowboy Corral, 202 W. Main, (970) 675-8986
Magalino's Restaurant, 124 W. Main, (970) 675-2321

SPORTING GOODS, GUNS, AND GUNSMITHS

Continental Supply, 15777 Hwy 64, (970) 675-2187

AUTO REPAIR

Poor Boy Garage Tire and Auto, 221½ E. Main, (970) 675-2500
Professional Touch, 112 E. Main, (970) 675-2025
Widmer Automotive, 739 E. Main, (970) 675-8664

MEDICAL

Rangely District Hospital, 511 S. White Ave., (970) 675-5011

FOR MORE INFORMATION

Rangely Chamber of Commerce, 209 E. Main, Rangely, CO 81648, (970) 675-5290

Rifle
Population — 6,784 · Elevation — 5,345'

Rifle, which is located in Garfield County, is another Colorado community that caters to big game hunters. With its close proximity to the White River National Forest, the Grand Mesa National Forest, and BLM lands, there are literally thousands of acres of public land at Rifles door step. Garfield County is also a well-known producer of trophy mule deer, and there are also large numbers of elk in the area. This area also holds good opportunities for hunters interested in pursuing mountain lion and black bear.

Notable features in the Rifle area include the Roan Plateau, which is located to the northwest of town. This area offers exceptional deer and elk hunting. Rifle Gap Reservoir and the associated State Recreation Area are located a few miles north of town. This is a popular fishing and camping destination that many people take advantage of during the various hunting seasons. Big game hunters should also keep Garfield Creek State Wildlife Area in mind when they are in the area. This 13,000-acre property is located in GMU 42 to the east of town and offers good opportunities for deer and elk.

ACCOMMODATIONS

Red River Inn, (970) 625-3050, 718 Taughenbaugh Blvd.
Rusty Cannon Motel, (970) 625-4004, 701 Taughenbaugh Blvd.
Winchester Motel, (970) 625-1777, 520 Railroad Ave.

RESTAURANTS

Rio Grande Mexican Restaurant, (970) 625-0358, 160 E 26th St.
Sammy's On Park Avenue, (970) 625-8008, 412 Park Ave.
Audrey's Cafe, (970) 625-1311, 17 W 4th St.
Base Camp Cafe, (970) 625-0374, 129 E 3rd St.

SPORTING GOODS

Timberline Sporting Goods, (970) 625-4868, 101 East 3rd Street

TAXIDERMISTS

Sportsman's Barn Taxidermy, (970) 625-1949, 1601 Railroad Ave # B
White River Taxidermy, (970) 625-0441, 1301 Arabian Ave.

VETERINARIANS

Antlers Veterinary Hospital, (970) 625-2874, 30239 Highway 6
Carter, Zane R DVM, (970) 625-2874, 30239 Highway 6
Green, John A DVM, (970) 625-2874, 1595 Railroad Ave.
Hamilton, Don DVM, (970) 625-2729, 11749 County Road 320
Town & Country Veterinary Hospital, (970) 625-2971, 1595 Railroad Ave

Meat processors

Rifle Packing Plant, (970) 625-1745, 2140 Whiteriver Ave.

Auto repair

T & G Auto & Diesel Repair, (970) 625-4783, 28485 Highway 6, # 5
Master Automotive, (970) 625-3820, 2100 Access Rd.

Hospital

Grand River Hospital District, (970) 625-1510, 701 E 5th St.

Fort Collins
Population — 118,652 · Elevation — 5,003'

Fort Collins is probably best known as the home of Colorado State University. This bustling college town is often a jumping off point for big game hunters headed into the northern reaches of the state. Fort Collins can offer any service you require for your hunting pursuits. If you need any additional hunting equipment or supplies before you head into the backcountry, stop by Sportsman's Warehouse located just off Interstate 25 a few miles south of Fort Collins in the town of Loveland.

From Fort Collins, Colorado State Highway 14 follows the Cache La Poudre River to the west. This route provides access to large expanses of the Roosevelt National Forest, several wilderness areas, and the Colorado State Forest. In addition to the good big game hunting in this area, the river is well known for quality fishing. On a side note, the agricultural areas surrounding Fort Collins provide some of the best goose hunting in the state.

ACCOMMODATIONS
Comfort Inn, 1638 East Mulberry, (970) 484-2444, 25 rooms
Mulberry Inn, 4333 East Mulberry, (970)493-9000, 121 rooms, Dogs allowed for a fee
Inn at Fort Collins, 2612 South College Avenue, (970) 226-2600, 60 rooms, Dogs allowed
Holiday Inn, 425 West Prospect Road, (970) 482-2626, 253 rooms, Dogs allowed
Trout Lodge, 1078 Ramona Drive, Red Feather Lakes, (970) 881-2964

BED AND BREAKFAST
Gypsy Terrace B and B, 4167 Poudre Canyon Highway, Bellvue, (970) 224-9389, Located in the beautiful Poudre Canyon
Scorched Tree B and B, 31601 Poudre Canyon Highway, Rustic, (970) 881-2817, Innkeeper: Brenda Way, Also in the Poudre Canyon

CAMPING
Beaver Meadows Resort Ranch, Red Feathers Lakes, (970) 881-2450
Columbine Lodge, 9940 Poudre Canyon Highway, Bellvue, (970) 484-3013

RESTAURANTS
The Breakfast Club, 121 West Monroe Drive, (970) 223-7193, Open 6AM for breakfast
Charco Broiler, 1716 East Mulberry, (970) 482-1472, Opens Monday–Saturday 6AM, Sunday 11AM, Cocktails
Silver Grill Cafe, 218 Walnut, (970) 484-4656, Open 6AM–2PM
Hickory House South, 6013 South College Avenue, (970) 226-5070, Open Monday – Saturday 6:30AM–10PM, Sunday 7:30AM, Cocktails
Perkins Restaurant, 310 South College Avenue, (970) 484-5981, Open 24 hours
Canino's Italian Restaurant, 613 South College Avenue, (970) 493-7205

Sporting Goods

Alkire's Sporting Goods, 1211 9th Street, Greeley, (970) 352-9501
Betty's Bait and Tackle, 429 West Wilcox Lane, (970) 484-7459
Discount Fishing Tackle, Inc., 1793 S. College Ave, (970) 472-1911
Don's Pro Shop, 3121 Old Highway 287, LaPorte, (970) 493-0534
Dusty Bait and Tackle, 2020 North College Avenue, (970) 495-9880
First Stop Sporting Goods, 1006 North College Avenue, (970) 493-3525
Fort Collins Outdoor World, 1611 South College Avenue, (970) 221-5166
Gart Sports, 215 East Foothills Parkway, (970) 226-4913
Gart Sport Superstore, 425 South College Avenue, (970) 482-5307
Jax Surplus, 1200 North College Avenue, (970) 221-0544
Outback Sports, 328 South Link Lane, (970) 484-6582
Vern's Place, 4120 West CR 54G, LaPorte, (970) 482-5511
Sportsman's Warehouse, (970) 461-5000, 1675 Rocky Mtn. Ave.

Hospitals
Poudre Valley Hospital, 1024 Lemay Avenue, (970) 495-7000

Airports
Denver International Airport, (970) 342-2000, (970) 342-0400, United: 800-241-6522, Delta: 800-221-1212, American: 800-433-7300, TWA: 800-221-2000
Ft. Collins/Loveland Airport, 4824 Earhart Road, Loveland, (970) 667-2574, United Express: 800-241-6522
Fort Collins Downtown Airport, 2200 Airway Avenue, (970) 484-4186, Private planes

Auto Rental
Advantage Rent-A-Car, 2539 South College Avenue, (970) 224-2211
Avis Rent-A-Car, 344 East Foothills Parkway, (970) 229-9115, 800-831-2847
Dollar Rent-A-Car, 7704 South College Avenue, (970) 226-6855
Enterprise Rent-A-Car, 2100 South College Avenue, (970) 224-2592, 800-325-8007
Price King Rent-A-Car, 203 Mulberry, (970) 490-2000

Auto Service
King's Auto Service, 203 West Mulberry, (970) 490-2000
Poudre Valley Automotive, 3020 East Mulberry, (970) 221-2054, Towing, repairs
Import Car Service and Repair, 1943 East Lincoln Avenue, (970) 221-4700

Locksmith
Pop-A-Lock, (970) 484-0025
Dave's Locksmithing, 208 South Mason, (970) 221-5397, (970) 482-6050

For More Information
Chamber of Commerce
225 South Meldrum
Fort Collins, CO 80522
(970) 482-3746

Region 1 Outfitters

The following list includes outfitters registered with the Colorado Outfitters Association who provide big game hunting services in one or more of the Game Management Units within Region 1. Information concerning the outfitters company name, license number, address, phone, species, GMU numbers, type of land hunted (national forest, regional area, private vs. public), and facilities are provided below.

LARRY AMOS
Winterhawk Outfitters #187
P.O. Box 425, Silt, CO 81652
(970) 876-2623
Deer, elk, bear, lion, 25, 26
Lion 31, 22, 23, 33, 34, 35, 42, 25, 26
White River, BLM, Glenwood Springs
Tent camps

BOB ANDERSON
Quarter Circle A Outfitters # 1296
P.O. Box 402, Buena Vista, CO 81211
(719) 395-2914
Deer, elk, antelope, 28, 57, 58
BLM-Salida/Canon City
Private property
Tent camps/cabins

LARRY ARNOLD
Beaver Creek Outfitters #1506
Rt. 1, Box 24, Wiseman AR 72587
(870) 322- 7191
Deer, elk, 12
Routt, tent camps

RANDALL BAIRD
Yampa River Outfitters #1198
634 Barbara Dr., Craig, CO 81625
(970) 824-2455
Deer, elk, antelope, 301, 13
All private property

JIM BEALL
J-B Guiding and Outfitting # 1625
P.O. Box 1, Craig, CO 81626
(970) 824-7369
Deer, elk, bear, antelope, 301,
211, 11, 15, 3. Routt, BLM-Craig.
Private property, trespass fee,
Tent camps, cabins, trailers

CADE BENSON
Colo. High Guide Service #598
P.O. Box 1430, Elizabeth, CO 80107,
(303) 646-9890
Deer, elk, 24, 25
White River, tent camps, cabins

DEAN BILLINGTON
Bull Basin Guides Outfitters #1037
6097 W. 86th Ave., Arvada,CO 80003
(303) 423-1539
Deer, elk, bear, antelope, sheep, 26, 28,
35. Arapahoe, BLM-Glenwood &
Kremmling, private property,
Tent camps, cabins

LARRY BISHOP
Rocky Mtn Ranches #1543
1563 Quivira Drive, Thornton, CO 80229
(303) 286-8656
Deer, elk, antelope. 3, 301, 13, 15
Private property, trespass fee
Tent camps, cabins, trailers

SHAWN BOLTON
Sundown Guide and Outfitters #1908
P.O. Box 251, Meeker, CO 81641
(970) 878-4079
Deer, elk, bear, lion, 23, 24, 12, 11, 211
Private property, cabins

MARION BRICKER
K and K Outfitters #1421
P.O. Box 1002, Granby, CO 80446
(970) 887-2301
Deer, elk, bear, moose, 18
Arapaho, tent camps

JIM BRINK
AJ Brink Outfitters #370
Glendevey Route Colo Jelm, WY 82063
(970) 435-5707. Deer, elk, bear, antelope,
goat, sheep, lion, moose, 6, 7, 8, 25, 43,
S58, Roosevelt, White River, Routt, tent
camps, cabins

THOMAS BULLOCK
Saddle Tramp Outfitters #491
4668 311 Road, New Castle, CO 81647
(970) 876-2960
Deer, elk, bear, sheep, 33, 42,43
White River, tent camps
Springs Resource Area, private property
Motel

STEVE CHIN
Colorado Mountain Adventures #1926
4255 W 92nd Place, Westminster, CO
80031. (303) 430-1567
Deer, elk, bear, 4, 41, 171
Grand Mesa, private property
Tent camps, cabins

BRYAN CLARK -
High Voltage Outfitters #1886
6750 County Rd. 301
Parachute, CO 81635
(970) 285-7470
Deer, elk, antelope, lion, 31, 32, 33, 421,
42; BLM-Glenwood

M. BRUCE COTTRELL, DVM
All Seasons Ranch #884
6135 Templeton Gap Rd.
Colorado Springs, CO 80918
(719) 596-2047
Deer, elk, 12
Routt, tent camps

ROBERT COULTER
Snake River Outfitters #1931
1404 Sandray Dr, Opelika AL 36801
(334) 749-8132
Deer, elk, antelope
Hat Hill, Nine Mile, Deer Creek
Private property

TOM COX
Meadows Vega #69
P.O. Box 441, Collbran, CO 81624
(970) 487-3750
Deer, elk, 421, 31, 21, 22
Private property, cabins, trailers

WES DUBOIS
Purple Sage Outfitters #1629
73179 Hwy 64, Meeker, CO 81641
(970) 878-4486 or (970) 878-5273
Deer, elk, 22, 23, 211
BLM-Meeker, private property
Tent camps

MARK DAVIES
Chuck Davies Guide Service #56
P.O. Box 8, Loma, CO 81524
(970) 858-0370 or (970) 858-7079
Deer, elk, bear, antelope, lion. 10, 11, 21,
30, 31, 40, 41, 42, 421, 521, 60, 61, 62
Grand Mesa, White River, Gunnison
BLM-Grand Junction, Meeker, Montrose
Private property
Tent camps, trailers, cabins

ELMER DUARTE
Duarte Guide Service #595
2656 G Road, Grand Junction, CO 81506
(970) 243-5362
Deer, elk, bear, antelope
Private property, trespass fee
Cabins, resort

EAGLES NEST OUTFITTERS #1870
1670 Broadway, Ste. 3300
Denver, CO 8020
(303) 831-4673
Deer, elk; White River, tent camps

WILLIAM ELDER
Hunting and Fishing World #1117
P.O. Box 130, Bull Shoals, AR 72619
(870) 445- 4148
Deer, elk, 17
BLM-Kremmling, private property,
Bunk houses

FRED ELLIS
Rawhide Adventures #623
P.O. Box 1161, Meeker, CO 81641
800-838-7256
Deer, elk, 11, 22
White River, BLM
Tent camps, house

WILLARD FORMAN
Summit Trail Adventures #794
6150 Hwy 73, Evergreen, CO 80439
(303) 670-9758
Deer, elk, 371, 37, 28, 43
Arapaho, White River
Private property, tent camps

TOM FRITZLAN
Family Guide and Outfitters #950
0391 CR 332, Rifle, CO 81650
(970) 625-2743
Deer, elk, bear, lion, 23, 24, 33, 42
White River, tent camps, trailers

MARY FUNKHOUSER
The Craig Wild Bunch #1121
P.O. Box 64, Craig, CO 81626
(970) 824-0340
Deer, elk ; Routt, private property, tres-
pass fee ; Tent camps, trailers

KYLE REVELLE , SKEETER GINGERY
S and K Outfitting and Guide Service #63
7434 S. Monroe Ct., Littleton, CO 80122
(303) 796-8669 or (970) 824-4932
Deer, elk, antelope, lion, 3, 4, 12, 13, 301,
441, 211, 11
Private property, trespass fee
Tent camps, cabins

KEITH GODDARD, VICKY SPAULDING
Magnum Outfitters #1760
2417 24th Place, Rifle, CO 81650
(970) 625-4436
Deer, elk, lion, 32,
BLM, Glenwood Springs
Tent camps

ART GURULE
Old Time Outfitting Serv. #15
4660 CR 311, New Castle, CO 81647
(970) 876-5466
Deer, elk, bear, 44, 45, 47, 444
White River, tent camps

GUS, REGAS AND JOHN HALANDRAS
H&H Outfitting #1208
P.O. Box 677, Meeker, CO 81641
(970) 878-3394 or (970) 878-5126
Deer, elk, antelope, 22, 23
White River, BLM-Rio Blanco
Private property, trespass fee
Cabins, bed & breakfast

TIM HAMILTON
Badger Creek Guide and Outfitter
#1319790 Hwy 317, Hamilton, CO 81638
(970) 824-7436
Deer, elk, antelope, 12, 13, 131, 211, 4, 441
BLM-Little Snake, private property
Tent camps, bed and breakfast, motel

JACK HARRISON
White River Resort #377
21679 E. Otero Pl., Aurora, CO 80016
(303) 690-6627
Deer, elk, 24, 25, 34
White River; tent camps, cabins, resort

MARIE HASKETT
JML Outfitters #288
300 CR 75, Meeker, CO 81641
(970) 878-4749
Deer, elk, bear, 24
White River; tent camps, cabins

RAY HEID
Del's Triangle 3 Ranch #22
P.O. Box 333, Clark, CO 80428
(970) 879-3495
Deer, elk, 5, 14, 161, 214,
Routt; tent camps, cabins

RON HILKEY
Adams Lodge #1159
2400 RBC Rd 12, Meeker, CO 81641
(970) 878-4312
Deer, elk, 24
White River; private property
Tent, camps, cabins

MILES HOGAN
Eagle Spirit Outfitters #1592
P.O. Box 775792
Steamboat Springs, CO 80477
(970) 870-8241
Deer, elk, bear, 131, 15
Private property; lodge

MARK LUMPKINS
High Lonesome Outfitters #1656
110 quartz, Bailey, CO 80421
(303) 838-9756; Deer, elk, 33
White River; tent camps

SCOTT LIMMER
Comanche Wilderness Outfitters #1165
P.O. Box 1965, Fort Collins, CO 80522
(970) 223-5330
Deer, elk, bear, antelope, sheep, moose,
6-9, 19, 20, 87, 91, 92, 93, 95, 98, 101, 102,
136, 143, 14, S1, S19, S37, S48, S57, S58
Roosevelt, Arapahoe, private property
Tent camps, cabins, ranch house

PAT LUARK
Luark Ranch and Outfitters #761
Box 25, 2834 Luark Road
Burns, CO 80426
(970) 653-4324
Deer, elk, bear, lion, 26
Private property; tent camps, cabins,
trailers, resort

DEAN MANTLE
Outlaw Adventures #1681
25600 CR 5, Rifle, CO 81650
(970) 878-4311
Deer, elk, bear, antelope, 10, 22,
BLM, Craig, private property
Tent camps, trailers

JEANNE AND RANDY HORNE
Bar-H Outfitters #1913
3631 Gypsum Creek Road,
Gypsum, CO, 81637
(970) 524-7280
Deer, elk, 12, 24; White River, Routt,
BLM-Meeker; Tent camps, bed and
breakfast

BILL HUELSENBECK, WAYNE THOMAS
WW Adventures #1810, 426 Dock Road,
West Creek, NJ 08008, (888) 494-2722 or
(609) 294-0329, deer, elk, 131
BLM-Craig, tents

DANNY JEFFCOAT
Jeffcoat Ranch & Outfitters #953
P.O. Box 97, Hamilton, CO 81638
(970) 824-3757
Deer, elk, 12
Private property

KEN JETT
Ripple Creek Lodge #330
39020 CR 8, Meeker, CO 81641
(970) 878-4725 or (303) 989-4950
Deer, elk, bear, antelope, 23, 24
White River, cabins, resort

ROD AND GAIL JOHANSEN
Nakota Outfitters #1690
627 Barclay, Craig, CO 81625
970) 824-2263 or (970) 326-8060
Deer, elk, bear, antelope, lion, 3, 301, 12,
13, 4; Routt, BLM-Little Snake, private
property, trespass fee, tent camps,
trailers, cabins

DAVID JOHNSON HUNTING #1637
4851 MCR 57, Meeker, CO 81641
(970) 272-3279
Deer, elk, 11
BLM-White River, private property
Trespass fee, bunkhouse

DR. ALLAN JONES
Winslett Ranch (Lic # Not Listed)
1616 RBC Rd 42, Meeker, CO 81641
(970) 272-3279
Deer, elk
White River; private property, cabins

NOWELL MAY
Black Mountain Ranch #1343
P.O. Box 219, McCoy, CO 80463
800-967-2401
Deer, elk, bear, 15
Routt, BLM, Glenwood Springs
Private property; cabins, resort

JARREL MASSEY
NW Colorado Ranching for Wildlife #1186
P.O. Box 212, Meeker, CO 81641
(970) 878-5436
Deer, elk, Ranching for Wildlife

DAVIS MCDONALD
Carr Creek Ranch #1872
P.O. Box 2991, Grand Junction, CO 81501
(970) 283-5573 or (970) 245-1234
Deer, elk, bear, 31
Private property; cabins

MIDDLE CREEK RANCH OUTFITTERS #1618
27460 RCR 31, Oak Creek, CO 80467
(970) 871-9036
Deer, elk, 131; Private property; resort

TOM MIKESELL
M&M Outfitters #296
P.O. Box 1020, Craig, CO 81626
(970) 824-5812
Deer, elk, lion, 12, 13, 2, 201
BLM-Little Snake, private property
Trailers

DON MYERS
Myers Hunting Services #1229
6148 State Hwy 317, Hamilton, CO
81638-9602
(970) 824-9317
Deer, elk, lion, 12, 13, 131, Little Snake,
private property, cabins, trailers, ranch
house

KENNETH OSBORN
Colorado Big Game Outfitters #1686
6736 CR 41, Hamilton, CO 81638
(970) 824-6434
Deer, elk, antelope, 12, 211
Private property, cabins, trailers

LARRY OSBORN
Triple-O-Outfitters #994
P.O. Box 99, Hamilton, CO 81638
(970) 824-6758
Deer, elk, bear, antelope, 12
White River; tent camps, cabins, resort

RUSS PAPKE
Coulter Lake Guest Ranch #73
P.O. Box 906, Rifle, CO 81650
(970) 625-1473
Deer, elk, 33; White River, cabins, resort

DAVE PARRI
Outfitting & Guide Service #1243
P.O. Box 254
Hot Sulphur Springs, CO 80451
(970) 725-3531
Deer, elk, bear, 18
Routt, Arapahoe; tent camps

HARLEY PETERS
Peters Hunting Service #175
P.O. Box 268, Rangely, CO 81648-0268
(970) 675-2574
Deer, elk, bear, 21, 30
BLM-Grand Junction, Meeker
Private property; tent camps, trailers

SETH PETERS
Bearcat Outfitters #38
P.O. Box 110, Craig, CO 81626
(970) 824-7958, deer, elk, 12
White River, tent camps, cabins

PHIL PHILLIPS
Phil's Colorado Adventures #977
P.O. Box 786, Montrose, CO 81402
(970) 249-8068
Deer, elk, antelope, 11, 64,
Uncompahgre; private property, cabins

PINNACLE PEAK ADVENTURES #1841
CR 18 N, Craig, CO 81625
(970) 824-9269
Deer, elk, 4, private property
Modular lodging

GARTH PETERSON
Old Glendevey Ranch #287
3219 CR 190, Glendevey CO Rt.,
Jelm, WY 82063
(970) 435-5701
Elk, antelope, 6, 7, 8
Roosevelt, BLM-Kremmling
Private property; tent camps, resort

JOHN PICKERING
Elk Mountain Guides & Outfitters #670
44157 Hwy 6, Glenwood
Springs, CO 81601
(970) 984-2707
Deer, elk, 24, 25
White River, Flat Tops; tents

SAM POTTER
Big Mountain Outfitters #942
P.O. Box 148, Rifle, CO 81650
(970) 625-2192
Deer, elk, bear, 23, 32, 33
White River, private property, trespass
fee, tent camps, cabins, resort

LOUIS RABIN
5-Springs Ranch Guide
and Outfitters #1513
P.O. Box 1582
Steamboat Springs, CO 80477
(970) 879-0868
Deer, elk, bear, antelope, 15, 131, 231, 3,
301, 214, private property, trailers, ranch
house

MICHAEL REID
Pack Country Outfitters #329
P.O. Box 3511, Vail, CO 81658
(970) 476-2793
Deer, elk, bear, 231
Routt, private property
Tent camps, cabins

TIM RESCH
Aspen Lodge @ Estes Park #1409
6120 Hwy 7 LPR, Estes Park, CO 80517
(970) 586-8133, ext. 412
Deer, elk, 20; Roosevelt, Arapaho, private
property, trespass fee, cabins, resort

DENNIS RODEBAUGH
D&S Guide&Outfitter
#897—24767 CR 8, Meeker, CO 81641
(970) 878-5108
Deer, elk, 23, 24, 33
White River BLM-Rio Blanco, cabins,
trailers

RALPH ROYSTER
R and R Ranch #1372
P.O. Box 250, Maybell, CO 81640
(970) 326-3068
Deer, elk, antelope, lion, 11, 211
BLM-Little Snake River, private property
Cabins, resort, lodge

RICHARD SAMUELSON
Samuelson Outfitters
#729, P.O. Box 868, Fraser, CO 80442
(970) 726-8221
Deer, elk, moose, 18, 28; Arapaho
Medicine Bow, Routt, tent camps

JOHN SANDELIN
Big Creek Reserve #1146
45965 RCR 129
Steamboat Springs, CO 80487
(970) 879-0173
Deer, elk, bear, lion, 4, 5, 14, 15
Routt; cabins

ARNIE SCHLOTTMAN
Red Feather Guides & Outfitters #666,
P.O. Box 935, Gypsum, CO
(970) 524-5054
Deer, elk, 6, 171, 161, 16
Routt, private property
Tent camps, cabins

DEREK SIGNORELLI
Flying diamond Outfitters #1658
30110 Hwy 131, Oak Creek, CO 80467
(970) 870-3074
Elk, lion, 15, 131,
Private property, ranch houses, resort

DENNIS STAMP
High Meadows Ranch #1247
P.O. Box 771216
Steamboat Springs, CO 80477
(970) 736-8416, elk, 15, 231
Routt, tent camps, cabins, resort

RUDY STEELE
Guides and Outfitters #392
P.O. Box 2503
Glenwood Springs, CO 81602
(970) 945-8100
Deer, elk, antelope, 32, 33
BLM-Glenwood Springs
Private property
Tent Camps, cabins, trailers

BOYD TALLENT
Yampa valley Outfitters #1385
P.O. Box 910, Craig, CO 81626
(970) 824-2102
1624 So. Courtland Dr., or
Thompson, GA 30824
(706) 595-1717
Deer, elk, lion, 3, 4, 12, 441
Routt, BLM-Little Snake
Private property, cabins, trailers

DALE THOMPSON
Pinon Ridge RFW #1944
P.O. Box 1082, Craig, CO 81626
(970) 824-4117
Deer, elk, antelope, 11, 13, 211, BLM-
Little Snake, private property, resort

HOWARD TIEDEN
Arrowhead Outfitters #1072
32325 Goldenrod St. NW
Cambridge, MN 55008
612) 689-0672
Deer, elk, 441, 24, 22
Private property, cabins, houses

TOM TIETZ
Natural Adventures #532
3517 Green Mountain Circle
Parker, CO 80138
(303) 805-8804
Whitetail, mule deer, elk, antelope, goat,
sheep, 2, 39, 102, 103, 105, 107, 109, 111,
112, 113, 114, 201, 391, Arapaho, BLM-
Craig; private property, motel accommodations

CRAIG TOMKE
4 + 2 Ranch #868
Box 896, Hayden, CO 81639
(970) 276-4283
Deer, elk, antelope, lion, 3, 13, 301, 441,
Routt, BLM-Little Snake, private property, drop camps, trespass fee, cabins,
resort

TOM TUCKER
Buford Guide Service #890
24284 CR 8, Meeker, CO 81641
(970) 878-4596
Deer, elk, 23, 24
White River, private property, cabins

GLEN YOUNGER
Younger Brothers #834
302 S. 7th St., Grand Junction, CO 81501
(970) 242-5759
Deer, elk, 15, cabins

BILL AND FRED WALLACE
Wallace Guides and Outfitters #394—
Box 380, Collbran, CO 81624
(970) 487-3235. Deer, elk, bear, ante-
lope, lion, 41, 40, 30, 31, 32, 33, 21, 22,
60, 61, 421, 42, 62
White River, Grand Mesa
BLM-Grand Junction, Glenwood
Springs; private property, tent camps,
cabins, resort

JIM WALMA
Buffalo Horn Ranch #1616
13825 CR 7, Meeker, CO 81641
(970) 878-5450
Deer, elk, lion, 11, 22, 211
BLM-White River, private property
Cabins, resort, guest ranch, private
property, tent camps, cabins, resort

PATSY WILHELM
Sunset Ranch #76
Box 876, Steamboat Springs, CO 80477
(970) 879-0954
Deer, elk, 14, Routt, tent camps

CHUCK WISECUP
Mill Creek Outfitters#1456
Box 458, Oak Creek, CO 80467
(970) 736-8150
Deer, elk, lion, 15, 131, 231, 25, 26, 36,
37, Routt, Medicine Bow, BLM-
Glenwood Springs, camps, cabins,
trailers

JIM YOST
Latigo Ranch #877
201 CR 1911, Box 237
Kremmling, CO 80459
(970) 724-9008, deer, elk, 27, Routt
Private property, cabins, resort

JOHN ZIEGMAN
Whistling Elk Outfitters #828
P.O. Box 2, (4164 JCR 27
Rand, CO 80473
(970) 723-8311
Deer, elk, antelope, moose, 17, 171, 6
Routt, BLM-Kremmling
Private property, cabins, resort

Region 2 Major Roads, Rivers & Hub Cities

© WILDERNESS ADVENTURES PRESS, INC.

REGION 2

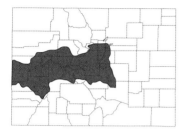

Located in the central and western portion of the state, Region 2 may be the most mountainous area in Colorado. Beginning at I-25 (the eastern boundary of the region) Pikes Peak dominates the landscape when looking to the west. Pikes Peak is one of many mountains in the region rising above 14,000 feet. The highest mountain in the state (Mount Elbert, at 14,433 feet) is also found in Region 2. The area has several important river systems, vast areas of montane and subalpine forest, and large tracts of public land.

There are several areas in Region 2 that offer exceptional opportunities to hunt bighorn sheep and mountain goat. In fact, eleven of the thirteen mountain goat units in the state are found in Region 2. Notable goat areas include Mount Evans and the Collegiate Peaks in the Sawatch Range. Furthermore, nearly one-third of all the bighorn sheep units are concentrated in Region 2. Desert bighorns are also found along the Uncompahgre Plateau area near the southwest part of the region. Drawing a tag for one of these rare animals will be comparable to winning the lottery, but several lucky hunters do it each year.

Elk and mule deer are very abundant across the entire region. Antelope are not nearly as plentiful as in other parts of the state, but there are a few herds scattered across Region 2 that should not be overlooked. Also, good opportunities for black bear and mountain lion exist locally. In terms of spectacular scenery and an abundance of big game hunting opportunities, Region 2 has it all.

The Flatirons and Pikes Peak above Boulder.

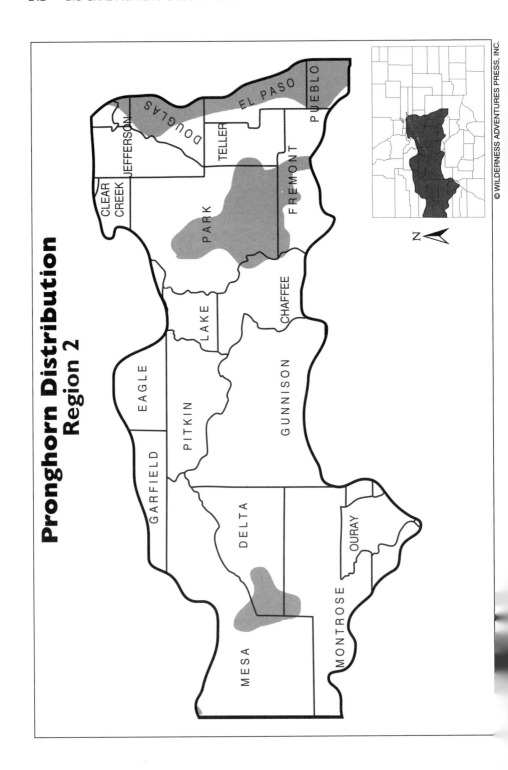

Pronghorn Distribution
Region 2

© WILDERNESS ADVENTURES PRESS, INC.

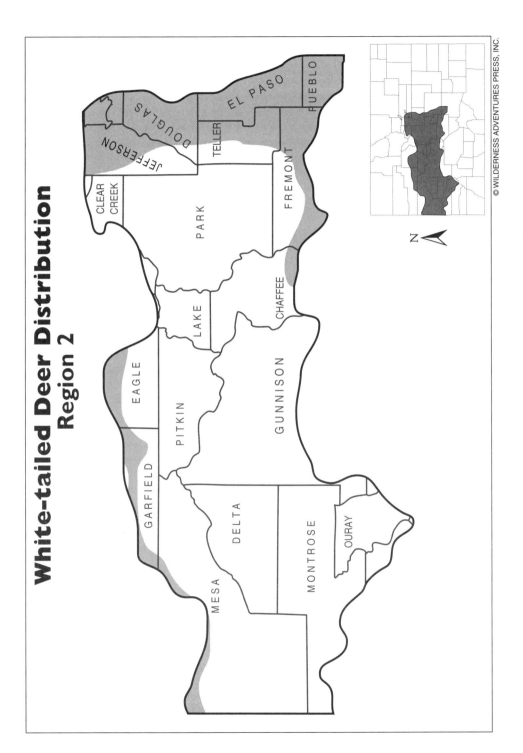

White-tailed Deer Distribution
Region 2

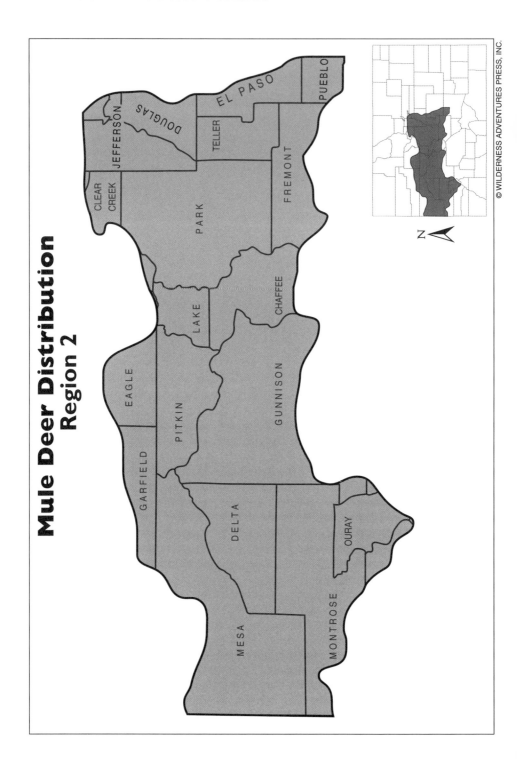

Mule Deer Distribution
Region 2

© WILDERNESS ADVENTURES PRESS, INC.

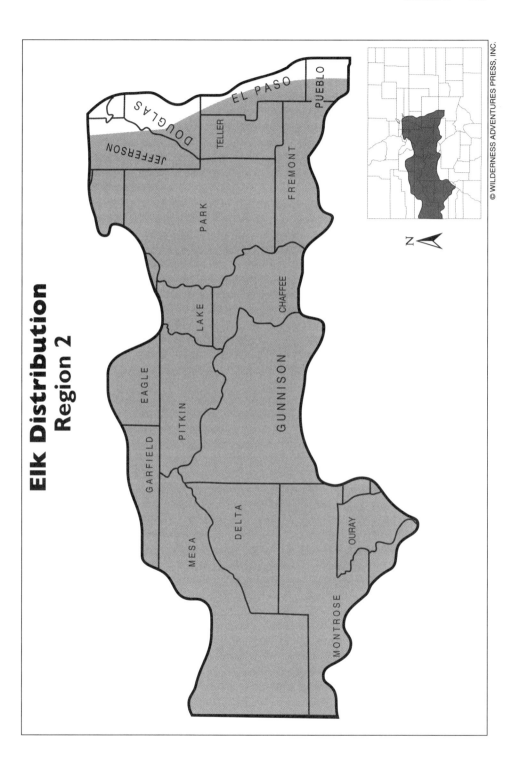

Elk Distribution
Region 2

© WILDERNESS ADVENTURES PRESS, INC.

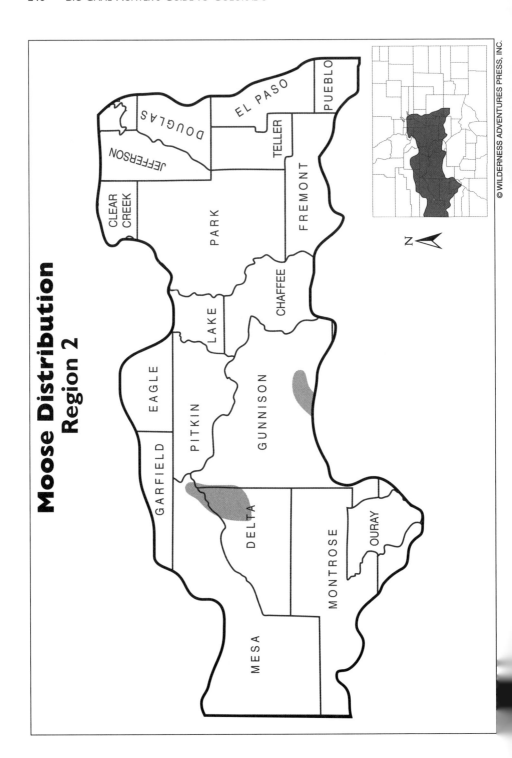

Moose Distribution Region 2

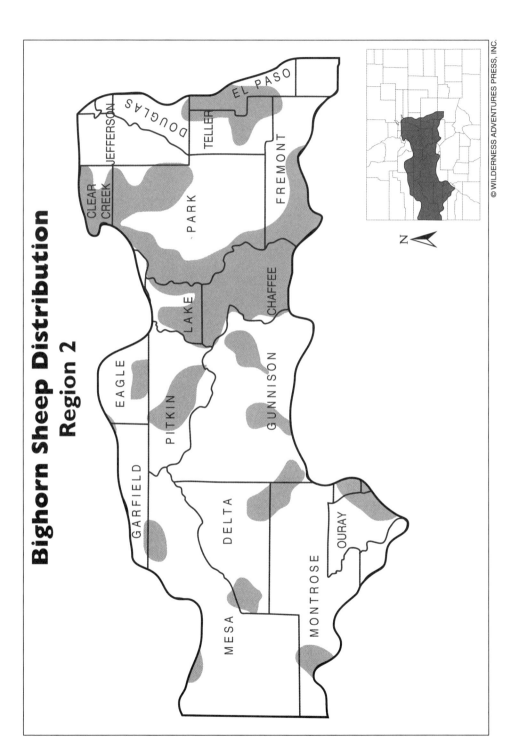

Bighorn Sheep Distribution
Region 2

© WILDERNESS ADVENTURES PRESS, INC.

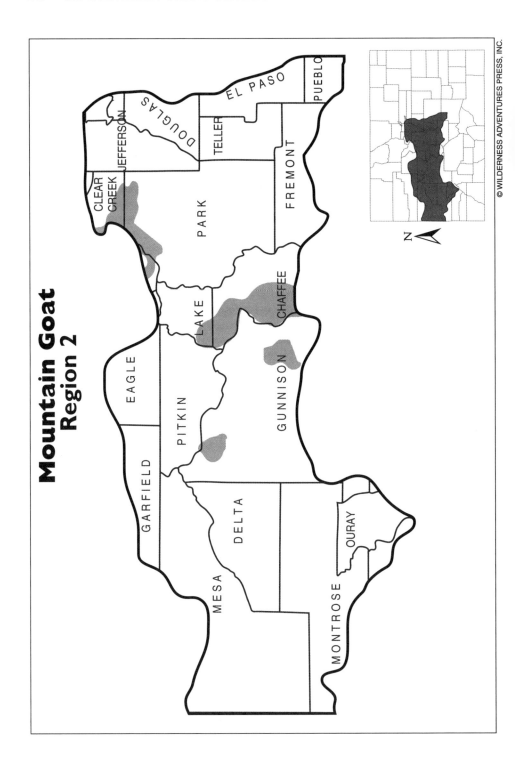

Mountain Goat
Region 2

© WILDERNESS ADVENTURES PRESS, INC.

Black Bear Distribution
Region 2

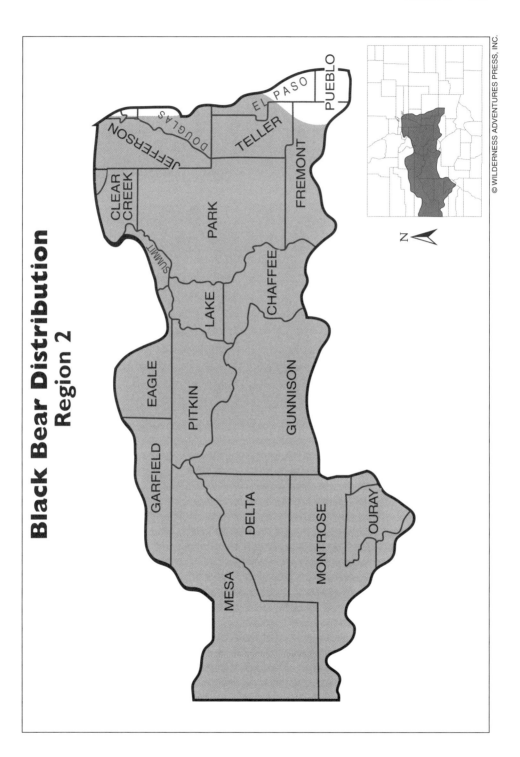

© WILDERNESS ADVENTURES PRESS, INC.

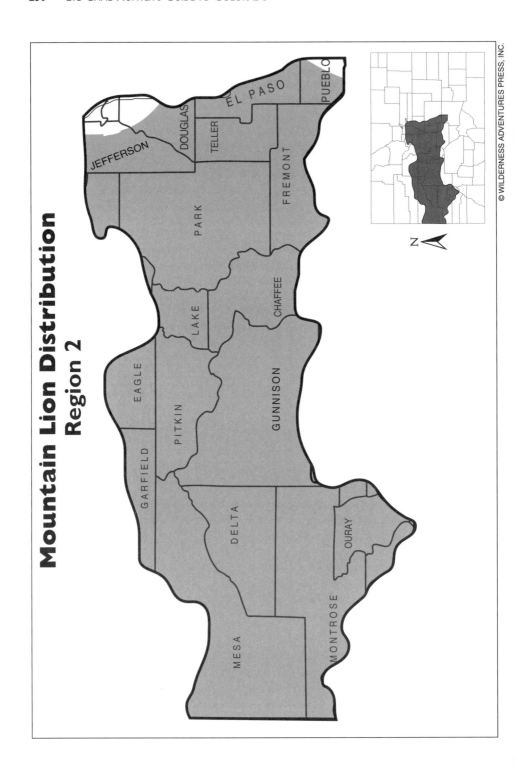

Mountain Lion Distribution
Region 2

© WILDERNESS ADVENTURES PRESS, INC.

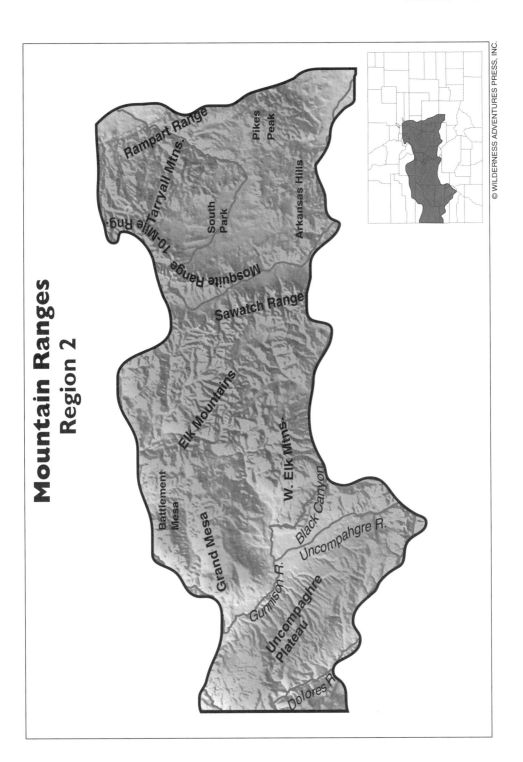

Mountain Ranges
Region 2

Rampart Range

Pikes Peak

Tarryall Mtns.

Arkansas Hills

South Park

Mosquite Range 10-Mile Rng.

Sawatch Range

Elk Mountains

W. Elk Mtns.

Battlement Mesa

Grand Mesa

Black Canyon

Uncompahgre R.

Gunnison R.

Uncompahgre Plateau

Dolores R.

© WILDERNESS ADVENTURES PRESS, INC.

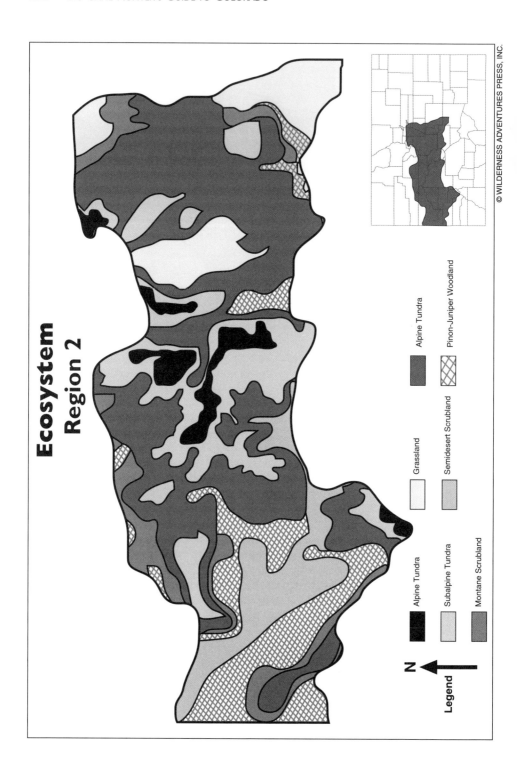

Ecosystem
Region 2

Legend

Alpine Tundra

Subalpine Tundra

Montane Scrubland

Grassland

Semidesert Scrubland

Alpine Tundra

Pinon-Juniper Woodland

N

© WILDERNESS ADVENTURES PRESS, INC.

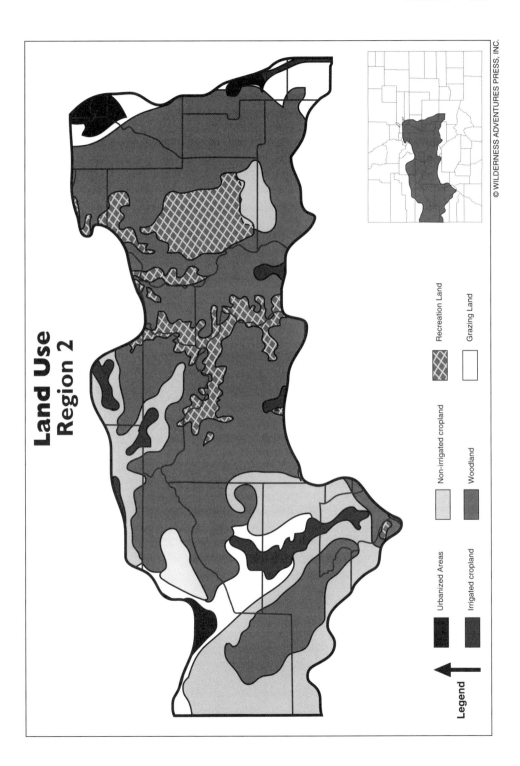

**Land Use
Region 2**

Legend

Urbanized Areas

Irrigated cropland

Non-irrigated cropland

Woodland

Recreation Land

Grazing Land

© WILDERNESS ADVENTURES PRESS, INC.

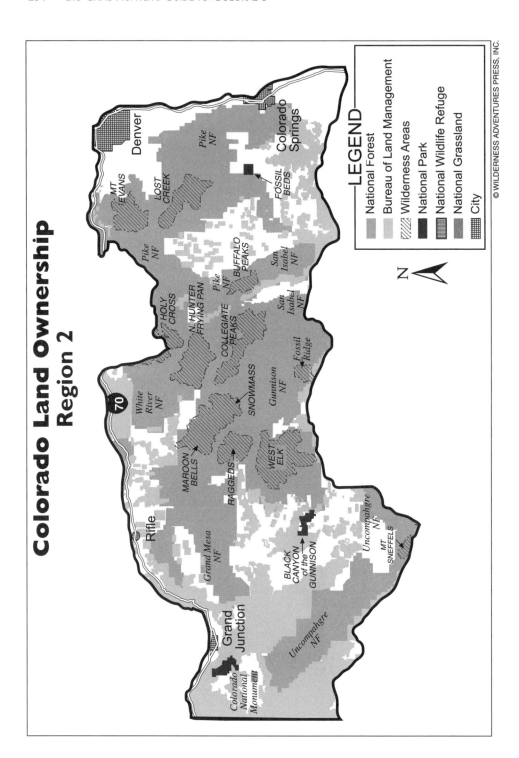

Colorado Land Ownership
Region 2

LEGEND

- National Forest
- Bureau of Land Management
- Wilderness Areas
- National Park
- National Wildlife Refuge
- National Grassland
- City

© WILDERNESS ADVENTURES PRESS, INC.

N

Denver

Pike NF

Colorado Springs

MT EVANS

LOST CREEK

FOSSIL BEDS

Pike NF

BUFFALO PEAKS

San Isabel NF

HOLY CROSS

N. HUNTER FRYING PAN

Pike NF

COLLEGIATE PEAKS

San Isabel NF

Fossil Ridge

White River NF

SNOWMASS

Gunnison NF

70

MAROON BELLS

RAGGEDS

WEST ELK

Uncompahgre NF

Rifle

Grand Mesa NF

BLACK CANYON of the GUNNISON

MT SNEFFELS

Grand Junction

Uncompahgre NF

Colorado National Monument

GAME SPECIES AND NUMBERS

There are fifteen recognized elk herds in Region 2 with a combined population over 67,000 animals, based on recent DOW statistics. The Grand Mesa elk herd alone boasts a population over 11,000 animals. There is a good distribution of deer throughout the region with over 170,000 animals. The Uncompahgre deer herd takes honors as the largest in the region with recent population estimates at 37,000 animals. Most of the mountain goats in Colorado are found in Region 2 as well as large populations of black bear and mountain lion.

The following tables provide the herd name, the GMUs where the herd ranges, and the population of the herd for elk, deer, and antelope. This information is current at the time of publishing, but populations change over time. Still, the distribution of populations in each area has remained relatively consistent over the years.

ELK HERD	UNITS	POPULATION
Mt. Evans	39, 46, 461	3,140
Glade Park	40	2,710
Grand Mesa	41, 42, 52, 411, 421, 521	11,670
Avalanche Creek	43, 471	5,850
Frying Pan	44, 45, 47, 444	7,920
Collegiate Range	48, 56, 481, 561	2,460
Buffalo Peaks	49, 57, 58	3,810
Kenosha Pass	50, 500, 501	1,740
Coal Creek/Fruitland Mesa	53, 63	3,840
Sapinero	54	3,850
Fossil Ridge	55, 551	3,820
Eleven Mile	59, 511, 581	1,830
Paradox	60	700
Uncompahgre	61, 62	9,110
Cimarron	64, 65	5,390
TOTAL ELK POPULATION REGION 2 = 67,840		

DEER HERD	UNITS	POPULATION
Bailey	39, 46, 41, 461	7,570
Glade Park	40	7,820
N. Grand Mesa	41, 42, 421	29,720
Maroon Bells	43, 47, 471	12,280
Red Table	44	7,840
Cottonwood Creek	48, 56, 481, 561	6,290
Cripple Creek	49, 57, 58, 59, 581	12,950
South Park	50, 500, 501	2,650
S. Grand Mesa	52, 411, 521	6,580
Crawford	53	5,240
West Elk	54	4,300
Taylor River	55, 551	5,660
Paradox	60	2,620
Uncompahgre	61, 62	37,000
Fruitland Mesa	63	3,260
Cimarron	64, 65	13,660
Basalt	444	2,650
Rampart Range	511, 512	3,030
TOTAL DEER POPULATION REGION 2 = 171,120		

ANTELOPE HERD	UNITS	POPULATION
Delta	41, 52, 62, 63, 411	260
South Park	49, 50, 57, 58, 501, 511, 581	710
Fort Carson	59, 591	220
Collegiate	48, 56, 481	130
Doyleville	66, 67, 551	330
TOTAL ANTELOPE POPULATION REGION 2 = 1,650		

Populations of bear and mountain lion are not as well documented. There is specific statewide information for the other big game species.

SPECIES	STATEWIDE POPULATION
Black Bear	Unknown (estimates from 8,000 to 12,000)
Mountain Lion	Unknown (estimates from 1,500 to 3,500)
Desert Bighorn	400
Rocky Mtn. Bighorn	6,500
Mountain Goat	1,100
Moose	1,175

Harvest Trends

Hunter success rates vary greatly from year to year, season to season, and unit to unit. The Colorado Division of Wildlife publishes the big game hunting statistics each year, which includes success rates for each season in each unit. This information is available online at http://wildlife.state.co.us/huntrecap/index.asp.

The following success rates are based on 2001 DOW statistics averaged for all seasons and manners of take statewide.

SPECIES	SUCCESS RATE	TOTAL ANIMALS HARVESTED
Elk	21%	42,630
Deer	42%	31,634
Antelope	61%	6,417
Black Bear	6%	759
Desert Bighorn	100%	9
Rocky Mtn. Bighorn	51%	175
Mountain Goat	92%	169
Moose	84%	102

It is not possible to estimate the mountain lion success rate because the harvest is based on a quota system instead of limited licenses; however, 315 of the big cats were harvested in Colorado during the 2000 hunting season.

Physical Characteristics

From Denver south to the city of Colorado Springs, the land between Interstate 25 and the mountains to the west is almost entirely private. Although this 70-mile corridor has not been entirely developed yet, the sprawl associated with the two cities has consumed much of the land. From Denver south along Highways 85 and 105 to the town of Monument, the foothills and valleys have been almost entirely consumed by "mini-ranches" and trophy homes. Hunters will have to work hard to get permission to hunt this area, but it could be worth the trouble. There are some tremendous mule deer in this area as well as trophy-caliber elk. Continuing south along I-25 from Colorado Springs to Pueblo, a large amount of land between the Interstate and Highway 115 to the west is occupied by the Fort Carson Military Reservation.

Moving west from the I-25 corridor, the Rampart Range trends in a southerly direction towards Pikes Peak. The Arkansas Hills flank Pikes Peak to the south and form an important watershed for the Arkansas River. Continuing west, South Park is an important feature bounded by the Tarryall Mountains to the north, the Ten Mile Range and the Mosquito Range to the west. The headwaters of the South Platte River originate in the Mosquito Range. Moving still farther to the west, the Sawatch Range trends north to south and rises above the Arkansas River valley. The Elk Mountains, and West Elk Mountains are located west of the Sawatch Range near the center of Region 2. Battlement Mesa, Grand Mesa, the Gunnison River, and the Uncompahgre Plateau wrap up the most important features of the region.

With over 10 million acres of public land, big game hunters will have no problem finding places to hunt in Region 2. Six national forests cover the area with eleven wilderness areas and a large amount of BLM property. There are also numerous state wildlife areas and state trust lands open to hunting.

Region 2 has a broad diversity of ecosystems due to the great variability in elevation across the area. Tracts of grassland are found along the I-25 corridor, but are disrupted by a large area of montane forest on the Platte-Arkansas Divide located between Denver and Colorado Springs. Montane forest is also the predominant ecosystem along the Rampart Range, Pikes Peak, and south into portions of the Arkansas Hills. The north side of the divide is bounded by montane shrubland; pinon-juniper woodland bound the south edge. Moving to the west, South Park forms a large island of intermountain grasslands. To the north and west of South Park is one of the largest areas of alpine tundra found anywhere in the state, or in the western United States. The Ten Mile Range, Mosquito Range, Sawatch Range, and Elk Mountains all contain relatively large areas above 11,400 feet in elevation. As would be expected, the areas of tundra are surrounded by subalpine forest, and montane forest at lower elevations.

The Gunnison River forms an important riparian system and flows through large areas of semi-desert shrubland. The Uncompahgre Plateau is primarily montane forest at the higher elevations ringed by montane shrubland and large areas of pinon-juniper woodland to the northeast and southwest. Finally, the Grand Mesa area has large tracts of subalpine forest on top with montane forest, and montane shrublands at the lower elevations. The north and south sides of Grand Mesa are bounded by pinon-juniper woodland. All of the major ecosystem designations used in this book are found in Region 2. The broad diversity of ecosystems equates to a broad diversity of wildlife.

The Uncompahgre National Forest.

Land Use

As discussed in Region 1, the I-25 corridor is the most heavily populated area in the state. Denver, Colorado Springs, Pueblo, and the communities surrounding these cities account for most of the population in the state. The land in these areas has been developed to a large extent. Land use in those areas that remain undeveloped between the three cities is used for agricultural purposes. Some irrigated farmland is found south of Colorado Springs with larger areas of dry land used for farming and grazing.

Land use in the large areas of national forest to the west of the I-25 corridor includes ranching, logging, recreation, and mining. Cattle operations are found throughout Region 2 with grazing occurring in large part on national forest and BLM properties. The Gunnison area is known for its large ranching operations and numerous hay meadows along the rivers in the area. Recreational opportunities abound throughout the region with several major ski resorts, including Keystone, Breckenridge, Aspen, and Crested Butte to mention a few. Historically speaking, mining has had a large influence on western Colorado. Both the miners and the towns that they built make up a colorful part of the state's history. To a limited extent mining is still going on. Large quarry operations exist just west of Colorado Springs and the largest gold mining operation in the state is located between the towns of Cripple Creek and Victor. The Climax Mine north of Leadville was a huge molybdenum producer, although it is now in a maintenance mode with no active mining. The Black Cloud Mine in Leadville recently closed and was one of the last operating underground mines in the state.

In the western portion of Region 2 there is more oil and gas production on the BLM properties. While there are numerous farms with irrigated cropland in Delta and Mesa Counties, there are also many orchards and vineyards unique to this region of the state. More specifically, the area surrounding Grand Junction has several vineyards. The towns of Paonia, Hotchkiss, Orchard City, and Cedaredge are well known for apple, peach, and cherry orchards. These towns are fun to visit in the fall, as there are numerous stands set up where you can sample delicious fresh fruit and ciders.

Weather

The weather in Region 2 (as with all of western Colorado) is greatly affected by the high mountain ranges. Similar to Region 1, the summer weather pattern is one of afternoon thunderstorms. Early season hunters will likely experience comfortable hunting conditions with moderate highs and lows. It is a nice time of the year to hunt Colorado. The thunderstorm weather pattern will generally tail off in September. As the Jet Stream is deflected south from cold arctic air, snow can begin to accumulate as early as mid-September in the high country. Region 2 is sometimes spared from the early winter storms because of its southern declination, but generally the weather patterns will be very similar to those described for Region 1.

It cannot be stated too many times that the high mountain ranges experience extremes in weather conditions at any time of the year. If you're hunting at high elevations in the Rampart Range, Pikes Peak, Mosquito Range, Sawatch Range, Elk

Mountains, or any other location in Region 2, pay attention to the weather. The high ranges will often capture large quantities of moisture from Pacific fronts moving across the state. If one of these fronts moves through the state when you are hunting at 10,000 feet, you could be in for a lot of snow.

While bowhunting for elk in the Pike National Forest near the town of Fairplay in 1997, I experienced one of the most violent storms of my life. I learned two important lessons on that hunt. The first lesson was that sometimes there is no reason to camp at extremely high elevations. The second lesson was that you should pay attention to instinct. Even though it is a pain to pick up camp and move, sometimes it makes good sense.

I scouted the area thoroughly before the season and found elk on a high ridge. In order to get within reasonable walking distance, I camped near a trailhead at an elevation over 10,000 feet. On a weeklong hunt I ambushed elk within 100 yards of my camp three separate times after returning from long treks on the higher ridge. This taught me the first lesson; you don't always have to go higher and farther to find elk. I would have been better off staying a thousand feet lower and hunting the area where I was camped.

Weather can change rapidly in the Rockies.

The second lesson was learned one night when a terrible thunderstorm hit. I could see huge clouds building up over the mountains and I knew it was going to get nasty. I had a camper on my truck and felt confident that my shelter would be secure no matter how bad the storm, but the thought did cross my mind to move to a lower camping area. I ignored my instincts and stayed put. At about 8:00 that night it started to rain, and sleet, and then hail. The wind blew and the thunder crashed. Storms generally move through this area quickly, but this storm stayed put on the continental divide and hammered the area. Several times lightning flashed like a blue strobe light immediately followed by a resounding boom that shook the truck. It felt like mortar shells were detonating all around my camp. You truly gain respect for Mother Nature in this kind of storm. Near midnight it stopped briefly, but it was too late to consider leaving. The steep road had become muddy and covered in hail. In fact, the whole landscape was white with hail. The storm started back up and lasted until 2:00 in the morning. I was exhausted by the time I finally went to sleep. The next morning it looked like a blizzard had hit. Several inches of hail covered the area and portions of the road had almost been completely washed out. I was able to get down the mountain (or I should say I slid down the mountain) later that afternoon. I stayed in a hotel in Fairplay that night and the storm was the center of conversation. At a much lower elevation, the town had still been hit savagely by the storm. People lost roofs off barns and sheds blew down. Pastures were flooded and livestock had to be rescued. Localized flash flooding destroyed dirt roads and undermined small overpasses. The storm definitely left its mark.

The following table provides average temperatures, precipitation, and snowfall for Buena Vista, Colorado. Buena Vista is located in the eastern half of Region 2 at an elevation of 7,955 feet above mean sea level.

MONTH	AVERAGE HIGH (°F)	AVERAGE LOW (°F)	AVERAGE PRECIPITATION (Total inches)	AVERAGE SNOW FALL (Total inches)
August	78.4	45.7	1.93	0.0
September	72.6	37.9	0.94	1.0
October	62.8	28.4	0.83	2.8
November	48.6	19.0	0.56	5.3
December	40.8	11.4	0.43	5.0

Temperature ranges were based on National Weather Service data for Buena Vista. Period of record 8/01/1948 to 7/31/2000.

Be aware that average temperature ranges along the I-25 corridor will generally be higher than those listed above. Also, the temperatures along the western slope (west of the continental divide) especially in the western third of the region will be significantly higher than listed on the table. Furthermore, total snowfall will be much greater in the higher elevations of the surrounding mountain ranges.

Public Lands and Acreage

Region 2 has nearly ten million acres of public land in the form of six national forests, BLM properties, and state lands. Over three million acres are found in the Pike National Forest alone—the biggest national forest in the state. Twelve federally designated wilderness areas are located in the region with over one million acres. The acreage of these areas is tabled below to help identify the amount of wilderness area in the region; however, these acreages are part of the total listed for the national forests.

As discussed in Region 1, not all of the acres listed are necessarily within the boundaries of the region. Some of the national forests extend beyond the Region 2 boundary. Most notably, an estimated 50 percent of the White River National Forest is in Region 1. In addition, approximately 50 percent of the San Isabel N.F. and 30 percent of the Gunnison N.F. extend into Region 3. These approximations are noted in the following table. BLM acreage is given by county, and some of the counties also cross the Region 2 boundary. There are also private lands within the national forests and areas on the BLM lands that are sometimes closed to the public due to various land uses and lease agreements.

PUBLIC LAND DESCRIPTION	ACREAGES
Grand Mesa National Forest	360,000
Gunnison National Forest (70 percent)	1,190,000
Pike National Forest	3,106,000
San Isabel National Forest (50 percent)	619,000
Uncompahgre National Forest (80 percent)	911,200
White River National Forest (50 percent)	1,000,000
Curecanti National Recreation Area	42,000
Bureau of Land Management	2,745,764
TOTAL PUBLIC LANDS IN REGION 2	*9,973,964*

WILDERNESS AREAS (NATIONAL FOREST)		ACREAGES
Buffalo Peaks	(Pike/San Isabel)	43,410
Collegiate Peaks	(Gunnison/San Isabel/White R)	167,994
Fossil Ridge	(Gunnison)	33,060
Holy Cross	(White River/San Isabel)	121,883
Hunter-Frying Pan	(White River)	82,729
Lost Creek	(Pike)	120,700
Maroon Bells-Snowmass	(White River/Gunnison)	180,962
Mount Evans	(Arapaho/Pike)	74,401
Mount Massive	(San Isabel)	30,540
Mount Sneffels	(Uncompahgre)	16,505
Raggeds	(Gunnison/White River)	65,019
West Elk	(Gunnison)	176,092
TOTAL WILDERNESS AREA REGION 2		*1,113,295*

REGION 2 HIGHLIGHTS

Pikes Peak (GMUs 59, 511, 512, 581)

For over three years I lived near Pikes Peak and got to know the area very well. Pikes Peak is located on the western edge of El Paso County, adjacent to Teller County, within the Pike National Forest. For purposes of discussion GMU 59 covers most of the Pikes Peak area, but GMUs 511, 512, and 581 will also be addressed.

In terms of deer, GMUs 59 and 581 are two of five units that make up the Cripple Creek deer herd. The population estimate for this herd has varied from 10,000 to almost 13,000 animals over the past few years. The buck-to-doe ratio for the herd was very low at 7 to 100; however, I always saw good numbers of bucks when hunting the area. (Of course, my observations were limited to areas where the buck-to-doe ratio might not have been representative of the entire population). GMUs 511 and 512 make up the Rampart Range deer herd with a population that generally approaches 3,000 animals with a strong buck-to-doe ratio in the 60 to 100 range. GMUs 59, 511, and 581 make up the Eleven Mile elk herd with nearly 2,000 animals. There are also a few antelope in GMU 59 in the Fort Carson herd, which generally numbers over 200.

Region 2 has good populations of mule deer.

Rudy Meyers with a lion taken in the Pikes Peak GMU. (Rudy Meyers)

If you're interested in hunting predators, the area holds good numbers of bear and mountain lions. In fact, the areas surrounding Canon City and Florence hold a large concentration of lions. The Rampart Range also has good numbers of lions and there are several outfitters in the area that can get you onto the big cats. Bighorn Sheep Unit S6 covers Pikes Peak and offers the most licenses in the area with a 2001 harvest of 10 rams and 26 ewes during all of the seasons. There are also opportunities to hunt sheep in Units S46, S34, S60, and S6A.

The predominant ecosystem found in the Pikes Peak area is montane forest with large aspen stands, various pines, fir, and spruce. If you're hunting national forest surrounding the peak, the terrain is steep and unforgiving. There is also an island of alpine tundra at the higher elevations of Pikes Peak surrounded by subalpine forest. As you move farther south in GMUs 59 and 581, the area becomes drier with pinon-juniper woodlands in a canyonland setting. As you would expect, the weather on Pikes Peak can be severe, but my experience during the early hunting seasons was one of mild weather patterns with little to no precipitation. Later, during the rifle seasons, there was usually some snow accumulation in October and November at elevations above 9,500 feet. Moving farther south in the area towards Canon City, temperatures were higher in all seasons with very little precipitation.

To access the area take Highway 24 west from Colorado Springs. There are several roads and trailheads off of 24 that will provide access to the east side of Pikes Peak. Continuing on Highway 24 to the town of Woodland Park will provide access via several county roads into GMUs 511 and 512. At Divide, located west of Woodland

Park on 24, take Highway 67 south to Cripple Creek. Highway 67 forms the boundary between GMUs 581 and 59 and provides good access to the west side of Pikes Peak. Before reaching Cripple Creek take Teller County Road (CR) 81 south. There are at least two public roads off of CR 81 (that I'm aware of) that will provide access into the Pike National Forest on the southwest side of Pikes Peak. This area holds some good elk. Continuing south on CR 81 will take you to the Gold Camp Road—a historic railroad grade. This dirt road provides good access into large areas of national forest on the south side of Pikes Peak and will eventually take you all the way back to Colorado Springs (when it's open). From the town of Cripple Creek, CR 88 (better known as the Shelf Road) goes all the way to Canon City to the south. This road is less known to the general public and provides access into an area with good numbers of mountain lion and deer. From the town of Victor, Phantom Canyon road is a well-known tourist route in the summer that also allows access into good mountain lion areas.

While there is a large quantity of public land to hunt, be aware that almost all of the land immediately surrounding the towns of Cripple Creek and Victor is private. This historic gold mining district is plastered with patented mining claims. Patented mining claims are private property. Furthermore, there is a large active gold mining operation between the two towns. If you get caught on any of this property, you will likely get a chance to meet the local sheriff. Finding the right people to ask for permission to hunt mining claims is a tough proposition due to the dissected ownership. There are also several large ranches in the area that are off limits to the public. Don't let this discourage you, though. Instead, get the Pikes Peak, Colorado Springs, Canon City, and Pueblo Surface Management Status Maps from the Bureau of Land Management and spend some time scouting. Combining these maps with topographic maps should help you discern the public areas from the private. For GMUs 511 and 512 you will also need the Bailey and Castle Rock maps. There is plenty of quality hunting on the public lands in this area.

Late in the summer of 1990 I scouted an area in the Pike National Forest on the southwest side of Pikes Peak (east of Gillett). I found an area of stepped grassy meadows in a deep valley ending in a gulch that had been dammed by beaver. There was literally an elk highway next to the beaver pond that led through the gulch to a lower series of meadows. I planned on bowhunting the area that year and built a brush blind beneath a large spruce about 15 yards from the trail. It was the perfect set up as numerous tracks indicated many of the elk stopped to drink providing close range, stationary shots. Unfortunately, I was forced to work out of state for the entire bow season, and I never got a chance to occupy the blind I had so meticulously constructed. Even though I don't live in the area any longer, I've never forgotten about that spot. If you ever decide to hunt this area, you might find me sitting under a spruce tree next to a beaver pond waiting for elk.

A Mount Evans mountain goat.

Mount Evans Goats (GMUs 39, 46, 51, 461)

In addition to mountain goats, Mount Evans holds a large population of bighorn sheep, and the surrounding area is exceptional for deer and elk. At 14,264 feet, Mount Evans is visible from Denver and stands out as one of the most scenic regions in the state. It is located near the boundary of the Arapaho and Pike National Forests in the south part of Clear Creek County about ten miles south of Idaho Springs. The Mount Evans Wilderness Area includes over 74,000 acres with nearly 70 miles of trails. There is also a Mount Evans State Wildlife Area located to the east of the mountain that has over 3,400 acres of property open for big game hunting.

GMUs 39, 46, and 461 make up the Mount Evans elk herd with a population that is normally about 3,000 animals. The herd has a strong bull-to-cow ratio in the 40 to 100 range, with excellent trophy potential. All three of these GMUs have limited licenses so you will have to accumulate preference points to draw a tag. Bowhunters and muzzleloaders will generally draw a tag with 0 to 2 preference points. Rifle hunters may have to wait a little longer depending on the season and unit, but generally 1 to 3 preference points will get you a tag. Two or three years really isn't that long to wait to hunt a quality area like Mount Evans, and you can always hunt a GMU with unlimited licenses as a second choice during the years when you don't draw the limited tag. GMUs 39, 46, 51, and 461 make up the Bailey Deer herd with a recent population of over 7,500 animals and a good buck-to-doe ratio in the 40 to 100 range.

In terms of trophy species, Mount Evans can't be beat for mountain goats. In 2001 there were 35 rams and 27 ewes (over 35 percent of the state's total harvest) taken in Unit G7 alone. Unit G4 had a harvest of 8 rams and 5 ewes. Since the area is so well known for mountain goats, many of the 3,000+ applicants put in for tags in G4 or G7 each year. This is a lot of competition that will probably mean you have to wait 5 to 10 years before you draw a tag.

Bighorn Sheep Units S3 and S4 have several licenses available each year. In 2001, eighteen sheep were harvested from the two combined units. These are relatively popular units for sheep and it will take several years to draw a tag. Keep in mind that there are ways to hunt sheep before accumulating three points. This is a well-guarded secret by most Colorado hunters, but if you want to simply experience a sheep hunt and are willing to settle for a ewe, there are tags available for hunters with less than three preference points. This is variable from year to year depending on the number of applicants and management goals. You will have to do some research with the DOW to identify these opportunities.

When hunting the Mount Evans area you will find a great deal of the terrain extremely steep and rugged. Due to the high elevation there are vast areas above tree line made up of alpine tundra, and, locally, arctic tundra. If you're after mountain goats or sheep you will likely hunt this terrain. Besides the loose talus, sheer cliffs, and frequent storms, hunting here is a breeze. Needless to say, be prepared when hunting the area. Storms can build up fast, and lightning is a real threat at high elevations. I've heard that the chances of getting struck by lightning are less than winning the lottery. However, your odds go up tremendously if you're trapped at 12,000 feet by a severe thunderstorm. Tragically, in September of 1999, a herd of 56 elk were killed by a lightning strike just below Mount Evans at an elevation between 12,000 and 13,000 feet.If you are hunting near tree line, there are some relatively large stands of bristlecone pine. At lower elevations you will find a montane forest ecosystem with an abundance of lodgepole pine, spruce, fir, and aspen. The weather on Mount Evans is unpredictable regardless of the season you choose to hunt. Be prepared for the worst and enjoy it when it's nice. On a visit I made to Mount Evans in July of 1999 the temperature on the summit was 38 degrees.Due to its proximity to Denver, large numbers of tourists visit the area each year. Driving south from Idaho Springs on Highway 103 (Mount Evans Highway) will take you into the wilderness area to State Highway 5 (also known as the Mount Evans Highway or the Summit Highway). The summit highway was built before Mount Evans was designated as a wilderness area and was allowed to remain after the designation. This road allows thousands of visitors to reach the summit each year. As you travel to the summit you will likely see mountain goats along the way. These animals are nearly tame from all of the contact with people and offer excellent photo opportunities. Due to the high use, there are several areas along State Highway 5 that are closed to hunting. Please see the regulations for specific information concerning these closures. To access the Mount Evans State Wildlife Area take I-70 west from Denver to the El Rancho exit. Travel south on Highway 74 to the Upper Bear Creek Road. Turn right and proceed to County Road 480. Turn right again and stay on 480 to the property.

Jim Titchenell with a nice black bear taken in Unit 461. (Jim Titchenell)

Suburban Hunts (GMUs 46, 391, 461)

Located approximately 20 miles west of Denver is the mountain community of Evergreen. From the southwest side of Denver, Highway 285 leaves the urban area for several small mountain communities including Conifer and Bailey. Much of the Evergreen area and the 285 corridor between Denver and Bailey is slowly being chewed up by development. Houses and condos seem to spring up overnight and formerly large tracts of ranchland have been dissected. What has resulted is a rather large area of private land that still holds large numbers of deer and elk. In fact, a visit to these communities in the winter will often allow good opportunities to view deer and elk that are literally wintering in people's yards. Some of the homeowners in the area love the wildlife. Although you're not supposed to, some of the more ignorant homeowners even feed the wild animals. Others hate the deer and elk and consider them a nuisance.

Evergreen is located in GMU 391 and Highway 285 runs south through 391 and forms part of the boundary between GMUs 46 and 461. Most hunters, myself included, travel through this area each year without ever considering possible hunting opportunities. As I've learned more about big game hunting in Colorado, I'm amazed by the number of trophy deer and elk that are taken off small parcels (20 acres to 200 acres) of private land in these three units. I know of several people who have successfully gained permission to hunt private property in these areas and consistently harvest quality bucks and/or bulls.

It may take some legwork and persistence to gain access to private property, but it could be worth the trouble if you succeed. My advice is to scout the area just as you would public land. (Obviously, don't trespass without permission). You want to find a place that holds animals during the season you intend to hunt. Once you find a promising area identify the landowners. If there are houses in the area start knocking on doors. This is how you will start accumulating the information you need to find that honey hole. Even if a landowner won't let you hunt, he may be able to tell you of a neighbor who allows hunters or how to contact adjacent landowners. If there isn't a home on the property you're interested in, write down all of the identifying features you can find. These may include crossroads or addresses of nearby properties. You may even want to make a simple map of the area. Take this information to the county courthouse and search plat maps and tax records to find the property owner. As a rule it is generally illegal to discharge firearms (including bows) inside city limits, so focus your search on unincorporated areas.

What are the pros of hunting small tracts of private property in suburban areas? There are often large numbers of animals concentrated into small areas. Due to the lack of hunting pressure, there are often trophy-class animals. Also, many times these animals are more approachable because of the lack of hunting pressure. Hunting in these areas can also help reduce herd overpopulation locally, and it can reduce property damage complaints. Further, it can help reduce car accidents associated with big game where high densities of animals are found near heavily traveled roads.

What are the cons of hunting suburban areas? Hunting in a residential setting will definitely feel different than hunting remote wild country. Shot opportunities must be carefully considered. Nobody ever wants to wound an animal, but such an event in a suburban area could have grave consequences to hunters if the wounded animal were to expire on an anti-hunter's front step. Furthermore, safety of the non-hunting public is the most important consideration. You will have to know where neighboring homes are before you even think about shooting. Also, you may not be able to hunt safely with a firearm in such an area.

When talking to landowners try to be courteous and straightforward. Let them know from the start that you are seeking permission to hunt on their property. Let them know when you hope to hunt and what kind of weapon you intend to use. Obviously, landowners may be more willing to allow you to trespass if you plan on hunting with a bow versus a rifle. Furthermore, be prepared to offer something to the landowner. They may be looking for a trespass fee or it could be as simple as offering to share the meat if you are lucky enough to harvest an animal. If a prospective landowner turns you down, don't argue. Thank them for their time and move on. Also, do your door knocking well in advance of the season so you will have time to apply for the appropriate license. This also lets the landowner know that you're a serious hunter, not just another guy who happened to see a deer in his front yard on opening day and stopped to ask about shooting it.

It's an unfortunate fact of modern hunting that much of the quality opportunities exist on private lands. Many of these lands are being leased or purchased specifically for hunting. If you luck out and find that perfect spot, consider offering to lease the hunting rights to the land. This is exactly how outfitters secure large tracts of private land every year. If you have a few buddies, pool your resources. Three or four people throwing in a couple of hundred dollars each can add up pretty fast. This will benefit the landowner that has a resource you're interested in, and it can help secure your hunting spot for years to come. The Evergreen area and Highway 285 in GMUs 391, 46, and 461 are good places to start your search, but there are several areas throughout the state that offer good opportunities for quality hunting around suburban areas.

South Park (GMUs 49, 50, 57, 58, 500, 501)

The counterpart to North Park is South Park, an elongate intermountain park roughly 40 miles north to south and up to 20 miles east to west. Located in Park County, South Park is surrounded by the Pike National Forest. Although deer, elk, and antelope are found in the lower elevations (9,000 feet) of the park, a more descriptive name for this highlight area might be, "the mountains surrounding South Park." The park is bounded on the west by the Mosquito Range, the north/northeast by the Tarryall Mountains, and the south/southeast by the Arkansas Hills. The Lost Creek Wilderness Area is located to the east of South Park in the Pike National Forest.

The Kenosha Pass elk herd is found in GMUs 50, 500, and 501. The usual population of this herd varies from about 1,700 to 1,900 animals with very high bull-to-cow ratio that has been as high as 70 to 100 in recent years. GMUs 49, 57, and 58 make up the Buffalo Peaks elk herd that generally has about 3,800 animals. This herd also has a good bull-to-cow ratio of 47 to 100 in recent years. These six units cover the entire South Park area and most of the mountains surrounding the park and beyond. The area has good numbers of deer as well, with 2,300 to 2,700 animals in the South Park deer herd in GMUs 50, 500, and 501. This herd has had an estimated 26 bucks to every 100 does in past years. GMUs 49, 57, and 58 are three of five units that make up the Cripple Creek deer herd (discussed in the Pikes Peak highlight area). This herd reportedly has a population approaching 13,000 animals. There is also a significant antelope herd, also known as the South Park herd, which generally has over 700 animals. There are some good bucks in this herd with a buck-to-doe ratio of 24 to 100 in recent years.

Mountain goat hunting is limited in this area; however, portions of Units G7 and G4 extend to the north end of South Park where State Highway 285 forms the south boundary of both units. As discussed in the Mount Evans highlight area, these are the two most prolific mountain goat units in the state. Several bighorn sheep units surround South Park, including S23, S27, and S12. These units have several licenses available each year with variable harvests. If you're interested in hunting bears, talk to residents of Fairplay and Como who will undoubtedly have stories of problem bears. I've had my own experience with bears in the area and can assure you that they are plentiful. There are also a good number of mountain lions here.

The predominant ecosystem in South Park is grassland with relatively flat terrain. Much of the park is at an elevation of 9,000 feet surrounded almost completely by montane forest. Large areas of subalpine forest are also found at the higher elevations on all sides of the park. As you approach the continental divide on the west, there are numerous peaks rising above 13,000 feet with large areas above tree line consisting of an alpine tundra ecosystem. When hunting the area you will find numerous types of terrain in the mountains. Be prepared for anything from nice gentle hills to steep slopes covered with dark timber. Several of the drainages in the area open up into valleys with numerous beaver ponds. From a distance these valleys look lush and green with nice flat terrain. The reality is that they are often covered with head-high willow in peat bogs. Crossing 100 yards of this terrain on foot can leave you soaking wet and covered in black mud up to your waist.

The weather in South Park and the surrounding mountains can be extreme during the hunting season. There are often strong winds in the park, and the mountains along the continental divide capture large amounts of moisture. While bowhunting in GMU 500 over a three-year period (during September) I experienced one season with warm daytime temperatures in the 60s and blue skies almost everyday. The other two seasons consisted of rainy weather with relatively cold temperatures often in the 40s and low 50s. Rifle hunters can expect some snow in October with significant accumulations starting in November. As always, expect more severe weather conditions the higher you hunt.

As mentioned above, I bowhunted public land in GMU 500 with my friend Duane Redford over a three year period in the '90s. During that time I was able to take one elk and Duane connected two years in a row. That's a pretty fair success rate for bowhunting. Overall bowhunters had an 17 percent success rate in the most recent bow season and rifle hunters had exceptional success ranging from 29 percent in the first season to 54 percent in the third combined rifle season in recent years. I never saw any trophy bulls while hunting the area, but there were definitely an abundance of raghorns and spikes. I also found a shed in a high basin of a massive six-point bull, proving that the big ones do exist. I plan on hunting this area again in the future. If you're new to this area, try scouting the numerous drainages from Kenosha Pass to Fairplay. The Jefferson Lake area holds a good number of elk. Although deer are not plentiful in Unit 500 where I hunted, I did see a few big bucks. I also had two mountain goats walk right by my camp one year. This was in an area outside of Mountain Goat Unit G7. I don't know if it was an anomalous sighting or if the goats have increased their range and numbers in the area. Maybe there will be a new goat unit in the area, or an extension of G7 someday in the future.

Although most hunting techniques will work well for elk in the South Park area, don't overlook treestands when bowhunting. There are several areas where elk habitually use well-established trails. A treestand placed over one of these trails, or near an active wallow, might be your key to success.

When hunting any of the seasons in GMU 500 you will likely see many other hunters. Although there are limited licenses for elk in this unit, the DOW is very generous with the tags. The unit is one of the smallest GMUs in the state, and hunters tend to get concentrated in small areas. Once you learn the area and pattern the elk movements, you can definitely use hunter pressure to your advantage – especially during the rifle seasons.

To access the area, take Colorado Highway 285 from Denver. From Colorado Springs you can access the area via Highway 24. Depending on which unit you choose to hunt there are several county roads and logging roads off 285 and 24 that will get you into the national forest. While there is a great deal of public land in the area, most of it is found in the mountains surrounding South Park. The Bailey, Pikes Peak, Leadville, and Gunnison Surface Management Status BLM Maps will help you determine public lands in the area. Just because I have related my experiences about hunting in GMU 500 doesn't mean you should overlook the other units in the area for deer and elk. As an example, the Buffalo Peaks area is renowned for trophy-class mule deer.

As I alluded to earlier, I had my own run-in with a bear while hunting GMU 500. The year I took an elk I shot it near sunset and wasn't able to get it off the mountain that night. Unfortunately, a bear found the elk during the night and took out a good portion of the back quarters. I still got most of the meat, but I was disappointed to lose any of it after all of the hard work it had taken to harvest the animal. Since that time I have had two other instances where I was forced to leave animals overnight before packing them out. That free meal I donated to the bear taught me to take precautions. At a minimum, I now drag the animal as far as possible from the gut pile and cover the carcass with a few branches or logs. Then I place my shirt or an article of clothing over it so there is a lot of human scent in the area. I also urinate all around the carcass hoping to mark my territory and fend off any predators. So far I haven't lost any more elk meat to predators. If you can quarter out the animal before dark and get it hung in a tree, that is probably the best way to protect it. This also allows it to cool out quickly.

Maroon Bells Snowmass Wilderness (GMUs 43, 47, 471)

The town of Aspen had its beginning, as with many other mountain communities in Colorado, as a mining camp. It was one of the richest silver mining districts in the nation during the 1880s and 1890s. After silver prices dropped and mining tailed off, the natural beauty of the area kept the local economy alive through tourism and the development of world-class resorts. The area now boasts four ski resorts (Aspen Mountain, Aspen Highlands, Buttermilk, and Snowmass) and is a well-known home to the rich and famous. Located in Pitkin County west of Aspen, the Maroon Bells Snowmass Wilderness is the largest wilderness area in Region 2 at over 180,000 acres. Six mountains rise up over the 14,000-foot mark in the Elk Mountains within the wilderness area, including Pyramid Peak, which is a well-stratified mountain often used for calendar photos. Most of the wilderness area falls into the White River National Forest, but a small portion extends into the Gunnison National Forest to the south.

The Maroon Bells deer herd is located in GMUs 43, 47, and 471. At over 12,000 animals, and a good buck-to-doe ratio of 25 to 100 in recent years, there are exceptional opportunities for deer hunters in this area. Please note that GMU 47 is located to the north and east of Aspen and covers a large part of the Hunter-Frying Pan Wilderness Area. The Avalanche Creek elk herd occupies GMUs 43 and 471 with a population that has varied from 4,500 to nearly 6,000 animals in recent years. The bull-to-cow ratio has been in the range of 20 to 100. There is no antelope hunting found in the area, but bear hunters will find a high concentration of bruins in this part of Colorado. Furthermore, mountain goat hunters should look into opportuni-

The author with a 5x5 bull taken on public land during the archery season in Unit 43, Maroon Bells Wilderness.

ties in Units G11, G12, and G13. There are also several tags available for bighorn sheep in Units S12 and S25.

Due to the high elevations in the Elk Range (with over 7,000 feet of relief in some areas) there is great diversity in terms of habitat. At the high elevations above 11,400 feet there are large areas of alpine tundra. Large tracts of subalpine forest and montane forest surround the alpine tundra at the lower elevations. As the name Aspen implies, there are large aspen stands throughout the area in addition to spruce and fir. You will also find large areas of montane shrubland with an abundance of scrub oak. There are also some agricultural areas, mostly hay meadows, along some of the rivers at the lower elevations. These areas are all private, but most of the land outside of Aspen and Snowmass within the national forests is public and open to hunting. As a historic mining district there are patented mining claims in the area that constitute private property. The Leadville and Carbondale Surface Management Status BLM Maps will illustrate public versus private property in the area.

Weather conditions will play a big role when hunting the area. Deer and elk will migrate to lower elevations when significant snow accumulates. As you would expect in an area with several ski resorts, there is a great deal of snow every year. In fact, the area generally receives over 150 inches of annual snowfall. Snow will begin to accumulate in October and will greatly minimize vehicle travel at the higher elevations. If you plan to hunt one of the early seasons, I would concentrate on the higher elevations above 10,000 feet for both deer and elk. Once the snow begins to accumulate try the lower areas from 7,000 to 9,000 feet in elevation.

As a rule, the terrain in the area is steep and unforgiving. You will want to be in good physical condition before you tackle the Maroon Bells Snowmass Wilderness Area as a hunting venue. However, it is a spectacular place to hunt and the work will be rewarding regardless of the take. If you're interested in hunting this area you should consider applying for one of the High Country Rifle Deer tags. All three GMUs in the Maroon Bells deer herd (43, 47, and 471) offer licenses for this hunt. September is a good time to hunt this area, and depending on which unit you choose, you might luck out and draw a high country deer tag with only two or three preference points. This might be the chance to harvest a big timberline muley.

Holy Cross Wilderness (GMUs 44, 45, 47, 444)

Located to the north of the Maroon Bells Snowmass and Hunter-Frying Pan Wilderness Areas in the Sawatch Range, the Holy Cross Wilderness is another exceptional area for big game hunters within the White River National Forest. The namesake of the wilderness area, Mount of the Holy Cross, is a 14,003-foot peak that has a slightly leaning cross, formed by two snow-filled gulches on its east face. The snow remains year-round, and the cross forms a prominent landmark. The wilderness area is large, with over 120,000 acres and 164 miles of trails.

The Mount of the Holy Cross is located on the west side of the continental divide in GMU 45, adjacent to the eastern boundaries of GMUs 44 and 444. These three GMUs, and Unit 47, make up the Frying Pan elk herd with a large population that has varied between 6,500 and nearly 8,000 animals in the past few years. GMU 44 makes

Mount of the Holy Cross Wilderness.

up the Red Table deer herd (a well-known trophy deer area) and Unit 444 is known as the Basalt herd. The two units have a combined deer population well over 10,000 animals according to recent DOW statistics. Although sheep units surround the area, there are currently no bighorn sheep units that cover the immediate Mount of the Holy Cross area. As discussed previously, that could change in the future depending on the success of a recent bighorn transplant to the area. There aren't any mountain goat units in this area either, but if you are looking for bears this will be a good location to consider.

I had an interesting bear sighting in this area recently. Each summer the Colorado Bowhunters Association holds a jamboree at Camp Hale located in GMU 45. This is a well-attended event with over 1,000 people participating each year. In addition to seven 3-D ranges, there are several calling contests. After all of the elk and turkey callers have had their chance, the winners are announced at a ceremony Saturday evening. In 1997 there were between 200 and 300 people attending the awards ceremony when several people interrupted the speaker and began pointing and exclaiming in low voices. Directly across the valley from the camping area stood one of the biggest black bears I have ever witnessed in the middle of a meadow halfway up the opposite mountainside. I think he had come out to see what all of the commotion was about. He got up on his back legs and stood looking down on all of the bowhunters assembled in the valley. After a few minutes he began to get a bad feeling about something, and he dropped down on all fours and hurried off into the trees. It was an exciting moment for all of the bowhunters, and a good example of the high density of bears in the area.

If you plan to hunt in the wilderness area, be prepared for extremely rugged terrain. This is a good area to consider a pack-in hunt. As with the Maroon Bells Snowmass Wilderness, the weather will definitely play a role in your hunt. Although this is probably starting to sound redundant, be prepared for extreme weather conditions. Ecosystems here are diverse with the great amount of vertical relief in the area. Alpine tundra is abundant at the high elevations and is surrounded by vast areas of subalpine and montane forest. Because the area receives great amounts of snow in the winter, many of the valleys are flooded in early summer with a deluge of snowmelt. These areas often remain boggy well into the hunting seasons. There are also numerous creeks and small alpine lakes in the area.

For those big game hunters interested in rifle hunting cow elk in an early season, there were 100 licenses available in GMU 45 during a recent early season (September 15-30). There were only 138 applicants for those licenses during this particular year, so you had a very good chance to draw a tag without any preference points. The number of tags for this early season rifle hunt can vary from year to year, so please check the regulations if interested in this hunt. Also, GMUs 44, 45, and 444 had 25 tags available for the early season High Country Rifle hunt for bucks during a recent season. This is another good opportunity for those hunters who want to use a rifle during an early season and have a chance at a trophy timberline muley. It will probably take several years to draw the buck tag, so start applying for preference points if you are interested. Overall success rates for deer and elk hunters in the GMUs 44, 45, and 444 are generally at or above statewide average harvest rates.

The extensive trail system will allow you to access some truly remote country. As many people will recall, this is the area where an A-10 Thunderbolt disappeared in April of 1997. Even with all of their sophisticated surveillance technology, it took the military two weeks to find the wreckage of the plane near Gold Dust Peak.

To access the wilderness area travel Interstate 70 to Exit 171 and turn south on Highway 24. In addition to the trailheads right off of Highway 24, County Roads 707 (Tigawan Road) and 703 along Homestake Creek will take you into the east side of the wilderness. There are several trailheads and jeep trails that can be accessed from 707 and 703. A good way to get to the west side of the wilderness area is to take Frying Pan Road east from the town of Basalt. Continue past Ruedi Reservoir where several other county roads, trailheads, and jeep trails can be accessed.

If you ever decide to hunt in the Holy Cross Wilderness, plan on some serious scouting before hunting season. While deer and elk are abundant here, they can be hard to find. Preseason scouting will give you a chance to enjoy the area in the summer. Take your fishing rods along and take advantage of the plentiful cutthroats and brook trout in the creeks and lakes. Also, if you are scouting the area during July, plan on attending the Colorado Bowhunter Jamboree at Camp Hale. This is a great event for the entire family.

Collegiate Peaks (GMUs 48, 56, 481, 561)

The Collegiate Peaks are a spectacular group of mountains in the Sawatch Range found to the south of the Holy Cross and Mount Massive Wilderness Areas. This group of peaks is also the namesake for the third largest wilderness area in Region 2 containing 167,994 acres of land and over 100 miles of trails. Eight of the peaks within the wilderness area are over 14,000 feet in elevation, forming a spectacular skyline above the Arkansas River valley. If you drive south from Buena Vista to Salida along Highway 285 during the summer, you will likely see countless cars pulled over on the shoulder of the road as travelers record the scenery with film, video, and paint. GMUs 48, 56, 481, and 561 cover the Collegiate Peaks and a larger area to the south of the wilderness area. These four GMUs make up the Cottonwood Creek deer herd with a population that varies around 5,000 to 6,000 animals. The same GMUs make up the Collegiate Peaks elk herd with a current population of 2,470 animals and a strong bull-to-cow ratio of 37 to 100 in recent years.

Mountain goat hunters will want to take special interest in the Collegiate Peaks. The following five goat units cover the area: G13, G3, G2, G14, and G1. (Note that G13 is also referred to as G3N in the hunting regulations). Other than G7, Unit G13 offered more resident licenses in previous years than any other unit. There was also a substantial harvest of 28 rams and 14 ewes taken in G13 during 2001. Combined, there were 67 rams and ewes taken from these five units in 2001, accounting for nearly 40 percent of the total mountain goat harvest in the state. Bighorn sheep hunters should also take interest in this part of the state. Sheep Units S11, S17 (also known as S11S) and S20 cover the area. Several tags are available in these three units and 12 sheep were harvested from them in 2001.

If you choose to hunt this part of the state for goats or sheep you will be taking on a great challenge. This is truly rugged country, as rugged as anything you will come across while hunting the same species in the far north. With several thousand feet of vertical relief, sheer cliffs, huge talus fields, and year-round snowpack, this area defines the word challenge. I don't mean this to be a deterrent to interested hunters; I just want to be clear that this area is for serious, well-conditioned, and well-prepared hunters. If you are one of the fortunate few to get a tag for goats or sheep in this area, and you meet the challenge by taking one of these trophy animals, it will be one of the most rewarding hunts available in the state.

Due to the high elevations in the Collegiate Range there are large tracts of alpine tundra surrounded by subalpine forest. Large alluvial fans buffet the peaks on the east side and form highly dissected hills running down to the Arkansas River valley. This area is largely pinon-juniper woodlands and makes a good locale to spot-and-stalk mule deer. Most of the land in the river bottom is private, with numerous ranches and hay meadows. With all of the recreational opportunities in the valley (e.g. whitewater rafting) the greater public has discovered the area. As a result, there is a lot of new development in the valley and the land surrounding the river. Luckily, there are state lands in the hills and plenty of public land in the national forest for big game hunters to access.

The town of Buena Vista is located in Chaffee County and sits below the Collegiate Peaks next to the Arkansas River. There aren't many other towns in the state that can boast such scenic wonder. It makes a good jumping-off point to access

The Collegiate Range from the Arkansas River Valley.

The author with a 5x6 bull taken in Unit 56 in the Collegiate Peaks.

the Collegiate Peaks Wilderness Area and the high mountain peaks within the San Isabel National Forest to the south of the wilderness area. From Buena Vista you can travel Cottonwood Pass Road (County Road 306) west all the way over the continental divide and drop down into Taylor Park. Leaving Buena Vista to the north on Highway 24 will take you to numerous county roads that access trailheads. South from Buena Vista on 285 also accesses numerous county roads that will lead into the national forest. County Road 162 takes you west along Chalk Creek between Mount Princeton and Mount Antero. There are numerous trailheads and jeep trails off this road, and you can follow Chalk Creek past St. Elmo along the Tin Cup Pass Road over the continental divide. A good Colorado Atlas and the Gunnison Surface Management Status BLM Map will be helpful when trying to scout this area.

I bowhunted for elk in GMU 56 during the 2000 hunting season. Although this is a limited unit for archery, I was able to draw the tag without any preference points. This unit generally has low success rates for bowhunters as indicated by past statistics where only eight to 10 percent of the bowhunters took an elk. Still, there are plenty of elk in this area, and some excellent bulls to boot. I had never hunted the unit before and actually used information I compiled for this book to help me scout. After finding a good area with elk in the summer, I concentrated on that area during the archery season and ended up taking a nice 5x6 bull on public land. This is beautiful country to hunt, but much of the terrain is extremely steep. There are also a lot of off-road enthusiasts who use the jeep trails. I would recommend this area to anybody who is up for a good challenge.

Taylor Park (GMUs 55, 551)

South of the Maroon Bells Snowmass Wilderness and west of the Collegiate Peaks Wilderness is an area known as Taylor Park. Living in Gunnison for several years gave me the opportunity to hunt and fish this area extensively. Taylor Park Reservoir (as a map reference) is located centrally within GMU 55 in Gunnison County. GMUs 55 and 551 make up the Taylor River deer herd with a population that has been steadily near 5,500 animals over the past few years. According to DOW statistics the buck-to-doe ratio for this herd has been 20 bucks for every 100 does in recent years. Although the buck-to-doe ratio isn't especially high, if you're looking for a trophy mule deer this is still a very good area that holds some big bucks. GMUs 55 and 551 also make up the Fossil Ridge elk herd with a population that has varied from about 3,800 to over 4,500 animals in the past few seasons. Fossil Ridge is also the namesake of a small, but significant wilderness area made up of 33,060 acres within the Gunnison National Forest.

Other big game hunting opportunities in the area include bighorn sheep in Unit S26 and mountain goat in Units G8 and G9. There is a small herd of mountain goats in the Henry Mountain area within the Fossil Ridge Wilderness Area. During the 2001 hunting season there were eight bighorn rams taken in S26 and six mountain goats harvested from G8 and G9 collectively. There is also a very small herd of antelope in GMU 551 known as the Doyleville herd. It has had a population ranging between 130 and 330 animals over the past few years. There are only a few antelope tags available in Unit 551, so you will have to build up preference points for several years if you want to hunt it. Don't overlook the opportunity though, I know a hunter who shot a tremendous Boone and Crockett class buck from the Doyleville herd in 1997. There is also good bear hunting locally in the Taylor Park area.

The area in GMU 55 that makes up Taylor Park is unique in the fact that it is characterized as semi-desert shrubland. This area is much higher in elevation (10,000 feet) than other locales with the same classification. Another unique factor, resulting from the high elevation, is that this island of semi-desert shrubland is surrounded by subalpine forest. More commonly, semi-desert shrublands occupy lower elevations adjacent to montane forest, montane shrublands, or pinon-juniper woodland. The eastern portion of GMU 55, up to the continental divide, consists of large areas of alpine tundra. When hunting this area you can travel from open tracts of sagebrush, through dense subalpine forest, and up above timberline into alpine tundra in a relatively short drive. This means the terrain can vary from open rolling hills to steep wooded mountainsides to rugged alpine terrain with talus fields and year-round snowpack.

As you may have guessed, weather in Taylor Park and the surrounding portions of GMUs 55 and 551 can be quite extreme. Generally, roads will remain open and accessible well into November, but single storm events can close backcountry roads for the rest of the year. These storms may come at any time during the big game hunting seasons. Since there is so much area above 10,000 feet in elevation accessible to vehicle travel, hunters do get stranded by winter storms in this area. Pay attention to weather reports, and move to lower elevations when necessary. As in many other parts of Colorado, the weather will often play a key role in hunter success rates.

Heavy snowfall during the rifle seasons can move the deer and elk to wintering grounds at lower elevations. As an example, the Almont Triangle is a wintering area on the west side of GMU 55 between Crested Butte and Almont. This area is closed to public access from November 15 through March 31 every year. This allows deer, elk, and bighorn sheep a safe haven to make it through the extremely cold winter months in the Gunnison area. However, when heavy snows drive the elk into this area prior to the seasonal closure, it often results in a significant elk harvest for hunters.

If you haven't hunted this area before, you should understand that this is a very popular big game hunting venue in Colorado. In other words, it can be very crowded. I have seen opening days during various rifle seasons when there are literally traffic jams on dirt roads heading into the high country outside of Gunnison. You either need to accept the crowds and learn how to use hunter pressure to your advantage, or plan on expending the effort to get into the backcountry. This may mean backpacking or traveling by horse into remote areas. Don't let the popularity of the area dissuade you from hunting here, though, there are plenty of deer and elk to go around, and this is a beautiful part of Colorado.

There is a lot of BLM and national forest in GMUs 55 and 551, so you will have plenty of country to hunt. There are many ranches in the area as well, so get the Gunnison and Saguache BLM Surface Management Status Maps to help determine public versus private lands. Access to the area is good via Highway 50, which divides GMUs 55 and 551. As discussed in the Collegiate Peaks highlight area, Cottonwood Pass Road from Buena Vista crosses the continental divide and drops down into Taylor Park. From Gunnison to Crested Butte, Highway 135 forms the western boundary of GMU 55. There is good access into GMU 551 from Highway 114 located off of Highway 50 just east of Gunnison. From all of the major paved roads listed above, there are countless county roads and jeep trails that provide access into the backcountry.

A hunter takes aim near Fossil Ridge. (Scott Elnicki)

The Crested Butte area is home to elk and some large mulies.

Hunting Tip

Access the area east of Crested Butte by County Road 738, which takes you by the Crested Butte airport. This will lead you to several jeep trails and pack trails. Numerous creeks feed the East River here. Scout the Brush Creek tributaries and Deer Creek. This is a good elk area and holds a few big muleys, as well. Serious bear hunters should look at the Spring Creek drainage accessible by County Road 744. When I lived in the area there were numerous bear sightings along Spring Creek and the related side tributaries every year. Finally, if you're up to a challenge, try the Crystal Creek drainage within the Fossil Ridge Wilderness Area for elk. Access to this drainage is difficult, but Trail 430 off of County Road 742 from Taylor Canyon will get you close.

The Gunnison Country (GMUs 53, 54, 63)

The area surrounding the town of Gunnison holds exceptional opportunities for big game hunters. Located near the confluence of Tomichi Creek and the Gunnison River, the town of Gunnison is truly a jumping-off point for outdoor enthusiasts. The Gunnison National Forest, West Elk Wilderness Area, Curecanti National Recreation Area/Blue Mesa Reservoir, Black Canyon of the Gunnison, and Crested Butte Ski Area provide a wealth of recreational opportunities. As a side note, if you happen to be looking for prospective colleges to attend, or you have college-aged children who love outdoor pursuits, you should consider Western State College (WSC) in Gunnison. WSC is a relatively small school with a high teacher-to-student ratio and an excellent scholastic reputation.

Although the Gunnison Country represents a larger area to most locals, which includes the Taylor Park area, this highlight area covers big game hunting opportunities in GMUs 53, 54, and 63.

There are a lot of mule deer in the Gunnison area. GMU 54 is known as the West Elk deer herd with a strong population that generally has over 4,000 animals. The Crawford deer herd is made up by GMU 53 and currently has an estimated population of 5,240 animals, and GMU 63 is known as the Fruitland Mesa deer herd with 3,260 animals based on current DOW statistics. Buck-to-doe ratios for these three herds have been 22 to 23 bucks for every 100 does in recent years. I saw some out-

Jim Dawson with a tremendous bull taken with a muzzleloader in the Gunnison Country GMU. (Jim Dawson)

standing bucks taken from these units when I lived in Gunnison in the mid-1980s. Elk numbers are very strong in the three GMUs mentioned above. The Coal Creek/Fruitland Mesa elk herd (GMUs 53 and 63) has had a consistent population of approximately 3,800 animals over the past few years. GMU 54 is known as the Sapinero elk herd with a population that has varied from about 3,800 to 4,500 animals over the past few years. This herd has had a bull-to-cow ratio of 27 to 100 in recent years.

In addition to the exceptional deer and elk hunting in the Gunnison area, there are also limited opportunities to hunt bighorn sheep in Game Management S54. This unit had three ram tags available in 2001 and two were filled. There is also some exceptional bear hunting in GMU 53, 54 and 63. The area just west of Blue Mesa Reservoir on the north side of the Black Canyon of the Gunnison is known as Black Mesa. This area has large tracts of oakbrush and aspen, which make up the best bear habitat in the state.

During a period from 1979 to 1985, a bear survey was conducted by the DOW on Black Mesa in GMU 63 and portions of 53 and 54. A total of 129 bears were captured or handled in their dens during this survey. The study showed that there was a significant increase in bear population over the survey period and the population density was estimated at one bear for every 2.2 square miles. There was also a significant increase in population during the middle of August through September as bears migrated to the area to take advantage of the mast crop from Gambel oak.

Serious bear hunters may want to consider this area, as the survey showed there is ideal bear habitat with a good population density (at least at the time of the survey). There is also a large amount of public land in this part of Colorado. I should also mention that this can be an exceptional area for deer and elk. Bear hunters have a chance to time their hunt with the mast crop to take advantage of the increased number of bears migrating to Black Mesa. If you're interested in obtaining the survey contact the DOW and reference Technical Publication No. 39, *Black Bears of West-Central Colorado*, Thomas Beck, September 1991.

The Gunnison area has very diverse types of habitat, and if you have never been to the area, you may be surprised when you drive into the town of Gunnison. It is situated in a large area of semi-desert shrubland made up primarily of sagebrush. This habitat type is widespread surrounding the Gunnison River valley and Blue Mesa Reservoir. Not far from the town of Gunnison the habitat changes dramatically, and there are large tracts of montane shrubland and forest, as well as subalpine forest at the higher elevations. The terrain is also variable with rolling hills of sagebrush to areas with plateaus, and forested mountains. Some of the off-road trails provide good four-wheel-drive access into remote areas. However, these roads can be treacherous with even a small amount of snow accumulation.

The first year I lived in Gunnison (in 1983) was a severe winter in terms of temperature and snowpack. Snow came early, piled up, and lasted the entire winter. This resulted in mass migrations of deer and elk to lower elevations where they were still unable to meet their dietary needs. What resulted was a significant die off of deer, and to a lesser extent, elk, even with the efforts of the DOW to provide supplemental feed. I would say that this type of winter is the exception rather than the rule for the area. Since that severe winter, snow accumulations have been much more moderate and deer and elk numbers have rebounded.

Gunnison is still known as one of the coldest places in the nation. While I lived there it had the dubious honor of being the coldest town in the U.S. for two years in a row. Many of the mountain communities located in valleys have extremely cold winter temperatures. Cold air from the mountains flows down and accumulates in the valleys. These frigid conditions are most common after the hunting seasons in January and February. In fact, hunting in the Gunnison area during the early seasons can be very comfortable. Daytime temperatures are mild and enjoyable while lows are bearable. As the rifle seasons progress into late October and November, temperatures can decrease dramatically with highs in the 30s and lows in the single digits. Snows will usually hit the high country as early as September, and significant accumulations will start in late October and November.

The Gunnison area is home to numerous cattle operations. These private ranches occupy lands predominantly surrounding the river bottoms, but there is also a great deal of public land. Both BLM and national forest provide hunters the opportunity to access huge areas of quality deer, elk, and bear habitat. The West Elk Wilderness is located in the Gunnison National Forest a mere 15 miles northwest of Gunnison. This is a large wilderness area with over 176,000 acres of land and 200 miles of trails. Access into the east side of the wilderness area can be obtained from County Road 730 north of Gunnison along Ohio Creek. There are a few county roads and jeep trails from 730 that proceed west to the boundary of the wilderness area. Note that some of these roads are closed to public access. You will have to do some scouting. There are also several roads off of State Highway 50 on the north side of Blue Mesa Reservoir that provide access into the southern portion of the wilderness area.

For those of you interested in scouting out the Black Mesa area, exit off of Highway 50 at the Blue Mesa Reservoir Dam. Proceed across the dam on Highway 92 along the north side of the Black Canyon of the Gunnison. This narrow and winding road cuts through large tracts of oakbrush and aspen stands with good views of the Black Canyon. Not only is this a spectacular drive, there are a handful of county roads and jeep trails that will get you onto Black Mesa—look for Roads 717, 719, and 720. The BLM Montrose and Paonia Surface Management Status Maps will provide information concerning public versus private land for this part of Colorado.

Grand Mesa (GMUs 41, 42, 52, 411, 521, 421)

Located in Mesa and Grand Counties, Grand Mesa is a prominent geographic feature in western Colorado. The mesa covers a large area of roughly 1,000 square miles with elevations between 10,000 and 11,000 feet above mean sea level. It is heavily forested with subalpine forest on top surrounded by montane forest and montane shrubland at the lower elevations. At still lower elevations near the Colorado and Gunnison Rivers, the landscape changes dramatically with pinon-juniper woodland. The dense forests on top of the Mesa hide approximately 300 alpine lakes. This area is a sportsman's Disney Land with incredible big game hunting opportunities as well as excellent fishing.

The area is home to one of the largest populations of deer in one geographic area of Region 2. The North Grand Mesa deer herd is defined by GMUs 41, 42, 411, 421, 52, and 521, with a population that has contained approximately 30,000 animals during the past several years. In general, some of the bigger deer herds in the state have relatively low buck-to-doe ratios (less than 15 per 100), but the Grand Mesa herd has had a good population dynamic with 25 bucks for every 100 does in recent years. The herd is further broken down into the South Grand Mesa deer herd made up by GMUs 52, 411, and 521. The most recent deer population in these three units was estimated at 6,580.

The same six units that define the North Grand Mesa deer herd also make up the Grand Mesa elk herd. The DOW estimated that there were 11,670 elk in the herd after the 2001 hunting season. These units also have the distinction of holding the largest number of elk in one geographic area of Region 2. There is also a small, but recognized, antelope herd in GMUs 41, 62, and 411 located to the west of and between the towns of Grand Junction and Delta. This is known as the Delta herd with a nominal population that varies from about 250 to 350 animals. Although it is a relatively small population there were a handful of licenses available on a limited basis during the 2001 season. Sometimes trophy potential can be very good in the smaller herds of antelope and hunters should not overlook these opportunities. Other big game hunting opportunities in the Grand Mesa area include bears and mountain lions. In fact, bear numbers are believed to be very high on the mesa and surrounding area with good lion numbers in the lower country.

*The Grand Mesa area is home to one of the largest
populations of deer in Region 2.*

Elk licenses were unlimited for bulls in the regular rifle seasons during 2001 and the DOW was very liberal with cow licenses. Hunters had a good chance to draw a cow tag with 0 to 2 preference points depending on the unit and season they chose to hunt. As far as harvest rates, most of the units experience rates near the state average ranging from 9 percent to 24 percent, in recent years, depending on unit and season. GMU 521 generally had a slightly higher success rate for elk than the other five units that make up the Grand Mesa elk herd. Again depending on the season, success rates for 521 generally exceeded state averages. Although buck licenses were totally limited starting in 1999 there were more than enough licenses to go around. There are generally more buck licenses than applicants for all six of the units that make up the North Grand Mesa deer herd.

To access Grand Mesa take I-70 to De Beque and head south on County Road 45.50. This winding road will take you through some interesting country and eventually meets Highway 65. You can follow 65 all the way over Grand Mesa to the town of Cedar Edge on the other side. Highway 65 is the main road over the Mesa and the only one that is maintained during the winter (when it's not temporarily closed by blizzards). It passes numerous trailheads and other county roads and jeep trails. Access on to the Mesa can also be gained on county roads from the towns of Collbran on the north side and Paonia on the south side. Grand Mesa receives huge amounts of snow each year. The snowpack can often exceed 10 feet, making the window for backcountry access (without a snowmobile) relatively small. Most years you can plan on vehicle access during the months of June through October.

If you choose to hunt this area be prepared for dark timber on top of the Mesa.

Heavy snows in the fall often trigger mule deer migrations
to lower wintering grounds

Due to the abundant moisture Grand Mesa receives each year, the area is home to thick clouds of mosquitoes. If you hunt the lower elevations off the Mesa there is an abundance of thick oakbrush on relatively steep terrain. The areas outside of the national forest are mostly private. The property around Cedaredge, Orchard City, Paonia, and Delta is mostly oriented towards agriculture. The climate is much more moderate at the lower elevations and the area is known for orchards as well as irrigated cropland. While the town of Paonia has its share of orchards, it is also an active coal mining area. Mining companies control much of the land between Paonia and the national forest to the north. On the north side of Grand Mesa the area surrounding the town of Collbran is primarily used for cattle ranching and related feed production.

This part of the state holds fond memories for me. I took my first mule deer while bowhunting a ranch on the edge of Grand Mesa National Forest northeast of the town of Collbran. Three of my friends and I had gotten permission to bowhunt from a local rancher. We didn't know at the time what a sweet deal we had. For $50 each (and a bottle of Jack Daniels) the rancher let us stay in a well-furnished cabin located on the edge of a large hay meadow. When we weren't hunting we fished for the abundant cutthroat trout in the creeks and streams in the area. I built a brush blind on the edge of the meadow in the scrub oak not far from a prominent game trail. It was hit or miss hunting. If the animals entered or left the meadow on the trail you were set up on, you might get a shot. If they came into a different part of the meadow you were forced to sit and watch the animals feeding out of bow range until dark.

I had a small buck enter the meadow near my blind one September evening. He fed leisurely until he was standing broadside only 25 yards below me. The deer remained unaware of my presence as I got the bow to full draw. I took careful aim and thought the deer was mine. I neglected to compensate for the steep downhill shot, though, and I was incredulous as my arrow sailed right over the buck's back. The wind was in my favor and the buck never got my scent. He wasn't very spooked and only took a few short bounds into the corner of the meadow. After surveying the area for several minutes he resumed feeding and eventually came to a place where I had positioned a rock as a marker at 35 yards (the limit of my effective shooting range at the time). The deer was actually standing over the rock when I finally took the second shot and the arrow found its mark. Although the deer was only a 2x2, he was a beautiful buck in velvet and the hunt still stands out as an exceptional memory.

My friends and I were able to hunt the spot for three years. Unfortunately, the rancher passed away unexpectedly and his son started charging large amounts of money to hunt the property. Thus seems to be the trend with hunting in Colorado. When people have quality hunting opportunities on their property, they generally take advantage of it. After all, it is a resource and I don't begrudge them at all for trying to make some money from it. Especially if they also take steps to increase the quality of habitat on their property. Don't be discouraged, though, if you don't have thousands of dollars to hunt private land. Besides the abundance of quality big game hunting on public land in this part of Region 2, there are still a few generous landowners that have chosen to share the state's wildlife. If you can find these rare individuals you will have found the proverbial diamond in the rough. Treat them and their land with respect, and you may have a great place to hunt for many seasons to come.

Uncompahgre Plateau (GMUs 61, 62)

Another important geographic feature to big game hunters in western Colorado is the Uncompahgre Plateau. This area is covered by GMUs 61 and 62 and consists of large tracts of public land. The flat-topped mountains of the plateau are bounded on the east by the Uncompahgre and Gunnison Rivers and the west by the Dolores and San Miguel Rivers. For map reference, Highway 50 runs north and south from the town of Delta along the river valleys to the east of the Plateau. The south is bounded by Highway 62 between Ridgway and Placerville. Highways 145 and 141 form a western boundary, and Highway 141 also forms the northern boundary through Unaweep Canyon east from Gateway.

Most attractive to hunters in this area is a huge deer herd, considerable elk herd, good mountain lion and bear hunting, and one of only two units in the state that offers limited licenses for desert bighorns. The Uncompahgre deer and elk herds are both defined by the geographic area made up by GMUs 61 and 62. The deer population has grown from 28,922 in 1999 to 37,000 in 2001. The elk population has also grown from an estimate of 7,743 in 1999 to over 9,000 animals after the 2001 hunting season. Nine precious desert bighorn sheep tags were available in 2001 in Sheep Units S62 and S64. For predators, there is ideal habitat for bears in the abundant scrub oak areas in the lower reaches of the plateau. The pinon-juniper and canyon country combined with a large deer population also translates into a high mountain lion population density.

The word plateau may connote a high region of flat or level ground, but don't let the word mislead you. The terrain on the plateau and surrounding area is steep and rugged in certain locations. Numerous side canyons cut into the plateau on the east and west with sidewalls made up of sheer cliffs in numerous areas. In terms of habitat, this is another part of the state with a tremendous amount of vertical relief resulting in several ecosystems at different elevations. The river valleys surrounding the plateau have elevations in the 5,000- to 6,000-foot range. These areas make up important riparian systems, where agriculture hasn't altered the natural landscape. The east and west sides of the Uncompahgre Plateau consist of large tracts of pinon-juniper woodland. As the elevation increases above 8,000 feet there is a change to montane shrubland with an abundance of Gambel oak and mountain mahogany. Surrounded by the shrublands is an elongate island of montane forest which trends southeast to northwest along the higher elevations of the plateau.

The weather is generally mild, with relatively hot temperatures in the early seasons. Bowhunters will commonly experience highs in the 70s and even low 80s in September. Mild weather often lasts well into the rifle seasons in October. As a usual caveat, be prepared for extreme changes in temperature and weather. Winter storms can and do occasionally hit the area hard during the various hunting seasons. Many of the dirt roads are made up of fine-grained, clay soils that turn into slick mud with the slightest precipitation. Be prepared for bad road conditions. Always travel with a shovel and a good jack. A winch or come-along is a plus, but at a minimum keep a tow rope handy in case you need a pull out of a mud hole.

Since all deer licenses became limited starting with the 1999 hunting season, you will have to apply for a tag to hunt deer in either GMU 61 or 62. Prior to this change in season structure deer licenses were already limited in GMU 61. With such a large population of deer it will be interesting to see how the DOW decides to manage the Uncompahgre herd considering the relatively low buck-to-doe ratio. This will likely be an area where they try to bolster buck numbers. This could have an effect on the number of buck tags available for the area. Elk licenses are also completely limited in GMU 61 (at this time), and it will take several years to accumulate enough preference points to hunt this unit for bulls regardless of what season you choose. If your primary goal is to harvest an elk for meat, you will have better odds drawing a cow tag in GMU 61 depending on the season and year. In general, hunter success rates are at state averages or higher in GMU 62 and much higher in GMU 61. Although it will take several years to get that bull tag in GMU 61, this is another good area to build preference points. If you're fond of the area, hunt 62 in the off years as a second choice until you accumulate enough points for a tag in 61.

If you are curious about the origin of the word Uncompahgre, it comes from the Ute Indians who had (and still have) a strong presence in this part of Colorado. According to Borneman and Lampert in *A Climbing Guide to Colorado's Fourteeners* (1978), the word Uncompahgre means hot water spring. The word has been widely used as a place name in southwestern Colorado. Uncompahgre Peak is found within the Uncompahgre Wilderness Area (which is located to the southeast of the Uncompahgre Plateau) within the Uncompahgre National Forest.

The Uncompahgre Plateau has a diverse ecosystem, from sheer cliffs to riparian systems to pinon-juniper woodlands.

Region 2 Hub Cities

Grand Junction is the largest city in western Colorado with a population over 40,000. It is located at the boundaries of Region 1 and 2 not far from the Utah state line. If you are traveling into Colorado by air, the Grand Junction airport is a full service airport that receives direct flights from many cities, and numerous transfers from Denver and other western hubs. If you are hunting in GMUs 30, 31, 40, or 41, Grand Junction will make a good base of operations. It is a sportsman friendly community with a variety of accommodations too numerous to list, and all of the services a big game hunter will need. If you desire more information on Grand Junction, please contact the chamber of commerce at (970) 242-3214.

Grand Junction
Population — 41,986 · Elevation — 4,597'

Grand Junction is the largest city on the western slope of Colorado. It is located at the confluence of the Gunnison and Colorado Rivers and is surrounded by thousands of acres of public land. With a commercial airport, many hunters avoid the five-hour drive from Denver and fly straight in.

For those people hunting in the Grand Mesa National Forest or the Uncompahgre National Forest, Grand Junction will make a good starting point. The community can provide any service a big game hunter will require. There are also several outfitters who operate out of Grand Junction and the surrounding communities if you would like some assistance on your hunt. If you've filled your tags early and have some extra time, check out the Colorado National Monument when you're in the area.

ACCOMMODATIONS
Best Western Horizon, (970)245-1410, 800-544-3782, (970)245-4039, Indoor pool, hot tub, pets OK, comp continental breakfast

Best Western Sandman, (970)243-4150, Outdoor pool, hot tub, fridge

Budget Host Inn, (970)243-6050 800-888-5736 ,Outdoor pool, microwave, fridge, dataport phones, cable TV, guest laundry, in-room coffee maker, pets OK.

Days Inn of Grand Junction, (970)245-7200, (800)790-2661, (970)243-6709, Suites, outdoor pool, restaurant, fridge, microwave, hair dryers, in-room coffee maker, dataport phones, guest laundry, cable TV, USA Today, pets OK.

Holiday Inn Grand Junction, (970)243-6790, (888) 489-9796, (970)243-6790 Indoor and outdoor pools, hot tub, suites, restaurant, lounge, fridge, pets OK

LaQuinta Inn & Suites, (970)241-2929, (800) 531-5900, (970)241-2999, Suites, outdoor pool, hot tub, fridge, microwave, complimentary continental breakfast, pets OK

Super 8 Motel, (970)248-8080, (800) 800-8000, (970) 243-4522, Outdoor pool, fridge, microwave, pets OK.

Comfort Inn, 750 Horizon Drive, (970) 245-3335, 230 rooms

Days Inn, 733 Horizon Drive, (970) 245-7200, 108 rooms, Dogs allowed for a fee
Timbers Motel, 1810 North Avenue, (970) 245-7275, 28 rooms
Travelers Inn, 704 Horizon Drive, (970) 245-3080, 125 rooms

BED AND BREAKFAST

The Cider House B and B, 1126 Grand Avenue, (970) 242-9087, Innkeeper: Helen Mills

CAMPING

Junction West RV Park, 55 spaces, (970) 245-8531, Store, laundromat, showers, dump station, pets allowed.

KOA Campground of Grand Junction, 3238 East I-70 Business Loop, (970) 434-6644, 134 sites, Showers, groceries, and game room

Rose Park RV Campground, 2910 North Avenue, (970) 243-1292, 25 RV sites

RESTAURANTS

Bob and Jan's Prime Rib and Lobster House, 2500 North Avenue, (970) 243-6213, Open 11AM–10PM for lunch and dinner, Great food

The Crystal Cafe and Bake Shop, 314 Main Street,(970) 242-8843

Village Inn, 1910 North Avenue, (970) 243-5467, Open 24 hours

Bennett's Bar-B-Que & Steaks, 2440 US Hwy 6&50 (Mesa Mall), (970) 256-7427, Su-Th 11am-9pm; F-Sam 11am-10pm

Chelsea London Pub & Grill, Mesa Mal,l (970) 245-9767, 11am-10pm; M-W; 11am-midnight Th-Sa; 12pm-8pm

Wrigley Field Restaurant & Sports Bar, 1810 North Ave, (970) 245-9010, 10am-midnight daily

Dolce Vita Restaurant 336 Main, (970) 242-8482 M-F 11-10pm; Sa 11:30-10pm

Pantuso's Restaurant & Lounge, 2782 Crossroads Blvd., (970) 243-0000, 11:30am-1:30pm M-F; 4:30pm-10pm nightly

Dos Hombres Restaurant, 421 Brach Dr. (Redlands) (970) 242-8861, 11a-10p daily

Outback Steakhouse, 2432 Hwy 6 & 50, (970) 257-7550, 4p - 10pm M-Th; 4pm - 11pm F; 3pm - 11pm Sa; 2pm - 9pm Sun

The Winery Restaurant , 642 Main St., (970) 242-4100, 4:30p-10p daily

GB Gladstone's , 2531 N 12th St, (970) 241-6000, 11am-10pm M-Sa; 11am-9pm Su

SPORTING GOODS

B & H Sports, 599 Northgate Drive, (970) 245-6605
Gart Brothers Sports, 2424 Hwy 6 & 50, (970) 241-7977
Gene Taylor's Sporting Goods, 445 West Gunnison Avenue, (970) 242-8165
Outdoor Sports, 507 30 Rd #4, Grand Junction, Co 81504 , (970) 245-1502
Sportsman's Warehouse, 2464 US Hwy 6 & 50, (970) 243-8100

HOSPITALS

Community Hospital, 2021 North12th Street, (970) 242-0920
St. Mary's Hospital, 2635 North7th Street, (970) 244-2273

TAXIDERMISTS

MEAT PROCESSORS

Quality Meat Co, (970) 242-1872, 340 North Ave, Grand Junction, CO
Old World Meat Co, (970) 245-2261, 1755 Main St, Grand Junction, CO

AIRPORTS

Walker Field Airport, 2828 Walker Field Drive, Grand Junction, (970) 244-9100, About 40 miles north of Delta, United Express: 800-241-6522, Continental: (970) 243-8424, Sky West: (970) 242-5365, 800-453-9417, Delta: 800-221-1212, American West Express: 800-235-9292

AUTO RENTAL

Budget Rent-A-Car, 2828 Walker Field Drive, (970) 244-9155
National Car Rental, Walker Field, (970) 243-6626
Sears Rent-A-Car, 2828 Walker Field Drive, (970) 244-9157

AUTO SERVICE

Advanced Automotive, 2493 West Mesa Ct, (970) 242-0580
Bear Automotive Service Inc., 1315 Pitkin Avenue, (970) 245-2585
Ken's Auto Repair, 1801 I-70 Business Loop #C-2, (970) 241-6062

LOCKSMITH

Simmon's Lock and Key Inc., 322 South 2nd Street, (970) 242-5562

FOR MORE INFORMATION

Grand Junction Chamber of Commerce, 360 Grand Avenue, Grand Junction, CO 81501, (970) 242-3214

Buena Vista

Population — 2,040 • Elevation — 7,955'

Buena Vista (Spanish for "good view") is a picturesque town located at the base of the Collegiate Peaks next to the Arkansas River. Hunters interested in hunting in the San Isabel National Forest either to the east or west of town will do well to make Buena Vista a base of operations. County Road 306 (known as Cottonwood Pass Road) begins in Buena Vista and proceeds west over the continental divide and into Taylor Park (GMU 55). Not only a spectacular drive, this road skirts the southern boundary of the Collegiate Peaks Wilderness Area and provides access into a lot of excellent big game hunting country.

Strategically located south of Leadville and north of Salida, Buena Vista will be a good choice for hunters pursuing game in GMUs 49, 57, and especially 481. It is also a great town for outdoor enthusiasts in general. There is quality fishing in the Arkansas River and surrounding lakes as well as whitewater rafting, plus all kinds of backcountry pursuits during each season.

ACCOMMODATIONS

Adobe Inn, 303 Hwy. 24 N., (719) 395-6340
Alpine Lodge, 123845 Hwy. 24 and 285, (719) 395-2415
Arkansas Valley Adventure Cabins, 40671 Hwy. 24 N., (719) 395-2338
Blue Sky Inn, 719 Arizona, (719) 395-8862
Cottonwood Springs Inn and Health Spa, 18999 County Rd. 306, (719) 395-6434
Forest Creek Cabins, 16115 County Rd. 306, (719) 395-4819
Great Western Sumac Lodge, 428 Hwy. 24 S., (719) 395-8111
Lakeside Motel, 112 W. Lake, (719) 395-2994
Mountain View Motel, 406 Hwy. 24 N., (719) 395-8665
Pinon Court Motel, 227 Hwy. 24 N., (719) 395-2433
Silver Wheel Motel, Hwy 24 S., (719) 395-2955
Super 8 Motel, 530 Hwy 24 N., (719) 395-8888
Thunder Lodge, 207 Brookdale Ave., (719) 395-2245
Topaz Lodge, Main St. and Hwy. 24, (719) 395-2427
Trout City Inn, 7600 County Rd. 307, (719) 395-8433
Vista Court Cabins and Lodge, 1004 W. Main St., (719) 395-6557
Vista Inn, 733 Hwy. 24, (719) 395-8009
Woodland Brook Cabins, 226 S. San Juan, (719) 395-2922

CAMPGROUNDS AND RV PARKS

Collegiate Peaks Family Inn and RV Park, 516 Hwy. 24 N., (719) 395-2251
Arkansas River Rim Campground, 33198 Hwy. 24 N., (719) 395-8883
Buena Vista KOA, 27700 County Rd. 303, (719) 395-8318
Crazy Horse Camping and Cabin Resort, 33975 Hwy 24 N., (719) 395-2323
Mt Princeton Mobile Home and RV Park, 30380 County Rd. 383, (719) 395-6206
State Park Camping Reservations, 800-678-CAMP
Forest Services Camping Reservations, 877-444-6777

RESTAURANTS

Buffalo Bar and Grill, 710 Hwy. 24 N., (719) 395-6472
Casa Del Sol, 333 N Hwy 24, (719) 395-8810
Dinner Bell Café, 12985 Hwy. 24 and 285, (719) 395-2996
Elkhorn Woodfired Grill, 301 E. Main St., (719) 395-2231
Gunsmoke Café, 12950 Hwy. 24 and 285, (719) 395-2725
Jan's Restaurant, 304 Hwy. 24 S., (719) 395-6940
Paradise Restaurant, 708 Hwy. 24 S., (719) 395-9289
The Raspberry Patch, 218 E. Main St., (719) 395-4481
Shang Hai, 527 W. Lake, (719) 395-4950

VETERINARIANS

Buena Vista Veterinary Clinic, 30400 Hwy. 24 N., (719) 395-8239

SPORTING GOODS, GUNS, AND GUNSMITHS

Coast to Coast, 401 Hwy. 24 N., (719) 395-8067
Hi-Rocky Gift and Sport Store, 111 Cottonwood Ave., (719) 395-2258
The Trailhead, 707 Hwy. 24 N., (719) 395-8001

TAXIDERMISTS

Old West, Hwy. 24, (719) 395-2387

AUTO REPAIR/RENTAL

Foreman Sales and Service, 222 Hwy. 24 S., (719) 395-2902
Gunsmoke Truck Stop, 12916 Hwy. 24 and 285, (719) 395-2833
Swisher Automotive and Diesel, 31455 Hwy. 24 N., (719) 395-6461
Crazy Horse Jeep Rentals, 33976 Hwy. 24 N., (719) 395-2323

AIR SERVICE

Buena Vista Municipal Airport, 27960 County Rd. 319, (719) 395-2496

MEDICAL

Mountain Medical Center, 36 Oak Street, (719) 395-8632

FOR MORE INFORMATION

Buena Vista Chamber of Commerce, 343 Hwy. 24 South,
Buena Vista, CO 81211, (719) 395-6612

Gunnison

Population — 5,102 • Elevation — 7,703'

One of my favorite places in western Colorado is Gunnison, the home of Western State College. Predominantly an agricultural and college town, Gunnison also has a rich mining history. For those of you interested in hunting GMUs 54, 55, 551, 66, or 67, Gunnison will make a good base of operations. The community welcomes hunters and relies on the annual revenue that this seasonal activity brings each year. Any service a hunter could possibly need is available in Gunnison from sporting goods, outfitters, taxidermists, meat processors, lodging, food, and an airport. If you're in need of sporting goods or licenses, stop in at Gene Taylor's. They have everything you will need and more.

When you're in the area take some time to stop by the Crested Butte Chamber of Commerce, where the former world-record bull elk is on display. (The town of Crested Butte is 28 miles north of Gunnison.) John Plute took this massive bull west of Crested Butte in 1899. After changing hands several times, the antlers were finally scored in the 1950s. Finally in 1961, Boone and Crockett certified the antlers as the world-record bull elk with an incredible score of 442 3/8. This record stood well into the 1990s, and in my opinion, the antlers are still more impressive than any other rack I have seen to date. I like to believe that the genetics from this bull may still survive in a few of the elk that currently inhabit the area. Who knows, maybe you will run into a descendant of this great bull if you choose to hunt the area.

ACCOMMODATIONS

ABC Motel, 121 E. Tomichi, (970) 641-2400
Best Western-Tomichi Village, 41883 Hwy. 50 E., (970) 641-1131
Columbine Victorian Hotel, 136 W. Tomichi, (970) 641-6834
Days Inn, 701 W. Tomichi – Hwy. 50, (970) 641-0608
Econolodge, 37760 Hwy. 50, (970) 641-1000
Holiday Inn Express, 400 E. Tomichi, (970) 641-1288
Hylander Inn, 412 E. Tomichi, (970) 641-0700
Island Acres Motel, 38339 W. Hwy. 50, (970) 641-1442
Jordan Inn/Long's Holiday Motel, 1198 W. Hwy. 50, (970) 641-0536
Mountain View Lodge, 117 N. Taylor, (970) 641-1799
Ramada Limited, 1011 W. Rio Grande, (970) 641-2804
Super 8 Motel, 400 E. Tomichi Ave., (970) 641-3068
Water Wheel Inn, (970) 641-1650, West of Gunnison
Western Motel, 403 E. Tomichi, (970) 641-1722
Wildwood Motel, 1312 W. Tomichi Ave., (970) 641-1663
Almont Resort, 10209 Hwy. 135, Almont, CO (970) 641-4009
Blue Mesa Rec Ranch, (970)-641-5387
Harmel's Ranch Resort, Taylor River Rd., Almont, CO (970) 641-1740
Kreuger Ranch, 6794 Hwy. 114, (970) 901-0558
Lake Fork Resort, 0940 cove Rd., (970) 641-3564
Lazy K Resort, 1415 W. Tomichi Ave., (970) 641-5174

Lost Canyon Resort, 8264 Hwy. 135, (970) 641-0181
Rockey River Resort, 4359 County Rd. 10, (970) 641-0174
Shady Island Resort, 2776 Hwy. 135, (970) 641-0416
Spring Creek Resort, (970) 641-0217
Three Rivers Resort, Almont, CO (888) 761-3474
Waunita Hot Springs Ranch, 8007 County Rd. 887, (970) 641-1266
White Pine Ranch, 7500 County Rd. 887, (970) 641-6410
White Water Resort, County Rd. 742, Almont, CO (970) 641-1713

CAMPGROUNDS AND RV PARKS

KOA Kampground, (970) 641-1358
Ley-Z-B at Sapinero, 1620 Hwy. 50, (970) 641-2340
Mesa Campground, 36128 W. Hwy. 50, (970) 641-3186
Tall Texan Campground, 2460 hwy. 135, (970) 641-2927
State Park Camping Reservations 800-678-CAMP
Forest Services Camping Reservations 877-444-6777

RESTAURANTS

Blue Iguana, 303 E. Tomichi Ave., (970)-641-3403
Cattlemen Inn, 301 E. Tomichi Ave., (970) 641-1061
Firebrand, 108 N. Main St., (970) 641-6266
Garlic Mikes, 2674 N. Hwy. 135, (970) 641-2493
Gunnison Valley Bakery, 728 North Main, (970) 641-0381
House of China, 405 W. Tomichi, (970) 641-0667
Josef's Restaurant, 41883 E. Hwy 50, (970) 641-5032
Mario's Pizzaria, 213 W. Tomichi, (970) 641-1374
Trough, 1-mile west of Gunnison, (970) 641-3724

VETERINARIANS

Gunnison Veterinary Clinic, 98 County Rd 17, (970) 641-0460
Tomichi Animal Hospital, 106 S. 11th St., (970) 641-2460
Town and Country Animal Hospital, 1525 Hwy. 135, (970) 641-2215

SPORTING GOODS, GUNS, AND GUNSMITHS

All Sports Replay, 115 W. Georgia Ave., (970) 641-1893
Berfield's Stage Stop, 519 W. Tomichi Ave., (970) 641-5782
Eflin Sports, 701 N. Main St., (970) 641-6640
Gene Taylor's Sportsman's Supply, 201 W. Tomichi Ave., (970) 641-1845
Gunnison Sporting Goods, 133 E. Tomichi Ave., (970) 641-5022
High Mountain Drifters, 115 S. Wisconsin, (970) 641-4243
Rock 'N Roll Sports, 608 W. Tomichi Ave., (970) 641-9150
Traders Rendezvous, 516 W. Tomichi Ave., (970) 641-5077

MEAT PROCESSORS

Berfield's Stage Stop, 519 W. Tomichi Ave., (970) 641-5782

AUTO REPAIR/RENTAL

Duncan 4x4, 811 N. Main St., (970) 641-4444
H&H Towing and Auto Repair, 901 W. New York Ave., (970) 641-2628
John Marzolf Automotive, 212 W. Hwy 50, (970) 641-0051
John Roberts Motor Works, 231 W. Tomichi Ave., (970) 641-0920
Monty's Auto Parts, 223 W. Hwy. 50, (970) 641-1282
Precision Automotive, 510 A. W. Hwy. 50, (970) 641-4040
Standard Tire, 412 W. Tomichi Ave., (970) 641-0202
Tomichi Tire and Towing, 1-mile east of Gunnison, (970) 641-2314
Budget Rent-A-Car, 711 Rio Grande Ave., (970) 641-4403

AIR SERVICE

Alpine Express, Gunnison County Airport, (970) 641-5074

MEDICAL

Gunnison Valley Hospital, 711 N. Taylor St., (970) 641-1456

FOR MORE INFORMATION

Gunnison County Chamber of Commerce, 500 E. Tomichi Ave.,
Gunnison, CO 81230, (970) 641-1501

Black Canyon of the Gunnison.

Leadville
Population — 2,909 • Elevation — 10,152'

Leadville is famous for many reasons, but what immediately stands out is the elevation of the city – 10,152 feet. It is the highest city in the United States. At such an elevation summers are short and winters are long and cold, but that doesn't seem to bother the residents. It's easy to understand why people are drawn to Leadville when you take in the incredible alpine scenery that surrounds this historic mining community. Located in Lake County, Leadville is surrounded by the San Isabel National Forest. The Mosquito Range rises above the town to the east and the continental divide zigzags to the north and west. Just west of town are the Holy Cross and Mount Massive Wilderness Areas. Located in GMU 49, which is known as a trophy deer and elk area with high elk harvest success rates, Leadville has all of the services big game hunters require. If you're interested in mining heritage visit the National Mining Hall of Fame and Museum when you're in Leadville.

ACCOMMODATIONS

Timberline Motel, 216 Harrison Ave., (800) 352-1876
Apple Blossom Inn, 120 W. 4th St., (719) 486-2141
Avalanche Motel, 231 Elm St., (719) 486-0881
Columbine Inn and Suites, Hwy. 24, (719) 486-5650
Delaware Hotel, 700 Harrison Ave., (719) 486-1418
Hitchin Post Motel, 3164 N. Hwy. 91, (719) 486-2783
Longhorn Motel, 1515 Poplar St., (719) 486-3155
Mountain Peaks Motel, Harrison Ave., (719) 486-3178
Pan-Ark Lodge, 5827 Hwy. 24, (719) 486-1063
Silver King Motor Inn, 2020 N. Poplar St., (800) 871-2610

CAMPGROUNDS AND RV PARKS

Sugar Loaf'n Campground, 2665 County Rd. 4, (719) 486-1031
State Park Camping Reservations 800-678-CAMP
Forest Services Camping Reservations 877-444-6777

RESTAURANTS

Tennessee Pass Cookhouse, Ski Cooper at Leadville, (719) 486-1750
Buckeye Creek Restaurant, 4039 hwy. 91, (719) 486-2276
Columbine Café, 612 Harrison Ave., (719) 486-3599
Golden Burro Café and Lounge, 710 Harrison Ave., (719) 486-1239
Grill Bar and Café, 715 Elm St., (719) 486-9930
La Cantina Restaurant, 1942 Hwy. 24, (719) 486-9021
Matilda's Café, 323 E 4th St., (719) 486-1071
Mountain High Picnic Basket, 115 E. 5th St., (719) 486-9555
Old Glory Café, 222 Harrison Ave., (719) 486-8432
The Pizzeria, 715 Harrison Ave., (719) 486-0873
Quincys, 416 Harrison Ave., (719) 486-9765

Szechuan Taste II, 500 Harrison Ave., (719) 486-0484
Wild Bill's Hamburgers and Ice Cream, 200 Harrison Ave., (719) 486-0533

Veterinarians

Leadville Veterinary Clinic, Front St., and Dexter St., (719) 486-1487

Sporting Goods, Guns, and Gunsmiths

Charter Sports, 325 S. Main St., (970) 476-7517
Bill's Sport Shop, 225 Harrison Ave., (719) 486-0739
Buckhorn Sporting Goods, 616 Harrison Ave., (719) 486-3944
Melanzana Outdoor Clothing, 609 Harrison Ave., (719) 486-3246
Otto's Coast To Coast Hardware, 1902 Poplar St., (719) 486-2220

Auto Repair

Bart's Auto Repair Center, 201 Harrison Ave., (719) 486-1277
Cloud City Amoco, 2009 N. Poplar, (719) 486-2812
Coldfoot Foreign Car Repairs, 121 E. 3rd St., (719) 486-3907
K-F Auto Service and Repair, 1719 Poplar St., (719) 486-3008
Mike's Starter Alternator and Auto Repair, 300 Poplar St., (719) 486-9263

Medical

St. Vincent General Hospital, 822 W. 4th St., (719) 486-0230

For More Information

Leadville Chamber of Commerce, 809 Harrison Ave., Leadville, CO 80461
(719) 486-3900

Salida

Population — 5,517 • Elevation — 7,036'

Salida is strategically located where the boundaries of GMUs 56, 57, and 86 come together. The area immediately surrounding Salida is home to large numbers of deer and elk. There is also excellent mountain lion hunting to be had locally. There is an abundance of public land in the area, and good access into the San Isabel National Forest is available not far from town. All of the services a big game hunter will require are available in Salida, and it's a nice place to stay with its location adjacent to the Arkansas River.

If you plan to stay in Salida take some time to visit my friends Brad and Stan Love at Western Archery located on the west side of town near the fairgrounds. The business has been in their family for over 80 years. In 1994 Brad and Stan moved the business from Denver to Salida. Not only do they provide a full service archery pro shop and bow range; they also manufacture a popular line of sporting goods under the name Vista Products.

ACCOMMODATIONS

Apple Grove Motel, 192 W Rainbow Blvd., (719) 539-4722
Aspen Leaf Lodge, 7350 W US Hwy 50, (719) 539-6733
Budget Lodge, 1146 E US Hwy 50, (719) 539-6695
Circle R Motel, 304 E US Hwy 50, (719) 539-6296
Colorado Lodge Best Western, 352 W Hwy 50, (719) 539-2514
Comfort Inn, 315 E US Hwy 50, (719) 539-5000
Econo Lodge, 1310 E US Hwy 50, (719) 539-2895
Holiday Inn Express, 7400 W US Hwy 50, (719) 539-8500
Monarch Mountain Lodge, 22720 W US Hwy 50, (719) 539-2581
Poncha Lodge, 10520 W US hwy 50 and Hwy 285, (719) 539-6085
Motel Vidal, 8284 US Hwy 50, Howard, CO, (719) 942-3441
Rainbow Inn, 105 E US Hwy 50, (719) 539-4444
Ranch House Lodge, 5745 W US Hwy 50, (719) 539-6655
Redwood Lodge, 7310 W US Hwy 50, (719) 539-2528
Rocky Mountain Lodge and Cabins, 446 E US Hwy 50, Poncha Springs, (719)-539-6008
Silver Ridge Lodge, 545 US Hwy 50, (719) 539-2553
Super 8 Motel, 525 W US Hwy 50, (719) 539-6689
Woodland Motel, 903 W 1st St., (719) 539-4980
Bender's Log Cabin, 320 Ouray, Poncha Springs, (719) 539-4531
Colorado Vacation Homes, 845 Oak St., (719) 539-7211
Pinon Valley Ranch, 8309 Co. Road 250, (719) 539-9370

CAMPGROUNDS AND RV PARKS

Heart of the Rockies Campground, 16105 US Hwy 50, Poncha Springs, (719) 539-4051

State Park Camping Reservations 800-678-CAMP
Forest Services Camping Reservations 877-444-6777

RESTAURANTS

Antero Grill, 14770 US Hwy 285, (719) 530-0301
Crossroads Café, 139-141 W3, (719) 539-3939
Et's Landing, 1015 E US Hwy 50, (719) 539-1519
First Street Café, 137 E 1, (719) 539-4759
Gold Star Bar-B-Que and Beer Garden, 1220 E US Hwy 50, (719) 539-6964
Homestead Café, 11228 W US Hwy 50, Poncha Springs, (719) 539-6072
Il Vicino Wood Oven Pizza and Brewery, 136 E 2nd St., (719) 539-5219
Country Bounty, 413 W. Hwy. 50, (719) 539-3546
LaFrontera Restaurante, 128 N F, (719) 539-7919
Rocky Mountain Restaurant, 11346 W US Hwy 50, (719) 539-5082
Spaghetti Western, 122 N F, (719) 530-9909
Windmill Restaurant, 720 E rainbow Blvd., (719) 539-3594

VETERINARIANS

Aspen Veterinary Practice, (719) 539-2140
Friend's Animal Clinic, 7035 County Rd 210, (719) 539-4362
Mountain Shadows Animal Hospital, 9171 W US Hwy 50, (719) 539-2533
Hutchinson Veterinary Clinic, 9104 US Hwy 50, (719) 539-4093

SPORTING GOODS, GUNS, AND GUNSMITHS

Western Archery Sales, 150 Pahlone Pkwy., Poncha Springs, (719) 539-1295
Salida Sporting Goods, 511 E. Hwy 50, (719) 539-6221
American Outdoor Sports, 645 E Rainbow Blvd., (719) 530-0725
Headwaters Outdoor Equipment, 228 N F, (719) 539-4506
Homestead Sport and Ski, 11238 Hwy 50, Poncha Springs, (719) 539-7507
Shop and Pawn, 116 S F St., (719) 539-7777

TAXIDERMISTS

G&B Taxidermy, 3750 E. Hwy. 50, Swissvale, CO, (719) 530-4609
Amettis Taxidermy (Fish and Birds Only), 807 Poncha Blvd., (719) 539-7576

MEAT PROCESSORS

C&M Processing, 1248 F Street, (719) 539-6489
Perry Patterson Big Game Processing and Taxidermy, 13690 Hwy 291, (719) 530-0234

AUTO REPAIR/RENTAL

A-1 Auto Service, 445 W Rainbow Blvd., (719) 539-7251
Salida Auto Repair and Machine Shop, 118 North E St., (719) 539-4127
Intermountain Engine and Machine, 202 Oak St., (719) 539-4461
Brad's Automotive Repair, 249 F St., (719) 539-3419

Auto Repair/Rental

Johnson's Automotive, Corner 15th and F, (719) 539-6601
Ashley Automotive (Towing) 302 G St., (719) 539-1650
Ford Rent-A-Car, Salida Motors, 943 E US Hwy. 50, (719) 539-6633

Air Service

Salida-Harriet Alexander Field, 9255 County Rd. 140, (719) 539-3720

Medical

Heart of the Rockies Regional Medical Center, 448 East First Street, P.O. Box 429, Salida, CO 81201, (719) 539-6661

For More Information

Heart of the Rockies Chamber of Commerce, 406 West Hwy. 50, Salida, CO 81201, (719) 539-2068

Montrose
Population — 11,149 • Elevation — 5,806'

Located in the Uncompahgre River valley, east of the Uncompahgre Plateau, the town of Montrose is situated perfectly for hunters to pursue the vast numbers of deer and elk in the surrounding game management units. It will make a good jumping-off point for people hunting in GMUs 62, 64, and 65. These units include part of the Uncompahgre deer herd and the Cimarron deer herd. The two herds make up one of the largest and densest populations of deer in the state. Throw in the fact that the same three units also hold part of the Uncompahgre elk herd and the Cimarron elk herd with a combined population of 14,500 animals, and it's easy to understand why so many hunters spend time in this part of the state each year. For those of you lucky enough to fill your tag early, make sure you bring your rods and take advantage of the exceptional fishing in the area. Montrose has a good variety of accommodations and offers a full range of services, including an airport.

Depending on your exact hunting venue you may also want to consider some of the other towns in the area such as Olathe and Delta. Also, those interested in hunting on Grand Mesa may want to look at Orchard City, Cedaredge, Hotchkiss, or Paonia as hub cities.

ACCOMMODATIONS

Inn At The Arrowhead, 1100 E Main #E, (970) 862-8206
Best Western Red Arrow Motor Inn, P.O. Box 236, (970) 249-9641
Black Canyon Motel, 1605 E. Main Street, (970) 249-3495
Blue Fox Motel, 1150 N. Townsend Ave., (970) 249-4595
Country Lodge, 1624 E. Main, (970) 249-4567
Days Inn, 1655 E. Main, (970) 249-3411
El Rancho Lodge, P.O. Box 307, Cimarron, CO, (970) 249-5774
Holiday Inn Express Hotel and Suites, 1391 S. Townsend, (970) 240-1800
Montrose Comfort Inn, 2100 E. Main, (970) 240-8000
Prock Elk Ranch, 22710 Uncompahgre, (970) 249-7828
Red Barn Motel, 1417 E. Main St., (970) 249-4507
San Juan Inn, 1480 S. Townsend, (970) 249-6644
Super 8 Motel, 1705 E. Main St., (970) 249-9294
Trapper Motel, 1225 E. Main, (970) 249-3426
Western Motel, 1200 E. Main St., (970) 249-3481

CAMPGROUNDS AND RV PARKS

Cedar Creek RV Park and Mini Golf, 126 Rose Ln., (970) 249-3884
Ley-Z-B at Sapinero, 16020 Hwy 50, Sapinero, CO, (970) 641-2340
Montrose KOA Campground, 200 N. Cedar Ave., (970) 249-9177
State Park Camping Reservations 800-678-CAMP
Forest Services Camping Reservations 877-444-6777

RESTAURANTS

Backwoods Inn, 103 Rose Lane, (970) 249-1961
Camp Robber Café, 228 E. main St., (970) 240-1590
Casa de Mehas, 710 N. Townsend, (970) 249-9305
Cimarron Inn, (970) 249-6222
Colorado Burger Company, 16367 S. Townsend, (970) 240-9247
Daily Bread of Montrose, 346 Main St., (970) 249-8444
El Sombrero, 82 Rose Ln, (970) 249-0217
Elk ridge Restaurant, 12500 Bostwick Park Rd., (970) 249-5021
Glenn Eyrie Restaurant, (970) 249-9263
Marketa Munoz, (970) 249-8529
Pasta Garden, (970) 249-7896
Red Barn Restaurant and Lounge, 1413 E. Main St., (970) 249-9202
Skura, 411 N. Townsend Ave., (970) 249-8230
Sandtrap Restaurant, 66860 LaPlaza Ct., (970) 249-7369
Sicily's Italian Restaurant, 1135 E. Main St., (970) 240-9199
Starvin' Arvin's of Montrose, 1320 S. Townsend Ave., (970) 249-7787
Stockman's Café and Bar, 320 Main St., (970) 249-9946
The Whole Enchilada, 44S Grand, (970) 249-1881

VETERINARIANS

Alta Vista Animal Hospital, 1845 E. Main St., (970) 249-8185

SPORTING GOODS, GUNS, AND GUNSMITHS

Jeans Westerner, 147 N. 1st, (970) 249-8757
Cimarron Creek, Inc., 317 E. Main St., (970) 249-0408
Carlton Calls and Hunt'n Stuff, P.O. Box 3248, (970) 240-4474
Buck Stop Pawn and Gun, 113 W. Main, (970) 249-0867
Sportsman Surplus Liquidators, 427 N 1, (970) 249-8105
Stop N Save, 2291 S Townsend Ave., (970) 249-5043

TAXIDERMISTS

Big Horn Taxidermy, 1720 6450 Rd, (970) 249-7881
Hunters Taxidermy Center, 1654 Main, Delta, CO (970) 874-5593
Southwest Taxidermy, 1837 6400 Rd., (970) 249-0486
Wildlife Enterprise Taxidermy, 68195 Kinikin Rd., (970) 240-1556

MEAT PROCESSORS

Dave's Processing and Wild Game Meats, 1220 n. Townsend Ave., (970) 249-2228
Hanson's Wild Game Locker, 14272 5875 Rd, (970) 249-1013
Valley Processing, 15541 Shavano Valley Rd., (970) 249-9762

AUTO RENTAL

Budget Rent A Car, 2100 Airport Rd., (970) 249-6083
Enterprise Rent-A-Car, 2940 N. Townsend #B, (970) 240-3835
Thrifty Car Rental, 2100 Airport Rd., (970) 249-8741

AUTO REPAIR

Lionel's Auto Repair, 2171 E. Main St., (970) 249-6070
Midas, 2000 E. Main St., (970) 240-4711
Performance Center, 2488 Woodgate Road, (970) 249-6005
Rainbow Garage, 315 North 1st, (970) 249-3904
Montrose Auto Parts (NAPA), 400 N. Townsend, (970) 249-8074

AIR SERVICE

Montrose County Airport Authority, 2100 Airport Rd., (970) 249-3203

MEDICAL

Montrose Memorial Hospital, 800 S. Third St., (970) 249-2211

FOR MORE INFORMATION

Montrose Chamber of Commerce, 1519 E. Main St., Montrose, CO 81401
(970) 249-5000, Fax (970) 249-2907, 800-923-5515

Fairplay

Population — 512 • Elevation — 9,920'

In a time when many cities across the U.S. have the same architecture, the same strip malls, the same fast food restaurants, and no hint of historic or cultural value, it is refreshing to visit a town with character. If you want the standard McDonalds or a Holiday Inn, don't bother with Fairplay. But if you're looking for a nice place to stay where you can still feel a bit of the history in the air, then Fairplay might be a good choice. It is the county seat of Park County, situated in South Park, and makes a great hub city for people hunting in GMUs 49, 50, or 500.

Fairplay is a historic mining town where rich placer deposits were processed for gold. The huge spoil piles of gravel found in the area still stand as a monument to the once bustling mining town. In addition to the placer deposits, the surrounding mountains were home to numerous underground precious metal mines. The associated communities that evolved around these mines are now mostly ghost towns, but if you want a taste of the old mining days you can stop in at South Park City which is an outdoor museum depicting a late 1800s mining town. On more than one occasion I have sought refuge at the Southpark Lodge after elk hunting in the nearby mountains. This historic hotel has creaky wooden floors and a well-worn bar with friendly patrons and a pleasant atmosphere.

ACCOMMODATIONS

Southpark Lodge, 801 Main St., (719) 836-3278
South Park Motel and RV, 801 Main St., (719) 836-0500
Western Inn Motel and RV Park, 490 W. Hwy 285, (719) 836-2026
American Safari Ranch, Hwy. 285 and County Rd. 7, (719) 836-2431

CAMPGROUNDS AND RV PARKS

Campground of the Rockies, Hwy. 285, (719) 836-2533
State Park Camping Reservations 800-678-CAMP
Forest Services Camping Reservations 877-444-6777

RESTAURANTS

Brown Burro Café, 706 Main St., (719) 836-2804
Como Depot, Como, CO, (719) 836-2594
Friendship Inn, 411 Hwy. 285, (719) 836-4629
Front Street Café, 436 Front St., (719) 836-7031
J-J Bar and Grill, 21980 US Hwy. 285, (719) 836-2729
Park Bar and Grill, 511 Front St., (719) 836-3404
The Ranch At Fairplay, 771 Main St., (719) 836-2789

VETERINARIANS

Alma Animal Clinic, 112 N. Main St., Alma, CO (719) 836-3127
Fairplay Pet Clinic, 730 Main St., (719) 836-2972

SPORTING GOODS, GUNS, AND GUNSMITHS

Even In The End Sporting Goods, 889 Steinfelt Pkwy, (719) 836-2470
Fairplay Trading Post, 1150 Castello Ave., (719) 836-0230

AUTO REPAIR

Beaver Ridge Auto, 15 South Main St., Alma, CO (719) 836-1561
Fairplay Auto Supply, 22077 Hwy. 285, (719) 836-2014
Main Street Garage and Tire Center, 22077 Hwy. 285, (719) 836-0510
Mountain Mechanic, 39329 Hwy. 285, (719) 836-1563
Silverheels Towing, 22077 Hwy. 285, (719) 836-7000

MEDICAL

Silverheels Health Center, 824 Castello, (719) 836-4151

FOR MORE INFORMATION

South Park Chamber of Commerce, (719) 836-3410

Woodland Park
Population — 5,985 • Elevation — 8,437'

Located in Teller County, Woodland Park is the perfect jumping-off point for those interested in hunting the Pikes Peak region. Specifically, hunters with tags for GMUs 511, 581, or 59 should consider this town as a hub city. It has all of the amenities a hunter will require and more. The vast tracts of public land in the Pike National Forest that surround Woodland Park will provide ample opportunities for big game hunters. Those hunters with tags for GMU 59 may also want to consider the historic mining town of Cripple Creek as a hub city. This town is located about 20 miles southwest of Woodland Park (as the crow flies) and offers several hotels and dining establishments that sprang up literally overnight with the legalization of gambling in 1993.

ACCOMMODATIONS

Country Inn, 723 Hwy 24 W, (719) 687-6277
Lofthouse Inn, 222 E. Henrietta, (719) 687-9187
Town and Country Resort, 510 N Hwy 67, (719) 687-9518
Woodland Park Vacation Suites, 316 Hwy 67, (719) 686-0113
Alpine Lake Resort, 4145 Omar Rd., Divide, CO (719) 687-7337
Black Bear Inn of Pikes Peak, 5250 Pikes Peak Hwy, Cascade, CO (719) 684-0151
Eleven Mile Motel, 38122 Hwy 24, lake George, CO (719) 748-3931
Elwell's Guest Cabins, 2220 Lee Circle Dr., (719) 687-9383
Mariposa Cottage, 116 Lake Ave., (719) 527-6778
Rocky Mountain Lodge and Cabins, (719) 684-2421
Woodland Park Lodge, 777 E Hwy 24, (719) 687-5700

CAMPGROUNDS AND RV PARKS

Alpine Lake Resort, 4145 Omar Rd., Divide, CO (719) 687-7337
Campground at Woodland Park, 1125 West Bowman, (719) 687-7575
Colorado Campground, Hwy 67, 5 miles north of Woodland Park, (877) 444-6777
Diamond Campground and RV Park, 900 N. Hwy. 67, (719) 687-9684
Lake George Cabins and RV Park, 8966 County Rd. 90, Lake George, CO
    (719) 748-3822
Town and Country RV Park, 510 N. Hwy 67, (719) 687-9518
State Park Camping Reservations 800-678-CAMP
Forest Services Camping Reservations 877-444-6777

RESTAURANTS

Austin's of Woodland Park, 228 E. Hwy 24, (719) 687-1022
Circle H Smokehouse, 720 Browning, (719) 687-1828
Gold Hill Grill, 609 W. Midland Ave., (719) 687-3118
Grandmother's Kitchen, 212 E. Hwy. 24, (719) 687-3118
JR's Restaurant, 730 E Hwy 24, (719) 687-4406
Paradise Mountain Café, 209 W. Midland Ave., (719) 687-3821
Rocky Mountain Joe's, 10263 Hwy 24 and 67, (719) 686-1500

Tres Hombres, 116½ W. Midland, (719) 687-0625
The Ute Inn, 204-06 W. Midland, (719) 687-1465

VETERINARIANS

Animal Medical Center, 15226 W. Hwy 24, (719) 687-9201
Compassion Animal Hospital, 312 W. Hwy. 24, (719) 687-6000
Woodland Veterinary Clinic, (719) 687-1060

SPORTING GOODS, GUNS, AND GUNSMITHS

Great Outdoor Sporting Goods, 520 W. Midland Ave., (719) 687-0401
Grizzly Firearms, 210 W. Midland Ave., (719) 687-6464
Pikes Peak Polaris and Sporting Goods, 300 W. Hwy. 24, (719) 687-6694

TAXIDERMISTS

Angler's Gallery, (719) 687-8794
Wild West Taxidermy, 8815 US Hwy. 24 W., Chipita Park, CO (719) 684-2598

AUTO REPAIR

Byrne's RV Repair, 1125 Sundance St., (719) 687-6981
Darrell's Automotive, 570 E. Chester, (719) 687-3313
Schumacher's, P.O. Box 6206, (719) 687-2446

MEDICAL

Langstaff Brown Medical Center, 41 N. Hwy 67, (719) 687-6022
Woodland Park Medical Center, P.O. Box 9029, (719) 687-3071

FOR MORE INFORMATION

Greater Woodland Park Chamber of Commerce, P.O. Box 9022, Woodland Park, CO 80866, (719) 687-9885, Fax (719) 687-8216

Carbondale
Population — 5,196 · Elevation — 6,170'

Carbondale is located between Glenwood Springs and Aspen in the midst of some beautiful country. If you are hunting in the White River National Forest in GMUs 43, 47, or 444, Carbondale will be a convenient location to pick up supplies or find food and lodging. This area provides excellent opportunities for deer, elk, black bear, and mountain lion. It is also a well-known location for the quality fishing found on the Fryingpan and Roaring Fork Rivers. The Basalt State Wildlife Area is located a short drive to the east of Carbondale. This SWA provides big game hunting opportunities as well as access into the White River National Forest to the north and east.

ACCOMMODATIONS
Fire & Iron, 12954 Highway 133, (970)963-3902
Comfort Inn, 920 Cowen Dr, (970)963-8880
Days Inn, 950 Cowen Dr, (970)963-9111
Redstone Cliffs Lodge, 433 Redstone Blvd, (970)963-2691
Country Inn, 920 Cowen Drive, 963-8880, 42 units
Days Inn, Highway 82 and Highway 133, 963-9111, 69 units
Thunder River Lodge Inc., 0179 Highway 133, 963-2543, 10 units, Dogs allowed

BED AND BREAKFAST
Mt. Sopris Inn, 0165 Mt. Sopris Ranch Road, Box 126, 1-800-437-8675

RESTAURANTS
Blue Creek Grill, 68 El Jebel Road, El Jebel, 963-3946, Open for dinner and drinks from 5–9PM
Capitol Deli, 218 E Valley Rd # 110, (970)963-4333
Claddaugh Pub, 1374 Main St, (970)704-0923
Dos Gringos Burritos, 588 Highway 133, (970)704-0788
El Korita, 19218 Highway 82, (970)963-4600
Lone Wolfe Brewing Co, 403 Main St, (970)963-9757
Mambo Italiano, 1054 Highway 133, 970)704-1600
Palomino Grill, 343 Main St, (970)963-6161
Pour House, 351 Main St, (970)963-3553
Red Rock Diner, 155 State Highway 133, (970)963-4111
Redstone Inn, 82 Redstone Blvd, (970)963-2526
Rock Creek Grill, 303 River Valley Ranch Rd, (970)963-0223
Sezen Restaurant & Sushi Bar, 912 Highway 133, (970)963-2385
Ship of Fools, 348 Main St, (970)963-3606
Six 89 Main Kitchen & Wine Bar, 689 Main St, (970)963-6890
The Relay Station, 14913 Highway 82, 963-1334
Peppino's Pizza, 524 Main, 963-2993, Open 11AM-9PM

SPORTING GOODS

Western Sports, 400 East Valley Road, (970) 963-3030, email: wsport@rof.net, Web page: www.wsports.com, Owner: Robert Woods, Fly shop, sporting goods, and guide service, Float and wade trips

TAXIDERMISTS

T's Taxidermy & Wildlife Decor, 516 Highway 133, Carbondale, CO 81623-1536, (970) 963-1192

VETERINARIANS

Alpine Animal Hospital, 17776 Highway 82, (970) 963-2371
Carbondale Animal Hospital, 234 Main St, (970) 963-2826
Redhill Animal Health Ctr, 955 Cowen Dr, (970)704-0403

AIRPORT

See Aspen and Denver airports information

AUTO SERVICE

Jed's Automotive, 0762 Highway 133, (970) 963-8402

LOCKSMITH

Valley Lock and Key, 579 Main Carbondale, (970) 963-1235

FOR MORE INFORMATION

Carbondale Chamber of Commerce, 0590 Highway 133, Carbondale, CO 81623, (970) 963-1890

Colorado Springs
Population 360,890 · Elevation — 6,008'

Colorado Springs is the second largest city in the state in terms of population. It is often the starting point for big game hunters in Colorado. With a large commercial airport, many hunters travelling from out of state fly straight into Colorado Springs. Any services associated with big game hunting are available in the city, and State Highway 24 makes it convenient to access the Pike National Forest to the west of town.

Colorado Springs has a strong military presence with the United States Airforce Academy, the Fort Carson Military Reservation, and the North American Aerospace Defense Command (NORAD). One of the most prominent landmarks in the state, Pikes Peak, towers over the city. The Pikes Peak area is home to a large number and diversity of big game animals including deer, elk, black bear, mountain lion, and bighorn sheep.

ACCOMMODATIONS
Antlers Hotel, 4 South Cascade Avenue, (970) 473-5600, 800-222-8733, 290 rooms, Dogs allowed
Broadmoor Hotel, 1 Lake Circle, (970) 634-7711, 700 rooms, World famous
Hampton Inn, 7245 Commerce Center Drive, (970) 593-9700, 800-426-7866, Dogs allowed
Town and Country Cottage, 123 Crystal Park Road, Manitou Springs 80829, (970) 685-5427, Highly recommended, 10 rooms
Cascade Hills Motel, 7885 Highway 24, Cascade 80809, (970) 684-9977, 14 rooms and 2 cabins

BED AND BREAKFAST
Black Bear Inn, 5250 Pikes Peak Highway, (970) 684-0151, Host: Christi Heidenrich, At the bottom of Pikes Peak Highway, Caters to float tubing and canoeing for the lakes on Pikes Peak
Gray's Avenue Hotel, 711 Manitou Avenue, Manitou Springs 80829, (970) 685-1277, Inn Keepers: Tom and Lee Bray

CAMPING
Colorado Campground, 31013 Highway 67, Woodland Park, (970) 687-0678
Lone Duck Campground, 8855 West Highway 24, Chipita Park, (970) 684-9907
Travel Port Campground, 39284 Highway 24, Lake George, (970) 748-8191, 25 RV and 10 tent sites, Located near Elevenmile and Spinney Mountain Reservoirs

RESTAURANTS
Perkins, 5190 North Academy Boulevard, (970) 528-5993, Open 24 hours
The Briarhurst Manor, 404 Manitou Avenue, Manitou Springs 80829, (970) 685-1864, Open 5:30PM–9PM for dinner and cocktails
Grandmother's Kitchen, 212 Highway 24, Woodland Park, (970) 687-3118, Open 6:00AM for breakfast
Mountain Shadows Restaurant, 2223 Colorado Avenue, (970) 633-2122

Sporting Goods

Great Outdoors Sporting Goods, 520 West Midland Avenue, Woodland Park, (970) 687-0401

Sports Hut, 719 Dale, Fountain, (970) 382-7646

Tackle Shack, 430 West Fillmore, (970) 635-1359

Tricos, 535 Lionstone Drive, (970) 574-5480

All American Sports, 3690 North Academy Boulevard, (970) 574-4400

Blick's Sporting Goods, 119 North Tejon, (970) 636-3348

Gart's Sports, 106 North Tejon, (970) 473-3143

Gart's Sports, 1409 North Academy Boulevard, (970) 574-1400

Gart's Sports, 7730 North Academy Boulevard, (970) 532-1020

Great Outdoors Sporting Goods, 520 E. Midland Ave, Woodland Park, (970) 687-0401

Grand West Outfitters , 3250 North Academy Boulevard, (970) 596-3031

Mountain Chalet, 226 North Tejon, 633-0732

Hospitals

Penrose Hospital, 2215 North Cascade Avenue, (970) 776-5000

Memorial Hospital, 1400 East Boulder, (970) 365-5000

Airports

Colorado Springs Airport, 7770 Drennan Road, 550-1900, United: 800-241-6522, American: 800-433-7300, Delta: 800-221-1212, Western Pacific: 800-722-5775

Ellicott Airport, 1757 Log Road, Ellicott, (970) 683-2701, Private planes

Auto Rental

Advantage Rent-A-Car, 1645 North Newport Road, Colorado Springs Airport, (970) 574-1144

Avis Rent-A-Car, 7770 Drennan Road, Colorado Springs Airport, (970) 596-2751

Thrifty Car Rentals, (970) 380-9800, www.thrifty.com

Auto Service

AA Auto Repair, 602 West Colorado Avenue, (970) 471-2067

Darrell's Automotive, 570 East Chester Avenue, Woodland Park, (970) 687-3313

Mobile Car Repair, (970) 338-1777

Locksmith

Action Locksmith Services, (970) 339-8400, 1-888-235-4545

Colorado State Safe and Lock Co., 3013 North Hancock Avenue, (970) 471-0096

Slim Jim's Auto Locksmiths, (970) 598-5940

For More Information

Colorado Springs Chamber of Commerce, 2 North Cascade, Colorado Springs,CO 80903, (970) 635-1551

Ouray
Population — 813 · Elevation — 7,811'

This town is named after one of the most revered leaders of the Ute Indian Tribe, Chief Ouray. Big game hunters are drawn to this area for many reasons. Not only are there exceptional hunting opportunities, but there are all types of recreational activities available here. The area surrounding Ouray was a center for mining starting in the 1800s. Most notably, the Camp Bird mine produced millions of dollars in gold over several decades of production. When you're hunting this area, keep in mind that there are numerous patented mining claims in the area that comprise private property.

Ouray is surrounded by incredible alpine scenery, and most hunters who have made the drive from Ouray to Silverton over Red Mountain Pass in the winter probably have a story about their white-knuckle drive along this narrow, steep, and winding road. Anyone hunting in the Uncompahgre National Forest in GMU 65 will do well to use Ouray as a base of operations. The Hot Springs is an added bonus if you choose to stay in Ouray during your hunting trip.

ACCOMMODATIONS

Alpine Motel, 645 Main St, (970)325-4546
Best Western Inn, 125 3rd Ave, (970)325-4427
Box Canyon Lodge & Hot Springs, 45 3rd Ave, (970)325-4981
Damn Yankee Country Inn, 100 6th Ave, 970)325-4219
Elkhorn Log Cabins, 1904 N Main # 1, (970)325-0431
Matterhorn Motel, 201 6th Ave, (970)325-4938
Timber Ridge Motel, 1515 N Main St, (970)325-4856

RESTAURANTS

Ouray Coffee House, 960 Main, (970)325-0401
Bon Ton, 426 Main St, (970)325-4951
Cecilia's, 630 Main St, (970)325-4223
Coachlight Restaurant, 118 W 7th Ave, (970)325-4361
Historic Western Hotel, 210 7th Ave, (970)325-4645
Outlaw Restaurant, 610 Main St, (970)325-4366
Papa's Restaurant, 800 Main St

SPORTING GOODS

Ouray Mountain Sports, 722 Main St, (970)325-4284

CAMPING

KOA Kampgrounds, 225 Highway 23, (970)325-4736

FOR MORE INFORMATION

Ouray Chamber Resort Association, (970) 325-4746, 800 228-1876, 1230 Main. Box 145, Ouray 81427 web: ouray@ouraycolorado.com

Region 2 Outfitters

The following list includes outfitters registered with the Colorado Outfitters Association who provide big game hunting services in one or more of the GMUs within Region 2. Information concerning the outfitters company name, license number, address, phone, species, GMUs, type of land hunted (national forest, regional area, private vs. public), and facilities are provided below.

LARRY ALLEN
Hubbard Creek Outfitters #1115
P.O. Box 25, Hotchkiss, CO 81419
(970) 872-3818
Deer, elk, bear, 521, 53
Gunnison, Uncompahgre
BLM Montrose; Private property
tent camps, cabins

ROBERT ASHLEY
High Park Lodge #1611
1733 F Road, Delta, CO 81416
(800) 345-8436
Deer, elk, 411, 51; BLM-Uncompahgre
Montrose, private property, resort

ROD BLACK
Coal Creek Outfitting #1262
P.O. Box 903, Gunnison, CO 81230
(970) 641-1227
Deer, elk, bear, sheep, 54
Gunnison, tent camps

GORDON BLAY
Western Colo. Outfitters #227
18315 6500 Rd, Montrose, CO 81401
(336) 643-4455
Deer, elk, bear, sheep, lion, 61, 62, 63
Gunnison, Uncompahgre
Private property, tent camps
Cabins, resort

JOE BOUCHER
Horn Fork Guides #70
P.O. Box 776, Buena Vista, CO 81211
(719) 395-3665
Deer, elk, goat, sheep
481, 49, G1, G2, G3, G3N, S20, S11S,
S11N, S12, S66
San Isabel, tent camps

CLYDE BRUTON
Bruton's Guide Service #89
1241 Hwy. 65, Box 42, Mesa, CO 81643
(970)268-5232
Deer, elk, lion, 421,41,42
Grand Mesa, private property,
Tent Camps, trailers, bunkhouse

JACK CASSIDY
Prof. Big Game Guide and Outfitter #229
1640 M Rd., Fruita, CO 81521,
(970) 858-3352
Deer, elk, bear, antelope, goat, sheep, 64,
65; Private property, tent camps, cabins

STU CHAPPEL, TODD RICHARDSON
#1341 San-Pahgre Outdoor
Adventures/Outfitting
65465 Sunridge Ct., Montrose, CO 81401
(970) 252-1389 or 1-888-288-2659
tbaecker@gwe.net
Deer, elk, bear, 61, 62, 65, 74, Gunnison,
BLM-Montrose, Cabins

BELLE CHESNICK
2V Outfitters #959
P.O. Box 57, Glade Park, CO 81523
(970) 245-4636
Deer, elk, 40
Private property, Ranching for Wildlife

TOM COLANDER
Colorado Trophies #1782
P.O. Box 249, Redvale, CO 81431
(970) 327-4678
Deer, elk, bear, lion, 60, 61, 62, 70, 711
Uncompahgre, BLM-Montrose
Private property, guest ranch

GARY EATON
Rainbow Lake Lodge and Outfitters
1231 Brick Church Rd.
Ontario, NY 14519
(315) 524-8467
Deer, elk, goat, sheep, 54
West Elk Wilderness, tent camps, cabins

DELLIS FERRIER
Ferrier Outfitters/Bar Diamond
Ranch #315, P.O. Box 688
Hotchkiss, CO 81419
(970) 527-3010
Deer, elk, bear, sheep, 53, 54
Gunnison; tent camps

DELNOR FLYNN
Flynn and Sons Outfitter #645
3827 Hwy. 92, Carwford, CO 81415
(970) 921-5221
Deer, elk, bear, 53, 63, 54
Gunnison, tent camps

RONALD FRANKS
J&Ray Colorado High Country #727
8360 6400 Road, Montrose, CO 81401
(970) 323-5155
Deer, elk, bear, 64, 65
Uncompahgre, BLM-Montrose
Tent camps

STAN AND DOYLENE GARVEY
Garvey Bros.Outfitting #606, P.O. Box 555
Nucla, CO 81424
(970) 864-2243
Deer, elk, bear, lion, 61
Uncompahgre, BLM-Montrose,
Grand Junction, private property
Tent camps, cabins

BILL GUERRIERI
Lazy F Bar Outfitters #188
P.O. Box 383, Gunnison, CO 81230
(970) 641-0193
Deer, elk, sheep, 54, 55

ANDY HARRIS
Cache Creek Outfitters #1550
P.O. Box 533, Parachute, CO 81635,
(888) 770-0601
Deer, elk, bear, 42
White River, BLM-Glenwood
Private property
Tent camps, bunk houses

DON HAWKINS OUTFITTING #782
2046 Hwy. 92, Delta, CO 81416
(970) 874-8892
Deer, elk, bear, lion
421, 63, 64, 62
BLM-Montrose
Tent camps, trailers

CLIFFORD AND JANICE HILL
Hills Guide Service
#105, Rt.#1, Box 189, Collbran, CO 81624,
(970) 487-3433
Deer, elk, bear, 421
Grand Mesa, private property
Cabins, trailers

DENNIS HOEFER
Dick Pennington Guide Service #145
P.O. Box 285, Norwood, CO 81423
888-336-3728
Deer, elk, 42, 43, 521
White River, BLM-Gunnison
Tent camps

TONY HOZA
Hoza Guide and Outfitters #294
P.O. Box 285, Norwood, CO 81423,
(970) 327-4305, deer, elk, bear, lion, 60,
61, 71; San Juan, Uncompahgre, BLM-
Durango Grand Junction, private
property; trespass fee, cabins

H. BRUCE HYATT
Hyatt Guides and Outfitters #34
Box 1288, Montrose, CO 81402
(970) 249-9733
Deer, elk, 61,62
Uncompahgre, cabins

JOHN JODRIE
Gypsum Creek Outfitters #1253
Box 157, Gypsum, CO 81637
(970) 524-7738
Deer, elk, bear, 44, 444
White River, private property
Tent camps, cabins

JOHN JUDSON
Quarter-Circle Circle Ranch #669
26100 County Road 17GG
Gunnison, CO 81230
(970) 641-3616
Deer, elk, antelope, sheep, 67, 68, 551
Gunnison, Rio Grande, BLM-Montrose,
Private property, tent camps, cabins

TIM KEMPFE
Adventure Experiences #1206
#2 Illinois Co. C.R. 742
Almont, CO 81210
800-595-2945, deer, elk, goat, sheep, 54,
55, 56; Gunnison, private property
Tent camps, cabins

ALLEN KENNON
Wild West Outfitters #1419
P.O. Box 232, Montrose, CO 81402
(970) 240-4134
Deer, elk, bear, 65
Private property, lodge

JON AND DORI LEE -
Pomotawh Naamtam Ranch #1172
26767 C. R. 12, Somerset, CO 81434
(970) 929-5917
Elk, 521
Gunnison, private property, cabins

CAMERON LEWI
4 Powderhorn Primative Outfit. #1556
78 C. R. 50, Gunnison, CO 81230
(970) 641-3654
Deer, elk, bear, lion, 66
BLM-Gunnison, tent camps

TONY MALDARELLA
Rendezvous Outfitters & Guides #1729
P.O. Box 25, Parlin, CO 81239
888-349-2459
Deer, elk, bear, goat, sheep, 53, 521, G11,
S54; Gunnison, BLM-Montrose
Tent camps

DAVE MAPES
4 Quaking Aspen Outfitters #83
P.O. Box 485, Gunnison, CO 81230
(970) 641-0529
Deer, elk, 43, 521
White River, BLM-Gunnison; Tent camps

MATT MUNYON
Big Cimarron Outfitters#1091
P.O. Box 802, Olathe, CO 81425
(970) 874-3921
Deer, elk, bear, 65
Uncompahgre, Gunnison
BLM-Montrose
Tent camps

JOHN NELSON
Gunnison Country Guide Service #249
P.O. Box 1443, Gunnison, CO 81230
(970) 651-2830
Deer, elk, bear, goat, sheep, 54, 55, 66,
67, 551; Gunnison, BLM-San Juan
Tent camps

DAVE PARK OUTFITTING #1043
726 N. Main #128, Gunnison, CO 81230
888-332-6075
Deer, elk, bear, antelope, 68, 82, 551, 681
Rio Grande, Gunnison, private property
Tent camps, cabins

ROBERT PORT
Cowboy Camp Outfitters #1114
5460 Ward Rd., Suite 160
Arvada, CO 80002
(303) 384-9724
Deer, elk, bear, antelope, 50
BLM-Canon City, private property
Tent camps, cabins

RYAN PRINGLE
Waunita Hot Springs Ranch #146
8007 CR 887, Gunnison, CO 81230
(970) 641-1266
Deer, elk, 551
Gunnison, Resort

STEVE REISER
Capitol Peak Outfitters #741
0554 Valley Road, Carbondale, CO 81623
(970) 963-0211
Deer, elk, sheep, 43, 47, 444
White River, Gunnison, BLM-Glenwood
Springs; private property, tent camps
cabins

RON ROLL
Silver Fox Outfitters #1560
1107 W. Tomichi #4, Gunnison, CO 81230
(970) 641-2242
Deer, elk, 55, 551
Gunnison, Tent camps

ED PUGH
Bar X Bar Ranch #1584
625 Lincoln Ave., P.O. Box 138
Wamego, KS
66547, (785) 456-9377
Deer, elk, bear, 53
Gunnison, tent camps, cabins
Resort, trailers, lodge

DUANE AND DALE PURCELL
Purcell Brothers Outfitting #845
30259 County Farm Road
Pueblo, CO 81006
(719) 948-4714
Deer, elk, lion, bear, antelope, sheep,
goat, 61, 62, 69, 84, 86, S-9, S-7, S-49,
S-20, S-11S, S-12, G-3N, G-3
Uncompahgre, San Esabel, Rio Grande,
BLM-Canon City, Grand Junction
Tent camps, cabins

RUDY AND DEB RUDIBAUGH
Fossil Ridge Guide Service
#251, 711 Ranch, Parlin, CO 81239
(970) 641-0666,
Deer, elk, goat, sheep
Horse Rental, 551, 55, 66, 67
Gunnison, Tent camps, cabins, trailers

TERRY SANDMEIR
Geneva Park Outfitters
#732, P.O. Box 771, Conifer, CO 80433
(303) 838-6311
Deer, elk, goat, sheep, 46, G4, G7, S3,
S3A, S12, S23N, S23S, S32, S34
Pike, San Isabel, Arapaho,
Tent camps, trailers

MIKE SCHILLING
Avalanche Outfitters #529
11382 Hwy. 133, Carbondale, CO 81623
(970) 963-2942
Deer, elk, bear, goat, sheep, 43, S13W,
G11, G12
White River, tent camps

LEE SELLS
Outfitters and Guide #1282
P.O. Box 896, Eufaula, AL 36072
(334) 687-7451
Deer, elk, 42, 421
Private property, cabins, motel

PAUL SINNER
The Flying M Ranch #1839
13508 M 73 road, Montrose, CO 81401
(970) 240-3467
Deer, elk, lion, 64
Private property, cabins, resort

JOE SPERRY-SPERRY'S #437
2015 F Road, Delta, CO 81416
(970) 874-3102
Deer, elk, bear, 411, 521
Gunnison, tent camps, cabins

JOHN AND STEVE STAJDUHAR
Stajduhar Ranches #254
998 21 Road, Fruita, CO 81521
(970) 858-3760
Deer, elk, bear, goat, sheep, 43, 47, 55,
471, 444,
Gunnison, White River
BLM-Glenwood Springs
Tent camps, cabins, trailers

JAMES TALBOT
Fantasy Ranch Outfitters #1285
P.O. Box 236, Crested Butte, CO 81224
(970) 349-5425
Deer, elk, 55
Horse rental, Gunnison, White River,
BLM-Gunnison, tents, cabins, resort

DOYLE WORBINGTON II
J&D Outfitters and Guide Service
#1877, P.O. Box 313
Cripple Creek, CO 80813
(719) 599-8545
Deer, elk, bear, antelope, sheep, 59, 581
Pike, private property
Tent camps, cabins

ROBERT MILLER
Big Cimarron Outfitters
1959, 609 S. 11th St., Montrose, CO 81401
(970) 249-6947
Deer, elk, bear, 65
Uncompahgre, tent camps

SEAN OLSON
Hecoma Partners #1910
P.O. Box 1798, Montrose, CO 81402
(970) 249-4700, deer, elk, bear, 411, 55,
62, 65
Private property, tent camps, cabins,
resort

GARY POPE
Soap Mesa Venture #1905
20600 Solitude Roa
Montrose, CO 81401
(970) 249-1569
Deer, elk, bear, 54,
Gunnison, private property, cabins,
trailers

Region 3 Major Roads, Rivers & Hub Cities

© WILDERNESS ADVENTURES PRESS, INC.

REGION 3

Located in the southwest portion of Colorado, Region 3 makes up one of the most beautiful and unspoiled areas in the state. Starting at Interstate 25 at the eastern boundary of the region, the Wet Mountains rise above the grassy plains. Farther to the west across the Wet Mountain Valley stands the Sangre de Cristo Range, one of the most distinct and spectacular mountain ranges in Colorado. Moving still farther to the west across the San Luis Valley is the most prominent geographic feature of the region, the San Juan Mountains. The San Juans make up a vast area comprised of a mountain system rather than a distinct range. This mountain system contains vast areas of alpine tundra and the greatest concentration of subalpine forest in the state. Several rivers derive their origin from snowmelt generated in the San Juans. Finally, in the far southwest corner of the state is Mesa Verde, famous for its Anasazi Indian ruins, but also an area that contains a significant deer herd.

Region 3 has vast areas of public land consisting of BLM, national forest, and state properties. Among the public land is some of the most pristine and remote wilderness in the state. Although there are many popular hunting areas that can be crowded during the big game rifle seasons, Region 3 may provide the best chance to find areas with low hunting pressure. There are large herds of deer and elk in this part of Colorado as well as several herds of antelope with huntable populations. Numerous opportunities exist for hunters interested in pursuing bighorn sheep. There are also a few desert bighorn sheep tags available in Sheep Management Units S62 and S64. There is one mountain goat unit in Region 3 plus the opportunity to hunt moose in two areas. If you are interested in hunting bear or mountain lion, Region 3 may hold the largest concentration of black bears in the state. Excellent opportunities to hunt mountain lion also exist locally.

The southwest corner of Region 3 supports a sizeable deer herd in rugged terrain near Mesa Verde.

Pronghorn Distribution
Region 3

© WILDERNESS ADVENTURES PRESS, INC.

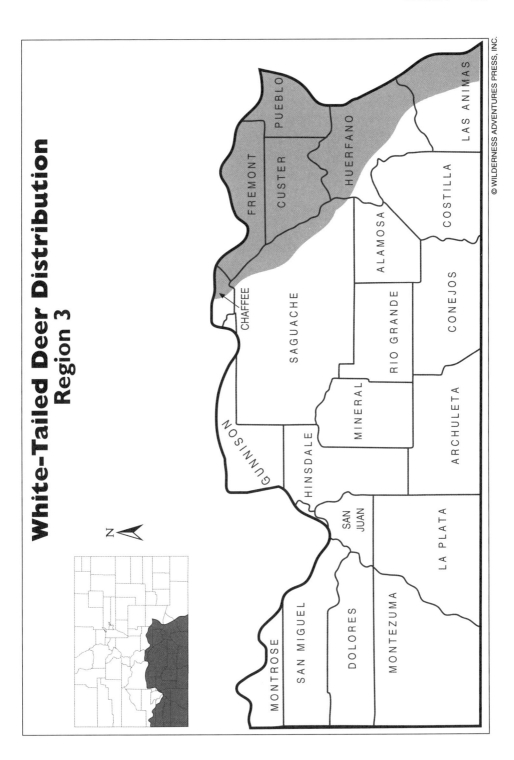

White-Tailed Deer Distribution
Region 3

© WILDERNESS ADVENTURES PRESS, INC.

Mule Deer Distribution
Region 3

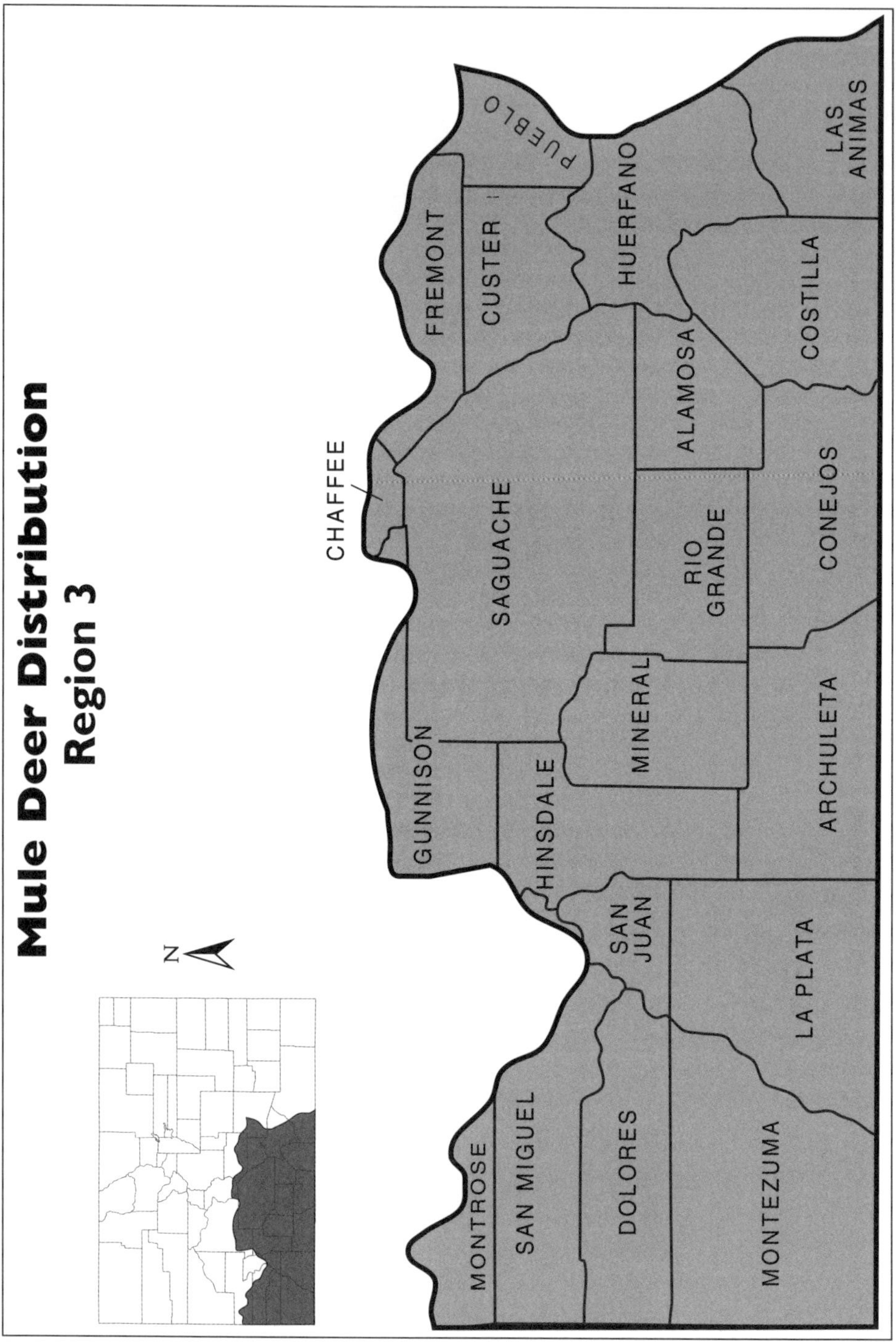

MONTROSE

SAN MIGUEL

DOLORES

MONTEZUMA

LA PLATA

SAN JUAN

HINSDALE

GUNNISON

ARCHULETA

MINERAL

RIO GRANDE

CONEJOS

SAGUACHE

ALAMOSA

COSTILLA

CHAFFEE

FREMONT

CUSTER

PUEBLO

HUERFANO

LAS ANIMAS

© WILDERNESS ADVENTURES PRESS, INC.

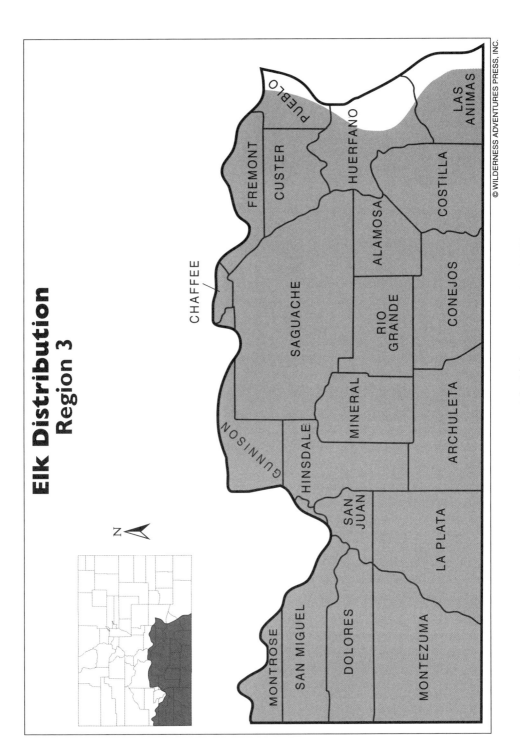

Elk Distribution
Region 3

© WILDERNESS ADVENTURES PRESS, INC.

Moose Distribution
Region 3

© WILDERNESS ADVENTURES PRESS, INC.

Bighorn Sheep Distribution
Region 3

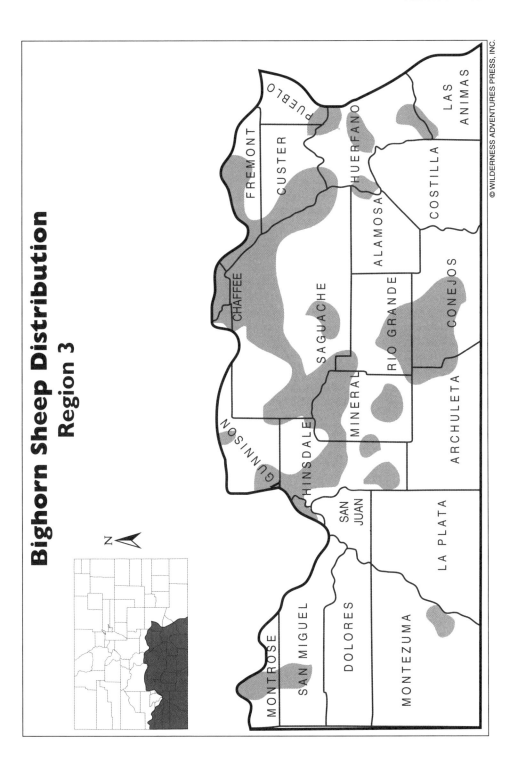

© WILDERNESS ADVENTURES PRESS, INC.

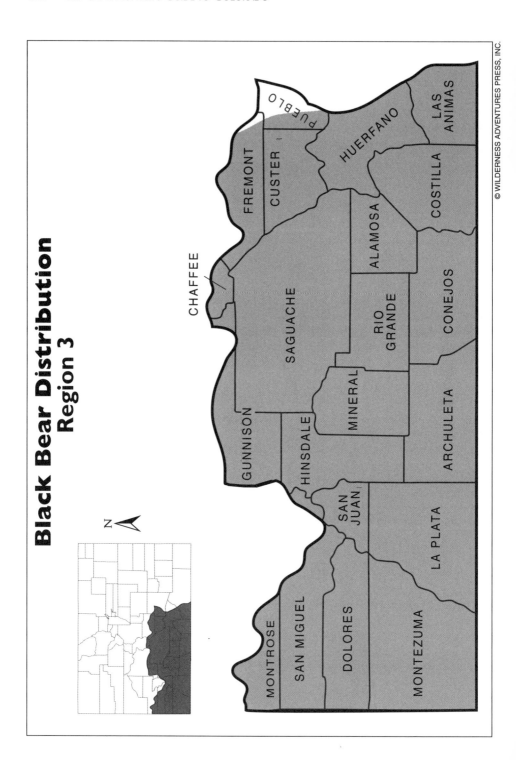

Black Bear Distribution
Region 3

© WILDERNESS ADVENTURES PRESS, INC.

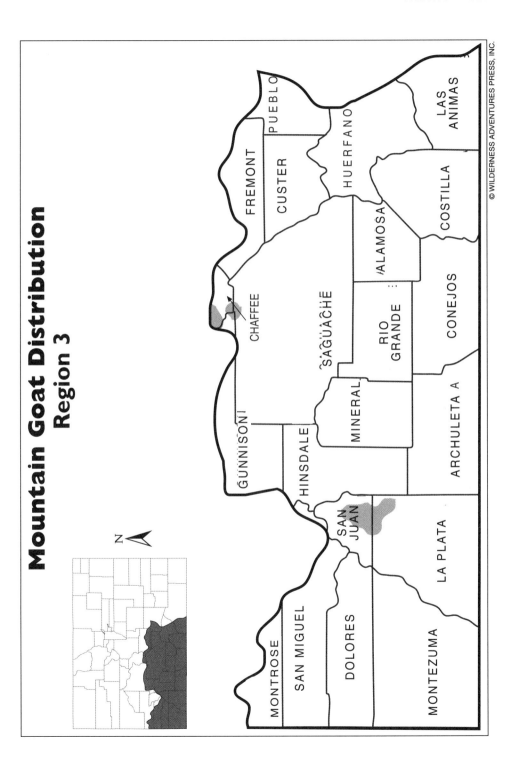

Mountain Goat Distribution
Region 3

Mountain Lion Distribution
Region 3

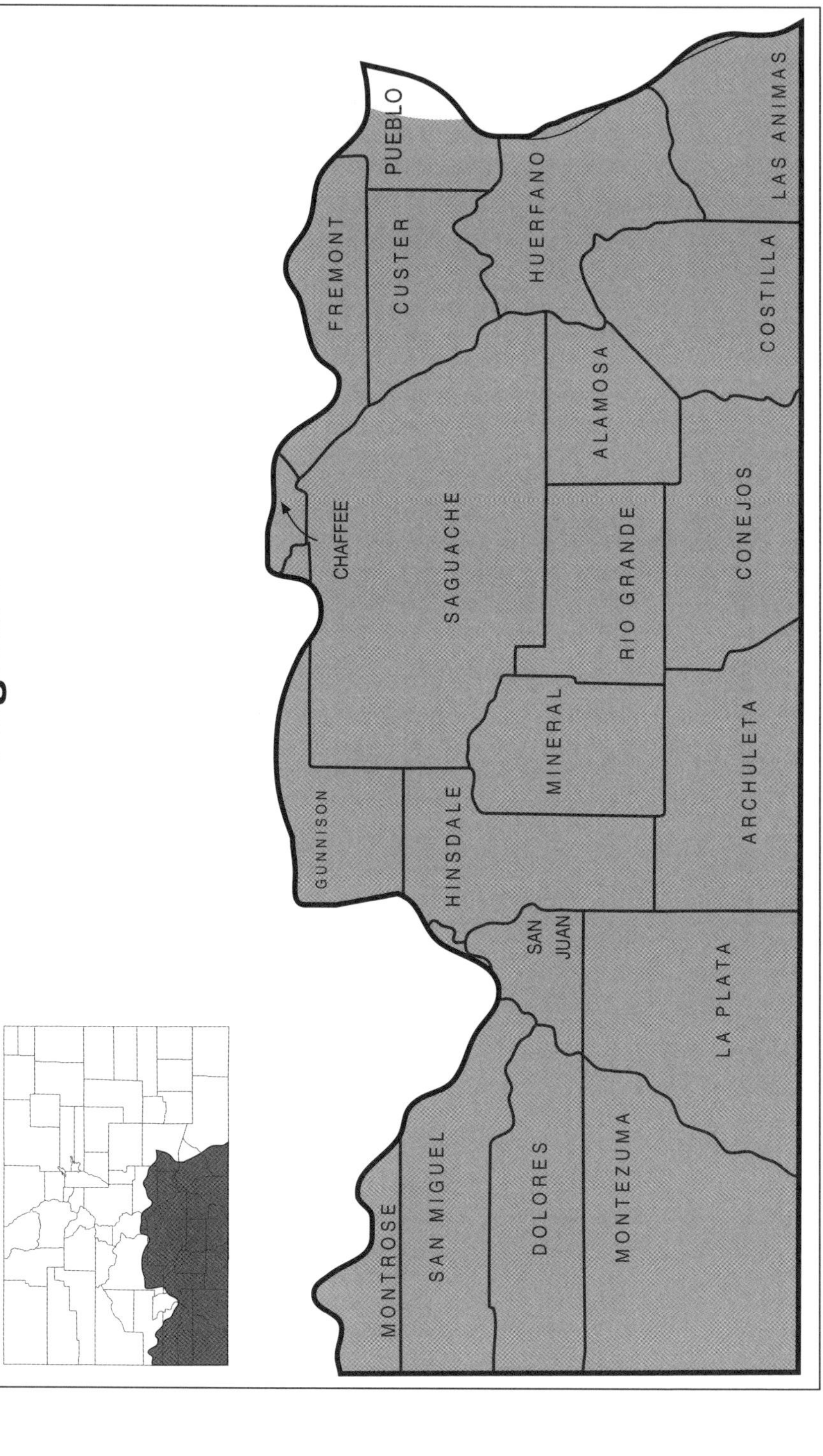

© WILDERNESS ADVENTURES PRESS, INC.

PUEBLO

FREMONT

CUSTER

HUERFANO

LAS ANIMAS

COSTILLA

ALAMOSA

CHAFFEE

SAGUACHE

RIO GRANDE

CONEJOS

MINERAL

ARCHULETA

GUNNISON

HINSDALE

SAN JUAN

LA PLATA

MONTROSE

SAN MIGUEL

DOLORES

MONTEZUMA

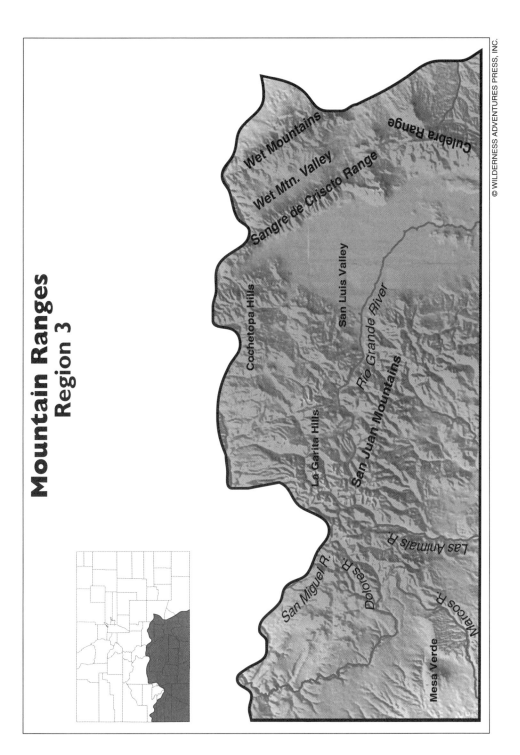

Mountain Ranges
Region 3

Wet Mountains

Culebra Range

Wet Mtn. Valley

Sangre de Criscto Range

Cochetopa Hills

San Luis Valley

Rio Grande River

La Garita Hills

San Juan Mountains

Las Animais R.

San Miguel R.

Dolores R.

Matcos R.

Mesa Verde

© WILDERNESS ADVENTURES PRESS, INC.

Game Species and Numbers

The thirty GMUs in Region 3 hold eleven recognized herds of elk that have grown to a combined population over 100,000 animals in recent years. Mule deer are distributed throughout the region with a total population over 120,000 animals. In addition to good numbers of deer, Region 3 has some of the best trophy-quality deer hunting in the state, as suggested by the high buck-to-doe ratios in several of the prominent herds. A large percentage of the bighorn sheep population is found in Region 3, within approximately one-third of the total sheep management units. Black bears are found throughout the region with large concentrations in the Trinidad area as well as the San Juans and Sangre De Cristos. Although there aren't large populations of antelope in this part of the state, there are several herds that sometimes produce exceptional trophies. There are also two GMUs with moose tags available to big game hunters. Finally, there are large numbers of mountain lions in Region 3.

Population statistics are a valuable asset to the hunter and the Colorado Division of Wildlife prepares official population and harvest statistics that are available to the public each year. This information is gathered from license sale statistics, field research, including aerial population counts, and hunter harvest surveys. Obviously, it would be impossible to count every animal in the state, so the populations are to some extent estimated using population models.

The following tables provide the herd name, the GMUs where the herd ranges and the population of the herd for elk, deer and antelope. This information is current at the time of publishing, but populations change over time. Still, the distribution of populations in each area has remained relatively consistent over the years.

ELK HERD	UNITS	POPULATION
Lake Fork	66, 67	5,510
Saguache	68, 681	4,770
Grape Creek	69, 84	1,650
Disappointment Creek	70, 71, 711	14,260
Hermosa	74, 741	5,290
San Juan	75, 751, 77, 78, 771	15,590
Upper Rio Grande	76, 79	5,500
Lower Rio Grande	80, 81	9,470
Sand Dunes	82	5,000
Trinchera	83, 85, 140, 851	34,280
Sangre de Cristo	86, 691, 861	1,810
TOTAL ELK POPULATION REGION 3 = 103,130		

DEER HERD	UNITS	POPULATION
Powderhorn Creek	66, 67	5,490
Saguache	68, 681	5,660
Wet Mountain	69, 84, 86, 861	15,000
Groundhog	70, 71, 711	30,500
Mesa Verde	72, 73	9,970
Hermosa	74, 741	7,330
San Juan	75, 77, 78, 751, 771	23,210
Upper Rio Grande	76, 79	3,890
Lower Rio Grande	80, 81	7,620
Sand Dunes	82	1,840
Costilla	83	3,200
Trinidad	85, 140, 851	6,600
TOTAL DEER POPULATION REGION 3 = 120,310		

DEER HERD	UNITS	POPULATION
Saguache	68, 681W	450
Wet Mountain	69, 84, 85, 86, 861	1,520
Del Norte	79	630
Monte Vista	80	560
Magote Peaks	81	570
Villa Grove	82, 681E	1,170
TOTAL ANTELOPE POPULATION REGION 3 = 4,900		

Populations of bear and mountain lion are not as well documented. There is specific statewide information for the other big game species.

GAME SPECIES	STATEWIDE POPULATION
Black Bear	Unknown (estimates from 8,000 to 12,000)
Mountain Lion	Unknown (estimates from 1,500 to 3,500)
Desert Bighorn	400
Rocky Mtn. Bighorn	6,500
Mountain Goat	1,100
Moose	1,175

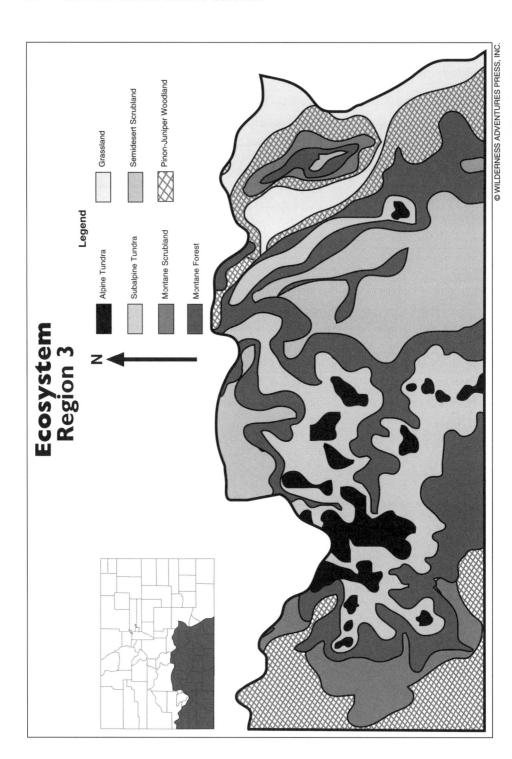

© WILDERNESS ADVENTURES PRESS, INC.

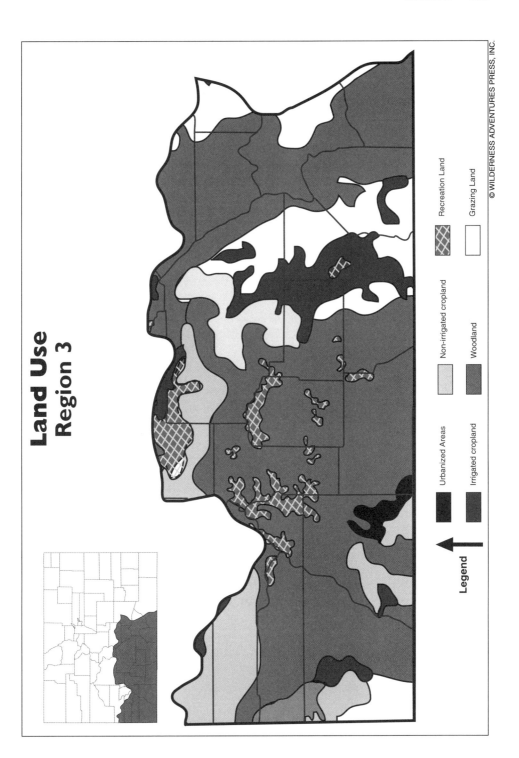

Land Use
Region 3

Legend

Urbanized Areas

Irrigated cropland

Non-irrigated cropland

Woodland

Recreation Land

Grazing Land

© WILDERNESS ADVENTURES PRESS, INC.

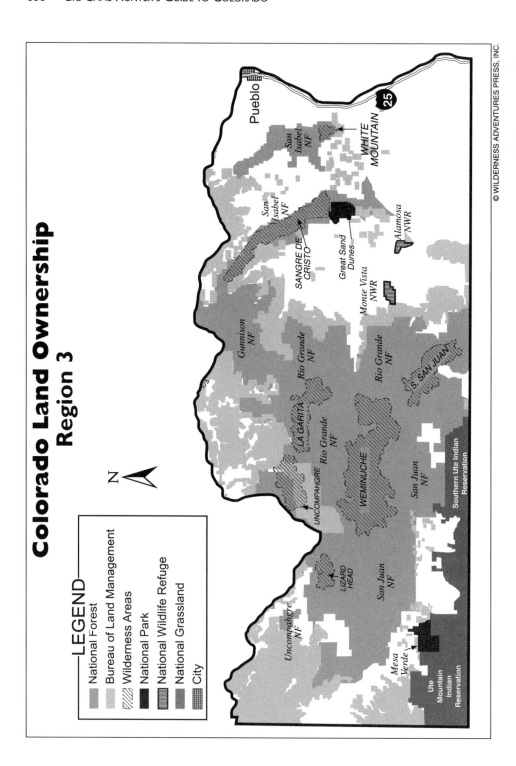

Colorado Land Ownership
Region 3

© WILDERNESS ADVENTURES PRESS, INC.

Harvest Trends

Hunter success rates vary greatly from year to year, season to season, and unit to unit. The Colorado Division of Wildlife publishes the big game hunting statistics each year, which includes success rates for each season in each unit. This information is available online at http://wildlife.state.co.us/huntrecap/index.asp.

The following success rates are based on 2001 DOW statistics averaged for all seasons and manners of take statewide.

SPECIES	SUCCESS RATE	TOTAL ANIMALS HARVESTED
Elk	21%	42,630
Deer	42%	31,634
Antelope	61%	6,417
Black Bear	6%	759
Desert Bighorn	100%	9
Rocky Mtn. Bighorn	51%	175
Mountain Goat	92%	169
Moose	84%	102

It is not possible to estimate the mountain lion success rate because the harvest is based on a quota system instead of limited licenses; however, 315 of the big cats were harvested in Colorado during the 2000 hunting season.

Physical Characteristics

Interstate 25 marks the eastern boundary of Region 3. From the city of Pueblo south along the I-25 corridor to the New Mexico state line is an area made up of grasslands. Almost all of the land along the I-25 corridor is private property used for farming and cattle grazing. Moving west into Region 3 the first prominent geographic feature is the Wet Mountains and, farther to the south, the Culebra Range, which extends into New Mexico. Continuing west into Region 3 is the Wet Mountain Valley, an area of intermountain grassland roughly 10 miles wide by 35 miles long. The Sangre de Cristo Range parallels the Wet Mountain Valley to the west. This spectacular, narrow range of snowcapped mountains contains several peaks over 14,000 feet in elevation. The phrase Sangre de Cristo is Spanish for "Blood of Christ," which may have been chosen as a name due to the reddish-glow sometimes associated with the mountains during sunrise and sunset.

To the west of the Sangre de Cristo Range is the San Luis Valley, a large area of mostly private property used for agriculture. The Great Sand Dunes National Monument is located adjacent to the Sangre de Cristo Range on the east side of the valley. Moving still farther west into Region 3 are the La Garita Hills and the San Juan Mountains. The San Juans have the distinction of being the single largest mountain complex in the state. This area also contains the Weminuche Wilderness Area, the largest in the state at nearly half a million acres. The headwaters of the San Juan River and the Rio Grande River originate in the San Juan Mountains, as well as other important rivers such as the Animas and the Dolores to name a few. South of the San Juans adjacent to the New Mexico state line is the Southern Ute Indian Reservation. Abutting this reservation to the west is the Ute Mountain Indian Reservation. The Four Corners area is rich in Indian history. Not far from the town of Cortez to the east is Mesa Verde National Park and to the west is Hovenweep National Monument.

With over six million acres of public land, big game hunters will find countless areas to hunt in Region 3. Five national forests cover the area with eight wilderness areas and huge tracts of BLM property. There are also numerous state wildlife areas and state trust lands open to hunting.

As with the other two western regions in Colorado, there is a great deal of variability in ecosystems across Region 3 due to the large changes in elevation. The I-25 corridor is predominantly made up of grasslands, which extend into the Wet Mountain Valley. The Wet Mountains are characterized by subalpine forest at the highest elevations surrounded by montane forest, montane shrubland, and pinon-juniper woodland at the lower elevations. The Sangre de Cristo Range attains higher elevations resulting in several areas of alpine tundra. Due to the narrowness of the Sangre de Cristo Range the alpine tundra ecosystem is surrounded on both sides by relatively thin tracts of subalpine forest followed by montane forest. At the lower elevations above the valleys thin tracts of pinon-juniper woodland flank the Sangre de Cristos.

The San Luis Valley is one of the largest areas of semi-desert shrubland in the state. Pinon-juniper woodlands ring the valley and give way to montane forests that abut the eastern edge of the San Juan Mountains and the La Garita Hills. The San Juans comprise the largest continuous tracts of subalpine forest in the state. Due to the abundance of land above 11,400 feet in elevation in the San Juans there are large areas of alpine tundra. Stepping down in elevation along the west side of the San Juans is montane forest followed by large areas of montane shrubland. The shrublands give way to pinon-juniper woodland at lower elevations. Dispersed within the pinon-juniper woodland are several distinct areas of semi-desert shrubland in the far southwest portion of Region 3. Several major rivers, including the San Juan and the Rio Grande, form important riparian systems in the region. Region 3 has representative areas of all eight of the major ecosystem designations used in this book. As with the other western regions of Colorado, this broad diversity of ecosystems equates to a rich diversity of wildlife.

Land Use

With a population over 100,000 people, the city of Pueblo is the most heavily populated area in Region 3. There are only one or two other cities in the region with populations over 10,000, although the towns of Trinidad, Alamosa, Durango, and Cortez represent the largest population centers across the region (even though they are relatively small by today's standards.) Development associated with urbanization is most prevalent in the Pueblo area, but there is also increasing development in the form of summer homes, mini-ranches, and commercial businesses in and surrounding many of the communities throughout Region 3. Still, Region 3 represents the most sparsely populated and least developed region in the state. It is also home to Hinsdale County, the least populated county in the state, which has only one town with a year-round resident population (Lake City, population 322).

Land use along the I-25 corridor from Pueblo to the New Mexico state line is primarily agricultural with dryland farming and some irrigated cropland as well as cattle grazing. The eastern third of Region 3 consists of the largest areas of private property. Most of the land in the Wet Mountain Valley and the San Luis Valley is private. The San Luis Valley contains important wetland areas and vast areas of irrigated cropland. Moving into the San Juan Mountains there are huge areas of public land and federally designated wilderness. Most of the forested areas in the San Juan National Forest and the Rio Grande National Forest outside of the wilderness areas have multiple uses including forestry, recreation, and watershed.

As with much of western Colorado, many of the small towns got their start as mining camps. Places such as Silverton, Creede, Lake City, Telluride, and Ouray all originated because of precious metals mines. Currently, there is no significant production of precious metals in the region. There were also large coal-mining operations, especially in the Trinidad area, and uranium mining, most notably in the Uravan area. The only significant mining in the region now consists of sand and gravel operations and aggregate quarries that produce construction materials.

Much of the land south and west of the San Juan Mountains is private with various agricultural uses and oil and gas production. The area south of Colorado State Highway 160 from Pagosa Springs west to the Utah state line is in large part Indian Reservations consisting of the Southern Ute and Ute Mountain tribes.

Weather

As discussed in Region 1 and 2, the summer weather pattern is one of afternoon thunderstorms. While early season hunters will likely encounter comfortable hunting temperatures in the 60s and 70s, severe thunderstorms can still be prevalent well into September. As arctic air in the far north causes the Jet Stream to move south, snowstorms can hit the high country as early as September, but more commonly in October. Due to its southern latitude, Region 3 is sometimes spared from early storms that dump snow on the mountains in northern Colorado.

People hunting at high elevations in the Wet Mountains, Sangre de Cristo Range, La Garita Mountains, Culebra Range, or the San Juan Mountains are advised to pay attention to local weather forecasts. Weather in the high mountains is unpredictable. The high ranges receive large amounts of moisture when Pacific fronts move across the state. The mountains in Region 3, especially the Sangre de Cristo Range and the San Juan Mountains receive large amounts of snow. Most years the snowpack in the San Juans will exceed 100 inches, and even 150 inches at the higher elevations. Luckily, much of this snow accumulates in the winter months after most of the big game hunting seasons have ended.

The following table provides average temperatures, precipitation, and snowfall for Durango, Colorado. Durango is located in the southwest corner of Region 3 at an elevation of 6,523 feet above mean sea level.

MONTH	AVERAGE HIGH (°F)	AVERAGE LOW (°F)	AVERAGE PRECIPITATION (Total in.)	AVERAGE TOTAL SNOW FALL (in.)
August	83.1	48.9	2.32	0.0
September	76.7	40.6	1.75	0.0
October	65.7	30.9	1.87	1.0
November	52.1	21.3	1.34	5.3
December	41.4	12.9	1.78	15.4

Temperature ranges were based on National Weather Service data for Durango. Period of record 1/01/1900 to 3/31/1991

As with other areas in western Colorado, this information should only be used as a rule of thumb. Temperatures across Region 3 can vary dramatically, especially at the higher elevations. Snowfall will be much greater in the surrounding mountains than in the valleys.

The San Juan Mountains receive a great deal of snow each winter. Hunter's should stay in tune to the local weather forecasts to avoid getting stranded in the high country.

Public Lands and Acreage

Region 3 has over six million acres of public land with five national forests, over a million acres of BLM properties, and state lands. The San Juan and Rio Grande National Forests are of comparable size and contain a combined area over 3.6 million acres. Some of the most remote and hard-to-access wilderness areas in the state are found in Region 3. There are eight federally designated wilderness areas, including the Weminuche, which is the biggest in the state at nearly half a million acres. Although there is less public land overall in Region 3 when compared to Regions 1 and 2, there is more wilderness area.

Please note that some of the acreages listed in the tables below extend beyond the Region 3 boundaries. Most notably half of the San Isabel National Forest extends into Region 2 and large percentages of the Gunnison and Uncompahgre National Forests extend beyond the boundary. These approximations are accounted for on the table below. Furthermore, BLM acreages are given by county, and some of the counties cross the Region 3 boundary. Still this represents a good estimate of the public lands available in Region 3.

PUBLIC LAND DESCRIPTION	ACREAGES
Rio Grande National Forest	1,800,000
Gunnison National Forest (30 percent)	510,000
San Juan National Forest	1,870,000
Uncompahgre National Forest (20 percent)	227,800
San Isabel National Forest (50 percent)	619,000
Bureau of Land Management	1,199,024
Monte Vista and Alamosa National Wildlife Refuges	24,469
TOTAL PUBLIC LANDS IN REGION 3	*6,250,293*

WILDERNESS AREAS (NATIONAL FOREST)		ACREAGES
Lizard Head	(San Juan/Uncompahgre)	41,496
La Garita	(Gunnison/Rio Grande)	129,626
Uncompahgre	(Uncompahgre)	102,668
Powderhorn	(Gunnison)	60,100
Weminuche	(San Juan/Rio Grande)	492,418
South San Juan	(San Juan/Rio Grande)	158,790
Sangre de Cristo	(Rio Grande/San Isabel)	226,455
Greenhorn Mountain	(San Isabel)	22,040
TOTAL WILDERNESS AREA REGION 2		*1,233,593*

REGION 3 HIGHLIGHTS

The Trinidad Area (GMUs 83, 85, 851, 140)

Located at the juncture of GMUs 85, 851, and 140, Trinidad sits amid some of the best deer and elk hunting in the state. These three units plus GMU 83 make up the Trinchera elk herd, the largest herd in Region 3 with over 34,000 animals. In addition to a large population, this herd has bragging rights to the highest bull-to-cow ratio in the state with over 70 bulls for every 100 cows in recent years. As you would expect, trophy quality is very good in this part of the state. This four-unit area also boasts a large deer population with two recognized herds. GMUs 85, 140, and 851 make up the Trinidad deer herd that has varied in population over past few years from about 6,500 to nearly 10,000 animals. GMU 83 is known as the Costilla deer herd that generally contains over 3,000 animals. These two herds generally have very good buck-to-doe ratios sometimes exceeding 40 bucks for every 100 does.

Hunters interested in pursuing antelope will find that a portion of the Wet Mountain herd roams in Unit 85. Furthermore, there are a handful of tags available for bighorn sheep in Units S50 and S51. If you're interested in hunting predators, the area offers some of the best bear hunting in the state. There is also a high density of mountain lions in the area.

This four-unit portion of Region 4 sounds like a hunter's dream, but before you start filling out your license applications you need to be aware of the downside to this area. It is in large part private property. More specifically, almost all of GMU 83 in Costilla County is private, as well as GMU 851 in Costilla and Las Animas Counties. If you do not have access to private land in these two units, your hunting opportunities will be severely limited. The same is true for GMU 140 within Las Animas County. Still, I would not have included this highlight area if I didn't believe it held adequate opportunities for big game hunters. There is a large section of the San Isabel National Forest located in GMU 85 in the southwest corner of Huerfano County and a small portion of Las Animas County north of Monument Park and south of La Veta. This area includes a portion of the Culebra Range and Spanish Peaks. Although it is not designated as a wilderness area, the Spanish Peaks are currently being studied for federal "wilderness" designation. The area includes nearly 20,000 acres of wildlands with 228 miles of trails on the east side of State Highway 12, north of Cucharas Pass. Hunters will also find good access to public lands on the west side of Highway 12 in the San Isabel National Forest.

In addition to public lands in the national forest, there are currently five state trust lands found in GMU 85 that are open to big game hunting. These include the Black Hawk, Little Sheep Mountain, Schultz Canyon, South Middle Creek, and Guillermo Ranch properties. Although they are all relatively small (585 acres to 2,118 acres) they all provide opportunities to hunt one or more of the big game species. There are also limited licenses available for deer and elk in several of the Ranching for Wildlife properties in the area. However, it will generally take several preference points to draw these licenses. (Please refer to the Ranching for Wildlife section for more details.)

Another prospect for hunters seeking opportunities on public land is the Bosque

Region 3 offers some of the best deer and elk hunting in the state.

del Oso State Wildlife Area in GMU 851. This 30,000-acre property was recently purchased by the Division of Wildlife and is open, on a limited basis, to deer, elk, bear, and mountain lion hunting. Although there are a few other SWAs (such as the Spanish Peaks SWA) scattered between the four-unit area, the Bosque del Oso probably provides the best opportunity for the general public to hunt trophy-quality animals. Although it is a new SWA, it hasn't been kept a secret. If you want a deer or elk tag for this area you will have to be persistent and apply for the appropriate license for several years before accumulating enough preference points.

Other opportunities to hunt in this part of Region 3 include guided hunts through outfitters and trespass fees to access private properties. A word of warning, trespass fees and guided hunts in this area are likely to be very expensive. If you're willing to put in the effort, I also know of at least one hunter who has obtained permission to hunt private property for elk without having to pay a trespass fee. It will take some digging, but there may be a couple of landowners in the region that will still let you hunt for free.

If you are lucky enough to get the chance to hunt this part of Colorado, you will find pinon-juniper woodland in the foothills west of Trinidad. As you continue higher into the foothills and lower elevations of the Culebra Range you will find large areas of montane shrubland. This area makes up excellent habitat for black bears and is responsible for the dense bear population. As you continue to higher elevations in the Spanish Peaks you will find montane and subalpine forest. There is also a small area of alpine tundra at the highest elevations in the southern portion of the Culebra Range.

Terrain will vary greatly depending on elevation from gently rolling hills to deeply eroded foothills to steep mountainous terrain with meadows and valleys. Weather conditions in this part of Colorado are generally mild in the early seasons. Even with its southern latitude the Culebra Range can pick up considerable amounts of snow as early as October. Some of the high mountain valleys can also have very low temperatures (in the single digits) as early as November. For public land information see the Blanca Peak, Trinidad, and Alamosa BLM Surface Management Status Maps.

While public property and licenses are limited, the Trinidad area may hold one of the best chances for hunters to collect a trophy of a lifetime. Although it will take some planning, and some scouting, persistent hunters will find opportunities here. This is a good area to save up preference points and hunt second choice units in the meantime. It may take several years to get the tag you want, but it could be well worth the wait.

The Wet Mountains and Sangre De Cristo Range (GMUs 69, 84, 86, 861)

Located on the east side of Region 3, the Wet Mountains make up a relatively low and broad range. To the west of the Wet Mountains is the Sangre De Cristo Range, a narrow band of picturesque mountains that divide the San Luis Valley from the Wet Mountain Valley. The range contains eight 14,000-foot peaks, four of which are found in the Sangre De Cristo Wilderness Area. The wilderness area encompasses over 226,000 acres of wildlands along the range.

Four GMUs (69, 84, 86, and 861) cover the Wet Mountains area and Sangre De Cristo Range. These four units make up the Wet Mountain deer herd, which is the third largest in Region 3 with over 15,000 animals and a strong buck-to-doe ratio. GMUs 86 and 861 cover the Sangre De Cristo Range and comprise the Sangre De Cristo Elk herd, which has contained 1,600 to 1,800 animals over the past few years. Units 69 and 84 make up the Grape Creek elk herd that generally has about 1,600 animals with a strong bull-to-cow ratio that has been as high as 38 to 100 in recent years.

In addition to excellent deer and elk hunting, the area also offers abundant opportunities to hunt bighorn sheep. Sheep Management Units S8 and S9 cover the Sangre De Cristo Range, which may hold the largest population of sheep in the state. There were 60 bighorn sheep licenses available in S9 for all seasons in 2001 with 25 animals harvested. Although not as plentiful, there are also several sheep licenses available in Units S35 and S49, which cover the Wet Mountains. In addition to good bear hunting, the Wet Mountain antelope herd is the largest in Region 3, with over 1,500 animals and a good buck-to-doe ratio that has been 30 to 100 in recent years. There are also opportunities to hunt in the early High Country Rifle Deer season; GMUs 82, 86, and 861. If you want to draw one of these tags it will probably take a minimum of six preference points, but these units produce some tremendous bucks.

The Wet Mountains are surrounded by pinon-juniper woodlands at the lower elevations followed by montane shrubland as you move higher. At still higher elevations you move into montane forest and subalpine forest. Elevation in the Wet Mountains varies from about 8,000 to 11,000 feet with the highest peaks pushing up over 12,000 feet. The terrain can be steep, but in general it is more forgiving than most of the other mountainous areas in Colorado. Vehicle access is good via State Highways 165 and 96. There are numerous forest service roads, campgrounds, and trails that can be accessed from both highways. There is a lot of private land in the area, but there is also a lot of public land in the San Isabel National Forest that offers good hunting for deer and elk. The Canon City and Blanca Peak BLM Surface Management Status Maps will be useful when trying to determine public from private land.

Weather in this part of Colorado will be variable but often milder than many of the higher mountain ranges in the state. Mild conditions with little precipitation can last well into the rifle seasons. The Wet Mountains make up an excellent area for deer hunters with several hundred animals harvested from GMUs 69 and 84 each year. Elk hunters also have relatively good success in the area.

The Sangre De Cristo Range is much different from the Wet Mountains in terms of habitat and terrain. This is in large part due to the extreme elevation differential. From the San Luis Valley there is over 7,000 feet of vertical elevation gain in portions of the range in as little as three horizontal miles. Since the range is so narrow, 7 to 8 miles wide in places, the extreme changes in elevation over short distances account for abrupt changes in the ecosystems. At the base of the range there is a thin tract of pinon-juniper woodland that extends along each side of the mountains. In succession, thin tracts of montane forest and subalpine forest are found at higher elevations. Finally, there is a relatively large area of alpine tundra at the highest elevations in the range. The result of a narrow, high mountain range is extremely steep and rugged terrain. Many of the drainages are very steep-sided, and the higher elevations have year-round snowpack. Although the Sangre De Cristo Range is not far from the Wet Mountains, the weather can be much more severe. The high peaks tend to capture a lot of moisture, although hunting in the early seasons can be reasonably mild and comfortable.

Unlike some of the other wilderness areas in the state, there are two roads that cut through the Sangre De Cristo Wilderness allowing for access to both sides of the range. From the San Luis Valley side, County Road LL57 leaves Highway 285 at Villa Grove and crosses the range over Hayden Pass and drops down into Coaldale. In the southern portion of the range County Road 235 follows Medano Creek over Medano Pass and drops down the east side of the range via County Road 406. There are several other county roads and jeep trails that will provide access into the mountains. There are also 180 miles of foot trails in the wilderness area that allow hunters the opportunity to get into remote areas of the range. Since the prominent access points tend to concentrate hunters in small areas, this is another location that is well-suited for people looking to find a less crowded hunting situation by backpacking.

While hunters in GMUs 69 and 84 will generally experience good success rates, GMUs 86 and 861 often have below average harvest rates for deer and elk. But the low harvest rates are offset by good trophy potential for both species and incredible scenic beauty. As an added bonus, big game hunters pursuing deer and elk in this area will also have good chances to find bears. In fact, a huge black bear was taken during the 1999 hunting season north of the town of Westcliffe on the east side of the Sangre De Cristo mountains. The bear weighed in at an incredible 575 pounds and measured 8 feet 4 inches with paws that were 8.25 inches wide. This is remarkable when compared to the average Colorado black bear that weighs between 200 and 250 pounds. Roger McQueen was the lucky hunter who bagged the bruin while spot-and-stalk hunting. He used a .300 Winchester magnum to harvest the bear.

Please note that a large part of the southern Sangre De Cristo Range, especially in GMU 861, is private property consisting of large ranches. Several of these ranches are accessible through various outfitters in the region who offer guided hunts. Refer to the Canon City and Blanca Peak BLM Maps for public land information.

The Sangre de Cristos offer trophy potential and incredible beauty.

Saguache (GMUs 68, 681)

The small town of Saguache (which is a Ute word for "blue water") is located at the north end of the San Luis Valley between GMUs 68 and 681. These two units make up a relatively small but important area for big game hunters in Region 3. Although it was once a busy supply town for nearby mining areas such as Bonanza, Saguache is now a quiet and somewhat isolated town. Most of the land to the south and east of town within the San Luis Valley is private, but hunters will find abundant public lands to the north and west.

Units 68 and 681 make up the geographic area that holds the Saguache deer, elk, and antelope herds. Based on recent DOW statistics there are over 5,600 deer in the two units. Elk numbers are also good in the area with over 4,700 animals and a bull-to-cow ratio of 23 to 100 in recent years. The antelope herd in this area is small at 450, but there are generally several tags available. Although opportunities are very limited, hunters familiar with the area may want to consider bighorn sheep hunting in Units S10 or S55. There is also the occasional black bear in the area.

When hunting the area you will find that the terrain west of Saguache along State Highway 114 is wide-open sagebrush country consisting of a large quantity of BLM land. (The Saguache and Del Norte BLM Surface Management Status Maps will be helpful in determining public land in the area.) This is where you will often see antelope and deer. The low sagebrush country also provides wintering areas for deer and elk later in the year. There is some pinon-juniper woodland at the lower elevations surrounding the sagebrush areas that makes up good deer hunting venues. Proceeding west on 114 takes you to the Cochetopa Hills within the Rio Grande National Forest. Here you will climb in elevation from about 7,600 feet in the sagebrush areas to over 10,000 feet at North Pass where Highway 114 crosses the continental divide. The divide makes up the western boundary for Units 68 and 681, and several of the higher peaks along the divide to the north approach 12,000 feet in elevation. The Cochetopa Hills consist of montane and subalpine forest with ponderosa pines, spruce, fir, and aspen. In general, the landscape in the lower areas is made up of hills with mountainous areas and moderate to rough terrain at the higher elevations.

There is good access to the area via Highway 285 from Salida or Monte Vista and Highway 114 from the Gunnison area. There are many county roads and jeep trails that can be accessed from the two highways. Weather conditions are generally mild with little snow accumulations through the first and sometimes second rifle seasons.

The pinon-juniper woodlands provide
good hunting for mule deer.

By the late rifle season temperatures can be downright cold (in the 20s and 30s) with strong winds in the open country. Hunters seem to have the best success in this area during the late rifle season, but this is also when you will find the most elk hunters in the field. In recent years well over 1,000 hunters pursued elk in Unit 68 during the third rifle season. Although it is a relatively isolated geographic area, hunting pressure is moderate to high. This is another region where learning the terrain and understanding deer and elk movements may help you utilize hunter pressure to your advantage. This may take a few hunting seasons, but be patient.

From a hunting standpoint, the appealing qualities of GMUs 68 and 681 are the large quantities of public land, good numbers of deer and elk, excellent access, and the geographic isolation. Although hunting pressure can be high, you probably won't have to compete with many other recreationalists. The general public really hasn't found the area yet like other parts of Colorado, where multiple types of recreation sometimes result in conflict. There have also been several trophy-caliber animals harvested in this region. Although it has been some time ago, a hunter killed a tremendous typical mule deer in Saguache County that scored 209. This buck is still ranked 32nd in the Boonc and Crockett *Records of North American Big Game*.

The Lake City Area (GMUs 66, 67)

Moving west in Region 3 from the Saguache area you go from a remote and isolated area to an even more remote and undeveloped part of the state. Lake City is the only town in Hindsdale County with a year-round population. It is located centrally in the southern half of GMU 66 and is surrounded by a tremendous amount of public land. Due north of Lake City is the Big Blue Wilderness Area and the Powderhorn Primitive Area. Immediately south and west are vast amounts of BLM lands, and due east of Lake City is the La Garita Wilderness Area. With abundant forest service land in the Rio Grande National Forest surrounding the area, Lake City makes a great jumping-off point for people interested in hunting the vast amount of public land in this remote section of Colorado.

Lake City is another town with a prominent mining heritage, and although there is a tremendous amount of public land here, you still need to watch for private property including mining claims. The town is situated on the Lake Fork of the Gunnison River and much of the property on the river bottoms is also privately owned. In addition to its mining heritage, Lake City is famous for Alferd Packer who was prospecting in the Lake City area in 1874. His group was stranded in a snowstorm and Alferd survived by eating his five companions. The flat-topped mountains above the Lake Fork of the Gunnison River northeast of Lake City became known as the Cannibal Plateau.

Units 66 and 67 make up the Powderhorn Creek deer herd, which generally has a population over 5,000 animals. These two units also comprise the Lake Fork elk herd that has contained 5,500 to 6,000 animals in recent years. There is also a small antelope herd in GMU 67 known as the Chance Gulch herd that normally contains over 200 animals. In addition to bear and mountain lion hunting, there was also one tag available for bighorn sheep in Unit S22. As a bonus there are also moose in the area. During the 2000 hunting season the DOW started allocating several moose licenses for residents in Unit 66 for the archery, muzzleloader, and rifle seasons. Basically, every big game animal (with the exception of desert bighorns) is available to hunters in this part of Colorado.

When hunting this area you will find a wide variety of terrain and habitat. Elevation ranges from 8,658 feet at Lake City to over 14,000 feet in the highest peaks in the area. As a result you will experience everything from open sagebrush to montane and subalpine forest as well as alpine tundra. The weather is as variable as the terrain. You will want to be well prepared for all types of weather, and make sure your four-wheel-drive is in good running condition. Don't forget the chains for your rig and a good shovel as well as a towrope. Some of the jeep trails in the area are rough and unforgiving.

You will find the Lake City area a beautiful part of Colorado. Although there are a good number of summertime visitors to the area, in general it still has an unspoiled quality. Hunting pressure is moderate, and hunters are rewarded with good harvest rates. Access is very good in the area with a number of county roads and forest service roads in the national forest. A wide variety of hunting opportunities exists here. Those that wish to car camp off of public roads will find plenty of space. Those in search of more remote destinations by vehicle will also find abundant four-wheel-drive roads. For those of you interested in pack-in trips there is also a tremendous amount of remote backcountry available for your use. I would recommend the La Garita Wilderness area where there are 175 miles of trails and good numbers of elk. If you get far enough off the beaten path, the La Garita Wilderness will reward you with an absence of other hunters.

The Lake City area offers a good amount of public access, scenic beauty, and a rich mining heritage.

Upper and Lower Rio Grande Herds (GMUs 76, 79, 80, 81)

The four units that comprise the upper and lower Rio Grande deer and elk herds make up an important area to big game hunters in Colorado. Units 76 and 79 contain the Upper Rio Grande deer herd that generally has a population over 3,500 animals. The Upper Rio Grande elk herd usually contains 5,000 to 5,500 animals. Units 80 and 81 are known as the Lower Rio Grande deer herd, and they generally contain 7,000 to 7,600 animals. The Lower Rio Grande elk herd has a strong population of over 9,000 animals based on recent DOW statistics.

In addition to good populations of deer and elk the area also contains three antelope herds. GMU 79 is known as the Del Norte herd and contains over 600 animals. GMU 80 makes up the Monte Vista herd at 560 animals, and GMU 81 contains the Magote Peaks herd with 570 animals. This is a significant concentration of antelope in Region 3. GMU 76 also contains a huntable population of moose. There are also opportunities to hunt bighorn sheep in Units S29 and S30.

The four units that make up the Rio Grande herds cover a large portion of the San Juan Mountains, especially that portion of the San Juans on the east side of the continental divide. Although much of the eastern portions of GMUs 79, 80, and 81 contain private property within the San Luis Valley, there is abundant public land in the Rio Grande National Forest in the western portions of these units. At the margin between the San Luis Valley and the national forests to the west there is also a significant amount of BLM land and some scattered state properties. Moving west into these units you will find that GMU 81 contains a large percentage of the South San Juan Wilderness on the east side of the continental divide. Unit 76 contains a significant portion of the Weminuche Wilderness Area, also on the east side of the divide.

In terms of habitat the four-unit region is very diverse. Starting in the San Luis Valley there is abundant agricultural lands and, where natural vegetation remains, large areas of semi-desert shrublands. The valley is bounded to the west by a margin of pinon-juniper woodlands that gives way to montane forest. The montane forest penetrates the San Juan Mountains parallel to the Rio Grande River drainage where there are also areas of montane shrubland. These shrubland areas make up some of the best black bear habitat in the San Juans. The Rio Grande River drainage is also an important riparian system. Surrounding the montane forests at higher elevations are large tracts of subalpine forest and relatively large areas of alpine tundra at the highest elevations.

Elevations range from 7,500 to over 14,000 feet at the highest peaks. As with all other mountainous areas in Colorado hunters will need to pay special attention to wind direction when hunting areas with vast elevation changes over short distances. As a rule of thumb, start at lower elevations in the early morning and work your way up. Air currents are usually falling from the high elevations to the low elevations at this time of day. This is due to the relative temperature and density of the air. The greatest cumulative heat loss from the earth's surface is generally just prior to sunrise. The cold air at the higher elevations generally flows downhill because it is denser, and when hunting big game, you always want the wind in your favor. Following this method means that you will generally be hunting uphill early with a nice cold breeze hitting you in the face. The animals above you won't pick up your scent until it's too late.

As warming occurs throughout the morning, air currents will begin to change direction by late morning and into the afternoon. The heated air in the valleys will often begin to rise, causing a complete switch. If you have planned out your hunt accordingly, you should be working your way back downhill when this switch starts to happen. Many hunters overlook the wind and don't give big game animals due credit for their ability to smell. This one oversight can lead to an unsuccessful hunt where no animals are spotted. Keep the wind in your favor, and also understand that this rule of thumb is often thwarted by weather systems and unusual geographic features that can cause wind currents to shift in unusual patterns.

While all four of the GMUs discussed here are known for good elk hunting, Unit 76 stands out above the rest. Elk licenses are only available on a limited basis for this unit, but drawing a tag here will be worth the wait. Depending on the season you choose to hunt, most rifle hunters can expect to draw a tag with three preference points. The area also offers good opportunities to draw cow elk tags in all four of the units with 0 to 2 preference points. Bowhunters will generally pull a bull license for Unit 76 with two points, and success rates are very good. A total of 104 bowhunters harvested 30 bull elk in Unit 76 during the 2001 archery season. This translates to a solid 29 percent success rate, which is very good for bowhunters when compared to state averages of about 14 to 15 percent in recent years. Although this region of Colorado is not touted as a productive deer hunting area, don't let it discourage you. It will take some scouting, but there are some very good deer hunting locations. I would also suggest talking to some of the private landowners in this area.

The four-unit area that comprises the Rio Grande deer and elk herds is an excellent place for big game hunters in Colorado. The diversity of terrain and good access to abundant public lands creates a multitude of opportunities for all types of hunters. Backcountry hunts are available as well as good day hunting from access points easily obtainable from public roads. Hunters will find services available in towns such as Del Norte, Monte Vista, Alamosa, and Antonito when hunting this area.

The San Juan Mountains (GMUs 75, 751, 77, 78, 771)

The San Juan Mountains make up a large area in the western half of Region 3. GMUs 75, 77, 78, 751, and 771 comprise the San Juan deer and elk herds and cover a large part of the San Juan Mountains including those portions of the Weminuche and South San Juan Wilderness Areas that lie on the west side of the continental divide. Although this is a large area there are plenty of deer and elk to go around. The DOW estimated that there has been over 20,000 deer in this five-unit region for the past few years. Elk were also very abundant, with a population that has varied from approximately 15,000 to over 18,000 animals in recent years.

In addition to a very strong bear population the area holds a good number of bighorn sheep in Management Units S15, S16, S28, and S31. In 2001 there were nine sheep harvested from the four combined units. The San Juans also hold the only mountain goat unit in Region 3. Management Unit G5 had six tags issued and six animals harvested in the most recent hunting season. Although there are only a few goat tags for G5 it's still a good opportunity to consider, especially for hunters who live nearby.

Although mule deer have been declining, the area still offers very good deer hunting. Harvest rates for deer in the five units is generally good, with rifle hunters normally exceeding average success rates. Most notably, 191 hunters in the third rifle season in a recent year harvested a total of 121 deer in GMU 771, equating to an incredible 66 percent success rate. This included does and bucks. Of course, each season will vary depending on weather conditions and hunting pressure. Elk hunters generally meet state average success rates in the area, and more importantly, there are an abundance of tags available. Bull tags are still available over the counter in the five units (at the present time) and several of the units had leftover cow tags in recent years. So if you're strictly looking to get some meat, there are very good chances to draw cow elk tags without preference points. The DOW has also been generous with deer tags in the area over the past few years. Although the number of doe tags has been reduced recently there are still opportunities to draw doe licenses in Units 751 and 771.

In terms of habitat and terrain there is a great deal of variability between the five units that make up the San Juan deer and elk herds. Those individuals hunting in the southern portions of Units 75, 751 and 771 will find hills of pinon-juniper woodland and dry, open landscapes with large areas of sagebrush. It should be noted that this area contains a large amount of private land as well as a portion of the Southern Ute Indian Reservation, where hunting is currently restricted to tribal members only. (The Durango BLM Surface Management Status Map will provide public versus private land information.) Farther north in Units 75 and 751 as well as all of Unit 77 and large parts of 78 contain mountainous areas of montane forest, and at the higher elevations, large tracts of subalpine forest consisting of spruce, fir, aspen, and pine. At

The San Juan Mountains from Ignacio.

Craig Hopkins with a 6x6 bull taken in the San Juan Mountains. (C. Hopkins)

still higher elevations there are relatively large areas of alpine tundra. Hunters tackling the remote mountainous areas will want to be in good physical condition and well prepared with survival gear.

The northern portions of Units 75, 751, and 77 cover much of the Weminuche Wilderness Area on the west side of the continental divide. Unit 78 consists of about half of the South San Juan Wilderness Area, also on the west side of the continental divide. These two wilderness areas combined contain over 650,000 acres of the most unspoiled and tough to access wildlands in Colorado. Although many visitors use the trails that are easy to reach, those hunters looking for a true backcountry experience can find it if they put in the effort. This will mean backpacking in or using animal power.

The South San Juan Wilderness is well known to Colorado hunters as the place where the last known grizzly bear in the state was killed. In 1979 a bowhunter killed a sow grizzly in the Navajo River Basin. Although no grizzly sightings have been confirmed since 1979, there have been frequent sightings by hunters and hikers in the Weminuche and the South San Juan Wilderness. The sightings are most likely black bears, but the best chance of a remnant population of grizzly bears exists in one of these wilderness areas. In fact, bear surveys conducted by volunteer groups have turned up hair and scat samples that may indicate there are a few grizzlies still inhabiting the area (*The Complete Guide to Colorado's Wilderness Areas*, Fielder and Pearson, 1994).

Access into the wilderness areas is difficult due to the absences of roads, but good access is attainable via forest service roads into the San Juan National Forest outside of the wilderness. Another way to get into the Weminuche is to take the Durango-Silverton Narrow Gauge, which parallels the Animas River. The Animas River forms the boundary between GMUs 74 and 75. The train runs through the western portion of the wilderness area and makes stops at two locations (Needleton and Elk Park) to drop and pick up backpackers. Most years these trips are available when the train runs between Durango and Silverton from May 6 to October 28. Hunters are welcome, and the train carries several bowhunters into the backcountry each year. If you are fortunate enough to harvest an animal, the train will carry your meat back in a freight car. Just be sure to wrap the meat well and be courteous to the other passengers who are likely to be non-hunting tourists. For more information concerning the Durango-Silverton Narrow Gauge, call (970) 247-2733.

I am very fond of the San Juan Mountains region of Colorado. My grandparents lived in Durango for many years and my family made numerous visits to the area when I was growing up. These visits often included rides on the Durango-Silverton Narrow Gauge, and although I haven't done a hunt in the Weminuche yet, it is on my list of things to do. So if you ever decide to load up the backpack and ride the train into the Weminuche, you might find me on the same train-car.

Craig Hopkins with a trophy mule deer taken in the Durango area, San Juan Mountains. (C. Hopkins)

The Four Corners Region (GMUs 72, 73, 74, 741)

This area might be notable because Colorado, Utah, Arizona, and New Mexico meet at a common point, but it is remarkable for much more. It is an area of important cultural significance, especially to the Ute Indians. Both the Ute Mountain and Southern Ute Indian Reservations are found in this part of Colorado. Mesa Verde National Park is an incredible venue for viewing the ancient cliff dwellings of the Anasazi Indians, and Hovenweep National Monument makes up another important archeological site. More relevant to this book, though, is the fact that the area contains a tremendous mule deer population. It also offers big game hunters good opportunities at elk, mountain lion, and bears.

There are over 17,000 deer in this four-unit region made up by two recognized herds. Units 72 and 73 are known as the Mesa Verde deer herd which numbers 9,970 animals based on recent DOW estimates. Units 74 and 741 make up the Hermosa deer herd that has grown from about 5,000 in 1999 to over 7,000 by most recent DOW estimates. Although there are elk in Units 72 and 73, these two GMUs are not incorporated into any recognized herd by the DOW. The more important elk units here are 74 and 741, which make up the Hermosa elk herd. This herd has stayed consistent at about 5,000 animals over the past few years.

Starting at the far southwest corner of the state, GMU 72 covers a large area of pinon-juniper woodland. In addition to the pinon pines and juniper, you will encounter a great deal of red cedar. Unit 72 also contains semi-desert shrubland and large areas of montane shrubland. Moving east into Units 73 and 741 you will also find large areas of pinon, juniper, and cedar to the south. As you move north into the units you will pass through montane shrubland and into montane forest at the higher elevations. Unit 74 is markedly different from the other three because of its alpine terrain. With elevations over 11,000 feet there is a large amount of montane and subalpine forest consisting of various pine, fir, aspen, and spruce.

Excluding the mountainous alpine terrain of GMU 74, you will find widespread high-desert, canyon terrain in the southwest part of Colorado. There are relatively large areas with sparse groundcover, and the arid climate results in intermittent drainages that stay dry for much of the year. There are also large areas with hills and scenic locations with high rimrock and deep canyons. Weather conditions during the hunting seasons are generally warmer and drier than in other parts of western Colorado. Hunters can use the dry climate to their advantage. Scouting out good water sources in areas where water is scarce can lead to good concentrations of deer. The heat can also be a problem for those hunters who fill their tags. Make preparations prior to your hunt to properly care for your meat. This may mean identifying local meat processors or facilities that have coolers. If these aren't available you will have to be prepared with ice and coolers of your own. This is an especially important consideration for early season hunters. Your window of opportunity to get your meat cooled will be very limited before spoilage and flies ruin it. One of my hunting companions built a small trailer specifically to store his meat after productive hunting trips. The trailer consists of a storage area for the meat that is kept dry and cool. Compartments that are filled with blocks of ice surround the storage area. Drainage holes channel the melt water out of the trailer. Even during the hottest conditions, he can keep his meat cold for several days if necessary.

As is often the case with productive big game areas, there is a downside. The downside to the Four Corners region is the large amount of private property. The Ute Mountain Indian Reservation covers a large part of the southern half of Units 72 and 73. This land is closed to the general public for big game hunting. A large area in the southern portion of Unit 741 contains Southern Ute Indian lands. This land is also currently closed to the general public for hunting. The Southern Ute Tribe has offered limited hunts with Indian guides on reservation lands in the past, but these are currently not available. Furthermore, the area along Highway 160 from Durango to Cortez is in large part private. Areas along the La Plata River and in Montezuma Valley contain irrigated farms, orchards, and cattle operations that are off limits to hunters.

The upside is that serious hunters can find good opportunities on public lands if they spend enough time scouting in the area. There is a good deal of BLM land in the north half of GMU 72. There are also scattered BLM lands surrounding the north and east sides of Mesa Verde National Park. (Please note there is no hunting allowed in the National Park). There are also scattered state lands surrounding Durango, including state wildlife areas such as BODO and Perins Peak. Unit 74 extends from Durango north to Silverton and is primarily National Forest Service land open to hunting. Regardless of the unit, you always want to be very careful to avoid trespassing on private lands without permission. This is one of the most common hunting violations in Colorado. To help prevent this problem, purchase the Cortez and Durango Surface Management Status Maps available through BLM.

If you are new to this area and interested in elk hunting, I would recommend hunting GMU 74. While harvest rates aren't unusually high here, there are good numbers of elk and some big bulls. I would concentrate on the namesake of the elk herd and hunt the Hermosa Creek drainage located north of Durango. Be sure to check out some of the side tributaries that run into Hermosa Creek. Units 72, 73, and 741 are all very good deer hunting GMUs. Statistically hunters often exceed 40 percent harvest rates in any of these units. Harvest rates are generally higher in the later seasons. For example, in a recent year, 68 percent of the 419 rifle hunters that hunted the third season in GMU 741 bagged a deer. If you're willing to pay for a high quality hunt, there are also several outfitters in the area that have access to private property.

Disappointment Creek (GMUs 70, 71, 711)

Disappointment Creek originates in the San Juan National Forest and flows along the northern portion of Dolores County and into San Miguel County in GMUs 70 and 71. The Disappointment Creek elk herd is made up by GMUs 70, 71, and 711. Elk numbers are anything but disappointing, with over 14,000 animals in the three combined units. This makes up the third largest elk herd in Region 3. The same three units make up the Groundhog deer herd which ranks as the largest deer herd in Region 3 with a population just over 30,000, based on recent DOW statistics. If the numbers didn't get your attention, it might even sound more appealing to learn that many of these animals roam public lands in the San Juan and Uncompahgre National Forests. There is also a large amount of BLM land, predominantly in the western half of San Miguel County in GMU 70 that extends into portions of Dolores

County to the south. The area is also home to the Lizard Head Wilderness Area.

This part of Colorado is rich with wildlife. Not only are deer and elk numbers good, but predators are abundant, with good black bear and mountain lion populations. As an added bonus there is also a very limited opportunity to hunt desert bighorn sheep in the area. Sheep Management Units S62 and S64 are the only two units with huntable populations of desert bighorns. There were nine precious licenses available (six in S62 and three in S64) during the most recent hunting season.

With all of the deer in the area you would think that trophy potential would be high, and you would be right. The DOW estimates that there are about 14 bucks for every 100 does in the Groundhog herd. This doesn't sound that exceptional, but when you consider the total number of animals in the herd (over 30,000), it translates into a lot of bucks. In fact, the world record typical mule deer was harvested in Dolores County in 1972. According to the Boone and Crockett records this buck scored an astounding 226 4/8 points and was taken in Proven Canyon within the San Juan National Forest. This 5x6 muley far outclasses the competition, beating the number two buck in the world by over 9 points. The area is also responsible for more records, as if the number one mule deer wasn't enough. According to the fourth edition of the *Colorado Bowhunting Records of Big Game,* the largest bear and the second largest mountain lion were both taken in San Miguel County. Wrapping up the records resume of the area, the second largest typical mule deer taken by a bowhunter came out of Dolores County.

Terrain and habitat are very diverse in this part of Colorado. The western portions of GMUs 70 and 711 consist of large areas of pinon-juniper woodland and semi-desert shrubland. The Dolores River and numerous tributaries contain important riparian zones. As you move east into the higher elevations of the San Juans you will find large areas of montane shrubland before moving into montane forest. At still higher elevations in the eastern portion of GMU 70 and most of 71 you will find large stands of subalpine forest and alpine tundra at the highest elevations. The Lizard Head Wilderness Area contains three peaks over 14,000 feet in elevation. Below timberline the areas of alpine tundra are surrounded by large stands of aspen, spruce and fir. Terrain varies from mountainous to plateau and canyons to hills and flatter farm country.

Due to the large variance in elevation across this region weather can also be extremely variable. As an example, someone rifle hunting at lower elevations near 6,000 feet in GMU 711 during the first rifle season might experience warm temperatures in the 60s. Another person hunting the same day at a higher elevation near 11,000 feet in the Lizard Head Wilderness in GMU 71 might be experiencing cold temperatures in the 30s and snow. The leading edge of the San Juans can intercept a lot of moisture moving in from the west. This results in early snows at the high elevations.

The DOW is very liberal with elk tags in all three units. Bull licenses are currently unlimited and there are generally enough cow tags available that you will have good chances to draw without preference points. Although deer tags are currently all limited, the DOW has been liberal with licenses in this region in the past few hunting seasons. Unless management practices change drastically here in the near future you should be able to draw a deer tag each year and hunt elk in the same unit. The icing on the cake is that you will probably have a very good opportunity to fill both tags. Success rates for both species are very good, unlike other units where hunting is better for one animal when compared to the other.

With the large numbers of deer and elk this region of Colorado has become a popular area with big game hunters. Access is very good on state highways, county roads, forest service roads, and jeep trails. The one drawback is that hunting pressure can be high, but with the abundance of public land there are still places where you can escape from the crowds. (The Silverton and Dove Creek Surface Management BLM Maps will be helpful to determine public lands in this region.) If you are new to hunting in Colorado or just looking for a new hunting spot, this may be one of the best deer and elk areas in Region 3, if not in the entire state.

Bighorn sheep tracks.

Region 3 Hub Cities
Trinidad
Population — 9,546 • Elevation — 6,025'

If you are driving south on Interstate 25 towards New Mexico, you will find the town of Trinidad to be the last major stop before heading over Raton Pass and crossing the state line. Trinidad straddles the Purgatoire River and is situated among some of the best deer, elk, and bear hunting areas in the state. Although there is a lot of private land in the vicinity of Trinidad, good big game hunting opportunities exist nearby in the San Isabel National Forest to the west of town. There are also several State Trust Properties west of town, and state wildlife areas such as the Spanish Peaks and Bosque del Oso provide additional public lands for hunters to access.

Trinidad originated as an encampment along the Santa Fe Trail. Later it became a center for large cattle ranches. Numerous coal mines also operated in the area. The town has a historic atmosphere and many of the existing buildings were constructed around the turn of the 20th century. Hunters pursuing game in GMUs 85, 851, 134, 140, or 141 will do well to use Trinidad as a resource center for their hunts.

ACCOMMODATIONS

Best Western Inn, I-25 and Exit 13A, (719) 846-2215
Holiday Inn, I-25 and Exit 11, (719) 846-4491
Royal Motel, 1115 E. Main St., (719) 846-3361
Savoy Hotel and Café, 311 N. Commercial, (719) 846-2532
Trail's End Motel, 616 E. Main St., (719) 846-4425
Picketwire Lodge and Store, 7600 Hwy. 12, Stonewall, CO, (719) 868-2265

CAMPGROUNDS AND RV PARKS

Biggs RV Park, 10301 Santa Fe Trail Dr., (719) 846-3307
Cawthon Park, 1701 Santa Fe Trail Dr., (719) 846-3303
Trinidad Lake State Park, 32610 Hwy. 12, (719) 846-4730
State Park Camping Reservations 800-678-CAMP
Forest Service Camping Reservations 877-444-6777

RESTAURANTS

Black Jacks Saloon and Steakhouse, 225 W. Main St., (719) 846-9501
Bob and Earl's Café, 1118 Robinson Ave., (719) 846-0144
C&H Restaurant, 443 N. Commercial, (719) 846-3851
Country Kitchen, I-25 and Exit 11, (719) 846-4500
El Capitan, 321 State St., (719) 846-9903
El Paso Café, 1101 E. Main St., (719) 846-8522
Elm Street Station, 516 Elm Street, (719) 846-1400
La Victoria Mexican Restaurant, 525 San Juan Ave., (719) 845-8792
Lee's Bar-B-Q, 825 San Pedro, (719) 846-7621

RESTAURANTS, CONTINUED

Lone Star Café, 200 W. Main St., (719) 846-6101
Mission At The Bell Restaurant, 134 W. Main St., (719) 845-1513
Trinidad Diner, 734 E. Main St., (719) 846-7798
Twin Pines Lounge, 1415 Nolan Dr., (719) 846-0458

VETERINARIANS

Fisher's Peak Veterinary Clinic, 1617 Santa Fe Trail, (719) 846-3211
Trinidad Animal Clinic, 1701 E. Main St., (719) 846-3212

SPORTING GOODS, GUNS, AND GUNSMITHS

Leisure Time Sports, 134 W. Main St., (719) 846-4749
Corral Pawn and Trading Post, 114 E. Main St., (719) 846-6043
The Gun Shack, 113 E. Main St., (719) 845-8011

TAXIDERMISTS

Huffman Bird Taxidermy, 36740 Freedom Dr., (719) 846-4567
Steve Huffman Taxidermy, 123 E. Main St., Aguilar, CO (719) 941-4125

MEAT PROCESSORS

Bob's Processing, 2261 N. Linden Ave., (719) 846-6432

AUTO RENTAL AND REPAIR

A-1 Automatics, 2500 E. Main St., (719) 846-6193
Bowie Automotive, 224 Elm St., (719) 846-7871
Circle Chevrolet-Buick, I-25 and exit 11, (719) 846-9805
Pioneer Motors of Trinidad (Auto Repair and Rental), 426 E. Main St., (719) 846-2264
Cordova's Towing, 307 E. 2nd St., (719) 846-9620
Jolly's Towing, 39277 County Rd. 42, (719) 846-3028
Kelly's Towing and Automotive Repair, (719) 845-1810
M&M Towing, 138 E. Plum St., (719) 846-8546
J&J Motors (Rental) 732 N. Commercial, (719) 846-3318

AIR SERVICE

Las Animas County Government Airport (Municipal Airport), (719) 846-6271

MEDICAL

Mt. San Rafael Hospital, 410 Benedicta Ave., (719) 846-9213

FOR MORE INFORMATION

Trinidad Las Animas County Chamber of Commerce
309 Nevada Ave., Trinidad, CO 81082-2557, (719) 846-9285

Walsenburg

Population — 3,787 • Elevation — 6,182'

Walsenburg is the county seat of Huerfano County. It makes a good place to stay for people hunting in the San Isabel National Forest to the west of town in GMUs 84 and 85. More specifically it will put you in close proximity to the Wet Mountains and the Spanish Peaks. It's also a convenient location to access GMUs 128 and 133 on the east side of I-25. Highway 160 is an important route that traverses the southern Sangre De Cristo Range via La Veta Pass, providing access into the San Luis Valley from Walsenburg. The community originated as a Spanish settlement in the early 1870s. Large coal deposits made it an important mining center in southern Colorado for much of its history.

ACCOMMODATIONS

Anchor Motel, 1001 Main St., (719) 738-2800
Best Western Rambler Motel, I-25 and Exit 52, (719) 738-1121
Cuchara Inn, 73 Cucharas Ave., Cuchara, CO 81055, (719) 742-3685
Plaza Inn, 118 W. Sixth St., (719) 738-5700

CAMPGROUNDS AND RV PARKS

Country Host Motel and RV Park, 553 US Hwy. 85 and 87, (719) 738-3800
Dakota Campground, 1079 US Hwy 85 and 87, (719) 738-9912
State Park Camping Reservations 800-678-CAMP
Forest Service Camping Reservations 877-444-6777

RESTAURANTS

Alpine Rose Café, 522 Main St., (719) 738-1157
Alys' Fireside Café, 606 Main St., (719) 738-3993
Corine's Mexican Food Restaurant, 822 Main St., (719) 738-1231
Huerfano Café, 904 W. Seventh St., (719) 738-2882
Iron Horse Restaurant and Lounge, 503 W. Seventh St., (719) 738-9966

VETERINARIANS

Rio Cucharas Veterinary Clinic, 22540 U.S. Hwy. 160, (719) 738-1427

SPORTING GOODS, GUNS, AND GUNSMITHS

Hollow Point Gun Shop, 342 W. 7th St., (719) 738-3426
Pawn Shop, 434 W 7th St., (719) 738-2530
Lock Stock and Barrel, 10232 I-25, (719) 738-6181

TAXIDERMISTS

Story Creek Outfitters and Taxidermy, 1054 C.R. 318, (719) 738-3704

AUTO REPAIR

Harp Motor, 1018 W. Seventh St., (719) 738-2842
J M Tire Inc., 928 Main St., (719) 738-2150

Auto Repair, Continued

Jordan's Service, 359 E. 5th St., (719) 738-3833
Price Wrecker and Radiator Service, 110 E. 5th St., (719) 738-1640
Rambler 66 Service Center, 729 Main St., (719) 738-3500

Medical

Huerfano Medical Center, 23500 U.S. Hwy. 160, (719)-738-1500

For More Information

Walsenburg Chamber of Commerce, Railroad Depot, Walsenburg, CO 81089
(719)-738-1065

Del Norte
Population — 1,809 • Elevation — 7,880'

Del Norte is the county seat of Rio Grande County. It is centrally located at the common boundary of GMUs 79 and 80 (two of four units that comprise the Lower and Upper Rio Grande deer and elk herds). Although Del Norte is a small community it caters to big game hunters. It makes a good jumping-off point to the Rio Grande National Forest and the eastern extremities of the San Juan Mountains as well as the La Garita Mountains. Depending on your exact hunting venue, the nearby towns of Monte Vista (to the east) and Creede (to the northwest) also offer the common services required by hunters. Some services available in these two towns have also been listed below for your reference.

ACCOMMODATIONS

Del Norte Motel and Café, 1050 Grand Ave., (719) 657-3581
El Rancho Motel, 1160 Grand Ave., Del Norte, CO (719) 657-3332
La Garita Creek Ranch, 38145 CR Rd. E 39, Del Norte, CO (719) 754-2533
Best Western Movie Manor, 2830 W US Hwy. 160, Monte Vista, CO (719) 852-5921
Comfort Inn Of Monte Vista, 1519 Grand Ave., Monte Vista, CO (719) 852-0612
El Campo Motel, 401 Ulysses Blvd., Monte Vista, CO (719) 852-5952
Snowshoe Motel, Creede, CO (719) 658-2315
Willow Creek Cabins, Creede, CO (719) 658-2322

CAMPGROUNDS AND RV PARKS

State Park Camping Reservations 800-678-CAMP
Forest Service Camping Reservations 877-444-6777

RESTAURANTS

Boogies Restaurant, 410 Grand Ave., (719) 657-2905
Del Norte Motel and Café, 1050 Grand Ave., (719) 657-3581
La Fuente, 540 Grand Ave., (719) 657-0629
The Wright Place, 13319 US Hwy. 160, (719) 657-3512

VETERINARIANS

Del Norte Animal Hospital, 630 Grand Ave., (719) 657-3440

SPORTING GOODS, GUNS, AND GUNSMITHS

Casa De Madera Sports, 660 Grand Ave., (719) 657-2723

TAXIDERMISTS

Valley Taxidermy, 4128 W US Hwy 160, Monte Vista, CO (719) 852-2636
Daniel Keith Taxidermy Studio, 9186 S CR 4 E., Monte Vista, CO (719) 862-5865
Ernest's Taxidermy and Crafts, 3596 W US Hwy 160, Monte Vista, CO
  (719) 852-3277

AUTO RENTAL AND REPAIR

Bailey's Automotive, 12160 US Hwy. 160, (719) 657-0742
Eriksen Motors, 775 Grand Ave., (719) 657-2772
Den's service Center, 810 Grand Ave., (719) 657-2880
Precision towing and Automotive, 10728 US Hwy. 160, (719) 657-3466

MEDICAL

Rio Grande Clinic, 1280 Grand Ave., (719) 657-2510

FOR MORE INFORMATION

Del Norte Chamber of Commerce, 140 Spruce, Del Norte, CO 81132
(719) 657-2845
Monte Vista Chamber of Commerce, 1035 Park Ave., Monte Vista, CO 81144
(719) 852-2731
Creede-Mineral County Chamber of Commerce, Creede Ave., Creede, CO 81130
(719) 658-2374

Pagosa Springs
Population — 1,462 • Elevation — 7,105'

Pagosa Springs is the county seat of Archuleta County. Hunters familiar with Region 3 have probably spent some time in Pagosa Springs. It is a popular town for big game hunters due to its location right in the middle of large concentrations of deer and elk. The town sits at the juncture of GMUs 77, 78, and 771, three of five units that make up the San Juan deer and elk herds. This is another town where you are likely to see large orange banners that read "Welcome Hunters" during the big game seasons. There is good access into the San Juan National Forest from Pagosa Springs and several roads lead to trailheads that provide access into the west side of the South San Juan Wilderness Area.

Pagosa Springs has a long history due to its natural hot springs. Ute and Navajo Indians used the area extensively prior to white settlement. The word Pagosa is derived from a Ute word that means healing waters. The geothermally heated waters are still used as a heat source for local business as well as recreation. There is nothing better than relaxing in a hot mineral spring after a long day of hunting another advantage to staying in Pagosa Springs.

ACCOMMODATIONS

Pagosa Lodge, (970) 731-4141
First Inn of Pagosa, 260 E Hwy 160, (970) 264-4161
Holiday Inn, 2 Solomon Dr., (970) 731-5101
Best Western Oak Ridge Lodge, 158 Hot Springs Blvd., (970) 264-4173
High Country Lodge, Hwy 160 E., (970) 264-4181
Pinewood Inn, 157 Pagosa St., (970) 264-5715
San Juan Motel, 191 E. Pagosa St., (970) 264-2262
Sky View Motel, W Hwy 160, (970) 264-5803
Spring Inn Motel, (970) 264-4168
Super 8 Motel, 34 Piedra Rd., (970) 731-4005

CAMPGROUNDS AND RV PARKS

The Spa Motel and RV Resort, 317 Hot Springs Blvd., (970) 264-5910
Elk Meadows Camping and Recreation Area, Hwy. 160, (970) 264-5482
Pagosa Riverside campground, 2270 E Hwy 160, (970) 264-5874
Wolf Creek Valley Campground, (970) 264-4853
State Park Camping Reservations 800-678-CAMP
Forest Service Camping Reservations 877-444-6777

RESTAURANTS

Amore's House of Pasta, 121 Pagosa St., (970) 264-2822
Bavarian Inn, 90 Piedra Rd., (970) 731-5944
Branding Iron Bar-B-Que, Hwy 160 E., (970) 264-4268
The Cottage, 110 N 4, (970) 264-4555
Elkhorn Café, (970) 264-2146

RESTAURANTS, CONTINUED

Greenhouse Restaurant and Bar, 505 CR 600, (970) 731-2021
Hogs Breath Saloon, 157 Navajo Trail Dr., (970) 731-2626
JJ's Upstream Restaurant, 356 E. Hwy 160, (970) 264-9100
Junction Restaurant, US 160 and 84, (970) 264-5729
Long Horn Sandwich and Steak House, 4760 W Hwy 160, (970) 731-9060
Los Amigos Mexican Grill, 4760 W Hwy 160, (970) 731-2188
Moose River Pub, 20 Village Dr., (970) 731- 5451
Ole Miner's Steakhouse, NE on Hwy 160, (970) 264-5981
The Rose, (970) 264-2955
Seafood Café, 755 San Juan St. #4, (970) 264-9007
Spanish Inn Restaurant, 358 E. Pagosa St., (970) 264-4676
The Three Pines, (970) 731-4141

VETERINARIANS

Aspen Tree Animal Caring Center, 137 CR 250, (970) 382-0100
Pagosa Veterinary Clinic, 550 Hot Springs Blvd., (970) 264-2148
San Juan Veterinary Services, 102 Pike Dr., (970) 264-2629

HORSE RENTAL

Astraddle A Saddle, (970) 731-5076
Diamond Hitch Stables, 2404 N Piedra Rd., (970) 731-7433

SPORTING GOODS, GUNS, AND GUNSMITHS

Pagosa Springs Trading Post, 169 Pagosa St., (970) 264-2185
Ponderosa Do It Best Home Center, Hwy 160 W and Piedra Rd., (970) 731-4111
Sideline Sports, 468 N. Pagosa Blvd., (970) 264-6141

MEAT PROCESSORS

The Buck Stop, 10501 Hwy 160 W., (970) 731-3535

AUTO RENTAL AND REPAIR

Bill's Garage, W 14th St., (970) 264-5326
Blackwood Automotive, 2147 A hwy 160, (970) 731-4993
Lauffer Bros Garage, 2345 W Hwy 160, (970) 731-5523
NAPA Autocare Center, Hwy 160 W, (970) 264-4159
Sutton Automotive, 298 Bastille Dr., (970) 731-4331
Foster Motor and Machine, (970) 264-4769

MEDICAL

Centura Health-Mercy Medical Center, 375 E. Park Ave., Durango, CO
(970) 247-4311

FOR MORE INFORMATION

Pagosa Springs Chamber of Commerce, 402 San Juan St., Pagosa Springs, CO
81147, (970) 264-2360

Durango
Population — 13,722 • Elevation — 6,523'

Durango is a thriving center for tourism in southwest Colorado. It is also the county seat of La Plata County and the largest city in the southwestern corner of the state. It provides a good starting point for access into the San Juan National Forest and the west side of the Weminuche Wilderness Area. Most attractive to big game hunters is the fact that Durango is located near some of the most productive GMUs in Region 3. Hunters who have tags in Units 74, 75, and 741 will find Durango to be a good resource center for their hunt.

As discussed in the San Juan Mountains Highlight, Durango is also home to the Durango and Silverton Narrow Gauge Railroad. Steam-fired train engines built in the early 1920s pull passenger cars along the edges of sheer cliffs adjacent to the Animas River. The scenery is spectacular, and of importance to hunters, this is one route that allows access to the interior of the Weminuche Wilderness Area.

If you've had a successful hunt in the Durango area and you need a good taxidermist, stop in and see my friend Craig Hopkins at AA Taxidermy. Craig is an accomplished big game hunter and excellent taxidermist. His business is located in the small town of Bayfield, Colorado, a short drive from Durango.

ACCOMMODATIONS

Best Value Four Winds Hotel, 20797 US Hwy 160, (970) 247-4512
Best Western Rio Grande Inn, 400 E 2 Ave., (970) 385-4980
The Comfort Inn, 2930 Main Ave., (970) 259-5373
Dollar Inn, 2391 Main Ave., (970) 247-0593
Double Tree Hotel Durango, 501 Camino Del Rio, (970) 259-6580
Durango Inn Best Western, 21382 US Hwy 160, (970) 247-3251
Durango Lodge, 150 E 5th St., (970) 247-0955
Econo Lodge of Durango, 2002 Main Ave., (970) 247-4242
End O Day Motel, 350 E 8 Ave., (970) 247-1722
Ferringway Condominiums, 6 Ferringway Cir., (970) 247-0441
General Palmer Hotel, 567 Main Ave., (970) 247-4747
Hampton Inn, 3777 Main Ave., (970) 247-2600
Hawthorn Suites, 401 E 2nd Ave., (970) 385-4980
Holiday Inn of Durango, 800 S Camino Del Rio, (970) 247-5393
Jarvis Suite Hotel, 125 W 10, (970) 259-6190
Needles Townhomes, 46850 Hwy 550 N., (970) 259-5960
Quality Inn and Suites, 455 S. Camino Del Rio, (970) 259-7900
Ramada Limited, 3030 Main Ave., (970) 259-1333
Residence Inn by Marriott, 21691 US Hwy 160, (970) 259-6200

CAMPGROUNDS AND RV PARKS

Alpen Rose RV Park, 27847 Hwy 550 N., (970) 247-5540
Cottonwood Camper Park, 21636 US Hwy 160, (970) 247-1977
Durango North/Ponderosa KOA, 13391 CR 250, (970) 247-4499

CAMPGROUNDS AND RV PARKS, CONTINUED

Hermosa Meadows Camper Park, 31420 US Hwy 550, (970) 247-3055
KOA Durango East, 30090 US Hwy 160, (970) 247-0783
Lightner Creek Campground, 1567 CR 207, (970) 247-5406
Sundown Acres Year-round RV Park, 5875 US Hwy 550, (970) 247-5199
United Campgrounds of Durango, 1322 Animas View Dr., (970) 247-3853
State Park Camping Reservations 800-678-CAMP
Forest Service Camping Reservations 877-444-6777

RESTAURANTS

Farquahrts, 725 Main Ave., (970) 247-5442
Mama's Boy, 3690 Main Ave., (970) 247-0060
Chelsea London Pub and Grill, 862 Main Ave., (970) 247-2432
Francisco's Restaurante Y Cantina, 619 Main Ave., (970) 247-4098
A'Roma Restaurant and Tavern, 2659 Main Ave., (970) 259-0019
Bar D Chuckwagon Suppers, 8080 CR 260, (970) 247-5753
Bayou Doc's, 701 E 2nd Ave., (970) 259-6486
Bogies Joint 5800 Main Ave., (970) 382-3881
The Buzz House, 1019 Main Ave., (970) 385-5831
Café Durango, (970) 259-3423, 21382 Hwy 160
Carver's Restaurant and Brewery, 1022 Main Ave., (970) 259-2545
Cascade Grill, 50827 US Hwy 550, (970) 259-3500
Catalyst Coffeehouse, 601 E 2 Ave., (970) 385-4041

VETERINARIANS

Alpine Animal Hospital, 2910 Main Ave., (970) 247-5771
Animas Equine, 837 Oso Grande Dr., (970) 259-0129
Baker's Bridge Veterinary Clinic, 13225 CR 250, (970) 247-4701
Durango Animal Hospital, 2461 N. Main, (970) 247-3174

HORSE RENTAL

Adventures Beyond, 4140 CR 234, (970) 247-1694
Buck's Livery, 1 Skier Place, (970) 247-9000
Miller Mountain, Lemon Lake-4748 CR 243, (970) 247-8325
Red Mountain Ranch, 27846 US Hwy 550, (970) 247-9796
Southfork Riding Stables, 28481 US Hwy 160 E., (970) 259-4871

SPORTING GOODS, GUNS, AND GUNSMITHS

Backcountry Experience, 12th and Camino Del Rio, (970) 247-5830
Butler's Wildcat Canyon Traditional Archery, 145 E College Dr., (888) 495-9159
Clayton's Goods for the Woods, Durango Mall, (970) 247-5725
Duranglers Flies and Supplies, 801-B Main Ave., (970) 385-4081
Durango Guns, 2145 Main Ave., (970) 259-9204
Durango Sporting Goods, 863 Main Ave, Durango, Co 81301 , (970) 247-2660
Gardenswartz Outdoors, 8th and Main Ave., (970) 259-6696
Rocky Mtn. Pawn and Gun, 157 CR 250, (970) 247-5226

TAXIDERMISTS

AA Taxidermy and Antler Traders, 39728 Hwy 160 W, Bayfield, CO (970) 884-4194
Antlers, 1996 CR 205, (970) 247-7815
Morningstar's Wildlife Studio, 817 Rainbow Rd., (970) 259-5393
Trophy Taxidermy, 65 CR 207, (970) 247-2201
Wildlife Expressions, 559 E 6 Ave., (970) 247-2013

MEAT PROCESSORS

Bane's Custom Packing, 11063 Rd. 25, (970) 565-3011
Doc's Packing, East of Bayfield, CO (970) 884-2211,

AUTO RENTAL AND REPAIR

AJ Automotive, 799 E 3rd St., (970) 247-4729
AA American, 28753 US Hwy 160 E, (970) 247-4651
Affordable Automotive, 113 CR 250, (970) 247-9786
Basin Towing and Repair, 25823 US Hwy 160 E, (970) 247-2444
Durango Tire, 67 Suttle, (970) 247-1311
Durango Truck 4x4 Outfitters, 29465 Hwy 160 E, (970) 259-5953
Enterprise Rent-A-Car Iron Horse Inn, 5800 N Main Ave., (970) 385-6860
Avis Rent A Car, La Plata Airfield, (970) 247-9761
Budget Car and Truck Rental, La Plata Airfield, (970) 247-9761
Rent-A-Wreck, 21698 US Hwy 160 W., (800) 682-5858

AIR SERVICE

La Plata County Airport, (970) 247-8143

MEDICAL

Centura Health-Mercy Medical Center, 375 E. Park Ave., (970) 247-4311

FOR MORE INFORMATION

Durango Area Chamber Resort Association, 111 S. Camino Del Rio, Durango, CO 81301, (970) 247-0312

Cortez
Population — 8,105 • Elevation — 6,201'

Cortez is the county seat of Montezuma County, centrally located among several important archaeological sites. Most notably, Mesa Verde National Park and Hovenweep National Monument are located nearby, as well as several smaller sites. In addition to the historical significance of the area, Cortez still acts as a cultural center for Native Americans in the area, especially Ute and Navajo tribes.

Deer hunters with licenses for Units 72 and 73 will find that Cortez is a good resource center. From Cortez hunters will find good access into BLM lands to the west and the San Juan National Forest to the north. McPhee Reservoir, located north of Cortez, is also a popular recreation area for visitors.

ACCOMMODATIONS

Holiday Inn Express Cortez, 2121 E. Main, (970) 565-6000
Aneth Lodge-Budget Six, 645 E. Main, (970) 565-3453
Budget Host Inn, 2040 E. Main, (970) 565-3738
Travelodge, 440 S. Broadway, (970) 565-3755

CAMPGROUNDS AND RV PARKS

A&A Mesa Verde RV Park Resort, 34979 US Hwy 160, (970) 565-3517
Cortez KOA Kampground, 27432 E. US Hwy 160, (970) 565-9301
Days Inn and Lazy G Campground, E Of Cortez, (970) 565-8577
Mesa Oasis Campground, 5608 US Hwy 160, (970) 565-8716
State Park Camping Reservations 800-678-CAMP
Forest Service Camping Reservations 877-444-6777

RESTAURANTS

Cortez Creamery Theatre and Restaurant, 24 N. Chestnut, (970) 565-1910
Homesteaders Restaurant, 45 E. Main St., (970) 565-6253
Anasazi Motor Inn Restaurant, 640 S Broadway, (970) 565-9617
Bosco's Pit Bar-B-Q and Steak House, 2707 E. Main, (970) 565-6363
Catfish Cottage, 332 E. Main, (970) 565-9677
Dry Dock Restaurant, 200 W Main, (970) 564-9404
El Grande Café, 28 E. Main, (970) 565-9996
Glade Restaurant and Sports Lounge, 925 S Broadway, (970) 565-3171
Main Street Brewery, 21 E Main, (970) 564-9112
Pippo's Diner, 100 W Main, (970) 565-6039
Purple Sage Rib Company, 2811 Mancos Rd., (970) 565-1233

VETERINARIANS

Adobe Animal Hospital, 11314 Hwy 145, (970) 565-4458
Cedarwood Animal Clinic, 1819 E. Main, (970) 565-6531
Montezuma Veterinary Clinic, 10411 US Hwy 666, (970) 565-7567

SPORTING GOODS, GUNS, AND GUNSMITHS

Howard's Sporting Goods, 16 W. Main, (970) 565-9371
Jerry's Sporting Goods, 15 W. Main, (970) 565-7561
Little Bear Indian Trading Post, 220 W. Main, (970) 565-9372
Shooters World, 1220 E. North, (970) 565-8960
Stagecoach Trading Post, 7399 US Hwy 666, (970) 565-2523

TAXIDERMISTS

AA Taxidermy and Antler Traders, 39728 Hwy 160 W, Bayfield, CO (970) 884-4194
A to Z Taxidermy, 202 S 2, Dolores, CO (970) 882-7705
Kibel Taxidermy, Dove Creek, CO (970) 677-2942
Spikes Taxidermy, 15301 CR 25, Dolores, CO (970) 882-2473

MEAT PROCESSORS

Bane's Custom Packing, 11063 Rd 25, (970) 565-3011

AUTO RENTAL AND REPAIR

Quality Rental, 410 W. Main, (970) 565-2106
U-Save Auto Rental of Cortez, Cortez Municipal Airport, (970) 565-9168
Autoworks, 237 N Broadway, (970) 564-5170
D and L Service, 725 E Main, (970) 565-8109
Dave's Auto Repair, 501 N Broadway, (970) 564-0336
H&T Auto Repair, 725 E Main, (970) 565-7600

AIR SERVICE

Cortez Municipal Airport, County Road F, (970) 565-9510

MEDICAL

Southwest Memorial Hospital, 1311 N. Mildred Rd., (970) 565-6666

FOR MORE INFORMATION

Cortez Chamber of Commerce, 928 E. Main, Cortez, CO 81321, (970) 565-3414

Lake City
Population — 322 • Elevation — 8,658'

Lake City is the county seat of Hinsdale County, the most sparsely populated county in Colorado. It is surrounded by vast amounts of national forest. Included in the national forest not far from Lake City are three wilderness areas: Big Blue, Powderhorn, and La Garita. In addition to excellent big game hunting, Lake City is also a popular fishing destination. Lake San Cristobal and the Lake Fork of the Gunnison River both offer quality fishing.

Although Lake City is a small community, the local retailers gear up for the big game hunting seasons each year. You will find most the services you need to carry out a successful hunt in the area. Besides, if you are hunting this area, Lake City is the only town within the southern half of Unit 66.

ACCOMMODATIONS

Lake City Resort, 307 S. Gunnison Ave., (970) 944-2866
Matterhorn Lodge, (970) 944-2210
Pleasant View Resort, 549 S. Gunnison Ave., (970) 944 2262
Silver Spur Motel, 301 N. Gunnison Ave., (970) 944-2231

CAMPGROUNDS AND RV PARKS

Henson Creek RV Park, Hwy 149, (970) 944-2394
Highlander RV Campground, 3445 CR 30, (970) 944-2878
Lake City Campground, 8th St. and Bluff, (970) 944-2920
State Park Camping Reservations 800-678-CAMP
Forest Service Camping Reservations 877-444-6777

RESTAURANTS

Lake City Café and Bar, 3rd and Gunnison Ave., (970) 944-2733
Olde Rocking Horse Inn, Silver St., (970) 944-2383
Tubb's Smokey Deli, 8th and Gunnison Ave., (970) 944-2521
Western Belle Lodge, Silver St., (970) 944-2415

SPORTING GOODS, GUNS, AND GUNSMITHS

The Tackle Box, 144 S. Gunnison Ave., (970) 944-2306

AUTO RENTAL AND REPAIR

Lake City Auto and Sports Center, 809 N Hwy. 149, (970) 944-2311
Sportsman's Texaco Station and Garage, (970) 944-2525

MEDICAL

Lake City Area Medical Center, 700 Henson St., (970) 944-2331

FOR MORE INFORMATION

Lake City Chamber of Commerce, (970) 944-2527

Creede

Population — 377 · Elevation — 8,838'

Historically, Creede is probably best known for its silver mines, but today it is known for all of the recreational opportunities that abound in the area. Creede is surrounded by the Rio Grande National Forest with the La Garita Wilderness to the north and the Weminuche Wilderness to the south. This area comprises some of the most unspoiled and remote backcountry in Colorado. Anyone hunting in GMUs 76 or 79 will do well to use Creede as a base of operations.

ACCOMMODATIONS

Wason Ranch Company, Box 220, 658-2413, Hosts: Rod and Marilyn Wintz, Two bedroom cabins and three bedroom cottages on the Rio Grande, No pets, kennel available in Creede, Highly recommended

Snowshoe Motel, Highway 149 in town, 658-2315, Owners: Mark and Julia Viergutz, 14 rooms, 2 kitchenettes, Small dogs allowed

Creede Hotel, Box 284, 658-2608, Hosts: Rich and Kathy Ormsby, Restaurant and 7 rooms, Open 7AM–10:30AM for breakfast, 4PM–9PM for dinner

4UR Ranch, 1238 FR 605, 658-2202, Managers: Rock and Christen Swenson, Private fishing on the Rio Grande River and Goose Creek, Reservations needed well in advance, Package deals

BED AND BREAKFAST

The Old Firehouse, Main Street, 658-0212, Innkeeper: Katherine Brennand

RESTAURANTS

Creede Hotel Dining Room, 658-2608, Hosts: Rich and Kathy Ormsby, Open 7AM for breakfast, 4AM–9PM for dinner

Mucker's Bucket Saloon, Highway 149, 658-9997, Hosts: Chuck and Kathy Lehman, Open 7AM–9PM daily, 8AM on Sunday, Bar open until 2AM

Old Miner's Inn, Highway 149, 658-2767, Open 11AM–9PM, Cocktails

SPORTING GOODS

Ramble House, 116 Creede Avenue, Creede, CO 81130, (719) 658-2482

San Juan Sports, Creede, CO 81130, (719) 658-2359

HOSPITALS

Los Piños Health Center, 1280 Grande Avenue, Del Norte, 657-3342, Del Norte is 40 miles southwest of Creede on Highway 160

AIRPORTS

Alamosa San Luis Valley Regional Airport, 2500 State Avenue, 589-6444, United Express: 800-241-6522

Mineral County Airport, Creede, 658-9962, Private planes

FOR MORE INFORMATION

Creede-Mineral County Chamber of Commerce, Creede Avenue, Creede, CO 81130, 658-2374

Region 3 Outfitters

The following list includes outfitters registered with the Colorado Outfitters Association who provide big game hunting services in one or more of the GMUs within Region 3. Information concerning the outfitters company name, license number, address, phone, species, GMUs, type of land hunted (national forest, regional area, private versus public), and facilities are provided below.

LEE BOLIN
Bugle Basin Outfitters #1697
P.O. Box 16095
Colorado Springs, CO 80935
(719) 638-8072
Deer, elk, bear, sheep, lion, 681
Private property, tent camps, horse rental

GARY BRAMWELL
Astraddle A Saddle #117
P.O. Box 1216, Pagosa Springs, CO 81147
(970) 731-5076
Deer, elk, bear, 77, 78, San Juan NF

JOHN BRENNAN
Steward Ranch Outfitters #440
4385 C.R. 207, Durango, CO 81301
(970) 247-8396
Deer, elk, bear,
Private Ranch, drop camps,
San Juan NF; Tent camps, cabins

CADWELL OUTFITTERS #302
1582 C.R. 52, Powderhorn, CO 81243
(970) 641-0773
Deer, elk, sheep, 66, 67
Gunnison, private property, tent camps, cabins, resort

ALLEN CANNON
Circle K Ranch #332
27758 Hwy. 145 Dolores, CO 81323
(970) 562-3808
Deer, elk, bear, 71,73, 74
San Juan, tent camps, cabins, lodge

WILLIAM DEAN
Lost Canyon Ranch #1731
5817 Cypress Point
Fort Worth, TX 76132
(970) 882-7176
Deer, elk, bear, 73, 711,
San Juan, private property, cabins

LARRY EHARDT
Wilderness Adventures #647
P.O. Box 265, South Fork, CO 81154
(719) 873-5216
Deer, elk, bear, lion, 76, 82, 80
Rio Grande, tent camps, campground resort

OBBIE DICKEY
Diamond-D-Bar Ranch #13
8018 North 6 West, Del Norte, CO 81132
(719) 657-2293
Deer, elk, bear, antelope,goat, sheep, 76, 79, 681, 80, 81
Rio Grande, tent camps

KIRK ELLISON
Lazy FF Outfitter #760
Freemon's Ranch, Creede, CO 81130,
(719) 658-2250
Deer, elk, 76, Rio Grande
Tent camps, cabins, resort

BOB FERTSCH
B7B Outfitters of Durango #1017
P.O. Box 20, Cortez, CO 81321
(970) 564-1706
Deer, elk, antelope, 711, 72
San Juan, private property, tent camps, cabins

JIM FLYNN
Red Mountain Outfitters #900
P.O. Box 893, Alamosa, CO 81101,
(719) 589-4186
Deer, elk, bear, antelope, sheep, lion,
moose, 80, 81, 82, 79, 681, 68, 76
Rio Grande, San Juan, private property,
tents, cabins

SAMMY FRAZIER
Frazier Outfitting #1738
HC 70, Box 6C, Creede, CO 81130
(719) 588-3386
Elk, 76, Rio Grande, private land, tent
camps, cabins

GREGORY GEELHOED
Timber Basin Outfitters #902
256 E. Danbury Ct.
Grand Junction, CO 81503
(970) 243-9781
Deer, elk, antelope, 66, 67
BLM-Gunnison, private property, cabins

DAYSON GOETZ
D Bar G Outfitters #1704
971 D Bar K Drive, Durango, CO 81301
(970) 385-6888
Deer, elk, bear, 74, private property,
Tent camps

DAVID GRIGGS
Bugle Mountain Outfitters #1800
120 Beaver Meadows Rd.,
Bayfield, CO 81122
(970) 884-2730
Deer, elk, bear, lion, 74, 75, 77, 751, 771
San Juan, private property, tent camps
trailers

WALTER HEADY
Conejos River Outfitters #597
P.O. Box 404, Alamosa, CO 81101
(719) 376-2226
Deer, elk, bear, 81, Rio Grande,
Tent camps, cabins, resort, horse rental

ROY HUTT
Little Cone Outfitter #962
P.O. Box 296, Norwood, CO 81423,
(970) 327-4620, deer, elk, bear, 70,
Uncompahgre, private property, cabins

SUE JAMESON AND WALTER TYCKSEN
T&J Outfitters#1545
P.O. Box 1101, Dolores, CO 81323
(970) 882-7179
Deer, elk, bear, 711, 77
San Juan, private property, trespass fee,
Tent camps, trailers

JOHN JUDSON
Quarter-Circle Circle Ranch #669
26100 C.R. 17GG, Gunnison, CO 801230
(970) 641-3616
Deer, elk, bear, antelope, sheep, 67, 68,
551; Gunnison NF, Rio Grande NF
BLM-Montrose, private property
Tents, cabins

JIM LAMKE
Lake City Outfitters #1986
24669 Pleasant Park Road
Conifer, CO 80433
800-481-6401
Deer, elk, bear, 66, BLM-Gunnison,
Lake City, tent camps

HARRY LANDERS
Wildhorse Outfittes #1727
P.O. Box 1736, Pagosa Springs, CO 81147
(970) 883-2356
Deer, elk, bear, 77, 78, 80, 81,
South San Juan Wilderness
Tent camps, cabins, chalets, guest ranch

JOHN KNOLL AND KEVIN WELLS
KW Wapiti Outfitters
#1620, P.O. Box 3463
Evergreen CO 80437
(303) 674-4027
Deer, elk, bear, sheep, 54, 67,
Gunnison NF, tent camps

JOHN AND BOBBIE MARTIN
Mineral Mountain Outfitters #209,
8568 H.C. 50, Powderhorn,CO 81243,
(970) 641-2673
Deer, elk, bear, 66, 67
Gunnison, BLM-Montrose
Cabins, trailers

SEVEN MAZZONE
7M Guide Service #1276
P.O. Box 1933, Durango, CO 81301
(970) 259-2170
Deer, elk, bear, sheep, 75
San Juan, tent camps

FRANK MORNINGSTAR andMICHAEL
PATCHECK,
Hermosa Creek Outfitters #998
817 Rainbow Rd., Durango, CO 81301,
(970) 259-5393
Deer, elk, antelope, 74, 741
San Juan, BLM-SW; Private property,
Tent camps

DAN NEWMAN
Great Divide Outfitters #1014
8696 C.R. 502, Bayfield, CO 81122
(970) 884-2372
Deer, elk, bear, 75, 751
San Juan, private property, cabins

ALAN PALMER
Palmer Outfitters #1714
58919 C.R. E.E. 2, Moffat, CO 81143,
(719) 256-4817
Deer, elk, bear, antelope, sheep, 82, 681
San Juan, Rio Grande, BLM-Canon
City/Saguache, private property, tent
camps, cabins

RANDY AND TERRY PALMER
Over the Hill Outfitters #1832
4140 C.R. 234, Durango, CO 81301,
(970) 247-1694
Deer, elk, bear, 75, 751
San Juan, private property, tent camps

DAVID PARK OUTFITTING #1043
14950 Roling Hills Dr.
Montrose, CO 81401
(970) 252-8835
Deer, elk, bear, antelope, sheep, 68, 681,
82, 551, Rio Grande, Gunnison, private
property, tent camps, cabins

RON PFEFFER
Ron-D-View Outfitting #752
1151 Anna Rd., Ignacio, CO 81137
(970) 563-9270
Deer, elk, bear, 74
San Juan, private property,
Trespass fee, tent camps, horse rental

DAVID POWELL
Jake's Rio Grande Outfitting #724
P.O. Box 57, Creede, CO 81130-0057,
(719) 658-0926
Elk, moose, 76, Rio Grande NF
Tent camps

BUTCH RAWLS
Mountain Trails Outfitters and Toneda
Outfitters #954, 7129 C.R. 4 W,
Del Norte, CO
(719) 852-3870
Deer, elk, bear, lion, high country
Trophy buck, sheep, 80, 81, 82, 500, S9,
S9N; tent camps, cabins

TODD RICHARDSON AND RICK BAECKER
San-Pahgre Guides and Outfitters #1341
21700 Hwy 550, Montrose, CO 81401
(970) 240-8183
Deer, elk, bear, 65, 74, 75, 61, 62
Uncompahgre, Gunnison, BLM,
Montrose, cabins

RICHARD RAY
Lobo Outfitters #147
4821A Hwy. 84
Pagosa Springs, CO 81147
(970) 264-5546
Deer, elk, bear, sheep, lion, 75, 751,
77, 771, 78, 79, 80, 81, 82, 83, 68, 681

DENNY SCHILTHUIS
Vallecito Lake Outfitters #1885
1545 C.R. 302, Durango, CO 81301,
(970) 247-1275
Deer, elk, bear, 75, 751, San Juan
Tent camps, horse rental

BILL AND TOM SCHULZE
Sangre De Cristo Outfit. #417
P.O. Box 586, Westcliffe, CO 81252,
(719) 783-2265
Deer, elk, bear, antelope, sheep, lion, 69,
84, 691, 59, San Isabel, Ranching for
Wildlife, private property, tent camps,
cabins

EUGENE STORY
West Fork Outfitters #571
P.O. Box 300, Dolores, CO 81321
888-882-8001, deer, elk, 71, 711
San Juan, cabins

BART TRAYNOR
Cow Creek Outfitters #1909
651 230th, Osceola, WI 54020
(715) 294-3908
Deer, elk, bear, sheep, 65
Uncompahgre, tent camps

PETE TURNER
Colorado Mountain Holiday
dba Rapps Guide Service #1975
3635 C.R. 301, Durango, CO 81301
(877) 600-2656
Deer, elk, 74, San Juan, Rio Grande

TOM AND CHERI VANSOELEN
San Juan Outfitting #997
186 C.R. 228, Durango, CO 81301
(970) 259-6259
Deer, elk, bear, sheep, 75, 751, 77
San Juan, BLM-San Juan Basin
Tent camps

JASON WARD
Wolf Creek Outfitters #1138
P.O. Box 1918, Pagosa Springs, CO 81147
(970) 264-5332
Deer, elk, bear, sheep, 771, 78,
San Juan, tent camps, cabins, trailers

L.F. WILT
East Fork Outfitters and Guides #1774
P.O. Box 64, Pagosa Springs, CO 81147,
(970) 264-6696
Deer, elk, bear, 78, South San Juan
Wilderness, tent camps

D.J. WINTERS
Dolores River Outfitters #1917
P.O. Box 366, Dolores, CO 81323
(970) 882-3099
Deer, elk, bear, 70, 71, 711, 741
BLM-Dolores and Cortez
Private property, trespass fee, tent
camps, cabins

WIT'S END GUEST RANCH AND
RESORT #1004
254 CR 500, Bayfield, CO 81122
(970) 884-4113
P.O. Box 8019
Glendale, AZ 85312-8019,
Deer, elk, 751
San Juan-Weminuche Wilderness
Private property, tent camps, cabins,
resort

ED ZINK
Waterfall Ranch Outfitters #1101
4166 C.R. 203, Durango, CO 81301,
(970) 247-8758, elk, 74
San Juan, tent camps

Region 4 Roads, Rivers, Hub Cities

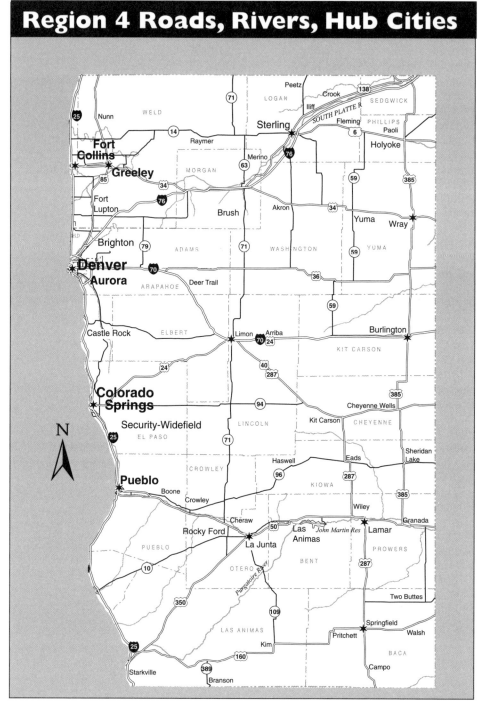

© WILDERNESS ADVENTURES PRESS, INC.

REGION 4

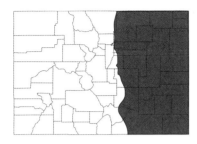

The eastern plains of Colorado make up Region 4. This vast area of grassland and farmland is completely different from the three mountainous regions previously discussed. In fact, hunters pursuing game in the eastern plains may feel like they are hunting in a different state. The eastern plains consist of wide-open spaces with nearly flat terrain to rolling hills. The Interstate 25 corridor from the Wyoming state line to the New Mexico state line is the most heavily populated and developed area in the state, especially from Fort Collins to Pueblo. Moving east from I-25, the plains are dotted with small farming communities. The larger towns are found on the major river drainages such as Sterling on the South Platte River and Lamar on the Arkansas River. There are several large reservoirs scattered across the plains. Most of these are also proximal to the South Platte and Arkansas River drainages.

Public lands are minimal on the eastern plains. The largest areas open to public access are the Pawnee National Grasslands in the north and the Comanche National Grasslands in the south. Besides these areas there are scattered state lands that include several state wildlife areas that offer big game hunting opportunities. The downside to hunting the eastern plains is that access to the good big game areas is often difficult to obtain. The upside is that the difficult access often deters many hunters. This results in quality hunting, often with uncrowded conditions. Deer and antelope are the primary big game species of concern here. The plains hold the largest number of antelope in the state and good numbers of deer. This is also the area where hunters will find significant numbers of whitetail deer. The DOW estimates that 40 percent of the eastern plains deer population is made up of whitetails.

Pronghorn Distribution
Region 4

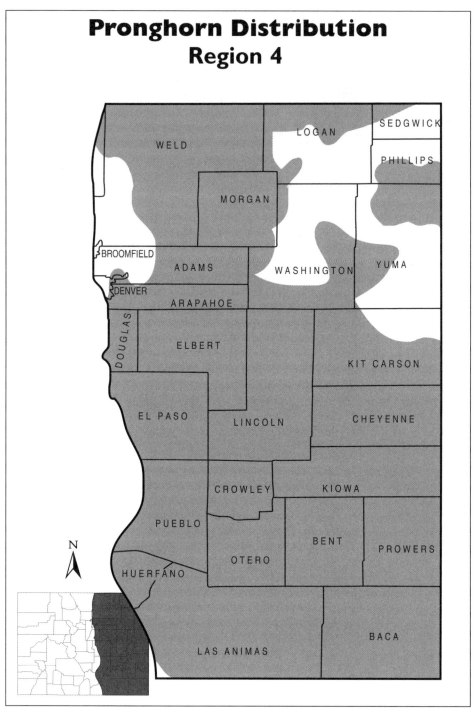

© WILDERNESS ADVENTURES PRESS, INC.

White-tailed Deer Distribution
Region 4

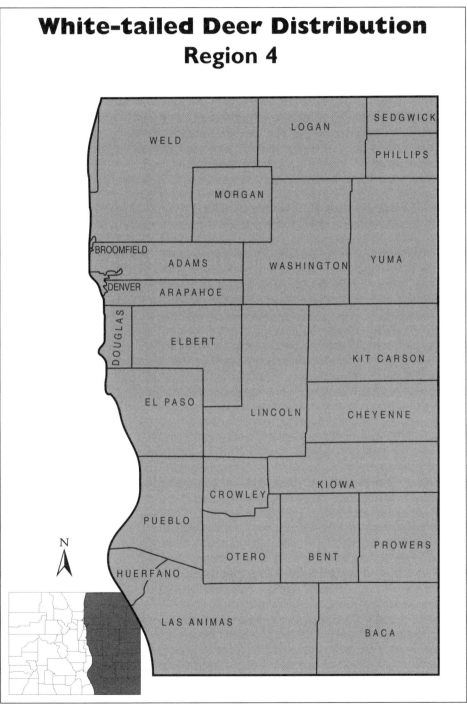

© WILDERNESS ADVENTURES PRESS, INC.

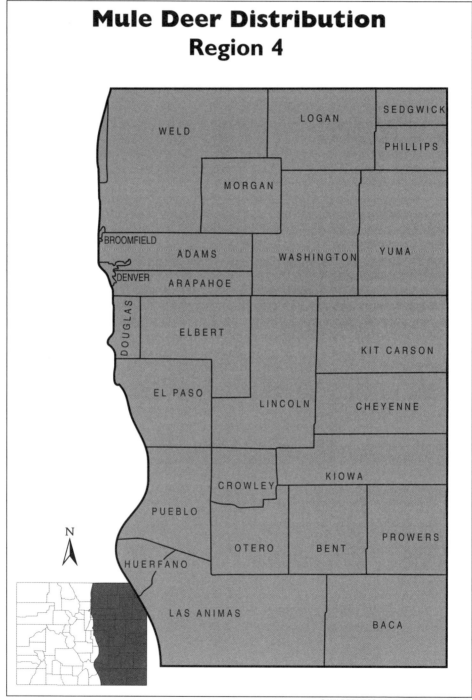

Mule Deer Distribution
Region 4

© WILDERNESS ADVENTURES PRESS, INC.

Bighorn Sheep Distribution
Region 4

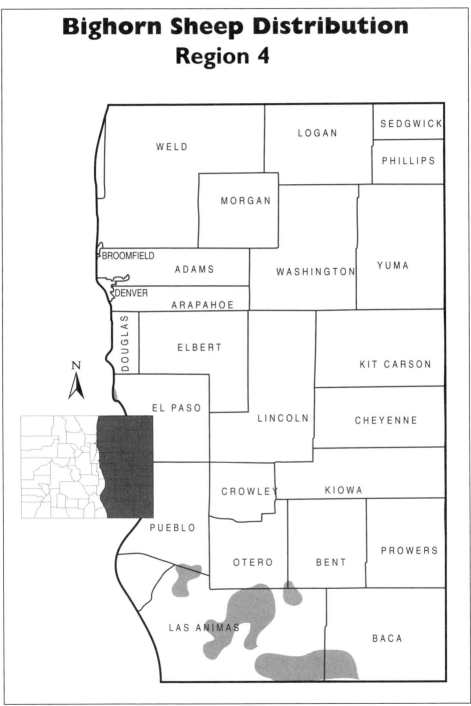

© WILDERNESS ADVENTURES PRESS, INC.

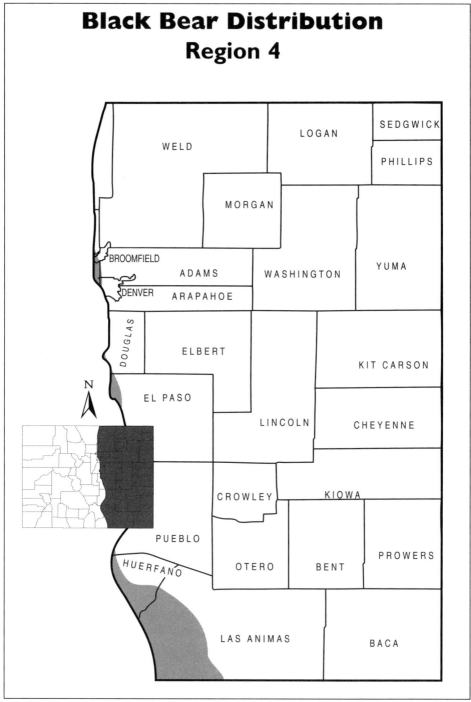

Black Bear Distribution
Region 4

© WILDERNESS ADVENTURES PRESS, INC.

Mountain Lion Distribution
Region 4

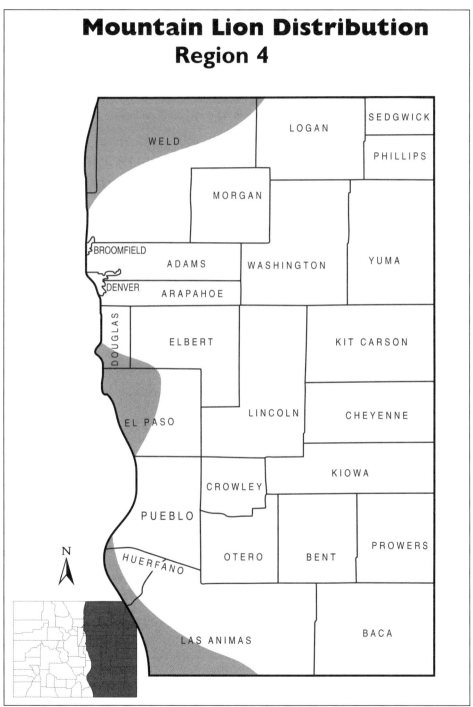

© WILDERNESS ADVENTURES PRESS, INC.

Mountain Ranges
Region 4

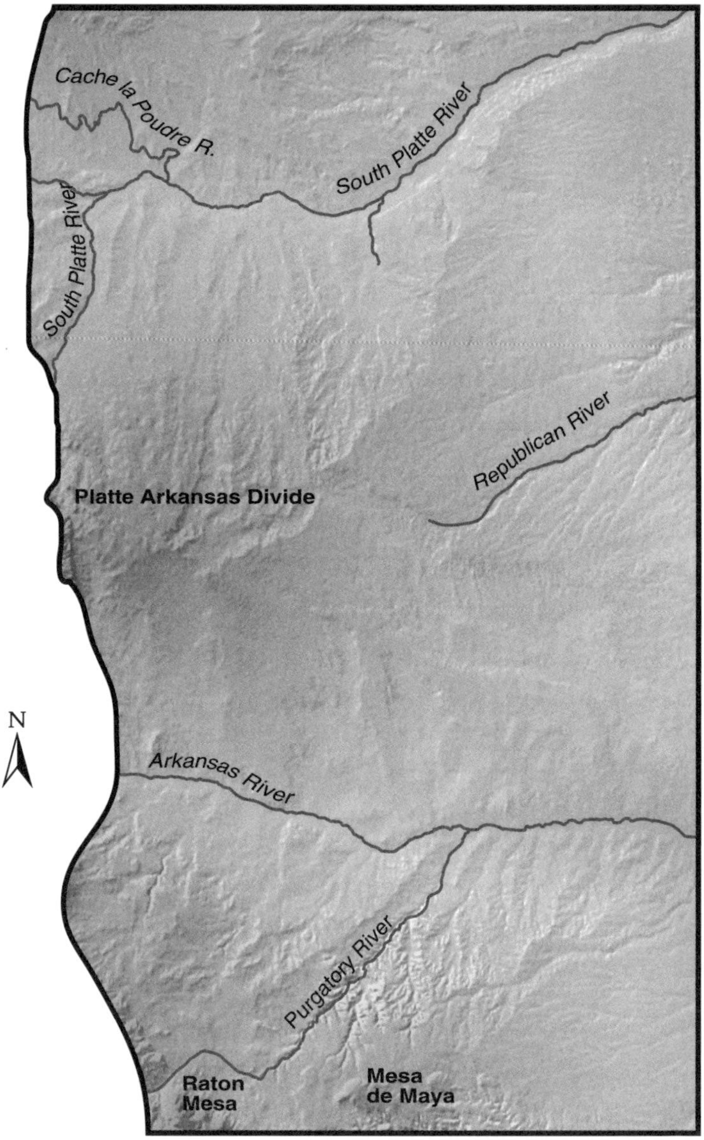

Cache la Poudre R.

South Platte River

South Platte River

Republican River

Platte Arkansas Divide

N

Arkansas River

Purgatory River

Raton Mesa

Mesa de Maya

© WILDERNESS ADVENTURES PRESS, INC.

Ecosystem
Region 4

Legend

N

- Alpine Tundra
- Subalpine Tundra
- Montane Scrubland
- Grassland
- Semidesert Scrubland
- Pinon-Juniper Woodland
- Montane Forest

© WILDERNESS ADVENTURES PRESS, INC.

Region 4 Land Use

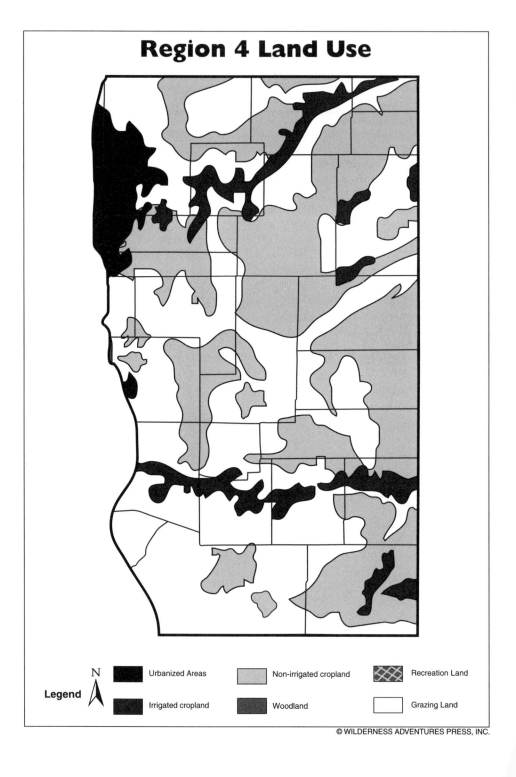

Legend

N

Urbanized Areas	Non-irrigated cropland	Recreation Land
Irrigated cropland	Woodland	Grazing Land

© WILDERNESS ADVENTURES PRESS, INC.

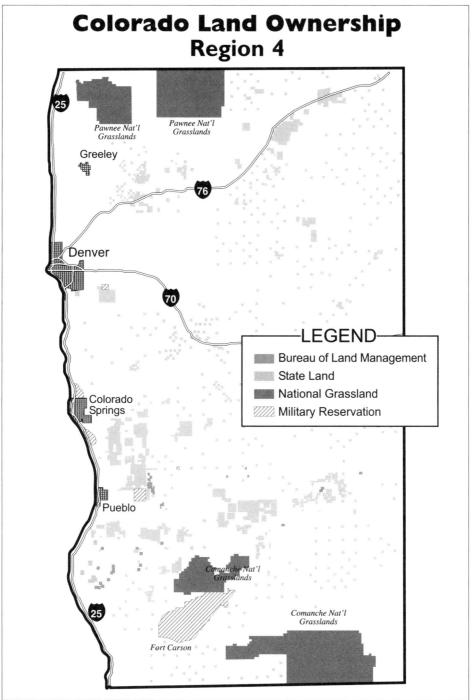

Colorado Land Ownership
Region 4

Game Species and Numbers

Region 4 is home to over 28,000 antelope and a slightly higher number of deer based on recent DOW population statistics. Although there are a few whitetail deer found in the western portion of Colorado, the most significant populations exist along the major river drainages of the eastern plains. The 40 percent of the deer in Region 4 that consists of whitetails translates to a population estimate of about 12,000. This doesn't sound like very many deer for such a large area, but when you consider that they are concentrated into relatively small areas along the rivers, it takes on a different meaning. Some of the best trophy whitetail and mule deer taken in Colorado each year come from the eastern plains. This adds an incentive to hunters who are after big bucks. Although there are three elk herds east of I-25, big game hunting in Region 4 is almost completely comprised of deer and antelope hunting.

As discussed in the other regions, the Colorado Division of Wildlife prepares official population and harvest statistics that are available to the public each year. This information is gathered from license sale statistics, field research, including aerial population counts, and hunter harvest surveys. Since it is impossible to count every animal in the state, the populations are to some extent estimated using population models.

The following tables provide the herd name, the GMUs where the herd ranges and the population of the herd for elk, deer and antelope. This information is current at the time of publishing, but populations change over time. Still, the distribution of populations in each area has remained relatively consistent over the years.

ELK HERD	UNITS	POPULATION
Castle Rock	51, 104, 105, 106, 110, 111	1,420
Cedarwood	128	300
Elkheart	145	40
TOTAL ELK POPULATION REGION 4 = 1,760		

DEER HERD	UNITS	POPULATION
Table Lands	87, 88, 89, 90, 93, 95, 97, 98, 99, 100, 101, 102	6,310
South Platte River	91, 92, 94, 96, 951	2,260
South Republican	103, 109, 116, 117	2,100
Bijou Creek	104, 105, 106	5,070
Big Sandy	107, 112, 113, 114, 115, 120, 121	2,570
Chico Basin	110, 111, 118, 119, 123, 124	1,890
Arkansas River	122, 125, 126, 127, 128, 130, 132, 137, 138, 139, 146	4,010
Las Animas	128, 129, 133, 134, 135, 136, 141, 142, 147	3,600
Mesa de Mayo	143, 144, 145	2,450
TOTAL DEER POPULATION REGION 4 = 30,260		

ANTELOPE HERD	UNITS	POPULATION
Escarpment	87, 88, 89, 90, 95, 951	5,390
Sandhills	93, 97, 98, 101, 102	570
Hardpan	99, 100	1,300
Last Chance	103, 106, 107, 109	1,850
Kiowa Creek	29, 38, 51, 104, 105, 391	2,910
Yoder	110, 111, 118, 119, 123, 124	4,550
Hugo	112, 113, 114, 115	2,210
Cheyenne	116, 117, 122, 127	1,040
Haswell	120, 121, 125, 126	2,070
Thatcher	128, 129, 133, 134, 135, 140, 141, 142, 147	4,400
Tobe	130, 136, 137, 138, 143, 144, 146	1,990
Two Buttes	132, 139, 145	280
TOTAL ANTELOPE POPULATION REGION 4 = 28,560		

The primary big game species that occupy Region 4 are deer and antelope. Statewide population estimates for the other big game species are provided in Regions 1, 2, and 3.

Harvest Trends

Hunter success rates vary greatly from year to year, season to season, and unit to unit. The Colorado Division of Wildlife publishes the big game hunting statistics each year, which includes success rates for each season in each unit. This information is available online at http://wildlife.state.co.us/huntrecap/index.asp.

The following success rates are based on 2001 DOW statistics averaged for all seasons and manners of take statewide.

SPECIES	SUCCESS RATE	TOTAL ANIMALS HARVESTED
Elk	21%	42,630
Deer	42%	31,634
Antelope	61%	6,417
Black Bear	6%	759
Desert Bighorn	100%	9
Rocky Mtn. Bighorn	51%	175
Mountain Goat	92%	169
Moose	84%	102

Physical Characteristics

The eastern plains of Colorado are made up in large part by flat to hilly terrain consisting of grasslands as well as large acreages of dry and irrigated farmland. Several rivers account for prominent variances in terrain and make up important riparian systems. The largest rivers are the South Platte and the Arkansas. These two drainages are separated by a highland known as the Platte-Arkansas Divide. The South Platte River originates in South Park and flows northeast between the Tarryall Mountains and the Rampart Range, where it breaks out onto the eastern plains. The South Platte is joined by the Cache la Poudre River near the town of Greeley where it turns east and continues on across the northern portion of Region 4. The Arkansas River also originates in the mountains, between the Sawatch and Mosquito Ranges. It flows south towards the town of Salida where it turns east and flows between the Arkansas Hills and the Wet Mountains. Once it makes its way onto the plains several important tributaries including the Apishapa River, the Purgatoire River, and the Big Sandy River join it. It continues east along the southern portion of the region to the Kansas state line. Other important rivers on the plains include the Arikaree and the North and South Forks of the Republican, which all originate in the eastern half of the region between the South Platte and Big Sandy.

There are several areas on the eastern plains where the typical terrain is dominated by more geographic relief in the form of small canyons and plateaus. Most notable is the Mesa de Maya area in the southern portion of Region 4. The Purgatoire River flows through a significant canyon on the eastern edge of the Pinon Canyon Military Reservation where you will find a relatively large area of pinon-juniper woodland. Just east of the Purgatoire River is Mesa de Maya, and farther to the east Black Mesa. This area contains numerous creeks and intermittent streams that have resulted in countless small canyons and deeply eroded washes. This area extends into the Comanche National Grasslands to the east and south near the Colorado, New Mexico, and Oklahoma borders.

Moving to the north there is an area of montane forest, known as the Black Forest, which extends across I-25 just northeast of Colorado Springs. Relatively large areas of montane shrubland bound the forests on the north. Another area that varies from the flat grasslands of the plains is the central, eastern portion of Region 4 where the North Fork of the Republican River flows through the town of Yuma. Here you will find small canyons and deep washes eroded away by the river and smaller side tributaries. Most of the area north of the river in Yuma County consists of hilly terrain accurately named the Sand Hills. The areas surrounding the Arikaree and South Fork of the Republican Rivers also contain varied terrain with deeply eroded washes and small canyons.

The last major derivation from the flat terrain of the plains exists in the northern reaches of Region 4 in the Pawnee National Grasslands. Just south of the Nebraska state line you will find an area known as the Chalk Bluffs. Numerous creeks and intermittent streams have eroded this area. You will find several small canyons, such as Sand Canyon, Chimney Canyon, and Lewis Canyons. A popular attraction in the Pawnee National Grasslands in Weld County is Pawnee Buttes. There is also one prominent butte south of the Chalk Bluffs in Logan County, known as Flat Top Butte, along with some lesser buttes and tablelands.

The predominant flora of the eastern plain grasslands consists of blue grama, buffalo grass, and western wheatgrass. According to Fitzgerald, Meaney, and Armstrong in *Mammals of Colorado* (1994), there are no undisturbed grasslands remaining in Colorado. Even areas that were never cultivated were heavily impacted by cattle grazing. Still, there are relatively large areas of grassland that have been preserved in the Pawnee and Comanche National Grasslands.

Elevations in the eastern plains generally decrease with distance away from the mountains. The I-25 corridor commonly has elevations over 5,000 feet. In the eastern plains near the Kansas border elevations are generally in the 3,500- to 4,000-foot range.

Land Use

Land use in eastern Colorado is predominantly agricultural. You will find large acreages of irrigated croplands along the South Platte and Arkansas Rivers. Irrigated lands are also dispersed throughout the region along lesser river drainages and where reservoirs and groundwater sources provide adequate water for irrigation. Major crops include corn, wheat, sugar beets, alfalfa, milo, vegetables, and melons. There are also large acreages of dryland farming of winter wheat, where the success of the crop is dependent upon precipitation. Cattle operations (often associated with the farms) utilize most of the uncultivated land on the plains for grazing. There are also large feedlots adjacent to the prominent towns and big hog farms at various locations. Besides the agricultural uses, Region 4 also accounts for significant oil and natural gas production in the state. There are also large sand and gravel operations adjacent to many of the rivers.

Weather

When compared to the mountainous areas of western Colorado the eastern plains are dominated by a very arid climate. Depending on elevation, the mountain ranges can receive anywhere from 20 to 60 inches of precipitation each year. This includes over 300 inches of snow in some of the highest ranges. The eastern plains normally receive less than 16 inches of total precipitation in a year, generally consisting of less than 50 inches of total snowfall. Depending on the density of the snow, one inch of precipitation is roughly equivalent to 14 inches of fresh snowfall on average. As an example, 140 inches of snowfall and 10 inches of rain in a year would equate to total precipitation of 20 inches for a given area.

The summer weather pattern of afternoon thunderstorms continues in the early hunting seasons in August and into September. This weather pattern can often cause severe thunderstorms and occasionally tornados as these systems gain energy late in the day and move onto the plains. Most tornadoes occur earlier in the summer, but while deer hunting in southeast Colorado in October of 1997, I experienced some very strong thunderstorms that resulted in several small tornadoes. Two friends and I were staying in my camper on a wooded river bottom during the night of October 11. The weather hadn't been that bad during the day, but as evening approached dark clouds were building and the wind began to pick up. After the sun set large thunderstorms illuminated the landscape with bright flashes of lightning. The wind was blowing hard and gusting so badly that it rocked my truck violently. I began to get concerned that the wind might blow trees or large branches onto the camper, but we decided to stay put and stick the storm out. Unbeknownst to us, tornados had been spotted a few miles away near the town of La Junta. Not until the next day did we learn from news reports that the storm had been so severe it had forced an Amtrak train to make an unscheduled stop in La Junta to offload the passengers until the tornados had passed. Fortunately, nobody was hurt and there was very little property damage. Still, we felt lucky that the twisters had missed us; we wouldn't have stood a chance in the camper.

From my experience while hunting big game on the eastern plains, temperatures are generally warm with little precipitation well into October. In fact, there have been several occasions when I actually hoped for cooler weather while bowhunting for whitetail deer in late October and early November. In 1999 the first appreciable snowfall occurred on September 28, but more commonly the first snow usually comes in October. Although infrequent, heavy rains may be of more concern to hunters on the plains because they can leave dirt roads impassable. Another weather related problem that will affect hunting on the plains is the wind. Winds can be strong and persistent at any time.

As you hunt later in the year temperatures can reach frigid lows, and although snow accumulation is usually minimal, be prepared for the worst. October of 1997 had a lot of extreme weather. The weekend after I experienced the severe thunderstorms I went back to southeast Colorado and was fortunate to fill my deer tag. If I hadn't gotten my deer I would have gone back again the next weekend of October 24. This turned out to be the date of one of the worst snowstorms in recent history to hit the eastern plains. After it was over there was two to three feet of snow piled up across much of the east. This resulted in huge drifts that stranded many motorists. Ranchers lost large numbers of cattle to the storm, and if I had been camped out on the river bottom where I hunt, it probably would have been several days before I could have gotten out.

When listening to weather reports key into "southeast low pressure systems." If you hear that a southeast low is approaching, the eastern plains are likely to get a snowstorm. In *The Colorado Weather Book* (1999), Mike Nelson gives us a good phrase to remember the difference between the two major storm makers in Colorado, "…Pacific front, mountains bear the brunt; southeast low, Denver gets the snow."

In order to get a better cross section of temperature ranges and precipitation from north to south, data from two representative towns in Region 4 are presented below. The following tables provide average temperatures, precipitation, and snowfall for Sterling and La Junta, Colorado. Sterling is located in the north portion of Region 4 at an elevation of 3,939 feet and La Junta is located in the south part of the region at an elevation of 4,066 feet above mean sea level.

MONTH	AVERAGE HIGH (°F)	AVERAGE LOW (°F)	AVERAGE PRECIPITATION (Total in.)	AVERAGE TOTAL SNOW FALL (in.)
August	87.9	56.8	1.79	.0
September	78.5	46.1	1.12	0.2
October	66.8	33.7	0.88	0.2
November	50.9	22.1	0.51	3.3
December	41.1	13.5	0.31	3.4

Temperature and precipitation data were based on National Weather Service data for Sterling.
Period of record 8/01/1948 to 7/31/2000

MONTH	AVERAGE HIGH (°F)	AVERAGE LOW (°F)	AVERAGE PRECIPITATION (Total in.)	AVERAGE TOTAL SNOW FALL (in.)
August	92.4	61.7	2.13	0.0
September	84.4	51.9	1.05	0.2
October	72.6	36.9	1.05	2.0
November	58.5	26.3	0.80	4.2
December	48.2	17.2	0.47	5.9

Temperature ranges were based on National Weather Service data for La Junta. Period of record 8/01/1982 to 7/31/2000.

Public Lands and Acreage

If there is a drawback to hunting Region 4 it is the lack of public lands. When compared to the western regions, there is only a fraction of public land available on the eastern plains. Still, the opportunities are there if you are willing to spend the time looking for them. Region 4 has slightly over 849,000 acres of public land open to big game hunting. This land is made up in large part by the Pawnee and Comanche National Grasslands. State wildlife areas (SWAs), state trust lands, and BLM land account for the remainder. SWAs and state trust lands are not broken out separately in the other regions because most of those properties are located within national forest acreages. However, most of the acreages in the SWAs in the eastern plains are not accounted for anywhere else. By my calculations, there are currently 44 SWAs in 20 counties adjacent to and east of I-25 that offer big game hunting opportunities. (There are several more SWAs on the eastern plains, but they do not provide big game hunting.) These SWAs vary from about 70 acres to slightly over 13,000 acres in size.

There are also several state trust lands that have deer and antelope hunting. You should note that state trust lands change public status from time to time, and depending on lease arrangements and use requirements, certain properties may revert back to private ownership or be closed to hunting. The trust land acreage listed below is based on the 1997 to 2000 supplement to the Colorado Wildlife Property Directory for the 14 properties east of I-25 that currently offer big game hunting opportunities.

PUBLIC LAND DESCRIPTION	ACREAGES
Pawnee National Grasslands	193,000
Comanche National Grasslands	419,000
State Wildlife Areas	115,146
State Trust Lands	59,633
Bureau of Land Management	62,317
TOTAL PUBLIC LANDS IN REGION 4	849,096
TOTAL PUBLIC LANDS IN REGION 4	*849,096*

Another significant amount of acreage is open to big game hunting on a limited basis at the Pinon Canyon Maneuvers Site (GMU 142). This U.S. military land has special access requirements, and hunting licenses are very limited; as a result it was not included in the public land acreages listed above. However, it does offer another 230,000 acres of land in southeast Colorado to hunters who are persistent enough to draw the license and obtain the required permits for access. (Please see the section on United States Military Lands for more details.)

Cropland adjacent to riparian land is excellent deer habitat.

Region 4 Highlights

South Platte River Drainage (GMUs 91, 92, 94, 96, 951)

The South Platte deer herd contains mule deer and whitetail deer in GMUs 91, 92, 94, 96, and 951. These GMUs cover the area from I-25 along the river northeast to the Nebraska state line. Several of the GMUs (91, 92, and 96) are long units that encompass narrow sections of land adjacent to the river in Morgan, Logan, and Sedgwick Counties. The South Platte herd has a population over 2,000 deer with a strong buck-to-doe ratio of 50 to 100, in recent years. Trophy quality is very good in this herd with several nice mule deer and whitetail bucks harvested each year. The South Platte GMUs are known primarily for deer hunting, but GMU 951 is one of six units that make up the Escarpment antelope herd. There are a few antelope licenses available to hunters in Unit 951 each year.

The upside to hunting the South Platte River drainage is that success rates are very good in most of the units. For example, bowhunters generally average between 15 and 20 percent for deer across the state. In comparison, bowhunters in Unit 96 far exceeded the average with a 38 to 52 percent success rate for deer in recent years. Rifle hunters also did well. The state average success rate for rifle hunters during the eastern plains deer season is generally over 50 percent. Unit 91 was a standout for rifle hunters in a recent year with a success rate of 63 percent. The good news is that if you have a tag for one of the units along the South Platte River you stand a very good chance of harvesting a deer. The bad news is that almost all of the property along the river is private.

Much of the land along the river consists of large cottonwood trees, various willow, sedges, and tamarack. Land adjacent to the South Platte River is primarily irrigated farmland, although there are some uncultivated areas that are unsuitable for farming. These areas are generally used for cattle grazing. The combination of abundant grain crops, natural food sources, water, and good cover equates to an abundance of wildlife, especially deer. Bucks can grow large racks in a relatively short time, translating to good trophy quality. Not surprising, many of the largest whitetail deer taken in Colorado have come from the South Platte deer herd in Morgan and Logan Counties. In fact, the number one typical whitetail deer listed in the *Colorado Bowhunting Records of Big Game* (1997), is a 194-point bruiser harvested by Stuart Clodfelder in Logan County. Both Logan and Morgan Counties are scattered throughout the list of Pope and Young entries for whitetail deer in Colorado.

If you're used to hunting the mountainous areas of Colorado, you will probably need to try some new strategies for deer hunting the eastern plains. Land in the river bottoms is often covered with dense foliage (depending on grazing management) making spot-and-stalk hunting difficult at best. Rifle hunters and bowhunters will find that treestands and ground blinds are effective tools when hunting the river bottoms. If you are concentrating on the farmlands surrounding the river, spot-and-stalk hunting may be effective depending on the terrain and crops, but stands and blinds will also be extremely useful. Hunters who can pattern deer movements between feeding and bedding areas will have good luck when setting up ambush points along these travel corridors. Also, when the rut kicks in, rattling, grunting, and the use of decoys can be effective for Colorado whitetail. (For obvious safety reasons, decoys should only be used by bowhunters.)

Since all deer tags are currently limited you will have to apply for a specific unit. If you want to bowhunt for deer in any of the GMUs that make up the South Platte herd you will stand a good chance of drawing a tag with 0 to 1 preference points. Rifle hunters will have to be more patient, it will generally take 1 to 3 points to draw a tag depending on which unit you choose. If you have a young hunter or you are only interested in harvesting a deer for meat consider applying for a doe tag. Most of the GMUs that make up the South Platte deer herd have many antlerless tags allocated each year. It may be possible to draw a doe tag without any preference points.

A common theme to the highlight areas of the eastern plains will be the lack of public lands available to hunt. Although most of the quality hunting opportunities are found on private lands, there are several state trust lands and SWAs scattered along the South Platte River. Many big game hunters stay away from the public lands on the eastern plains because they believe that upland bird and waterfowl hunters will interfere. This can be true, especially on some of the smaller properties, but can also help. Bird hunters will sometimes push deer into areas that aren't suitable for bird hunting. The result is that deer can get concentrated into smaller areas or areas that you wouldn't normally expect to find them. Deer hunters who find these locations often have very good success on public lands. To identify public lands open to big game hunting along the South Platte River you will need to obtain the *Information and Wildlife Property Directory* and the *State Trust Lands Supplement* published by the Colorado DOW. These two directories are available at DOW offices and most retail locations that sell hunting licenses. You can also obtain maps of these areas at DOW offices. Once you have identified potential areas, the only way to know for sure how the deer hunting will be is to scout.

If you don't want to hunt public land, but you don't have any connection to landowners on the plains there are two ways to proceed. First you can start knocking on doors. There may be some landowners that will simply give you permission to hunt, or they might ask for a trespass fee. Second, you can book a hunt through an outfitter that offers hunts in the area. (Refer to the list of outfitters for Region 4.)

Table Lands/Pawnee National Grasslands
(GMUs 87, 88, 89, 90, 93, 95, 97, 98, 99, 100, 101, 102)

The Table Lands deer herd consists of a large area covered by 12 GMUs (87, 88, 89, 90, 93, 95, 97, 98, 99, 100, 101, 102). Geographically this area extends on both the north and south sides of the South Platte River and makes up nearly one third of Region 4 in the north. The DOW estimates that there are over 6,300 deer in this broad area. Some good areas to concentrate on for deer are the Arikaree River in Unit 102 and the North Fork of the Republican River near the town of Wray, Colorado (Units 98 and 101). Yuma County covers a large portion of these three units. Both of the river drainages are almost completely in the hands of private landowners, so you will have to spend time to get access. If you decide to hunt this area don't overlook the smaller side tributaries to the rivers. Many of these tributaries are dry much of the time, but they can hold some good bucks. The *Colorado Bowhunting Records of Big Game* lists numerous Pope and Young whitetail entries for Yuma County.

This area also holds three separate antelope herds. GMUs 87, 88, 89, 90, 95, and 951 comprise the Escarpment antelope herd, which is consistently the largest herd in Region 4 with a current population of 5,390. Hunters interested in pursuing antelope on the eastern plains should note that most of the Pawnee National Grasslands are found in GMUs 87, 88, and 89. The importance is obvious; the second largest area of public land in the region is home to the largest antelope herd. The area also holds the Sandhills antelope herd in GMUs 93, 97, 98, 101, and 102. This small herd has nearly 600 antelope and a good buck-to-doe ratio of 48 to 100 in recent years. The third antelope herd in this part of Region 4 is the Hardpan herd in GMUs 99 and 100. This herd generally has 1,200 to 1,300 animals with with a strong buck to doe ratio.

Hunters who draw a tag for antelope or deer in one of the twelve units discussed above generally have good success rates. That's not to say that hunting will be easy in this area. Antelope have been educated here and they will commonly bolt at the first sign of a vehicle approaching, even at a distance of several hundred yards. A good strategy is to find vantage points and glass for antelope. The idea is to see the animals from a distance before they are alarmed by your presence. Once located, you can plan your stalk accordingly and move into adequate range. Rifle hunters will want to use fast, flat- shooting rifles, and they will want to be prepared for windy conditions.

Pawnee Butte in the Pawnee National Forest.

Antelope are small targets, so spend a good deal of time at the shooting range before you head out hunting. Accurate shots at small targets over wide-open flat terrain can be deceivingly difficult. Still, a moderate amount of patience and hard work will probably get you an antelope.

Bowhunters in pursuit of antelope in this part of the state have a real challenge. There is generally more surface water here than in the good antelope areas in Region 1. This takes away the effectiveness of hunting waterholes. With more available water antelope will not come in as consistently as they might in drier areas. This doesn't mean you should give up on watering areas, though. It means you may have to do more scouting to find productive watering locations. If your schedule won't allow you to camp out at a waterhole for several days take a more active approach. Stalking will be difficult, but there are areas of broken terrain where you may be able to move into bow range. The key is always patience. Take your time, get the wind right, move cautiously, and only proceed when the animals are feeding or have their heads turned away from you. It will probably take numerous stalks before you get into bow range of these wary animals. Still another approach (for bowhunters only) is decoys. If you hunt in September during the rut, dominant antelope bucks become aggressive when protecting does. This can be an exciting way to hunt antelope, but it takes skill to use the decoy properly and to identify susceptible bucks. This approach usually works best with two hunters, one to handle the decoy and one to shoot. Another more passive method is simply to use a doe antelope decoy. I know of hunters who have had very good success just setting up a doe decoy next to a watering location and waiting. The decoy may draw in a buck during the rut, or it may simply act as a confidence mechanism when a herd finally comes in to drink.

Rifle hunters will generally draw an antelope tag with 1 to 3 preference points, depending on which unit they choose. Deer hunters will need to be more patient. Depending on the season and the unit, it will take 1 to 4 points to get a tag. Whether you're after antelope or deer there are usually plenty of doe tags available in this area. This is a great opportunity for less experienced hunters to get some time in the field. Or if you simply want some meat, applying for a doe tag will allow you to hunt the area more frequently.

Arkansas River Drainage
(GMUs 122, 125, 126, 127, 130, 132, 137, 138, 139, 146)

To the chagrin of many big game hunters who frequent the southeastern plains of Colorado, the Arkansas River is becoming known as a trophy whitetail and mule deer producer. Magazine articles and word of mouth have spread the news. Even though the word is out you probably won't have to worry about crowds of hunters in this region of the state. Access is going to be the key component to a hunt in this area. If you put in the time to gain access to quality river bottom property, you will likely be rewarded with the chance to harvest an exceptional deer. The amount and diversity of wildlife along the Arkansas River is incredible. I have been fortunate to hunt near the town of La Junta for the past few years. During countless days spent in treestands near the Arkansas River I have witnessed some truly big whitetails. I have even harvested a mule deer during one hunting season and a whitetail deer the next from the same treestand.

The group of ten GMUs that the DOW recognizes as the Arkansas River deer herd encompasses a large portion of southeast Colorado. The DOW estimates that these ten units hold slightly over 4,000 deer based on recent population statistics. Although all ten of the units have deer, the six units (125, 126, 127, 130, 146, and 132) that surround the Arkansas River contain a large percentage of the deer population in this region of the state. You can even narrow down the most productive areas by concentrating on river bottom and farmlands that surround the river.

Rifle deer hunters have very good success rates when hunting in the units that make up the Arkansas River herd. The six units that surround the river had harvest rates between 58 percent and 80 percent in recent years. If you want to hunt bucks in any of these units you will need a minimum of two preference points. Bowhunters can also have good success rates, although the harvest is much more variable. The positive side is that bowhunters will generally draw a tag without any preference points. Deer hunters can approach their hunt in a variety of ways in this part of the state. If you want a big mule deer, concentrate on the farmlands and the prairie regions surrounding the river bottom. Big mule deer will come into the river bottoms, especially to escape bad weather and later in the season when food is less abundant. But you're more likely to find big whitetails on the river bottom.

There are also good numbers of antelope in this part of the state. Portions of the Haswell, Thatcher, Tobe, and Two Buttes antelope herds share GMUs with the Arkansas River deer herd. Statistically, bowhunters have a tough time in this part of

The author with a river-bottom whitetail.

The author with a river bottom mule deer taken from the same stand the next year.

the state when hunting antelope, but rifle hunters do better with success rates commonly over 50 percent.

For those people interested in hunting public land in this part of the state there are several SWAs in the area, especially in Bent County. Refer to the DOW *Information and Wildlife Property Directory*. Access to the area is very good. Highway 50 parallels the Arkansas River from Pueblo all the way to the Kansas state line. From the highway you can access any number of county roads.

Comanche National Grasslands (GMUs 135, 139, 143, 144, 145)

The U.S. Forest Service administers the national grasslands in Colorado. At 419,000 acres the Comanche National Grasslands make up nearly half of the public land in Region 4. Most statewide maps depict the Comanche National Grasslands as two large areas in southeast Colorado, a northern section in Otero County and a southern portion in Baca and Las Animas Counties. However, these maps are somewhat misleading. The grasslands consist of numerous parcels of public land separated by relatively large tracts of private land. In fact, the distribution of the public land is somewhat complicated. In order to avoid trespassing, you will need to obtain the Forest Service map for the Comanche National Grasslands before hunting in the area. This map provides a detailed breakdown of the sections that are included within the national grasslands boundary. It also depicts pasture numbers on many of the sections in the southern portion of the grasslands. The pasture numbers (e.g. 16BW) correspond to signs that are visible on fences along the county roads in the area. Once you start to locate these signs in the field it is relatively easy to distinguish private from public land.

The northern portion of the Comanche National Grasslands is located just south of the town of Rocky Ford. Most of this area is covered by GMU 135. The southern portion of the grasslands is located south of the town of Springfield. Here most of the grasslands are within GMUs 139, 143, 144, and 145. Both areas are important to people who are interested in hunting deer on public lands in southeastern Colorado. There is a lot of public land and good numbers of deer and antelope. Units 143, 144, and 145 make up the Mesa de Mayo deer herd that generally has about 2,400 animals. The buck-to-doe ratio for this herd has been good in recent years with 41 bucks to every 100 does. Unit 135 is one of nine units that comprise the Las Animas deer herd that has had an excellent buck-to-doe ratio of close to 70 to 100 in years past. Bowhunters will have to work hard to harvest a deer in these units, but it can be done. Rifle hunters have very good success rates in this part of the state. In past years rifle deer hunters connected between 50 percent and 80 percent of the time depending on which unit they hunted.

The Comanche National Grasslands also offer good chances for antelope hunters. The five units that cover most of the grasslands make up portions of the Thatcher, Tobe, and Two Buttes antelope herds. In general, bowhunters have very low success rates for antelope in this part of the state. Rifle hunters will have much better success in southeast Colorado, generally filling their tags over 50 percent of the time. As an example, there was an 80 percent success rate for rifle hunters who pursued antelope in GMU 135 in the most recent hunting season. Due to the presence of so much public land, Unit 135 attracts a lot of attention. Rifle hunters will need a minimum of two points before drawing a buck tag and one point for a doe tag. Bowhunters can buy an archery license over the counter for antelope in Unit 135.

Access into the area is very good. If you plan on hunting the northern portion of the grasslands in Unit 135, US Highway 350 cuts right through the middle of the public lands. From the highway you can access the area by any number of county roads. To access the southern portion of the grasslands, Highway 160 crosses the northern portion between the towns of Tobe and Springfield. Highway 285 provides north to south access along the eastern portion of the grasslands. Again there are countless county roads off both of these highways. If you are new to this area and trying to scout portions of the southern grasslands, be aware that there are sections of land that are only accessible through private roads. In fact, some of these roads pass right by ranch houses and through associated gates that appear to be private. The only way to identify these roads is to pay careful attention to the maps, and when in doubt, ask the ranchers. Don't assume you can drive through their property, and always be sure to leave gates the way you found them. Hunters often get a bad rap for leaving gates open—even when it's not our fault.

In addition to deer and antelope, there is also a small herd of elk in Unit 145 known as the Elkhart herd. This herd was originally planted in the area several years ago to try and re-establish elk as a plains animal. The only problem was that elk and farmland don't mix. The elk took advantage of the abundant corn and milo in the area and played havoc on the farm fences. The result was disputes for property damage between both Colorado and Kansas landowners in the area and the corresponding wildlife offices. In hindsight it may not have been such a good idea, but some of the farmers have begun to realize that the elk represent a cash crop that is more valuable than anything they can grow. In the past few years several outfitters have leased farms in the area and offered elk hunts for trophy bulls. I can assure you it is a strange sight to see a big bull elk in a milo field adjacent to a river bottom. But before you start buying your elk license for the area, be aware that this herd lives almost entirely on private land along the Cimarron River to the east of the Comanche National Grasslands. It also moves in and out of Colorado into Kansas from time to time. If you want to hunt one of the big bulls in this region it will probably cost you several thousand dollars. While helping an outfitter guide a whitetail hunter on the Cimarron River in 1998, I got to stalk some of these flatland elk just for the fun of it. They were relatively easy to get close to with the abundant cover on the river bottom, and there were some excellent bulls. The Cimarron River is also home to some huge whitetail deer. Again, your only access to this river bottom will most likely be through an outfitter.

There are also a few bighorn sheep in the southern portion of the Comanche National Grasslands area within Sheep Unit S48. There has only been one ram tag available for this unit during the past few seasons.

The Comanche National Grasslands are a special part of Colorado. Although most of the area is made up of vast reaches of flat to hilly terrain, the areas along the Oklahoma state line and into the Mesa de Maya area to the west are significantly different. Here you will find small canyons, deep washes, tablelands, and numerous intermittent streambeds. Many of the canyon areas contain pinon and juniper trees.

*David Blanton with a big whitetail taken in the
southeast corner of the state.*

The area holds some trophy-class mule deer, and the idea of hunting them in the rimrock of the canyons is very appealing. I have also heard stories of mountain lions in this part of the state. The habitat is right, and the deer numbers are good, so I don't doubt these stories for a moment. Lastly, the grasslands contain some important Indian sites that give an added attraction. The most notable of these sites is Picture Canyon and Crack Cave, both of which are located to the southwest of Campo. If you plan to hunt the southern portion of the Comanche National Grasslands take some time to visit these sites and enjoy the views of this vast unspoiled landscape.

South Fork of the Republican River (GMUs 103, 109, 116, 117)

The Republican River is a well-known whitetail deer and turkey hunting venue for many sportsmen in Nebraska. Colorado hunters are starting to find out that the South Fork of the Republican River is a similarly good destination in eastern Colorado. The South Fork of the Republican has its origin in Lincoln County not far from the town of Hugo. It runs northeast through Unit 109 into the southeast corner of Yuma County in Unit 103. Most of the drainage is privately owned up to Unit 103 where Bonny Reservoir and the South Republican State Wildlife Area are located. This SWA provides over 13,000 acres of land open to the public for various types of recreation, including hunting. The DOW recognizes GMUs 103, 109, 116, and 117 as the South Republican deer herd. The most recent post-hunting season population estimate for this herd is 2,100. As previously discussed, Yuma County has produced a large number of Pope and Young class bucks. To a lesser extent, Kit Carson County is also listed several times throughout the *Colorado Bowhunting Records of Big Game* for Pope and Young whitetail deer entries.

If the combination of public land and big bucks has your interest, you will be relieved to find out that it won't take years of preference points to draw a tag here. Depending on which season you choose to hunt, you may be able to draw a rifle buck tag with as few as two preference points for Unit 103, and bowhunters will generally draw a tag with one or two points. Surprisingly, in recent years there were left over muzzleloader tags available for Unit 103. Unit 109 has also been undersubscribed for muzzleloader hunters in past years. If you hunt with a muzzleloader, this could be a very good opportunity to pursue deer in a quality area and draw the tag on your first attempt.

In addition to the excellent deer hunting along the South Fork of the Republican River there are also two antelope herds that occupy a larger area. The Last Chance herd is made up by GMUs 103, 106, 107, and 109. It generally has a population of about 1,800 animals over the past few years. The Cheyenne antelope herd occupies GMUs 116, 117, 122, and 127, and had a population slightly over 1,000 animals in recent years. Most of the good antelope areas will be found on private land in this part of the state, so start seeking access well before you start applying for tags. If you do have access to land in the area you will generally be able to draw a rifle buck tag on a regular basis with zero to one preference points.

Las Animas Deer (GMUs 128, 129, 133, 134, 135, 136, 141, 142, 147)

From the town of Trinidad the Purgatoire River spills out onto the plains and runs a northeasterly course through Las Animas County. It eventually joins the Arkansas River to the east of La Junta near the inlet to John Martin Reservoir. The Purgatoire River, as well as the Apishapa River, the Pinon Canyon Military Reservation, and the northern section of the Comanche National Grasslands are important features within the area that comprises the Las Animas deer herd. This large area (inclusive of GMUs 128, 129, 133, 134, 135, 136, 141, 142, and 147) generally holds between 3,500 and 4,000 deer with an excellent buck-to-doe ratio of 69 to 100 in recent years. The same general area makes up the Thatcher antelope herd. This is one of the biggest herds in Region 4 with over 4,000 animals after the most recent hunting season.

Similar to many other regions of the eastern plains, the nine GMUs that make up the Las Animas DAU seems to be a very large area to support a rather nominal population of deer. The explanation is in part due to large areas of land that comprise poor habitat for deer. This means that the deer are concentrated into areas with more suitable habitat, such as riparian areas along the rivers and pinon-juniper woodlands associated with the tablelands and canyons.

As with many other parts of Region 4, public land is going to be difficult to find in this part of the state. In addition to the Comanche National Grasslands in Unit 135 (previously discussed in the Comanche National Grasslands Highlight Area) there are also some state lands adjacent to the northeast boundary of the Pinon Canyon Military Reservation. The Military Reservation (GMU 142) also offers a significant amount of property that is open to the public for hunting, but special access requirements apply and licenses are very limited. If you want a buck tag for GMU 142 for the Late Plains Rifle season you will probably need eight preference points to draw it. (See the Military Lands section for specific details concerning the Pinon Canyon Military Reservation.)

In addition to the grasslands and GMU 142, there are a few SWAs scattered across the region that provide public access. A good one to note is the Apishapa SWA located in Las Animas County. At almost 8,000 acres this SWA provides big game hunting opportunities for deer and antelope in GMUs 134 and 135, as well as bighorn sheep in Unit S38. Sheep Unit S61 is located adjacent to S38 to the east and also offers a few tags for sheep. In 2001 there were three rams harvested in Unit S61.

One of the three elk herds found east of I-25 is also present in this part of the state. Unit 128 holds the Cedarwood elk herd with a population of 128 based on recent DOW statistics. Opportunities to hunt these elk are extremely limited.

If you have never hunted this region of the state you can expect a variety of terrain, from wide-open prairie to deep canyons and mesas. The elevation varies from about 4,500 feet to 5,700 feet at the higher reaches. The weather is generally hot and dry in the early seasons. Even during the later seasons in October and November the weather can be very mild. As a standard caveat concerning the weather in Colorado, you should still be prepared for bad weather and cold temperatures regardless of the season you choose to hunt.

If you don't have connections to private property in this part of Colorado your hunting opportunities will be limited. With that said, the area still offers excellent big game hunting to those individuals willing to spend the time to identify public lands or procure access on private lands. The reward for persistent hunters who find places to hunt will be the chance to pursue deer and antelope with very high trophy potential.

Bijou Creek (GMUs 104, 105, 106)

Bijou Basin holds Bijou Creek, which is the geographical feature used to name the population of deer that occupies GMUs 104, 105, and 106. The Bijou Creek deer herd generally contains over 5,000 deer with an incredible buck-to-doe ratio that has been as high as 88 to 100 in recent years. Trophy quality, mostly for mule deer, is very good in this area. It is located on a geographic highland above the plains known as the Platte-Arkansas Divide. Montane forests spill out away from the Front Range Mountains. Areas of montane shrubland rim these forests before they merge with the grasslands of the plains. Other important drainages in the area include Kiowa Creek and Cherry Creek.

This area is also notable for elk and antelope. The Castle Rock elk herd is made up of GMUs 51, 104, 105, 106, 110, and 111. This herd has a current population of 1,420 with a high bull to cow ratio. Units 51, 104, and 105 make up the Kiowa Creek antelope herd, which contains nearly 3,000 animals based on recent DOW estimates.

The major setback to this area is its proximity to Denver and Colorado Springs. These units are located in portions of Douglas, Arapahoe, and Elbert Counties. Douglas County has experienced more growth in the last few years than any other county in the United States. The urban sprawl is spilling eastward and the small

*Portable blinds work well in many situations—such
as hunting deer on river bottoms in Region 4.*

towns in the area are feeling the growth. Housing developments are pressing the towns of Franktown, Elizabeth and Parker. Mini-ranches abound and exclusive golf course communities seem to spring up overnight. I'm not going to mislead you, if you don't have permission to hunt private land in Units 104, 105, or 106; it will be difficult to hunt this area. It is worth noting, though, because of the quality of the animals in this part of Region 4.

Although the populations of the Bijou Creek deer herd and Kiowa Creek antelope herd have been relatively steady over the past ten years, the Castle Rock elk herd population has declined dramatically. From a high population in the mid-1990s of over 3,200 animals, it has slid over the past few years to its current population of 1,420. Elk are big animals that need a lot of country to support them, and the unbridled development has started to take its toll. As new fences, roads, and structures dissect the countryside, it is likely that all of the big game populations in this area will be affected by the changing landscape.

Big Sandy (GMUs 107, 112, 113, 114, 115, 120, 121)

The units that make up the Big Sandy deer herd are located in the central region of the eastern plains. The namesake of the deer herd is Big Sandy Creek, which is a tributary of the Arkansas River. This persistent creek originates some 40 miles southwest of Limon. At Limon it changes course and turns to the southeast where it eventually joins the Arkansas River to the east of Lamar. Other rivers that are important to big game hunters also have their beginnings in this area. The Arikaree River originates just to the northeast of Limon in Unit 107 and flows northeast. The South Fork of the Republican River also has its headwaters in this area, originating just east of the town of Hugo in Unit 114. There are countless other creeks and intermittent streams that cross this relatively flat landscape of farmland and grasslands.

The Big Sandy deer herd contains 2,570 animals based recent DOW statistics. This herd has had a good buck-to-doe ratio of 44 to 100 in recent years. The Hugo antelope herd is also found in this region (Units 112, 113, 114, and 115). It had a post-hunting season population estimated of 2,210.

The DOW has been relatively liberal with licenses for the units that make up the Big Sandy deer herd. Most rifle hunters will draw a Plains Season rifle buck tag with zero to two preference points depending on which unit they choose to hunt. A rifle doe tag is almost a sure bet without any preference points. The same is true for rifle antelope licenses in these units. Most hunters will draw with zero to one point, and most rifle doe antelope tags are undersubscribed. Bowhunters will generally draw a buck deer tag in this area without any points and antelope licenses are unlimited.

This part of the state is dominated by flat, open country, making the hunting difficult. There are areas of broken terrain along the numerous drainages where deer hunters will have the most success. The majority of the antelope will be found in the middle of wide-open terrain. You will have to plan your stalks carefully and exercise all of the patience you can muster to get into adequate range.

Although most of the land in this region is privately owned, it receives less pressure than the more popular areas along the South Platte and Arkansas Rivers on the eastern plains. Some landowners will give permission to hunt antelope in this area, although you may have to work harder to access private land for deer. Generally, it seems that many of the farmers would just as soon see hunters take a few antelope off their land. The deer, however, seem to be more highly regarded.

If you don't have luck getting permission to hunt private property in this area there are a few SWAs that offer big game hunting. To identify these refer to the DOW *Information and Wildlife Property Directory.* Some suggestions would include the Hugo SWA in Lincoln County, which consists of 2,560 acres in two separate tracts of land open to deer and antelope hunting. The Flagler Reservoir SWA in Kit Carson County consists of 400 acres of land with some opportunities for deer. Remember that many of the SWAs in Colorado have special restrictions concerning big game hunting. Please check the restrictions, and scout the SWAs before you plan to hunt them.

Chico Basin (GMUs 110, 111, 118, 119, 123, 124)

The Chico Basin deer herd is made up by six GMUs that extend from Interstate 25 into the eastern plains between Colorado Springs and Pueblo. These units (especially 110 and 118) are also feeling the effects of growth, but not nearly as much as the neighboring units to the north near Denver. The Chico Basin deer herd generally contains 1,800 to 2,100 animals over the past few years. The same six units make up the Yoder antelope herd, which is one of the biggest in Region 4 with an estimated population of 4,550. Units 110 and 111 are two of the six GMUs that make up the Castle Rock elk herd (previously discussed in the Bijou Creek Highlight Area).

The area north of Colorado Springs within Unit 110 contains a forested area (known as the Black Forest) that extends onto the east side of I-25. This area represents the southern extension of the Platte-Arkansas Divide. South of this area the landscape along the I-25 corridor consists of gentle to steep hills that give way to flatter terrain to the east. Fountain Creek is the major drainage in this region. It flows south from Colorado Springs to Pueblo on the east side and parallel to I-25. This drainage holds good numbers of both mule deer and whitetail deer. I have even seen some very nice whitetail bucks just off of I-25 along Fountain Creek near the town of Security. Most of this region is privately owned, but the area does offer Front Range residents in proximity to Colorado Springs and Pueblo good opportunities on the eastern plains for both deer and antelope. Just like other locations on the eastern plains you will have to do some legwork to find places to hunt here.

Although this six-unit region is fairly large, I am only aware of one SWA in the area. The Colorado Springs SWA includes 3,200 acres of property with opportunities for deer hunting. There is also a state trust property in Unit 118, about 14 miles east of the town of Fountain, that big game hunters should be aware of. It is known as the Turkey Track Ranch and includes 8,887 acres open to public access for big game hunting.

Mulies do not run as other deer, but have a peculiar and distinctive bounding leap (stotting) over distances up to 8 yards, with all 4 feet coming down together.

Region 4 Hub Cities

Most of the towns on the eastern plains are within a one- to five-hour drive from the Front Range cities of Denver, Colorado Springs, and Fort Collins. Hunters who are traveling from out of state to hunt units on the plains will find that there is an abundance of services available in all of the cities along the Front Range, including accommodations, car rental, taxidermists, and meat processing. Air travel into the area is relatively easy through either Denver International Airport or the Colorado Springs airport.

Sterling
Population — 11,295 • Elevation — 3,939'

As with most of the towns on the eastern plains, Sterling is largely an agricultural community. Farms and cattle ranches predominate in the countryside surrounding Sterling. It is the largest community in northeast Colorado and is the county seat of Logan County. It is located adjacent to the South Platte River, and the area is known for excellent waterfowl and upland bird hunting. It is also known for producing big bucks, both whitetail and mule deer. If you are hunting in Units 89, 95, 96, 97, or 98, Sterling will make an excellent base of operations. There are also several SWAs near Sterling that provide chances to hunt deer on public land. Most notable is the Tamarack Ranch SWA consisting of over 10,000 acres of property, much of which is located adjacent to the South Platte River. Tamarack Ranch offers exceptional bird hunting to the public as well as opportunities for deer.Sterling is just a short drive of less than an hour to Sydney, Nebraska from Sterling. Sydney is home to one of the Cabela's sporting good stores. This huge store is a sportsman's paradise with every conceivable piece of equipment and clothing imaginable. The excellent collection of big game trophies in the store is worth the trip in itself.

ACCOMMODATIONS

Best Western Sundowner Motel, Overland Trail, (970) 522-6265
Colonial Motel, 915 Division Ave., (970) 522-3382
Crest Motel, 516 S. Division Ave., (970) 522-3753
Days Inn, I76 and Hwy. 6, (970) 522-1234
First Interstate Inn, 20930 E Hwy. 6, (970) 522-7274
Fountain Lodge, 619 N 3rd St., (970) 522-1821
Lontine's Inn, Logan St. and Hwy 138, (970) 522-5353
The Oakwood Inn, 810 S. Division Ave., (970) 522-1416
Plains Motel, 1005 S. Division Ave., (970) 522-7394
Ramada Inn, Hwy 6 and I76, (970) 522-2625
Sterling Motor Lodge, 731 N 3 St., (970) 522-2740
Super 8 Motel, 12883 Hwy 61, (970) 522-0300

CAMPGROUNDS AND RV PARKS

Buffalo Hills Campgrounds, 22018 US Hwy. 6, (970) 522-2233
State Park Camping Reservations 800-678-CAMP
Forest Service Camping Reservations 877-444-6777

RESTAURANTS

Coach's, 630 Sidney Ave., (970) 522-2950
Cocina Alvarado, 715 W Main St., (970) 522-8884
Country Kitchen, US Hwy. 6 and I76, (970) 522-2625
Delgado's Dugout, 116 Beech, (970) 522-0175
Fergies West Inn Pub, 324 W. Main St., (970) 522-4220
Fireside Inn Restaurant, 229 N. Front St., (970) 522-6318
J&L Café, 423 N 3rd St., (970) 522-3625
Kyotees, 118 Poplar St., (970) 522-7777
Lontine's Restaurant, Logan and Hwy 138, (970) 522-5353
Momma Conde's, Broadway Plaza Shopping Center, (970) 522-0802

VETERINARIANS

Sterling Animal Clinic, 1331 W. Main St., (970) 521-0333
Veterinary Medical Clinic, 211 El Camino, (970) 522-3321

SPORTING GOODS, GUNS, AND GUNSMITHS

Wal-Mart, 1510 W. Main, (970) 522-3012
Pro Sports, 119 N. 3rd St., (970) 522-8545
Unique Cameras and Guns, 105 Main St., (970) 522-4939

MEAT PROCESSORS

Sterling Steak and Sausage, 315 W. Main St., (970) 522-0208

AUTO RENTAL AND REPAIR

TLC Automotive, 507 Iris Dr., (970) 522-9683
Larson Motors (Dodge Authorized Service), 520 E. Chestnut, (970) 522-2523
Foxhoven Tire Center Sales and Service, 1020 W. Main St., (970) 522-4141
Herzog Automotive, 415 S. 10th Ave., (970) 522-0957
LH&M Garage, 105 Poplar St., (970) 522-3904
Sterling Auto Service Center, 524 W. Main, (970) 522-9500
Tower Automotive, 220 S 3rd Ave., (970) 522-0597
Holloway Toyota (for Car Rental), 1200 W. Main St., (970) 522-0450

AIR SERVICE

Sterling Municipal Airport, 16562 Hwy. 14, (970) 522-0417

MEDICAL

Sterling Regional MedCenter, 615 Fairhurst, (970) 522-0122

FOR MORE INFORMATION

Logan County Chamber of Commerce, 109 N. Front St., Sterling, CO 80751
(970) 522-5070

Wray

Population — 2,073 · Elevation — 3,522'

Wray is the county seat of Yuma County. The town is situated along the North Fork of the Republican River about 10 miles from the Nebraska state line, and the Arikaree River is only a few miles south of town. Both of these rivers and their numerous side tributaries have resulted in a relatively large area of broken terrain with deeply eroded washes. The area surrounding Wray is a popular destination for pheasant hunters, but the numerous draws and tributaries associated with the rivers hold good numbers of deer. You will find both mule deer and whitetail deer here, as well as a nominal population of antelope in the Sandhills herd.

Be aware that nearly all of the land in the area surrounding Wray is privately owned. But if you have managed to gain permission to hunt somewhere in Units 98, 101, or 102, Wray will make a good hub city for your hunt.

ACCOMMODATIONS
Butte Motel, 330 E 3rd St., (970) 332-4823
Four-U Motel, 710 E 3rd St., (970) 332-4875
Sandhiller Motel and Restaurant, 411 N W Railway, (970) 332-4134
Traveler's Inn, 240 E 3rd St., (970) 332-4848
Sunset Motel, 420 E. 3rd St., (970) 332-4871

CAMPGROUNDS AND RV PARKS
State Park Camping Reservations 800-678-CAMP
Forest Service Camping Reservations 877-444-6777

RESTAURANTS
Big Red, 369 W 2nd St., (970) 332-5864
Wray Dairy Queen, 233 N. Dexter St., (970) 332-2070
La Familia Restaurant, Wray Shopping Center, (970) 332-5157
Sandhiller Restaurant, 411 N W Railway, (970) 332-4134

VETERINARIANS
Sun Prairie Veterinary Clinic, 151 E. Badger St., (970) 332-3116

MEAT PROCESSORS
Wray Meat Packing, 137 E. Badger Way, (970) 332-5538

AUTO REPAIR
Bonanza Ford-Mercury, 341 Adams, (970) 332-4838
Eveready's Auto Center, 36605 Hwy. 385, (970) 332-4650

AIR SERVICE
Wray Airport, 36391 Hwy. 385, (970) 332-9997

MEDICAL
Wray Community District Hospital, 1017 W. 7th St., (970) 332-4811

FOR MORE INFORMATION
Wray Chamber of Commerce, 245 W. 4th St., Wray, CO (970) 332-4431

Burlington
Population — 3,024 · Elevation — 4,160'

For hunters who have a tag to hunt deer or antelope in Units 103, 109, 116, or 117, Burlington will be a good choice to find accommodations and other services that may be required. The area covered by the four units listed above is home to the South Republican deer herd. There are also good numbers of antelope in this part of the state in the Last Chance and Cheyenne herds. Roughly 30 miles north of Burlington is the Bonny Reservoir State Recreation Area (GMU 103), an area known to produce some exceptional bucks. The reservoir is fed by the South Fork of the Republican River and offers excellent fishing for warmwater species. In addition to deer and antelope hunting, the area surrounding Burlington has very good pheasant hunting.

ACCOMMODATIONS

Burlington Super 8, 2100 Fay St., (719) 346-5627
Burlington Travel Lodge, 450 S. Lincoln St., (719) 346-5555
Comfort Inn, 282 Lincoln St., (719) 346-7676
Hi-Lo Motel, 870 Rose Ave., (719) 346-5280
Sloans Motel, 1901 Rose Ave., (719) 346-5333
Super 8 Motel, 2100 Fay St., (719) 346-5627
Western Motor Inn Motel, 2222 Rose Ave., (719) 346-5371
Chaparral Budget Host, 405 S. Lincoln, (719) 346-5361
Kit Carson Motel, 700 Rose Ave., (719) 346-8513

CAMPGROUNDS AND RV PARKS

State Park Camping Reservations 800-678-CAMP
Forest Service Camping Reservations 877-444-6777

RESTAURANTS

Burlington Country Club, 300 S. Lincoln, (719) 346-7266
Del Sol Mexican Restaurant and Bakery, 474 14th St., (719) 346-7420
Eastern Plains Café, 102 Rose Ave., (719) 346-8322
Hoof Horn Restaurant, 46277 Hwy. 24, (719) 346-5015
Mr. A's Interstate House Restaurant, 415 S. Lincoln, (719) 346-8010
Western Motor Inn Restaurant and Lounge, 123 Lincoln, (719) 346-8115

VETERINARIANS

Vondy Powell Veterinarians, 11675 US Hwy 385, (719) 346-7341

SPORTING GOODS, GUNS, AND GUNSMITHS

Glenmark Enterprises, (970) 354-7342, 34607 Yuma County Rd 35

MEAT PROCESSORS

Bonny Locker, 2445 Hwy. 385, (970) 354-7404

Auto Rental and Repair

Ford Sales and Service, 1847 Rose Ave., (719) 346-5336
Vince's Chevrolet Olds Cadillac, 1332 Senter, (719) 346-5326
Rush Bill Pontiac Buick GMC Truck, 1697 Rose Ave., (719) 346-5541
Hi-Tech Auto and Tire Service, 463 15th St., (719) 346-5329
Joe's Garage, 1980 Colorado Ave., (719) 346-7752
Johnnie's Repair, 18107 CR 40, (719) 346-8896

Medical

Kit Carson County Memorial Hospital, 286 16th St., (719) 346-5311

For More Information

Burlington Chamber of Commerce, 415 15th St., Burlington, CO 80807
(719) 346-8070

Limon
Population — 2,208 · Elevation — 5,365'

Limon is another agriculturally-based town centrally located on the eastern plains of Colorado. Geographically, the town makes up a common point for several GMUs, including 105, 106, 107, 111, 112, and 114. Units 105 and 106 are two of three GMUs that make up the Bijou Creek deer herd. This herd of over 5,000 deer usually has an outstanding buck-to-doe ratio commonly in the range of 80 to 100. The area surrounding Limon is also home to good numbers of antelope. Not far to the north of town is the headwater of the Arikaree River. With good access from the Denver area via Interstate 70, Limon will make a good jumping-off point for anybody hunting the central eastern plains.

ACCOMMODATIONS

Holiday Inn Express, 2425 6th St., (719) 775-0700
Midwest Country Inn, 795 Main St., (719) 775-2373
Safari Motel, 637 Main St., (719) 775-2363
Best Western Limon Inn, 925 US Hwy. 24, (719) 775-0277
Bonn's Motel, 1510 Main St., (719) 775-2074
Dovers Inn, 1650 main St., (719) 775-8818
Econo lodge of Limon, 985 US Hwy. 24, (719) 775-2867
K S Motel, 385 Main St., (719) 775-0700
Limon Comfort Inn, 2255 9th St., (719) 775-2752
Limon Inn-4-Less, 250 Main St., (719) 775-2821
Preferred Motor Inn, I-70 exit 361158 E. Main, (719) 775-2385
Silver Spur Motel, 514 Main St., (719) 775-2807

CAMPGROUNDS AND RV PARKS

Limon KOA Campground, 575 Colorado Ave., (719) 775-2151
State Park Camping Reservations 800-678-CAMP
Forest Service Camping Reservations 877-444-6777

RESTAURANTS

Country Fare Restaurant, I-70 and Hwy. 24, (719) 775-2811
Flying J Restaurant, 198 Main St., (719) 775-2725
Lou's Place, 197 East Ave., (719) 775-8836
Pizza Hut, 220 E. Main St., (719) 775-2844
South Side Restaurant, 680 Main St., (719) 775-9593

VETERINARIANS

High Plains Veterinary Clinic, 521 Indiana Ave., (719) 775-2151
Limon Veterinary Clinic, 1005 Immel St., (719) 775-9773

SPORTING GOODS, GUNS, AND GUNSMITHS

Verns Sport Shack, 354 East Ave., (719) 775-9572

AUTO REPAIR

Limon Chrysler Plymouth Dodge Jeep, 1155 Hwy. 71, (719) 775-2881
Connie's Mechanic Shop, 286 Main St., (719) 775-8880
George's Repair Shop, 199 Main St., (719) 775-8828
Limon Tire Diesel/Automotive and Towing, 474 North Hwy. 71, (719) 775-2093
Rods Repairs, 1307 Colorado Ave., (719) 775-9734
Rip Griffin Diesel Shop, I-70 and Hwy. 24, (719) 775-9389

MEDICAL

Plains Medical Center, 820 1st Street, (719) 775-2367

FOR MORE INFORMATION

Limon Chamber of Commerce, 1062 Main St., Limon, CO 80828
(719) 775-9418

La Junta
Population — 8,040 · Elevation — 4,066'

La Junta is the county seat of Otero County. It is situated in an area rich with wildlife in southeast Colorado. One of the most important features of the La Junta area is the Arkansas River. The riparian ecosystem and farmlands adjacent to the river are becoming known as a trophy whitetail producer. As with other areas on the plains, access to quality lands will be difficult to obtain, but it will be worth it. Even if you can't get on private land there are several SWAs in the area that offer big game hunting opportunities. These include the McClelland, Purgatoire River, and Rocky Ford SWAs, but most notable may be John Martin Reservoir SWA to the east of town. La Junta is also located just north of the northern portion of the Comanche National Grasslands, which provide additional public lands for deer and antelope hunters. As a bonus to the good big game hunting the area is also well known for quality upland bird hunting and excellent waterfowl hunting. Services are also available in the nearby town of Rocky Ford.

ACCOMMODATIONS

Mid-Town Motel, 215 E 3rd St., (719) 384-7741
Stagecoach Motel, 905 W. 3rd St., (719) 384-5476
Travel Inn, 110 E. 1st St., (719) 384-2504
Westerner Motel, 1502 E 3rd St., (719) 384-2591
Holiday Inn Express, 27994 US Hwy. 50, (719) 384-2900
Super Eight Motel, 27884 US Hwy. 50, (719) 384-4408

CAMPGROUNDS AND RV PARKS

La Junta KOA, 26680 Hwy. 50, (719) 384-9580
State Park Camping Reservations 800-678-CAMP
Forest Service Camping Reservations 877-444-6777

RESTAURANTS

Café Grandmere, 408 W. 3rd St., (719) 384-2711
Carducci's, 114 Santa Fe Ave., (719) 384-6659
Carmen's 9 To 5, 500 W. 1st St., (719) 384-5403
Chiaramonte's, 208 Santa Fe Ave., (719) 384-8909
Copper Kitchen Café, 116 Colorado Ave., (719) 384-7216
Cristina's Mexican Food, 101 Dalton Ave., (719) 384-7508
El Azteca Mexican Restaurant, 710 W. 3rd St., (719) 384-4215
El Camino Inn, 816 W 3rd St., (719) 384-2871
El Patio, 315 Colorado Ave., (719) 384-6787
Hickory House, 1220 E. 3rd St., (719) 384-9250
Hogs Breath Saloon, 808 E. 3rd St., (719) 384-5089
Mexico City Café, 1617 Raton Ave., (719) 384-9818

Veterinarians

Colorado Veterinary Clinic, 30488 Hwy. 50, (719) 384-8111
La Junta Veterinary Clinic, 2917 San Juan, (719) 384-2471

Sporting Goods, Guns, and Gunsmiths

Sports World, 214 Santa Fe Ave., (719) 384-5546
Wal-mart, 27332 Hwy. 50, (719) 384-5951

Taxidermists

Trails End Taxidermy, 25213 CR 25, (719) 384-4292

Auto Rental and Repair

Big Valley Ford Chrysler, 26730 US Hwy. 50, (719) 384-5421
Downtown Auto Service, 121 W 2nd St., (719) 384-2901
East Side Garage, East of La Junta, (719) 384-5897
La Junta Valley Tire, 1000 W 3rd St., (719) 384-5497
Maler's Garage, 614 Daniels Ave., (719) 384-7818
McBee's Auto Repair, 610 N. Main St., (719) 384-4959
Menges Auto Repair, 1100 Barnes Ave., (719) 384-7676

Medical

Arkansas Valley Regional Medical Center, 1100 Carson Ave., (719) 384-5412

For More Information

Chamber of Commerce, 110 Santa Fe Avenue, Burlington, CO (719) 384-7411

Lamar
Population — 8,487 · Elevation — 3,622'

Lamar is located due east of La Junta and is also situated adjacent to the Arkansas River. It is the county seat of Prowers County and provides an excellent hub city for hunters pursuing game in GMUs 126, 127, 132, and 146. Much like La Junta, the area surrounding Lamar offers excellent deer hunting in addition to upland bird and waterfowl hunting. John Martin Reservoir is a short drive to the west of Lamar and the Queens SWA is located to the north of town. Both areas offer limited deer hunting on public land.

Accommodations

Stockman's Motor Inn, 201 S. Main St., (719) 336-2271
Super 8 Motel, 1202 N. Main St., (719) 336-3427
Best Western Cow Palace Inn, 1301 N Main St., (719) 336-7753
Blue Spruce Motel, 1801 S Main St., (719) 336-7454
Economy Inn, 1201 N Main St., (719) 336-7471
El Mar Budget Host Motel, 1210 S Main St., (719) 336-4331
El-Donna Motel, 404 N Main St., (719) 336-2286
Golden Arrow Motel, 611 E Olive St., (719) 336-8725
Motel 7, 113 N Main St., (719) 336-7746

Campgrounds and RV Parks

State Park Camping Reservations 800-678-CAMP
Forest Service Camping Reservations 877-444-6777

Restaurants

BJ's Burger and Beverage, 1510 S Main St., (719) 336-5386
Blackwell Station, 1301 S Main St., (719) 336-7575
Broken Spoke Coffee Shop and Deli, 1201 N Main St., (719) 336-4177
Green Garden, 601 E Olive St., (719) 336-3264
Oasis Restaurant at Cow Palace Inn, 1301 N Main St., (719) 336-7753
The Main Café by Dora Hernandez, 114 S Main St., (719) 336-5736

Veterinarians

Big Timbers Veterinary Hospital, 7415 US Hwy. 50, (719) 336-2253
Eaton Veterinary Clinic, 1004 E Maple St., (719) 336-5068

Sporting Goods, Guns, and Gunsmiths

Colorado Gunsmithing Academy of Lamar, 27533 US Hwy. 287, (719) 336-4099
Jandro's Gun Sports and Pawn, 7495 US Hwy. 50, (719) 336-7836
Wal-mart, 1432 East Olive St., (719) 336-5287

Meat Processors

K&K Custom Meats, 13th and Pearl St., (719) 336-5287

AUTO REPAIR

Adkins Repair, 105 S. 13th St., (719) 336-2263
Anything Automotive, 414 N Main St., (719) 336-9765
Arkansas Valley Auto Service, 516 E Olive St., (719) 336-2174
Ron Austin Repair Shop, 402 N Main St., (719) 336-2542
Dieterle Repair and Salvage, 37029 CR 7, (719) 336-2142
Dougs One Stop Auto, 113 E Olive St., (719) 336-3894
K&S Auto Repair, 203 S 4th St., (719) 336-7306
Tri-County Ford Lincoln Mercury, 7240 US Hwy. 50, (719) 336-3268
Woller Auto Parts and Salvage, (719) 336-2108

MEDICAL

Prowers Medical Center, 401 Kendall Drive, (719) 336-4343

FOR MORE INFORMATION

Chamber of Commerce, 109-A East Beech, Lamar, CO 81052, (719) 336-4379

Springfield

Population — 1,421 · Elevation — 4,365'

The town of Springfield is the county seat of Baca County. For big game hunters it makes up one of the few choices available for lodging and services in the far southeast corner of the state (GMUs 138, 139, 144, 145). The southern portion of the Comanche National Grasslands is easily accessible from Springfield and provides good deer and antelope hunting on public land. Although the landscape around Springfield is predominantly flat farmland, the area to the south near the Oklahoma state line is much more diverse with several small canyons and mesas. An interesting attraction in this area is Picture Canyon where several Indian carvings can be found on canyon walls. This is another area on the eastern plains that offers excellent upland bird hunting.

Accommodations

Crawford Motel, 288 Colorado St., (719) 523-6276
J's Motel, 265 Main St., (719) 523-6257
Stage Stop Hotel, 1033 Main St., (719) 523-4737
Starlite Motel, 681 Main St., (719) 523-6236

Campgrounds

State Park Camping Reservations 800-678-CAMP
Forest Service Camping Reservations 877-444-6777

Restaurants

Bar Four Corral, 27080 US Hwy. 287, (719) 523-4065
Main Café, 973 Main St., (719) 523-9926

Veterinarians

Southeast Colorado Veterinary Clinic, 1500 Main St., (719) 523-6828

Sporting Goods

Gambles, 189 E 9th Ave., (719) 523-6229
Best Way Sales, 1189 Main St., (719) 523-4731

Auto Rental and Repair

Deen's Automotive, 149 E 10th St., (719) 523-4531
Joe's Eastside Automotive, 380 Main St., (719) 523-9954
Wes' Auto Repair, 525 Main St., (719) 523-4353

Medical

Southeast Colorado Hospital, 373 E. 10th Ave., (719) 523-4501

For More Information

Chamber of Commerce, 948 Main St., Springfield, CO 81073, (719) 523-4061

Pueblo
Population — 102,121 · Elevation — 4,662'

For those hunters pursuing game in the southern portion of the state, Pueblo is a good starting point. State Highway 50 transects most of the state from east to west with Pueblo near its midpoint. This route provides good access into the mountains to the west or the eastern plains along the Arkansas River.

Pueblo was formerly an industrial center in Colorado, but has changed with the times. It is home to the Colorado State Fair each year, and with consistent growth, Pueblo has evolved into one of Colorado's thriving cities on the Front Range. Any services a big game hunter may require are available in Pueblo.

ACCOMMODATIONS

Hampton Inn, 4703 North Freeway, (719)544-4700, 112 rooms, Dogs allowed for a fee

Ramada Inn, 2001 North Hudson, (719)542-3750, 180 rooms, Dogs allowed

Super 8 Motel, 1100 West Highway 50, (719)545-4104, 60 rooms, Dogs allowed

CAMPING

Country Bunk Inn Motel & RV Park, 3369 S Interstate 25, Pueblo, CO 81004-9710, (719) 564-1840

Fort's RV Park, 3015 Lake Ave, Pueblo, CO 81004-5832, (719) 564-2327

Haggards RV Campground, 7910 W US Highway 50, Pueblo West, CO 81007-3303, (719) 547-2101

KOA Kampgrounds, 4131 N Interstate 25, Pueblo, CO 81008-9626, (719) 542-2273

RESTAURANTS

Ianne's Whiskey Ridge, 4333 Thatcher Avenue, (719) 564-8551, Open 4PM–10PM, Cocktails, Highly recommended

Jorge's Sombrero Restaurant and Lounge, 1319 East Evans Avenue, (719) 564-6486, Open 11AM–9PM, Cocktails

The Pantry Restaurant, 107½ East Abriendo Avenue, (719) 543-8072, Open 6AM for breakfast

Two and Nine Bar, 2912 North Elizabeth, (719)544-5507, Open evenings for sandwiches and drinks

SPORTING GOODS

Athlete's Foot, 3417 Dillon Dr, Pueblo, CO 81008-1007, (719) 542-7403

Edge Ski Paddle & Pack, 107 N Union Ave, Pueblo, CO 81003-4206, (719) 583-2021

Gart Sports, 3261 Dillon Dr, Pueblo, CO 81008-1005, (719) 544-7793

Great Divide Ski Bike & Hike, 400 N Santa Fe Ave, (719) 546-2453

Herb's Sport Shop, 729 W 8th St, Pueblo, CO 81003-2375, (719) 544-4008

Johnson Sport & Ski, 315 Court St, Pueblo, CO 81003-3288, (719) 542-6012

Pueblo Sporting Goods, 703 W 9th St # 2, Pueblo, CO 81003-2266, (719) 543-7755

Sports Hut, 332 South McCulloch Boulevard, (719) 547-2848

T & M Sporting Goods, 2023 Lakeview Ave, Pueblo, CO 81004-2723, (719) 564-0790

TAXIDERMISTS

Trails End Taxidermy, 1108 W Broken Bow Dr, Pueblo West, CO 81007-2073, (719)6 47-1211

Valentine Taxidermy the Art, 65 N Laser Dr, Pueblo West, CO 81007-1400, (719) 547-3404

HOSPITALS

Proactive Medical Care Center, 431 Quincy, (719) 583-2273

AIRPORTS

Colorado Springs Airport, 7770 Drennan Road, 550-1900, United: 800-241-6522, American: 800-433-7300, Delta: 800-221-1212, Western Pacific: 800-722-5775

Pueblo Municipal, (719)948-4423, United Express: 800-241-6522

AUTO RENTAL

Avis Rent-A-Car, (719) 948-9665

Budget Rent-A-Car, (719) 948-3363

AUTO SERVICE

Scottie's, 615 South Main, (719) 545-7557

Car Doctor, 2205 East 4th, 542-0457, Mobile service and towing

FOR MORE INFORMATION

Pueblo Chamber of Commerce
302 North Santa Fe Avenue
PO Box 697
Pueblo, CO 81002
Toll Free: 800-233-3496
Fax: (719) 542-1624

Denver
Population — 554,636 · Elevation — 5,280'

Known as the "Mile High City" Denver is the state capital of Colorado and the most populous city. The Denver Metropolitan area is home to well over half of the state population. Denver is a great sports town and offers a wide variety of arts and entertainment. Interstate 25 and Interstate 70 meet in Denver. A large number of big game hunters travel the I70 corridor west into the mountains as the first leg of their journey into the Colorado high country.

Many hunters who travel into Colorado from out of state will arrive at Denver International Airport. From here you will be able to obtain ground transportation or continue on to any of the small regional airports across the state. Denver has everything you need to get your hunt started. There are countless sporting goods stores, restaurants, and hotels. If you are spending an extra night in Denver and are looking for an interesting restaurant, I would recommend the Buckhorn Exchange. This fine dining establishment is adorned with countless mounted heads of big game, and the menu includes elk and other wild game entrees.

ACCOMMODATIONS (NEAR DENVER INTERNATIONAL AIRPORT DIA)

Holiday Inn DIA, I-70 exit 283, 15500 E 40th Ave, 257 rooms, dining room, cocktails, pets allowed, (303) 371-9494

Comfort Suites DIA, I-70 exit 286, 6210 Tower Road, some two bedrooms, (303) 371-9300

Courtyard by Marriott at DIA, I-70 exit 278, 7415 East 41st ave, 146 rooms, restaurant, cocktails, (303) 333-3303

Denver Airport Marriott, I-70 exit 283, 16455 E 40th circle, 238 rooms, restaurant, cocktails, (303) 371-4333

Fairfield Inn DIA, I-70 exit 286 6851 Tower Rd, 161 rooms, (303) 576-9640

Hampton Inn DIA, I-70 exit 186 Tower Rd., 122 rooms, (303) 371-0200

Holiday Inn Express, I-70 exit 186 tower Rd., 87 rooms, (303) 373-4100

La Quinta Inn & Suites DIA, I-70 exit 286 6801 Tower Rd, 169 rooms, (303) 371-0888

BED AND BREAKFAST

Cliff House Country Inn, 121 Stone Street, Morrison, (303) 697-9732, Innkeeper: Peggy Hahn, Great place for couples, very nice accommodations

RESTAURANTS

There are limited dining establishments near the airport. Your best bet is one of the larger motel/hotels listed above. Below I've listed a few of my favorites in and around the city.

Barolo Grill, 3030 E 6th Ave, Great northern Italian food. Rustic décor, cocktails and a great wine selection, Open for dinner, closed Sun/Mon, (303) 393-1040

RESTAURANTS, CONTINUED

The Buckhorn Exchange, I-25 exit 210 , 1000 Osage, Denver's oldest restraurant— a historic landmark., The Buckhorn features wild game. The walls are lined with game heads and great old hunting and western photos. This is a must-stop for the hunter. Open for lunch and dinner, (303) 534-9505

Denver Chophouse & Brewery, I-25 exit 205B, 2076 University Blvd, Great steaks, big selection of beers, cocktails. Open for lunch and dinner, (303) 296-0800

Wynkoop Brewery, 1445 Larimer St. The nation's largest microbrewery in an 1880s warehouse, American cuisine. Open for lunch and dinner, (303) 534-5140

Celtic Tavern, 1801 Blake Street, (303) 308-1795. A great Irish restaurant and pub. A great bar with beers, wines and spirits. Irish and Celtic cuisine and, of course, dart boards. Open for lunch Mon through Thurs. Dinner daily.

The Wellshire Inn, I-25 exit 204, 3333 Colorado Blvd, (303) 759-3333. American food served in an English Tudor atmosphere, cocktails. Open lunch and dinner.

Fresh Fish Company, 7800 East Hampden Avenue, (303) 740-9556. Open 5PM– 11PM for dinner and cocktails. Best seafood in town. Reservations recommended

The Chart House, 25908 Genesee Trail Road, Golden, (303) 526-9813, Open 5PM– 10PM, Located in the foothills west of Denver, Great steaks

Beau Jo's Pizza, Idaho Springs, (303) 573-6924. Home of the Colorado Mountain Pie. Awesome pizza

Perkins Family Restaurant, 1495 Simms Street, Lakewood, (303) 237-1339, Open 24 hours. Good place to stop on the west side of town for breakfast before a day of hunting.

Village Inn, 4775 Kipling Street, Wheatridge, (303) 420-9792, West side of town, Open 24 hours on Saturday and Sunday, 5AM–12AM weekdays

SPORTING GOODS AND GUN SHOPS

Army and Navy Surplus Store, 3524 South Broadway, Englewood, (303) 789-1827

Bait and Bullet Shop, 59 South 1 Avenue, Brighton, (303) 659-3286

Colorado Sport and Tackle, 5385 Quebec, Commerce City, (303) 287-2111

Dave's Guns, 1842 S Parker Rd #15, Denver, CO 80231, (303) 337-9494

Jumbo Sports, 7848 County Line Road, Littleton, (303) 792-3374, Fly Fishing, backpacking, and departments

Big R of Greeley, 310 8th St., Greeley, CO 80631, (970) 352-0544

Cal's Sporting Armory, 3431 S Federal Blvd.,Englewood, CO 80110, (303) 806-0357

Gart Brothers Sports,
   Arvada, 7400 A West 52nd Avenue, Arvada, CO 80002, (303) 431-8537
   Aurora, 14401 E. Exposition, Aurora, CO 80012, (303) 340-3524,
   Boulder, 3320 N. 28th, Boulder, CO 80301, (303) 449-9021
   Denver, 1000 Broadway, Denver, CO 80203, (303) 861-1122
   Denver, 2496 S. Colorado Blvd., Denver, CO 80222, (303) 692-0121
   Denver, 50 S Kalamath St, Denver, CO 80201, (303) 861-1122

Gart Brothers Sports (continued),
 Glenwood Springs, 3216 S. Glen Avenue, Glenwood Springs, CO 81601, (970) 928-0858
 Greeley, 1727 Greeley Mall, Greeley, CO 80631, (970) 351-0386
 Greenwood Village, 9000 E. Peakview Blvd., Greenwood Village, CO 80111, (303) 741-9621
 Littleton, 8501 W Bowles, Littleton, CO 80123, (303) 972-0350
 Littleton, 8055 - 4 West Bowles, Littleton, CO 80123, (303) 933-9005
 Longmont, 2251 Ken Pratt Blvd, Suite C, Longmont, CO 80502, (303) 772-0133
 Littleton, 7848 County Line Road, Littleton, CO 80120, (303) 792-3374
 Northglenn, 251 W. 104th, Northglenn, CO 80234, (303) 920-2226
 Westminster, 5403 W 88th, Westminster, CO 80003, (303) 429-9311
 Westminster, 9219 Sheridan Blvd., Westminster, CO 80003, (303) 426-0202
Grand West Outfitters, 801 Broadway, (303) 825-0300
Cal's Sporting Armory, 3431 S Federal Blvd.,Englewood, CO 80110, (303) 806-0357
Dave's Guns, 1842 S Parker Rd #15, Denver, CO 80231, (303) 337-9494
Green Mountain Guns Inc , 11078 W Jewell Ave B-4, Lakewood, Co 80232 , (303) 985-7240
Gunworks, 3355 S Yarrow #E 113, Lakewood, Co 80227, (303) 986-9412
L & M Firing Line, Inc., 20 S. Potomac St., Aurora, Co 80012, (303) 363-0041
Orchard's Hardware , 269 E 29th St., Loveland, Co 80538, (970) 663-2230
The Gun Room Lakewood, 1595 Carr St, Lakewood, Co 80215, (303).237-1300
Ward's Shootin' Shop,, 5042 N. Federal Blvd., Denver, Co 80221 (303).433-5153
High Country Bass'n Shop, 1126 South Sheridan Boulevard, (303) 934-4156
Sportsman's Warehouse, Aurora, Opening Fall 2002
Sportsman's Warehouse, (970) 461-5000, 1675 Rocky Mtn. Ave.
ICS Mountaineering, 278 Steele, (303) 322-8646

MEAT PROCESSORS

Steve's Meat Market, 5751 Olde Wadsworth Blvd, Arvada, CO 80002-2534, (303)422-3487

TAXIDERMY

Tanglewood Taxidermy, 8035 Federal Blvd, Westminster, CO 80031-4115, (303)429-8298

AIRPORTS

Denver International Airport, (303) 342-2000, (303) 342-0400, United: 800-241-6522, Delta: 800-221-1212, American: 800-433-7300, TWA: 800-221-2000
Arapahoe County Airport, 7800 South Peoria, Englewood, (303) 790-0598, Private planes
Front Range Airport, 5200 Front Range Parkway, Watkins, (303) 261-9100, Private planes
Jefferson County Airport, (303) 466-2314, Private planes

Auto Rental

Avis Rent-A-Car, (303) 342-5500, 800-831-2847

Enterprise Rent-A-Car, Denver International Airport, (303) 342-7350, 800-325-8007

Thrifty Car Rental, Denver International Airport, (303) 342-9400, 800-367-2277

For More Information

Aurora Chamber of Commerce
3131 South Vaughn Way
Aurora, CO 80014
755-5000

Greater Englewood Chamber
770 West Hampden Avenue
Englewood, CO 80110
789-4473

Northwest Metro Chamber
7305 Grandview Avenue
Arvada, CO 80002
424-0313

Denver Metro Chamber
1445 Market Street
Denver, CO 80202
534-8500

Wheatridge Chamber
P.O. Box 280748
Wheatridge, CO 80228-0748
233-5555

Region 4 Outfitters

The following list includes outfitters registered with the Colorado Outfitters Association who provide big game hunting services in one or more of the GMUs within Region 4. Information concerning the outfitters company name, license number, address, phone, species, GMUs, type of land hunted (national forest, regional area, private versus public), and facilities are provided below.

JACK CASSIDY
Prof. Big Game Guide & Outfitters #229
1640 M Rd., Fruita, CO 81521
(970) 858-8985
Deer, elk, bear, antelope goat,sheep,
61,62,64,65,137,138,143,144,145,125,
126,127,128,109,140
Private property, tent camps, cabin

GARY JORDAN
Pikes Peak Outfitters #1405
P.O. Box 9053, Woodland Park, CO 80866
800-748-2885
Deer, elk, bear, antelope, goat, sheep,
59,581,511,681,105,133,500,501,46,49,12,
8,130, Pike and Rio Grande, BLM-Royal
Gorge, private property, tent camps,
cabins

SCOTT LIMMER
Comanche Wilderness Outfitters #1165
P.O. Box 1965, Fort Collins,CO 80522
(970) 223-5330
6, 7, 8, 9, 19, 20, 87, 91, 92, 93, 95, 98,
101, 102, 136, 143, 144, S1, S18, S 19,
S32, S37, S48, S57,S58, G 7, Roosevelt
/Arapaho, private property, tents, cabins

FRANKIE MENEGATTI
Story Creek Outfitters #364
1054 CR 318, Walsenburg, CO 81089,
719-738-3704
Deer, elk, bear, antelope, lion, 85, 851,
140, 58, 59, 69, 861, 133, 134, 141
BLM-Royal Gorge, private property,
trailers

CRAIG OCEANAK
Timberline Outfitters #1530
9602 W Milliron Rd.
Cheyenne, WY 82009
307-635-7288
Antelope, 87, BLM, private property,
Tents, cabins, motel

ROBERT THOMPSON
Rock Creek Outfitters #1601
10523 Hwy 125, P.O. Box 39
Rand, CO 80473
970-723-4211
Deer, elk, antelope, sheep, moose, 17,
171, 16, 106, BLM-Kremmling
Private property,cabins, resort

TOM TIETZ
Natural Adventures #532
3517 Green Mtn Circle
Parker, CO 80138
303-805-8804
Whitetail and mule deer, elk, antelope,
goat, 2,39,102,103,105,107,109,111,
112,113,114,201,391, Arapaho, BLM-
Little Snake, private property, motel
accommodations

DOYLE WORBINGTON
J&D Outfitters and Guides #1877
P.O. Box 313, Cripple Creek, CO 80813
719-599-8545,
Deer, elk, bear, antelope, lion, 59, 64,
110, 111; private property, cabins

Hiring an Outfitter or Guide

There are many quality outfitters in Colorado that can provide you with fully guided hunts and any combination of services you desire. The first step in booking a hunt is to determine exactly what services you require and what your expectations are. Some common things to consider include what level of assistance you want. Maybe you would prefer to hunt on your own in a quality area. This may mean you are looking for an outfitter to provide a drop camp. Maybe you want one on one guiding service and hope to shoot the trophy of a lifetime. This may mean a more expensive hunt on private property. Do you want lavish accommodations and fancy meals, or will a tent camp with no running water and camp-stove meals be sufficient? These are some of the things you need to ask yourself and talk to the outfitter about before booking a hunt.

Once you have narrowed down your search a common practice is to ask an outfitter for references. Most of the time the outfitter will give you a list of successful hunters, who will probably tell you how great the hunt was. See if the outfitter will give you the names of any unsuccessful hunters to contact. Also, it's important to find out how much repeat business an outfitter gets and how long he has been in business. Lastly, be sure to ask about the experience of the guides and the rate of success their clients have had in the past.

Once you've settled on an outfitter it is a good idea to determine if they are properly registered with the State Office of Outfitters Registration. Each outfitter who operates in Colorado is required to meet the following criteria:

- Must be eighteen years of age or older;
- Must hold a valid instructor's card in first aid or standard first aid card issued by the American Red Cross or evidence of equivalent training;
- Possess minimum liability insurance coverage in the amount of $50,000 for bodily injury to one person in an accident and $100,000 for bodily injury to all persons in an accident;
- Possess a surety bond in the minimum sum of ten thousand dollars.

A prospective outfitter is required to submit an application to the office, and if all criteria are met, he receives an outfitter's license. You can contact the office at 303-894-7778, or via the Internet at www.dora.state.co.us/Outfitters/INDEX.htm, with an outfitter's license number to determine if the outfitter has ever had any violations or if the outfitter license is still valid. In addition to the state licensing requirements outfitters who operate on United States Forest Service land must have a special use permit. If you are hunting USFS land make sure the outfitter has the appropriate permit.

Once you've found an outfitter that can provide the services you require, and who is in good standing with the Office of Outfitters Registration, it's time to book a hunt. Part of the guidelines for operating as an outfitter in Colorado include providing you with a written contract. At a minimum the contract must describe the following items:

The type of services to be provided;

- The dates of service;
- Transportation arrangements;
- The costs of the services;
- The ratio of clients to guides;
- Cancellation policy including deposit refunds.

Most outfitters will require you to pay a deposit to book the hunt. The deposit is usually 50 percent of the total cost of the hunt, and in many situations is not refundable. In my experience licenses and gratuities are almost always extra costs not covered in the price of the hunt.

If you're traveling to Colorado from out of state, an item that is often overlooked is meat processing and trophy care if you have a successful hunt. Most outfitters will dress the animal and cape the head, but there will be extra costs for shipping and processing. Be sure to ask the outfitter how these items are handled.

The costs of guided big game hunts in Colorado are extremely variable. After reviewing information from numerous outfitters it seemed that a common price range for week-long guided hunts for deer and elk where adequate accommodations, food, and services were provided cost in the neighborhood of $2,500 to $3,000. Again, it should be understood that the cost of guided hunts is extremely variable. I also know of lodges that provide luxury accommodations on large private ranches that charge $9,000 a week for one person to hunt deer and elk. Drop camps where an outfitter sets up a camp and provides provisions, but no guide, often start at $1,000. Again, prices are variable depending on location and services.

Many of the outfitters in Colorado belong to the Colorado Outfitters Association. This group, which is separate from the state agency of registration, provides information on outfitters and the services they provide. The outfitters listed within each regional write up of this book were obtained from the Outfitters Association. For more information you can contact them at 970-876-0543, or on the Internet at www.colorado-outfitters.com.

Hunting Public and Private Lands

Colorado contains over 25 million acres of public land in the form of national forest, state lands, and Bureau of Land Management property. Almost all of my big game hunting has taken place on public land in Colorado. From first-hand experience I can tell you that very good opportunities still remain for persistent hunters who take the time to scout out areas of public land. This is not to say that public areas are not often overcrowded with hunters, and sometimes the quality of hunting is marginal. You need to either accept these conditions, or forge farther into remote areas away from the crowds.

Without a doubt private lands hold some of the highest quality hunting grounds in the state. Most of these are large ranches where outfitters operate. However, it is still possible to find landowners that will let courteous individuals hunt. Sometimes they ask for a trespass fee, and other times they may just let you hunt for free. If you are targeting private land, be sure to start researching well in advance of the upcoming hunting season. Due to the limited license structure in many areas, you may need to get permission to hunt private land well in advance of the season in order to apply for the appropriate big game management unit. If you get permission to hunt private property be sure you understand the boundaries of the land, and ask the landowner if he knows neighboring property owners. If you should have to trail a wounded animal onto neighboring private property you will have to get their permission first, before accessing their property. Also, try to get permission directly from the landowner in writing.

Hunting without permission on private land is one of the most common violations big game hunters receive in Colorado. In a recent hunting season it was the third most common violation, with 203 citations handed out. If you get caught trespassing, depending on circumstances, you will probably receive a $137 fine and lose all 20 points on your hunting license, which boils down to losing your right to hunt in Colorado for a period of time. Since landowners aren't required to post their property, the responsibility for determining property boundaries is incumbent upon the hunter. In most settings on large tracts of national forest or BLM land, trespassing can easily be avoided. In areas where there are parcels of private property be sure to research the area well before hunting season. This can best be accomplished with quality maps, especially the BLM Surface Management Status Maps that show public and private land boundaries. Finally, don't be afraid to stop and ask a local resident if you are unsure about a property boundary. If all else fails ask local officials for help. You may want to stop at the local forest ranger station, or at a DOW office.

STATEWIDE OVERVIEW MAPS

One of the most useful tools to big game hunters in Colorado is a state atlas of topographic maps. Several companies offer these products. Two good ones that I have used extensively for Colorado and other states are the *Colorado Atlas and Gazetteer* by the DeLorme Mapping Company and *The Roads of Colorado* by Shearer Publishing. Both products provide a complete set of topographic maps for the state at a scale of 1:160,000, which boils down to one inch equivalent to 2.5 miles. Both products contain an abundance of information including national forest boundaries, wilderness boundaries, BLM land, state land, rivers, lakes, roads, trails, campgrounds, and state wildlife areas to name a few.

TOPOGRAPHIC MAPS

For modern hunters utilizing computers there are several retail software products that provide state topographic packages. One that I have used is Map Academy, a trademark product of King's Outdoor World. For less than $100 you can purchase a complete set of 7.5-minute USGS topographic maps on CD for the state. Hunters who cover large areas of Colorado will find this product very helpful. It includes a GPS feature that allows you to type in coordinates and mark exact locations on the map. This feature allows you to integrate GPS data that you have gathered in the field and develop customized maps. With the ability to change scales and print specific parts of a topographic map (or the whole map) you can make tailored maps of your specific hunting area for use in the field.

For residents of Colorado who live in the Denver area there is a great source of information nearby. At the Denver Federal Center in Lakewood, Colorado is the USGS map center in Building 810. Here you can walk in and buy any topographic map in the state for $4.50. If you are heading out of state you can also get topos for any other state at this location. They also provide county maps, which cover larger areas than the 7.5-minute series topographic maps, and BLM maps. If you are outside of the Denver area you can reach the USGS at 1-888-ASK-USGS. They also have an Internet site at www.usgs.com. If you're unsure of which topo map you need, you can contact the USGS and request a Colorado Index to be sent to you free of charge. The index provides a state overview map that depicts all of the topos in the state so you can narrow down your request. It also provides ordering information for the various maps.

The 7.5-minute series of topographic maps is probably one of the best tools to help hunters navigate and scout in the outdoors. Before ever leaving for an area to scout you can locate drainages, trails, saddles, wetland areas, etc…and determine what the terrain will be like. Once you have targeted likely areas on the map you can use it in the field to help you get around.

For and quick, easy and free topographic reference maps on the internet:
www.topozone.com
www.terraserver.com

State School Lands (State Trust Lands)

State school lands were originally set aside by the Federal Government to help states generate money for school systems. In Colorado there are almost 3.2 million acres of property administered by the State Land Board. In 1993 the DOW entered into an agreement to lease state lands for wildlife management and public use. Currently the DOW leases about 430,000 acres from the State Land Board. Many of these properties are open to various types of hunting and fishing. For a complete list of these properties contact the DOW at (303) 297-1192 and request the *Supplement to the Colorado Wildlife Property Directory: STATE TRUST LANDS*. This directory is broken down by county, providing all of the state properties, where they are located, how many acres, and what type of activities are allowed. The directory was updated in 2001. The DOW also offers maps of the various state trust properties.

Please keep in mind that most of the state school lands are closed to public use. Many of these properties are leased by other entities, often ranches for cattle grazing. In these cases you can contact the leaseholder and ask permission to hunt, but they are not obligated to grant it. Furthermore, state lands often have seasonal use restrictions even when they are open to hunting.

State Wildlife Areas

The Colorado Division of Wildlife administers 241 state wildlife areas (SWA). Almost all of these properties are open to various types of hunting and/or fishing. Properties vary in size from less than 100 acres to several thousand acres. Many of the SWAs provide big game hunting opportunities. For a complete list of SWAs contact the DOW at (303) 297-1192 and request a copy of the *Colorado Fishing Season Information and Wildlife Property Directory*. These are also available, free of charge, at most sporting goods stores and retail venues that sell hunting and fishing licenses. The directories provide detailed information, including types of hunting or fishing allowed, restrictions, directions to properties, and types of facilities. You can also obtain a complete map set of the SWAs from the DOW for a fee.

For a listing of those SWAs that provide big game hunting, see the map opposite and listing on the following pages.

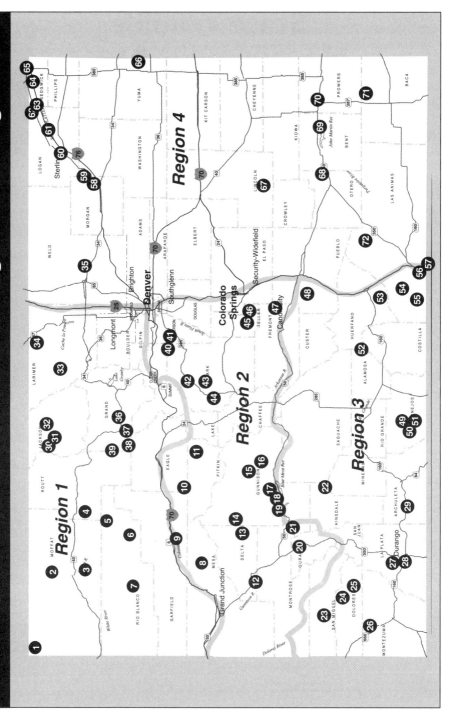

State Wildlife Management Areas

Colorado has 241 State Wildlife Management Areas, but only 72 permit big game hunting. Those are listed below and correspond with the map on the previous page.

	North-Central Colorado				
	SWA	SPECIES	ACRES	ELEV.	PHONE
1	Brown's Park	trophy-sized elk, deer	2,000	6000-8000	970-878-4493
2	Little Snake	deer, antelope	5,000	6000	970-878-4493
3	Bitter Brush	elk, deer, antelope	5,700	6000	970-878-4493
4	Indian Run	elk, deer, black bear	2,000	6700-7500	970-870-2197
5	Jensen	elk, deer	6,000	7500-8200	970-878-4493
6	Oak Ridge	big-game (elk, deer)	9,000	6000-7000	970-878-4493
7	Piceance	big-game (elk-deer)	(large)	6200-7500	970-878-4493
	West-Central Colorado				
	SWA	SPECIES	ACRES	ELEV.	PHONE
8	Plateau Creek	big-game (elk-deer)	1,350	6200	970-255-6100
9	Garfield Creek	big-game (elk-deer)	13,000	6000-9000	970-947-2920
10	Basalt	big-game, black bear	sev. hund.	7500-9000	970-947-2920
11	Coke Oven	elk, deer, black bear	330	85000	970-947-2920
12	Escalante	elk, deer, antelope	7,500	5000-7500	970-252-6000
13	McCluskey	elk, deer, black bear	1,600	6100-6800	970-641-7060
14	Beaver Reservoir	elk, deer, black bear	40	8500	970-641-7060
15	Almont Triangle	elk, deer	640	8000	970-641-7060
16	Cabin Creek	elk, deer	unk	9000-10500	970-641-7060
17	Gunnison	elk	2800	8500	970-641-7060
18	Centennial	elk, deer	1800	8000	970-641-7060
19	Sapinero	elk, deer	7000	7500-9000	970-641-7060
	Southwest Colorado				
	SWA	SPECIES	ACRES	ELEV.	PHONE
20	Billy Creek	elk, deer	5,000	6300-9000	970-252-6000
21	Cimarron	elk	6,000	7500-9500	970-252-6000
22	Cebolla Creek	elk, deer, bighorn sheep	1400	8800-10,000	970-641-7060
23	Dry Creek Basin	elk, deer	8,000	6000-8000	970-252-6000
24	Lone Cone	elk, deer	5,000	8000-9000	970-247-0855
25	Fish Creek	elk, deer	300	9000	970-247-0855
26	Lone Dome	deer, elk, black bear	1,700	7,000	970-247-0855
27	Perins Peak	elk, deer, black bear	13,000	7000-8500	970-247-0855
28	Bodo	elk, deer	7,500	7000-7500	970-247-0855
29	Devil Creek	deer	560	6800-7500	970-247-0855

North-Central Colorado				
SWA	SPECIES	ACRES	ELEV.	PHONE
30 Richard	elk, deer, antelope	2000	8100	970-870-2197
31 Delaney Butte	deer	2132	8100	970-870-2197
32 Diamond J	deer	3129	8100	970-870-2197
33 Bliss	bighorn sheep	352	7700-9000	970-472-4300
34 Cherokee	elk, deer, lion	19,022	6200-8600	970-472-4300
35 Nakagawa	deer	158	4600	970-472-4300
36 Hot Sulphur Spgs	elk, deer	1,200	7500	970-725-6200
37 Junction Butte	elk, deer	1,450	7700-8500	970-725-6200
38 Radium	elk, deer, bear, lion	1200	7000-87000	970-725-6200
39 Rock Creek	elk, deer, black bear	200	8500	970-870-2197
Central Colorado				
SWA	SPECIES	ACRES	ELEV.	PHONE
40 Mount Evans	elk, deer, bighorn sheep	3500	8300-10,500	303-291-7227
41 Bergen	elk, deer	500	8500-9600	303-291-7227
42 Teter	elk	950	9500	303-291-7227
43 Reinecker Ridge	elk, deer, antelope	12,000	9000	303-291-7227
44 Tomahawk	elk, deer	3,400	9000	303-291-7227
45 Dome Rock	elk	6,980	8000-9000	719-227-5200
46 Pikes Peak	bighorn sheep	640	10200-11000	719-227-5200
47 Beaver Creek	deer, bighorn sheep	2,740	6000-9000	719-561-5300
South-Central Colorado				
SWA	SPECIES	ACRES	ELEV.	PHONE
48 Pueblo Reservoir	deer	4,000	4600	719-561-5300
49 Hot Creek	elk, deer, bighorn sheep, lion	3,500	8000	719-587-6900
50 La Jara Reservoir	elk, deer, antelope, bighorn sheep, lion, bear	635	9700	719-587-6900
51 La Jarra	elk, deer, antelope, bighorn sheep, lion, bear	3,320	8400-9000	719-587-6900
52 Huerfano	deer	544	7600	719-561-5300
53 Wahatoya	elk, deer, bighorn sheep	200	7000	719-561-5300
54 Spanish Peaks	elk, deer	6,450	7000-8000	719-561-5300
55 Bosque del Oso	elk	30,000	7200-8800	719-561-5300
56 James M. John	bear, lion	8,200	7500-10000	719-561-5300
57 Lake Dorothy	elk, deer	4,804	7000	719-561-5300

Northeast Colorado					
	SWA	**SPECIES**	**ACRES**	**ELEV.**	**PHONE**
58	Elliott	deer	2,576	4100	970-842-6300
59	Messex	deer	680	4100	970-842-6300
60	Bravo	deer	1,081	3890	970-842-6300
61	Tamarack Ranch	deer	10,500	3700	970-842-6300
62	Red Lion	deer	1,300	3700	970-842-6300
63	Sedgewick Bar	deer	885	3569	970-842-6300
64	Julesburg	deer	1,100	3500	970-842-6300
65	Pony Express	deer	1,101	3500	970-842-6300
66	Simmons Ranch	deer	2,170	3600	970-842-6300
Southeast Colorado					
	SWA	**SPECIES**	**ACRES**	**ELEV.**	**PHONE**
67	Karval Reservoir	deer	235	5100	719-336-6600
68	Oxbow	deer	405	4000	719-336-6600
69	John Martin Res.	deer	22,325	3,850	719-336-6600
70	X-Y Ranch	deer	3,672	3400	719-336-6600
71	Two Buttes Res.	deer	6,793	4400	719-336-6600
72	Apishapa	deer, antelope, bighorn sheep	8,000	5400	719-561-5300

Forest service ranger stations are excellent sources of information.

UNITED STATES FOREST SERVICE

Colorado is home to eleven of the nation's national forests (see map in the introduction section of the book.) Together these lands comprise a large percentage of the public land available to hunters. In addition to the national forests, Colorado has two national grasslands that are also administered by the U.S. Forest Service. There are maps available for each national forest and grassland that depict a great deal of information useful to hunters. To obtain maps you can contact the U.S. Forest Service, Rocky Mountain Region Headquarters at (303) 275-5350. Maps are available for $4 each. It is also a good idea to contact district offices for local information concerning road closures, wood cutting permits, fire reports, and sometimes even tips on productive hunting areas. For more information call the numbers listed below.

U.S. FOREST SERVICE, ROCKY MOUNTAIN REGION HEADQUARTERS
740 Simms Street, Lakewood, CO 80225
(303) 275-5350, www.fs.fed.us/recreation

ARAPAHO/ROOSEVELT NF
240 W. Prospect Rd.
Ft. Collins, CO 80526
(970) 498-1100

GRAND MESA NF
2250 Hwy 50
Delta, CO 81416
(970) 887-4100

GUNNISON NATIONAL FOREST
2250 Hwy 50
Delta, CO 81416
(970) 887-4100

PIKE NATIONAL FOREST
1920 Valley Drive
Pueblo, CO 81008
(719) 545-8737

RIO GRANDE NF
1803 W. Hwy 160
Monte Vista, CO 81144
(719) 852-5941

ROUTT NF
29587 West U.S. 40, Ste. 20
Steamboat Springs, CO 80487
(970) 879-1870

SAN ISABEL NF
1920 Valley Dr.
Pueblo, CO 81008
(719) 545-8737

SAN JUAN NF
701 Camino del Rio, Rm. 301
Durango, CO 81301
(970) 247-4874

UNCOMPAHGRE NF
2505 S. Townsend
Montrose, CO 81401
(970) 874-7691

WHITE RIVER NF
9th St. and Grand
Glenwood Springs, CO 81601
(970) 945-2521

COMANCHE NATIONAL GRASSLAND
27162 Hwy 287, P.O. Box 127
Springfield, CO 81073
(719) 523-6591

PAWNEE NATIONAL GRASSLAND
660 O Street
Greeley, CO 80631
(970) 363-5004

Although many camping spots within national forest service campgrounds are first come first serve, it is possible to make reservations at certain campgrounds in the state. To make a reservation call 1-800-280-2267.

Bureau Of Land Management Map Index

Canyon of Lodor	Craig	Walden	Fort Collins	Eaton	Sterling	Julesberg
Rangely	Meeker	Steamboat	Estes	Greeley	Fort Morgan	Wray
Douglas	Glenwood Spring	Vail	Denver West	Denver East	Last Chance	Bonny Reservoir
Grand Junction	Carbondale	Leadville	Bailey	Castle Rock	Limon	Burlington
Delta	Paonia	Gunnison	Pikes Peak	Colorado Springs	Karval	Cheyenne Wells
Nucla	Montrose	Saguache	Canon City	Pueblo	Las Animas	Lamar
Dove Creek	Silverton	Del Norte	Blanca PEak	Walensberg	La Junta	Two Buttes Reservoir
Cortez	Durango	Antonito	Alamosa	Trinidad	Kim	Springfield

© WILDERNESS ADVENTURES PRESS, INC.

Bureau of Land Management

Based on a 1998 statistical report prepared by the U.S. Department of the Interior, Colorado contains 8,354,636 acres of federal lands administered by BLM. This land is widespread throughout western Colorado with the largest quantities in the northwest. While small isolated tracts make up some of this land, the land in the western quarter of the state is often found in large contiguous tracts of several thousand acres. Most of these lands are open to the public, and they comprise an important asset to big game hunters in the state.

The BLM publishes Surface Management Status Maps that are invaluable to hunters, especially in western Colorado. These maps depict private and public land controlled by various entities. When used alone or in combination with smaller scaled topographic maps, they can help you recognize public property boundaries. Be sure to obtain the most recent version of these maps when hunting since land status can and does change periodically. Maps are available from the Colorado State Office for $4 each. For ordering information call (303) 239-3600. District offices and Resource Area offices also have maps on a limited basis.

COLORADO STATE OFFICE
2850 Youngfield Street, Lakewood, CO 80125, (303) 239-3600

CANON CITY DISTRICT
3170 East Main St.
Canon City, CO 81212
(719) 269-8500

CRAIG DISTRICT
455 Emerson St.
Craig, CO 81625
(970) 824-8261

GRAND JUNCTION DISTRICT
2815 H Road
Grand Junction, CO 81506
(970) 244-3000

MONTROSE DISTRICT
2465 South Townsend
Montrose, CO 81401
(970) 249-7791

BLM SURFACE MANAGEMENT STATUS MAPS

The following list, as compiled by the Colorado Division of Wildlife, provides the name of the BLM Edition Surface Management Status Map you will need to obtain for the various big game management units in Colorado. Many of the units require more than one map.

MAP NAME	BIG GAME UNITS
Canyon of Ladore	1, 2, 3, 201
Rangely	10, 11, 21, 22
Douglas Pass	21, 22, 30, 31, 32
Grand Junction	30, 31, 40, 41, 42
Delta	40, 41, 411, 60, 61, 62
Nucla	60, 61, 62, 70
Dove Creek	70, 711, 71, 72
Cortez	72, 73, 74, 741
Craig	3, 4, 5, 301, 441
Meeker	12, 13, 231, 211, 301
Glenwood Springs	23, 24, 25, 26, 33, 34
Carbondale	42, 43, 421, 521
Paonia	52, 53, 54, 64, 521
Montrose	54, 62, 63, 64, 65, 66
Silverton	65, 66, 70, 71, 74, 75, 76
Durango	74, 75, 741, 751, 77, 771
Walden	14, 16, 161, 17, 171, 6, 7
Steamboat Springs	14, 16, 17, 171, 15, 27, 181, 18
Vail	26, 28, 35, 36, 37, 371, 44
Leadville	37, 43, 44, 444, 45, 47, 471, 48, 49
Gunnison	55, 481, 49, 56, 57
Saguache	551, 561, 681, 67
Del Norte	67, 68, 76, 79, 80
Antonito	78, 80, 81
Fort Collins	8, 9, 19, 191
Estes Park	18, 19, 20
Denver West	28, 29, 38, 39, 391
Bailey	46, 462, 50, 500, 501, 51
Pikes Peak	50, 511, 57, 58, 581, 59
Canon City	57, 58, 581, 59, 69, 82, 84, 86, 691
Blanca Peak	82, 84, 85, 86
Alamosa	80, 81, 82, 83, 85, 851
Eaton	87, 88
Greeley	94, 95, 951, 96
Denver East	99, 104, 105, 106
Castle Rock	104, 105

MAP NAME	BIG GAME UNITS
Colorado Springs	59, 110, 111, 512, 118, 119
Pueblo	59, 84, 118, 119, 123, 124, 128, 591
Walsenburg	84, 128, 129, 133, 135
Trinidad	85, 851, 133, 134, 140, 141, 142
Sterling	88, 89, 90, 91, 96, 97
Fort Morgan	95, 96, 97, 99, 100
Last Chance	99, 100, 106, 107
Limon	105, 106, 107, 111, 112, 114, 115
Karval	111, 112, 113, 114, 115, 119, 121
Las Animas	120, 121, 124, 125, 126
La Junta	125, 129, 130, 135, 146
Kim	126, 137, 142, 143, 147
Julesburg	90, 91, 92, 93
Wray	98, 101
Bonny Reservoir	101, 102, 103, 109
Burlington	109, 116, 117
Cheyenne Wells	116, 117, 122
Lamar	122, 126, 127
Two Buttes Reservoir	132, 138, 139, 146
Springfield	138, 139, 144, 145

HUNTING ON INDIAN RESERVATIONS

There are two Indian Reservations in Colorado. Both are located in southwest Colorado (Region 3). The Ute Mountain Tribe occupies a large area south of the town of Cortez, Colorado. At the present time hunting on tribal lands is closed to the general public. For more information you can contact the Ute Mountain Tribe, Towaoc, Colorado 81334, (970) 565-3751.

The second reservation is the Southern Ute Indian Tribe. The Southern Utes occupy a large area of land south of Durango to the east of the Ute Mountain Tribe. Hunting has been open on tribal lands in the past through Indian guides. However, hunting has been closed to the general public for the past few years. The tribe determines if hunting will be allowed on an annual basis. It is possible that some guided hunts could be available again in years to come. For more information contact the Southern Ute Indian Tribe, P.O. Box 737, Ignacio, CO 81137, (970) 563-0100.

As a side note, if you happen to be in Southwest Colorado hunting, or just passing through, the Southern Ute Indian Tribe operates a casino in the small town of Ignacio, Colorado. This is a first-class operation with a nice hotel and reasonable rates. It is a great place to stay if you are visiting surrounding attractions such as Navajo Reservoir or Mesa Verde National Park.

Ute Canyon.

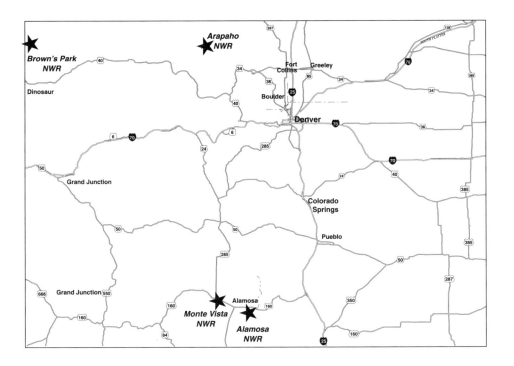

NATIONAL WILDLIFE REFUGES

There are four national wildlife refuges within Colorado. Where hunting is allowed, there are often special rules and regulations in addition to applicable state and federal regulations, when hunting on a refuge. For specific information concerning hunting opportunities, contact each refuge directly.

ALAMOSA NATIONAL WILDLIFE
REFUGE – 10,300 acres
P.O. Box 1148
Alamosa, CO 81101
(719) 589-4021

MONTE VISTA NATIONAL WILDLIFE
REFUGE – 14,169 acres
C/O Alamosa National Wildlife Refuge
P.O. Box 1148
Alamosa, CO 81101
(719) 589-4021

BROWNS PARK NATIONAL WILDLIFE
REFUGE – 13,500 acres
1318 Hwy 318
Maybell, CO 81640
(970) 365-3613

ARAPAHO NATIONAL WILDLIFE
REFUGE – 24,804 acres
P.O. Box 457
Walden, CO 80480
(970) 723-8202

Ranching for Wildlife

In order to better manage the state's wildlife on private land, the DOW initiated a program known as Ranching for Wildlife in 1985. Landowners who have a minimum of 12,000 contiguous acres can participate in this program with the DOW. As an incentive to perform habitat improvement landowners are guaranteed a certain number of big game licenses. They can then sell these licenses to outfitters or directly to hunters. These hunts are usually very expensive, but the revenue obtained by the landowner can help fund certain habitat projects. The landowner receives several benefits through this program. They have a 90-day hunting season to work with and can often use rifles during the early archery and muzzleloader season.

The public also benefits from this program. Not only are important wildlife projects undertaken in cooperation with the landowner, but also 10 percent of the buck/bull tags are earmarked for the public and all of the doe/cow tags are given to the public. The landowner must allow hunters who obtain the appropriate license in the public drawing access to hunt their property. There is a lot of competition for the buck and bull licenses. In fact, it will probably take you a minimum of seven preference points to successfully draw one of these tags. Still, if you save the points and draw the tag, you will likely be in for the hunt of a lifetime. For new hunters, young hunters, or meat hunters in general these ranches offer excellent opportunities to take does or cows. Most doe and cow tags can be drawn with 0 to 2 preference points. If you have a young hunter who hasn't ever had the chance to harvest an animal, this is the perfect opportunity to get a high percentage chance to fill a tag.

There are currently 27 individual ranches in the program accounting for over one million acres of land. Each ranch has its own hunt code for the various seasons, species, and sex of animal to be hunted. The hunt codes are listed in the annual hunting brochure and must be applied for like any other limited license. In 2000 the Wildlife Commission made a ruling that designated all public ranching for wildlife licenses to Colorado residents. For non-residents who are interested in hunting these ranches, it will probably be pricey, but you can contact the ranches directly to obtain a landowner tag.

United States Military Lands

There are three military lands in Colorado that offer big game hunting opportunities to the general public. They include the Air Force Academy in Colorado Springs (18,000 acres), the Fort Carson Military Reservation (136,000 acres), and the Pinon Canyon Maneuvers Site (230,000 acres), which is also administered by Fort Carson. The Pinon Canyon site is located in Las Animas County east of Walsenburg in GMU 142, and Fort Carson is located south of Colorado Springs in El Paso and Pueblo Counties in GMU 591.

Fort Carson and Pinon Canyon

If you're interested in hunting the Fort Carson properties they offer some exceptional opportunities for deer and antelope, but be aware, Fort Carson can close areas for training. If you happen to hold a license for either the reservation or the maneuvers site, training closures may prevent you from hunting. With that said, don't write Fort Carson off as a hunting venue. I would especially recommend it for people who live in the area. This will allow them to use proximity to their advantage when scouting and obtaining permits. All Colorado Division of Wildlife regulations are applicable to Fort Carson, and hunters must obtain the appropriate license from the DOW before hunting.

The first step in hunting Fort Carson is to obtain a recreation permit. To do this you must visit the base. At the Outdoor Recreation Complex (Building 2429) you can obtain the permit for $5. This will allow you to access portions of the base or maneuver site that are currently open, that is, where training is not being conducted. When you pick up your permit you can obtain a map to both areas. In order to determine what areas are open you must call an information line (719-576-8074) that will tell you where training is currently taking place. This recording lists numbers that correspond to the map. Once you have your permit you will still be required to get a range pass prior to entering the areas open to hunting each day you wish to obtain access. This pass is free and obtained by presenting the recreation permit at the perimeter gates. Now you're ready to go scouting.

After you complete your scouting and have successfully drawn the appropriate hunting license you must go back to the base to the same building and obtain a hunting permit. The permit is $20 a year. With the hunting permit you will receive a Safety Briefing Packet that is required reading for all hunters. This covers access, operations, and firearm issues among other things. Again, you will have to call the recording to determine what areas are currently open, and then you will have to present the Hunting Permit at the perimeter gates to obtain a range pass each day you go hunting. Finally you're ready to go hunting. Is all of the trouble worth it? According to the Fort Carson personnel that I spoke with there are abundant deer and big bucks. In a recent year a total of 32 lucky hunters obtained tags for the eastern plains rifle deer season in GMU 142. All 32 of them filled their tags harvesting 28 bucks and 4 does. Hunters also had a 90 percent success rate for antelope in the rifle season in GMU 142 in a recent year. For more information about hunting opportunities at Fort Carson call (719) 576-8074.

The Air Force Academy

The Air Force Academy offers special hunts each year, and just like at Fort Carson, all Colorado DOW regulations apply. There are also specific rules that only apply to the Academy. The first step in hunting at the Academy is to successfully obtain a limited license for GMU 512 through the DOW drawing. For the most recent hunting season there were 28 licenses available, and all 28 were filled. If you are one of the lucky hunters to draw a tag, the Air Force Academy will contact you through the mail. Generally a week or two before the season you must attend a pre-hunt briefing at the Air Force Academy. This briefing covers access, firearm issues, and safety. In addition to your license you will also be required to obtain an access permit for $20. You can get this at the base during the pre-hunt meeting.

Although the DOW big game hunting brochure says the season for the Air Force Academy hunt is December 1-31, it is actually held over a three day period presently December 21, 22, 23. When interviewing Air Force personnel about hunting opportunities they assured me that three days was more than enough time to harvest a deer, and almost every hunter usually fills his tag. They also indicated that there were many large bucks. The final consideration you should keep in mind if you intend to hunt the Academy is that high-powered rifles are currently not allowed. This could change in upcoming years, but currently you will only be allowed to hunt with muzzleloaders or shotguns. (Archery equipment is not allowed, either.) Hunts at the Air Force Academy are also escorted; that is, someone from the DOW or military personnel will accompany you on the hunt.

Hunting at the Academy started several years ago when deer populations were very high. At the time there were as many as 200 deer/vehicle collisions at the Academy each year. Since the deer numbers were decreased there are now only about 30 such incidents per year. Presently the hunts are intended to manage current populations on the Academy, not necessarily reduce numbers substantially. Depending on populations, license numbers may fluctuate up or down each year.

COLORADO OUTDOORS MAGAZINE

Colorado Outdoors is a bi-monthly magazine published by the Colorado Department of Natural Resources, Division of Wildlife. The magazine is, "...dedicated to the conservation and enjoyment of Colorado outdoors – its animals, fish, soil, forests, prairies and water." With excellent photography and informative articles, the magazine provides a wealth of information to hunters, anglers, and all wildlife enthusiasts. In addition to the articles, the "Outdoor Highlights" section presents current news related to wildlife. At $10.50 per year, a subscription to *Colorado Outdoors* is a great value. For more information call 800-417-8986.

A comfortable wall-tent camp. (Doug Egging)

Equipment Checklists

Regardless of whether you backpack into a remote wilderness area or hunt from a lavish RV, there is a multitude of equipment that will be needed on a big game hunt. If you have already been hunting for years, you probably have a good handle on all of the items you need. Still, it always seems like there is some small item that is forgotten. The following checklists will give you a good guideline to follow for assembling gear, and hopefully keep you from forgetting those small but important items.

CAMPING GEAR

We are lucky in Colorado because there are so many well-maintained campgrounds. The only problem is that many of them are closed for the year by the time hunting season rolls around. It is legal to camp in undesignated areas on U.S. Forest Service land and BLM land where it isn't otherwise posted. Just be sure you are on public land before setting up camp. Also, please remember to leave your camping spot just as clean or cleaner than you found it. Hunters take the blame for many other recreationalists misbehavior, so there is no reason to add fuel to the fire by leaving a trashy campsite.

Camps vary greatly from one group of hunters to another. Depending what kind of vehicle you have, where you plan to set up camp, or if you use an RV will all dictate what kind of gear you need. The following checklist is a generalized look at the basics.

____ Tents. The quality of your shelter will often determine how comfortable you will be on a hunting trip. A two-man dome tent, in my opinion, will not suffice as the only shelter for two grown men. Get the best gear you can afford and take into consideration the ability of the tent to withstand rain and snow. Dome tents with vestibules are nice, but quality canvas wall tents with a sheet metal, wood burning stove will provide warmth, space, and stability. Cabela's line of Alaskan Guide Model Tents and Outfitter Wall Tents are excellent choices if you're looking for a new tent.

____ Campers and RVs. There are many public and private campgrounds in good hunting areas that offer full RV hook-ups. Depending on where you want to go, though, some places will be inaccessible to RVs. You must also consider the weather when pulling large trailers into remote areas on bad roads.

____ Tarps. Take at least two extra tarps. One is used for another shelter outside of the tent where you can stay out of the weather, and one to cover extra gear or firewood. Tarps can also come in handy for dragging game, or lining vehicle interiors when you're ready to haul an animal home.

____ Poles, stakes, and extra ropes. Use poles with a tarp where trees are unavailable to make another shelter outside of your tent. Plenty of extra rope in different sizes will come in handy for dragging or hanging game and supporting tarps.

____ Sleeping bag, sleeping pad, cot, and pillow. Get the best sleeping bag you can afford and remember much of your body heat will be lost to the ground when sleeping on a tent floor. Get a quality pad to insulate you from the ground.

____ Frying pan or skillet, pots, spatula, plates, bowls, spoons, forks, knives can opener.

____ Coffee pot

____ Cooking accessories. Vegetable oil, butter, salt, pepper, season-salt, breadcrumbs, foil, plastic wrap, paper towels.

____ Cook stove and self-contained barbecue

____ Lanterns, flashlights, headlamps

____ Heater. Wood burning or gas. Be sure to utilize according to instructions where ventilation is adequate and tent materials will not ignite. Be aware of the hazards of carbon monoxide poisoning.

____ Coolers for food and game meat

____ High-density plastic containers are great for packing cooking supplies and dry foods.

____ Water jugs

____ Extra salt for cape and hides. Extra pepper to keep flies off game meat.

____ Hatchet, axe, wood saw, and or chainsaw.

____ Miscellaneous tools: Hammer, screwdriver, pliers, wrenches, meat saw.

____ Duct tape, bailing wire, and bubble gum.

____ Sun Shower. Even when it's too cold to get a sun shower bag warmed up, they can be useful to wash hands, or even rinse off dishes.

____ Camp table and chairs

____ Insect repellant

____ Trash bags

____ Frame pack if you need to pack out an animal.

____ Food. When hunting early in the morning and late in the evening it's often hard to find the time to cook. Prepackage meals or prepare them before the hunt so all you have to do is heat and serve. For example, you can make chili or stew at home and easily heat it up in a pot at camp. Convenience foods such as oatmeal and pop tarts can start you off in the morning. Take plenty of snacks, and nutritious foods to replenish those energy stores. Rearranging your eating schedule can also help maximize time spent hunting. If you take a break at midday, eat your biggest meal of the day then before you head out to hunt in the afternoon.

SURVIVAL GEAR

It's hard to believe that many hunters still take to the woods without any survival gear. Once your camp is set up and it's time to pursue game, make sure you have an adequate survival kit with you whenever you enter the field. Even if you think you're only going 100 yards into the trees, take a survival kit. The one time you leave it in the truck is the one time you will need it. Besides functioning as survival gear, much of the equipment you carry will also be useful when you get an animal down. Use a backpack or fannypack to carry the following items.

____ Compass and map of hunting area. Learn how to navigate with a compass and use it as you go.

____ Multipurpose tool such as a Leatherman

____ First-aid kit

____ Space blanket or survival blanket

____ Raingear

____ Fire starting kit – matches, lighter, and or steel

____ Mirror or rescue strobe

____ Compact folding saw or wire saw

____ Knife

____ Flashlight

____ Adequate water

____ Energy bar or snacks

____ Toilet paper

____ Nylon utility rope

____ Extra clothing as needed – gloves, hat, socks, sweater

____ Flagging tape

Essential items for your hunting trip.

Vehicle Emergency Kit

When traveling on back roads and four-wheel-drive roads in Colorado during the hunting seasons, conditions can be difficult. Mud, snow, and rough terrain can leave you stranded. A good emergency kit will help you avert a situation that might otherwise leave you on foot.

Your best bet for backcountry travel during the hunting seasons is a well-maintained four-wheel-drive vehicle. I've learned some hard lessons while traveling with friends who owned jalopies they kindly referred to as their "hunting rigs." These rigs often left us stranded due to a variety of problems. A very common occurrence is getting a flat tire when traveling off-road. Invest in quality mud and snow tires with a heavy sidewall. If you still get a flat a quality jack in addition to the one that came with the vehicle will be helpful. Flats always seem to occur in mud holes, deep snow, or on steep terrain. If you have ever tried to jack up a truck in a mud hole with a standard jack, you know why I recommend a heavy-duty jack with plenty of clearance and displacement. A couple of trash bags or a tarp will come in handy as a ground cloth when you pull the spare or are forced to crawl underneath a vehicle. Be prepared for slow leaks in tires with a can of Fix-A-Flat or a tire plug kit. After plugging a hole, a small compressor capable of running off the cigarette lighter can get you back on the road with hardly any downtime.

Also available in many auto supply stores are starter cables attached to a battery supply, so that you don't need an extra vehicle to jump-start your rig.

Although you can get much more elaborate with extra spare tires, electric winches, and spare parts, the following list is a good start for an emergency vehicle kit.

____ Heavy-duty jack	____ Tool kit
____ Shovel	____ Rags
____ Tow rope	
____ Jumper cables	____ Lighter
____ Fix-A-Flat and/or tire plug kit	____ Fuse kit
____ Small compressor	____ First-aid kit
____ Flashlight	
____ Water – for drinking or the engine	____ Work gloves
____ Blanket or sleeping bag	____ Trash bags
____ Extra fan belt or any other parts	
____ Duct tape, wire	____ Come-along
____ Spare tire	____ WD40 or penetrating oil

BACKPACK CAMPS

The activity of backpacking on its own is a very rewarding pursuit. Combine it with big game hunting and you take on one of the most challenging and rewarding pursuits in hunting. Challenges include packing in adequate gear to have a safe and comfortable camp. If you do get an animal, it can be a great deal of work to pack it and all of your gear out. Most people that hunt this way would probably tell you that all of the work is worth it. The rewards include getting farther into remote areas where animals are often more abundant and less pressured. There is usually less hunter crowding, and the gratification of being completely self sufficient in the outdoors is rewarding in itself.

The following list includes suggested items for a basic backpack camp.

____ Spare tire

____ Backpack. I prefer an external frame pack when hunting big game. The frame better supports heavy loads of meat after you get an animal down. I use a pack that easily detaches from the frame and use just the frame to pack out meat. Invest in a quality pack that fits you properly with well-padded shoulder and waist straps.

____ Tent. This is one of the most important items when backpacking. Camping in remote areas in Colorado at elevation often means severe weather. Get the best tent you can afford. Quality tents with a good rain-fly that will withstand strong wind, rain, and snow are a must.

____ Water purification pump. It's almost impossible to pack enough water while backpacking. Better than purification tablets, a pump capable of removing all harmful impurities will keep you going in areas with adequate surface water sources. Don't risk getting *giordosis* or other water-borne ailments, use a quality pump designed for backpacking – simple household water filters are not adequate.

____ Two-gallon collapsible water container. Fill it up using the pump when you get to camp.

____ Plastic water bottles as needed. Start with two, one for water while hiking. It's also nice to use one for powdered drink mixes.

____ Sleeping bag and insulating pad.

____ Lightweight tarp. Use for a ground tarp or as an additional overhead shelter or lean-to.

____ Food. Prepackaged dehydrated meals are ideal for backpacking. After a while they all taste the same, but they are easy to prepare.

____ Mess kit and utensils

____ Game bags

____ Trash bags

____ Multiuse tool

____ Skinning/gutting knife

____ First-aid kit

____ Head lamp

____ Lighter and matches

____ Backpacker gas stove, extra fuel

____ Nylon rope

____ Compact folding or wire saw

____ Compass, maps, and GPS

____ Extra shoes or sandals in addition to hunting boots

____ Clothing

____ Rifle and ammo, or bow and arrows

____ Hunting license and tag(s)

____ Big Game Hunter's Guide to Colo.

*A well-equipped pack can make or
break a hunting expedition.*

First Aid

Statistically speaking, hunting is a very safe sport. Still, accidents can and do happen. Serious hunters who spend a lot of time in the outdoors should invest some time in basic first-aid training and CPR. Wilderness medicine and a survival class are also a good idea. The better prepared you are for an injury or an illness, the better you will respond when the need arises.

When I hunt I carry a small first-aid kit in my daypack with other survival gear. It contains essential items such as bandages, gauze, antiseptic, antibacterial ointment, and aspirin in case of common injuries or illness. Back at camp, or in the vehicle, I keep a more comprehensive kit with additional items to treat more serious injuries. I also travel with a cellular phone in case I need to call for help. If you are depending on a mobile phone keep in mind the fact that many of the remote regions of Colorado don't have adequate cellular coverage yet. The larger first-aid kit I keep at camp contains the following items.

____ First-aid guide/manual

____ Numerous bandage materials

____ Burn ointment and non-adherent dressings

____ Scissors

____ Tweezers

____ Thermometer

____ Irrigation syringe

____ Povidine iodine for irrigating deep wounds

____ Antiseptic wipes

____ Wound closure strips

____ Tincture of benzoin to increase adhesiveness of bandages and tape

____ Antibiotic ointment

____ Tape

____ Cotton tip applicators

____ Sling

____ Ace bandage

____ Moleskin

____ Nitrile gloves

____ Safety pins

____ Immodium A-D antidiarrheal medicine

____ Tylenol

____ Motrin

____ Benadryl – antihistamine

____ Antacid medicine

____ Pocket mask CPR barrier

____ Snake bite kit

____ Eye wash solution

Clothing

Most hunters are fairly sophisticated when they dress for the outdoors. If you haven't hunted in Colorado before, you need to be prepared for extreme changes in weather conditions. This is especially true when hunting in the high country. In a given day the weather can be sunny, warm, cold, windy, overcast, raining, sleeting, or snowing. Dressing in layers is the way to stay warm and comfortable. There are numerous high-tech synthetic fibers used to make an ever-expanding array of fabrics and insulating materials. If you prefer natural products, wool is still a great option for hunting clothes, although I find many of the synthetic fabrics lighter in weight and more comfortable. I always use a daypack to keep survival gear, raingear, and extra clothing when hunting.

In a typical day of hunting in the high country when temperatures are in the 20- to 40-degree range I would wear a lightweight pair of long underwear under mid-weight fleece, wool, or saddlecloth hunting pants. Over my long underwear top I wear a long sleeved turtleneck or mock-turtle neck with a long sleeve, button-down chamois or canvas shirt on top. For the final layer I usually wear a mid-weight fleece jacket or vest. In my pack I carry quality rain gear consisting of Gore-Tex pullover pants and a Gore-Tex lined shell with a hood. I use two socks; first a thin liner made of Dacron polyester to keep moisture away from the skin. For the second layer I prefer socks that use combinations of wool, polyester, and/or nylon instead of pure wool socks. Combined with my high country hunting boot with 400-grams of thinsulate insulation my feet stay comfortable in a wide range of temperatures.

In addition to raingear, I keep an extra pair of socks in my daypack. I also keep an extra shirt that I can add as another layer or replace a sweat-soaked undershirt. On any given day when hiking long distances, I am constantly adjusting layers. If it gets too hot I will usually take a break to remove my long underwear bottoms. I also often end up shedding my fleece jacket and chamois shirt when hiking, then when I set up to glass or watch a certain area I put my heavy shirt and/or jacket back on before I get a chill. I always carry a stocking cap in my pack in addition to whatever brim-type hat I happen to be wearing. Neck gaiters are also nice additions on a cold day and don't take up much extra room in a pack. I also have light and heavy gloves.

If you end up on a hunt where temperatures are extremely low it's a good idea to use insulated coveralls and a heavy parka. This is also a good time to opt for pac boots with 1,000 grams or more of insulation. In windy conditions with blowing snow it's nice to have a face mask along.

Before investing in high-price hunting clothing take some time to consider what type of hunting you will do and where you will be hunting. Obviously it's much easier to wear heavy parkas and coveralls when hunting with a rifle from a blind, but if you need more mobility; cumbersome garments will be a burden when hiking and climbing over rugged terrain. Furthermore, if you choose to bowhunt or hunt with a muzzleloader you will want quiet clothing that doesn't rustle when you move. Once you've outfitted yourself with quality clothing take some time to wear it when you practice shooting. Heavy jackets may change your field of view through your scope or make it difficult to shoot your bow. Make sure you are comfortable shooting in the clothing you plan to hunt in.

FOOTWEAR

Hunting big game in Colorado necessitates a variety of quality footwear. The wrong boots can significantly hamper mobility, comfort, and safety. The season and terrain all play a role in selecting the right boot. Three basic classifications of boots that will work well in Colorado are listed below.

Boots made with Vibram™ soles make good choices on high country hunting boots.

High Country Boots

If you are hunting in the high country you have to have sole, that is, hard deep lugged soles. Vibram soles are without a doubt the best. They bite into hard surfaces and provide gripping traction on wet rocks. I prefer a shanked sole to help give the boot rigidity when climbing. This prevents unnecessary flexing that can fatigue the foot on arduous climbs. In addition to a quality sole, I look for mid-height boots starting at a 9- to 10-inch minimum height. In addition to tough double-stitched seams and leather or heavy cordura construction, I almost always use boots with a Gor-Tex liner when hunting in the high country. Invariably, you will cross streams, creeks, or boggy areas that will saturate unlined boots. There's nothing worse than wet feet when hiking all day. Lastly, insulation should be considered. I personally prefer lighter boots with 200 to 400 grams of Thinsulate insulation when actively hunting in the high country. I even prefer the lighter insulation when hunting during the late seasons when temperatures can be extremely cold. I use quality socks to adjust insulation as needed. However, if you will be sitting for long periods of time in cold conditions and your feet are prone to getting cold, you may want to consider purchasing boots with at least 800 grams of insulation. For extremely cold conditions in the high country, pac boots with a Vibram sole are a good combination. Although boots are expensive, it's a nice luxury to have two pair of quality hunting boots on any given trip.

Plains Boots

When hunting antelope or deer on the eastern plains or in semi-desert shrubland areas during the early season temperatures can be warm and the terrain is usually made up of dry, hilly landscapes. This type of terrain is not usually difficult in terms of footing, but heat and cactus can be a problem. I generally opt for a light boot with a softer, rubberized sole. I prefer an unlined boot that still provides good ankle support in the 7-inch height range. A breathable boot in Cordura that is still heavy enough to protect you from cactus is optimal. Many hunters wear tennis shoes when hunting antelope during the early seasons. This sounds like a good idea on a hot day until your first encounter with a prickly pear cactus.

River Bottom/Wetland Boots

River bottoms and wetland areas present a challenge in terms of footwear. Wet and cold conditions require waterproof boots with good insulation. Because surfaces are usually sand, dirt, mud, snow, ice or combinations, I go with a rubberized sole. When hunting river bottoms I'm often in treestands or blinds during the cold winter months. For extreme cold, I like a pac boot designed specifically for winter conditions at least 12 inches in height. I look for waterproof construction and temperature ratings of -25 degrees to -40 degrees. Due to unpredictable weather conditions I usually have two pair of boots in different heights and insulation ratings to span a wide range of temperature conditions. If you know you will be hunting in areas where you will have to cross shallow water or deep snow, you're better off to get high pac boots in the 15- or 16-inch range. Sometimes insulated hip waders or 18-inch insulated rubber boots are the best bet when hunting wetland areas. Obviously weather conditions can vary greatly on a river bottom, so make sure to pack a lighter boot in case temperatures are higher. Nobody would enjoy sitting in a treestand in a pair of pac boots in 60-degree temperatures.

Finally, don't buy new hunting boots right before the season. Do some planning ahead of time. If you need a new pair of boots, buy them several months before you will

be hunting so there is ample time to break them in. Stiff, unconditioned boots can make a hunting trip miserable. Even more important than breaking in your boots, though, is conditioning your feet. Hunters often overlook this issue when preparing for hunting season. Even with well-worn boots, if you haven't hiked at all, then suddenly start tromping several miles a day, your soft white feet will likely be adorned with painful blisters at the end of the day. Condition your feet before hunting season! Wear your boots before the season and hike over terrain and distances that will approximate hunting conditions.

GPS and the Compass

In today's modern world, the advancement of technology is an incredible and sometimes frightening thing. Through military technology we now have the ability to link up to satellites using handheld devices commonly referred to as Global Positioning Systems (GPS). More and more sportsmen use GPS units each year. They are very useful tools for the hunter. With the aid of GPS you can map out hunting locations; enter and save locations of interest; and navigate in remote areas without trail systems. If there is one group of outdoor enthusiasts that need to have good navigational ability it is definitely hunters. We are often off the beaten path far from roads and trails. But should GPS be the cure-all for finding your way in the outdoors?

GPS was developed by the Department of Defense (DOD) to help the military navigate anywhere in the world. GPS works by receiving location transmissions from satellites. Once the receiver acquires a signal it times the interval between transmissions, allowing it to calculate the distance to the satellite. Once three or more satellites have been acquired, the receiver converts the information to a coordinate system such as latitude/longitude, and we are able to use the information to determine our location on earth. The great thing about GPS is that the information is real-time, that is, as you move the receiver tracks the movement and continually updates the location. As a result, you can enter a location into the receiver's memory, and like magic, use the receiver to actually steer you along to the destination.

Back to the primary question, should GPS be a cure-all for finding your way in the outdoors? Absolutely not! Like any other tool, GPS has limitations. The compass is still the most dependable tool for orienting and navigating in the outdoors. It is also essential to have a compass to orient direction when using GPS. You will be much better off if you develop good navigation skills with the compass and supplement those skills with the technology of GPS.

In my experience GPS units are very good, but they have the following weaknesses. Since they depend on a signal to fix location, interruption of the signal will stop it from providing accurate information. This can happen for a number of reasons. Stormy weather can affect performance, tree cover can block signals, and occasionally the geometric array of the satellites will not allow for accurate fixes. In addition, just like any electronic device, it will stop working properly if the circuitry gets wet or if the batteries go dead. If you drop it on the rocks, it's probably going to be out of service, and if you're relying on it to get back to camp, it might make for a long night spent in the woods.

Every year many hunters get lost while hunting in Colorado. Even with the advent of GPS, many hunters will still get lost. This happens for a number of reasons, several of which I have experienced myself. First of all, when pursuing big game such as elk, it's very easy to lose track of time, direction, and distance traveled. The following steps are basic rules for orienting in the outdoors.

Before heading off on a hike, take the time to get your compass out of your pack and take a bearing. Keep track of the direction traveled. That means using the compass periodically as you go. A compass will provide very meaningless information if you wait to use it only after you become lost. Also, if you're using a GPS unit, enter a location fix at the start of the hike. It will do no good to have a GPS if you're not willing to wait a couple of minutes to acquire satellites so you can enter a point to return to.

Keep track of time. It's amazing how time flies when in pursuit of an animal. Two hours can feel like 20 minutes, and then the trip out is just the opposite – 20 minutes can seem like two hours.

Take the time to periodically look at your back-trail. Terrain has a way of looking completely different when traveled through in the opposite direction. If possible, pick a landmark behind you so there is a point of reference for the return trip. The best scenario is to identify three points of reference. One in front of you in the line of travel. One behind as a reference point to return to, and if possible, one on either side. What make good reference points? A mountain peak in the distance, a bluff, a valley, a radio antenna, a clear cut, or any other distinguishable landmark within view.

Keep track of geographic features as you travel. If you cross two ridges and one creek, make a mental note. If you're not paying attention, these landmarks won't help on the trip out.

Don't depend on other people! The worst feeling you can have is one of helplessness. If you trust somebody else to find your way, and suddenly they announce they're lost, you're going to know that feeling first hand.

Lastly, do some preparation before you go hunting. Get a good map of the hunting area and study it. Pay attention to the direction of major drainages. Note roads and prominent landmarks. Take the map with you and use it in the field. If you're using a GPS unit, know how to use it. Become confident of its operation and understand its functions before having to depend upon it.

This is not meant to be a comprehensive study of navigating in the outdoors, but these are a few tips that have helped me. Armed with a good map, GPS, and a compass, you will dramatically decrease the chance of getting lost. If you do get lost, you better have a survival kit. This will give you the piece of mind and confidence to avoid panic and find your way out in a logical and patient manner. If you don't have a basic survival kit, and no means of navigating, especially in a new area, you're asking for trouble.

To sum it up, GPS is an incredible navigational aid, but it should not replace basic orienting skills established with the use of a compass and a map. The combination of all three items (compass, map, and GPS) is the best approach for finding your way in the outdoors.

A few of the navigational aids available to hunters.

Rifles, Ammunition, and Scopes

Like any endeavor it is possible to get so deeply involved in something that you lose sight of the big picture. The big picture in high-power rifles for big game hunting is that even a novice, with no hunting or shooting experience, can purchase a mass- produced rifle from a sporting goods store and with practice quickly become efficient enough to hunt big game in Colorado. When I first started hunting big game I had very little knowledge about firearms, so when I purchased my first rifle I defaulted to the bandwagon approach. I knew many people who used the .30-06, and I found that there was an abundant selection of factory ammunition at every sporting goods store for the caliber. In retrospect my uneducated approach at selecting a big game rifle was pretty good. Although my inventory of hunting rifles has increased over the years my first big game rifle, a Remington Model 700 ADL .30-06, is still the most versatile rifle I own for every hunting situation and species the state has to offer.

Regardless of whether you are an experienced hunter looking for a custom-made, species-specific rifle, or a novice, there are some fundamental considerations before purchasing a hunting rifle. First, you want to determine what animal or animals you intend to hunt, the type of terrain, and at what type of ranges you will be shooting. Once you have answered these simple questions spend some time looking over ballistics tables. Compare the various calibers with the same weight and type of bullets in terms of velocity, energy, and trajectory. Depending on bullet weight, most rounds that carry over 1,000 foot-pounds of energy out to 400 or 500 yards will be efficient when hunting any big game animal in Colorado.

Colorado has minimum requirements for centerfire rifles that you should be aware of. The smallest caliber legal to hunt big game with in Colorado is .24-caliber or 6mm. The barrel of a rifle must be at least 16 inches in length, and the overall length of the gun must be 26 inches or longer. If you choose to use a semiautomatic rifle it can hold no more than 6 rounds in the magazine and chamber combined. Regarding bullet standards, in order to hunt deer, antelope and bear you must use an expanding bullet that weighs at least 70 grains. For elk and moose you must use a bullet of at least 85 grains. In both cases the bullet must carry a minimum impact energy of 1,000 foot-pounds at 100 yards as rated by the manufacturer.

Rifle Actions and Styles

While hunting big game in Colorado I have observed that the bolt action rifle is by far the most commonly used gun in the field. There is good reason for this trend. Bolt action rifles are produced in a large number of popular models and calibers by every major gun manufacturer. The bolt action is not only dependable but also extremely accurate in most models and brands, and it allows a relatively quick cycling time between shots.

In terms of popularity, it's probably a tie for second place between pumps, semi-automatic, and lever action rifles. All of these rifle actions offer faster cycling times between shots than a bolt action, but dependability and accuracy are sometimes sacrificed. Still, there are some excellent big game rifles available in pump action and semi-automatics. With a great deal of historic value, lever action rifles continue to be popular for hunting. Generally not as accurate as other rifles, lever actions still offer very fast cycling times between shots, and if used within their reasonable limits, they are extremely efficient. I have more fun shooting a Marlin model 336CS in .30-30 Winchester than any other rifle I own, but I would only hunt with it in certain situations. It is ideal for deer in brushy river bottoms or heavy timber where shots are likely to be 100 yards or less. It is also a good choice for someone pursuing mountain lions with dogs where the shot is likely to be very close. But if I'm apt to be pushing longer shots, past 200 yards, the effectiveness of a 170-grain, .30-30 Win. (for example) is going to be marginal for most big game animals.

Probably the least common rifle action I have observed while hunting big game in Colorado is the single shot. Single shots often offer superior accuracy, but accuracy is a relative thing. If you can consistently group your shots inside a 3-inch circle at 200 yards with a bolt action, is it worth going to a single shot to nominally improve your group under shooting range conditions? The obvious downside to a single shot is the amount of time to get a bullet chambered for a follow-up shot should you need one. Still, single shot rifles such as the Ruger No. 1 Series are often finely crafted, and many gun enthusiasts find the accuracy, style, and feel of these weapons more than adequate to offset quick cycling times between shots.

In addition to the action of a rifle, hunters should be concerned about the style. Although I have always been fond of traditional wood stocks, I have come to realize that the synthetic materials used for composite stocks combined with the extreme durability of stainless steel actions and barrels equates to a rugged and dependable firearm. The durability of a firearm is very important when you consider the rough terrain and severe weather conditions that often accompany big game hunting in Colorado. Furthermore, the overall weight of a firearm should be considered. Carry a 10-pound rifle around in the high country after elk and it will feel like a howitzer by the end of the day. You might be better of with a "mountain rifle" that starts off at less than 7 pounds without a scope. However, if you are sitting in a blind all day overlooking a winter wheatfield hoping to shoot a deer, that ten-pound rifle might be the ticket.

Lastly, consider the recoil of a firearm. If possible shoot some different rifles before committing to one. This is especially important for youngsters. If you start a youngster off with a rifle that packs too much punch, he/she may develop bad shooting habits from the start. Dad's old hunting rifle is not always the best choice for a beginner. Better to combine a medium weight rifle with an adequate caliber for the species they intend to pursue than to start them off with a big-bore that turns their shoulder to jelly.

Ammunition

There are several basic fundamentals to consider when choosing bullets for big game hunting. The shape, construction, and weight of a bullet will affect the downrange velocity, trajectory, and energy on impact. These variables will also affect expansion and weight retention on impact.

A light, frangible bullet might break up on impact and penetrate poorly, sometimes referred to as cratering. This could result in a wounded animal. The opposite would be a pointed, solid bullet that doesn't have the chance to expand at close range, or a bullet shot at an extreme distance where the downrange energy isn't enough to cause complete expansion. In these situations the bullet could pass through the animal without transferring its energy, or shocking power, resulting in a clean, small hole. This is still lethal if the bullet passes through internal organs, but a big animal like an elk can cover a lot of country with such a wound. The last thing to avoid is using a soft bullet that, under certain situations, could expand so much on impact that the penetration is poor.

The shape of the bullet can greatly affect the ballistics. Pointed bullets, which are more aerodynamic than a round-nose bullet, will often retain better downrange velocity and perform more accurately at long ranges. On the other hand a soft round-nose bullet might be optimal for close range shots (less than 100 yards) at thin-skinned animals such as whitetail deer where you want the bullet to mushroom rapidly.

With the aforementioned concerns when choosing a hunting bullet, it should be understood that most quality bullets fired from a high-powered rifle would result in a swift kill, especially on deer-sized or smaller animals if you hit the vitals. What I look for in a hunting bullet is balance. Since I often hunt deer and elk in the same season in the high country where shots could be very close, or long range, I want a bullet that is designed for accuracy without compromising expansion and weight retention. I look for a bullet that will expand to 1.5 to 2 times its original diameter, but still retain most of its weight. To accomplish this I use bullets such as the Nosler Partition, the Swift A-Frame, or the Barnes X-Bullet, but there are numerous quality bullets available to choose from.

Recommended Cartridges

The table opposite presents a list of commonly used cartridges for different game in different types of terrain. In terms of "long range" versus "close range," I make the distinction at 200 yards based on ballistics. Although this is a generalization, many high-powered rifles shoot very flat out to 200 yards, but beyond that significant changes in trajectory and energy begin to occur. Cartridge choice is also very important when you plan on hunting the biggest animals like elk and moose. If you want a rifle versatile enough to hunt all of the big game species in Colorado, I personally wouldn't start with a caliber smaller than the .260 Remington using at least a 140-grain bullet. Still better would be the .270 Winchester with at least a 150-grain bullet. Most calibers larger than the .270 will work well for elk and moose, although there will be variability in the effective ranges.

GAME ANIMAL	HABITAT	CARTRIDGES	
Pronghorn, sheep, mule deer, whitetail, mountain goat, cougar	Open country, long range	.243 Win., 6.5 x 55 Swedish .264 Win. Mag. .270 Wby. Mag. 7mm-08 Rem 7mm Rem. Mag. 308 Win. .30-06 Spring 300 Wby. Mag. .300 H&H Mag. .338 Win. Mag. .35 Whelen	.25-06 Rem. .260 Rem. .270 Win. 7mm Mauser, 7x64 .280 Rem. 7mm STW. 6mm Rem. .300 Win. Mag. .300 Rem.Mag. 8mm Rem. .338 Rem. Mag.
Pronghorn, sheep, mule deer, whitetail, mountain goat, cougar	Forests—heavy cover, close range	The cartridges listed above and: .250 Savage .30 Rem. .300 Savage .307 Win. .303 British 8 mm Mauser .35 Rem. .358 Win.	.257 Rbrts .30-30 Win. .30-40 Krag .303 Savage .32 Win Special .348 Win. 356 Win. 7-30 Waters
Elk, black bear, moose	Open country, long range	Calibers listed under long range — open country, larger than: .260 Rem. Also: .375 H & H Mag. .416 Rem. Mag. .30-378 Wby. Mag.	
Elk, black bear, moose	Forests—heavy cover, close range	Long range cartridges listed above and: 7-30 Waters .30 Rem. .30-30 Win. .300 Savage .30-40 Krag .307 Win. .303 Savage .303 British .32 Win. Special 8mm Mause 340 Wby Mag .348 Win. .35 Rem. 356 Win. .358 Win. .350 Rem. Mag. .75 Win. .375 H&H Mag .378 Weath. Mag. .416 Rem. Mag. .416 Rigby .416 Weath. Mag. .444 Marlin .45-70 Govt. .458 Win. Mag.	

Scopes

Almost without exception, modern rifle hunters use scopes when hunting big game. Most hunters who spend adequate time practicing can shoot very accurately out to 200 or even 300 yards with a modern scoped rifle. The quality and selection of scopes is almost overwhelming. A few things to consider when choosing a hunting scope include magnification, objective size, field of view, and lens coating. Most scopes use a nitrogen filled tube. Good scopes are generally waterproof to some degree, but most scopes will still fog up in bad conditions. Variable scopes are often less weather resistant than single magnification scopes due to the extra moving parts. It is very easy to spend more money on a quality scope than you spent on your rifle. Since most of us don't have unlimited funds, the best approach is to purchase the highest quality scope you can afford.

Magnification is the first thing most hunters look at when buying a scope. If you are setting up rifles for specific animals in specific terrain, most hunters will use a single magnification scope in the 4x to 8x ranges. Magnification of 6x is very versatile for most hunting situations in Colorado. If you want a set up for close range conditions, but it is likely that you might take some long shots as well, then a variable power scope might be the answer. Many manufacturers build variable scopes that range from 3x to 9x magnifications.

In addition to magnification an important quality of a scope is the ability to gather light. The size of the front lens determines how much light the scope will collect. For example, a 6x40 scope would indicate six-power magnification and a front objective lens of 40mm. The larger the front objective, the more light-gathering power. The trade off is that once you get up to a 40mm front objective or larger, scopes become large and heavy.

Other considerations when choosing a scope include lens coating and field of view. Multi-coated lenses reduce glare and reflection, providing clear, bright, sharp images. The field of view determines the size of the image, usually rated at 100 yards. The smaller the field of view, the more difficult it will be to find things in your scope.

Examples of good scopes in the lower price ranges (usually less than $250) include brands like Tasco and Simmons. Stepping up in price to quality scopes in the $100 to $600 range include brands such as Leupold, Nikon, Bushnell, Bausch and Lomb, Pentax, and Burris. From here it is easy to spend $500 to $1500 for a high-quality scope such as a Zeiss, Kahles, or Swarovski.

The last consideration for hunting scopes is the kind of mounts to attach the scope to the rifle. Don't spend a fortune on a scope then buy some cheap mounts. You want quality mounts that will lock the scope into place. Find out what mounts will work with your scope/rifle set up and don't skimp on quality.

TRAVELING WITH GUNS

If you are traveling through Colorado with a firearm in your vehicle you should be aware of the following state regulations. Concerning rifles or long-guns, it is legal to carry them in a vehicle in plain view or concealed as long as they are unloaded. Unloaded means no ammunition in the magazine or chamber. Concerning pistols or handguns, it is legal to carry a pistol in a vehicle in plain view or concealed that is loaded or unloaded; however, it is illegal to carry a concealed pistol or rifle on your person unless you have the appropriate permit. Understand that Colorado does not honor concealed weapons permits from other states.

Obviously you need to use common sense when transporting firearms in your vehicle. The best approach is to keep any weapon cased and unloaded during transport with the ammunition stored separately from the firearm. Furthermore, if by chance you are pulled over for a traffic violation while traveling with a firearm, be considerate to the officer. Let them know that you are traveling with a firearm for the purpose of hunting.

One final common sense issue deserves your attention. It is not only illegal to hunt while under the influence of alcohol, but it is strictly illegal to possess a firearm if you have been drinking. So if you've had a few drinks with dinner at the local bar after a long day of hunting and you have a gun in your vehicle, you could get yourself in some serious trouble, even if there is a designated driver and you are transporting the firearm properly.

Be aware that certain municipalities may have stricter regulations regarding firearms. For example, the city of Denver currently requires Denver residents to transport guns in the trunk of their car. This regulation does not apply to non-Denver residents.

New as of the 2000 hunting season hunters who use off highway vehicles such as 4-wheeler ATVs must transport rifles, muzzleloaders, and bows in a fully enclosed soft or hard case. Open-ended cases or scabbards do not meet the requirements. Furthermore, firearms must be completely unloaded with no ammunition in the magazine or chamber.

Airlines

Most airlines follow similar procedures for passengers who need to transport guns. The gun must be unloaded and in a locked hard case without any ammunition in the case. If you are taking ammunition with you place it in your luggage to be checked. Don't try to carry ammunition onto the plane or you probably won't be making your flight. When you check your baggage tell the airline attendant that you have a firearm to check. Each time I have traveled with a gun I have been asked to open the case. So if you are in the habit of taping your cases shut for extra security, you may want to do it at the check-in counter after they have had a chance to look in the case. The airline will provide you with a firearm card that must be signed and dated. The card usually reads "Firearm(s) Unloaded, I declare, as required by the code of federal regulation 108.11, that the firearm(s) being checked as baggage is (are) unloaded." After you sign and date the card you place it in the case, lock it shut, and you're good to go. The whole process only takes a few more minutes than checking in normal baggage. Many times when I have traveled with only a bow the airlines treated it as any other firearm, asking me to open the case and sign and date a firearm card. You are allowed to have arrows in the same case as your bow.

As we all know airlines can be very hard on checked luggage. The better case you can afford the better chance you'll have of getting your gun or bow to their destination without damage. It should go without saying, but you should always shoot your gun or bow before hunting to make sure it wasn't damaged in transit.

MUZZLELOADERS

If you draw one of the limited muzzleloader licenses to hunt big game in Colorado there are some specific guidelines that you should be aware of. Muzzleloading rifles and smoothbore muskets must be single-barrel and fired from the shoulder. They can only fire a single round-ball or conical projectile the length of which does not exceed twice the diameter. Sabots are illegal in Colorado. Cloth patches are not considered to be sabots. There are also minimum caliber requirements as follow: minimum of .40-caliber to hunt deer, antelope, bear, sheep and goat. A minimum of .50-caliber is required to hunt elk or moose. There are also bullet weight stipulations. A bullet must weigh at least 170 grains if fired from a .40-caliber to .50-caliber gun. A bullet must weigh at least 210 grains if fired from a gun larger than.50-caliber. Although popular in many other states, pelletized powder systems are currently not legal to use in muzzleloaders when hunting big game in Colorado. Also, muzzleloaders that load from the breech are not legal to use. In-line muzzleloaders that meet the requirements listed above are legal to use during the muzzleloader and rifle seasons in Colorado. Lastly, you cannot use scopes on muzzleloaders when hunting in Colorado. Only open or iron sights are legal.

Don't let the muzzleloader regulations deter you from taking advantage of this season. The muzzleloader season gives hunters the chance to enjoy an early season hunt with a firearm, and the regulations really aren't that complicated. If you're interested in hunting with a muzzleloader and you haven't purchased one yet, just keep the caliber requirements in mind before purchasing a new gun. I use a .54-caliber Hawken rifle manufactured by Cabela's, Inc.

ARCHERY EQUIPMENT AND INFORMATION

There are two basic classifications of archery equipment: traditional bows and compound bows. Traditional bows generally refer to longbows and recurve bows. These bows don't use any mechanical means to reduce the amount of weight the archer must hold back at full draw. Compound bows use wheels or cams to reduce the tension on the string at full draw. For example a 60-pound compound with 50 percent let-off means the archer would only be holding 30 pounds of weight at full draw. Modern compound bows are available in 50 percent to 80 percent let-off depending on what brand and model you choose. In addition to the different types of bows there are different styles of shooting. Many archers use sights to aim with while others (usually using traditional bows) shoot instinctively without sights.

The muzzleloader season gives hunters the chance to enjoy an early season hunt with a firearm.

(Jim Dawson photo.)

Using trees for makeshift blinds is very effective when bowhunting for elk.

Another distinction in styles of shooting is whether an archer uses a release aid to hold the string or whether they shoot with their fingers. Factor in the different types of arrows from traditional cedar to aluminum to high-tech carbon arrows, and there are literally endless combinations of archery equipment that people can use to pursue big game.

The advantage of utilizing compound bows with sights is that many people can use a heavier bow in terms of draw weight that generates greater velocity and energy on impact while maintaining accuracy at longer distances. The advantage of traditional bows is that their simple design of a bow and a string means there is very little chance for mechanical failure. In addition, instinctive shooters using traditional bows are often able to draw, aim, and shoot much faster than a person using a compound with a sight. Most bowhunters will agree, though, that it takes much more time to become proficient with a longbow or recurve for hunting.

If you would like to try bowhunting but don't know what type of equipment to start off with, my advice is to visit a local archery pro shop and try some different bows out. A good pro shop will be able to properly fit you with a quality hunting bow. You will want to make sure you get a bow that is matched to your draw length and strength. It's better to sacrifice a few pounds of draw weight than to sacrifice accuracy.

In terms of minimum requirements for legal hunting bows in Colorado there are some new regulations. Hand-held bows or compound bows with a string cannot be drawn mechanically or held mechanically under tension. The minimum draw weight to legally hunt big game in Colorado is 35 pounds and the maximum let off allowable on compound bows is 80 percent. No part of the bow's riser (handle) or track, trough, channel, arrow rest or other device (excluding cables and bowstring) that attaches to the riser can contact support and/or guide the arrow from a point rearward of the bow's brace height. Bows can propel only a single arrow at a time, and no mechanism for automatically loading arrows is permitted. Electronic or battery-powered devices cannot be incorporated into or attached to the bow. Hydraulic or pneumatic technology cannot be used to derive or store energy to propel arrows. Finally, it is illegal to use explosive arrows. (Please note, that it is legal to use hand held release aids to draw and release the string.)

Although the minimum poundage to hunt big game with a bow is 35, most bowhunters would probably agree that you would be much better off starting with at least 45 pounds of draw weight. If you're going after elk you would probably be better off to use a bow with at least 50 or 55 pounds of draw weight. Most adults have no problem pulling a 55 or 60 pound compound bow, and most of the bowhunters roaming the woods with compounds are probably using bows over 60 pounds in draw weight.

Another important consideration for bowhunters is the type of arrow to use. Most bowhunters that I know use either aluminum or carbon arrows. There are also arrows that use combinations of aluminum and carbon, and, of course, more traditional wood arrows. Aluminum arrows, such as those manufactured by Easton, are extremely straight, and depending on wall thickness, durable. Carbon arrows are usually much more durable than aluminum arrows, and they are often much lighter depending on the size. Carbons are much more expensive than aluminum, but can pay for themselves due to durability. Arrows are sized to match certain types of bows and draw weights. Lighter arrows result in faster velocities, which can help reduce error in range estimation. Heavier arrows tend to have more arcing trajectories, but may penetrate better. The bottom line is that just like rifle cartridge ballistics tables, you can compare certain bow set ups based on velocity, trajectory, and downrange energy at impact. It is very possible to set up a modern compound bow with a light carbon arrow that will achieve speeds over 300 feet per second, but a heavier aluminum arrow that shoots much slower may achieve the same foot-pounds of energy as the fast arrow. Again, if you are new to bowhunting seek the help of a local pro shop to get you set up with the right arrows.

Broadheads are one of the most important elements in bowhunting equipment. There are countless types of broadheads that will effectively take big game. Without exception you always want broadheads that are razor sharp. Never practice with a broadhead and then use it for hunting unless you have sharpened it or replaced the blades. Replaceable blade broadheads such as those produced by Muzzy or New Archery Products are excellent choices. Fixed blade broadheads such as the Bear Super Razorhead are also a good choice. Finally, there are more and more mechanical broadheads available on the market. These broadheads have blades that fold out on impact. The advantage here is a more streamlined point that provides better flight. The disadvantage is that it takes more energy on impact to open the blades, which can result in less penetration. I have used New Archery Products Spitfire mechanical broadheads to take all types of big game from antelope to elk and have never had a problem with performance or penetration. Still, I prefer to use a replaceable blade broadhead such as the Muzzy, 100-grain, three-blade. Keep in mind that broadheads can affect the flight of the arrow, changing the point of impact. When using a compound bow you may have to sight in with your broadheads or tune your bow differently.

Another consideration for bowhunters is whether to shoot with their fingers or with a release aid. Most people who use traditional bows shoot with their fingers. A lot of compound bow shooters have switched over to a release aid. If you want to shoot a compound with your fingers make sure you consider the overall length before purchasing a bow. A short string results in a deep valley at the nocking point that can pinch your fingers. Releases can usually help archers increase accuracy and consistency. The drawback (pardon the pun) is that it is one more mechanical item that could break or get lost on a hunting trip.

A final consideration when choosing bowhunting equipment is the eligibility requirements for entering trophies in the Pope and Young Club. The Pope and Young Club is an excellent organization involved in conservation and hunting. One of the major activities of the club is recording big game trophies harvested in North America. Among other requirements, an animal is not eligible for entry in to the record book if a bow with greater than 65 percent let-off was used. Keep this in mind if you're interested in entering a trophy animal into Pope and Young.

Whether you decide to shoot a basic longbow or the most advanced compound, the act of drawing a bow and releasing an arrow at a target is one of the simplest and most pleasing recreational activities I know of. One of the best ways to get involved in bowhunting is to join a bowhunting organization such as the Pope and Young Club. The Colorado Bowhunters Association (CBA) is also an excellent statewide organization that promotes bowhunting. The organization holds several archery events every year including an annual jamboree where several 3-D ranges are set up. This annual event draws over a thousand bowhunters every year. If you are interested in finding out more about the CBA give them a call at (303) 697-9660, or check out their web site at www.coloradobowhunting.org.

For people interested in becoming involved with a traditional bowhunters organization, the Compton Traditional Bowhunters was recently formed. Marv Clyncke, a well-known Colorado bowhunter who helped found the CBA, is the current president of the Compton Traditional Bowhunters. The organization was formed to help preserve and promote the use of traditional bowhunting equipment. If you are interested in finding out more, or joining, please phone (303) 494-0601 or look at the web site at www.comptontraditional.com.

SHOT PLACEMENT

One of the most important considerations in big game hunting is shot selection. Most premium bullets fired from a high-powered rifle carry a great deal of energy to the point of impact and can easily penetrate heavy muscle and bone. Still, even when hunting with a rifle you must consider what will be the most efficient kill shot without wasting large amounts of meat. For me the best shot every time is tight behind the shoulder at animals standing broadside or quartering away. For quartering away shots aim at the opposite shoulder or opposite front leg to align the shot properly. Try to visualize a horizontal line midway through the body of a big game animal and aim for the lower half. If you keep your shots low and in the rib cage, you will make a quick, clean kill.

Muzzleloaders are extremely efficient weapons to cleanly kill big game animals with, but many people shoot them beyond their effective ranges. To assure clean kills with a muzzleloader, only take broadside or quartering away shots within the effective range of the weapon. Shoot behind the shoulder as described above. The shoulder bone of an elk or even a deer-sized animal can stop a ball or conical bullet fired from a muzzleloader. This will result in a wounded animal that probably won't be recovered by even the best trackers.

When using archery equipment to hunt big game shot placement is extremely critical. Even with modern bows capable of launching arrows at speeds over 300 feet per second, penetration can be poor unless you hit the right spot. Again the best scenario is to shoot at stationary, broadside or quartering away animals. Aim for the rib cage area, low and behind the shoulder. An arrow with a sharp broadhead shot through both lungs of a big game animal is as effective as any other projectile. The drawback with archery equipment is that there isn't enough energy on impact to produce any shocking power. If you only hit meat with an arrow, it will most likely result in a wounded animal. Furthermore, the shoulder bone of an elk will stop an arrow almost every time. The shoulder bone of even smaller big game animals will also often stop an arrow from penetrating to the vitals. Remember, if an animal is quartering away line up on the opposite shoulder. You will have to aim farther back in the rib cage so the arrow passes through both lungs. If you shoot too far forward at an extreme angle when an animal is quartering away, you may only hit one lung. This is generally a lethal shot, but the animal may be able cover a lot of ground before going down. You should also consider the angle when shooting from a tree stand. If you hit too low on a broadside animal at a steep angle, the arrow will only catch one lung. Adjust your point of impact higher to compensate for the angle.

In addition to shot placement it is important to consider the overall situation when shooting at big game animals with a bow. If an animal is alert and looking at you, it is possible that it will jump before your arrow hits the target. This is commonly referred to as "jumping the string," and it is very common with whitetail deer. This could result in a clean miss or a bad hit. Furthermore, an animal that is alerted to the hunter's presence will likely run farther after even a good hit. I can't stress enough that the best shot scenario for archery is at stationary game, broadside or quartering away, where the animal is completely unaware of the hunter's presence. It's also important when rifle hunting. A spooked animal will almost always run farther after a good hit than an animal that was calm regardless of the weapon.

There are other shot angles for big game animals. Most of them will take extreme skill and accuracy in order to make a clean kill. The odds of wounding an animal can increase dramatically if you don't hit the perfect spot in these situations. For example, if you shoot specifically for the neck on a big animal like an elk, there is a lot of meat surrounding the vital arteries and the spinal column. If you only hit muscle in the neck it could very well end in a lost animal. This isn't a high-percentage kill shot.

On a frontal shot it is possible that the sternum and ribs could deflect a bullet or an arrow if the shot isn't perfect. Again, this would result in a muscle hit and a wounded animal. Animals that are quartering to you are difficult to take cleanly with a bow. Depending on the angle you may be able to slip the arrow just behind the shoulder and still get both lungs. If the angle is more extreme you will have to aim inside of the front shoulder to penetrate the chest cavity. In both situations hitting the shoulder with the arrow will probably stop it from penetrating to the lungs. Even though it's not a bad shot with a rifle, it often results in a great deal of wasted meat if the bullet penetrates the front of the shoulder. Straight away shots at the rump are also risky. In my book this is a no- shot situation for bowhunters. Even with a rifle, if you don't hit the base of the spinal column, the shot could result in a long tracking job. This angle will also result in a lot of ruined meat.

Finally, if all you have is a shot at the back flank, don't take it. There are probably very few people that could actually pinpoint the exact location of the femoral artery, and hitting it in on purpose will take luck. If you do luck out and hit it the animal will bleed out very quick, but intentionally shooting for the femoral artery is a low percentage way to cleanly kill a big game animal.

Aim behind the shoulder and you will take out both lungs, and sometimes the heart. This will result in a rapid kill regardless of which legal weapon you choose to hunt with.

Bracing against a tree can steady your aim.

Effective Range

The best way to make a good shot is to take ethical shots, and know the limits of your weapon and your ability. Even a high-powered rifle fired at extreme range may lack penetration to quickly bring down a big game animal. Each weapon has its advantages and disadvantages. Obviously, with rifles, the advantage is the accuracy, range, and extreme amount of energy that the bullet delivers to the target. This can result in an animal going down on the spot, but most of the time an animal will run at least a short distance before going down. The disadvantage with a rifle is that people tend to shoot beyond their effective range. It is possible to take a 500-yard shot and not even realize an animal has been hit. Personally, I try not to shoot past 200 yards, but I know hunters who are very competent with their rifles out to 400 yards. Still, if you are over 400 yards away, it might be better to try and cut the distance than to take a risky shot.

Muzzleloaders are capable of delivering plenty of energy to the target as long as reasonable shots are taken. I use a .54-caliber Hawken rifle and can consistently hit a paper plate at 80 yards. Once I move the target beyond 80 yards my accuracy falls off drastically. I know many other hunters who are accurate at distances well over a 100 yards with their muzzleloaders, but if you are shooting at animals at 150 or 200 yards and beyond with a legal muzzleloader with open sights, you're asking for trouble.

Effective range is extremely important with a bow and arrow. I pride myself on my ability to shoot a bow, but I learned an interesting lesson a few years ago. At the beginning of a bowhunter education course the instructor asked everyone in the class to write their effective hunting range with a bow on an index card. On the last day of the class we were asked to perform a proficiency test with our bows. Most of us had forgotten about the index card by that time. I had written down 40 yards and felt confident that if a deer were standing broadside and unspooked at that distance, I could make a clean kill shot. The instructor placed a metal silhouette target with a hole that represented the size of a very small kill zone on a deer at the range I had listed on the index card. He told us that we had to shoot three consecutive arrows through the kill zone in order to pass the class. I can assure you the hole in that target looked very small at 40 yards. Luckily, the instructor didn't hold us to our original claims, and I was able to pass the class without breaking any arrows. If you hunt with a bow you need to practice diligently and know your limits. Most of the animals I have taken with a compound bow have been at 30 yards or less. I will take longer shots, but the situation has to be perfect. I also practice at much longer ranges in case I ever have the chance to take a follow up shot at a wounded animal. I'm also fond of shooting a recurve bow. Currently, my effective range with my recurve would be about 15 to 20 yards under hunting conditions. Regardless of whether your effective range is longer or shorter than mine, try to stay within that range when hunting. Nobody wants to see a wounded animal.

Caring for Meat

After all of the time, money, and effort it has taken to get a big game animal, you want to be prepared to properly care for the meat. The first consideration should be getting the animal cleaned and skinned. Don't clean the animal and wait several hours to skin it. The meat will retain a great deal of heat for hours, especially the meat next to the bone. The best approach is to quickly skin the animal and hang it in a cool, shaded place where it can air-dry, forming a crust on the outside. Even when flies are absent during the colder months in the late rifle seasons I still use game bags. Not only do they keep flies from laying eggs on the carcass, but they also help to keep dirt and debris off the meat. If flies are a problem get the meat secured in game bags as soon as practical. Hunters often apply black pepper to the outside of the carcass to deter flies, although I'm not sure how much it really helps.

If temperatures are too warm to allow the meat to cool out naturally you need to be ready to artificially cool it down. Most hunters do this by cutting up the meat and placing it in a cooler with ice. The biggest mistake you can make is to allow the meat to get saturated with water—this will ruin it. If you are using coolers, either thoroughly bag the ice so it won't leak, or bag the meat so it doesn't get saturated. If you don't have coolers you can always buy blocks of ice, bag them up in trash bags and place them inside the carcass until you can get it butchered or to cold storage.

In addition to getting the meat cooled down quickly, you want to keep it clean through the gutting, skinning, and storage process. The long hair on the belly of a bull elk during the rut is often saturated with urine. If you get this on your hands and knife while skinning you will taint the meat when handling it and cutting it. You can use separate knives for different tasks, or at a minimum, be sure to frequently wash your hands and tools before handling the meat. The metatarsal gland on deer and the scent gland in the cheek of an antelope can also contaminate your hands and knives when skinning. A good way to avoid contaminating meat during the skinning process is to wear thin disposable latex or nitrile gloves. I usually have four or five pairs of these in my pack when hunting. I change them out after I gut the animal and after I've handled areas where urine or scent glands are present.

Pillowcases make good game bags if you have to pack out an animal. They are heavier than most game bags you can buy, but still allow air exchange to the meat. When packing an animal out I start by skinning half of the animal. I position it on its side and start with the legs. Then I skin out the shoulder, side, and flank until the skin is laid out on the ground like a tablecloth. Then I either remove all of the meat from the bone if I have a long pack out, or I take the shoulder and flank off with the bone intact for shorter distances. I cut the rest of the meat from the bone and place it into pillowcases or game bags for the pack out. During the whole process you can use the skin as a ground cloth to set pieces of meat on as you work. Once one side is complete, roll the animal over and carry out the same process on the other side. This whole thing can be done with a knife, but it's also nice to have a saw along to remove the lower portion of the legs if you plan on packing the shoulder and flank out with the bone in. It is not necessary to gut the animal using this approach, but it makes it easier to get to the tenderloins if the entrails have already been removed.

I always carry a sharpening hone in my pack. It's amazing how fast even a quality knife will dull when cleaning an animal, especially a thick-skinned animal like an elk. Accidents are also more apt to happen if you're trying to cut with a dull knife. Also, if an arrow breaks off inside of an animal be very careful not to cut yourself on the broadhead when removing the entrails.

If you've flown in for a hunt and you have to ship the meat back home you can use coolers or insulated boxes. In both cases it's best if the meat has already been processed and frozen. In this situation you will be fine to pack the cooler with very little or no ice if you know it will take less than 24 hours to get it home. I use oversized trash bags to line the inside of the cooler or box. Then place the meat, and ice if necessary, and tie off the trash bag when the cooler is loaded. This will stop any leakage from occurring. Then I secure the whole package by taping it closed. If you're traveling via the airlines remember they usually have a 70-pound cutoff for luggage. If you get a person who is a stickler for the rules at the check-in counter they will probably charge a minimum of $50 if the cooler is over 70 pounds.

Steve's Meat Market in Arvada, Colorado (303-422-3487) is the finest big game processor in the state. The owner, Steve Hein, specializes in wild game processing. When you take an animal in they immediately weigh it, thoroughly clean any dirt from the carcass, and send it into cold storage until it is processed. They de-bone all of the meat prior to cutting so you don't end up with bone fragments in your cuts. The steaks are shrink-wrap sealed in clear heavy plastic that prolongs the freezer life. They also have a full line of sausage and jerky available for people seeking custom products from their game meat. Be aware that Steve's has a broad reputation for quality butchering and he has as much business as he can handle. If you get an animal during any of the rifle seasons, call ahead before taking it in. You may have to make a reservation to drop it off.

The taste of your game meat depends a lot on the care taken when field dressing. Be sure to cool the animal quickly.

TROPHY CARE

The first step in preparing an animal for a shoulder mount is to remove the cape. The most common mistake made by hunters in the field is to not leave enough skin. To avoid this, leave all of the skin from the back of the legs forward. Start by cutting around the animal behind the front legs from the chest to the back. Then skin out the legs, being sure to cut down along the back of the legs to the cut around the chest. Make a cut along the back of the neck to the top of the head. From here, cut to each antler or horn, making a "Y" in the top of the head; or cut to one horn or antler and straight across to the other. Skin around the base of the horns or antlers and continue skinning forward. Detach the ears by cutting the cartilage close to the skull. Be careful when skinning forward from the eyes that you don't make big holes where the tear ducts are. Here you need to cut deeply to remove the skin. It's best to have someone show you how if you haven't ever done it. Continue skinning forward until you have removed all of the skin from the upper and lower jaw. Cut the nose well back from the outer skin to remove the cape. Remove all of the fat from the skin and as much of the meat as possible before salting. If you're not comfortable caping the head, skin as far up the neck as you can and remove the head. Keep the head and skin cold until you get it to the taxidermist. It's okay to freeze the entire head and skin if you can't get it to the taxidermist in a timely fashion. They will let it thaw and then finish caping it out.

If a cape is not properly salted or kept cold and the skin is allowed to spoil, the hair will slip from the hide, making it unusable for a mount. Most taxidermists can

get replacement capes if this happens. Keep in mind that if you are taking a cape or hide into a taxidermist to get it tanned, the hide can still slip in areas where there is a lot of fat, even if you have thoroughly salted it. This is often referred to as grease burning. Salt can penetrate into meat and skin, but it won't penetrate through fat. This results in a rotten area on the skin. Keep this in mind for both capes and "hair-on" hides.

Game bags help keep the flies off and keep the meat clean until it can be processed.

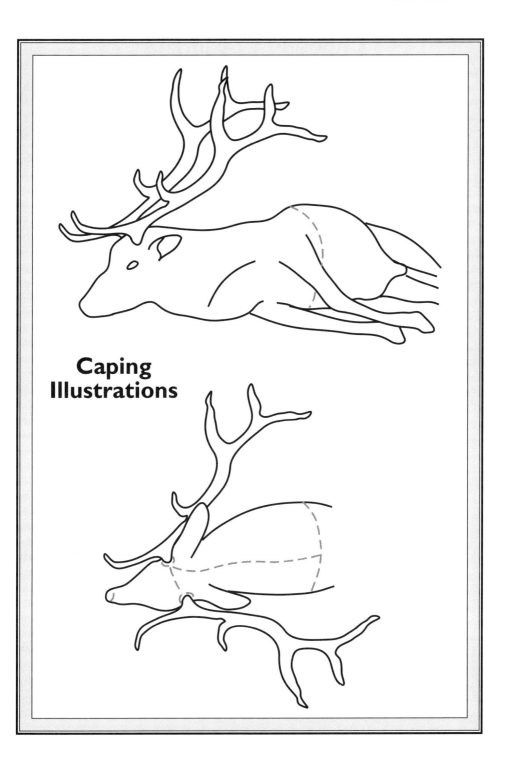

**Caping
Illustrations**

Choosing a Taxidermist

You can't be too careful when choosing a taxidermist. Many of them go in and out of business each year, and others only practice the occupation on a part-time basis. There is also great variability in the end product. Some taxidermists take painstaking care to render museum-quality work. If that's the kind of product you're after you will pay for it. Others do assembly-line work resulting in fair representations of the animal.

When you take your trophy into a taxidermist the first thing he should do is go over the type of mount you want. Most taxidermists have catalogs showing various forms for different mounts or they will show you a catalog of their own work depicting various mounts. You will want to consider which way the head is turned so it looks good on the wall where you intend to place it. Also, the taxidermist should take some measurements of the cape so he can get the right-sized form. Make sure the taxidermist tans the cape instead of using a pickling fluid. A tanned cape results in a leather product that will last for decades. Pickling fluids are acidic baths that don't have any tanning agents. A pickled cape is more likely to crack over time. Most taxidermists who do substantial business will send capes off to commercial tanners instead of doing it themselves. You also want to make sure that they will boil the horns/antlers to remove all remaining tissue before mounting.

Before you settle on a taxidermist find out what their turnaround time is. Many taxidermists have a backlog of work and it may take them over a year to get to your trophy. Most taxidermists require a 50 percent deposit when you drop off the animal to cover the costs of materials. The balance is usually due when you pick up the finished product.

Remember that taxidermists aren't miracle workers. If you bring in a spoiled cape the taxidermist will probably have to use another one. When this happens they usually charge an additional $30 to $100 for the extra cape depending on the species and size of the animal. If the cape is too short, cut up, or rubbed badly from dragging the quality of the mount could be compromised.

It's a good idea to bring a picture of the animal with you when you drop off the antlers and cape. When putting on the finishing touches the taxidermist can refer to the picture to make the best representation of your animal. Also, if the taxidermist has a display of his work to view there are some telltale signs of quality work. If the ears look good and aren't cracked or curling on older mounts this is probably a good indication of quality work. Also, the skin around the base of the horns will often pull away over time. If the taxidermist is good the skin will stay flush with the horns or antlers. If the eyes look natural and the ears seem to be in good position in relation to the antlers or horns, you're probably looking at some nice work.

If you are in need of a good taxidermist in the Denver area, Rudy Meyers has operated Tanglewood Taxidermy in Westminster, Colorado (303-429-8298) for nearly 30 years. Rudy has prepared thousands of big game mounts during his career. He can provide a quality representation of your animal for a reasonable price. He provides a full- service taxidermist shop specializing in big game, birds, fish, and tanning.

CONSERVATION

In March of 1948 a far-seeing, forward-thinking man penned the following words: "There are some who can live without wild things, and some who cannot." In the foreword of *A Sand County Almanac*, Aldo Leopold went on to say, "Like winds and sunsets, wild things were taken for granted until progress began to do away with them. Now we face the question whether a still higher 'standard of living' is worth its cost in things natural, wild, and free."

With the passage of over 50 years since Mr. Leopold gave us his thoughts on a "land ethic," there has never been a more applicable time in Colorado to consider his teaching. Unbridled growth and development in the form of urban sprawl, including housing developments, strip malls, mega malls, resorts, and mini-ranches, are quickly consuming large chunks of the wild places in Colorado. This situation is exemplified on the Front Range of Colorado where the largest population centers are found.

Recently, another huge shopping mall was built between the cities of Denver and Boulder. In an area where many people used to hunt small game, there is now nothing but concrete. It is ironic that a few short years ago the media negatively sensationalized an annual prairie dog shoot that was held on private property in Colorado. The "anti" groups jumped on this annual event, rallying opposition. Meanwhile, the wheels of development turned, and where there were once-thriving prairie dog towns there are now only scattered remnants in the medians and on the shoulders of busy roads surrounding this latest wonder of the world. Interestingly enough, whether you agree with shooting prairie dogs or not, there are still thriving prairie dog towns where the annual shoot was held.

While sportsmen, in general, are often misunderstood by the public at large and misrepresented by the media, we continue to pay the bill for wildlife management. More than any other group we strive to conserve the remaining wild places because we understand the value that these places hold. In future generations, if there is going to be the chance for the average person to hunt wild animals on public land in natural settings, we must continue to support organizations that protect and restore wild places. Organizations such as the Rocky Mountain Elk Foundation and Ducks Unlimited are fine examples. Not only do they convert your monetary donations directly into wildlife habitat, but they also fight to protect the remaining wild places and the animals that reside there. The list of conservation-oriented organizations that sportsmen fund is endless. As a group we should be proud of our efforts, but we should acknowledge that there is much more to be done. If we don't take it upon ourselves to protect the wild places for future hunters, nobody else will.

To quote Aldo Leopold one last time, he may have summed up my own sentiments best when he wrote, "Man always kills the thing he loves, and so we the pioneers have killed our wilderness. Some say we had to. Be that as it may, I am glad I shall never be young without wild country to be young in. Of what avail are forty freedoms without a blank spot on the map?"

When using archery equipment to hunt big game, shot placement is extremely critical. Practice diligently before the hunt!

Practice shooting at different ranges, in different terrain, and in different weather and light conditions.

Hunter Success

In order to define success, you must first know what a hunter considers as success. We all have different expectations and goals when in pursuit of big game. I have read others attempt to categorize hunters, but it's really not that easy. After all, hunters are dynamic people who change with time. Just like other recreational pursuits, there are hunters who spend a small amount of time and effort on hunting, while there are those that live a totally committed hunting lifestyle.

Some people are happy to just experience the outdoors and consider a hunt successful regardless of the take. To the opposite extreme, others won't consider a hunt successful unless they kill a trophy animal. Many hunters, including me, fall into several categories. In a given year I might hunt one species where my only expectation is to enjoy the company of good friends and experience the splendor of nature. If I happen to luck out and take an animal, it's an added bonus to the hunt. In the same year, on another hunt for a different species, I might find the hunt successful only after harvesting an animal for meat. Still in the same year, I might hunt another species in hopes of taking a mature representative animal.

Regardless of your definition of success, there are some universal keys that can help hunters take game on a more consistent basis. Whether you're out for a walk in the woods or after the trophy of a lifetime, the following points will help you become a more successful hunter.

Scouting

Long before hunting season I am usually busy scouting my hunting areas. Scouting often starts well before I ever get into the field. When I hunt a new location, I always assemble as much information and as many maps of the area as I can get my hands on. Using this information I can target certain areas to start scouting. Then armed with maps and a game plan, I head out to try to find good areas to hunt. Sometimes the activity of scouting alone is very rewarding. When you start to learn an area and actually begin to find animals on a regular basis, a preliminary success is already realized. Scouting is one of the most important keys to success. Without sufficient preseason work, many hunting trips turn into scouting trips.

Practice

When I'm not scouting, I try to practice shooting on a regular basis. When I first started hunting I was one of those guys that would blow the dust off the rifle and take it to the range a few weeks before hunting season. After a box of shells I usually felt that the gun was sighted in and it would be no problem to hit an animal. As I became more avid, I realized how important it was to shoot on a regular basis. Practicing at different ranges, in different geographic settings, and in different weather conditions made me a better shot.

For bowhunters and muzzleloaders practice is even more critical. There are numerous variables that go into making a good kill shot—especially with a bow. Picking up your bow and shooting it a few times before the season just isn't going to cut it. You need to practice year-round until the mechanics of drawing, anchoring, and shooting are just as natural as breathing. When that moment of truth comes, you don't want to be thinking about the process of shooting. It should happen naturally, with confidence that can only come with regular practice. Shoot 3-D, shoot the Dart System, shoot in ranges, shoot uphill, shoot downhill, shoot from treestands and blinds, but most importantly shoot a lot.

Patience and Persistence

Although these are two distinct concepts, they fit together well. Good hunters are patient. This usually comes from a great deal of time spent hunting. Most of us had a hard time sitting still when we were younger. It was more fun to hike through the woods with our gun than it was to sit in a blind and wait for an animal. Then many hunters realized that it is much easier to take an animal when it comes to you instead of the other way around. Treestands, blinds, still-hunting, and even stalking require extreme patience. If you're not sitting quietly and still in the blind or stand, you will spook the animal. If you don't still-hunt slowly enough, you will never see the animal before it sees you, and if you rush the stalk, the opportunity will be blown. Patience is hard to learn, but it is a successful hunter's virtue.

Persistence is slightly more abstract, but it is an important key to success. I can't tell you how many times something went wrong with a hunt that made me want to throw in the towel. But on those hunts when I stubbornly persisted and continued to hunt skillfully, I was often rewarded. Hunting, by nature, is a tough proposition. It can take both mental and physical toughness. That's why there are so many people that "used to hunt." It is not a lazy man's sport. When the hunt goes bad, don't give up. Things often happen for a reason. If you miss that buck after several days of hard hunting, don't let it ruin your hunt. A bigger buck might step out during the last five minutes of the last day of the season and give you a second chance. It has happened to me many times.

Visualization and Positive Attitude

When I hunt I often try to visualize every scenario before it actually happens. This is especially true when I'm bowhunting from a blind or a stand. I try to see in my minds-eye where an animal might come from, where it will travel, and where my shot opportunities will occur. Often when choosing stand locations for whitetail I visualize these scenarios before choosing the perfect tree. More often than not the hunt unfolds just as I visualized it.

If you have a bad attitude about the hunt, go back to camp and play cards because you're wasting your time. A positive attitude is more than a state of mind. It is mental motivation that sustains the ability to stay alert, and hunt cautiously. Sometimes it's hard to keep that good attitude going. The weather might be bad and you haven't seen an animal for several days. You start to lose hope and begin to believe that you won't ever get a chance. When you get in that frame of mind the hunt is over. You won't pay attention to detail, and you're likely to spook animals through sloppy hunting before you even know they are there.

Visualization can help maintain a positive attitude. If you are constantly running scenarios through your mind while you hunt, it is much easier to believe that something is going to happen. This will keep you sharp and alert. Lastly, if you have a bad attitude, keep it to yourself. How many times have you hunted with someone who constantly points out how bad everything is going? These people will pull everybody into a bad frame of mind and ruin the hunt.

Luck

I have often heard it said that a very small percentage of hunters are the ones that consistently take the largest percentage of the game. If this is true, is it because they are lucky? Luck probably has something to do with it, but I bet there is a little more to it. Hunters who have good equipment and take care of their equipment are lucky. Hunters who spend time scouting are lucky. Hunters who practice until they are proficient with their chosen weapons are lucky. Hunters who are patient and persistent are often lucky. Finally, hunters who visualize the hunt and maintain a positive attitude are lucky. There are many unskilled hunters who get lucky and bag a big game animal every now and then. Personally, I would rather make my luck than depend on it blindly.

Resources

COLORADO DIVISION OF WILDLIFE

DENVER HEADQUARTERS
6060 Broadway
Denver, CO 80216
(303) 291-7227

LAMAR SERVICE CENTER
1204 E. Olive
Lamar, CO 81052
(719) 336-6600

FORT COLLINS SERVICE CENTER
317 West Prospect Avenue
Fort Collins, CO 80526
(970) 472-4300

MONTE VISTA SERVICE CENTER
0722 South Road 1 East
Monte Vista, CO 81144
(719) 587-6900

WEST REGION SERVICE CENTER
711 Independent Ave.
Grand Junction, CO 81505
(970) 255-6100

BRUSH SERVICE CENTER
122 E. Edison, Box 128
Brush, CO 80723
(970) 842-6300

GLENWOOD SPRINGS SERVICE
CENTER
50633 Hwys. 6 and 24
Glenwood Springs, CO 81601
(970) 947-2920

MONTROSE SERVICE CENTER
2300 S. Townsend Ave.
Montrose, CO 81401
(970) 252-6000

DURANGO SERVICE CENTER
151 E. 16th St.
Durango, CO 81301
(970) 247-0855

GUNNISON SERVICE CENTER
300 W. New York Ave.
Gunnison, CO 81230
(970) 641-7060

HOT SULPHUR SPRINGS SERVICE
CENTER
346 Grand County Rd. 362
Hot Sulphur Springs, CO 80451
(970) 725-6200

MEEKER SERVICE CENTER
Box 1181
Meeker, CO 81641
(970) 878-4493

STEAMBOAT SPRINGS SERVICE
CENTER
925 Weiss Drive
Steamboat Springs, CO 80477
(970) 870-3324

PUEBLO SERVICE CENTER
600 Reservoir Rd.
Pueblo, CO 81005
(719) 561-4909

SALIDA SERVICE CENTER
7405 Hwy. 50
Salida, CO 81201
(719) 530-5520

COLORADO STATE PARKS

1313 Sherman Street, Room 618
Denver, CO 80203
(303) 866-3437
www.dnr.state.co.us/parks

UNITED STATES FOREST SERVICE

U.S. FOREST SERVICE, ROCKY MOUNTAIN REGION HEADQUARTERS
740 Simms Street, Lakewood, CO 80225
(303) 275-5350, www.fs.fed.us/recreation

ARAPAHO/ROOSEVELT NF
240 W. Prospect Rd.
Ft. Collins, CO 80526
(970) 498-1100

GRAND MESA NF
2250 Hwy 50
Delta, CO 81416
(970) 887-4100

GUNNISON NATIONAL FOREST
2250 Hwy 50
Delta, CO 81416
(970) 887-4100

PIKE NATIONAL FOREST
1920 Valley Drive
Pueblo, CO 81008
(719) 545-8737

RIO GRANDE NF
1803 W. Hwy 160
Monte Vista, CO 81144
(719) 852-5941

ROUTT NF
29587 West U.S. 40, Ste. 20
Steamboat Springs, CO 80487
(970) 879-1870

SAN ISABEL NF
1920 Valley Dr.
Pueblo, CO 81008
(719) 545-8737

SAN JUAN NF
701 Camino del Rio, Rm. 301
Durango, CO 81301
(970) 247-4874

UNCOMPAHGRE NF
2505 S. Townsend
Montrose, CO 81401
(970) 874-7691

WHITE RIVER NF
9th St. and Grand
Glenwood Springs, CO 81601
(970) 945-2521

COMANCHE NAT'L. GRASSLAND
27162 Hwy 287, P.O. Box 127
Springfield, CO 81073
(719) 523-6591

PAWNEE NATIONAL GRASSLAND
660 O Street
Greeley, CO 80631
(970) 363-5004

Although many camping spots within national forest service campgrounds are first come first serve, it is possible to make reservations at certain campgrounds in the state. To make a reservation call 1-800-280-2267.

BUREAU OF LAND MANAGEMENT

COLORADO STATE OFFICE
2850 Youngfield Street, Lakewood, CO 80125, (303) 239-3600

CANON CITY DISTRICT
3170 East Main St.
Canon City, CO 81212
(719) 269-8500

CRAIG DISTRICT
455 Emerson St.
Craig, CO 81625
(970) 824-8261

GRAND JUNCTION DISTRICT
2815 H Road
Grand Junction, CO 81506
(970) 244-3000

MONTROSE DISTRICT
2465 South Townsend
Montrose, CO 81401
(970) 249-7791

COLORADO STATE FOREST

2746 JACKSON COUNTY ROAD 41
Walden, CO 80480
(970) 723-8366

OFFICE OF OUTFITTERS REGISTRATION
Colorado Department of Regulatory Agencies
1560 Broadway, #1340
Denver, CO 80202
(303) 894-7778
www.dora.state.co.us/outfitters

COLORADO OUTFITTERS ASSOCIATION
P.O. Box 1949
Rifle, CO 81650
(970) 876-0543
www.colorado-outfitters.com

US GEOLOGICAL SURVEY

UNITED STATES GEOLOGICAL SURVEY
P.O. Box 25286 D.F.C.
Denver, CO 80225
1-800-435-7627, (303) 202-4700
www.usgs.gov

Maps

No matter where you're hunting in Colorado, you'll need a good map or two. Here are some sites to the U.S. Forest Service, Bureau of Land Management and U.S. Geological Survey, so you can find the maps you need. Also included is a link to guides and outfitters in Colorado. (Since the DOW does not regulate this industry, we must direct your inquiries about guide and outfitting services to the private organizations listed at the end of each Region, or to the Department of Regulatory Agencies.)

www.state.co.us/maps/index.html for Maps of Colorado including: Local, State and Federal Government; Colorado Counties, Political and Administrative Districts; Commercial Map Sites and GIS Related links;

www.fs.fed.us/r2/maps.htm for U.S. Forest Service Information and maps;

http://mapping.usgs.gov/ for purchasing USGS Topographical maps on-line;

http://mapping.usgs.gov/esic/usimage/test/co.html for USGS Topographical map dealers in Colorado;

www.co.blm.gov/ for Colorado Bureau of Land Management information and maps;

www.colorado-outfitters.com for a listing of outfitters who belong to the Colorado Guides and Outfitters Association (about 1/3 of the outfitters in Colorado belong to this organization);

www.topozone.com, a site for free topo maps.

www.terraserver.com, a site that provides photo relief maps as well as topo maps.

COLORADO DEPARTMENT OF TRANSPORTATION

LOCATION	EMERGENCY PHONE	ROAD/WEATHER PHONE
Alamosa	(719) 589-5807	(719) 589-9024
Burlington	(719) 346-8703	(719) 346-8778
Canon City	(719) 275-1558	(719) 275-1637
Colorado Springs	(719) 635-3581	(719) 635-7623
Cortez	(970) 565-8454	(970) 565-4511
Craig	(970) 824-6501	(970) 824-4765
Denver	(303) 239-4501	(303) 639-1111
Durango	(970) 247-4722	(970) 247-3355
Frisco	(970) 668-3133	(970) 668-3133
Fort Collins	(970) 484-4020	(970) 482-2222
Glenwood Springs	(970) 945-6198	(970) 945-2222
Grand Junction	(970) 245-7911	(970) 245-8800
La Junta	(719) 336-3444	(719) 336-4326
Limon	(719) 775-2354	(719) 775-2000
Montrose	(970) 249-9611	(970) 249-9363
Pueblo	(719) 544-2424	(719) 545-8520
Sterling	(970) 522-4693	(970) 522-4848
Trinidad	(719) 846-2227	(719) 846-9262

ADDITIONAL NUMBERS OF IMPORTANCE

COLORADO STATE PATROL	(303) 239-4500
EMERGENCY DIRECT DISPATCH	(303) 239-4501
Colorado Lodging and Hotel Assn.	(303) 297-8335
Colorado Assn of Campgrounds	(888) 686-8549
American Camping Assn.	(303) 778-8774
Colorado Outfitters Assn	(303)878-4043
Colorado Llama Outfitters & Guides Assn	(303) 526-0092
Colorado Restaurant Assn	(303)830-2972
Colorado Off-Highway Vehicle Coalition	(800) 318-3395
Colorado Dept of Transportation (Road Conditions)	(303) 639-1234
Colorado Travel and Tourism Authority	(800) COLORADO

Limited License – Preference Point Statistics

As part of the Colorado Division of Wildlife's management plan, the harvest of elk, deer, antelope, bear, moose, bighorn sheep, mountain goat and turkey is controlled by limiting the number of licenses that are sold each year for some or all of the hunts, depending on the species. If you participated in one of the limited license drawings and were unsuccessful, you were issued a preference point. Preference points provide the applicant an edge in the drawing the next time he/she applies. There are a few things to remember about preference point:

- Preference points are awarded to the first-choice hunt code only. The second-choice option does not use or generate preference points.

- The DOW offers a preference point hunt code for some species, which is listed in the regulations brochures. Use this hunt code if your goal is just to accumulate preference points for future drawings.

- Preference point records are maintained by Conservation Certificate numbers, name and date of birth. Use you CC number when applicable. Or use the exact name and date of birth you have always used when applying and our program will automatically reference your preference points.

- Remember to check the preference point box on you application if it applies.

- Preference points are by species only; they do not pertain to a specific method of take or season. A preference point that you gained last year by being unsuccessful in an archery elk draw can be used for a rifle cow elk tag the same year.

- It is possible to accumulate an unlimited number of preference points for deer, elk, antelope, bear and turkey, Preference points for these species will continue to accumulate until you are successful in drawing a first-choice license.

- For bighorn sheep, mountain goat and moose, a maximum of three preference points can be accumulated. After you have accumulated three points, you are placed in an applicant p9l where everyone has the same chance of drawing. If a person with three points is unsuccessful in drawing their first-choice license, they will be given one additional chance the following year. A person will continue to accumulate weighted points until they successfully draw a first-choice license or if they do not apply for a period of 5 years.

- Preference point information is based on the hunting statistics accumulated by the Colorado Division of Wildlife for the current hunting season. These statistics are published each year in a Special Edition of the Colorado Outdoors publication.

- One preference point is awarded to hunters who apply properly and are unsuccessful in drawing a license for their first-choice hunt code.
- Preference points are for individual hunters and species, i.e.preference points for elk are only for elk. Preference points aren't awarded by hunt codes or method of take. No one else can use your points.
- Priority goes to the hunter with the most points except when the license quota or nonresident limitation would be exceeded.
- Group applications receive priority on the basis of the group member with the fewest points except when there are not enough licenses left to fill the entire group's application.
- Second-choice hunt codes do not generate or use preference points. Licenses issued to successful second-choice applicants will list accumulated preference points.
- If unsuccessful for your first choice, you will be notified of accumulated points on your refund stub or your second-choice license.
- When you draw a first-choice license, your preference points drop to zero.
- Preference points accumulate until you draw a license as a first choice. If you don't apply at least once within five consecutive years for any species, your file will be purged. Applying for preference points will keep your file active.
- The most points you can accumulate for moose is 3. An applicant who already has 3 preference points for moose and fails to draw a first-choice.

It is also possible to view the most current statistics available on the DOW web site at www.wildlife.state.co.us.

Sporting Goods Stores by City
(Area Codes Listed with City Name)

Alamosa - 719
Alamosa Sporting Goods, 1114 Main / 589-3006
Kristi Mountain Sports, Villa Mall / West Highway 160 / 589-9759
Spencer Sporting Goods, 616 Main / 589-4361

Almont - 970
Three Rivers Resort, 130 Country Road / Almont, CO 81210 /641-1303

Antonito - 719
Fox Creek Store 26573 Hwy 17 / Antonito, CO 81120 / 719-376-5881

Aspen - 719
Elkstream Outfitters Inc., 6400 Highway 82 / 928-8380, 800-287-9656 / Fax:
    945-5455
Aspen Outfitting Company, 315 East Dean Avenue / 925-3406
Aspen Taylor Creek At Aspen Sports, 408 E. Cooper St. Mall / Aspen. CO 81611 /
    970-925-6331
Highlands Outfitting 4102 Trailhead Lodge / 0133 Prospector Road / Aspen,
    CO81611 / 970-920-9080
Mark Justin Outdoor, 217 S Galena ,Aspen, CO81611 / 925-1046
Mountains and Streams, 424 E. Cooper Street / 970925-5580
Oxbow Outfitters Co., 623 East Durant Avenue / 925-1505, 800-421-1505
Western Sports, 555 East Durant / 963-0696
The Outfitters, Snowmass Village Mall / 923-5959
Pomeroy Sports 614 E. Durante Ave. Aspen, CO/ 81611 / 970-925-7875

Aurora - 303
Sportsman's Warehouse, Opening Fall 2002
Garts, 7400 A West 52nd Avenue, (303) 431-8537
Garts, 14401 E. Exposition, (303) 340-3524

Avon - 970
Dixon Outfitters, 142 Beaver Creek Pl / Avon, CO 81620 / 949-1985
Gorsuch Outfitters, 0097 Main, Unit E102 / 926-0900

Berthoud - 970
Bennett's Inc. 121 Bunyan Ave Berthoud, CO 80513 / 532-2213

Boulder - 303
Boulder Outdoor Center, 2510 47th / 444-8420, 1-800-364-9376
Bucking Brown Trout Company, 26 East 1st Street, Nederland 80466 / 258-3225 /
    email: buckingb@earthnet.net
Gart Sports, 2525 Araphoe Ave. / 449-6180

Boulder, continued

Gart Sports 3320 N. 28th Boulder, CO 80301/ 449-9021
Kinsley and Company / 1155 13th Street / 442-6204, 800-442-7420
McGuckin Hardware, 2525 Arapahoe Avenue / 443-1822
Mountain Sports, 821 Pearl Street / 443-6770
Rocky Mountain Outfitters, 1738 Pearl / 444-9080
Southcreek Ltd., 415 Main Street, Lyons 80540 / 823-6402
Army and Factory Surplus, 1545 Pearl St / 442-7616

Broomfield - 720

Galyan's, 31 West FlatIron Circle, 720-887-0900

Buena Vista - 719

Between the Lines, 17920-YS Highway 285, Nathrop / 539-2067
Good Brothers Inc., 320 Charles Street / 395-9348
Hi-Rocky Gift and Sport Store, 111 Cottonwood Avenue / 395-2258
The Trailhead, 707 Highway 24 North / 395-8001
Coast to Coast, 401 Hwy. 24 N., (719) 395-8067

Cañon City - 719

Bubba's Sporting Goods, 723 Main Street / 275-4626
Capricorn Sports, 275-4351
Jimmy's Sport Shop, 311 Main Street / 275-3685

Carbondale - 970

Western Sports, 400 East Valley Road / 963-3030 / email: wsport@rof.net /
    Web page: www.wsports.com
Capital Peak Outfitters, 0554 Valley Road / 963-0211

Colorado Springs - 719

Broadmoor Sporting Classics, P.O. Box 1439, 80901 / 577-5832
Gart Sports 7730 N. Academy Colorado Springs, CO 80920 / 532-1020
Sports Hut, 719 Dale, Fountain / 382-7646
All American Sports, 3690 North Academy Boulevard / 574-4400
Blick's Sporting Goods, 119 North Tejon / 636-3348
Gart's Sports, 1409 North Academy Boulevard / 574-1400
Great Outdoors Sporting Goods, 520 E. Midland Ave, Woodland Park / 687-0401
Grand West Outfitters , 3250 North Academy Boulevard / 596-3031
Mountain Chalet, 226 North Tejon / 633-0732

Cortez - 970

Howard's Sporting Goods, 16 W. Main, (970) 565-9371
Jerry's Sporting Goods, 15 W. Main, (970) 565-7561
Little Bear Indian Trading Post, 220 W. Main, (970) 565-9372
Shooters World, 1220 E. North, (970) 565-8960
Stagecoach Trading Post, 7399 US Hwy 666, (970) 565-2523

Craig - 970

Cashway Distributors, 385 Ranney, (970) 824-3035
Craig Sports, 124 W. Victory Way, (970) 824-4044
Outdoor Connections, 34 E. Victory Way, (970) 824-5510
Sport Stop, Centennial Mall, (970) 824-8661

Creede - 719

The Ramble House, 116 Creede Avenue / 658-2482 / email: rambhse@rmi.net
Wason Ranch Company, Box 220 / 658-2413
San Juan Sports, 658-2359

Crested Butte - 970

Alpine Outside, 315 6th Street / 349-5011
The Alpineer, 419 6th Street / 349-6286
The Colorado Boarder, 32 Crested Mountain Lane / 349-9828
Critter Mountain Wear, 318 Elk Avenue / 349-0450
Efflin Sports, 10 Crested Butte Way / 349-6121
Gene Taylor's Sports, 19 Emmons Rd / 349-5386

De Beque - 970

High Lonesome Lodge 0275 222 Road Po Box 88 / De Beque 81630 / 283-9420

Del Norte - 719

Jaho True Value Hardware, 616 Grande Avenue / 657-3666
Casa De Madera Sports, 660 Grand Ave., (719) 657-2723

Delta - 970

Gunnison River Pleasure Park, Highway 92 at the confluence of the North Fork of
the Gunnison with the Gunnison / 907 2810 Lane, Lazear 81420 / 872-2525
The Sports Network, 252 Main Street / 874-7811

Denver Area - 303

Boxwood Gulch Ranch / 838-2465 / Owner: Dan Mauritz / email: boxwood@fly-
fishers.com
Colorado Sports & Tackle, 5385 Quebec St / Commerce City, CO 80022 / 287-2111
Duck Creek Sporting Goods, 400 S Boulder Rd / Lafayette, CO 80026 / 665-8845
Galyan's 31 West Flatiron Circle Broomfield, CO 80020 / 720-887-0900
Gart Sports, 1000 Broadway Denver, CO 80203 / 861-1122
Gart Sports, 14401 E. Exposition Aurora, CO 80012 / 340-3524
Gart Sports, 7400 A West 52nd Avenue Arvada, CO 80002 / 431-8537
Gart Sports, 5403 W 88th Westminster, CO 80003 / 429-9311
Gart Sports, 251 W. 104th Northglenn, CO 80234 / 920-2226
Gart Sports, 7848 County Line Road Littleton, CO 80120 / 792-3374
Gart Sports, 8055 - 4 West Bowles Littleton, CO 80123 / 933-9005
Gart Sports, 8501 W Bowles Littleton, CO 80123 / 972-0350
Gart Sports, 9000 E. Peakview Blvd.Greenwood Village, CO 80111 (303) 741-9621

Denver Area, continued

Gart Sports ,9219 Sheridan Blvd. Westminster, CO 80003 (303) 426-0202
Outdoor Sports Supply, 822 E 19th Ave ,Denver, CO 80218 / 861-1218
Army and Navy Surplus Store, 3524 South Broadway, Englewood / 789-1827
Bait and Bullet Shop, 59 South 1 Avenue, Brighton / 659-3286
Colorado Sport and Tackle, 5385 Quebec, Commerce City / 287-2111
Jumbo Sports, 7848 County Line Road, Littleton / 792-3374
Gart Sports, 1000 Broadway / 861-1122
Grand West Outfitters, 801 Broadway / 825-0300
ICS Mountaineering, 278 Steele / 322-8646
Sportsman's Warehouse, Aurora, Opening Fall 2002
Sportsman's Warehouse, (970) 461-5000, 1675 Rocky Mtn. Ave.

Dillon - 970

Gart Sports 306 U.S. Highway 6 Dillon, CO 80435 / 468-1340

Durango - 970

Colorado Trails Ranch, 12161 County Road / 240 Durango, CO 81301
Durango Sporting Goods (Gardenswartz), 780 Main Ave / Durango, CO 81301
Outfitter Sporting Goods, 341 Railroad Avenue / 882-7740
Animas Sporting Goods, 1444 Main Avenue / 247-3898
Durango Sporting Goods, 863 Main Avenue / 259-6696
Gardenswartz Sporting Goods, 863 Main Avenue / 247-2660
Backcountry Experience, 12th and Camino Del Rio, (970) 247-5830
Butler's Wildcat Canyon Traditional Archery, 145 E College Dr., (888) 495-9159
Clayton's Goods for the Woods, Durango Mall, (970) 247-5725
Duranglers Flies and Supplies, 801-B Main Ave., (970) 385-4081
Durango Guns, 2145 Main Ave., (970) 259-9204
Gardenswartz Outdoors, 8th and Main Ave., (970) 259-6696
Rocky Mtn. Pawn and Gun, 157 CR 250, (970) 247-5226

Eagle - 970

Eagle Pharmacy, 301 Broadway / 328-6875
The Sports Recycler, 34510-A6 Highway 6, Edwards 81632 / 926-3867

Edwards - 970

Gorsuch Outfitters, 0097 Main Street Unit E102 Edwards, CO 81632 / 926-0900

Estes Park - 970

Colorado Wilderness Sports, 358 East Elkhorn Avenue / 586-6548
Rocky Mountain Adventures Inc., 1360 Big Thompson Avenue / 586-6191
Coast to Coast/Ben Franklin Stores, 461 East Wonderview Avenue / 586-3496
Outdoor World, 156 East Elkhorn Avenue / 586-2114
Scott's Sporting Goods, 870 Moraine Avenue / 586-2877

Fairplay - 719

Even In The End Sporting Goods, 889 Steinfelt Pkwy, (719) 836-2470
Fairplay Trading Post, 1150 Castello Ave., (719) 836-0230

Fort Collins - 970

Rocky Mountain Adventures, 1117 North Highway 287 / 493-4005
Rocky Ridge Sporting and Conservation Club, 633 Gait Circle / 221-4868
Gart Sports, 215 E Foothills Parkway Ft. Collins, CO 80525 / 970-226-4913
Gart Sports 425 S. College Drive Ft. Collins, CO 80524 / 970-482-5307
Longs Drug Store #226, 743 S Lemay Ave, Fort Collins, CO 80524 / 482-3503
Outdoor World, 1611 S College Ave / 221-5166

Glenwood Springs - 970

Gart Sports, 3216 S. Glen Avenue / 928-0858
Elkstream Outfitters Inc., 6400 Highway 82 / 928-8380, 800-287-9656 / Fax: 945-5455
Colorado Canoe and Kayak, 910 Grand / 928-9949
K-Mart, 51027 Highway 6 Glenwood Springs 81601 / 945-2357
Payless/Center Drugs, 945-7401
Relay Sports, 715 Grand Avenue / 928-0936
Summit Canyon Mountaineering, 732 Grand Ave / Glenwood Sprgs 81601 / 945-6994
Timberline Sporting Goods, 101 East 3rd, Rifle 81650 / 1-800-625-4868
Army and Factory Surplus, 2828 Glen Ave., (970) 945-7796
Roaring Fork Anglers, 2114 Grand Ave., (970) 945-0181
Roaring Fork Outfitters, 2022 Grand Ave., (970) 945-5800
Summit Canyon Mountaineering, 307 8th Street, (970) 945-6994

Granby - 970

Devil's Thumb Ranch Resort, P.O. Box 750, Tabernash 80478 / 800-933-4339 / Web site: rkymtnhi.com/devthumb
Fletcher's Sporting Goods, 217 West Agate Avenue / 887-3747
Budget Tackle, (970) 887-9344
Fletcher's, (970) 887-3747

Grand Junction - 970

B & H Sports, 599 Northgate Drive / 245-6605
Gene Taylor's Sporting Goods, 445 West Gunnison Avenue / 242-8165
Eddy Sport, 580 32 Rd Unit E / Grand Junction, CO 81504 / 434-4811
Gart Sports, 2424 Hwy 6 & 50 Grand Junction, CO 81505 / 241-7977
Sportsman's Warehouse, 2464 US Hwy 6 & 50, (970) 243-8100

Greeley - 970

Garretson Sport Center, 3817 W 10th Greeley, CO 80634 / 353-8068
Gart Sports, 1727 Greeley Mall Greeley, CO 80631 / 970-351-0386
Stone Creek, Ltd., 2645-6th Avenue ,Greeley, CO 80634-8906 / 330-7476,

Greenwood Village - 970

Gart Sports, 9000 E. Peakview Blvd., (303) 741-9621

Gunnison - 970

High Mountain Outdoors, 115 South Wisconsin / 641-4243 or 800-793-4243
Adventure Experiences, Inc., #2 Illinois, CR 742, Almont / 641-4708, 641-0507
All Sports Replay, 115 W. Georgia Ave., (970) 641-1893
Berfield's Stage Stop, 519 W. Tomichi Ave., (970) 641-5782
Gene Taylor's Sportsman's Supply, 201 W. Tomichi Ave., (970) 641-1845
Gunnison Sporting Goods, 133 E. Tomichi Ave., (970) 641-5022
High Mountain Drifters, 115 S. Wisconsin, (970) 641-4243
Rock 'N Roll Sports, 608 W. Tomichi Ave., (970) 641-9150
Traders Rendezvous, 516 W. Tomichi Ave., (970) 641-5077

Kremmling - 970

Sportsman Quick Stop, 200 Park Center Avenue / 724-9523
Fishin' Hole Sporting Goods, 310 Park Ave., (970) 724-9407
Middle Park Baits, 412 South 5th, (970) 724-0530

Lake City - 970

The General Store, Box 143 Highway 149 / 944-2513 / John and Karen Roose
The Sportsman, Box 340 Highway 149 / 944-2526 / Lynn Hudgeons
Timberline Craftsman, 227 Silver St / Delta / 944-2334 / Betty Houston
Back Country Navigator, 811 N Hwy 149 / 944-6277
The Tackle Box, 124 S. Gunnison Ave., (970) 944-2306

Lamar - 719

Colorado Gunsmithing Academy of Lamar, 27533 US Hwy. 287, (719) 336-4099
Jandro's Gun Sports and Pawn, 7495 US Hwy. 50, (719) 336-7836
Wal-mart, 1432 East Olive St., (719) 336-5287

La Junta - 719

Sports World, 214 Santa Fe Ave., (719) 384-5546
Wal-mart, 27332 Hwy. 50, (719) 384-5951

Leadville - 719

Charter Sports, 325 S. Main St., (970) 476-7517
Bill's Sport Shop, 225 Harrison Ave., (719) 486-0739
Buckhorn Sporting Goods, 616 Harrison Ave., (719) 486-3944
Melanzana Outdoor Clothing, 609 Harrison Ave., (719) 486-3246
Otto's Coast To Coast Hardware, 1902 Poplar St., (719) 486-2220

Limon - 719

Verns Sport Shack, 354 East Ave., (719) 775-9572

Littleton - 719

Galyan's, Park Meadows Mall, 8435 Park Meadows Center Dr., (720) 479-0600
Garts, 8501 W Bowles, (303) 972-0350
Garts, 8055 4 West Bowles, (303) 933-9005
Garts, 7848 County Line Road, (303) 792-3374

Longmont - 719
Gart Sports 2251 Ken Pratt Blvd Suite C Longmont, CO 80502 / 772-0133

Loveland - 719
Brown's Corner Sporting Goods, 1310 East Eisenhower Boulevard / 663-4913
Sportsman's Warehouse, (970) 461-5000, 1675 Rocky Mtn. Ave.

Meeker - 970
Buffalo Horn Ranch, 13825 County Road #7 / Meeker, CO 81641 / 878-5450
Cherokee Outfitters, P.O. Box 537 / 878-5750
Elk Creek Lodge, Llc Po Box 130 / Meeker / CO 81641 / 878-5454
Wyatt's Sport Center, 223 West Market / 878-4428
Rocky Mountain Archery Pro Shop, 654 Main / 878-4300
Lone Tom Outfitting, 12888 RBC 8 / 878-5122
Marvine Outfitters, P.O. Box 130 / 878-4320
Downing's Hardware, 624 Market / 878-4608
Rio Blanco Ranch Company, 3050 Trappers Lake Road / Meeker / 81641 /
    878-3444
Rocky Mountain Bowstrings and Guns, 240 7, (970) 878-4300

Montrose - 970
Montrose Sporting Goods, 245 West Main Street / 249-9292
Jeans Westerner, 147 N. 1st, (970) 249-8757
Cimarron Creek, Inc., 317 E. Main St., (970) 249-0408
Carlton Calls and Hunt'n Stuff, P.O. Box 3248, (970) 240-4474
Buck Stop Pawn and Gun, 113 W. Main, (970) 249-0867
Stop N Save, 2291 S Townsend Ave., (970) 249-5043

Northglenn - 970
Gart Sports, 251 W. 104th, (303) 920-2226

Pagosa Springs - 970
Ski and Bow Rack Inc., East end of Pagosa Springs / 264-2370
Lake Capote, 17 miles west of Pagosa on Highway 160 / 731-5256 / Private fishing
Pagosa Clay and Trout Ranch, 731-9830
Pagosa Sports, 432 Pagosa Street / 264-5811
Pagosa Springs Hardware, 543 San Juan Street / 264-4353
Ponderosa True Value Home Center, Highway 160 and Piedra Road / 731-4111
Ponderosa Do It Best Home Center, Hwy 160 W and Piedra Rd., (970) 731-4111
Sideline Sports, 468 N. Pagosa Blvd., (970) 264-6141

Pueblo - 719
Pueblo Sporting Goods, 703 W. 9th St #2 / 543-7755
Sports Hut, 332 South McCulloch Boulevard / 547-2848
T and M Sporting Goods, 2023 Lakeview Avenue / 564-0790
Gart Sports 3261 Dillon Road / Pueblo, CO 81008 / 719-544-7793

Rangley- 719

Continental Supply, 15777 Hwy 64, (970) 675-2187

Salida - 970

American Outdoor Sports, 645 East Rainbow Boulevard / 530-0725
G and G Sporting Goods, East Highway 50 / 539-4303
Good Brothers Inc., 116 South F Street / 539-7777
Western Archery Sales, 150 Pahlone Pkwy., Poncha Springs, (719) 539-1295
Salida Sporting Goods, 511 E. Hwy 50, (719) 539-6221
American Outdoor Sports, 645 E Rainbow Blvd., (719) 530-0725
Headwaters Outdoor Equipment, 228 N F, (719) 539-4506
Homestead Sport and Ski, 11238 Hwy 50, Poncha Springs, (719) 539-7507
Shop and Pawn, 116 S F St., (719) 539-7777

Silverthorne - 970

Columbine Outfitters, 247 Summit Place Shopping Ctr / Silverthorne, CO 80498 /
262-0966
Antler's, 908 North Summit Boulevard, Frisco 80443 / 668-3152
Eddie Bear's Sporting Good Store, 591 Blue River Pkwy / 468-9320
Wilderness Sports, 266 Summit Plaza / 468-5687

South Fork - 719

The Powder Connection Ski and Gift Shop, 31101 Highway 160 / 873-5644
Rainbow Grocery & Sporting, 30359 W Highway Us 160 / South Fork, CO 81154 /
873-5545

Springfield - 719

Gambles, 189 E 9th Ave., (719) 523-6229
Best Way Sales, 1189 Main St., (719) 523-4731

Steamboat Springs - 970

Blue Sky West, 435 Lincoln Ave / Steamboat Springs, CO 80477 / 879-8033
Buggywhip's, P.O. Box 770477 / 879-8033, 800-759-0343
Back Door Sport Ltd., 811 Yampa / 879-6249
Inside Edge Sports, 1835 Central Park Plaza / 879-1250
Lahaina Ski and Sport, Gondola Square / 879-2323
Sportstalker, 2305 Mt. Werner Circle / 879-0371
Spiro's Trading Post, 107 Main, Oak Creek 80467 / 736-2443
Christy Sports, 1835 Central Park Plaza, (970) 879-1250
Good Times Sports, 730 Lincoln Ave., (970) 879-7818
Shop and Hop Food Stores-Phillips 66, 35775 E US Hwy 40, (970) 879-2489
SportStalker, 36900 Steamboat Village Circle, (970) 879-0371
Straightline Outdoor Sports, 744 Lincoln Ave., (970) 879-7568
Wal-Mart, 1805 Central park Drive, (970) 879-8115

Sterling- 719
Wal-Mart, 1510 W. Main, (970) 522-3012
Pro Sports, 119 N. 3rd St., (970) 522-8545
Unique Cameras and Guns, 105 Main St., (970) 522-4939

Trinidad - 719
Leisure Time Sports, 134 W. Main St., (719) 846-4749
Corral Pawn and Trading Post, 114 E. Main St., (719) 846-6043

Vail - 970
Gorsuch Outfitters, 263 East Gore Creek Drive / 476-2294 / email: flyfish@vail.net
Fly Fishing Outfitters Inc., Box 2861 / 476-3474, 800-595-8090 / email: fish@vail.net /
Vail Rod and Gun Club, Box 1848 / 476-3639
Gart Sports, 2161 N. Frontage Road W., / 476-5453

Walden - 970
Corkle's Little Market, 1 mile north of Walden / 723-8211 / Fishing supplies & licenses
Sportsman Supply, 466 Main / 723-4343
High County Sports, 491 Main / 723-4648
Orvis Flies Only Tackle, 524 Main / 723-4215

Walsenberg - 970
Pawn Shop, 434 W 7th St., (719) 738-2530
Lock Stock and Barrel, 10232 I-25, (719) 738-6181

Westminster - 303
Gart Sports, 5403 W 88th, (303) 429-9311

Woodland Park - 719
Grizzly Firearms, 210 W. Midland Ave., (719) 687-6464
Pikes Peak Polaris and Sporting Goods, 300 W. Hwy. 24, (719) 687-6694

Selected List of References

Armstrong D.M., Meaney, C.A., Fitzgerald, J.P., *Mammals Of Colorado.* Niwot, Colorado: Denver Museum of Natural History and University Press of Colorado 1994.

Beck, Thomas, *Black Bears Of West-Central Colorado.* Technical Publication No. 39, Colorado Division of Wildlife 1991.

Bettas, George and Byers, Randall, editors, Boone and Crockett Club *Records Of North American Big Game 11th Edition.* Missoula Montana: Boone and Crockett Club 1999.

Dodson, Douglas, editor, *Colorado Bowhunting Records Of Big Game Fourth Edition.* Denver, Colorado: Colorado Bowhunters Association 1997.

Jacobs, Randy, editor, *Guide To The Colorado Mountains, Revised Ninth Edition.* Boulder, Colorado: Johnson Books 1997.

Fielder, John and Pearson, Mark, *The Complete Guide To Colorado's Wilderness Areas.* Englewood, Colorado: Westcliffe Publishers 1994.

Nelson, Mike, *The Colorado Weather Book.* Englewood, Colorado: Westcliffe Publishers 1999.

Spomer, Ron, *Big Game Hunter's Guide To Montana.* Belgrade, Montana: Wilderness Adventures Press 1999.

Spomer, Ron, *Big Game Hunter's Guide To Idaho.* Belgrade, Montana: Wilderness Adventures Press 2000.

Index

NOTES

NOTES

NOTES

NOTES